Knowledge & Information

Knowledge & Information

Studies in Information Science

Edited by

Wolfgang G. Stock (Düsseldorf, Germany)
and
Ronald E. Day (Bloomington, Indiana, U.S.A.)
Sonja Gust von Loh (Düsseldorf, Germany) – Associate Editor
Richard J. Hartley (Manchester, U.K.)
Robert M. Hayes (Los Angeles, California, U.S.A.)
Peter Ingwersen (Copenhagen, Denmark)
Michel J. Menou (Les Rosiers sur Loire, France, and London, U.K.)
Stefano Mizzaro (Udine, Italy)
Christian Schlögl (Graz, Austria)
Sirje Virkus (Tallinn, Estonia)

Knowledge and Information (K&I) is a peer-reviewed information science book series. The scope of information science comprehends representing, providing, searching and finding of relevant knowledge including all activities of information professionals (e.g., indexing and abstracting) and users (e.g., their information behavior). An important research area is information retrieval, the science of search engines and their users. Topics of knowledge representation include metadata as well as methods and tools of knowledge organization systems (folksonomies, nomenclatures, classification systems, thesauri, and ontologies). Informetrics is empirical information science and consists, among others, of the domain-specific metrics (e.g., scientometrics, webometrics), user and usage research, and evaluation of information systems. The sharing and the distribution of internal and external information in organizations are research topics of knowledge management. The information market can be defined as the exchange of digital information on networks, especially the World Wide Web. Further important research areas of information science are information ethics, information law, and information sociology.

De Gruyter Saur

Katrin Weller

Knowledge Representation
in the
Social Semantic Web

De Gruyter Saur

D 61

ISBN 978-3-598-25180-1
e-ISBN 978-3-598-44158-5
ISSN 1868-842X

Library of Congress Cataloging-in-Publication Data

Weller, Katrin.
  Knowledge representation in the social semantic Web / Katrin Weller.
    p. cm. -- (Knowledge & information, ISSN 1868-8144)
  Includes bibliographical references and index.
  ISBN 978-3-598-25180-1 -- ISBN 978-3-598-44158-5 (ebook)
  1. Semantic Web. 2. Knowledge representation (Information theory) I.
Title.
  TK5105.88815.W45 2010
  025.042'7--dc22
                                                          2010030140

Bibliographic information published by the Deutsche Nationalbibliothek
The Deutsche Nationalbibliothek lists this publication in the Deutsche
Nationalbibliografie; detailed bibliographic data are available in the Internet
at http://dnb.d-nb.de.

Printing: Hubert & Co. GmbH & Co. KG, Göttingen
∞ Printed on acid-free paper

Printed in Germany

www.degruyter.com

Contents

Introduction

In 2009, the publicly accessible World Wide Web celebrated its 18th Birthday[1]. During its childhood and adolescence it has grown to become an enormous accumulation of information, entertainment, and spam – in a variety of forms and formats and with differing quality. All this has become part of our daily life. And never before have such an amount and such a variety of information been as easily accessible. On the other hand, navigating through a collection of documents and finding just the right piece of information has probably never been a greater challenge. We are experiencing an enormous "information overload" (e.g., Neill, 1992) on the WWW, a phenomenon also referred to as "infosmog" (e.g., Shadbolt, Burke & Friedland, 2003) or the "data deluge" (e.g., Gershon & Miller, 1993).

Web search engines are doing a fine job, but difficulties remain in finding appropriate information in suitable formats and within a moderate time period. One challenge is the lack of either recall or precision in search results – achieving a simple and exact overview on retrieved documents is another one. Thus in the time of Google the precise and effective retrieval of information is still one of the biggest challenges for information societies. But although we can hardly imagine life without the WWW, its development is still far from being finished. Optimization of Web technologies and Web contents are a constant issue.

In very recent years, however, a huge development has happened which has revolutionized the WWW: the users have conquered the Web. *Social software* such as *wikis, blogs, podcasts* and *vodcasts, social networking services* and *social media sharing platforms* have enabled common Web users without any background in computer science or skills in programming languages to publish content on the Web and to share it with others. This revolutionary development has been called *Web 2.0* (O'Reilly, 2005). Due to the significant new dimensions that were added to the 'former' Web it was acclaimed as a new release version. Sometimes it is also referred to as the *Social Web*, because its figureheads are broad communities of users. The power of Web 2.0 applications lies in these *social* communities rather than in any *technical* innovations. Huge groups of people are able to contribute Web content on a variety of topics; they may ensure the coverage of minority issues (the so-called "long tail"; see Anderson, 2006) as well as mutual quality control.

---

[1] Whereas several technical preconditions and the underlying Internet have been available before the "birth" of the public WWW in August 1991.

By now, Web 2.0 principles and tools are no longer an innovation for many users, but have become a matter of fact. Services like Wikipedia[2], Facebook[3] and Flickr[4] are already part of many people's daily life.

In scientific discourse on the topic, the initial enthusiasm has been dampened. What promised to be the manifestation of the "wisdom of the crowds" (Surowiecki, 2004), or "collective intelligence" (Weiss, 2005), has by now also revealed its weaknesses and posed a variety of new challenges for Web developers and researchers in this field, for example concerning antisocial behavior like spamming, cyber stalking or misuse of personal data. Furthermore, with everybody contributing, the Web is growing even faster than it already had done in its previous form – and so is the information overload and the challenge to find the right information at the right time. But the Social Web has also introduced its own approach to this problem of finding and retrieving information: *folksonomies*.

Folksonomies are collections of keywords (called *tags*), which users of certain Web 2.0 services may freely add to documents such as photos, videos or bookmarks to describe their contents and make them manageable and retrievable. Users are *tagging* the documents. With this, folksonomies have transferred a fundamental idea of library and information science to the Web: *indexing* documents with *content-descriptive metadata*. For decades, librarians, information specialists and professional indexers have assigned keywords to library holdings, digital document collections or archives in order to apply some structured access to the respective information. But there has never been enough capacity to do so for the huge amounts of documents on the Web. Now the Web users have taken over this challenge themselves, in a rather intuitive manner and without any rules.

Folksonomies enable the searching of and browsing through large social document collections in a novel way, but they also show different problems and shortcomings – and thus are not the ultimate solution for accessing information on the Web. One major shortcoming of folksonomies is the complete lack of *vocabulary control*. This means, for one, that synonyms are not bound together and a user searching for New York in a folksonomy-based system will have to think of alternative denotations, such as NY or Big Apple, and add them to his search query. This problem and other effects of free tagging have been heavily reduced in *controlled vocabularies*, which are used for indexing in library and information science.

Such methods of vocabulary control for indexing and retrieval are essentials in the field of *knowledge representation* as it is perceived in information science. Realized in the form of *classifications, thesauri, nomenclatures* or other *knowledge organization systems* (KOS), they have long been applied in different practical settings. Thus it seems only natural that years of expertise in this discipline should now be combined with novel indexing approaches in social tagging appli-

---

[2]   Wikipedia: http://www.wikipedia.org.
[3]   Facebook: http://www.facebook.com.
[4]   Flickr: http://www.flickr.com.

cations: The classical knowledge representation techniques are among the first aspect that should be considered for use within the context of the (Social) Web.

There is another ongoing research area which is of high interest for the problem of handling the enormous growth of information on the Web: the *Semantic Web* (Berners-Lee, Hendler & Lassila, 2001). The principles of Semantic Web and of Web 2.0 differ not only in their particular goals and features, but also fundamentally in their origins: The term 'Web 2.0' describes a kind of movement on the Web which emerged independently over a period of time and was first and most prominently noticed and reported by Tim O'Reilly. The Semantic Web, on the other hand, has not really become a reality yet. It is based on a vision (most popularly expressed by Tim Berners-Lee, James Hendler and Ora Lassila) of how the current WWW could be improved by adding a supportive layer of machine-readable, semantic metadata and by enhancing the topical linkage of Websites, in order to make navigation, information retrieval and information integration easier and more effective. The aim is to close the *semantic gap* (e.g. Ehrig, 2007) between the words as symbols and their meanings; between computers that match word strings and humans who interpret meanings of words. An enormous research community has developed around this basic idea in order to create whatever technical background would be needed to achieve this goal. Presently, the Semantic Web is still rather an enormous research goal than a real experience on the Web. But, as we will see throughout this book, these efforts have yielded first results in the form of several semantic applications and, what is more, have already resulted in a sophisticated technical infrastructure. In this research field, one major point of emphasis is the development of *ontologies*.

Ontologies are complex forms of knowledge organization systems represented in a machine-readable formal language. They are needed to provide the semantic layer for the Web. Principally, ontologies can represent a vocabulary for a domain of interest in form of general *concepts* in this domain, particular *instances* that embody these concepts, *relations* which describe the properties of concepts, and *axioms* that capture general facts about them. If an ontology makes appropriate use of all these elements, it can become an elaborate form of controlled vocabulary for indexing Web documents. However, ontologies may further include general facts and statements (which is not the case in traditional KOS). And, as they make use of formal representation languages, they can include explicit concept definitions that may be interpreted by machines and can thus even be used to infer implicit knowledge.

Apart from a specific technical infrastructure, the Semantic Web thus urgently requires a set of high-quality ontologies for different domains of interest, which provide a shared vocabulary and place concepts from a domain of interest into semantic contexts. The practical realization of the Semantic Web will heavily depend on future ideas for providing such semantic knowledge models. Due to their complexity, the development of ontologies is rather costly and laborious. This is one of the reasons why their distribution over the Web is only proceeding slowly. But if we succeed in spreading ontologies comprehensively thoughout the Web, the idea of the Semantic Web can become reality. Previous approaches have not succeeded, yet. But recent developments in the Social Web represent a highly promising opportunity for the Semantic Web: with the help of broad user communities, lots of manpower could be gathered for the creation and application of ontologies on the Web.

This leads us right to the main objective of this book: we want to explore the opportunities and challenges of combining Social Web activities with the efforts to establish a semantic layer for the Web. We focus particularly on the development of rich semantic knowledge representations and on ways in which user communities may (directly or indirectly) contribute to this process.

Ontologies on the Semantic Web, folksonomies on the Social Web, and classical methods of knowledge representation in information science principally all share the same aim: to index documents with content-descriptive metadata in order to reduce semantic ambiguity and to improve retrievability. They are all manifestations of knowledge representation; yet they all differ in their particular characteristics, features and problems. Classical approaches mainly rely on vocabulary control, ontologies add aspects of machine-readability and automatic reasoning, while folksonomies do the complete opposite and make use of uncontrolled, but socially collected keywords. All these different approaches should not be used in isolation, but must become interrelated on the Web, if a benefit is to be drawn from their particular advantages.

Similarly, the research communities of the Social and the Semantic Web are increasingly collaborating and converting, in order to discuss what has been named the *Social Semantic Web*. The term 'Social Semantic Web' refers to the effect that the boundary between social software on the one hand, and the development of semantic applications on the other, is becoming increasingly blurred. Web tools of the future should consider focusing both on communities, interaction and communication as well as on navigation based on meanings and the semantic interlinking of data collections. The aim is to profit both from broad user communities with their collected knowledge and manpower and from semantic technologies, along with navigation based on meanings, in order to make navigation and retrieval on the WWW more effective. For example, semantic layers can be added to large community-based document collections and help to structure their contents and establish meaningful links between single pieces of information. On the other hand, user communities can help to construct novel ontologies and combine their skills and expertise in order to put these knowledge models to practice. Since 2008, the number of (announced or released) tools that focus particularly on combining social and semantic technologies has been rising; the most popular examples are *semantic wikis* and *semantic blogs* which interlink community-created contents with simplified (lightweight) ontologies. These tools can be viewed as the herald of the Social Semantic Web. Although the combination of social and semantic applications now seems so fundamental, it has only started to be addressed quite recently and still has a long way to go.

The development of the Social Semantic Web up to now will be recapitulated in this book, and application scenarios of social semantic tools will be discussed. We will not, however, describe the technical backgrounds and computational aspects of the Social Semantic Web in more detail. Instead, the general focus of this book is directed at a more specific sub-topic: it will address the problem of knowledge representation as one particular challenge in the emerging Social Semantic Web. We will comprehensively address the question of what knowledge representation in a Social Semantic Web might look like, which includes both rich semantic structures and community contributions. This book starts mainly from the Semantic Web point of view and explores in detail, how Social Web activities contribute to ontology development – rather than a Social Web perspective, which might, for example, focus on the question of how semantic models can be applied to enhance navigation in social communities. The latter aspect will only be addressed briefly.

State of Research

This book touches on a variety of different research areas from the field of information science and related disciplines (e.g. knowledge representation models and their development, social interaction on the Web, collaborative ontology engineering and semantic upgrades) – and, unfortunately, we cannot provide a comprehensive overview on the state of research for every single sub-topic. Some of these relevant topics are already very well investigated; others are only just beginning to attract broad interest. We have sought to provide useful references for additional readings throughout the single chapters and sections. Additionally, we will now present a short overview on the state of research for the most important related topics and highlight some of the most pertinent related publications.

Knowledge Representation and Knowledge Organization Systems in Information Science

The topic of knowledge representation has been a priority in information science for a long time. Consequently, various publications on this topics exist, both in the form of both scientific articles (in journals, proceedings or edited volumes) and monographic books. Of the latter, some provide a broad overview on different knowledge representation and indexing methods, e.g. Cleveland and Cleveland (2001), Lancaster (2003), Stock and Stock (2008). Others focus on one particular method, e.g. Aitchison, Gilchrist and Bawden (2000) on thesauri and Batley (2005) on classifications. And some consider methods of knowledge representation in a certain application setting, like Caplan (2003) and Taylor (1999) in the context of libraries and library science, Foulonneau and Riley (2008) in digital document collections and Lambe (2007) in corporate knowledge management. More detailed publications on single knowledge organization systems and their application will be cited in the respective sections throughout the book.

Knowledge representation is still an important research topic in information science, library science and documentation today and has also made its way into scientific fields related to the Web. Among the recent research trends in this field are: the interoperability of different representation systems, structural enrichments of KOS and the involvement of user communities into knowledge representation activities. This book refers to these aspects and considers knowledge organization systems in the broader setting of Social Web and Semantic Web technologies.

Web 2.0 Technologies and Knowledge Representation in Web 2.0

The developments in the WWW which are referred to as 'Web 2.0' or 'Social Web' have recently started to become a sizeable new research area with a very broad spectrum of sub-topics. Literature in this domain of interest is highly scattered among a variety of conference proceedings and journals – in disciplines ranging from computer science (technical and computational aspects of social software services) to economics (application of social software in organizational settings like knowledge management or marketing), also including social sciences (e.g. user behavior, media reception) and humanities (e.g. considerations on new text genres like blogs and microblogging). Monographic scientific considerations and broad topical collections on Social Web technologies are still rare. One relatively broad overview can be found in Dumova and Fiordo (2009). One example for a quite different perspective on the Web 2.0 phenomenon is presented by Giltrow and Stein (2009), who have collected different discussions on new (literary) genres in the Social Web environment.

In analogy to the phrase 'Web 2.0', several application scenarios for social software services have been announced by adding the '2.0'; such as 'enterprise 2.0', 'library 2.0' or 'e-learning 2.0'. Literature exists for several application areas (e.g., Koch & Richter, 2007), focusing also on individual social software services like wikis (e.g., Klobas, 2006) or blogs (e.g., Blood, 2002).

Due to the great public interest, a variety of popular science books are available as well. And apart from scientific conferences and journals, a lot of innovation takes place directly on the Web: online publications, in the form of blog posts or comments, also play an important role for scientific discussions in this field. The same goes for the particular aspect of indexing and retrieval in Web 2.0 using folksonomies. The most comprehensive overview on this topic is found in Peters (2009). A less scientific point of view on social tagging systems is presented by Smith (2008).

Many of the latest research questions on the Social Web concern aspects of how different types of social software can be interrelated (or *mashed-up*). With respect to the overall topic of this book, we will consider some aspects of how social applications (e.g. wikis and blogs) can be enhanced with semantic technologies. Then, we will have a closer look at the role of social tagging in a Social Semantic Web scenario. To wit, we will investigate how social tagging applications can interact with ontologies or other semantic approaches, and show that folksonomies may profit from additional semantic structures, providing a useful starting point for the development of ontologies.

Ontologies and Semantic Web Technologies

Ontologies and ontology engineering have established themselves as prominent research topics, mainly in the field of computer science and related disciplines where particular emphasis is placed on ontologies as a new means for finding and managing information on the Web. And yet there also exist other points of view on this topic, e.g. basic questions of knowledge modeling with philosophical traditions and considerations on formal representation languages and their complexity.

One of the most important publications on ontologies in the context of Semantic Web research is surely the "Handbook on Ontologies", a collection of articles covering a wide range of topics (including ontology languages, engineering methods, exemplary ontologies and applications), edited by Staab and Studer (2004). It is now also available in a revised version (Staab & Studer, 2009). Another true classic amongst publications on ontologies is the book on "Ontology Engineering" by Gómez-Pérez, Fernández-López and Corcho (2004). It provides a useful overview on the theoretical foundations of ontologies as well as technical backgrounds in ontology engineering, from representation languages to engineering tools. Several other important books with slightly different foci are available. Stuckenschmidt (2009) focuses on the expressiveness of ontologies and discusses conceptual definitions, methods for representing meaning and the capacities of different ontology languages. Allemang and Hendler (2008) present a broad overview on issues of modeling ontologies in the representation languages OWL, RDF and RDF(S). Davies, Studer and Warren (2006) cover a broad spectrum of technical background on ontology engineering and usage. Additional general literature on ontologies includes books by Breitmann, Casanova and Truszkowski (2007) as well as Sharman, Kishore and Ramesh (2007).

The broad variety of scientific articles also deals with very specific subdisciplines of ontologies and ontology engineering, which will not be listed here. Similarly, a sheer endless number of journal articles and conference proceedings deal with the different aspects of developing a technological infrastructure for the Semantic Web, with the International Semantic Web Conference (ISWC) as well as the European (ESWC) and Asian Semantic Web Conferences (ASWC) as the leading discussion forums for recent developments. Important overviews on technological achievements in this field are (amongst others) given by Antoniou and van Harmelen (2004), Hitzler, Krötzsch et al. (2008), and Stuckenschmidt and van Harmelen (2005). Kashyap, Bussler and Moran (2008) and Yu (2007) focus on the development of Semantic Web Services. Pellegrini and Blumauer (2006) have collected a variety of research papers on personal and organizational usage of semantic approaches. Other collections were published by Fensel (2004), Hepp, de Leenheer et al. (2008), and Taniar and Rahayu (2006).

All these renowned publications indicate that the research on ontologies has reached a remarkable level. The same holds for the more general topic of Semantic Web research. Still, there are lots of open research challenges – the Semantic Web has not yet become a reality. Over the last years, the fundamental technological infrastructure as well as several basic technologies (like representation languages, inference engines, ontology editors, methodologies for creating, merging and mapping ontologies) have been developed, and future work will be dedicated to the practical realization of the Semantic Web and the establishing of ontology-based applications in various contexts.

Important research interests in the area of the Semantic Web are, for instance, practical applications for certain contexts (e.g., semantic search and semantic desktop tools), the further development of standards and supportive technologies, data integration and exchange as well as the interlinking of different tools and data.

This book focuses intensively on ontologies as the most complex form of KOS that we know so far. But it addresses the topic of ontologies and ontology engineering from an information scientist's perspective and with respect to the general topic of knowledge representation in the Social Semantic Web. This means that little to no attention is paid to some of the topics that are of great importance in computer science, such as the technical realization of tools for ontology engineering, reasoning or information extraction or the development of formal ontology languages. Instead, we will elaborate on the conceptual challenges in ontology engineering (including questions such as how to properly model concepts, instances and relations in ontologies) in order to outline their semantic capabilities. We will discuss the spectrum of traditional and novel knowledge organization systems and place ontologies into this context. And we will consider ontology engineering in the social context of Web communities, in order to demonstrate the potential of the Social Web for the creation of the Semantic Web.

The Social Semantic Web

After the individual topics of Web 2.0 and Semantic Web had started to be intensively discussed, research on the potential of combining both principles began to follow. Conferences and workshops have started to address this intersection (e.g., Auer, Bizer et al., 2007); single applications have been developed and published. The Journal of Web Semantics had a special issue on "Semantic Web and Web 2.0" (Mika & Greaves, 2008). And, very recently, books have been published for the first time presenting a general introduction to the Social Semantic Web, most impotantly Breslin, Passant and Decker (2009), which describes how social software tools make use of semantics and how different applications are increasingly interlinked on the Web. Furthermore, Blumauer and Pellegrini (2008), Cardoso and Lytras (2009), Cunha (2009), and Lytras and Ordonez de Pablos (2009) have collected a variety of practical examples of enhanced Social Web applications. Kinsella, Passant et al. (2009) discuss semantic extensions for wikis and blogs and describe how semantic data can be added to software projects and may be aggregated over the Web.

All in all, this combined research area is still in its infancy and the full potential of social semantic technologies has not yet been fully unleashed; more publications are to follow. The literature available provides a useful overview on current initiatives and approaches. Our book focuses on one particular aspect within this emerging Social Semantic Web, namely knowledge representation.

Objectives and Main Research Questions of this Book

The book intends to help closing the gap between knowledge representation methods in the Social and the Semantic Web. This is, currently, the gap between user-created uncontrolled tags in folksonomies on the one side, and highly formalized ontologies created by trained experts on the other. To bridge this particular gap, we will incorporate background knowledge from classical knowledge representation initiatives. At first sight, the differences between folksonomies and ontologies may seem enormous. But a comprehensive consideration of folksonomies, nomenclatures, classifications, thesauri and ontologies already reveals a scale of step-by-step semantic enrichments. So we already have the means to bridge folksonomies and ontologies. Yet in many current studies, knowledge representation methods are not considered in their full spectrum. This book provides an overview on classical and novel approaches in knowledge representation, with a detailed view on ontologies as the most elaborate of these methods. It highlights the differences of several methods as well as their similarities, points of contact and interactions. By combining several approaches, the Social Semantic Web will be able to profit from long traditions in knowledge representation for document indexing: from user collaboration in folksonomies and from rich semantics in ontologies.

Nevertheless, this book will not solve the information overload problem or close the semantic gap. But it might act as another little step on the long path towards this ultimate goal. The main purpose of this book is to sum up the vital and highly topical research issue of knowledge representation on the Web and to discuss novel solutions by combining some advantages of folksonomies and Web 2.0 approaches with ontologies and semantic technologies. We discuss the structure of ontologies in order to explain the complexity of semantic models for the Web and to investigate ways in which Web users may contribute to respectable rich KOS.

A broad range of questions and challenges are centered on this topic, the most important ones for our perspective being the following:

- What knowledge organization systems are already available on the Web or in other application settings? What are their characteristics and features?
- What kind of knowledge can be represented in knowledge organization systems? Which degrees of structural complexity have to be distinguished to characterize different KOS types?
- How can complex KOS (ontologies) be built? Which tools are available? Which functionalities will be needed in the Social Semantic Web?
- How can users participate in ontology engineering processes? How can they be motivated and taught to contribute to structured KOS?
- Can pieces of KOS be created through little effort? Can particular knowledge bases be reused? Can users even help to create ontologies without noticing it?
- Which resources on the Web can be reused for ontology engineering?
- How can different approaches learn from each other?
- How and in which context can different KOS be combined? What is needed to let them interact?

In this book, we have addressed these questions as detailed as possible.

Outline of this Book

This book is organized into three main chapters, which capture the topic of knowledge representation in the Social Semantic Web as follows:

Chapter 1

In this chapter, we will provide an introduction to the importance of knowledge representation in information science. We will explain the correlations between knowledge representation, knowledge organization systems, document indexing, metadata and information retrieval. The different types of classical knowledge organization systems are introduced (mainly: nomenclature, classification and thesaurus), and we will present several examples of how these KOS are put into practice and applied to different domains and usage scenarios, e.g. for intellectual property or medical information.

With this background in knowledge representation traditions we will then proceed to the Semantic Web. We will explain the underlying ideas of the Semantic Web and demonstrate how they are related to the aims of classical KOS – and how they go beyond classical approaches. We will give an initial short introduction to ontologies as the key elements of knowledge representation in the Semantic Web (a more detailed discussion of ontologies will follow in Chapter 2) and discuss the Semantic Web's state of development.

Next, the Social Web or Web 2.0 will be introduced as another recent development in the WWW that has also brought forward a novel approach to knowledge representation and indexing: folksonomies. This section comprises considerations of the advantages and shortcomings of folksonomies, and of general aspects of user communities and Web collaboration as propagated under the Web 2.0 paradigm.

Finally, this first chapter concludes with the explanation of the novel term 'Social Semantic Web'. We will provide a definition for the Social Semantic Web and explain how aspects of semantic indexing and social Web collaboration are already converging and what new developments can be expected in the near future.

Chapter 2

After this comprehensive overview on the past, present and future of knowledge representation, the second chapter focuses primarily on the aspect of *semantics* of the Social Semantic Web. We will discuss the elements and structure of ontologies in detail, as they provide the richest semantic structures of all current knowledge organization systems. This is mainly done on an abstract level, i.e. without explaining the capabilities of single ontology languages. For some aspects, illustrative examples are provided, based on the ontology language OWL or the ontology editor Protégé. Yet it is not the aim of the book to compare characteristics of individual ontology languages. Instead, we want to highlight the novel features of ontologies in comparison with other KOS and hint at the complexity of possibilities for knowledge representation – in order to sensitize the growing community within the Social Semantic Web to these difficulties and challenges. We thus introduce the most important elements of ontologies: concepts, instances, properties/relations and axioms, and see how they make up the structure of an ontology and how they can be used for representing knowledge in general. A particular focus is placed on semantic relations as KOS elements.

While the core of this chapter is the detailed analysis and introduction of ontology elements and their role in semantic knowledge representation, it also features a brief introduction to the history of ontology in computer science, some discussions on ontology definitions, and a comparison of structural differences across several KOS and other knowledge resources.

Chapter 3
In the last chapter, the aspect of *semantics* for the Web is now combined with *social* dimensions. We will discuss the principles of ontology engineering, i.e. the construction of semantic models, which have to be placed into the context of the Social Semantic Web. Two different points of view will be considered: a) how broad user communities may participate in processes of developing ontologies (or other KOS) and b) how general activities of Web users may be exploited to improve the state of knowledge representation on the Web.

To provide an initial overview on the current state, different tools that support ontology engineering activities are collected and the general dimensions of ontology engineering outlined. We will then address the specific question of how social communities may be involved in the engineering process. Collaborative vs. community-based approaches in ontology engineering will be distinguished, novel tools and utilities described. Furthermore, a variety of current approaches will be discussed that have the potential to reuse the activities of broad Web communities and to transfer them to the development of semantic knowledge representations; among them are *community knowledge bases, controlled natural languages* and *games with a purpose*. A particular focus is placed on the potential of folksonomies as user created index terms. We will discuss how tag gardening can be applied to improve the performance of folksonomies and to enrich their semantic structure. On the other hand, folksonomies may also be used as a source for creating richer KOS.

Finally, the chapter addresses a topic of high importance for the Social Semantic Web: the co-existence of several knowledge organization systems. Different types of interactions between KOS as well as single application scenarios are outlined. Attempts to enable easy access at available KOS are discussed and the Knowledge Organization Systems Ontology (KOSO) is introduced as a suggested *meta model* for classifying and describing existing KOS. We will conclude this chapter with a visionary view on KOS interactions in the Social Semantic Web.

Acknowledgements

This book could not have been written without the inspiring collaboration with my colleagues and the interesting and motivating discussions with fellow researchers. I particularly thank all my colleagues at the Department of Informaton Science, Heinrich-Heine-University Düsseldorf: many thanks to Wolfgang G. Stock for his constant support and advice. Thanks to Isabella Peters, Jasmin Schmitz, Violeta Trkulja and Sonja Gust von Loh – and also to all other members of the department and those students who worked with me in several projects. Further thanks go to all my co-workers in the Ontoverse project (funded by the BMBF) for insights into their disciplines and interdisciplinary discussions; thanks to Indra Mainz, Dominic Mainz, Ingo Paulsen. Thanks to James Kilbury. Thanks to Paul Becker for proofreading this book. Of course, there are many more people I met during the writing of this book and who helped me with advice and inspiration. Hopefully, I will manage to thank all of them in person one day.

This book is dedicated to my family with many thanks for all the years of loving support.

Formal Remarks

The three main parts of this book, as well as both introduction and conclusion, all have their own list of references. If not indicated otherwise, all Web sources cited in the reference sections and in other parts of this book (e.g. in footnotes and captions) have last been accessed on November 20, 2009.

References

Aitchison, J., Gilchrist, A., & Bawden, D. (2000). Thesaurus Construction and Use (4th Edition). London: Aslib.

Allemang, D., & Hendler, J. A. (2008). Semantic Web for the Working Ontologist: Modeling in RDF, RDFS and OWL. Amsterdam: Morgan Kaufmann/Elsevier.

Anderson, C. (2006). The Long Tail: Why the Future of Business is Selling Less of More. New York: ACM.

Antoniou, G., & van Harmelen, F. (2004). A Semantic Web Primer. Cambridge: MIT Press.

Auer, S., Bizer, C., Müller, C., & Zhdanova, A.V. (Eds.) (2007). The Social Semantic Web: Proceedings of the 1st Conference on Social Semantic Web (CSSW), Leipzig, Germany. GI-Edition Proceedings, 113. Bonn: Gesellschaft für Informatik.

Batley, S. (2005). Classification in Theory and Practice. Oxford: Chandos.

Berners-Lee, T., Hendler, J., & Lassila, O. (2001). The Semantic Web. Scientific American, 284(5), 34–43.

Blood, R. (2002). The Weblog Handbook: Practical Advice on Creating and Maintaining your Blog. Cambridge: Perseus Pub.

Blumauer, A., & Pellegrini, T. (Eds.) (2008). Social Semantic Web: Web 2.0 – Was nun? Berlin: Springer.

Breitman, K., Casanova, M. A., & Truszkowski, W. (2007). Semantic Web: Concepts, Technologies and Applications. London: Springer.

Breslin, J. G., Passant, A., & Decker, S. (2009). The Social Semantic Web. Berlin: Springer.

Caplan, P. (2003). Metadata Fundamentals for All Librarians. Chicago: ALA Editions.

Cardoso, J., & Lytras, M. D. (Eds.) (2009). Semantic Web Engineering in the Knowledge Society. Hershey: Information Science Reference.

Cleveland, D. B., & Cleveland, A. D. (2001). Introduction to Indexing and Abstracting (3rd Edition). Englewood: Libraries Unlimited.

Cunha, M. M. (Ed.) (2009). Handbook of Research on Social Dimensions of Semantic Technologies and Web Services. Hershey: Information Science Reference.

Davies, J., Studer, R., & Warren, P. (Eds.) (2006). Semantic Web Technologies: Trends and Research in Ontology-Based Systems. Chichester: Wiley & Sons.

Dumova, T., & Fiordo, R. (Eds.) (2009). Handbook of Research on Social Interaction Technologies and Collaboration Software: Concepts and Trends. Hershey: IGI Publishing.

Ehrig, M. (2007). Ontology Alignment: Bridging the Semantic Gap. New York: Springer.

Fensel, D. (2004). Ontologies: A Silver Bullet for Knowledge Management and Electronic Commerce (2nd Edition). Chichester: Springer.

Foulonneau, M., & Riley, J. (2008). Metadata for Digital Resources: Implementation, Systems Design and Interoperability. Oxford: Chandos Publishing.

Gershon, N. D., & Miller, C. G. (1993). Dealing with the Data Deluge. IEEE Spectrum, 30(7), 28–32.

Giltrow, J., & Stein, D. (Eds.) (2009). Genres in the Internet: Issues in the Theory of Genre. Amsterdam: John Benjamins Publishing.

Gómez-Pérez, A., Fernández-López, M., & Corcho, O. (2004). Ontological Engineering: Advanced Information and Knowledge Processing (3rd Print). London: Springer.

Hepp, M., de Leenheer, P., de Moor, A., & Sure, Y. (Eds.) (2008). Ontology Management: Semantic Web, Semantic Web Services, and Business Applications. Boston: Springer.

Hitzler, P., Krötzsch, M., Rudolph, S., & Sure, Y. (2008). Semantic Web. Berlin, Heidelberg: Springer.

Kashyap, V., Bussler, C., & Moran, M. (2008). The Semantic Web: Semantics for Data and Services on the Web. Berlin, Heidelberg: Springer.

Kinsella, S., Passant, A., Breslin, J. G., Decker, S., & Jaokar, A. (2009). The Future of Social Web Sites: Sharing Data and Trusted Applications with Semantics. Advances in Computers, 76, 121–175.

Klobas, J. (2006). Wikis: Tools for Information Work and Collaboration. Oxford: Chandos Publishing.

Koch, M., & Richter, A. (2007). Enterprise 2.0: Planung, Einführung und erfolgreicher Einsatz von Social Software in Unternehmen. München: Oldenbourg.

Lambe, P. (2007). Organising Knowledge: Taxonomies, Knowledge and Organisational Effectiveness. Oxford: Chandos.

Lancaster, F. W. (2003). Indexing and Abstracting in Theory and Practice. Champaign, Ill.: University of Illinois, Graduate School of Library and Information Science.

Lytras, M. D., & Ordonez de Pablos, P. (Eds.) (2009). Social Web Evolution: Integrating Semantic Applications and Web 2.0 Technologies. Hershey: Information Science Reference.

Mika, P., & Greaves, M. (2008). Editorial: Semantic Web & Web 2.0. Journal of Web Semantics, 6(1), 1–3.

Neill, S. D. (1992). Dilemmas in the Study of Information: Exploring the Boundaries of Information Science. New York: Greenwood Press.

O'Reilly, T. (2005). What is Web 2.0: Design Patterns and Business Models for the Next Generation of Software. Retrieved from http://www.oreilly net.com/pub/a/oreilly/tim/news/2005/09/30/what-is-web-20.html.

Pellegrini, T., & Blumauer, A. (Eds.) (2006). Semantic Web: Wege zur vernetzten Wissensgesellschaft. Berlin, Heidelberg: Springer.

Peters, I. (2009). Folksonomies: Indexing and Retrieval in Web 2.0. Berlin: De Gruyter Saur.

Shadbolt, N., Burke, M. A., & Friedland, N. S. (2003). Panel Discussion on Knowledge Acquisition Projects (Halo, RKF, and AKT). In J. H. Gennari; B. Porter, & Y. Gil (Eds.), Proceedings of the KCAP'03 Workshop on Knowledge Capture and Semantic Annotation, Florida, USA (pp. 2–3). New York: ACM.

Sharman, R., Kishore, R., & Ramesh, R. (Eds.) (2007). Ontologies: A Handbook of Principles, Concepts and Applications in Information Systems. Boston: Springer.

Smith, G. (2008). Tagging: People-powered Metadata for the Social Web. Berkeley: New Riders.

Staab, S., & Studer, R. (Eds.) (2004). Handbook on Ontologies. Berlin, Heidelberg, New York: Springer.

Staab, S., & Studer, R. (Eds.) (2009). Handbook on Ontologies (Second Edition). Dordrecht et al.: Springer.

Stock, W. G., & Stock, M. (2008). Wissensrepräsentation: Informationen auswerten und bereitstellen. München, Wien: Oldenbourg.

Stuckenschmidt, H. (2009). Ontologien: Konzepte, Technologien und Anwendungen. Berlin, Heidelberg: Springer.

Stuckenschmidt, H., & van Harmelen, F. (2005). Information Sharing on the Semantic Web. Berlin, Heidelberg: Springer.

Surowiecki, J. (2004). The Wisdom of Crowds: Why the Many are Smarter than the Few and How Collective Wisdom Shapes Business, Economies, Societies and Nations. New York: Anchor Books.

Taniar, D., & Rahayu, J. W. (Eds.) (2006). Web Semantics and Ontology. Hershey: Idea Group Publishing.

Taylor, A. G. (1999). The Organization of Information. Englewood, CO: Libraries Unlimited.

Weiss, A. (2005). The Power of Collective Intelligence. netWorker, 9(3), 16–23.

Yu, L. (2007). Introduction to the Semantic Web and Semantic Web Services. Boca Raton: Chapman & Hall/CRC.

Chapter 1

Knowledge Representation and Indexing: Background and Future

1.1 Knowledge Representation

The term knowledge representation is defined differently in various scientific fields. A sophisticated overview with largely theoretical background (philosophical and logical) is given by Sowa (2000). Research in Artificial Intelligence (AI) discusses methods of knowledge modeling or knowledge engineering (e.g. Studer, Benjamins & Fensel, 1998). Another different point of view is obtained through linguistic studies and their elucidation of knowledge representation (e.g. Löbner, 2002).

The considerations within this book are placed in the specific and practical context of information science and its particular definition of knowledge representation (Cleveland & Cleveland, 2001; Lancaster, 2003; Stock & Stock, 2008). This discipline has its origins in philosophy and, to a greater extent, in library-related developments. The latter can be traced back to the libraries in Egypt and Mesopotamia in the pre-Christian era. A comprehensive historical review is provided by Stock & Stock (2008). While philosophical approaches have always aimed at representing or organizing world knowledge on a *theoretical* level, the *practical* aim of providing access to knowledge was central within the context of libraries. Thus, systematic catalogues for organizing library holdings can be regarded as the first practical methods of knowledge representation; they formed the basis for a long tradition of classification schemes[5].

1.1.1 Metadata, Indexing and Retrieval

Today, knowledge representation has to be viewed as an approach to handling the key problems of the information society: how to structure and store information and, how to find and retrieve it precisely and effectively. Huge research efforts are

---

[5] In this book we will also use the term 'classification' as a synonym for 'classification scheme' and 'classification system'. Yet we must point out that this is not unambiguous; classification may also refer to the acts of classifying and classing (Wellisch, 2000).

concentrating on these challenges, many of them in the field of information re-trieval (Chu, 2007; Frakes & Baeza-Yates, 1992; Lewandowski, 2005; Stock, 2007a). These studies focus on methods and algorithms to enable the precise and comprehensive searching of document collections.

Methods of knowledge representation have been established as a complemen-tary approach to tackling the problem (Belkin & Croft, 1997). They are applied to provide a better basis for information retrieval tools and are based on the represen-tation of document *contents*, and thus offer an alternative or additional approach to *text statistics* and *content-based retrieval*[6]. Figure 1.1 shows how information re-trieval is based on document indexing and on the development of methods and models of knowledge representation.

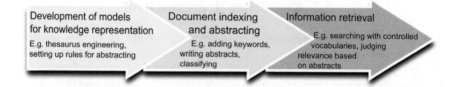

Figure 1.1.   Value chain of knowledge representation, document indexing and information retrieval.

Providing information about a document's content may be done in two ways: by *abstracting* the topics of a document, i.e. writing an abstract which captures the main contents of a document (Stock & Stock, 2008, Chapter 21), and by document *indexing*, i.e. assigning content-descriptive keywords to a document or placing it into a classification scheme (Cleveland & Cleveland, 2001; Lancaster, 2003).

Both approaches enhance retrieval techniques and aid users in deciding on a document's relevance in different ways. Indexing is used to represent certain *ob-jects* from a document's content by means of keywords; abstracting is used to rep-resent *facts and statements* from a document's content in the form of complete sentences (Stock & Stock, 2008).

Both indexing and abstracting must be distinguished from *formal metadata*[7], i.e. information about the characteristics of a document which do not involve its content (or its *aboutness*) (Stock & Stock, 2008). This might be the document's author, its title, publication year or publishing company. Both formal and content

---

[6]   The term 'content-based retrieval' can easily be misunderstood: it is particularly used for image retrieval and denotes retrieval based on characteristics of the document file itself, e.g. colors, shapes, textures (Lew, Sebe et al., 2006; Rasmussen, 1997). This approach does not make use of metadata and knowledge representation. These studies speak of *concept-based* approaches when index terms are assigned to documents.

[7]   Also known as *bibliographic metadata*.

descriptive metadata should ideally be used in combination. Professionally generated metadata are usually segmented into different fields, separating content-descriptive metadata from different types of formal metadata. In general, metadata can very broadly be defined as 'data about data', or, more precisely, as quoted below:

> "Metadata is here used to mean structured information about an information resource of any media type or format." (Caplan, 2003)

> "Traditionally, librarians and archivists have used the term metadata for descriptive information used to index, arrange, file, and improve access to a library's or museum's resources." (Gilliland-Swetland, 1998)

A pragmatic and comprehensive discussion of metadata for document collections is found in Foulonneau and Riley (2008).

In this book, we will mainly focus on the use of knowledge representation for the purpose of indexing. Indexing techniques typically rely on the use of controlled vocabularies, i.e. they provide a predefined set of concepts that are used to describe documents as well as for query formulation in information retrieval. Applying methods of vocabulary control for indexing and retrieval helps to enhance consistency in the choice of index terms and to unify the user's and the indexer's vocabularies. As controlled vocabularies typically make use of explicit concept interrelations (hierarchical structures, synonymy and associations, which will be discussed intensively in Chapter 2.2), they can also provide suggestions for query expansions and modifications, and reduce semantic ambiguity (Lancaster, 1986).

Indexing is a process made up of different phases. A general precondition is the availability of an appropriate knowledge representation model, e.g. a domain-specific classification or a thesaurus. Furthermore, indexing is always done for a certain collection of *documents*. Documents may be textual documents (e.g. books, articles, patents), but also pretty much anything that can be collected and stored, that carries a message or information and should thus be made searchable (e.g. videos, images, artistic works). The ISO definition (ISO 5963:1985) for 'document' is: "any item, printed or otherwise, which is amenable to cataloguing or indexing". Wellisch (2000) provides a more detailed definition:

> "Document. A medium on or in which a message is encoded; thus, the combination of medium and message. The term applies not only to objects written or printed on paper or on microforms (for example, books, periodicals, maps, diagrams, tables, and illustrations) but also to non-print media (for example, artistic works, audio and video recordings, films, machine-readable records, and multimedia) and, by extension, to naturally occurring or humanly made objects intended to convey information (for example, zoo animals, plants in botanical gardens, museum collections of hand tools, etc.)." (Wellisch, 2000)

Another extended definition is given by Buckland (1997). Furthermore, one often distinguishes documents and *documentary units*. One document may consist of several documentary units that should be indexed independently, e.g. one journal volume consisting of several articles. Also, several documents may form one documentary unit that should be indexed as a whole, e.g. a complete series of books. In the context of the WWW the definition of 'document' might have to be refined in future, particularly in Social Web environments with their variety of user-generated content.

Mai (2000) aptly sums up the elements of the indexing process:

> "The first step, the document analysis process, is the analysis of the document for its subjects. The second step, the subject description process, is the formulation of an indexing phrase or subject description. The third step, the subject analysis process, is the translation of the subject description into an indexing language. The three steps link four elements of the process. The first element is the document under examination. The second element is the subject of the document. This element is only present in the mind of the indexer in a rather informal way. The third element is a formal written description of the subject. The fourth is the subject entry, which has been constructed in the indexing language and represents the formal description of the subject." (Mai, 2000)

The indexing of professional and commercial services is typically (and ideally) done by professional *indexers*, i.e. people trained in the fields of knowledge representation and documentation and familiar with the use of controlled vocabularies. *Intellectual indexing* is a time-consuming and thus cost-intensive task. This way of professional, intellectual indexing provides high-quality indexing results. Yet it cannot guarantee perfection. Inconsistent indexing behavior may still occur on the inter-indexer level, if different indexers assign different index terms, as well as on an intra-indexer level, if one indexer uses an index vocabulary inconsistently over time (Lancaster, 2003; Stock & Stock, 2008).

Failures in indexing lead to deteriorating quality in information retrieval. If the quality and consistency of indexing fail, shortcomings in recall and precision will follow:

> "If an indexer fails to assign X when it should be assigned, it is obvious that recall failures will occur. If, on the other hand, Y is assigned when X should be, both recall and precision failures can occur. That is, the item will not be retrieved in searches for X, although it should be, and will be retrieved for Y, when it should not be." (Lancaster, 2003)

To reduce the costs of intellectual indexing, the development of automatic techniques to assist the classification and indexing of digital resources has been a research field for several years (Lancaster, 2003; Mani, 1999; Moens, 2000). Several approaches can be distinguished, particularly those that work with a form of knowledge representation and those that try to 'classify' documents based on similarities (Stock & Stock, 2008, Chapter 20). In practical application, automatic approaches have not yet displaced intellectual indexing.

1.1.2 Classical Knowledge Organization Systems

Different types of *knowledge organization systems* (KOS) have been developed for the indexing of documents with content-descriptive keywords. In this chapter, we will introduce three of them: *nomenclatures*, *classifications* and *thesauri*. These traditional KOS are well established in practical contexts of library, archive and documentation sciences. For classifications and thesauri, national or international standards exist.

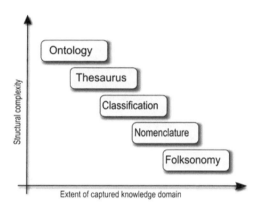

Figure 1.1. The three most prominent classical KOS arranged according to complexity and broadness – with ontologies and folksonomies extending the spectrum at both sides. Source: Modified from Weller, 2007.

All three are structured – *controlled* – vocabularies. They comprise the concepts relevant for a certain domain of interest (the vocabulary) and impose a structure by interrelating the concepts with different semantic relations. The foundation of a KOS is usually in the form of a concept hierarchy that may be enriched with further semantic relations, e.g. relations of equivalence and concept associations (we will discuss different types of relations and their importance for distinguishing different types of KOS in Sections 2.2 and 2.3.2). The more a knowledge organization system makes use of semantic relations, the more complex it is in semantic structure. But the more complex the structure, the smaller the captured *knowledge domain* will have to be[8], due to reasons of feasibility in knowledge engineering (Figure 1.2).

Recently, two new approaches, which will be discussed in the following sections, have joined classical KOS: ontologies and folksonomies. They also address issues of document indexing and knowledge representation and have thus contributed a revival in discussions about metadata on the Web (Madhavan, Halevy et al.,

---

[8] Either in terms of the broad coverage of domains or in terms of the in-depth representation of a domain.

2006; Safari, 2004). Their use has led to an increasing awareness of knowledge representation issues in scientific areas and even within the common Web-user community.

Both embody different principles and complement traditional techniques from opposite sides (Figure 1.2). Folksonomies are based on the social approaches of Web 2.0 and include novel, user-centered (collaborative) dimensions while renouncing the use of vocabulary control[9]. Ontologies extend the possibilities of formal vocabulary structuring in the sense of a Semantic Web.

NORMDATEN: *Schlagwort (7548364-6)*

s| **World Wide Web 2.0**

> Q *Wikipedia (als Web 2.0)* ; D *Bezeichnung für die Weiterentwicklung und die veränderte Wahrnehmung oder Nutzung des WWW. Das "neu" Web basiert technisch auf der großflächigen Verfügbarkeit einer Vielzahl von breitbandigen Internetzugängen, die es den Nutzern u. a. ermöglichen, die im Internet bereitgestellten Inhalte selbst zu erstellen und/oder zu bearbeiten. Typische Beispiele hierfür sind Wikis, Weblogs, Podcasts sowie Bild- und Video-Sharing-Portale. Das "neue" Web ist nicht mehr eine bloße Ansammlung von Web-Seiten, sondern eine Plattform für eine Reihe neuer interaktiver Techniken und Dienste des Internets.* ; SYS 30

BF Web 2.0

    WWW 2.0

VB Semantic Web

    Soziale Software

3.

Figure 1.2.   The keyword 'World Wide Web 2.0' in the SWD, with synonyms (BF) and associated keywords (VB). Source: http://z3950gw.dbf.ddb.de/z3950/zfo_ get_file.cgi?file Name=DDB/searchForm.html.

Nomenclature
A nomenclature (Stock & Stock, 2008) is a comparatively simple form of knowledge organization system that works with controlled keywords extracted from natural language. These keywords are structured via the precise identification and labeling of synonyms, sometimes enriched by associative cross-references within

---

[9]   It may thus be argued about whether they should be regarded as knowledge organization systems or not. If one considers the existence of a concept structure as prerequisite for KOS, folksonomies have to be regarded as a different kind of knowledge representation technique (like for example citation indexing which also cannot be regarded as KOS but is used for indexing). However, in this book we will regard folksonomies as a very lightweight form of KOS. As we will see below folksonomies at least contain some forms of implicit (statistical) connections between tags, due to their social dimensions.

the vocabulary. Homonyms are distinguished for unambiguous term definitions. The tradition of nomenclatures goes back to C.A. Cutter's "dictionary catalog" from 1876 (Foskett, 1982).

A nomenclature is often accompanied by a set of rules, which directs the indexing process. One example is the *Schlagwortnormdatei* (SWD) with its rule system *Regeln für den Schlagwortkatalog* (RSWK)[10] (RSWK, 1998; Umlauf, 1999). They were developed in the 1980s, and are still used in scientific and public libraries in Germany and German-speaking countries.

The SWD lists preferred keywords to be used for document indexing, together with their synonyms which must not be used as index terms. Figure 1.3 shows the SWD account for the keyword 'World Wide Web 2.0': the abbreviation BF (which stands for 'benutzt für' = 'used for') points to synonyms, the abbreviation VB ('Verwandter Begriff' = 'related term') can be used for navigating to thematically related terms in the vocabulary. Furthermore, we find a definition (D) and indication of source (Q).

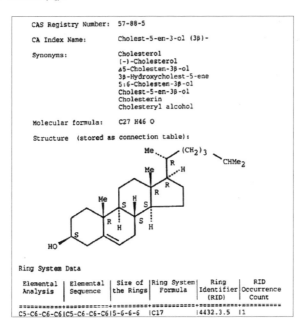

Figure 1.4. CAS Registry file entry example. Source: Weisgerber, 1997.

10   Regeln für den Schlagwortkatalog (RSWK), 3rd Edition:
http://deposit.ddb.de/ep/netpub/89/96/96/967969689/_data_stat/www.dbiberlin.de/dbi_
pub/einzelpu/regelw/rswk/rswk_00.htm.

The RSWK provide guidance for proper indexing based on the vocabulary. They contain, for instance, the instruction to use the most specific index terms and to avoid pleonasms in indexing (RSWK, 1998). The system envisions syntactic indexing in the form of keyword chains. Several chains are used to separate different topics appearing in a document. For this purpose, different categories of keywords are distinguished from general content-descriptive keywords: persons, geographic specifications, time specifications and formal keywords (regarding document types) (Umlauf, 2007).

The SWD is constructed for a universal domain, not for domain-specific library collections. As an example of a nomenclature with a specialized, delimited domain, we will look at the leading database for chemical literature, Chemical Abstracts Services (CAS)[11], and its registry file (*CAS Registry*) (Weisgerber, 1997). In the domain of chemistry, synonyms may not only be natural language words but also the molecular or structural formula of a chemical compound. The CAS Registry provides a unique identifier, the CAS Registry Number[12], to explicitly identify every chemical substance. These identifiers are linked with the compound's name and synonyms, such as the chemical formula, generic names or colloquial expressions, as depicted in Figure 1.4 (Stock & Stock, 2008).

Classification

Classification systems (Batley, 2005; DIN 32705:1987; Foskett, 1982; Stock & Stock, 2008, Chapter 12) have a long tradition in knowledge representation, both for indexing library collections and for use in online databases. They focus particularly on the structuring of knowledge in the form of concept hierarchies. Thus the main effort in creating a classification lies in choosing the appropriate classes to capture a domain of interest, and establishing a suitable hierarchical structure.

The most important peculiarity of classifications is that they work with *notations*. These are sets of characters that represent concepts in a language-independent way. For example, in the International Patent Classification (IPC), which is used for world-wide patent indexing)[13] the class 'shoe lacing fastenings' is represented by the notation A43C 1/00 (Figure 1.5). Some notations reflect the concepts' position in the classification hierarchy and thus enable hierarchical query expansions with truncations (Stock & Stock, 2008). With notations as unique identifiers, the classes' names may be more easily translated into different languages for international usage, while consistent indexing is still possible across languages. For the long-term usage of a classification, it is important that the notation system is able to incorporate new classes. This capability is called *hospitality*.

---

[11]   Chemical Abstracts Services (CAS): www.cas.org.
[12]   A unique identifier is needed in addition to the molecular formula, because one molecular formula may denote different substances. The structural formula is unique but difficult to handle.
[13]   International Patent Classification (IPC), English version:
       http://www.wipo.int/classifications/ipc/en/.

IPC	Definitions	Illustrations	RCL	Catchwords	Compilation	Corrigendum	Help	Options

	A	SECTION A — HUMAN NECESSITIES	
		PERSONAL OR DOMESTIC ARTICLES	
	A43	FOOTWEAR	
	A43C	FASTENINGS OR ATTACHMENTS FOR FOOTWEAR; LACES IN GENERAL	
	A43C 1/00	Shoe lacing fastenings (garment fastening devices A41F)	
	A43C 1/02	· with elastic laces	
	A43C 1/04	· with rings or loops	
	A43C 1/06	· tightened by draw-strings	
	A43C 3/00	Hooks for laces (making from sheet metal B21D 53/46); Guards for hooks	
	A43C 3/02	· Lacing-hooks with guide-rollers	
	A43C 3/04	· Spring safety-hooks	

Figure 1.5.   An excerpt from the International Patent Classification. Source:
http://www.wipo.int/classifications/ipc/ipc8/?lang=en.

We must distinguish between several specific forms of classification systems: A *decimal classification* is based on the principle that every class is divided into ten subclasses. The classical example for this type of classification is the *Dewey Decimal Classification* (DDC)[14] (Chan & Mitchell, 2006; DDC, 2003). The highest hierarchical level of the DDC consists of ten classes; each of them has ten subclasses, which are again subdivided into ten subclasses and so on. The ten top level classes of the DDC are:

> 000 Computers, Information & General Reference
> 100 Philosophy & Psychology
> 200 Religion
> 300 Social Sciences
> 400 Language
> 500 Science
> 600 Technology
> 700 Arts & Recreation
> 800 Literature
> 900 History & Geography

The DDC (Figure 1.6) is also an example for another type of classification: the *universal classification*. The approach of universal classifications is to capture the entire domain of human knowledge. They are primarily used for the systematic shelf arrangement of library holdings, but are also of interest for classifying web-

---

[14]   Dewey Decimal Classification (DDC): http://www.oclc.org/dewey/.

sites, e.g. in the Yahoo! Directory[15] and the Open Directory Project[16] (see below). The DDC is the most important and most widely used universal classification, several more specific and refined versions having been derived from it for the use in some (European) countries, e.g. the Universal Decimal Classification (UDC) (McIlwaine, 2000; UDC, 2005).

```
Main Classes
500   Science
579-590    Natural history of specific kinds of organisms
580-590        Plants and animals
590                Animals (Zoology)
592-599                Specific taxonomic groups of animals
597                        *Cold-blooded vertebrates  Pisces (Fishes)
597.9                        *Reptilia (Reptiles)
597.948-597.96                Squamata (Scaly reptiles)
597.95                        *Sauria (Lizards)
597.955                        *Agamidae
```

Figure 1.6.   Excerpt from the Dewey Decimal Classification. Source:
http://www.oclc.org/dewey/resources/tutorial/.

Faceted classifications are another interesting type of classification systems (Broughton, 2002; Stock & Stock, 2008). A faceted classification is not one continuous classification system but comprises several sub-classifications: the *facets*. Facets should represent the fundamental categories of a domain of interest.

The idea is to enable the *combination* of a fixed set of simple basic concepts to produce a multitude of complex concepts. In this way, it is not necessary to decide on one hierarchical system for the entire domain, but only to structure the concepts within one category or facet. Consider the following example, provided by Broughton (2006; see also Stock & Stock, 2008): an excerpt from a hierarchical classification of the simple domain of "socks".

Grey socks
    Grey wool socks
        Grey wool work socks
            Grey wool hiking socks
                Grey wool ankle socks for hiking
                Grey wool knee socks for hiking
                    Grey spotted wool knee socks for hiking

---

[15]   Yahoo! Directory: http://search.yahoo.com/dir.
[16]   Open Directory Project: http://www.dmoz.org.

As this pre-combined approach is rather complicated and would lead to much overhead in the classification system (i.e. one would certainly end up with classes that are never used); one might rather identify the basic categories of the domain and their subclasses (for this purpose, the single facets have to be disjoint; a concept cannot be part of more than one facet). This could look like the following faceted scheme proposed by Broughton (Broughton, 2004; Broughton, 2006):

Colour	Pattern	Material	Function	Length
Black	Plain	Wool	Work	Ankle
Grey	Striped	Polyester	Evening	Calf
Brown	Spotted	Cotton	Football	Knee
Green	Hooped	Silk	Hiking	
Blue	Checkered	Nylon	Protective	
Red	Novelty	Latex		

By combining these facets we may then represent things like 'blue striped cotton socks for football'. The individual complex concepts are only created via combination at the time they are needed (and not in advance within a complete hierarchy). This principle is called post-coordination (Bertram, 2005; Stock & Stock, 2008). The *citation order* defines the order in which the elements of different facets have to be arranged, which is needed for the construction of notations based on facet combinations. Specific symbols may be used to separate the faceted elements from each other within notations.

The first (and still prevalent) example of a faceted classification system is the Colon Classification (CC) (Ranganathan, 1965; Ranganathan 1987[1933]). Other examples are the Bliss Bibliographic Classification, 2nd Edition (BC2) (Mills & Broughton, 1977) and the Classification of Library and Information Science (Daniel & Mills, 1975). The faceted approach to knowledge organization has also been adopted by other KOS.

Some classifications partly make use of additional facets, without relying entirely on this combinatory approach (Stock & Stock, 2008). They contain additional tables with aspects that often co-occur with other concepts. For example, the DDC has auxiliary tables for geographical information that can be attached to the concepts from the main thematic classification.

Thesaurus

The last major type of classical knowledge organization system is the thesaurus (Aitchison, Gilchrist & Bawden, 2000; Foskett, 1981; Lancaster, 1986, Stock & Stock, 2008; Taylor, 1999). While in some contexts as well as in colloquial language the term 'thesaurus' denotes a lexicon of synonyms, in the field of knowledge representation it describes a complex controlled vocabulary. Thesauri in the latter sense are standardized by national as well as international norms (BS 5723:1987; ISO 2788:1986; DIN 1463/1:1987). They pay a lot of attention to the collection of synonyms, but also use hierarchical concept structures and associative relations between related terms to represent domain knowledge. Aitchison, Gilchrist and Bawden (2000) define a thesaurus as

> "[…] a vocabulary of controlled indexing language, formally organized so that a priori relationships between concepts are made explicit, to be used in information retrieval systems, ranging from card catalogue to the Internet." (Aitchison, Gilchrist & Bawden, 2000)

Concepts in thesauri are typically not supported by complete definitions (as in a dictionary). Yet thesauri may contain (short) definitions for concepts – and more and more thesauri do make use of this feature. Aitchison, Gilchrist and Bawden (2000) point out:

> "Definitions tend to be necessary most frequently in social science and humanities thesauri, to clarify imprecise terminology, which occurs more often in these subject areas." (Aitchison, Gilchrist & Bawden, 2000)

Furthermore, *scope notes* are used in thesauri to indicate restrictions on meaning or the range of concepts, to give instructions to indexers, to provide examples for usage or to document the term history (Aitchison, Gilchrist & Bawden, 2000).

For the purpose of vocabulary control, most thesauri work with *preferred terms* in a set of synonyms. These preferred terms are sometimes called *descriptors*. Descriptors are exclusively used for indexing and retrieval; all their synonyms (the *non-preferred terms*) are only used as pointers to the preferred terms. In thesauri that do not make use of preferred terms, all synonyms are regarded as equal and may be used for indexing.

The typical way of displaying a thesaurus is in the form of an alphabetical list of all terms[17], with additional information on concept interrelations and usage: the *term records*. A prototypical entry for a preferred term in the alphabetical display of term records has the following form:

PREFERRED TERM
   SN "Scope Note"
   D   "Definition"
   UF "Used For": References to equivalent non-preferred terms.
   BT "Broader Term": References to broader terms.
   NT "Narrower Term": References to narrower terms.
   RT "Related Term": References to related terms.

An entry for a non-preferred term only contains the pointer to the respective preferred terms, e.g.:

Non-preferred term
   USE PREFERRED TERM

---

[17] Another frequently chosen display option is an additional hierarchical list of terms. For additional display approaches see Aitchison, Gilchrist & Bawden (2000).

An example for a preferred term ('deprived families') and non-preferred term ('underprivileged families') may look like this (Aitchison, Gilchrist & Bawden, 2000):

DEPRIVED FAMILIES
SN	Socially disadvantaged and underprivileged
UF	Underprivileged families
BT	Families
NT	Homeless families
	One parent families
RT	Deprivation

Underprivileged families
USE	DEPRIVED FAMILIES

Figure 1.7 shows some more examples taken from the alphabetical term records in the ASIS&T Thesaurus of Information Science, Technology and Librarianship (Redmond-Neal & Hlava, 2005).

The term records may also contain more detailed information. For example, the quality of broader and narrower terms may be specified according to partitive and generic hierarchical structures (e.g. BTP = broader term partitive, BTG = broader term generic). A list of these abbreviations used in term records in English and German thesauri is provided by Stock and Stock (2008).

Types of thesauri are mainly distinguished based on the depicted domain. Faceted approaches to thesauri are also available but rather rare (Aitchison, Gomersall & Ireland, 1969; Spiteri, 1999; Stock & Stock, 2008). Furthermore, we may consider multilingual thesauri, for which specific guidelines have been developed (e.g. ISO 5964:1985).

The main problems in providing multilingual thesauri are due to the fact that concepts often cannot be translated exactly. Thus terms in two languages may not have one hundred per cent overlapping meanings. A prominent example is the German term 'Wissenschaft' which has a broader meaning than the English 'science'.

A common method for establishing multilingual thesauri is to choose one *source language* that serves as a starting point and provides the basis for the translations, and one or more *target languages* that are mapped to the first (Aitchison, Gilchrist & Bawden, 2000). For the connection of several languages, one source thesaurus is mostly used as standard reference:

> "In practice, and more happily in some systems than in others, the target thesauri are not directly related to each other, leaving the source thesaurus in the hub position of a radial network." (Aitchison, Gilchrist & Bawden, 2000)

information entropy (cont.)
  information.
BT (information and data processes)
RT information theory

information exchange
USE information transfer

information exchange formats
USE interchange formats

information explosion
UF publication explosion
BT (information and data processes)
RT information overload
  publishing

information extraction
USE data mining

information filtering
UF filtering, information
BT information operations
NT collaborative filtering
  content filtering
RT boundary spanners
  censorship
  gatekeepers
  information overload
  invisible colleges
  SDI services
  social networking

information flow
SN *Passive and unintentional spread of
  information; contrast with "information
  dissemination."*
BT (information and data processes)
NT cross disciplinary fertilization
  transborder data flow
RT boundary spanners
  gatekeepers
  information channels
  information dissemination
  information resources management
  information transfer
  interdisciplinarity
  invisible colleges
  social networking

information gathering
USE information retrieval

information harvesting
USE knowledge discovery

information highway
USE telecommunications networks

information industry
BT (product and service providers)
NT online industry
RT database producers
  information brokers
  information infrastructure
  information sector
  information utilities
  publishers
  search services
  telecommunications industry

information infrastructure
BT socioeconomic aspects
RT abstracting and indexing service bureaus
  database producers
  information industry
  information utilities
  libraries
  publishers
  search services

information life cycle
BT (information and data processes)
RT aging of materials
  obsolescence

information literacy
UF information skills
BT literacy
RT bibliographic instruction
  computer literacy
  information and reference skills
  information needs
  information use
  user training

information management
USE information resources management

information mapping
SN *Use for, e.g., mapping of queries to
  documents, or of one vocabulary to another*
UF metamapping
  subject switching
BT information operations
RT controlled vocabularies
  cross matching
  searching
  switching languages

information models
BT analytic models

Figure 1.7.   Excerpt from the ASIS&T Thesaurus of Information Science, Technology and
Librarianship. Source: Redmond-Neal & Hlava, 2005.

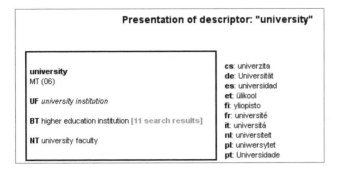

Figure 1.8. Excerpt from TESE: descriptor "university" with translations for ten
languages. Source: http://eacea.ec.europa.eu/portal/page/portal/Eurydice/TESE
Descriptor?descriptorId =2700.

> **Bilingualism**
> MT 3.30 Linguistics
> FR Bilinguisme
> SP Bilingüismo
> BT1 Language policy
> NT1 Multilingualism
> RT Biculturalism
> RT Foreign languages
> RT Intercultural communication
> RT Second language instruction
> RT Sociolinguistics

Figure 1.9. Term record for 'Bilingualism' in the UNESCO Thesaurus with translations
for French (FR) and Spanish (SP). Source: http://www2.ulcc.ac.uk/unesco/
terms/list13.htm.

The Eurydice Information Network on Education in Europe is currently developing the Thesaurus for Education Systems in Europe[18] (TESE) (partly based on existing thesauri). It is intended to be published in 14 languages, but currently descriptors are translated to ten European languages (Figure 1.8). Another important
example is the UNESCO Thesaurus[19] (UNESCO, 1995), which covers the topics
of education, science, culture, social and human sciences, information and communication, politics, law and economics. It includes French (FR) and Spanish (SP)
equivalents of English preferred terms (Figure 1.9).

---

[18]   Thesaurus for Education Systems in Europe (TESE):
      http://eacea.ec.europa.eu/portal/page/portal/Eurydice/TESEHome.
[19]   UNESCO Thesaurus: http://www2.ulcc.ac.uk/unesco/.

1.1.3 Knowledge Organization Systems in Practice

As we have seen, classical knowledge organization systems are developed for the practical aim of indexing certain document collections for retrieval purposes. Others also focus on the standardization of domain representations, e.g. for organizational or statistical purposes – and thus constitute a shared point of view on this domain. Let us have a look at some of the most important fields of application.

Library Catalogs and Publication Databases
Library catalogs are the traditional application area of classification schemes. We have already seen some universal classifications used in library indexing. Mitchell (2000) points out: "Today, the Dewey Decimal Classification is the world's most widely used library classification scheme."

While physical libraries require a knowledge organization system which considers the actual placement of books in the library shelves, this is not needed for digital publication databases. Most professional information providers focus on domain specific databases. These, in return, require specialized, domain specific KOS.

```
 1. ⊞ Anatomy [A]
 2. ⊟ Organisms [B]
        o Eukaryota [B01]  +
        o Archaea [B02]  +
        o Bacteria [B03]  +
        o Viruses [B04]  +
        o Organism Forms [B05]  +
 3. ⊞ Diseases [C]
 4. ⊞ Chemicals and Drugs [D]
 5. ⊞ Analytical, Diagnostic and Therapeutic Techniques and Equipment [E]
 6. ⊞ Psychiatry and Psychology [F]
 7. ⊞ Phenomena and Processes [G]
 8. ⊞ Disciplines and Occupations [H]
 9. ⊞ Anthropology, Education, Sociology and Social Phenomena [I]
10. ⊞ Technology, Industry, Agriculture [J]
11. ⊞ Humanities [K]
12. ⊞ Information Science [L]
13. ⊞ Named Groups [M]
14. ⊞ Health Care [N]
15. ⊞ Publication Characteristics [V]
16. ⊞ Geographicals [Z]
```

Figure 1.10. Highest hierarchical level of MeSH 2008 with subclasses for one of the top classes. Source: http://www.nlm.nih.gov/mesh/2010/mesh_browser/ MeSHtree.B.html.

The Medical Subjects Headings[20] (MeSH) are a *domain specific* thesaurus used for document indexing (Gaus, 2005). MeSH is produced and maintained by the National Library of Medicine, Bethesda, Maryland, USA. It has reached a considerable degree of popularity due to it being used for the reference database MEDLINE[21]. MeSH registers approximately 23.000 *headings* (which correspond to descriptors). The hierarchical structure starts with 16 top categories (Figure 1.10). The system is polyhierarchic, which means that every term may belong to more than one superordinate concept (Figure 1.11).

Figure 1.11. Polyhierarchy in MeSH. Source: http://www.nlm.nih.gov/cgi/mesh/
2008/MB_cgi.

MeSH headings may further be combined with qualifiers. Qualifiers are used to render the headings more precisely and to capture certain document features. Examples for MeSH qualifiers are 'Abnormalities' or 'Administration & Dosage'. Every qualifier can only be used in combination with a given division from the

---

[20]   Medical Subjects Headings (MeSH): http://www.nlm.nih.gov/mesh.
[21]   MEDLINE, accessible via PubMed: http://www.ncbi.nlm.nih.gov/sites/entrez.

whole thesaurus. This also imposes a certain form of implicit structure on concept interrelations.

Chapter	Blocks	Title
I	A00–B99	Certain infectious and parasitic diseases
II	C00–D48	Neoplasms
III	D50–D89	Diseases of the blood and blood-forming organs and certain disorders involving the immune mechanism
IV	E00–E90	Endocrine, nutritional and metabolic diseases
V	F00–F99	Mental and behavioural disorders
VI	G00–G99	Diseases of the nervous system
VII	H00–H59	Diseases of the eye and adnexa
VIII	H60–H95	Diseases of the ear and mastoid process
IX	I00–I99	Diseases of the circulatory system
X	J00–J99	Diseases of the respiratory system
XI	K00–K93	Diseases of the digestive system
XII	L00–L99	Diseases of the skin and subcutaneous tissue
XIII	M00–M99	Diseases of the musculoskeletal system and connective tissue
XIV	N00–N99	Diseases of the genitourinary system
XV	O00–O99	Pregnancy, childbirth and the puerperium
XVI	P00–P96	Certain conditions originating in the perinatal period
XVII	Q00–Q99	Congenital malformations, deformations and chromosomal abnormalities
XVIII	R00–R99	Symptoms, signs and abnormal clinical and laboratory findings, not elsewhere classified
XIX	S00–T98	Injury, poisoning and certain other consequences of external causes
XX	V01–Y98	External causes of morbidity and mortality
XXI	Z00–Z99	Factors influencing health status and contact with health services
XXII	U00–U99	Codes for special purposes

ICD
Version 2007

Figure 1.12. The highest hierarchical level of the ICD-10. Source: http://www.who.int/ classifications/apps/icd/icd10online/.

Health Care
Some classifications have been established in the sectors of medicine and public health service. They are used as standardized representations to enable comparability for health statistics (e.g. causes of death) or for the use in administrative fields (e.g. accounting in hospitals) (Stock & Stock, 2008). The World Health Organization oversees the following classifications for diseases, health and disability, and health interventions (Gaus, 2005):

- International Classification of Diseases (ICD, currently the tenth version: ICD-10[22]): It classifies diseases and other health problems and is used in different types of health records, e.g. death certificates. It starts with 22 classes on the highest level (called chapters, Figure 1.12) and currently contains around 64,000 classes. It provides unitary notations for diseases, like J32.2 for 'chronic frontal sinusitis' or S62.7 for 'multiple fractures of fingers', which are often enriched with synonyms and directions for appropriate usage. ICD-10 is available in six official languages of WHO (Arabic, Chinese, Eng-

---

[22]   International Classification of Diseases (ICD):
http://www.who.int/classifications/icd/en/.

lish, French, Russian and Spanish) as well as in 36 other languages. According to Gaus (2005) it is the most intensively used KOS in the world.

- International Classification of Health Interventions[23] (ICHI, formerly International Classification of Procedures in Medicine, ICPM): This classification covers medical interventions such as surgeries, therapies and diagnostics. It provides a standardized tool for reporting and analyzing the distribution and evolution of health interventions for statistical purposes.
- International Classification of Functioning, Disability and Health[24] (ICF): The ICF classifies the domain of health as described from a body, individual and societal perspective. For this purpose it contains two lists: a list of body functions and structure, and a list of domains of activity and participation. Additionally, the ICF includes a list of environmental factors.
- The Diagnosis Related Groups (DRG): The DRG is a classification system developed for classifying hospital patients. It was created in the early 1980s for statistical purposes and to compare hospital costs for different types of patients. The DRG consists of approximately 500 classes (called *groups*). Based on the US version, translations have been created for use in other countries (e.g. the German G-DRG). Furthermore the DRG has provided the basis for more specific classification systems in health care politics. The DRG is updated yearly. In 2007 major changes where performed for the 25th version of DRG, including the re-sequencing of groups. As of October 1, 2008 the 26th version is available with only minor changes.
- TNM Classification of Malignant Tumours[25] (TNM) (Sobin & Wittekind, 2002): The TNM is a faceted classification for classifying the state of cancer in a patient's body. Its development began in the early 1940s and it has been constantly updated since, in accordance with progress in the field of medicine. Since 1993, the *TNM Supplement* is available; a set of rules that should promote the uniform use of the TNM and lists practical examples. The TNM aims at providing a "common language" for oncologists all over the world in comparing their clinical material and in assessing the result of a treatment. The International Union against Cancer (UICC) therefore works in close cooperation with national and international organizations in order to maintain and promote the TNM.

The abbreviation TNM stands for the three different categories that are needed for cancer staging: T stands for 'primary Tumor' and is used to describe the size of the tumor (Figure 1.13); N stands for 'regional lymph Nodes' and classifies those regional lymph nodes which are involved in the disease to describe the absence or presence of regional lymph metastasis; and

---

[23] International Classification of Health Interventions (ICHI):
http://www.who.int/classifications/ichi/en/.

[24] International Classification of Functioning Disabilty and Health (ICF):
http://www.who.int/classifications/icf/en/.

[25] TNM Classification of Malignant Tumours: http://www.uicc.org/tnm.

M stands for 'distant Metastasis' and includes those regions where metastasis may appear to describe the absence or presence of distant metastasis.

One distinguishes between clinical classifications (pre-treatment, cTNM) and pathological classifications (post-surgical, pTNM). Other facets of describing tumors can be added, for example the 'histopathological Grading' (G), 'Lymphatic Invasion' (L), 'Venous Invasion' (V), and the 'Certainty Factor' (C-facor, C). The TNM includes mappings to ICD.

T – Primary Tumour
>
>| | |
>|---|---|
>| TX | Primary tumour cannot be assessed |
>| T0 | No evidence of primary tumor |
>| Tis | Carcinoma in situ |
>| T1, T2, T3, T4 | Increasing size and/or local extent of the primary |

tumor

Figure 1.3. General definitions for classifying primary tumours with TNM. Source: Sobin & Wittekind, 2002.

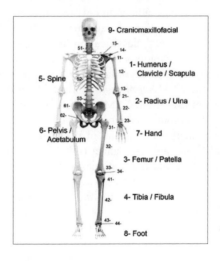

Figure 1.14. AO Classification of Fractures: Classification of body regions. Source: www.aofoundation.org.

- Müller AO Classification of Long Bone Fractures (AO Classification) (Murphy & Leu, 2000): The AO Classification is developed by the AO Foundation[26], an organization led by an international group of surgeons who specialize in the treatment of trauma and disorders of the musculoskeletal system. They also provide additional classifications for cranio-maxillofacial fractures (CMF classification), scapula fractures, and spinal fractures.

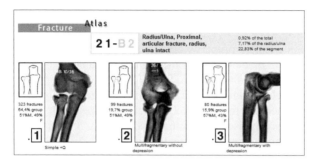

Figure 1.15. AO Classification: examples for fractures 21-B2.1 to 21-B2.3. Source: Fundación Maurice E. Müller, Fracture Atlas, from http://www.muller foundation.org/atlas/main/21/b2.htm.

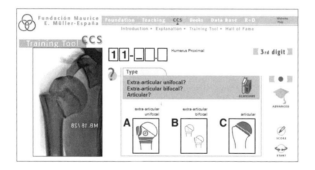

Figure 1.16. AO Classification Training Game. Source: http://www.muller foundation.org/ccs/tool/game.php.

The AO longbone fracture classification system describes the localization and morphology of fractures. Each type of fracture is represented by a five digit notation. The first digit is a number from 1 to 9, representing the body region (Figure 1.14). Each region is again divided into sections, numbered 1 to 3 (sometimes 4), which make up the second digit. The last three digits classify the type of fracture and the severity (always with three subtypes).

---

[26] AO Foundation: http://www.aofoundation.org.

Figure 1.15 shows examples of fractures classified 21-B2.1 to 21-B2.3. The Maurice E. Müller Foundation also provides a training game including about 1,000 cases to help young health professionals improve their fracture diagnosing skills (Figure 1.16).

Intellectual Property

In the field of intellectual property, classifications are used for indexing technical (patents and utility models) and non-technical documents (trademarks and designs) (Stock & Stock, 2006; Stock & Stock, 2008).

The following classifications for international usage in the intellectual property field are maintained by the World Intellectual Property Organization (WIPO). They are all intensively used on international levels and are supported by official agreements between international patent offices.

- International Patent Classification[27] (IPC) (IPC, 2005): The IPC is used for the thematic classification of patents and utility models (Figure 1.5, above). The current IPC (2009 edition) lists approximately 70,000 classes. The WIPO provides an English and a French version; translations into other languages are available from certain national patent offices.

  Based on the Strasbourg Agreement from 1971, international patent offices consistently classify patent literature according to the International Patent Classification. Commercial database producers for legal and technical information (like Derwent[28] and Questel[29]) have also adopted this standard. Figure 1.17 shows an excerpt from a US patent including the IPC number A63D 15/00 for 'Billiards; Billiard tables; Pocket Billiards'.

- Nice Classification[30] (International Classification of Goods and Services for the Purposes of the Registration of Marks under the Nice Agreement) (Nice Classification, 2007): The Nice Classification classifies goods and services for the purpose of registering trademarks and service marks. A trademark may be registered for one or more Nice classes (and thus for one or more product sectors). Thus the same product names may exist in parallel if they have been registered for different Nice classes.

  On the top level, the Nice Classification comprises 34 classes of goods (e.g. class 15: Musical Instruments) and 11 classes of services (e.g. class 35: Advertising; Business Management; Business Administration; Office Functions).

- Vienna Classification[31] (International Classification of the Figurative Elements of Marks under the Vienna Agreement) (Vienna Classification, 2008): Trademarks often consist of or contain figurative elements. To enable the

---

[27]   International Patent Classification (IPC): http://www.wipo.int/classifications/ipc/en/.
[28]   Derwent: http://www.derwent.co.uk.
[29]   Questel: http://www.questel.com.
[30]   Nice Classification: http://www.wipo.int/classifications/nice/en/index.html.
[31]   Vienna Classification: http://www.wipo.int/classifications/vienna/en/.

unified description of such figurative elements and thus the retrieval of these visual trademarks, the Vienna Classification is used. An exemplary class hierarchy is:

Category 21   Games, toys, sporting articles, roundabouts
  21.3   Sporting articles, roundabouts
    21.3.1   Footballs and other balls, shuttlecocks

- Locarno Classification[32] (Locarno Classification, 2004): The Locarno Classification provides classes of goods and products. Trademark offices use these classes for registering industrial designs (by naming the classes into which the goods incorporating the designs belong). The use of the Locarno Classification by national offices has the advantage of filing industrial designs with reference to a single classification system.

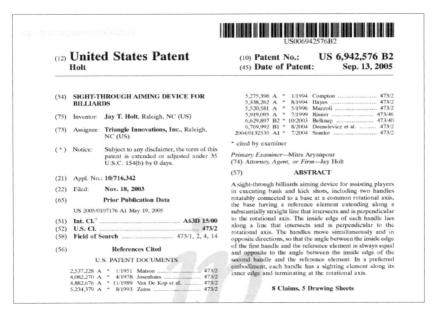

Figure 1.17. Excerpt from a US Patent (Patent Nr. 6942576), including notations from the IPC (51) and USPC (52).

For patent indexing, some individual other classifications are used in addition to the IPC. The European Patent Office uses the European Classification (ECLA), which provides a downward expansion of the IPC (Dickens, 1994). The United States Patent and Trademark Office (USPTO) also uses its own classification system; the US Patent Office Classification System (USPC). The USPTO has also es-

---

[32] Locarno Classification: http://www.wipo.int/classifications/locarno/en/.

tablished mapping tables that point from a class in the USPC to a comparable class in the IPC. The exemplary patent in Figure 1.17 includes both an IPC class and the USPC class 473/2 (class 473: 'Games using tangible projectile; 1. Billiards or pool; 2. Practice device or device to aid in aiming cue or cue ball during shots (e.g. to assist in bank shots, etc.)').

Economics
In the field of economics, several classification systems exist parallely in order to classify industrial sectors or products (Krobath, 2004; Stock & Stock, 2008). Some are provided by national or international institutions, others by commercial information hosts.

For the classification of industrial sectors, the most important models are NACE[33] (Nomenclature general des activités économiques dans les Communautés Européennes) and NAICS[34] (North American Industry Classification System). NACE is maintained and used by the European Union and its member states; NAICS is used for official statistics in North America. Yet, the NAICS' predecessor, the Standard Industrial Classification[35] (SIC), is also still widely used, particularly by commercial information providers. SIC was officially replaced by NAICS in 1997, as it was based on the structure of the USA as an industrial society in the 1930s and had thus become too out of date to be restructured. In its 2007 version, NAICS consists of the following 20 top level classes:

11	Agriculture, Forestry, Fishing, and Hunting
21	Mining, Quarrying, and Oil and Gas Extraction
22	Utilities
23	Construction
31-33	Manufacturing
42	Wholesale Trade
44-45	Retail Trade
48-49	Transportation and Warehousing
51	Information
52	Finance and Insurance
53	Real Estate and Rental and Leasing
54	Professional, Scientific, and Technical Services
55	Management of Companies and Enterprises
56	Administrative and Support and Waste Management and Remediation Services

---

[33] NACE : http://ec.europa.eu/eurostat/ramon/index.cfm?TargetUrl=DSP_PUB_WELC.
[34] NAICS : http://www.census.gov/epcd/www/naics.html.
[35] Standard Industrial Classification (SIC): http://www.census.gov/epcd/www/sic.html.

61	Educational Services
62	Health Care and Social Assistance
71	Arts, Entertainment, and Recreation
72	Accommodation and Food Services
81	Other Services (except Public Administration)
92	Public Administration

Figure 1.18 shows an excerpt from the subclasses of the information sector.

2007 NAICS Code	2007 NAICS Title
51	Information
511	Publishing Industries (except Internet)
5111	Newspaper, Periodical, Book, and Directory Publishers
51111	Newspaper Publishers
511110	Newspaper Publishers
51112	Periodical Publishers
511120	Periodical Publishers
51113	Book Publishers
511130	Book Publishers
51114	Directory and Mailing List Publishers
511140	Directory and Mailing List Publishers
51119	Other Publishers
511191	Greeting Card Publishers
511199	All Other Publishers
5112	Software Publishers
51121	Software Publishers

Figure 1.18. Excerpt from NAICS. Source: http://www.census.gov/naics/
2007/NAICOD07.HTM.

Industry classifications can be enriched with product classifications. Currently, additional representations of product groups are being developed for the NAICS in the North American Product Classification System[36] (NAPCS). So far it is available for products of service industries (sectors 51-81); an excerpt of product classes with references to the NAICS industries producing them (separated by countries) is depicted in Figure 1.19. NAPCS also contains cross-references to the

---

[36]   North American Product Classification System (NAPCS):
http://www.census.gov/eos/www/napcs/napcs.htm.

United Nations Central Product Classification[37], the product classification system hosted by the United Nations Statistics Division.

1	2	3	4	5	6	7	8		9
Industry Subject Area	Working Group Code	Tri-lateral Detail	National Product Detail				United States		NAICS Industries Producing the Product
			Can	Méx	US	Title	Definition		
51111	1					Newspapers	Publications issued daily, weekly, or at other regular intervals consisting mainly of current news together with editorials, features, correspondence and other information of current public interest. A considerable amount of space is devoted generally to photographs and advertisements. Includes: • newspapers published in print, online, or on electronic and other media. • subscription and single copy sales. Excludes: • published archives of newspapers. • providing back issues of newspapers is in product 3.9, Archive materials.		511110 511120 511130 516110
51111	1.1					General newspapers	Newspapers consisting of multiple topics with the intent of appealing to a broad audience. Includes: • newspapers published in print, online, or on electronic and other media. • community newspapers. • subscription and single copy sales. Excludes: • published archives of newspapers. • providing back issues of newspapers is in product 3.9, Archive materials.		511110 511120 511130 516110
51111	1.1.1					General newspapers, daily	Newspapers published at least four times a week consisting of multiple topics with the intent of appealing to a broad audience. Includes: • newspapers published in print, online, or on electronic and other media. • community newspapers. • subscription and single copy sales. Excludes: • published archives of newspapers. • providing back issues of newspapers is in product 3.9, Archive materials.		511110 511120 511130 516110

Figure 1.19. Excerpt from NAPCS. Source: http://www.census.gov/eos/www/napcs /napcstable.html.

The information producer Dun & Bradstreet (a provider of business records) has developed a product classification based on SIC: the D&B-SIC. They have multiplied the number of classes by more than 15 in order to enable detailed product representation.

Together with the United Nations Development Programme (UNDP), Dun & Bradstreet also developed the United Nations Standard Products and Services Codes[38] (UNSPSC); a classification of goods and services that can provide a unified set of descriptions for e-commerce.

---

[37]   United Nations Central Product Classification (CPC): http://unstats.un.org/unsd/cr/registry/regcst.asp?Cl=3.
[38]   United Nations Standard Products and Services Codes (UNSPSC): http://www.unspsc.org.

XX <u>Segment</u>
The logical aggregation of families for analytical purposes

    XX <u>Family</u>
    A commonly recognized group of inter-related commodity categories

        XX <u>Class</u>
        A group of commodities sharing common characteristics

            XX <u>Commodity</u>
            A group of substitutable products or
            services

                XX <u>Business Function</u>
                The function performed
                by an organization in
                support of the
                commodity

Figure 1.20. The five levels of UNSPSC. Source: http://www.unspsc.org/FAQs.asp#
        WhatistheUNSPC.

The classification consists of five levels (Figure 1.20), where the fifth level is different in function as it does not belong to the classification hierarchy, indicating instead the business function of a supplier (e.g. rental/lease, wholesale/retail). UNSPSC version 11.0501 registers more than 21,000 products and services identified by unique notations (Figure 1.21 shows an exemplary excerpt of UNSPSC). New versions are released regularly.

Hierarchy	Category Number	Name
Segment	44	Office Equipment and Accessories and Supplies
Family	44 12	Office supplies
Class	44 12 19	Ink and lead refills
Commodity	44 12 19 04	Ink refills

"Ink refills" - UNSPSC classification 44-12-19-04

Figure 1.21. Excerpt from UNSPSC. Source: UNSPSC 11.0501 Documentation.

Geography
Geographical information has also been subject to classification, resulting in KOS both from official statistical institutions and from commercial information producers.

The Nomenclature des unités territoriales statistiques[39] (NUTS) is produced by the Statistical Office of the European Communities (Eurostat). According to its Website[40], NUTS is used as a basis

- "for the collection, development and harmonization of Community regional statistics,"
- "for the socio-economic analyses of the regions,"
- and "for the framing of Community regional policies."

Code	Country	Level 1	Level 2	Level 3
BE	BELGIQUE-BELGIË			
BE1		RÉGION DE BRUXELLES-CAPITALE / BRUSSELS HOOFDSTEDELIJK GEWEST		
BE10			Région de Bruxelles-Capitale / Brussels Hoofdstedelijk Gewest	
BE100				Arr. de Bruxelles-Capitale / Arr. van Brussel-Hoofdstad
BE2		VLAAMS GEWEST		
BE21			Prov. Antwerpen	
BE211				Arr. Antwerpen
BE212				Arr. Mechelen
BE213				Arr. Turnhout
BE22			Prov. Limburg (B)	
BE221				Arr. Hasselt
BE222				Arr. Maaseik
BE223				Arr. Tongeren

Figure 1.22. Excerpt from NUTS. Source: http://ec.europa.eu/eurostat/ramon/ nuts/codelist_en.cfm?list=nuts.

NUTS originally treated the Member States of the European Union, but has been enriched with regional data on the candidate countries awaiting accession to the EU, the other European Economic Area (EEA) countries and Switzerland (in agreement with the countries concerned). Figure 1.22 shows an exemplary excerpt from NUTS. Countries are subdivided into regions, which again are split into sub-regions.

---

[39]   Nomenclature des unités territoriales statistiques (NUTS): http://ec.europa.eu/eurostat/ramon/nuts/splash_regions.html.

[40]   http://ec.europa.eu/eurostat/ramon/nuts/application_regions_en.html.

Figure 1.23. Excerpt from Gale CC for formulating queries in the industry database
PROMT. Source: Gale Group Promt Plus – Practice File (TRPT).

The Gale Group Country Codes (GaleCC, CC) are widely used in professional information services. In contrast to NUTS, they comprise world regions, confederations and countries. Single countries, apart from the U.S.A., are not subdivided into smaller geographical units. Figure 1.23 shows part of the search interface for a practice file of the industry database PROMT[41]: geographical regions can be selected from the GaleCC for query formulation. Figure 1.24 shows a search result within the same database, retrieved in a search by specifying the region to 'Paraguay'.

---

41 Gale Group PROMT, hosted by DIALOG:
http://library.dialog.com/bluesheets/html/bl0016.html.

```
☑ Dokument 10 von 444
GALE GROUP PROMT PLUS - Practice File (TRPT)

Accession number & update
       75020565 20010526.
Title
       nevirapine Boehringer Ingelheim marketed, Paraguay.
Source
       R & D Focus Drug News, 28 May 2001, p. NA, Publisher: IMS World Publications Ltd.
       ISSN: 1350-1135.
Text
       Boehringer Ingelheim's nevirapine (VIRAMUNE), a non-nucleoside HIV-1 reverse transcriptase inhibitor, has
       treatment of HIV infection.
       nevirapine, BIRG 587, VIRAMUNE, J5C, HIV Antivirals,
       Boehringer Ingelheim, marketed, Paraguay.
       THIS IS THE FULL TEXT: COPYRIGHT 2001 IMS World Publications Ltd.
Company
       Boehringer-Ingelheim-Group.
Classification codes
       US NAICS Codes:
       325412 Pharmaceutical-Preparation-Manufacturing
       US SIC Codes:
       2834 Pharmaceutical-preparations.
Product names and codes
       Antiinfective-Preparations-NEC (P2834890).
Event names and codes
       Product-introduction (E336).
Country names and codes
       Paraguay (C3PARA).
Special features
       COMPANY
```

Figure 1.24. Search result including the GaleCC code for Paraguay. Source: Gale Group
        Promt Plus – Practice File (TRPT).

Media Archives and Museums

Large document collections are also accumulating in most media companies, e.g.
editorial offices of newspapers, television and radio stations (Lu, 2001; Markkula
& Sormunen, 2000; Ornager, 1995), as well as in museums or other cultural heri-
tage institutions (Baca, 2002).

   The indexing of images, sound files, videos and other multimedia objects requires some different reflections compared to purely textual documents, e.g. regarding media-specific characteristics such as perspective, color and production
techniques, or regarding the interpretation of symbols or concerning the identification of the individuals and objects which are depicted. Thus, multimedia indexing
(and retrieval) has become established as an additional research field (Byrd &
Crawford, 2002; Lancaster, 2003), which also focuses more intensively on ways
for automating (in the sense of content-based retrieval, see footnote 2) and for
richer semantics in indexing (as will be discussed later). Yet so far, the results are
not sufficient.

   Greenberg (2001) reviews different metadata schemes applicable to image collections. One example of a classification system developed and used for image
collections in museums is Iconclass[42] (Hourihane, 2002). It is used by art histori-
ans, researchers and curators to examine and classify the subjects of different

---

42   Iconclass: http://www.iconclass.nl/.

types of images (e.g. paintings, drawings, photographs). Various institutions across the world use Iconclass to describe and classify their collections in a standardized manner. Iconclass consists of 28,000 hierarchically ordered classes divided into ten main divisions (Figure 1.25).

The 10 main categories - click one to start browsing and searching

0 · Abstract, Non-representational Art
1 · Religion and Magic
2 · Nature
3 · Human Being, Man in General
4 · Society, Civilization, Culture
5 · Abstract Ideas and Concepts
6 · History
7 · Bible
8 · Literature
9 · Classical Mythology and Ancient History

Figure 1.25. The ten main categories of the Iconclass classification. Source: http://www.iconclass.org/help/outline.

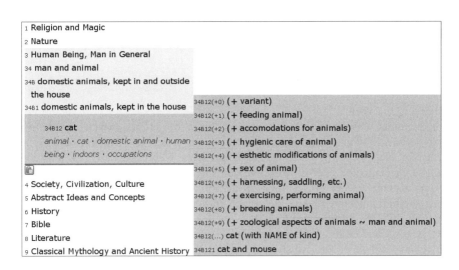

Figure 1.26. Excerpt from the Iconclass hierarchy. Source: http://www.iconclass.org /rkd/34B12/.

Each class is identified by a notation. From the Iconclass Libertas Browser[43], the concepts can directly be used for retrieval in the collections of the Medieval Illuminated Manuscripts Database (Koninklijke Bibliotheek, Den Haag), the National Gallery, London, the ARTCYCLOPEDIA, and the Getty Museum. Figure 1.26 shows the hierarchy of the image motif 'human with cat'; Figure 1.27 shows how each concept is illustrated with corresponding images, a feature that helps browsing the Iconclass classification.

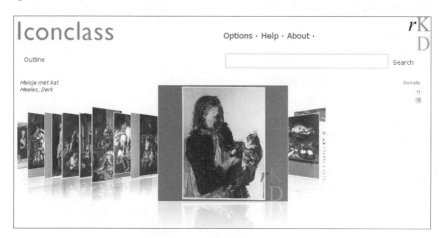

Figure 1.27. Exemplary images illustrating the class 34B12. Source: http://www.iconclass. org /rkd/34B12/

Indexing the Web

The examples described so far all address closed information systems or application scenarios with a limited scope and a certain degree of shared underlying structure. None of this is given for the World Wide Web in general. The Web contains enormous (and ever growing) amounts of information from all possible domains of interest. The presentation of this information is completely heterogeneous and non-uniform; in fact, heterogeneity can be found on different levels – starting with the various file formats, varieties in character coding and different languages – and ending with entirely individual site structures. There are no such things as field schemata and shared terminologies for the whole Web. While the mere size of the Web makes intellectual indexing impossible, its heterogeneity is the main obstacle for automatic approaches. Furthermore, internet contents are in constant development – and are thus permanently changing their form and contents. On the other hand, all this diversity requires particularly sophisticated methods for search and navigation in order to overcome information overload. Many

---

[43]   Iconclass Libertas Browser: http://www.iconclass.nl/libertas/ic?style=index.xsl.

postulate the organization of Web contents in the form of analytical indexes or classifications – all while pointing out the obstacles and apparently insurmountable difficulties (Casey, 1999; Lancaster, 2003; Safari, 2004; Trippe, 2001).

Arts & Humanities	News & Media
Photography, History, Literature, Performing Arts...	Newspapers, TV, Radio...
Business & Economy	**Recreation & Sports**
Products, Shopping, B2B, Finance, Jobs...	Sports, Travel, Autos, Outdoors...
Computers & Internet	**Reference**
Internet, WWW, Software, Games...	Phone Numbers, Dictionaries, Quotations...
Education	**Regional**
College and University, K-12...	Countries, U.S. States, Local...
Entertainment	**Science**
Movies, Actors, Humor, Music, TV...	Animals, Astronomy, Biology, Engineering...
Government	**Social Science**
Elections, Military, Law, Taxes...	Languages, Archaeology, Psychology...
Health	**Society & Culture**
Diseases, Drugs, Fitness, Medicine, Hospitals, Medical Centers...	People, Environment, Religion, Home & Garden, Food...

Figure 1.28. Main categories in the Yahoo! Directory. Source: http://help.yahoo.com/l/us/yahoo/directory/ctd/ctd-07.html.

One approach to providing structured access to the World Wide Web comes from *directories* that classify Websites according to their contents (Zins, 2002). Well-known examples aiming to cover the whole WWW and not focusing on single domains are the Yahoo! Directory and the Open Directory Project (ODP). Web directories are typically created and maintained by human editors. While Yahoo! offers places in their categories for sale, the ODP counts on the help of volunteers from an interested internet user community to collect and classify numerous Websites. Both have to face the general problem of coping with the enormous amount of sites on the Web and their constant change.

The Yahoo! Directory is structured hierarchically, starting with 14 top level categories (Figure 1.28). ODP currently comprises 4,614,295 sites classified in 590.000 categories[44], starting with 16 main categories on the top level (Figure 1.30), which are quite similar to those of Yahoo! Figures 1.29 and 1.31 show the category 'diseases and conditions' (subordinate to the category 'health') from Yahoo! and from the Open Directory Project. ODP is available and updated in numerous languages. Yahoo! is also available in other languages, but has already stopped maintenance on some of them (e.g. German).

The quality of Web directories has been subject to some debate (e.g. Lewandowski, 2005; Stock & Stock, 2000). The categories of the Yahoo! and the ODP directories have been developed from scratch and do not refer to established universal classification systems. Over time, they have been growing unchecked and are of a mixed quality by now. Sometimes, similar Websites are scattered among different categories.

---

[44] As stated on www.dmoz.org on Oct. 25th, 2008.

Figure 1.29. The Yahoo! Web directory, category 'diseases and conditions', subclass of 'health'. Source: http://dir.yahoo.com/Health/Diseases_and_Conditions/.

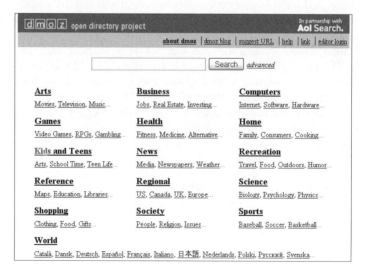

Figure 1.30. Main categories from the ODP. Source: http://www.dmoz.org/.

The practical importance of Web directories for navigating the Web is much lower than that of Web search engines (such as Ask.com[45], Google[46], Live Search[47]). Web search engines do not work with knowledge organization systems and indexing methods, they mainly rely on algorithms that involve link structures and text statistics (Hock, 2001; Lewandowski, 2005; Stock, 2007a).

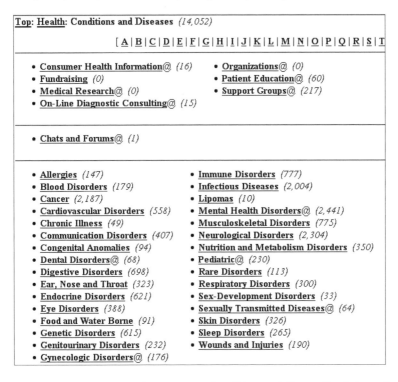

Figure 1.31. Open Document Project, category "conditions and diseases", subclass of "health". Source: http://www.dmoz.org/Health/Conditions_and_Diseases/.

A different approach to adding structures to the WWW comes from *metadata initiatives*, which aim at providing Web documents with standardized metadata. Most important is the Dublin Core Metadata Initiative (DCMI)[48]. The DCMI devotes itself to "promoting the widespread adoption of interoperable metadata standards and developing specialized metadata vocabularies for describing resources that

---

45 Ask.com: http://www.ask.com.
46 Google: http://www.google.com.
47 Live Search: http://www.live.com.
48 Dublin Core Metadata Initiative (DCMI): http://dublincore.org.

enable more intelligent information discovery systems"[49]. The heart of the DMCI efforts is the Dublin Core Metadata Element Set[50] (DCMES, or just DC) (ISO 15836:2003). In its latest release version, it consists of a vocabulary of fifteen properties for use in resource description with definitions and comments on appropriate usage (Figure 1.32).

Some of them regard formal aspects of document specification (creator, publisher, contributor, date, format, identifier, language). Others focus on content specifications (subject, title, description, type, source, relation, coverage). The Dublin Core elements are suggestions for the unitary description of Web pages. Yet they are rarely used by the millions of webmasters creating content on the WWW. Thus the unification of metadata on the Web is far from complete.

Term Name: subject	
URI:	http://purl.org/dc/elements/1.1/subject
Label:	Subject
Definition:	The topic of the resource.
Comment:	Typically, the subject will be represented using keywords, key phrases, or classification codes. Recommended best practice is to use a controlled vocabulary. To describe the spatial or temporal topic of the resource, use the Coverage element.

Figure 1.32. The label 'subject' as suggested in the Dublin Core elements. Source:
http://dublincore.org/documents/dces/.

Recently, another idea has become the starting point for new efforts in Web indexing: Instead of classifying complete Websites, the focus is on uniquely labeling single pieces of information. Information presentation on the WWW has traditionally been meant to be understandable for humans only. A human user may read a website, understand its meaning and relate contents to other pieces of information. Yet with the growing amounts of data on the Web, this task becomes almost unmanageable for human users. To enable automatic processing of information on the Web in order to collect distributed pieces of information and combine them to new meaningful units, a new dimension of information indexing on the Web is needed. This is where the vision of a *Semantic Web* begins.

---

[49]   As stated on their Website: http://dublincore.org/about/.
[50]   Dublin Core Metadata Element Set, Version 1.1: http://dublincore.org/documents/dces/.

1.2 The Semantic Web

1.2.1 The Vision of a Semantic Web

Tim Berners-Lee, James Hendler and Ora Lassila (2001) disseminated the term Semantic Web with their vision of an extended and enhanced World Wide Web: Data should be provided in such a way that not only humans can read it; computers should also be able to manipulate and recombine the information meaningfully[51]. They describe a scenario where "Web agents" help users to solve complex search queries such as 'find me a doctor who offers specific treatments, who is located close to my home and whose appointment times match my personal time schedule'. This vision goes far beyond the potential of conventional Web search engines:

> "If the world's knowledge is to be found on the Web, then we should be able to use it to answer questions, retrieve facts, solve problems, and explore possibilities. This is qualitatively different than searching for documents and reading them, even though text search engines are getting better at helping people do these things. Many major scientific discoveries and breakthroughs have involved recognizing the connections across domains or integrating insights from several sources. These are not associations of words; they are deep insights that involve the actual subject matter of these domains. The Semantic Web has the machinery to help address interoperability of data from multiple sources." (Gruber, 2008)

This vision of interoperability of data poses the challenge of *information integration*: The information a user needs may not be available all in one place (e.g. all on the same website), but may have to be collected from several sites and then presented in an integrated way. To handle complex search queries and to enable information integration and exchange across applications, technologies are being invented which allow for new ways of indexing information on the Web in order to finally facilitate information retrieval via the *meanings* of words, and not just spellings and character strings.

This requires detailed descriptions of information units that are not currently made explicit in websites (e.g. that 'Heinrich Heine' is the name of a *person* or that 'Düsseldorf' is the name of a *city*) plus additional background knowledge about the interrelation of different pieces of information (e.g. that Heinrich Heine *lived in* Düsseldorf). These information interrelations may be based on implicit knowledge of general facts and can be combined to derive new assumptions – such as: 'if a person A has a brother (person B) and a son (person C), then person B is the uncle of person C' (example modified from Daconta, Obrst & Smith, 2003) or 'as Dresden is a city in Germany and Samaipata is a city in Bolivia and

---

[51] This vision is not new. Tim Berners-Lee has discussed it before, e.g. at the first World Wide Web Conference in 1994 (Shadbolt, Berners-Lee & Hall, 2006), as well as in a keynote on the XML2000 conference (Berners-Lee, 2000).

as the time difference between Bolivia and Germany is five hours one should not make a phone call from Dresden to Samaipata before noon' (Hitzler, Krötzsch et al., 2008).

Information about the meanings of single words or of other information units should be integrated as supplements to the existing websites in order to provide an additional layer of the traditional Web, as Berners-Lee, Hendler and Lassila (2001) point out:

> "The Semantic Web is not a separate Web but an extension of the current one, in which information is given well-defined meaning, better enabling computers and people to work in cooperation." (Berners-Lee, Hendler & Lassila, 2001)

Visions of computers and people working together have led to the interpretation that the aim of the Semantic Web is to enable computers to actually *understand* the meaning of information. While this has long been a research challenge in the field of *Artificial Intelligence* (AI), the Semantic Web community today focuses on less far-reaching and more practical objectives (Hitzler, Krötzsch et al., 2008): methods and means should be developed to represent information in such a manner that machines may handle and modify it in ways that are useful and reasonable to humans[52]. Instead of providing machines with the intelligence to read and understand 'normal' Websites and process the information, the idea of the Semantic Web is to provide information in a way that can be processed by computers (Hitzler, Krötzsch et al., 2008).

> "The original idea of the Semantic Web was to bring machine-readable descriptions to the data and documents already on the Web, in order to improve search and data usage. [...] Humans can read Web pages and understand them, but the inherent meaning is not available in a way that allows interpretation by computers. [...] The Semantic Web aims at defining ways to allow Web information to be used by computers not only for display purposes, but also for interoperability and integration between systems and applications." (Cardoso, Lytras & Hepp, 2008)

This is done in the form of metadata or "semantic markups" (Pan, 2007), machine-understandable index terms associated with Web resources. While HTML has been developed to serve as a markup system for formatting issues on the Web, the next step is "[...] to provide metadata not just concerning the syntax of a Web resource (i.e., its formatting, its character strings) but also its semantics [...]" (Legg, 2007). This is the Semantic Web's equivalent to classical document indexing. In contrast to former metadata initiatives like Dublin Core, the new vision is that websites (and, even further: single elements within websites or single pieces of information) should be indexed with content-specific index terms with highest the possible specificity and based on a complex knowledge organization system.

---

[52]   Naturally, there are points of contact between research on AI and the Semantic Web (Shadbolt, Berners-Lee & Hall, 2006; Studer, Ankolekar et al., 2006).

Semantic Web indexing thus requires the development of markup languages in order to enable such new indexes – but there is also the need for shared KOS in the form of first-class vocabularies to facilitate this semantic indexing: *Ontologies*.

> "Annotations alone do not establish semantics of what is being marked-up. [...] In response to this need for more explicit meaning, ontologies have been proposed to provide shared and precisely defined terms and constraints to describe the meaning of resources through annotations [...]."
> (Pan, 2007)

The realization of a Semantic Web thus depends on interoperable technologies and standards on the one hand as well as on ontologies as sophisticated knowledge organization systems on the other.

This extension and improvement of the World Wide Web is a demanding task, as not only do the technologies have to be developed, but the community of Web users and webmasters has to be motivated to join in the actual application of such new technologies. Yet a substantial and highly engaged research community has formed up to accept the challenge, with the Semantic Web Science Association[53] (SWSA) as a leading institution. The World Wide Web Consortium[54] (W3C) has also committed itself to the development of technical standards for the Semantic Web. Altogether, the Semantic Web can be regarded as "the most ambitious project the W3C has scaffolded so far" (Legg, 2007).

1.2.2 Indexing the Semantic Web: Ontologies

Research on ontologies in computer science started before Tim Berners-Lee and his colleagues published their vision of a Semantic Web. Yet since then, efforts have increased and focused on a new practical aim.

> "For the semantic web to function, computers must have access to structured collections of information and sets of inference rules that they can use to conduct automated reasoning." (Berners-Lee, Hendler & Lassila, 2001)

What is needed are structured representations of world knowledge and concept interrelations with the ability to draw conclusions from them. Ontologies can provide this structured knowledge and they can be supported by *reasoning mechanisms* or *inference engines* that deduce implicit facts and can analyze over the explicit knowledge to check the logical consistency of the knowledge model (Gómez-Pérez, Fernández-López & Corcho, 2004). Ontologies have thus become a key component in research efforts to establish a Semantic Web (e.g. Alexiev, Breu et al., 2005; Breitman, Casanova & Truszkowski, 2007; Davies, Fensel & van Harmelen, 2003; Davies, Studer & Warren, 2006; Handschuh & Staab, 2003; Hendler & van Harmelen, 2008; Staab & Studer, 2004; Stuckenschmidt & van Harmelen, 2005; Taniar & Rahayu, 2006).

---

[53] The Semantic Web Science Association Web (SWSA): http://www.iswsa.org/.
[54] World Wide Web Consortium (W3C): http://www.w3.org. The W3C's main page for Semantic Web research is http://www.w3.org/2001/sw/.

Ontologies are formal conceptualizations of a knowledge domain (Gruber, 1993), expressed in systems of *concepts* (classes), *instances* (individuals) and the *relations* between them. Classes represent abstract concepts of a domain of interest, instances represent real-world individuals and relations represent interconnections of classes and thus specify their *properties* – as we will see in detail in Section 2.2. At first glance, ontologies tend to resemble traditional thesauri, but they include possibilities for defining new types of relations between concepts and allow the adding of rules and axioms that impose restrictions on concept interrelations, and thus explicitly define concepts. With a variety of freely defined concept interrelations, they provide new forms of navigation within a knowledge organization system and can thus be used for more precise document indexing as well as enhanced options in query expansion.

Generally, ontologies should be considered in the context of indexing the World Wide Web, yet they fundamentally differ from the previously discussed classical approaches on indexing, as indexing is not their only purpose (some do not even regard indexing as the primary focus of ontologies): They also aim at capturing facts and coherences. Based on the use of rules and axioms, formal definitions for classes can be provided and conditions for class membership may be formalized. Using complex ontology languages (such as OWL-DL[55]), deduction and reasoning processes are made possible.

Ontologies oscillate between KOS and knowledge bases. They may contain detailed, explicit information about (real-world) objects and contexts – for instance the fact that 'London' 'is capital of' 'England'[56]. Thus they may in some cases strongly resemble databases. In this sense they can become shared knowledge bases for communities and for computer-computer and human-computer interaction. Information can also be retrieved within ontologies, which in turn requires additional, specific query languages.

> "A particular usage of ontologies found in many semantic systems is the task of inferring new knowledge from facts and rules expressed in an ontology language. Another common task is the execution of search queries on data represented in an ontology language to retrieve semantically meaningful search results. The combination of both leads to semantic search applications that make full use of ontologies in order to provide complete and relevant answers to user queries." (Herzog, Luger & Herzog, 2007)

In Semantic Web research, the elements of ontologies are often discussed as and stored in the form of *triples*. These are tripartite entities in the form of subject, predicate and object (Hitzler, Krötzsch, et al., 2008). In the previous example, 'London' would be the subject, 'is capital of' the predicate, and 'England' the object.

---

[55]   Web Ontology Language (OWL): http://www.w3.org/2004/OWL/. OWL is available in three versions, OWL lite, OWL-DL (description logics) and OWL full.

[56]   In this case, London and England would have to be represented as instances of classes like 'City' and 'Country', which are themselves interrelated by an 'is_capital_of' property.

A First Example

As ontologies are the most advanced systems of knowledge representation, we will discuss them in detail in the following chapter. For now, we will exemplarily consider a single ontology for an introduction: eClassOWL[57].

eCl@ass[58] started as a broad classification for products and services, aiming to make e-business transactions easier. From this classification, an enhanced version was constructed containing properties specifying the classes, which then was turned into an ontology in OWL format: the eClassOWL (Hepp, 2006a). Today, it contains a hierarchical classification (Figures 1.33 and 1.34) of products and services.

Top-Level Category	Number of Product or Service Categories
Organic chemicals	5,312
Automation, electrical-engineering, PLT	2,659
Office supplies, furniture, equipment, and papeterie	1,992
Machines, apparatus	1,793
Inorganic chemicals	1,464
Laboratory materials and technology	1,327
Auxiliary supplies, additives, formulations	1,216
Services	1,064
Tools	1,033
Machine elements and fixings	964
Construction technology	802
Medicine, medical technology, life science	760
Polymers	726
Packing materials	620
Installations (complete)	521
Marketing	504
IT	489
Industrial piping	440
Equipment for mining, metallurgical plants, rolling mills, and foundries	432
Home economics, home technology	351
Energy, basic chemicals, aux. agents	258
Machines or devices (for special applications)	255
Occupational safety, accident prevention	247
Semi-finished products, materials	226
Automotive technology	203

Figure 1.33. Top level categories in eClassOWL. Source: Hepp, 2006b.

The single concepts in this hierarchy can also be enriched with additional information, such as 'has Net Weight in kg' (Hepp, 2006b). Such properties describing the concepts allow for advanced searches within the ontology, like "search for all agricultural machines in the ontology that weigh less than 160 kg" (Hepp, 2006b). The ontology can be browsed for concepts as well as for types of properties. Figure1.35 shows an extract from the list of properties concerning the term 'weight'.

---

[57] eClassOWL: http://www.heppnetz.de/projects/eclassowl/.
[58] eCl@ss: http://www.eclass.de.

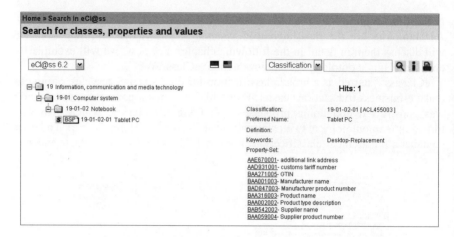

Figure 1.34. Excerpt from the eCl@ss classification. Concept hierarchy down to bottom
term 'Tablet PC', with associated properties for this concept. Source:
http://www.eclass.de/Home/Search-in-eCl@ss/3463,en.html?no=intro.

Property	☑ WEIGHt	🔍 ℹ 🔒

Hits: 49

Property	Fieldformat
AAA665002 - Weight of breathing mask	NR1..3
AAA666002 - Weight of heat and moisture exchanger	NR2..1.1
AAA667002 - Weight of basic apparatus	NR2..3.2
AAA668002 - Weight of mallet	NR2..3.1
AAA669002 - Weight of medical instrument	NR1..1
AAA670002 - Weight of unused heat and moisture exchangers	NR2..1.1
AAA912002 - maximum body weight	NR2..2.1
AAA949002 - minimum body weight	NR2..1.1
AAB107003 - Weight of glass	NR2..2.1
AAB108002 - Weight of glass	NR2..2.1
AAB163002 - maximum body weight	NR2..2.1
AAB166002 - minimum body weight	NR2..1.1
AAB713002 - Weight	NR2..5.5
AAC060002 - Net weight of the motor with brake	NR2..5.1
AAC061002 - Net weight of the primary part	NR2..3.1

Figure 1.35. Properties containing the word 'weight' in eCl@ss. Source:
http://www.eclass.de/Home/Search-in-eCl@ss/3463,en.html?no=intro.

Infrastructure

The realization of the Semantic Web is to a large degree an issue of developing the right technologies for the different goals (Antoniou & van Harmelen, 2004; Daconta, Obrst & Smith, 2003; Ding, Fensel et al., 2002; Hitzler, Krötzsch et al., 2008). The most famous sketch of the Semantic Web's underlying architecture is Tim Berners-Lee's Semantic Web Layer Stack[59] diagram (Figure 1.36) (Berners-Lee, 2000), which has by now been modified and amended several times. Though it has recently been criticized as being no longer adequate for representing the various needs of the Semantic Web and the interrelatedness of different technologies, during the first years of semantic technology development it was very stimulating.

Regarding the technical infrastructure, Semantic Web research has already achieved considerable results. Shadbolt, Berners-Lee and Hall (2006) name the following aspects as the most notable achievements by the Semantic Web community:

- Ontology languages for representing shared meaning. The most popular one is the Web Ontology Language OWL with its three dialects.
- Rules and inference mechanisms.
- Triple stores that allow large scale storage of ontologies based on triples (mainly needed to store RDF and RDFS data). A popular example is the Jena[60] framework.
- Query languages to retrieve information from ontologies.
- Methods to extract structured information from Websites and translate it into formats such as RDF, e.g. GRDDL[61] which makes it possible to extract RDF from XML and XHTML.

Ankolekar, Krötzsch, Tran and Vrandecic (2007) also sum up the achievements of Semantic Web research:

> "The Semantic Web vision has inspired a big community of researchers and practitioners, and they have achieved a number of goals: languages like RDF and RDF(S) were revised, the Web Ontology Language OWL was standardised. Academic research contributed methodologies for ontology engineering, evolution, debugging, and modularisation, and has led to a thorough understanding of the complexity and decidability of common ontology languages. These insights enabled the implementation of increasingly scalable solutions for inferencing, and of improved modeling tools for ontologies. Based on those achievements, major companies like Oracle and IBM are working on large scale data stores supporting Semantic Web standards, and a growing number of specialised companies such as Aduna, Altova, Ontoprise, and TopQuadrant provide industrial strength tool sets fa-

---

[59]   Also known as *Semantic Web Cake* and *Semantic Web Layer Cake*.
[60]   Jena Semantic Web Framework: http://jena.sourceforge.net/.
[61]   GRDDL, Gleaning Resource Descriptions from Dialects of Languages: www.w3.org/2004/01/rdxh/spec.

cilitating the use of semantic technologies in corporate settings."
(Ankolekar, Krötzsch et al., 2007)

Furthermore, the Semantic Web technologies are based upon some achievements of earlier Web technology research. Basic foundations are provided by *markup languages* like HTML and XML or the use of *uniform resource identifiers* (URI).

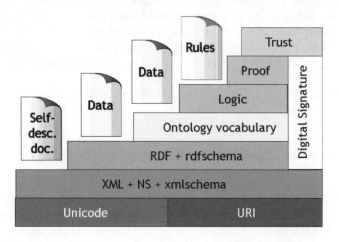

Figure 1.36. Original version of the Semantic Web Layer Stack model. Source:
http://www.w3.org/2000/Talks/1206-xml2k-tbl/slide10-0.html.

URIs

URIs are character strings created for the unambiguous identification of abstract or real-world objects (Berners-Lee, 1997; Berners-Lee, Fielding & Masinter, 2005). They are used particularly in order to identify Websites or other files on the WWW.

> "Associating a URI with a resource means that anyone can link to it, refer to it, or retrieve a representation of it. […] Much of the motivation for the Semantic Web comes from the value locked in relational databases. To release this value, database objects must be exported to the Web as first-class objects and therefore must be mapped into a system of URIs." (Shadbolt, Berners-Lee & Hall, 2006)

Often URLs (Uniform Resource Locators, identifying resources addressable via the Web) and URNs (Uniform Resource Names, envisioned for worldwide unitary and persistent object identification, comparable to ISBN or ISSN) are discussed as subtypes of URIs.

> "The generality (and hoped-for power) of the URN is such that it is not confined to Web pages but may be used to name any real-world object one

wishes to identify uniquely (buildings, people, organizations, musical re-
cordings). [...] In short, the push to develop URNs is a vast, unprecedented
exercise in *canonicalizing names* [...]. At the same time, however, the bap-
tism of objects with URNs is designed to be as decentralized as anything on
the Web – anyone may perform such naming exercises and record them in
'namespaces'. This tension between canonicalization and decentralization is
one of the Semantic Web's greatest challenges." (Legg, 2007)

In the context of the Semantic Web, URIs are an integral part of ontology languages and help to identify the conceptual elements of ontologies (concepts, properties, instances). For example, if a user starts to build a new ontology within the
ontology editor Protégé[62], a unique identification number is automatically created
for this file. In most cases one may also specify one's personal URI which may
look like this: http://my.domain.com/myOntology (Cuenca Grau, Motik & Patel-
Schneider, 2007). Such a basic URI is part of any ontology file saved in a standard
ontology language.

Furthermore, single elements of the ontology are provided with a URI based on
the ontology's original URI, e.g. a class 'person' in our example ontology would
be labeled with http://my.domain.com/myOntology#person. In this way every ontology is built in a standard format and all their elements can be uniquely identified. The identification numbers can be used to resolve problems for cross-
references between multiple ontologies.

From Markup Languages to Ontology Languages
Markup languages are used to provide parts of textual documents with additional
information. In computer science, this activity is also referred to as *annotating*; the
resulting annotations are also called metadata, as they provide data about data
(Hitzler, Krötzsch et al., 2008). HTML (Hypertext Markup Language) is a markup
language that enables us to specify information about how documents should be
displayed on the Web. Parts of a textual document are annotated with *tags*[63] (also
called *metatags*), which are predefined symbols in angle brackets. Web browsers
can interpret them and format the text accordingly. For example, the tag <i> can
be used for formatting text in italics. A start tag <i> and an end tag </i> enclose
the part of a text which should be displayed in italics. HTML is a fixed collection
of such tags with definitions for their effects, also called a *vocabulary*. This basic
principle of HTML markup was one of the Web's great successes; together with
the interconnections in the form of hyperlinks it has considerably shaped the appearance of the WWW.

The next stage of development was reached with XML (Extensible Markup
Language; Yergeau, Bray et al., 2004). XML is another markup language that
works with tags for document markup. It does not define the layout of a document
but rather its logical structure. More generally, XML can also be used to create

---

[62] Protégé: http:// protege.stanford.edu/.
[63] Tags in markup languages are not to be confused with tags used in folksonomies. The
latter will be discussed in detail in section 1.3.2.

and define new markup languages (Hitzler, Krötzsch et al., 2008). With XML one can thus create the actual vocabulary for document annotation. XML documents consist of elements. A start tag and an end tag enclose the elements' content. The tags themselves are self-defined labels written in angle brackets. One example would be <Person>Queen Elisabeth II</Person>. This gives us a way of labeling all person names inside a document. These elements can also be arranged into nested structures, as in the following example:

```
<catalog>
<cd>
<title>A Hard Day's Night</title>
   <artist>The Beatles</artist>
   <year>1964</year>
</cd>
<cd>
<title>Achtung Baby</title>
   <artist>U2</artist>
<year>1991</year>
</cd>
</catalog>
```

XML enables Web designers to add structure and metadata (tags) to the Web – but this does not include information on what the structure means (Berners-Lee, Hendler & Lassila, 2001). As anyone is free to define XML tags himself, and as there are no definitions, explanations or meanings associated with the tags, XML annotation alone does not provide semantics for the Web. From a Semantic Web perspective, XML tags are merely words that are neither unambiguously defined nor interrelated with one another (Hitzler, Krötzsch et al., 2008).

> "XML is the syntactic foundation layer for the Semantic Web. All other technologies providing features for the Semantic Web will be built on top of XML. Requiring other Semantic Web technologies (like the Resource Description Framework) to be layered on top of XML guarantees a base level of interoperability. [...] Is XML enough? The answer is no, because XML only provides syntactic interoperability. In other words, sharing an XML document adds meaning to the content; however, only when both parties know and understand the element names. For example, if I label something a <price>$12.00 </price> and you label that field on your own invoice <cost> $12.00</cost>, there is no way that a machine will know those two mean the same thing unless Semantic Web technologies like ontologies are added [...]." (Daconta, Obrst & Smith, 2003)

Another important development that comes closer to the Semantic Web's aim of capturing the meanings of documents (documents' elements) is RDF[64] (Resource

---

[64]   Resource Description Framework (RDF): http://www.w3.org/RDF/.

Description Framework; Hjelm, 2001; Manola & Miller, 2004). It has been developed as a formal language for describing structured information and for information exchange across applications.

RDF works with URIs and stores information in the form of RDF triples. A subject-predicate-object triple makes up a statement, and so an RDF document is always a collection of statements about a domain of interest.

> "In RDF, a document makes assertions that particular things (people, Web pages or whatever) have properties (such as 'is a sister of', 'is the author of') with certain values (another person, another Web page). This structure turns out to be a natural way to describe the vast majority of the data processed by machines. Subject and object are each identified by a Universal Resource Identifier (URI), just as used in a link on a Web page. (URLs, Uniform Resource Locators, are the most common type of URI.) The verbs are also identified by URIs, which enables anyone to define a new concept, a new verb, just by defining a URI for it somewhere on the Web. [...] Because RDF uses URIs to encode this information in a document, the URIs ensure that concepts are not just words in a document but are tied to a unique definition that everyone can find on the Web." (Berners-Lee, Hendler & Lassila, 2001)

RDF triples are not arranged in hierarchies but form a directed graph (Hitzler, Krötzsch et al., 2008). By now, RDF is frequently used as the formalization format of ontologies. More sophisticated ontology languages have been built on top of RDF, e.g. RDFS (McBride, 2004) and OWL.

> "RDF Schema became a recommendation in February 2004. RDFS took the basic RDF specification and extended it to support the expression of structured vocabularies. It has provided a minimal ontology representation language that the research community has adopted fairly widely." (Shadbolt, Berners-Lee & Hall, 2006)

In addition to the development of markup languages for the Web and formal resource descriptions (and temporarily running in parallel), first efforts for the implementation of sophisticated ontology languages have been made. These languages make use of different types of logic and axiomatization.

Ontology Languages
First approaches in computational ontologies (in the beginning of the 1990s) were based on frames and first-order logic (Gómez-Pérez, Fernández-López & Corcho, 2004). By and by, new knowledge representation languages were developed, based on description logics (Baader, Calvanese et al., 2003; Nardi & Brachman, 2003; Sattler, 2003), such as OIL[65] (Fensel, Horrocks et al., 2000; Fensel, Hor-

---

[65]   Ding, Fensel et al. (2002) point out one peculiarity of OIL: "One of the central design ideas in OIL is its onion model [...]. No single language will ever satisfy all human requirements. OIL's onion model offers languages of varying complexity; this allows applications to select the degree of complexity they require."

rocks et al., 2001; Horrocks, Patel-Schneider & van Harmelen, 2003) or DAML+OIL (Fensel, Ding et al., 2001; van Harmelen, Patel-Schneider & Horrocks, 2001). These languages all differ in their methods of explicitly stating information within the ontology. Thus the actual character of an ontology is always influenced by the ontology language in use. It is beyond the scope of this book to present the structure of the different ontology languages in detail. We will discuss the structure and elements of ontologies exemplarily for OWL in Section 2.2. Overviews, comparisons and more information on important ontology languages are provided by Fensel, Lassila et al., 2000, Gómez-Pérez & Corcho (2002), Gómez-Pérez, Fernández-López and Corcho (2004), Staab and Studer (2004), among others.

Today, the most important development in this regard is the Web Ontology Language (OWL) (Dean & Schreiber, 2004; Hendler, 2004; Horrocks, 2005), which is very popular for ontology engineering and is fast becoming the most propagated standard. It is available in three dialects, with different degrees of complexity: *OWL lite* as the simplest version with limited expressiveness, *OWL-DL*, based on description logics, and *OWL full* with maximum expressiveness but with no guarantee for logical consistency.

> "For those who required greater expressivity in their object and relation descriptions, the OWL [...] specification integrated several efforts. The W3C recommendation presents three versions of OWL, depending on the degree of expressive power required. OWL's core idea is to enable efficient representation of ontologies that are also amenable to decision procedures. It checks an ontology to see whether it's logically consistent or to determine whether a particular concept falls within the ontology. [...] Ontologies can become distributed, as OWL allows ontologies to refer to terms in other ontologies. In this way OWL is specifically engineered for the Web and Semantic Web." (Shadbolt, Berners-Lee & Hall, 2006)

Yet in some cases, OWL has turned out to be too complex even for the actual end user. In consequence, some ontologists have returned to simply using RDF as an easier way of formalizing the information in triple units[66]. In addition, simpler ontology languages are developed:

> "Recently, this research has led both to an extension of the expressiveness of OWL DL [...], and to the identification of a number of much simpler but still useful ontology languages, such as EL++ [...] or RDFS++ [...]." (Ankolekar, Krötzsch et al., 2007)

The W3C is currently developing an enhanced version of OWL, called OWL 2 (Motik, Cuenca Grau, et al., 2008). This has already inspired new discussions about whether highly formalized ontology languages are actually needed – par-

---

[66]   OWL and RDF have different semantics and overlapping expressive powers. From an ontological point of view, OWL DL is more expressive than RDF. A comparison as well as a discussion of interrelations between both languages is provided by Pan (2007), for example.

ticularly during a panel discussion at the International Semantic Web Conference 2008[67] entitled "An OWL 2 Far?"

Queries, Automatic Reasoning and Information Extraction

To retrieve information within ontologies, *query languages* have been developed. This means, that one may formulate queries in a specific syntax in order to retrieve all the elements from an ontology that fulfill certain requirements. Relatively new yet already quite popular is SPARQL[68] (Beckett & Broekstra, 2007; Hitzler, Krötzsch et al., 2008, chapter 7; Prud'hommeaux & Seaborne, 2008), which is used for querying RDF. SPARQL enables queries with varying degree of complexity. Similarly, the query language OWL-QL can be used for querying OWL files (Fikes, Hayes & Horrocks, 2003; Pan, 2007). On the other hand, *reasoners* (also called inference engines) have been developed with the primary aim of detecting logical inconsistencies within ontologies.

> "A side effect of the axiomatic specification of conceptual elements in an ontology is that it increases the likelihood that modeling errors can be spotted, because an inference engine is empowered to find logical inconsistencies. [...] it must be stressed that only logical inconsistencies can be spotted this way, while other types of modeling errors remain undetected." (Hepp, 2008)

Furthermore, reasoners can analyze the whole structure of the ontology and derive information that has not been inserted directly (e.g. Gómez-Pérez, Fernández-López & Corcho, 2004). For example, based on class properties a reasoner may specify an individual which possesses these properties to be a member of that class: a given ontology includes a class 'capital city' defined, as a city which is the seat of government of a country (with 'country' being another class of the ontology, and 'is seat of government of' the relation between the two classes); the ontology also includes an individual 'London', which is characterized as being the seat of government of another individual 'England', which in is already classified as a 'country'. The reasoner may then infer that London is a 'capital city'. The use of a reasoner is particularly interesting for complex and highly axiomatized ontologies.

> "The axiomatic definition of conceptual elements as described in the previous section also empowers computational inferences, i.e., the use of a reasoner component to deduce new, implicit facts. An important contribution of this property is that it reduces redundancy in the representation of a knowledge base and thus eases its maintenance, because we do not need to assert explicitly what is already specified in the ontology." (Hepp, 2008)

Another direction of research in semantic technologies is the field of *information extraction* (Barnbrook, Danielsson & Mahlberg, 2006; Moens, 2006; Mooney &

---

[67]   International Semantic Web Conference 2008 (ISWC 2008), October 26-30, Karlsruhe, Germany. http://iswc2008.semanticweb.org/.

[68]   SPARQL is an acronym for Simple Protocol and RDF Query Language.

Bunescu, 2005; Pazienza, 1997). The aim of information extraction activities is to extract pieces of structured information from unstructured textual documents. Information extraction systems may use an ontology as internal knowledge base. Some also attempt to collect categorized and contextualized information (for example to identify people, companies, products or other named entities). Other approaches seek to detect candidates for new classes or relations to be integrated in a given ontology.

> "There are several promising techniques for the [...] approach, to extract structured data from unstructured user contributions [...]. It is possible to do a reasonable job at identifying people, companies, and other entities with proper names, products, instances of relations you are interested in (e.g., person joining a company) [...], or instances of questions being asked [...]. There are also techniques for pulling out candidates to use as classes and relations although these are a bit noisier [...]." (Gruber, 2008)

Achievements and Challenges

A variety of usage scenarios has been proposed for the Semantic Web, all with varying degrees of complexity. They vary from challenges in word-sense disambiguation and collections of synonyms for information retrieval to a gradually refined retrieval over growing ranges of data. The most ambitious vision comprises automatic information extraction, integration and processing over a variety of sources (Aufaure, Le Grand et al., 2006; Goble & de Roure, 2002; Hendler, 2001). Furthermore, *Expert Systems* with ontologies as their knowledge base were intended to be sophisticated information systems providing expert level answers and advice that help to answer users' questions on a certain domain (e.g. Giarratano & Riley, 2005; Jackson, 1998). The Semantic Web has been envisioned to revolutionize scientific work as well as business applications (e.g. Fensel, 2004).

> "Today, the Semantic Web is not only about increasing the expressiveness of Web information to enable the automatic or semiautomatic processing of Web resources and Web pages. Academia and industry have realized that the Semantic Web can facilitate the integration and interoperability of intra- and inter-business processes and systems, as well as enable the creation of global infrastructures for sharing documents and data, make searching and reusing information easier." (Cardoso, Lytras & Hepp, 2008)

Much of this is still an ambitious vision today. Some critics doubt that the Semantic Web will ever become reality. And yet, with the technical innovations described above, important steps have been achieved that provide a basis for future activities. It turns out that a single all-embracing Semantic Web will certainly not be created in the short term, requiring much more intensive research. But the focus has changed from one comprehensive Semantic Web to various single *semantic applications*. More and more applications that make innovative use of semantic technologies are coming up (Carstens, 2008); many very recent developments were tried out, e.g. during the International Semantic Web Conference's demo sessions[69]. Previous works have also revealed critical aspects on which Semantic Web research will have to focus in the future, e.g. the interconnection of data collections to avoid isolated data silos (Bizer, Heath et al., 2007; Heath & Motta, 2008) or the creation of high-quality ontologies with a view to depicting a shared view of a broad community. While the infrastructure for ontology engineering is well equipped, the actual development of premium ontologies and their application remains difficult. The problem of creating elaborated ontologies is often traced back to the *knowledge acquisition bottleneck* (or *ontology acquisition bottleneck*): one of the biggest challenges in ontology development (and thus for realizing the Semantic Web) is the collection and formalization of relevant knowledge in the form of ontologies. Additionally, the actual indexing of documents on the Web remains a challenging task (Corcho, 2006; Uren, Cimiano et al., 2006). Without a solution here, the so-called *semantic gap* will remain. The semantic gap denotes the problem of matching world conceptualizations or common knowledge with documents' contents. This match would be achieved if documents were intensively indexed with ontologies. Ramesh Jain (2008) has consequently posed the question of whether Semantic Web research is actually bridging the semantic gap – or "whether we are only improving techniques on both sides of the gap": by improving methods of knowledge representation on the one hand, and methods for detecting document contexts (e.g. via structural analysis of image features) on the other. Due to the enormous size of the WWW, both ontology development and semantic indexing require the contribution and assistance of Web users. Consequently, many recent efforts concentrate on incorporating user communities in these activities. Another recent development is thus of enormous interest for the Semantic Web: the Social Web with its new dimension of user contribution and collaboration on the Web.

1.3 The Social Web

In very recent years, the efforts of establishing a Semantic Web have come to be accompanied by another trend: the Social Web, the user-centered Web, or – as it is mostly called – the *Web 2.0*. This last phrase has gained enormous popularity, not only in scientific discussion. And although some soon got tired of the attachment "2.0" (Notess, 2006), which started to spread to other terms like "library 2.0" or "knowledge management 2.0", the underlying principles and ideas will remain of high importance for the future internet.

1.3.1 Web 2.0 and the Role of the User

The term Web 2.0 was coined during a discussion by Tim O'Reilly and Dale Dougherty from O'Reilly Media about what Web developments will be of long-term effectiveness (O'Reilly, 2005). Afterwards, the phrase soon began to spread

---

[69] For examples from the ISWC 2008 see Bizer & Joshi (2008).

widely. Though definitions may still vary slightly, the term Web 2.0 has generally been accepted to describe a new era of the World Wide Web, in which it is the users who are in the spotlight (Cormode & Krishnamurthy, 2008; Madden & Fox, 2006; Musser & O'Reilly, 2006). Users are enabled to easily contribute to the creation of Web content. Thus the borders between "consumers" and "producers" of content are blurring – we may talk of a new type of Web user: the "prosumer" as envisioned by Toffler (1980).

The term Web 2.0 arose as a description of past and present effects on the Web rather than as a vision of future perspectives. Therefore examples of what are regarded as Web 2.0 principles can be found in the era preceding this term. For example, Google's PageRank algorithm (Brin & Page, 1998) may be counted among social navigation techniques – it is based on analyses of Web links, which may be regarded as large-scale activities of Web prosumers. Applications such as instant messaging and peer-to-peer-networks can be considered early examples of this development; they have enjoyed large success before the actual hype around Web 2.0 began (Alby, 2007). Recent Web 2.0 services have moved on toward communication as well as interconnections between larger groups and communities; the focus is on many-to-many relationships. The collaboration of large communities enables the creation of content in new formats and of enormous scale. Thus apart from social networking and personal interconnections, the interlinking of topics and discussions plays a decisive role. Various new communication channels create a "matrix of dialogues" (Maness, 2006a) across different types of content and different data formats (e.g. blogs, wikis, podcasts, multi-media content, discussions, forums, personal profiles). The asynchronous character of most of these new communication channels allows the overcoming of barriers of space and time, creating versatile, heterogeneous communities: "We can now talk to anyone and learn from others' conversations without being there" (Gruber, 2008). The co-action of numerous users allows the generation of content of new quality and enormous extent.

> "Web 2.0 pages allow contributors to collaborate and share information easily. The emerging result could not have been achieved by each individual contributor, be it a music database like freedb[70], or an event calendar like upcoming[71]. Each contributor gains more from the system than she puts into it." (Ankolekar, Krötzsch et al., 2007)

Ideally, everyone will finally profit from the concentrated knowledge of a growing community. The Web should help to capture the *collective intelligence* (Surowiecki, 2004; Weiss, 2005). The fundamental idea here is that in a community large enough there will always be at least one expert on any given topic, and that bundled knowledge will help to correct mistakes and eliminate spam. Yet this vision is not without its problems and dangers (Lanier, 2006) – and it requires enough people willing to contribute, probably even to provide an insight into their

---

[70] Freedb: http://www.freedb.org.
[71] Upcoming: http://upcoming.yahoo.com.

privacy (Albrechtslund, 2008; Szugat, Gewehr & Lochmann, 2006; Zimmer, 2008).

A variety of programs and tools has been developed to specifically enable online collaboration, document collection and management, communication or networking, and it goes under the name of *social software*. Definitions for this term may also vary. By now, a variety of programs and services can be counted among social software tools and different approaches have been made to collecting, classifying and characterizing them (e.g. Alby, 2007; Bächle, 2006; Hannay, 2007; Löwenberg, 2008; Musser & O'Reilly, 2006; Peters, 2009; Warr, 2008; Weller, Mainz et al., 2007a).

With the help of the right social software, users can actively create content e.g. with *wikis* (Leuf & Cunningham, 2001; Klobas, 2006; Desilets, Paquet & Vinson, 2005) or *blogs* (Walker, 2005), they can maintain their contacts and find new interesting people on *social networking* portals (Boyd, 2007; Boyd & Ellison, 2007) and discuss arbitrary topics or share their experiences, e.g. with *rating systems* (i.e. by assigning ratings to single documents or products such as books or hotels). *Citizen journalism* and product reviews have become a substantial part of the Web (Gruber, 2008).

Tools are provided for publishing content in various media formats as well as for storing, organizing and sharing it, e.g. photos (Flickr), videos (YouTube[72]), bookmarks (Gordon-Murnane, 2006; Hammond, Hannay et al., 2005; Lund, Hammond et al., 2005) or events (Upcoming). In the form of *mash-ups*, Web 2.0 tools may also be recombined to create even more diverse applications (Weiss, 2005). The social networking platform Facebook directly allows its users to integrate their own small applications[73] into the network.

Many Web 2.0 services are mainly entertainment-oriented. Yet the underlying developments go beyond entertainment and influence various areas of life, e.g. socializing (via business networking portals like XING[74]), reading news (e.g. with Digg[75]), searching and browsing the Web (social navigation via bookmarking systems or recommender systems, e.g. Adomavicius & Tuzhilin, 2005; Goldbeck & Hendler, 2006; Linden, Smith & York, 2003; Perugini, Goncalves & Fox, 2004), and shopping (local exchange trading systems, user ratings and again recommender systems). Web 2.0 approaches outside the private internet have mainly been discussed for use in enterprises (Millen, Feinberg & Kerr, 2006; Koch & Richter, 2007; Peters & Stock, 2007a; Raabe, 2007; Schiller García, 2007), science and scientific work (Hannay, 2007; Waldrop, 2008; Weller, Mainz et al., 2007a and 2007b), libraries (Casey & Savastinuk, 2006; Danowski & Heller, 2006; Habib, 2006; Maness, 2006a and 2006b) and e-learning (Bruns & Hum-

---

[72]   YouTube: http://www.youtube.com.
[73]   Facebook Applications: http://apps.f8.facebook.com/apps/ (login required).
[74]   XING: http://www.xing.com.
[75]   Digg: http://digg.com.

phreys, 2005; Downes, 2005). Apart from the technical foundations[76] of Web 2.0 and Social Software (e.g. Alby, 2007; Johnson, 2006), research and discussions focus on sociological effects and communication structures (e.g. Birdsall, 2007; Gillmor, 2004; Eigner, Leitner & Nausner, 2003; Möller, 2005).

Social software services increase the range of products offered on the WWW and the way users navigate through the Web. Not only do the borders between users and producers become blurred, but due to the high degree of creative participation the borders between information systems and their users are also getting vague (Hapke, 2007). Facebook users, for example, create a significant part of the Facebook platform themselves by adding applications that everyone may use on the network.

The active user has a variety of new options in utilizing the Web – but will also need new competencies in handling it (Godwin, 2006; Godwin-Jones, 2006; Ockenfeld, 2008). The information overload, which has been subject to criticism before the Web 2.0 era, has reached a new dimension (Möller-Walsdorf, 2008) and it is becoming even more difficult to separate relevant from irrelevant and high-quality from untrustworthy information.

1.3.2 Indexing the Social Web: Folksonomies

There was thus a growing need for structure and accessibility for the large amounts of user-generated content on the Web. In this context, the well-known problem of indexing documents with content-descriptive metadata was rediscovered and addressed from a new, user-centered perspective. Users were enabled to index their document collections themselves – with their own keywords. In this way, even large amounts of image and multimedia files were meant to be made retrievable. Easy interfaces were provided for this purpose and the users broadly accepted this way of labeling documents with keywords (Figure 1.37).

In this context, the assigned keywords have been called *tags*[77]. The indexing process is called (*social*) *tagging*. And the totality of tags used within one platform is called *folksonomy* (Peters, 2009). The term 'folksonomy' (a combination of 'folk' and 'taxonomy') was introduced by Thomas Vander Wal and first cited in a blog post by Gene Smith (2004). The reference to taxonomies as well as pointing to "classification" (Smith, 2004) for paraphrasing folksonomies have led to misleading and wrong connotations. Folksonomies are neither classifications nor taxonomies; they lack the fundamental characteristics of these classical KOS (e.g. they work with neither notations nor with semantic relations). However, they serve a comparable purpose: they have become a new type of knowledge organization system, with its own advantages and disadvantages.

---

[76]   Among the major technological innovations are RSS feeds and Ajax, which will not be discussed in detail in this book.

[77]   The term *tag* in folksonomies has to be considered independently of the definition of *tag* in HTML.

Figure 1.37. A document in the photo sharing platform Flickr with tags added by a user. Source: www.flickr.com, photo uploaded by user 'Richard and Gill' on Feb. 17th 2007.

Put simply, a folksonomy is an indexing method allowing users to apply freely chosen index terms. Peter Merholz (2004) labels it "metadata for the masses"; the writer James Surowiecki (2004) refers to it as one example of "the wisdom of crowds". The most remarkable effect of folksonomies is that they have managed to incorporate broad communities in the process of indexing documents on the WWW and made the use of content-descriptive metadata tangible for non-experts in indexing.

Folksonomies have now become an essential part of many social software and Web 2.0 applications. They are used to organize various types of resources such as scientific articles (Hotho, Jäschke et al., 2006b), references, bookmarks, pictures (Beaudoin, 2007), videos (Paolillo & Penumarthy, 2007), audio files, blog posts (Brooks & Montanez, 2006), discussions, events, places (Kennedy, Naaman et al., 2007), people (Farell, Lau et al, 2007) etc. Tags can be used as an additional access point to data collections outside of traditional folder structures. They are particularly needed to improve the retrievability of non-textual documents, such as videos and photos. Also, they are probably the only way in which large data collections on the Web can be indexed in an intellectual yet cost-efficient manner.

Just like certain social software applications, folksonomies have found their way out of the Web 2.0. It is of course also possible to work with folksonomies outside of Social Web contexts, e.g. in company intranets (Fichter, 2006) or for indexing corporate blogs, podcasts and vodcasts (Peters, 2006a and 2006b), for corporate bookmarking services (Millen, Feinberg & Kerr, 2006) and message boards (Murison, 2005). With the advent of these approaches, folksonomies have to be considered as a serious candidate for knowledge organization implementations.

Also, the branches that traditionally rely on elaborated professional indexing methods have started to give folksonomies a try. Engineering Village[78] by Reed Elsevier was the first commercial online information supplier to implement social tagging, followed by GENIOS' WISO portal[79]. Folksonomies are suggested for broader use within professional databases (Stock, 2007b) as well as libraries (Kroski, 2005; Spiteri, 2006). Among the latter, the library of the University of Pennsylvania was a pioneer in allowing user-generated tags with its system PennTags[80]. Trant (2006a and 2006b) discusses folksonomies as a user-focused access point to art museum holdings.

All this shows that a process of rethinking is taking place in classical document indexing domains. And what is more, social tagging applications can be envisioned for other parts of everyday life, e.g. as an addition to classificatory folder approaches – for online shopping portals (Tschetschoning, Ladengruber et al., 2008) or for structuring files on a personal computer[81].

Folksonomies have made rapid progress in their way into various practical application scenarios. Within less than five years of their existence, folksonomy-based applications have outnumbered ontology-based applications by far. While semantic indexing based on formal ontologies is still mainly applied to narrow niche application scenarios, social tags can be found in a variety of practical settings, and the process of social tagging is performed by a large community. Yet apart from this success and their various advantages, folksonomies do entail certain problems and shortcomings – which have not remained unnoticed by both users and the research community (Figure 1.38).

The problems of folksonomies are well-discussed, and options for improvement are a focus of several current research efforts (Peters, 2009). The most obvious problem is their lack of vocabulary control, which becomes particularly visible in comparison with other KOS. In folksonomies, spelling variants, synonyms, trans-language synonyms and abbreviations are in no way interlinked; homonyms are not distinguished. Misspellings and encoding limitations[82] are serious problems for folksonomies (Guy & Tonkin, 2006). This leads us back to the long-known "vocabulary problem" (Furnas, Landauer et al., 1987), which has quickly come to be considered to be a main challenge for tagging systems (e.g. Golder & Huberman, 2006; Furnas, Fake et al., 2006; Mathes, 2004): different people use different words to describe the same object (or document). This all leads to a lack of preci-

---

[78]   Engineering Village: http://www.engineeringvillage.com.
[79]   WISO: http://www.wiso-net.de.
[80]   PennTags: http://tags.library.upenn.edu/.
[81]   Some software developers have already integrated the tagging principle into their products. With Windows Vista, Microsoft enables the tagging of several data formats, such as pictures, videos and Office files. A similar approach can be found with Apple's iPhoto. Yet as long as tagging is performed by single users within their personal workspace the social component is lacking entirely, and we cannot speak of folksonomies in a strict sense – only of *personomies* (Hotho, Jäschke et al., 2006a).
[82]   E.g. if compound words and phrases cannot be captured and have to be transferred to makeshifts such as "semantic_web" or "SemanticWeb".

sion and recall when executing a search. There have been speculations that users will notice these problems and change their tagging behavior accordingly developing some sort of "tag literacy" (Guy & Tonkin, 2006). Yet detailed studies on user behavior in social tagging are still rare (some exceptions are Ames & Naaman, 2007; Hammond, Hannay et al., 2005; Marlow, Naaman et al., 2006).

Benefits of Folksonomies	Problems of Folksonomies
Folksonomies • represent an authentic use of language, • allow for multiple interpretations, • recognize neologisms, • are cheap methods of indexing, • are the only way to index mass information on the Web, • leave the quality "control" to the masses, • allow for searching and – perhaps even better – browsing, • can help to identify communities, • are sources for collaborative recommender systems, • are sources for the development of ontologies, thesauri or classification systems, • make people sensitive to information indexing issues.	Folksonomies • have no vocabulary control and do not recognize synonyms or homonyms, • do not make use of semantic relations between tags, • mix up different degrees of specificity, • mix up different languages, • do not distinguish formal from content-descriptive tags, • include spam-tags, user-specific tags (which cannot be interpreted by users other than the author), and other misleading keywords.

Figure 1.38. Benefits and problems of folksonomies. Source: Modified from Peters & Stock, 2007b.

1.3.3 Collaboration vs. Collection

Web 2.0 is often described as a world of social efforts and collaborating communities – yet this is only one possible perspective. Many social software tools do not support explicit *collaboration* but are rather based on the *collection* of data. Wikipedia is the most popular example of a really collaborative approach: different users work together to create one shared representation of a topic in the form of an encyclopedic article. Of course, wiki articles may also be created by individual users without any interaction – and this is actually the fact for quite a lot of

Wikipedia topics. But the wiki software provides the means for interaction and collaboration, and in many cases there is a process of discussion and revision before a final version of an article is settled on. This of course does not always proceed without complications and some disagreements may be too strong to put aside. In contrast, there is no need at all to communicate and to agree on some point of view with some social software tools, such as bookmarking or photo-sharing platforms. These tools facilitate the collection, storage and exchange of data – on the basis that every user acts independently from the others. The value of a social software platform is to a large extent down to the amount of collected data. This holds for pure collective tools, where a user may access the whole collection and browse other users' documents, as well as for collaborative platforms like Wikipedia, which aim to establish a huge collection of knowledge. Gruber (2008) refers to the majority of Web 2.0 tools as providing "*collected* intelligence". *Collected knowledge systems* are characterized by user-generated content with large domain coverage including manifold perspectives; the more people contribute, the more useful the system gets (Gruber, 2008).

Similarly to the distinction between collaborative and collective systems, one may argue whether the expression 'social software' is appropriate, as users' intentions to contribute to those platforms do not have to be social but can be entirely focused on personal benefits (e.g. one may use a social bookmarking system with the mere intention to organize one's own personal bookmarks) (Pluzhenskaia, 2006). The same holds for social tagging. Users who tag documents do not necessarily do so with the objective of helping a community find relevant information. Many users simply use tags to organize their own private collection. Thus many tags in use are personal rather than social (Guy & Tonkin, 2006); including some tags which do not describe the content but give a judgment (like 'stupid'). Some tags "are virtually meaningless to anybody except their creators" (Pluzhenskaia, 2006) or can only be understood in a specific context (like the term 'me' on Flickr, which describes a photo of the document's author). Others can be called "performative"; a planned or performed activity is tagged, for example 'toread' on Delicious (Kipp, 2006).

Of course this also accentuates the openness of folksonomies, the flexibility in the personal choice of tags. This still is a valuable advantage of social tagging, particularly regarding timeliness and multiple perspectives. Folksonomy users are not bound to a certain point of view and can create tags quickly in response to new developments and changes in terminologies (Kroski, 2005). These effects can only work in systems that refer to collective principles.

architecture **art** australia **beach** birthday blue bw **california** canada **canon** china **christmas** **city** concert england **europe** **family** festival **flower** **flowers** food **france** **friends** fun germany green **italy** **japan** **london** **music** **nature** new **newyork** night **nikon** **nyc** **paris** **park** **party** **people** **portrait** red sanfrancisco **sky** **snow** spain street **summer** sunset taiwan **travel** **trip** uk **usa** **vacation** **water** **wedding** white **winter**

Figure 1.39. A tag cloud from Flickr which displays the most popular tags within the entire Flickr platform in alphabetical order. The bigger the font size of a tag, the more often a tag has been used. Source: www.flickr.com.

Vander Wal (2008) has pointed out the importance of a distinction between collective and collaborative systems for the interpretation of social tagging. Folksonomies originate in the collection of users' tags within one platform. There are no attempts by users to collaborate in finding the most appropriate tags for a document or in establishing consistent tagging vocabulary. The value of folksonomies is based on the collection of tags – where counting tag frequencies is the embodiment of the 'wisdom of crowds' principle in folksonomies (the implication being that 'if a tag is assigned various times by different people to the same document, it has to be meaningful and appropriate'). A *tag cloud* is the most popular method for displaying the most frequently applied tags of a folksonomy (Figure 1.39) (Sinclair & Cardew-Hall, 2008).

For counting tag frequencies two different types of folksonomies have to be distinguished according to Vander Wal (2005): *broad folksonomies* are systems in which every document can be tagged several times by different people, so that tags can be assigned more than once (e.g. in the bookmarking service Delicious[83]); on the other hand, systems where every tag can be assigned to a document only once are called *narrow folksonomies* (these are sometimes systems, where only the creator of a document may tag it, like the photo-sharing platform Flickr; in other cases, different people may tag the document but every tag is only recorded once). In broad folksonomies, tag clouds can be generated to display the popularity of tags within the entire folksonomy as well as a document-specific tag cloud, which shows tags that were assigned to one specific document. In narrow folksonomies, tag clouds, by definition, cannot be provided for single documents (as every tag can only be assigned to a document once).

Analysis and graphical displays of these tag frequencies reveal tag distributions (Peters & Stock, 2007b) (which can be computed for all tags within a platform, but are mainly used to analyze the tags for one single document within a broad folksonomy). The most popular tag distribution is the *power law distribution*

---

[83] Delicious (formerly del.icio.us): http://delicious.com.

(Shirky, 2005; Vander Wal, 2005), following a Lotka-like power law (Egghe & Rousseau, 1990; Egghe, 2005). In this case, we have a small number of tags with very high frequencies and a "long tail" (Anderson, 2006; Shirky, 2005) of numerous tags with low frequencies (Figure 1.40).

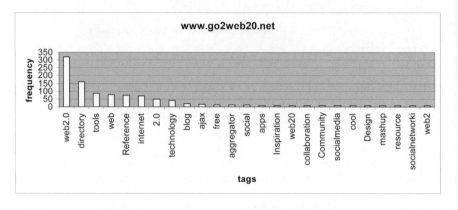

Figure 1.40. Power law distribution of tags. Based on tagging data from Delicious for http://www.go2web20.net, retrieved 2008-05-15. Source: Weller, Peters & Stock, 2009.

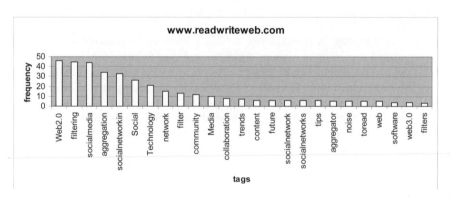

Figure 1.41. Inverse-logistic distribution of tags. Based on tagging data from Delicious for http://www.readwriteweb.com, retrieved 2008-05-15. Source: Weller, Peters & Stock, 2009.

Peters and Stock (2007b) point out the existence of at least one additional important prototypical distribution in folksonomies, the *inverse logistic distribution* (Stock, 2006). In this case, there are again many seldom-used tags forming the long tail of the distribution's graph, but there are also many high-frequency tags at the curve's left-hand side, which are called the "long trunk" (Figure 1.41) (Peters & Stock, 2007b). It is not always easy to distinguish these distributions at first sight. Both share the long tail characteristic, and high-frequency (and thus probably highly relevant) "power tags" can be determined for both cases:

> "There are two possibilities to emphasize "power tags": a) in case of an informetric [i.e. a power-law] distribution we pick the first n tags (e.g. the first three tags) and b) in case of an inverse-logistic distribution we pick all tags of the left-hand long trunk." (Peters & Stock, 2007b)

Peters and Stock (2007b) envision these power tags for use as additional search functionalities in folksonomy-based systems. For us, their integration into ontologies or other KOS may also be of interest (as will be discussed in Section 3.3.1). Yet for both of these aims, a closer analysis of and fundamental research on tag distributions and their emergence would be extremely beneficial. This would lead to a better understanding of community dynamics and assumed consensus in tag assignments. Currently, the evolution of such long tail tag distributions is explained by the well-known 'rich gets richer' or 'success breeds success' phenomenon (Egghe & Rousseau, 1995): Tags that are already popular and highly visible will be adopted by others and used even more often, other tags are only rarely used and will form the "long tail" (Cattuto, Loreto & Pietronero, 2007; Halpin, Robu & Shepherd, 2007). Several studies show that the characteristic shape of the distributions of document-specific tags (not the absolute number of tags) will remain stable at a certain point in time (Kipp & Campbell, 2006; Golder & Huberman, 2006; Halpin, Robu & Shepherd, 2007; Maass, Kowatsch & Münster, 2007).

Furthermore, statistics and metrics derived from folksonomies may be used for other purposes, e.g. for detecting user communities (Diederich & Iofciu, 2006). The Tagline Generator[84] also analyzes information inherently hidden in folksonomies by visualizing how popular terms within a topic-specific tag cloud change over time. The result is a timeline-based tag cloud, which can help to observe developments or opinions regarding certain events.

In a nutshell, folksonomies profit from the collective features of social software tools. Thus knowledge representation with folksonomies is entirely based on the sum of primarily individual ideas. These collections can be mined to obtain information for different purposes. For the context of this book, the most interesting aspects (which will be discussed in chapter 3) are: a) how folksonomy mining can be used for ontology maintenance and the enrichment of semantic representations and b) how collective principles can be combined most effectively with collaborative approaches in ontology engineering. These questions also mark an important next step in Web research: the fusion of Web 2.0 and Semantic Web aspects, the *Social Semantic Web*.

---

[84] Tagline Generator: http://chir.ag/tech/download/tagline/.

1.4 The Social Semantic Web

Recently, Semantic Web research has been accompanied by more and more Web 2.0 elements. The two formerly distinct (even regarded as competing by some) fields are increasingly merging (Ankolekar, Krötzsch et al., 2007 and 2008; Breslin, Passant & Decker, 2009; Greaves, 2007; Hoser & Hotho, 2007; Mika & Greaves, 2008), resulting in what has been called the *Social Semantic Web* or *Web 3.0*[85]. This convergence can be observed in scientific conferences' topics[86] and publications (Blumauer & Pellegrini, 2008) as well as in some applications already (see below). Mika and Greaves (2008) point out that both Web 2.0 and the Semantic Web "address the fundamental concept of socially shared meaning" and report a strong belief that the Social Semantic Web will "become a major application area of Semantic Web technology". The Social Web as an "ecosystem of participation, where value is created by the aggregation of many individual user contributions" and the Semantic Web as "an ecosystem of data, where value is created by the integration of structured data from many sources" (Gruber, 2008) complement each other. The Web and its users will profit from this combination of social and semantic approaches:

> "We believe that future Web applications will retain the Web 2.0 focus on community and usability, while drawing on Semantic Web infrastructure to facilitate mashup-like information sharing. [...] The Semantic Web can learn from Web 2.0's focus on community and interactivity, while Web 2.0 can draw from the Semantic Web's rich technical infrastructure for exchanging information across application boundaries." (Ankolekar, Krötzsch et al., 2007)

The resulting research questions also come from two perspectives and can be summed up as 'What lessons can Semantic Web technologies learn from the success of Web 2.0?' and 'How can semantic techniques be used to enhance the values of Web 2.0 sites?' (Mika & Greaves, 2008). Web 2.0 trends have produced (at least) four effects that are of high interest for Semantic Web efforts: a) user participation, and even user collaboration, has become a natural part of the World Wide Web, b) large collections of user-generated content are available and represent various perspectives and points of interest, c) the basic principles of document indexing have become easy to grasp due to social tagging applications, and d) networking structures support the interlinking of people as well as contents.

The tendency to recombine existing applications in order to generate mash-ups with additional benefits can be regarded as another positive effect of Web 2.0 (Ankolekar, Krötzsch et al., 2007).

---

[85]   We will prefer the term 'Social Semantic Web' because sometimes the term 'Web 3.0' is also used as a synonym for 'Semantic Web' (Markoff, 2006).

[86]   E.g. the panel discussion at WWW 2006 (http://www2006.org/programme/item.php?id=panelk01) and ISWC 2006 (http://iswc2006.semanticweb.org/program/webpanel.php).

On the other hand, Semantic Web technologies will help to provide a structure for the miscellaneous Web 2.0 services by adding structured metadata to the document collections and by interlinking the various individual data storage services (Gruber, 2008).

> "The challenge for the next generation of the Social and Semantic Webs is to find the right match between what is put online and methods for doing useful reasoning with the data. True collective intelligence can emerge if the data collected from all those people is aggregated and recombined to create new knowledge and new ways of learning that individual humans cannot do by themselves." (Gruber, 2008)

According to Gruber, machine support and inference systems are the key to turning collected information into instruments of collective intelligence. Computation and inference over collected information can lead to answers and discoveries that cannot be found in the individual contributions. In this way, new values are created from the collected data. He refers to this as "emergent knowledge" (Gruber, 2008).

Hendler and Goldbeck (2008) consider network effects as the critical factor of success of a Social Semantic Web.

> "The network effect describes the value of a service to a user that arises from the number of people using the service. At its core, it captures that value increases as the number of users increases, because the potential links increase for every user as a new person joins. This is best quantified by what has come to be known as Metcalfe's law." (Hendler & Goldbeck, 2008)

These networks in today's Web can belong to various types, as we will see in the next section. Interlinking efforts can be observed on different levels, originating in the fields of Web 2.0, Semantic Web and e-Science. They all help to create new and more effective navigation options on the Web.

1.4.1 A Networked World: Web 2.0, Semantic Web & e-Science

Joining the strengths of Social and Semantic Web is envisioned to enable a new networked Web infrastructure, with advantages for various areas of everyday life. A large application area that has aroused early interest is the support of networked scientific collaboration. Research co-operations are generally gaining in importance (Hendler, 2003; Sonnenwald, 2007), thus also requiring adequate communication channels and technical support.

Funding agencies in several countries[87] are searching for ways of providing a working environment which would release scientists from routine technical tasks, simplify scientific workflow and enable efficient infrastructures as well as a comprehensive interlinking of research institutes. These efforts have been classed under the keyword *e-Science* (Hey & Trefethen, 2003). The term stands for "en-

---

[87]   Mainly the UK and USA, but also, among others, Germany.

hanced science" and has been introduced by John Taylor (the former manager of Hewlett-Packard and Director General of the United Kingdom's Office of Science and Technology). In 2001, it was first used to name a large research funding program in Great Britain, the "UK e-Science Program"[88].

Projects and funding of *e-Science* started with attempts to establish a networked architecture for scientific work. They focused on interlinking data and resources; most of all on resources for distributed computing in *Grid* networks (Foster & Kesselmann, 2004). In this context, similar projects in the USA coined the term *cyberinfrastructures* (Hey & Trefethen, 2005). Large computing centers and physical networks provide the foundation for storage, processing, exchange and examination of primary research data.

Although this technical interlinking of scientific institutes and the distributed handling of computationally intensive tasks constitutes an important foundation for efficient research work, more aspects have to be combined in order to achieve a comprehensive restructuring of the scientific infrastructure. Apart from computer networks, the interlinking of knowledge (*knowledge networking*) is crucial. Knowledge networks can be provided on two levels: either they focus on the people who congregate to share their expertise (*human infrastructures* or *social networking*), or the focus is on providing highly interlinked and navigable data or knowledge units (*resource networks, data grid*) (Hey & Trefethen 2005; Lee, Dourish & Mark, 2006; Niederee, Risse et al., 2007; Paulsen, Mainz et al., 2007). Here we can find some first points of contact to Web 2.0 elements. Hendler and Goldbeck (2008) regard the social networks as particularly important not only for connecting people but also for navigation within the Social Web; searching and navigating in sharing portals is enhanced mainly through social contexts, not content-descriptive data.

Several social software applications can be used to facilitate knowledge sharing and management in (scientific) work groups as well support the establishing of overall virtual communities. Some social networking portals explicitly address scientists, e.g. the Nature Network[89] by the Nature Publishing Group. The shared collection, aggregation and analysis of knowledge units may also be accomplished using certain social software tools (Weller, Mainz et al., 2007a).

Goble, Corcho et al. (2006) sum up the different requirements that have to be combined for global scientific networking:

> "Scientific progress increasingly depends on pooling resources, know-how and results; making connections between ideas, people, and data; and finding and interpreting knowledge generated by others, in ways that may have not been anticipated when it was created. [...] It has as much to do with intelligent information management as with sharing scarce resources like large scale computing power or expensive instrumentation." (Goble, Corcho et al., 2006)

---

[88]   UK e-Science Program: http://www.rcuk.ac.uk/escience/default.htm.
[89]   Nature Network: http://network.nature.com.

We may further point out the aspect of availability of resources as discussed in the open access initiatives (e.g. Cram, 2005; Deutsche Forschungsgemeinschaft, 2005; Guédon 2004; Harnad, Brody et al., 2004). Within the Semantic Web community, the idea of open access to publications has been broadened to open access to data and – with regard to social applications – to social data collections for reuse in other applications (Bizer, Cyganiak et al., 2007), with the most notable efforts stemming from the Linking Open Data[90] project (see Section 3.4.3).

Finally, the aspect of 'intelligent information management' has to be considered. The collected knowledge resources have to be made retrievable and navigable. While an entirely free tagging of information units works well for photo sharing portals and other entertainment services, scientific contexts make higher demands on context indexing. Controlled and structured metadata are needed to enable context-sensitive information navigation and semantic integration. Knowledge should not only be easily findable but should also be integrated into contexts of other existing information. This is where ontologies and semantic annotation approach enter the scene[91].

A lot of the effort to establish ontologies for knowledge representation is made in the various fields of life sciences, additionally supported by activities in bioinformatics and related e-Science projects (Baclawski & Niu, 2006; Bodenreider & Stevens, 2006; Burger, Davidson & Baldock, 2008). In these areas, there is a particular need for sound shared vocabularies for indexing purposes. This is due to the vast amount of data produced in this field, as well as to inconsistent terminologies and definitions within this large research area, which make scientific exchange eminently difficult. Ontologies are also used to capture the actual standard of knowledge of a research community, in definitions that should be as unambiguous as possible (Neumann & Prusak, 2007). The most popular example of ontologies in the life sciences is the Gene Ontology (GO) project (Ashburner, Ball et al., 2000).[92] In this same context we also find some interesting approaches and discussions on scientific online communities (Clark & Kinoshita, 2007; Neumann & Prusak, 2007) and the combining of community collaboration with semantics.

In sum, the following levels of networking are of relevance for comprehensive knowledge management and collaboration in science (Figure 1.42): distributed computing, interlinked and collaborating communities, accessibility of resources and semantic interlinking of knowledge units.

---

[90] Linking Open Data:
http://esw.w3.org/topic/SweoIG/TaskForces/CommunityProjects/Linking OpenData.

[91] Furthermore, ontologies are used to enhance the interoperability of grid technologies within so-called semantic grid applications (Bachler, Buckingham Shum et al., 2004; Corcho, Pinar et al., 2006).

[92] Bio-ontologies will also be discussed in chapter 3.2.2.

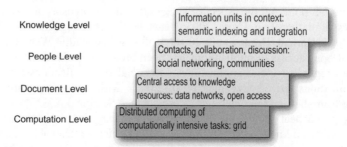

Figure 1.42. Levels of interconnectedness. Source: Modified from Weller, Mainz et al., 2007b.

The ideal composition of networks for e-Science would thus look something like this: technologies use distributed computation networks to handle scientific research data, the results are kept in universal and comprehensive archives (covering both primary data and publications). These archives are collaboratively administered and updated. Communities comment on and discuss available content, using the provided portals to organize and structure information; ontologies are used for semantic indexing. While this comprehensive scenario is only a distant vision so far, some smaller applications can already be found and used.

1.4.2 Approaches for Mashing-Up the Social and Semantic Web

Not all efforts to combine collaborative and collective principles with semantics are focusing particularly on scientific application scenarios. More and more projects envision the usage for generally all internet users. Among them are the following ideas.

Semantically Interlinked Communities

Some projects deal with the development of ontologies for capturing social networks (e.g. people, projects, events and activities) (Bachler, Buckingham Shum et al., 2004; Breslin, Harth et al., 2005). Most popular is the FOAF[93] project founded by Dan Brickley and Libby Miller (Brickley & Miller, 2003; Dodds, 2004; Goldbeck, 2007). The idea behind it is to enable social networking in a platform independent way. Networking platforms like Facebook or XING are closed systems which 'lock in' their users[94]; a user can only state his relationships to other users on the same platform. Web 2.0 consists of separated "silos", "leading to the un-Web-like situation where a friend on Facebook is a stranger on MySpace" (Heath

---

[93]   FOAF, Friend Of A Friend: http://www.foaf-project.org/.
[94]   Some small attempts have been started to reduce this, for example a Facebook's application is available that points to Xing profile pages.

& Motta, 2008). FOAF is an ontology – or, more precisely, an RDF vocabulary – that can represent information about people, their interests, relationships and activities. Anyone can create his own FOAF description including his name, contact details, interests etc. and then publish it (Figure 1.43). Tools like FOAF-a-matic[95] help non-experts in RDF to create a FOAF profile. Furthermore, the FOAF description may include information about "friends", which actually constitutes the networking effect.

> "The `foaf:knows` property is used to assert that there is some relationship between two people. Precisely what this relationship is, and whether it's reciprocal (i.e. if you know me, do I automatically know you?), is deliberately left undefined." (Dodds, 2004)

URIs are used to uniquely identify individuals and to disambiguate of people with the same name.

```
<rdf:RDF xmlns:rdf="http://www.w3.org/1999/02/22-rdf-syntax-ns#"
         xmlns:foaf="http://xmlns.com/foaf/0.1/"
         xmlns:rdfs="http://www.w3.org/2000/01/rdf-schema#">

<foaf:Person rdf:nodeID="harry">
  <foaf:name>Harry Osborn</foaf:name>
  <rdfs:seeAlso rdf:resource="http://www.osborn.com/harry.rdf"/>
</foaf:Person>

<foaf:Person>
  <foaf:name>Peter Parker</foaf:name>

  <foaf:knows rdf:nodeID="harry"/>

  <foaf:knows>
      <foaf:Person>
        <foaf:name>Aunt May</foaf:name>
      </foaf:Person>
  </foaf:knows>
</foaf:Person>

</rdf:RDF>
```

Figure 1.43. Two persons and their interrelatedness captured in the FOAF format. Source: Dodds, 2004.

As FOAF is based on RDF and is machine-readable, it may easily be used by other applications. The option of using FOAF for digital photo collections has already been considered by the developing community:

> "Digital cameras being all the rage these days, it's not surprising that many people are interested in capturing metadata about their pictures. FOAF provides for this use case in several ways. First, using the `foaf:depiction` property we can make a statement that says 'this person (Resource) is

---

[95] FOAF-a-matic: http://www.ldodds.com/foaf/foaf-a-matic.html.

shown in this image'. FOAF also supports an inverse of this property
(foaf:depicts) that allows us to make statements of the form: 'this image is a picture of this Resource'." (Dodds, 2004)

First projects have been started to integrate FOAF in other social semantic applications. Celma, Ramirez and Herrera (2005) describe their idea for a music recommendation system that combines user profiles via FOAF descriptions and content-based metadata. FOAF users can state their favorite music – as well as any
other hobby – via foaf:interest. These fields are checked with a music repository to see whether they match a band or artist's name – and are then used as the
basis for computing users with similar interests.

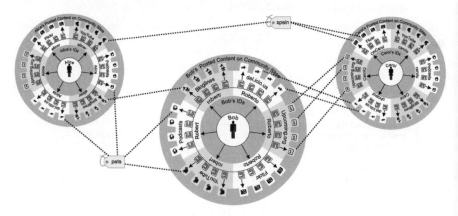

Figure 1.44. The SIOC approach to creating social networks via object-centered sociality.
Source: Bojars, Breslin et al., 2008.

Another valuable addition to FOAF is the SIOC[96] project. This project goes one
step further and addresses the problem of community interconnections as well as
the various contributions by users on Web 2.0 sites (Bojars, Breslin et al., 2008;
Breslin, Harth et al., 2005). Their motivation is to capture "an individual's entire
contribution to the Social Web" (Bojars, Breslin et al., 2008).

> "A combination of the FOAF (Friend of a Friend) vocabulary and SIOC can
> be used to describe content created by a person across several different sites
> by including a list of her social media site accounts in personal FOAF pro-
> files and using SIOC to express user-created content on these sites." (Bo-
> jars, Breslin et al., 2008)

In this way one can make exhaustive use of the "object-centered sociality"
(Engeström, 2004), of social networks that "are being formed through created content and things that people have in common" (Bojars, Breslin et al., 2008). This

---

[96]   SIOC, Semantically Interlinked Online Communities: http://sioc-project.org/.

idea is illustrated in Figure 1.44: a person is linked to the social platforms he uses (with his respective user names) and the types of content he creates there. Across the platforms, he is linked to other people connected by the content they create, co-annotate or for which they use similar tags.

The SIOC initiative has developed a core ontology[97] that defines the main concepts and properties required to describe information about online communities (Breslin, Harth et al., 2005). It was expanded by the SIOC Types module, which provides additional structures for describing different Web 2.0 objects and content items that people are creating, annotating or talking about in Web 2.0 platforms. Other RDF vocabularies describing possible Web 2.0 objects should be integrated by being applied as values for certain SIOC-specific relations. For example, vocabularies are needed to describe what a blog is about, and they can be integrated via the `sioc:about` relation (Bojars, Breslin et al., 2008).

This model could be used to retrieve information about all persons who have replied to posts created by a particular user. For this kind of query over the underlying RDF data, the Social SIOC Explorer[98] has been developed in order to extract social relations and context from online community sites.

Semantic Blogs

Blogs (short for *weblogs*) are among the most popular Web 2.0 developments. They are personal websites in the form of journals or diaries, created by people "to express personal or professional views on their world or on observed items that may be of interest to others" (Möller, Bojars & Breslin, 2006). Blogs can deal with any topic of personal interest. *Bloggers* habitually publish short texts to their personal blog website, where they are collected chronologically (with the newest blog post at the top of the page) and may often be commented on by others. Several Web-based blogging services are available to allow users to set up their own blog without any technical knowledge[99]. These services often provide integrated RSS feeds: xml documents containing information about new items on a Web site or content summaries that can be subscribed to by users. Users subscribing to the feed will be notified about new blog posts. Trackback[100] and permalink[101] are other features that have become popular with blogging. Hendler and Goldbeck (2008) consider these techniques to be critical for the development of a link space that enables the desired network effects for the Social Web. Many bloggers tag their blog posts with free keywords. Thus folksonomies (or rather personomies) are the state of the art in indexing blogs.

---

[97] SIOC core ontology: http://www.w3.org/Submission/2007/02/.
[98] SIOC Explorer: https://launchpad.net/sioc-ex.
[99] For example: Movable Type (http://www.movabletype.org), WordPress (http://wordpress.org), LiveJournal (www.livejournal.com/) and Blogger (https://www.blogger.com).
[100] The trackback feature notifies the owner of a blog if one of his posts is cited in another blog.
[101] A permalink is a URL that points to exactly one blog post. In this way, every blog post receives its own URL and can be linked directly.

Semantic blogging is intended for indexing single content items within a blog post with semantic information. A different approach is to establish structured formats for certain parts of a blog, e.g. by using specific forms with schematic fields. The idea of semantic blogging has been discussed earlier by Cayzer (2004 and 2006), Karger and Quan (2004) and Möller, Bojars and Breslin (2006). Current blogs do not provide any information about how the different posts relate to another (e.g. whether two blog posts are both discussing different actresses or if blog post A is about an actress who has also directed another movie which in turn is reviewed in blog post B). Formal and content-descriptive metadata should be added. Structured data in blogs can mainly be captured for clearly defined domains such as film or literature for which typical properties can be identified.

> "In structured blogging, structured data about people, reviews, events and other objects are becoming a part of blog posts. Sometimes a person will need for more structure in their posts (e.g. when doing a review) and may best be served by filling in an appropriate form during the post creation process. An advantage of microformats and structured blogging is that they can serve as an introduction to semantics for non-technical users: users simply choose their post type and some semantic content is generated in the background. A little bit of structure added by the user allows us to generate a lot more semantics." (Bojars, Breslin et al., 2008)

Ankolekar et al. (2007 and 2008) have presented an approach to semantic blogging in the domain of film reviews: A blogger who regularly blogs about movies could then be supported by a specific "movie plug-in". This plug-in should contain a form with fields for basic movie properties. Typical information about movies would then be explicitly provided by the blogger for every blog post, such as the director, runtime and official homepage of the film. Ideally, the film would also be uniquely identified by linking to an authoritative reference – like Wikipedia or the Internet Movie Database (IMDb[102]). The plug-in should then transfer the collected data into a machine readable format (e.g. RDF) without the blogger noticing. The information provided for every movie can then be used as semi-structured tags for navigation within the blog. In a next step towards the Semantic Web, these data would have to be directly interlinked, e.g. with information on cinemas, the respective films' runtimes, or online shops selling the DVDs (Ankolekar, Krötzsch et al., 2007).

Of course, other existing formal representations could also be used for the semantic enrichments of blogs, e.g. SIOC or FOAF for person identification (Möller, Bojars & Breslin, 2006; Passant, 2007). Structured Blogging[103] is a tool that can be installed to classical blogging software for capturing some basic structured data on blogging "reviews" (of events, journal articles, movies, restaurants, websites, etc.).

---

[102] IMDb: http://www.imdb.com/.
[103] Structured Blogging: http://structuredblogging.org.

Semantic Wikis

Quite a lot of research concerning the convergence of the Social and the Semantic Web is done in the field of *semantic wikis* (Buffa, Gandon et al., 2008; Lange, Schaffert et al., 2008). A *wiki* is a collection of editable and interlinked pages on the Web. Users can fill them with their own content, edit, modify and interlink pages and create new ones with little effort. The idea comes from Ward Cunningham, who developed the first wiki, the Portland Pattern Repository[104], in 1995 (Leuf & Cunningham, 2001). The editing and interlinking of wiki pages is done online in a Web browser using a simplified markup language.

> "Cunningham's biggest contribution from our point of view is the invention of WikiWords as a means to create hyperlinks, even to pages not yet created. Type a WikiWord (e.g., NewPage) and it will be saved as a link to a page whose URL ends with this WikiWord. If the page does not exist, clicking on the link creates it." (Buffa, Gandon et al., 2008)

Since then, several wiki engines have been developed, which slightly differ in user interfaces and functionalities, e.g. using a different wiki syntax for page editing. The most popular wiki application is the online encyclopedia Wikipedia (using the MediaWiki[105] engine).

There are two different ways in which wikis and semantic technologies can act together (though sometimes both directions are combined within one project): a) wiki principles and technologies can be adopted for ontology engineering tools in order to enable collaborative ontology creation; and b) wiki platforms are enriched with specific extensions to add structured semantics to the wiki articles. While the latter is more frequently referred to as the 'semantic wiki approach', we will discuss the first aspect in Section 3.2.2 on community-based ontology engineering.

Semantic knowledge in wikis is envisioned to enable better retrieval functions, identification of community networks, dynamic content update, detection of implicit connections etc.

Many semantic wikis are currently under development, as the community is still experimenting with different approaches on how to handle the integration of wikis and semantics. Sometimes semantic technologies are built on top of existing wiki engines, in other cases semantic wikis are developed from scratch. Different ways of integrating ontology editors and inference engines with wikis are being explored. Buffa, Gandon et al. (2008) provide a broad overview on current projects.

Much attention is also focused on the development of semantic enhancements for Wikipedia, as a semantic version of the MediaWiki engine is currently being developed (Krötzsch, Vrandecic & Völkel 2005 and 2006; Völkel, Krötzsch et al., 2006; Vrandecic & Krötzsch, 2006). Wikipedia is the largest online encyclopedia collaboratively developed by a community of volunteers and has become an enormously broad knowledge collection.

---

[104] Portland Pattern Repository's Wiki: http://www.c2.com/cgi/wiki?WelcomeVisitors.
[105] MediaWiki: http://www.mediawiki.org

> "Besides the encyclopedic articles on many subjects, Wikipedia also holds numerous articles that are meant to enhance the browsing of Wikipedia: rock'n'roll albums in the sixties; lists of the countries of the world, sorted by area, population, or the index of free speech; the list of popes sorted by length of papacy, their name or the year of inauguration. [...] As it is now, all these lists have to be written manually, introducing several sources of inconsistency, only maintainable through the sheer size of the community."
> (Völkel, Krötzsch et al., 2006)

At first there was no way to process structured information in Wikipedia, e.g. information about how different articles are related. Now, extensions are being established in order to create semantic links between articles and to specify single aspects within an article. The aim is to enable information compilations across multiple articles, like "Give me a table of all movies from the 1960s with Italian directors" (Völkel, Krötzsch et al., 2006). Although all the information (movie titles, directors and years of release) is already included in the traditional Wikipedia, there is no way of allocating this information automatically; it can only be received by browsing through articles and reading them. In a new semantic version of Wikipedia this will be handled by two additional approaches to already existing categories (for classifying articles according to their content): Typed links and attributes. Both have to be added intellectually by the users.

Typed links are links between articles which state the type of interrelation between both articles. Figure 1.45 shows a schematic depiction of the article 'London' and its links to certain other articles like 'England' or 'United Kingdom'. In Figure 1.46 some of these links have been typed with specific semantic relations:

> "As an example, one could type a link from the article 'London' to 'England' with the relation 'is capital of.' Even very simple search algorithms would then suffice to provide a precise answer to the question 'What is the capital of England?'" (Völkel, Krötzsch et al., 2006).

The decision of how the linking relations should be named will be left to the users, with respect to the basic principles of wiki usage. Links are typed within the editing page of the wiki articles. This could look like the following: London [[is capital of::England]].

Attributes can also be attached to an article in order to specify its properties directly, without linking to additional articles. This is particularly needed in cases where the property value is a number, like dates and coordinates, or the examples 'population' and 'area' in Figure 1.47.

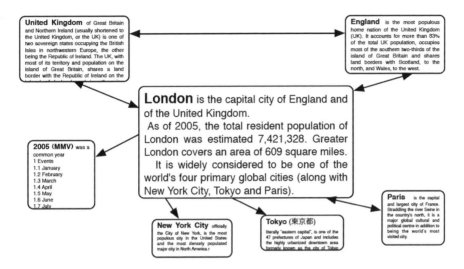

Figure 1.45. Linking structure between Wikipedia articles in the traditional version. Source: Völkel, Krötzsch et al., 2006.

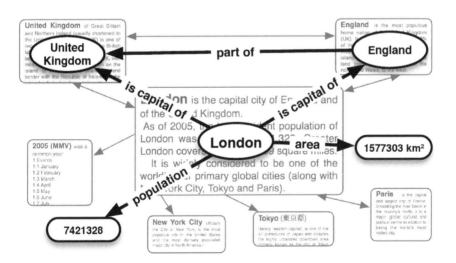

Figure 1.46. Approach for semantic relations to specify the types of interlinks between Wikipedia pages. Source: Völkel, Krötzsch et al., 2006.

The final application of these features is under development; an extension for the Semantic Media Wiki[106] can already be downloaded and used; further semantic extensions are planned. Considerations have to be made as to how the community can be provided with easy-to-handle mechanisms and with functionalities that directly demonstrate the benefits of these additional efforts. Currently, additional information can be displayed as semantic metadata for an article. To support machine processing, Semantic MediaWiki translates typed links and attributes into RDF and thus enables the use of external reasoners.

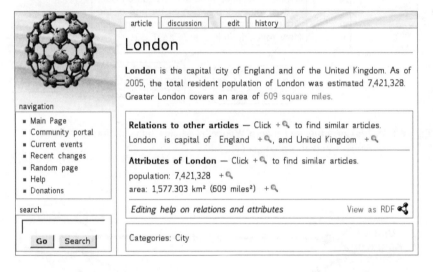

Figure 1.47. Displaying article relations and attributes for a wiki article with Semantic MediaWiki. Source: Völkel, Krötzsch et al., 2006.

A different but complementary approach is the DBpedia[107] project (Auer, Bizer et al., 2007; Auer & Lehmann, 2007; Bizer, Cyganiak, et al., 2007): it extracts structured information from Wikipedia and turns it into a machine-readable representation. DBpedia allows users to perform sophisticated queries over Wikipedia, e.g. 'Which cities in Germany have more than 100,000 inhabitants?' Different projects provide tools for formulating such queries against DBpedia, for example to find "all soccer players, who played as goalkeeper for a club that has a stadium with more than 40.000 seats and who are born in a country with more than 10 million

---

[106]   Semantic MediaWiki: http://semantic-mediawiki.org.
[107]   DBpedia: http://dbpedia.org.

inhabitants"[108]. In contrast to the Semantic MediaWiki approach, DBpedia does not require users to provide explicit semantics.

Semantic Knowledge Repositories, Semantic Desktops and Related Approaches

Besides wikis and blogs, other platforms also give social semantic technologies a try. So far the diversity of approaches is not easy to classify. One example is RealTravel[109], a portal for travel plans and travel experiences (Gruber, 2008). The domain of travel depends heavily on geographical information. This information can be well represented as ontologies, basically relying on hierarchical structures (meronymy, e.g. the state North Rhine Westphalia is_part_of Germany) and geospatial topology (e.g. the city of Düsseldorf is_next_to the river Rhine)[110]. If such a representation is available, inference mechanisms can be used to compute best-matching documents. RealTravel combines this kind of information with user-generated content, mainly blogs reporting travel experiences and different rating structures. Searching for content is then not only based on strings but on underlying geographical information, and query expansion mechanisms may be used.

Another example of a new Web application for the travel community is Dopplr[111]. Users publish their itineraries and share them with the community – to find out whether they have overlapping travel plans with others. Like RealTravel it uses a simple location ontology. If both Dopplr and RealTravel were combined, their users could profit from the new complementing contents. And if photos from Flickr or personal profiles from FOAF were added, we would end up with a new "mega application" (Hendler & Goldbeck, 2008).

The 2007 ISWC Semantic Web Challenge[112] was won by Revyu[113], a portal for user-generated reviews and ratings for all kinds of objects (Heath & Motta, 2008). The approach of Revyu is to provide an easy-to use interface for collecting various data – and to use this data to generate new RDF resources and thus to contribute to a Web of interlinked structured information (Bizer, Heath et al., 2007). The normal user is not aware of these activities and may simply tag his contributions as usual. Based on this tagging data, certain types of information can be turned into structured data; e.g. articles can be automatically classified as belonging to the categories 'film' or 'books' and are enriched with information from other Web sources or interlinked with other services such as DBpedia (by applying

---

[108] This and more examples as well as an overview on supportive tools can be found on: http://wiki.dbpedia.org/OnlineAccess.

[109] RealTravel: http://realtravel.com.

[110] For the domain of geographical information in general, the idea of *geotagging* is also an interesting alternative: Web resources may be tagged with geographical identification metadata, typically consisting of latitude and longitude coordinates, sometimes also additional information like altitude or place names.

[111] Dopplr: http://dopplr.com.

[112] Semantic Web Challenge: http://challenge.semanticweb.org.

[113] Revyu: http://revyu.com.

`owl:sameAs` statements). Revyu applies the metadata-schemes from FOAF, the Review RDF vocabulary[114] and the Tag Ontology[115].

The DBin[116] project aims at establishing a platform for collaborative knowledge collection supported by ontology structures (Tummarello, Morbidoni & Nucci, 2006). Communities of interest can form up and collect their knowledge (e.g. texts, commentaries, images) within a special kind of peer-to-peer network. The information units are coupled with different domain-specific ontologies, depending on the domain of interest. Also, templates for domain-specific annotations and for readily established domain queries are provided.

Lately, the idea of a semantic desktop has become a topic of interest in the Semantic Web community (Decker, Park et al., 2006; Groza, Handschuh et al., 2007; Nadeem & Sauermann, 2007, Sauermann, Bernardi & Dengel, 2005): personal information management (PIM) on personal computers should become more effective and interlinked with the help of (personal) ontologies. The semantic desktop should support the management of documents of everyday life – like e-mails, texts, video and audio files – which up to now have mainly been organized in folder structures (chiefly due to the propagation of this structural approach by the Windows Explorer). Thus the first step would be to make them interchangeable and manageable across programs.

> "A Semantic Desktop is a device in which an individual stores all her digital information like documents, multimedia and messages. These are interpreted as Semantic Web resources, each is identified by a Uniform Resource Identifier (URI) and all data is accessible and queryable as RDF graph. Resources from the web can be stored and authored content can be shared with others. Ontologies allow the user to express personal Mental Models and form the semantic glue interconnecting information and systems." (Sauermann, Bernardi & Dengel, 2005)

This idea can and should also be broadened to social semantic desktops, which is particularly needed for large projects and working groups. As currently documents are mainly exchanged via e-mail, every recipient has to solve the task of how to store and process the document – with the effect that "sending a document to 5–10 colleagues inside or outside an organization multiplies the effort of management of this document times the number of people it is being sent to" (Decker, 2006). Thus we broaden the scope from personal semantic document management to communities.

Currently the main project working on the realization of a semantic desktop is NEPOMUK[117] with its semantic desktop environment Gnowsis[118]. Sauermann, van Elst and Dengel (2007) have also presented the PIMO ontology framework for usage within semantic desktops.

---

[114]   Review RDF vocabulary: http://danja.talis.com/xmlns/rev_2007-11-09/index.html.
[115]   Tag Ontology: http://www.holygoat.co.uk/projects/tags/.
[116]   DBin: http://www.dbin.org.
[117]   NEPOMUK: http://nepomuk.semanticdesktop.org.
[118]   Gnowsis: http://www.gnowsis.org/.

1.4.3 Knowledge Representation in the Social Semantic Web

Indexing in the Social Semantic Web has the overall aim of enabling information integration on a large scale and harvesting the collected intelligence for other than the original purposes. So far, the strategies for achieving this have been:

- *Simple user interfaces plus semantics behind the scenes*: applications try to provide as easy-to-use as possible user interfaces in order to ensure contributions from numerous Web users. Users should not need to learn ontology languages to take part in the new kinds of semantic applications. Solutions are needed to transform the collected data into formal structures like RDF.

- *Practical approach to knowledge organization systems*: the model that serves a purpose best should be the one that is implemented. This may be an ontology, a thesaurus, a folksonomy or sometimes even a totally different knowledge resource like the Wikipedia hierarchy. The focus is less on formal semantics than on practicability.

- *Reuse and recombination of existing KOS resources*: the mash-up principle of Web 2.0 is also applied to metadata. If possible, existing structures should be reused and thus become distributed over the Web, which enhances integration of different applications. Existing informal knowledge models may also be transferred to RDF or OWL representations (like in the DBpedia project).

- *Interlinking of available KOS*: if no resources can directly be reused for an application they may still be interesting as additional references. Links to other available resources support the overall integrative approach.

- *Standard references*: widely accepted knowledge representations or other information collections with broad domain coverage are particularly valuable for interlinking and cross-referencing data. Wikipedia articles have already gained importance as object identifiers, e.g. for identifying movies in Revyu or in the semantic blog described by Ankolekar, Krötzsch et al. (2007). The linguistic thesaurus WordNet[119] (Fellbaum, 1999) is frequently used as a basis for mapping other vocabularies. The principle of standard references has to be related to the principle of assigning persistent, unique identifiers like URIs.

- *Data Portability and Open Access*: Data collected by communities must not end up in data silos where they cannot be accessed or exported freely. Not only should various documents be openly accessible, but also index terms in the form of social tags and newly created ontologies, for example in the form of RDF or OWL vocabularies.

Thus the Social Semantic Web will require different kinds of knowledge organization systems and novel approaches for them to interact. It will need social tagging as one easy approach for user involvement and data collection. It will need ontologies for the highest possible structure and ontology languages for exchange and standard integrations. It will need traditional KOS as qualitative and approved

---

[119] WordNet: http://wordnet.princeton.edu.

representations. And it will even need to access other knowledge collections and knowledge models as resources and referencing points. Although ontologies and formal knowledge representations are still the main focus of Social Semantic Web indexing, they are no longer to be viewed uncoupled from other KOS. So far, most of this is more of a vision than a reality. Yet considerable efforts to realize community-based semantics on the Web have begun.

Conclusion

This chapter has provided an overview on the past, present and future of methods for knowledge representation. Thesauri, classifications, nomenclatures and other classical KOS as well as folksonomies and ontologies all principally share the same aim: to enable better access to information by providing a vocabulary for associating documents with content-descriptive keywords. The more elaborated the KOS, the more users will profit from pre-established concept interrelations and richer semantics. Folksonomies take an exceptional position among knowledge organization systems as they are completely unstructured and thus do not provide any vocabulary control or features of semantic navigation at all. Ontologies not only enrich the expressivity of classical KOS by allowing for specified concept interrelations, but they are also formalized in specific ontology languages which enable machine-processing and the inference of knowledge.

We have introduced some examples for the practical application of knowledge organization systems. Nomenclatures, classifications and thesauri are well established in a variety of domains. In record time, folksonomies have made their way to large scale usage on the World Wide Web. Ontologies still lag behind the other KOS in terms of applicability and practical usage. To actually make use of the rich semantic power of ontologies, new approaches have to be found. The most promising idea seems to be the combination of user collaboration with rich semantics.

We have seen that the convergence of Web 2.0 and the Semantic Web has already begun and that it is proceeding rapidly with developments such as semantic wikis and semantic blogging. Finally, folksonomies and ontologies should not be viewed as rivaling systems (Gruber, 2005). They both play important roles in the new Social Semantic Web.

In the next section we will describe the most complex KOS in detail: we will explain the structure and elements of ontologies to enable a better understanding of the requirements of developing high-value semantic representations. This chapter will thus explicitly address the question of what is meant by semantics in the context of the Social Semantic Web. Ontologies are currently the most expressive way of handling semantics in computational contexts. After discussing the structure and elements of ontologies, we will once more take a look at the spectrum of different KOS.

All this provides the basis for the last chapter, where we will discuss the problems of knowledge representation in the Social Semantic Web with respect to: a) the process of creating appropriate knowledge models by including the collective power of the Social Web and b) the co-existence of various KOS.

References

Adomavicius, G., & Tuzhilin, A. (2005). Toward the Next Generation of Recommender Systems: A Survey of the State-of-the-Art and Possible Extensions. IEEE Transactions on Knowledge and Data Engineering, 17(6), 734–749.

Aitchison, J., Gilchrist, A., & Bawden, D. (2000). Thesaurus Construction and Use (4th Edition). London: Aslib.

Aitchison, J., Gomersall, A., & Ireland, R. (1969). Thesaurofacet: A Thesaurus and Faceted Classification for Engineering and Related Subjects. Rugby: Jolly and Barber.

Albrechtslund, A. (2008). Online Social Networking as Participatory Surveillance. First Monday, 13(3). Retrieved from http://www.uic.edu/htbin/cgiwrap/bin/ojs/index.php/fm/article/view/2142/1949.

Alby, T. (2007). Web 2.0: Konzepte, Anwendungen, Technologien. München, Wien: Carl Hanser Verlag.

Alexiev, V., Breu, M., de Bruijn, J., Fensel, D., Lara, R., & Lausen, H. (Eds.) (2005). Information Integration with Ontologies: Experiences from an Industrial Showcase. Chichester: Wiley & Sons.

Ames, M., & Naaman, M. (2007). Why We Tag: Motivations for Annotation in Mobile and Online Media. In B. Begole, et al. (Eds.). Proceedings of the SIGCHI Conference on Human Factors in Computing Systems. San Jose, California, USA (pp. 971–980). New York: ACM.

Anderson, C. (2006). The Long Tail: Why the Future of Business is Selling Less of More. New York: ACM.

Ankolekar, A., Krötzsch, M., Tran, T., & Vrandecic, D. (2007). The Two Cultures: Mashing Up Web 2.0 and the Semantic Web. In 16th International World Wide Web Conference (WWW 2007), Banff, Alberta, Canada (pp. 825–834). Red Hook: Curran.

Ankolekar, A., Krötzsch, M., Tran, T., & Vrandecic, D. (2008). The Two Cultures: Mashing Up Web 2.0 and the Semantic Web. Journal of Web Semantics, 6, 70–75.

Antoniou, G., & van Harmelen, F. (2004). A Semantic Web Primer. Cambridge: MIT Press.

Ashburner, M., Ball, C. A., Blake, J. A., Botstein, D., Butler, H., Cherry, J. M., et al. (2000). Gene Ontology: Tool for the Unification of Biology. Nature Genetics, 25, 25–29.

Auer, S., Bizer, C., Kobilarov, G., Lehmann, J., Cyganiak, R., & Ives, Z. (2007). DBpedia: A Nucleus for a Web of Open Data. In K. Aberer, & et al. (Eds.). The Semantic Web. 6th International Semantic Web Conference, 2nd Asian

Semantic Web Conference (ISWC 2007 + ASWC 2007), Busan, Korea (pp. 722–735). Berlin: Springer.

Auer, S., & Lehmann, J. (2007). What Have Innsbruck and Leipzig in Common? Extracting Semantics from Wiki Content. In E. Franconi, M. Kifer, & W. May (Eds.). The Semantic Web: Research and Applications. 4th European Semantic Web Conference (ESWC 2007), Innsbruck, Austria. Proceedings (pp. 503–517). Berlin, Heidelberg: Springer.

Aufaure, M. A., Le Grande, B., Soto, M., & Bannacer, N. (2006). Metadata- and Ontology-Based Semantic Web Mining. In D. Taniar, & J. W. Rahayu (Eds.). Web Semantics and Ontology (pp. 259–295). Hershey: Idea Group Publishing.

Baader, F., Calvanese, D., McGuinness, D., Nardi, D., & Patel-Schneider, P. F. (Eds.) (2003). The Description Logic Handbook: Theory, Implementation and Applications. Cambridge: Cambridge University Press.

Baca, M. (Ed.) (2002). Introduction to Art Image Access. Los Angeles: Getty Research Institute.

Bächle, M. (2006). Social Software. Informatik-Spektrum, 29(2), 121–124.

Bachler, M., Buckinham Shum, S., Chen-Burger, J., Dalton, J., de Roure, D., Eisenstadt, M., et al. (2004). Collaborative Tools in the Semantic Grid. In GGF11 Semantic Grid Applications Workshop, Honolulu, Hawaii, USA. Retrieved from http://eprints.ecs.soton.ac.uk/9439/.

Baclawski, K., & Niu, T. (2006). Ontologies for Bioinformatics. Cambridge: MIT Press.

Barnbrook, G., Danielsson, P., & Mahlberg, M. (Eds.) (2006). Meaningful Texts: The Extraction of Semantic Information from Monolingual and Multilingual Corpora. London, New York: Continuum.

Batley, S. (2005). Classification in Theory and Practice. Oxford: Chandos.

Beaudoin, J. (2007). Flickr Image Tagging: Patterns Made Visible. Bulletin of the ASIST, 34(1), 26–29.

Beckett, D., & Broekstra J. (2007). SPARQL Query Results XML Format: W3C Working Draft 14 June 2007. Retrieved from http://www.w3.org/TR/rdf-spargl-XMLres/.

Belkin, N., & Croft W.B. (1997). Information Filtering and Information Retrieval: Two Sides of the Same Coin? Communications of the ACM, 35(12), 29–39.

Berners-Lee, T. (1997). URI References: Fragment Identifiers on URIs. Retrieved from http://www.w3.org/DesignIssues/Fragment.html.

Berners-Lee, T. (2000). RDF and the Semantic Web. In XML 2000 Conference, Washington DC, USA. Retrieved from http://www.w3.org/2000/Talks/1206-xml2k-tbl/.

Berners-Lee, T., & Fielding, R. T. Masinter L. (2005). Uniform Resource Identifier (URI): Generic Syntax. Retrieved from http://www.ietf.org/rfc/rfc3986.txt.

Berners-Lee, T., Hendler, J., & Lassila, O. (2001). The Semantic Web. Scientific American, 284(5), 34–43.

Bertram, J. (2005). Einführung in die inhaltliche Erschließung: Grundlagen, Methoden, Instrumente. Content and Communication, Vol. 2. Würzburg: Ergon.

Birdsall, W. F. (2007). Web 2.0 as a Social Movement. Webology, 4(2). Retrieved from http://www.webology.ir/2007/v4n2/a40.html.

Bizer, C., Cyganiak, R., Auer, S., & Kobilarov, G. (2007). DBpedia: QueryingWikipedia like a Database. In Developers Track Presentations at the 16th International Conference on World Wide Web (WWW 2007), Banff, Canada.

Bizer, C., Heath, T., Ayers, D., & Raimond, Y. (2007) Interlinking Open Data on the Web. In Proceedings of the Demonstrations Track, 4th European Semantic Web Conference (ESWC2007), Innsbruck, Austria. Retrieved from http://www.eswc2007.org/ demonstrations.cfm.

Bizer, C., & Joshi, A. (Eds.) (2008). ISWC2008 Posters and Demonstrations: Proceedings of the Poster and Demonstration Session at the 7th International Semantic Web Conference (ISWC2008), Karlsruhe, Germany. CEUR Workshop Proceedings: Vol. 401.

Blumauer, A., & Pellegrini, T. (Eds.) (2008). Social Semantic Web: Web 2.0 – Was nun? Berlin: Springer.

Bodenreider, O., & Stevens, R. (2006). Bio-Ontologies: Current Trends and Future Directions. Briefings in Bioinformatics, 7(3), 256–274.

Bojars, U., Breslin, J. G., & Finn, A. Decker S. (2008). Using the Semantic Web for Linking and Reusing Data Across Web 2.0 Communities. Journal of Web Semantics, 6(1), 21–28.

Boyd, D. (2007). Social Network Sites: Public, Private, or What? The Knowledge Tree, 13. Retrieved from http://kt.flexiblelearning.net.au/tkt2007/?page_id=28.

Boyd, D., & Ellison, N. B. (2007). Social Network Sites: Definition, History, and Scholarship. Journal of Computer-Mediated Communication, 13(1). Retrieved from http://jcmc.indiana.edu/vol13/issue1/boyd.ellison.html.

Breitman, K., Casanova, M. A., & Truszkowski, W. (2007). Semantic Web: Concepts, Technologies and Applications. London: Springer.

Breslin, J. G., Harth, A., Bojars, U., & Decker, S. (2005). Towards Semantically-interlinked Online Communities. In A. Gómez-Pérez, & J. Euzenat (Eds.). The Semantic Web: Research and Applications. Proceedings of the 2nd European Semantic Web Conference (ESWC 2005), Heraklion, Greece (pp. 500–514). Berlin, Heidelberg: Springer.

Breslin, J. G., Passant, A., & Decker, S. (2009). The Social Semantic Web. Berlin: Springer.

Brickley, D., & Miller, L. (2003). FOAF Vocabulary Specification (Revision). Retrieved from http://xmlns.com/foaf/0.1/.

Brin, S., & Page, L. (1998). The Anatomy of a Large-Scale Hypertextual Web Search Engine. Computer Networks and ISDN Systems, 30, 107–117.

Brooks, C., & Montanez, N. (2006). Improved Annotation of the Blogosphere via Autotagging and Hierarchical Clustering. In L. Carr; D. de Roure, & A. Iyengar (Eds.), International World Wide Web Conference: Proceedings of the 15th

International Conference on World Wide Web. Edinburg, Schottland (pp. 625–632). New York: ACM.

Broughton, V. (2002). Faceted Classification as a Basis for Knowledge Organization in a Digital Environment: The Bliss Bibliographic Classification as a Model for Vocabulary Management and the Creation of Multidimensional Knowledge Structures. The New Review of Hypermedia and Multimedia, 7(1), 67–102.

Broughton, V. (2004). Essential Classification. London: Facet.

Broughton, V. (2006). The Need for a Faceted Classification as the Basis for all Methods of Information Retrieval. Aslib Proceedings, 58(1/2), 49–72.

Bruns, A., & Humphreys, S. (2005). Wikis in Teaching and Assessment: The M/Cyclopedia Project. In D. Riehle (Ed.), Conference Proceedings of the 2005 International Symposium on Wikis, San Diego, California, USA. (pp. 25–32). New York: ACM Press.

BS 5723:1987. Guidelines for the Establishment and Development of Monolingual Thesauri (2nd Edition). London: British Standards Institution.

Buckland, M. K. (1997). What is a "Document"? Journal of the American Society for Information Science, 48(9), 804–809.

Buffa, M., Gandon, F. L., Sander, P., Faron, C., & Ereto, G. (2008). SweetWiki. Journal of Web Semantics, 6(1), 84–97.

Burger, A., Davidson, D., & Baldock, R. (Eds.) (2008). Anatomy Ontologies for Bioinformatics: Principles and Practice. Goldaming: Springer.

Byrd, D., & Crawford, T. (2002). Problems of Music Information Retrieval in the Real World. Information Processing and Management, 38, 249–272.

Caplan, P. (2003). Metadata Fundamentals for All Librarians. Chicago: ALA Editions.

Cardoso, J., Lytras, M. D., & Hepp, M. (2008). The Future for the Semantic Web for Enterprises. In J. Cardoso, M. Hepp, & M. D. Lytras (Eds.). The Semantic Web. Real-World Applications from Industry (pp. 3–15). Boston: Springer.

Carstens, C. (2008). Semantic Web Applications In- and Outside the Semantic Web. In S. Auer, S. Schaffert, & T. Pellegrini (Eds.), Proceedings of I-SEMANTICS'08: International Conference on Semantic Systems, Graz, Austria (pp. 25–33). Graz: J.UCS.

Casey, C. (1999). An Analytical Index to the Internet: Dreams of Utopia. College & Research Libraries, 60, 586–595.

Casey, M. E., & Savastinuk, L. C. (2006). Library 2.0: Service for the Next-Generation Library. Library Journal. Retrieved from http://www.library journal.com/article/CA6365200.html.

Cattuto, C., Loreto, V., & Pietronero, L. (2007). Semiotic Dynamics and Collaborative Tagging. Proceedings of the National Academy of Sciences of the United States of America, 104(5), 1461–1464.

Cayzer, S. (2004). Semantic Blogging and Decentralized Knowledge Management. Communications of the ACM, 47(12), 47–52.

Cayzer, S. (2006). What Next for Semantic Blogging? Technical Report HPL-2006-149, Hewlett-Packard Laboratories, Bristol, UK.

Celma, O., Ramirez, M., & Herrera, P. (2005). Getting Music Recommendations and Filtering Newsfeeds from FOAF Descriptions. In Proceedings of the 1st Workshop on Scripting for the Semantic Web: 2nd European Semantic Web Conference (ESWC2005), Heraklion, Greece.

Chan, L. M., & Mitchell, J. S. (2006). Dewey Dezimalklassifikation: Theorie und Praxis. Lehrbuch zur DDC 22. München: Saur.

Chu, H. (2007). Information Representation and Retrieval in the Digital Age (3rd Printing). Medford, NJ: Information Today.

Clark, T., & Kinoshita, J. (2007). Alzforum and SWAN: The Present and Future of Scientific Web Communities. Briefings in Bioinformatics, 8, 163–171.

Cleveland, D. B., & Cleveland, A. D. (2001). Introduction to Indexing and Abstracting (3rd Edition). Englewood, Colo.: Libraries Unlimited.

Corcho, O. (2006). Ontology-Based Document Annotation: Trends and Open Research Problems. International Journal of Metadata, Semantics and Ontologies, 1(1), 47–57.

Corcho, O., Pinar, A., Kotsiopoulos, I., Missier, P., Bechhofer, S., & Goble, C. (2006). An Overview of S-OGSA: A Reference Semantic Grid Architecture. Journal of Web Semantics, 4(2), 102–115.

Cormode, G., & Krishnamurthy, B. (2008). Key Differences Between Web 1.0 and Web 2.0. First Monday, 13(6). Retrieved from http://www.uic.edu/htbin/cgiwrap/bin/ojs /index.php/fm/article/viewArticle/2125/1972.

Cram, H. R. (2005). Die Auswirkungen der Open-Access-Initiative auf die Wertschöpfungskette. In R. Ball (Ed.). Knowledge Extended. Die Kooperation von Wissenschaftlern, Bibliothekaren und IT-Spezialisten. 3. Konferenz der Zentralbibliothek. Schriften des Forschungszentrums Jülich (pp. 57–71). Jülich: Forschungszentrum Jülich.

Cuenca Grau, B., Motik, B., & Patel-Schneider, P. (2007). OWL 1.1 Web Ontology Language XML Syntax: W3C Editor's Draft of 23 May, 2007. Retrieved from http://www.webont.org/owl/1.1/xml_syntax.html.

Daconta, M. C., Obrst, L. J., & Smith, K. T. (2003). The Semantic Web. A Guide to the Future of XML, Web Services and Knowledge Management. Indianapolis: Wiley.

Daniel, R., & Mills, J. (1975). A Classification of Library and Information Science. London: Library Association.

Danowski, P., & Heller, L. (2006). Bibliothek 2.0: Die Zukunft der Bibliothek? Bibliotheksdienst, 40(11), 1259–1271.

Davies, J., Fensel, D., & van Harmelen, F. (Eds.) (2004). Towards the Semantic Web: Ontology-Driven Knowledge Management. Chichester: Wiley.

Davies, J., Studer, R., & Warren, P. (Eds.) (2006). Semantic Web Technologies: Trends and Research in Ontology-Based Systems. Chichester: Wiley.

DDC (2003). Dewey Decimal Classification and Relative Index (4 Volumes, 22nd Edition). Dublin, Ohio: OCLC Online Computer Library Center.

Dean, M., & Schreiber, G. (Eds.) (2004). OWL Web Ontology Language Reference: W3C Recommendation February 10, 2004. Retrieved from http://www.w3.org/TR/owl-ref/.

Decker, S. (2006). The Social Semantic Desktop: Next Generation Collaboration Infrastructure. Information Services & Use, 26(2), 139–144.

Decker, S., Park, J., Sauermann, L., Auer, S., & Handschuh, S. (Eds.) (2006). Semantic Desktop and Social Semantic Collaboration: Proceedings of the Semantic Desktop and Social Semantic Collaboration Workshop (SemDesk 2006). Located at the 5th International Semantic Web Conference ISWC 2006, Athens, GA, USA. CEUR Workshop Proceedings: Vol. 202.

Desilets, A., Paquet, S., & Vinson, N. (2005). Are Wikis Usable? In D. Riehle (Ed.), Conference Proceedings of the 2005 International Symposium on Wikis, San Diego, California, USA. (pp. 3–16). New York: ACM Press.

Deutsche Forschungsgemeinschaft (2005). Publikationsstrategien im Wandel? Ergebnisse einer Umfrage zum Publikations- und Rezeptionsverhalten unter besonderer Berücksichtigung von Open Access. Weinheim: Wiley VCH.

Dickens, D. T. (1994). The ECLA Classification System. World Patent Information, 16, 28–32.

Diederich, J., & Iofciu, T. (2006). Finding Communities of Practice from User Profiles Based on Folksonomies. In N. Karacapilidis (Ed.), Proceedings of the 1st International Workshop on Building Technology Enhanced Learning Solutions for Communities of Practice (TEL-CoPs'06). In Conjunction with the 1st European Conference on Technology Enhanced Learning (EC-TEL'06), Crete, Greece (pp. 288–297).

DIN 1463/1:1987. Erstellung und Weiterentwicklung von Thesauri: Einsprachige Thesauri. Berlin: Beuth.

DIN 32705:1987. Klassifikationssysteme: Erstellung und Weiterentwicklung von Klassifikationssystemen. Berlin: Beuth.

Ding, Y., Fensel, D., Klein, M., & Omelayenko, B. (2002). The Semantic Web: Jet Another Hip? Data and Knowledge Enginneering, 41(2-3), 205–227.

Dodds, L. (2004). An Introduction to FOAF. Retrieved from http://www.xml.com/pub/a/2004/02/04/foaf.html.

Downes, S. (2005). E-Learning 2.0. eLearn Magazine, 2005(10). Retrieved from http://www.elearnmag.org/subpage.cfm?section=articles&article=29-1.

Egghe, L. (2005). Power Laws in the Information Production Process: Lotkaian Informetrics. Amsterdam: Elsevier.

Egghe, L., & Rousseau, R. (1990). Introductions to Informetrics. Amsterdam: Elsevier.

Egghe, L., & Rousseau, R. (1995). Generalized Success-Breeds-Success Principle Leading to Time-Dependent Informetric Distributions. Journal of the American Society for Information Science and Technology, 46(6), 426–445.

Eigner, C., & Leitner, H. Nausner P. (2003). Online-Communities, Weblogs und die soziale Rückeroberung des Netzes. Graz: Nausner & Nausner.

Engeström, Y. (2004). Collaborative Intentionality Capital: Object-Oriented Interagency in Multiogranizational Fields. University of California, San Diego.

Retrieved from http://www.edu.helsinki.fi/activity/people/engestro/files/ Collaborative_intentionality.pdf.

Farrell, S., Lau, T., & Wilcox, E., Muller, M. J. (2007). Socially Augmenting Employee Profiles with People-tagging. In C. Shen; R. Jacob, & R. Balakrishnan (Eds.), Proceedings of the 20th Annual ACM Symposium on User Interface Software and Technology, Newport, Rhode Island (pp. 91–100). New York: ACM.

Fellbaum, C. (1999). WordNet: An Electronic Lexical Database (2nd Printing). Cambridge: MIT Press.

Fensel, D. (2004). Ontologies: A Silver Bullet for Knowledge Management and Electronic Commerce (2nd Edition). Chichester: Springer.

Fensel, D., Ding, Y., Omelayenko, B., Schulten, E., Botqin, G., & Brown, M., et al. (2001). Product Data Integration for B2B Commerce. IEEE Intelligent Systems, 16(4), 54–59.

Fensel, D., Horrocks, I., van Harmelen, F., Decker, S., Erdmann, M., & Klein, M. (2000). OIL in a Nutshell. In R. Dieng & O. Corby (Eds.), Knowledge Engineering and Knowledge Management: Methods, Models and Tools. Proceedings of the 12th International Conference (EKAW 2000), Juan-les-Pins, France (pp. 1–16). Berlin: Springer.

Fensel, D., Horrocks, I., van Harmelen, F., McGuinness, D., & Patel-Schneider, P. (2001). OIL: Ontology Infrastructure to Enable the Semantic Web. IEEE Intelligent Systems, 16(2), 38–45.

Fensel, D., Lassila, O., van Harmelen, F., Horrocks, I., Hendler, J., & McGuinness, D. L. (2000). The Semantic Web And Its Languages. IEEE Intelligent Systems, 15(6), 67–73.

Fichter, D. (2006). Intranet Applications for Tagging and Folksonomies. Online, 30(3), 43–45.

Fikes, R., Hayes, P., & Horrocks, I. OWL-QL (2003): A Language for Deductive Query Answering on the Semantic Web (KSL Technical Report No. 03-14). Stanford: Knowledge Systems Laboratory, Stanford University.

Foskett, A. C. (1982). The Subject Approach to Information (4th Edition). London: Clive Bingley; Hamden: Linnet.

Foskett, D. J. (1981). Thesaurus. In Encyclopedia of Library and Information Science: Vol. 30. New York: Marcel Dekker, Inc.

Foster, I., & Kesselmann, C. (2004). The Grid: Blueprint for a New Computing Infrastructure. San Francisco: Morgan Kaufmann; Elsevier.

Foulonneau, M., & Riley, J. (2008). Metadata for Digital Resources: Implementation, Systems Design and Interoperability. Oxford: Chandos Publishing.

Frakes, W. B., & Baeza-Yates, R. (Eds.) (1992). Information Retrieval: Data Structure and Algorithms. Upper Saddle River: Prentice Hall.

Furnas, G., Landauer, T., Gomez, L., & Dumais, S. (1987). The Vocabulary Problem in Human-System Communication: An Analysis and a Solution. Communications of the ACM, 30, 964–971.

Furnas, G. W., Fake, C., von Ahn, L., Schachter, J., Golder, S., Fox, K., Davis, M.; Marlow, C., Naaman, M. (2006). Why do Tagging Systems Work? In G. Olson & R. Jeffries (Eds.), Conference on Human Factors in Computing Systems (CHI '06): Extended Abstracts on Human Factors in Computing Systems (pp. 36–39). New York: ACM.

Gaus, W. (2005). Dokumentations- und Ordnungslehre (5th Edition). Berlin, Heidelberg: Springer.

Giarratano, J., & Riley, G. D. (2005). Expert Systems: Principles and Programming (4th Edition). Boston: Course Technology.

Gilliland-Swetland, A. J. (1998). Defining Metadata. In M. Baca (Ed.), Introduction to Metadata: Pathways to Digital Informatio. Los Angeles: Getty Information Institute.

Gillmor, D. (2004). We the Media. Sebastopol: O'Reilly Media.

Goble C, Corcho, O., Alper, P., & de Roure, D. (2006). E-Science and the Semantic Web: A Symbiotic Relationship. In L. Todorovski, N. Lavrac, & K. P. Jantke (Eds.), Discovery Science: 9th International Conference (DS 2006), Barcelona, Spain (pp. 1–12). Berlin: Springer.

Goble, C., & de Roure, D. (2002). The Grid: An Application of the Semantic Web. SIGMOD Record, 31(4), 65–70.

Godwin, P. (2006). Information Literacy in the Age of Amateurs: How Google and Web 2.0 Affect Librarians' Support of Information Literacy. ITALICS, 5(4). Retrieved from http://www.ics.heacademy.ac.uk/italics/vol5iss4.htm.

Godwin-Jones, R. (2006). Emerging Technologies: Tag Clouds in the Blogosphere. Electronic Literacy and Social Networking. Language Learning and Technology, 10(2), 8–15.

Goldbeck, J. (2007). Cross-Network Linkages with FOAF: Technical Report TRMS1292, MINDSWAP, University of Maryland.

Goldbeck, J., & Hendler, J. (2006). FilmTrust: Movie Recommendations Using Trust in Web-Based Social Networks. In Proceedings of the IEEE Consumer Communications and Networking Conference (CCNC2006), Las Vegas, Nevada, USA (pp. 282–286).

Golder, S. A., & Huberman B. A. (2006). Usage Patterns of Collaborative Tagging Systems. Journal of Information Science, 32(2), 198–208.

Gómez-Pérez, A., & Corcho, O. (2002). Ontology Languages for the Semantic Web. IEEE Intelligent Systems, 17(1), 54–60.

Gómez-Pérez, A., Fernández-López, M., & Corcho, O. (2004). Ontological Engineering: Advanced Information and Knowledge Processing (3rd Print). London: Springer.

Gordon-Murnane, L. (2006). Social Bookmarking, Folksonomies, and Web 2.0 Tools. Searcher. The Magazine for Database Professionals, 14(6), 26–38.

Greaves, M. (2007). Semantic Web 2.0. IEEE Intelligent Systems, 22(2), 94–96.

Greenberg, J. (2001). A Quantitative Categorical Analysis of Metadata Elements in Image-Applicable Metadata Schemas. Journal of the American Society for Information Science and Technology, 52, 917–924.

Groza, T., Handschuh, S., Möller, K., Grimnes, G., Sauermann, L., & Minack, E., et al. (2007). The NEPOMUK Project.: On the way to the Social Semantic Desktop. In K. Tochtermann, W. Haas, F. Kappe, A. Scharl, T. Pellegrini, & S. Schaffert (Eds.), International Conference on New Media Technologies and Semantic Systems: Proceedings of I-Media '07 and I-Semantics '07 (pp. 201–211). Graz: J.UCS.

Gruber, T. (1993). A Translation Approach to Portable Ontology Specification. Knowledge Acquisition, 2(5), 199–220.

Gruber, T. (2005). Folksonomy of Ontology: A Mash-up of Apples and Oranges. In First on-Line conference on Metadata and Semantics Research (MTSR'05). Retrieved from http://www.metadata-semantics.org/. Additionally Published in Internationall Journal on Semantic Web & Information Systems, 3(2), 2007.

Gruber, T. (2008). Collective Knowledge Systems: Where the Social Web meets the Semantic Web. Journal of Web Semantics, 6(1), 4–13.

Guédon, J. (2004). The Green and Gold Roads to Open Access: The Case for Mixing and Matching. Serials Review, 30(4), 315–328.

Guy, M., & Tonkin, E. (2006). Folksonomies: Tidying up tags? D-Lib Magazine, 12(1). Retrieved from http://www.dlib.org/dlib/january06/guy/01guy.html.

Habib, M. C. (2006). Toward Academic Library 2.0: Development and Application of a Library 2.0 Methodology. A Master's Paper for the M.S. in L.S. Degree, University of North Carolina at Chapel Hill.

Halpin, H., Robu, V., & Shepherd, H. (2007). The Complex Dynamics of Collaborative Tagging. In 16th International World Wide Web Conference (WWW 2007), Banff, Alberta, Canada (pp. 211–220). Red Hook: Curran.

Hammond, T., Hannay, T., Lund, B., & Scott, J. (2005). Social Bookmarking Tools (I): A General Review. D-Lib Magazine, 11(4). Retrieved from http://www.dlib.org/dlib/april05/hammond/04hammond.html.

Handschuh, S., & Staab, S. (Eds.) (2003). Annotation for the Semantic Web. Amsterdam: IOS Press.

Hannay, T. (2007). Web 2.0 in Science. CT Watch Quarterly, 3(3). Retrieved from http://www.ctwatch.org/quarterly/articles/2007/08/web-20-in-science/.

Hapke, T. (2007). Informationskompetenz 2.0 und das Verschwinden des Nutzers. Bibliothek Forschung und Praxis, 31(2), 137–149.

Harnad, S., Brody, T., Vallieres, F., Carr, L., Hitchcock, S., & Yves, G., et al. (2004). The Access/Impact Problem and the Green and Gold Roads to Open Access. Serials Review, 30(4), 310–314.

Heath, T., & Motta, E. (2008). Ease of Interaction plus Ease of Integration: Combining Web2.0 and the Semantic Web in a Reviewing Site. Journal of Web Semantics, 6(1), 76–83.

Hendler, J. (2001). Agents and the Semantic Web. IEEE Intelligent Systems, 16(2), 30–37.

Hendler, J. (2003). Science and the Semantic Web. Science, 299(5605), 520–521.

Hendler, J. (2004). Frequently Asked Questions on W3C's Web Ontology Language (OWL). W3C. Retrieved from www.w3.org/2003/08/owlfaq.

Hendler, J., & Goldbeck, J. (2008). Metcalfe's Law, Web 2.0, and the Semantic Web. Journal of Web Semantics, 6(1), 14–20.

Hendler, J., & van Harmelen, F. (2008). The Semantic Web: Webizing Knowledge Representation. In F. van Harmelen, V. Lifschitz, & B. Porter (Eds.). Handbook of Knowledge Representation (pp. 821–840). Amsterdam: Elsevier.

Hepp, M. (2006a). Products and Services Ontologies: A Methodology for Deriving OWL Ontologies from Industrial Categorization Standards. International Journal on Semantic Web & Information Systems (IJSWIS), 2(1), 72–99.

Hepp, M. (2006b). eClassOWL 5.1 Products and Services Ontology for e-Business: User's Guide, Version 1.0. Retrieved from http://www.heppnetz.de/projects/eclassowl/ eclassOWL-Primer-final.pdf.

Hepp, M. (2008). Ontologies: State of the Art, Business Potential, and Grand Challenges. In M. Hepp, P. de Leenheer, A. de Moor, & Y. Sure (Eds.). Ontology Management. Semantic Web, Semantic Web Services, and Business Applications (pp. 3–22). Boston: Springer.

Herzog, C., Luger, M., & Herzog, M. (2007). Combining Social and Semantic Metadata for Search in a Document Repository. In B. Hoser & A. Hotho (Eds.). Bridging the Gap between Semantic Web and Web 2.0 (SemNet 2007). International Workshop at the 4th European Semantic Web Conference, Innsbruck, Austria (pp. 14–21).

Hey, T., & Trefethen, A. (2003). The Data Deluge: An e-Science Perspective. In Berman F., & Fox C. G. (Eds.). Grid Computing. Making the Global Infrastructure a Reality (pp. 809–824). Chichester: Wiley.

Hey, T., & Trefethen, A. (2005). Cyberinfrastructures for e-Science. Science, 308, 817–821.

Hitzler, P., Krötzsch, M., Rudolph, S., & Sure, Y. (2008). Semantic Web. Berlin, Heidelberg: Springer.

Hjelm, J. (2001). Creating the Semantic Web with RDF. New York: Wiley.

Hock, R. E. (2001). The Extreme Searcher's Guide to Web Search Engines (2nd Edition). Medford: Information Today.

Horrocks, I. (2005). OWL: A Description Logic Based Ontology Language. Lecture Notes in Computer Science, 3709, 5–8.

Horrocks, I., Patel-Schneider, P., & van Harmelen, F. (2003). From SHIQ and RDF to OWL: The Making of a Web Ontology Language. Journal of Web Semantics, 1(1), 7–26.

Hoser, B., & Hotho, A. (Eds.) (2007). Bridging the Gap between Semantic Web and Web 2.0: Workshop located at the European Semantic Web Conference (ESWC 2007), Innsbruck, Austria. Retrieved from http://www.kde.cs.uni-kassel.de/ws/eswc2007/program.html.

Hotho, A., Jäschke, R., Schmitz, C., & Stumme, G. (2006a). Information Retrieval in Folksonomies: Search and Ranking. Lecture Notes in Computer Science, (4011), 411–426.

Hotho, A., Jäschke, R., Schmitz, C., & Stumme, G. (2006b). BibSonomy: A Social Bookmark and Publication Sharing System. In Proceedings of the Conceptual Structure Tool Interoperability Workshop: Located at the 14th International Conference on Conceptual Structures, Aalborg, Denmark (pp. 87–102).

Hourihane, C. (2002). It Begins with the Cataloguer: Subject Access to Images and the Cataloguer's Perspective. In M. Baca (Ed.). Introduction to Art Image Access (pp. 40–66). Los Angeles: Getty Research Institute.

IPC (2005). International Patent Classification (8th Edition). Genf: WIPO.

ISO 15836:2003. Information and Documentation: The Dublin Core Metadata Element Set. Genf: International Organization for Standardization.

ISO 2788:1986. Documentation: Guidelines for the Establishment and Development of Monolingual Thesauri. Genf: International Organization for Standardization.

ISO 5963:1985. Documentation: Methods for Examining Documents, Determining their Subjects, and Selecting Indexing Terms. Genf: International Organization for Standardization.

ISO 5964:1985. Documentation: Guidelines for the Establishment and Development of Multilingual Thesauri. Genf: International Organization for Standardization.

Jackson, P. (1998). An Introduction to Expert Systems (3rd Edition). Boston: Addison-Wesley.

Jain, R. (2008). Multimedia Semantic Web: Keynote Talk at ISWC2008, Karlsruhe, October 28, 2008. Retrieved from http://ngs.ics.uci.edu/ presentations/Multimedia_Semantic_ Web_081028.ppt.

Johnson, D. (2006). RSS and Atom in Action: Web 2.0 Building Blocks. Greenwich: Manning.

Karger, D. R., & Quan, D. (2004). What Would it Mean to Blog on the Semantic Web? In S. McIlraith, D. Plexousakis, & F. van Harmelen (Eds.), The Semantic Web. Proceedings of the 3rd International Semantic Web Conference (ISWC 2004), Hiroshima, Japan (pp. 214–228). Berlin, Heidelberg: Springer.

Kennedy, L., Naaman, M., Ahern, S., Nair, R., & Rattenbury, T. (2007). How Flickr Helps Us Make Sense of the World: Context and Content in Community-Contributed Media Collections. In R. Lienhart & A. R. Prasad (Eds.), Proceedings of the 15th International Conference on Multimedia, Augsburg, Germany. New York: ACM Press.

Kipp, M. E. I. (2006). @toread and cool: Tagging for Time, Task and Emotion. In 17th ASIS&T SIG/CR Classification Research Workshop: Abstracts of Posters (pp. 16–17).

Kipp, M., & Campbell, D. (2006). Patterns and Inconsistencies in Collaborative Tagging Systems: An Examination of Tagging Practices. In Proceedings of the 17th Annual Meeting of the American Society for Information Science and Technology, Austin, Texas, USA.

Klobas, J. (2006). Wikis: Tools for Information Work and Collaboration. Oxford: Chandos Publishing.

Koch, M., & Richter, A. (2007). Enterprise 2.0: Planung, Einführung und erfolgreicher Einsatz von Social Software in Unternehmen. München: Oldenbourg.

Krobath, A. (2004). Analyse von ausgewählten Wirtschaftsklassifikationen. Diploma Thesis from Karl-Franzens-University Graz, Institute for Information Science.

Kroski, E. (2005). The Hive Mind: Folksonomies and User-based Tagging [Blog Post: December 12, 2005]. Retrieved from http://infotangle.blogsome.com/2005/12/07/the-hive-mind-folksonomies-and-user-based-tagging.

Krötzsch, M., Vrandecic, D., & Völkel, M. (2005). Wikipedia and the Semantic Web: The Missing Links. In Proceedings of Wikimania 2005: The First International Wikimedia Conference. Wikimedia Foundation.

Krötzsch, M., & Vrandecic, D. (2006). Semantic Mediawiki. In I. Cruz, S. Decker, & et al. (Eds.), The Semantic Web. 5th International Semantic Web Conference (ISWC 2006). Athens, GA, USA. (pp. 935–942). Berlin: Springer.

Lancaster, F.W. (1986). Vocabulary Control for Information Retrieval (2nd Edition). Arlington: Information Resources Press.

Lancaster, F. W. (2003). Indexing and Abstracting in Theory and Practice. Champaign: University of Illinois, Graduate School of Library and Information Science.

Lange, C., Schaffert, S., Skaf-Molli, H., & Völkel, M. (Eds.) (2008). The Wiki Way of Semantics: Proceedings of the 3rd Semantic Wiki Workshop (SemWiki 2008) at the 5th European Semantic Web Conference (ESWC 2008), Tenerife, Spain. CEUR Workshop Proceedings: Vol. 360.

Lanier, J. (2006). Digital Maoism: The Hazards of the New Online Collectivism. In The Edge. Retrieved from http://www.edge.org/3rd_culture/lanier06/lanier06_index.html.

Lee, C. P., Dourish, P., & Mark, G. (2006). The Human Infrastructure of Cyberinfrastructure. In Computer Supported Cooperative Work: Proceedings of the 2006 20th Anniversary Conference on Computer Supported Cooperative Work (pp. 483–492), Banff, Canada. New York: ACM Press.

Legg, C. (2007). Ontologies on the Semantic Web. Annual Review of Information Science and Technology, 41, 407–451.

Leuf, B., & Cunningham, W. (2001). The Wiki Way: Quick Collaboration on the Web. Boston: Addison-Wesley.

Lew, M., Sebe, N., Djeraba, C., & Jain, R. (2006). Contentbased Multimedia Information Retrieval: State of the Art and Challenges. ACM Transactions on Multimedia Computing, Communications, and Applications, 2(1), 1–19.

Lewandowski, D. (2005). Web Information Retrieval: Technologien zur Informationssuche im Internet. Reihe Informationswissenschaft der DGI, Vol. 7. Frankfurt am Main: DGI.

Linden, G., Smith, B., & York, J. (2003). Amazon.com Recommendations: Item-to-Item Collaborative Filtering. IEEE Internet Computing, 4(1), 76–80.

Löbner, S. (2002). Understanding Semantics. London: Edward Arnold Publishers.

Locarno Classification (2004). International Classification for Industrial Designs under the Locarno Agreement (8th Edition). Genf: WIPO.

Löwenberg, B. (2008). Web 2.0: Prinzip, Technologien und Einsatzszenarien - ein Überblick. In M. Ockenfeld (Ed.). Informationskompetenz 2.0: Zukunft von qualifizierter Informationsvermittlung. Tagungsband des 24. Oberhofer Kolloquium zur Praxis der Informationsvermittlung, Barleben/Magdeburg (pp. 21–34). Frankfurt am Main: DGI.

Lu, G. (2001). Indexing and Retrieval of Audio: A Survey. Multimedia Tools and Applications, 15, 269–290.

Lund, B., Hammond, T., Flack, M., & Hannay, T. (2005). Social Bookmarking Tools (II): A Case Study – Connotea. D-Lib Magazine, 11(4). Retrieved from http://www.dlib.org/dlib/april05/hammond/04hammond.html.

Maass, W., Kowatsch, T., & Münster, T. (2007). Vocabulary Patterns in Free-for-all Collaborative Indexing Systems. In Chen, Cudré-Mauroux et al. (Eds.) Proceedings of International Workshop on Emergent Semantics and Ontology Evolution. Co-Located with ISWC 2007 and ASWC 2007, Busan, Korea (pp. 45–57). CEUR Workshop Proceedings: Vol. 292.

Madden, M., & Fox, S. (2006). Riding the Waves of "Web 2.0": More than a Buzzword but Still not Easily Defined. Washington, D.C.: Pew Internet and American Life Project. Retrieved from http://www.pewinternet.org/pdfs/PIP_Web_2.0.pdf.

Madhavan, J., Halevy, A., Cohen, S., Dong, X., Jeffery, S. R., Ko, D., & Yu, C. (2006). Structured Data Meets the Web: A Few Observations. IEEE Data Engineering Bulletin, 29(4), 19–26.

Mai, J. (2000). Deconstructing the Indexing Process. Advances in Librarianship, 23, 269–298.

Marlow, C., Naaman, M., Boyd, D., & Davis, H. (2006). HT06, Tagging Paper, Taxonomy, Flickr, Academic Article, To Read. In Proceedings of the 17th Conference on Hypertext and Hypermedia, Odense, Denmark (pp. 31–40). New York: ACM.

Maness, J. (2006a). Library 2.0 Theory. Web 2.0 and its Implications for Libraries. Webology, 3(2). Retrieved from http://www.webology.ir/2006/v3n2/a25.html.

Maness, J. (2006b). Library 2.0: The Next Generation of Web-based Library Services. LOGOS: Journal of the World Book Community, 17(3), 139–145.

Mani, I. (1999). Advances in Automatic Text Summarization. Cambridge: MIT Press.

Manola, F., & Miller, E. (2004). Resource Description Framework (RDF). Primer: W3C Recommendation, 10 February 2004. Retrieved from http://www.w3.org/TR/rdf-primer/.

Markkula, M., & Sormunen, E. (2000). End-User Searching Challenges Indexing Practices in the Digital Newspaper Photo Archive. Information Retrieval, 1(4), 259–285.

Markoff, J. (2006). Entrepreneurs See a Web Guided by Common Sense. New York Times, November 12, 2006.

Mathes, A. (2004). Folksonomies: Cooperative Classification and Communication Through Shared Metadata. Urbana, Ill.: University of Illinois Urbana-Campaign, Graduate School of Library and Information Science. Retrieved from http://www.adammathes.com/academic/computer-mediated-communi cation/folksonomies.html.

McBride, B. (2004). The Resource Description Framework (RDF) and its Vocabulary Descripton Loanguage (RDFS). In S. Staab, & R. Studer (Eds.). Handbook on Ontologies (pp. 51–65). Berlin, Heidelberg, New York: Springer.

McIlwaine, I. C. (2000). The Universal Decimal Classification: A Guide to Its Use. The Hague: UDC Consortium.

Merholz, P. (2004). Metadata for the Masses [Blog Post: October 19, 2004]. Retrieved from http://www.adaptivepath.com/publications/essays/archives/ 000361.php.

Mika, P., & Greaves, M. (2008). Editorial: Semantic Web & Web 2.0. Journal of Web Semantics, 6(1), 1–3.

Millen, D. R., Feinberg, J., & Kerr, B. (2006). DOGEAR: Social Bookmarking in the Enterprise. In R. Grinter; T. Rodden, et al. (Eds.), Proceedings of the SIGCHI Conference on Human Factors in Computing Systems (SIGCHI 2006), Montreal, Quebec, Canada (pp. 111–120). New York: ACM.

Mills, J., & Broughton, V. (1977 onwards). Bliss Bibliographic Classification (BC2) (2nd Edition). London: Butterworth.

Mitchell, J. S. (2000). The Dewey Decimal Classification in the Twenty-First Century. In R. Marcella & A. Maltby (Eds.), The Future of Classification (pp. 81–92). Aldershot: Gower.

Möller, E. (2005). Die heimliche Medienrevolution: Wie Weblogs, Wikis und freie Software die Welt verändern. Hannover: Heise.

Möller, K., Bojars, U., & Breslin, J. G. (2006). Using Semantics to Enhance the Blogging Experience. In Y. Sure & J. Domingue (Eds.), The Semantic Web Research and Applications: 3rd European Semantic Web Conference (ESWC 2006), Budva, Montenegro (pp. 679–696). Berlin, Heidelberg: Springer.

Möller-Walsdorf, T. (2008). Informationsflut und Web 2.0-Welle: Was bieten Web2.0-Technologien den Bibliotheken? In M. Ockenfeld (Ed.). Informationskompetenz 2.0 - Zukunft von qualifizierter Informations-vermittlung. Tagungsband des 24. Oberhofer Kolloquium zur Praxis der Informationsvermittlung, Barleben, Magdeburg (pp. 9–20). Frankfurt am Main: DGI.

Moens, M.-F. (2000). Automatic Indexing and Abstracting of Document Texts. The Kluwer International Series on Information Retrieval, Vol. 6. Boston: Kluwer Academic Publishing.

Moens, M.-F. (2006). Information Extraction Algorithms and Prospects in a Retrieval Context. Dordrecht: Springer.

Mooney, R., & Bunescu, R. (2005). Mining Knowledge from Text Using Information Extraction. SIGKDD Explorations Newsletteer, 7(1), 3–10.

Motik, B., Cuenca Grau, B., Horrocks, I., Wu, Z., Fokou, A., & Lutz, C. (2008). OWL 2 Web Ontology Language: Profiles: W3C Working Draft 08 October,

2008. Retrieved from http://www.w3.org/TR/2008/WD-owl2-profiles-20081008/.

Murison, J. (2005). Messageboard Topic Tagging: User Tagging of Collectively Owned Community Content. In R. Anderson; B. Blau, & J. Zapolski (Eds.), Proceedings of the 2005 Conference on Designing for User eXperience, San Francisco, California, USA (pp. Article No. 5). New York: American Institute of Graphic Art.

Murphy, W. M., & Leu, D. (2000). Fracture Classification: Biological Significance. In T. P. Rüedi; W. M. Murphy; M. Renner, & G. E. Fackelman (Eds.), AO Principles of Fracture Management (pp. 45–57). Stuttgart: Thieme.

Musser, J., & O'Reilly, T. (2006). Web 2.0: Principles and Best Practices. O'Reilly Media, Executive Report. Retrieved from http://www.oreilly.com/catalog/web2report/ chapter/web20_report_excerpt.pdf.

Nadeem, D., & Sauermann, L. (2007). From Philosophy and Mental-Models to Semantic Desktop. In K. Tochtermann; W. Haas; F. Kappe; A. Scharl; T. Pellegrini, & S. Schaffert (Eds.), International Conference on New Media Technologies and Semantic Systems: Proceedings of I-Media '07 and I-Semantics '07 (pp. 211–220). Graz: J.UCS.

Nardi, D., & Brachman, R. (2003). An Introduction to Description Logics. In F. Baader; D. Calvanese; D. McGuinness; D. Nardi, & P. F. Patel-Schneider (Eds.), The Description Logic Handbook: Theory, Implementation and Applications (pp. 1–40). Cambridge: Cambridge University Press.

Neumann, E., & Prusak, L. (2007). Knowledge Networks in the Age of the Semantic Web. Briefings in Bioinformatics, 8(3), 141–149.

Nice Classification (2007). International Classification of Goods and Services under the Nice Agreement (9th Edition). Genf: WIPO.

Niederee, C., Risse, T., Paukert, M., & Stein, A. (2007). An Architecture Blueprint for Knowledge-Based e-Science. In Proceedings of the German eScience Conference 2007. Max Planck Digital Library, ID 316509.0.

Notess, G. R. (2006). The Terrible Twos: Web 2.0, Library 2.0, and More. Online, 30(3), 40–42.

Ockenfeld, M. (Ed.). 2008. Informationskompetenz 2.0 – Zukunft von qualifizierter Informationsvermittlung: Tagungsband des 24. Oberhofer Kolloquium zur Praxis der Informationsvermittlung, Barleben/Magdeburg. Frankfurt am Main: DGI.

O'Reilly, T. (2005). What is Web 2.0: Design Patterns and Business Models for the Next Generation of Software. Retrieved from http://www.oreillynet.com/ pub/a/oreilly/tim/news/2005/09/30/what-is-web-20.html.

Ornager, S. (1995). The Newspaper Image Database: Empirical Supported Analysis of Users' Typology and Word Association Clusters. In E. Fox; P. Ingwersen, & R. Fidel (Eds.), Proceedings of the 18th Annual International ACM SIGIR Conference on Research and Development in Information Retrieval (pp. 212–218). New York: ACM.

Pan, J. Z. (2007). OWL for the Novice: A Logical Perspective. In C. J. O. Baker & K.-H. Cheung (Eds.), Semantic Web: Revolutionizing Knowledge Discovery in the Life Sciences (pp. 159–182). Boston: Springer.

Paolillo, J.; Penumarthy, S. (2007). The Social Structure of Tagging Internet Video on del.icio.us. In Proceedings of the 40th Annual Hawaii International Conference on System Sciences (HICSS) (p. 85).

Passant, A. (2007). Using Ontologies to Strengthen Folksonomies and Enrich Information Retrieval in Weblogs: Theoretical Background and Corporate Use-Case. In International Conference on Weblogs and Social Media (ICWSM), Boulder, USA. Retrieved from http://www.icwsm.org/papers/paper15.html.

Paulsen, I., Mainz, D., Weller, K., Mainz, I., Kohl, J., & von Haeseler, A. (2007). Ontoverse. Collaborative Knowledge Management in the Life Science Network. In Proceedings of the German eScience Conference 2007. Max Planck Digital Library, ID 316588.0.

Pazienza, M. T. (Ed.) (1997). Information Extraction: A Multidisciplinary Approach to an Emerging Information Technology. LNCS, Vol. 1299. Berlin: Springer.

Perugini, S., Goncalves, M. A., & Fox, E. A. (2004). Recommender Systems Research: A Connection-Centric Study. Journal of Intelligent Information Systems, 23(2), 107–143.

Peters, I. (2006a). Inhaltserschließung von Blogs und Podcasts im betrieblichen Wissensmanagement. In M. Ockenfeld (Ed.), Content: 28. Online-Tagung der DGI, 58. Jahrestagung der DGI, Frankfurt, Germany (pp. 143–151). Frankfurt am Main: DGI.

Peters, I. (2006b). Against Folksonomies: Indexing Blogs and Podcasts for Corporate Knowledge Management. In H. Jezzard (Ed.), Preparing for Information 2.0. Online Information 2006 Conference Proceedings (pp. 93–97). London: Learned Information Europe.

Peters, I. (2009). Folksonomies: Indexing and Retrieval in Web 2.0. Berlin: De Gruyter Saur.

Peters, I., & Stock, W. G. (2007a). Web 2.0 im Unternehmen. Wissensmanagement, 9(4), 22–25.

Peters, I., & Stock, W. G. (2007b). Folksonomy and Information Retrieval. In Joining Research and Practice: Social Computing and Information Science. Proceedings of the 70th Annual Meeting of the American Society for Information Science and Technology. Milwaukee, Wisconsin (pp. 1510–1542).

Pluzhenskaia, M. (2006). Folksonomies or Fauxsonomies: How Social is Social Bookmarking? In 17th ASIS&T SIG/CR Classification Research Workshop: Abstracts of Posters (pp. 23–24).

Prud'hommeaux, E., & Seaborne, A. (2008). SPARQL Query Language for RDF: W3C Recommendation, 15 January 2008. Retrieved from http://www.w3.org/TR/rdf-sparql-query.

Raabe, A. (2007). Social Software im Unternehmen. Wikis und Weblogs für Wissensmanagement und Kommunikation. Saarbrücken: VDM Müller.

Ranganathan, S. R. (1965). The Colon Classification. Rutgers Series on Systems for the Intellectual Organization of Information, IV. New Brunswick, NJ: Graduate School of Library Sercice, Rutgers – the State University.

Ranganathan, S. R. (1987 [1933]). Colon Classification (7th Edition). Madras: Madras Library Association.

Rasmussen, E. M. (1997). Indexing Images. Annual Review of Information Science and Technology, 32, 169–196.

Redmond-Neal, A., & Hlava, M. M. K. (Eds.) (2005). ASIS&T Thesaurus of Information Science, Technology, and Librarianship (3rd Edition). ASIST Monograph Series. Medford, NJ: Information Today.

RSWK (1998). Regeln für den Schlagwortkatalog (3rd Edition). Berlin: Deutsches Bibliotheksinstitut.

Safari, M. (2004). Metadata and the Web. Webology, 1(2). Retrieved from http://www.webology.ir/2004/v1n2/a7.html.

Sattler, U. (2003). Description Logics for Ontologies. In A. de Moor, W. Lex, & B. Ganter (Eds.), Conceptual Structures for Knowledge Creation and Communication. 11th International Conference on Conceptual Structures (ICCS 2003), Dresden, Germany (pp. 96–116). Berlin: Springer.

Sauermann, L., Bernardi, A., & Dengel, A. (2005). Overview and Outlook on the Semantic Desktop. In S. Decker, J. Park, D. Quan, & L. Sauermann (Eds.), Semantic Desktop Workshop: Proceedings of the ISWC 2005 Workshop on The Semantic Desktop. Next Generation Information Management & Collaboration Infrastructure, Galway, Ireland. CEUR Workshop Proceedings: Vol. 175.

Sauermann, L., van Elst, L., & Dengel, A. (2007). PIMO: A Framework for Representing Personal Information Models. In K. Tochtermann; W. Haas; F. Kappe; A. Scharl; T. Pellegrini, & S. Schaffert (Eds.), International Conference on New Media Technologies and Semantic Systems: Proceedings of I-Media '07 and I-Semantics '07 (pp. 270-277). Graz: J.UCS.

Schiller García, J. (2007). Enterprise 2.0: Web 2.0 im Unternehmen. Saarbrücken: VDM Verlag Dr. Müller.

Shadbolt, N., Berners-Lee, T., & Hall, W. (2006). The Semantic Web Revisited. IEEE Intelligent Systems, 21(3), 96–101.

Shirky, C. (2005). Ontology is Overrated: Categories, Links, and Tags. Retrieved from www.shirky.com/writings/ontology_overrated.html.

Sinclair, J., & Cardew-Hall, M. (2008). The Folksonomy Tag Cloud: When is it Useful? Journal of Information Science, 34(1), 15–29.

Smith, G. (2004). Folksonomy: Social Classification [Blog Post: August 03, 2004]. Retrieved from http://atomiq.org/archives/2004/08/folksonomy_social_classification.html.

Sobin, L. H., & Wittekind, C. (Eds.) (2002). TNM Classification of Malignant Tumours (6th Edition). New York: Wiley-Liss.

Sonnenwald, D. H. (2007). Scientific Collaboration. In B. Cronin (Ed.), Annual Review of Information Science and Technology, Vol. 41 (pp. 643–681). Medford, NJ: Information Today.

Sowa, J. F. (no date). Building, Sharing, and Merging Ontologies. Retrieved from http://www.jfsowa.com/ontology/ontoshar.htm.

Sowa, J. F. (2000). Knowledge Representation: Logical, Philosophical and Computational Foundations (Reprint). Pacific Grove, Calif.: Brooks/Cole.

Spiteri, L. F. (1999). The Essential Elements of Faceted Thesauri. Cataloging & Classification Quarterly, 28(4), 31–52.

Spiteri, L. F. (2006). The Use of Folksonomies in Public Library Catalogues. The Serials Librarian, 51(2), 75–89.

Staab, S., & Studer, R. (Eds.) (2004). Handbook on Ontologies. Berlin, Heidelberg, New York: Springer.

Stock, M., & Stock, W. G. (2000). Klassifikation und terminologische Kontrolle: Yahoo!, Open Directory und Oingo im Vergleich. Password, 14(12), 26–31.

Stock, M., & Stock, W. G. (2006). Intellectual Property Information: A Comparative Analysis of Main Information Providers. Journal of the American Society for Information Science and Technology, 57, 1794–1803.

Stock, W. G. (2006). On Relevance Distributions. Journal of the American Society for Information Science and Technology, 57(8), 1126–1129.

Stock, W. G. (2007a). Information Retrieval: Informationen suchen und finden. München, Wien: Oldenbourg.

Stock, W. G. (2007b). Folksonomies and Science Communication. A Mash-up of Professional Science Databases and Web 2.0 Services. Information Services & Use, 27(3), 97–103.

Stock, W. G., & Stock, M. (2008). Wissensrepräsentation: Informationen auswerten und bereitstellen. München, Wien: Oldenbourg.

Stuckenschmidt, H., & van Harmelen, F. (2005). Information Sharing on the Semantic Web. Berlin, Heidelberg: Springer.

Studer, R., Ankolekar, A., Hitzler, P., & Sure, Y. (2006). A Semantic Future for AI. IEEE Intelligent Systems, 21(4), 8–9.

Studer, R., Benjamins, V., & Fensel, D. (1998). Knowledge Engineering. Principles and Methods. IEEE Transactions on Data and Knowledge Engineering, 25(1-2), 161–197.

Surowiecki, J. (2004). The Wisdom of Crowds: Why the Many are Smarter than the Few and How Collective Wisdom Shapes Business, Economies, Societies and Nations. New York: Anchor Books.

Szugat, M., Gewehr, J., & Lochmann, C. (2006). Social Software. Blogs, Wikis & Co. Frankfurt am Main: Entwickler.press.

Taniar, D., & Rahayu, J. W. (Eds.) (2006). Web Semantics and Ontology. Hershey, PA: Idea Group Publishing.

Taylor, A. G. (1999). The Organization of Information. Englewood, CO: Libraries Unlimited.

Toffler, A. (1980). The Third Wave. New York: Morrow.

Trant, J. (2006a). Exploring the Potential for Social Tagging and Folksonomy in Art Museums. Proof of Concept. New Review of Hypermedia and Multimedia, 12(1), 83–105.

Trant, J. (2006b). Social Classification and Folksonomy in Art Museums: Early Data from the Steve Museum Tagger Prototype. In J. Furner & J. T. Tennis (Eds.), Proceedings of the 17th ASIS&T SIG/CR Classificaiton Research Workshop. Advances in Classification Research: Vol. 17

Trippe, B. (2001). Taxonomies and Topic Maps: Categorization Steps Forward. EContent, 24(6), 44–49.

Tschetschoning, K., Ladengruber, R., Hampel, T., & Schulte, J. (2008). Kollaborative Tagging-Systeme im Electronic Commerce. In B. Gaiser, T. Hampel, & S. Panke (Eds.), Medien in der Wissenschaft: Vol. 47. Good Tags – Bad Tags. Social Tagging in der Wissensorganisation (pp. 119–129). Münster: Waxmann.

Tummarello, G., Morbidoni, C., & Nucci, M. (2006). Enabling Semantic Web Communities with DBin: An Overview. In I. Cruz, S. Decker, et al. (Eds.), The Semantic Web. 5th International Semantic Web Conference (ISWC 2006), Athens, GA, USA. (pp. 943–950). Berlin: Springer.

UDC (2005). Universal Decimal Classification. London: BSI Business Information.

Umlauf, K. (1999). Regeln für den Schlagwortkatalog: Die Grundregeln der RSWK. Berlin: Berliner Handreichungen zur Bibliothekswissenschaft (Vol. 66).

Umlauf, K. (2007). Einführung in die Regeln für den Schlagwortkatalog SWK. Most recent amendment: 16. January, 2007. Retrieved from http://www.ib.hu-berlin.de/~kumlau/handreichungen/h66/.

UNESCO (1995). UNESCO Thesaurus: A Structured List of Descriptors for Indexing and Retrieving Literature in the Fields of Education, Science, Social and Human Science, Culture, Communication and Information. Paris: UNESCO Publishing.

Uren, V., Cimiano, P., Iria, J., Handschuh, S., Vargas-Vera, M., Motta, E., & Ciravegna, F. (2006). Semantic Annotation for Knowledge Management: Requirements and a Survey of the State of the Art. Journal of Web Semantics, 4(1), 14–28.

van Harmelen, F., Patel-Schneider, P. F., & Horrocks, I. (Eds.) (2001). Reference Description of the DAML+OIL (March 2001) Ontology Markup Language: Technical Report. Retrieved from http://www.daml.org/2001/03/reference.html.

Vander Wal, T. (2005). Explaining and Showing Broad and Narrow Folksonomies [Blog Post: February 02, 2005]. Retrieved from http://www.vanderwal.net/random/ category.php?cat=153.

Vander Wal, T. (2008). Welcome to the Matrix! In B. Gaiser, T. Hampel, & S. Panke (Eds.), Medien in der Wissenschaft: Vol. 47. Good Tags – Bad Tags. Social Tagging in der Wissensorganisation (pp. 7–10). Münster: Waxmann.

Vienna Classification (2008). International Classification of the Figurative Elements of Marks under the Vienna Agreement (6th Edition). Genf: WIPO.

Völkel, M., Krötzsch, M., Vrandecic, D., Haller, H., & Studer, R. (2006). Semantic Wikipedia. In L. Carr; D. de Roure, & A. Iyengar (Eds.), International World Wide Web Conference: Proceedings of the 15th

International Conference on World Wide Web, Edinburg, Schottland (pp. 585–594). New York: ACM.

Vrandecic, D., & Krötzsch, M. (2006). Reusing Ontological Background Knowledge in Semantic Wikis. In M. Völkel & S. Schaffert (Eds.), First Workshop on Semantic Wikis – From Wiki to Semantics (SemWiki2006). Proceedings of the First Workshop on Semantic Wikis, co-located with the ESWC2006. Budva, Montenegro. CEUR Workshop Proceedings: Vol. 206.

Waldrop, M. M. (2008). Science 2.0: Great New Tool, or Great Risk? Scientific American. Retrieved from http://www.sciam.com/article.cfm?id=science-2-point-0-great-new-tool-or-great-risk.

Walker, J. (2005). Weblog. In D. Herman; M. Jahn, & M. L. Ryan (Eds.), Routledge Encyclopedia of Narrative Theory (p. 45). London, New York: Routledge.

Warr, W. A. (2008). Social Software: Fun and Games, or Business tools? Journal of Information Science, 34(4), 591–604.

Weisgerber, D. W. (1997). Chemical Abstract Service Chemical Registry System: History, Scope and Impacts. Journal of the American Society for Information Science, 48, 349–360.

Weiss, A. (2005). The Power of Collective Intelligence. netWorker, 9(3), 16–23.

Weller, K., Mainz, D., Mainz, I., & Paulsen, I. (2007a). Wissenschaft 2.0? Social Software im Einsatz für die Wissenschaft. In M. Ockenfeld (Ed.), Information in Wissenschaft, Bildung und Wirtschaft: 29. Online-Tagung der DGI, 59. Jahrestagung der DGI, Frankfurt am Main, Germany (pp. 121–136). Frankfurt am Main: DGI.

Weller, K., Mainz, D., Mainz, I., & Paulsen, I. (2007b). Semantisches und vernetztes Wissensmanagement für Forschung und Wissenschaft. In R. Ball (Ed.), Wissenschaftskommunikation der Zukunft. 4. Konferenz der Zentralbibliothek Forschungszentrum Jülich (WissKom 2007), Jülich, Germany (pp. 33–46). Jülich: Forschungszentrum Jülich.

Weller, K., Peters, I., & Stock, W. G. (2009). Folksonomy: The Collaborative Knowledge Organization System. In T. Dumova & R. Fiordo (Eds.), Handbook of Research on Social Interaction Technologies and Collaboration Software: Concepts and Trends (pp. 132–146). Hershey, New York: IGI Publishing.

Wellisch, H. H. (2000). Glossary of Terminology in Abstracting, Classification, Indexing, and Thesaurus Construction. Medford: Information Today.

Yergeau, F., Bray, J., Paoli, J., Sperberg-McQueen, C. M., & Maler, E. (2004). Extensible Markup Language (XML) 1.0 (3rd Edition). W3C Recommendation, 4th February 2004. Retrieved from http://www.w3.org/TR/REC-xml.

Zimmer, M. (2008). The Externalities of Search 2.0: The Emerging Privacy Threats when the Drive for the Perfect Search Engine Meets Web 2.0. First Monday, 13(3). Retrieved from http://www.uic.edu/htbin/cgiwrap/bin/ojs/index.php/fm/article/view/2136/1944.

Zins, C. (2002). Models for Classifying Internet Resources. Knowledge Organization, 29, 20–28.

Chapter 2
Ontologies: Semantics for the Web

2.1 Ontologies: Definition and Background

The heterogeneous (scientific) communities dealing with ontologies all have different backgrounds and requirements. After several years of highly active ontology research, the question of how to precisely define 'ontology' has still not been answered satisfactorily. Even Gruber's constantly quoted definition, "an ontology is an explicit specification of a conceptualization" (Gruber, 1993), still leaves enough room for discussion. Comprehensive considerations on how ontologies relate to traditional knowledge representation and document indexing methods on the one hand and to relational databases on the other hand are rather underrepresented in scientific discussion. There are different reasons for this – as we will see in the following sections, where we will provide a short overview of how the term 'ontology' has entered computer science and related disciplines and how it has been perceived since then.

2.1.1 From Philosophy to Computer Science

In philosophy, Ontology is a field concerned with the nature of existence; e.g. in Aristotle's Metaphysics primitive categories were collected to account for All That Is (Gruber, 2009). Comparable studies are explicitly described as "ontologia" since the 17th century (Smith & Welty, 2001; Stock & Stock, 2008).

> "Ontology is a discipline of Philosophy that deals with what is, with the kinds and structures of objects, properties, and other aspects of reality. While much of the philosophical practice of ontology dates back to Aristotle and what his students called 'metaphysics', the term ontology (ontologia) was coined in 1613 by Rudolf Gockel and apparently independently by Jacob Lorhard. According to the OED [Oxford English Dictionary], the first recorded use in English was 1721. Today's ontology includes questions such as, 'what is a castle?' and 'what is a whole?' The way we answer these questions reflects the way we perceive and interact with the world." (Welty & Guarino, 2001)

Today's computational ontologies are still about capturing the nature of existence, and they still refer to their philosophical roots (Guarino, 1995; Gruber, 2009).

They describe concepts with respect to their specifications (comparable to Quine, 1974) and use relations between concepts to represent statements. By applying methods of formal logic (Sowa, 2000; Stock & Stock, 2008, Chapter 14) they facilitate mechanisms of reasoning and inference. Smith (2003) points out the foundations of ontologies with respect to philosophy:

> "The methods used in the construction of ontologies thus conceived are derived on the one hand from earlier initiatives in database management systems. But they also include methods similar to those employed in philosophy [...], including the methods used by logicians when developing formal semantic theories." (Smith, 2003)

But computational ontologies today care much less about well thought-out categories; they also often regard very limited and specialized domains instead of "all that is" in the world. In contrast to philosophical and theoretical studies, the new context of ontologies is coupled with practical applications and specific tasks – as also indicated by Gruber (2009):

> "In computer and information science, ontology is a technical term denoting an artifact that is designed for a purpose, which is to enable the modeling of knowledge about some domain, real or imagined." (Gruber, 2009)

This domain knowledge is then to be used for some computational purpose. Therefore the primary aim is to serve this purpose well and the actual knowledge model is often created with respect to its application – not to form a precise world model. This practical focus may even lead to the production of ontologies with entirely fictitious domains of interest:

> "Computational ontologies in the context of information systems are artifacts that encode a description of some world (actual, possible, counterfactual, impossible, desired, etc.), for some purpose. They have a (primarily logical) structure, and must match both domain and task: they allow the description of entities whose attributes and relations are of concern because of their relevance in a domain for some purpose, e.g. query, search, integration, matching, explanation, etc." (Presutti & Gangemi, 2008)

Sometimes computational ontology is viewed as a kind of *applied philosophy* (Sowa, 1984). Some of the well-known projects that develop so-called *upper* or *top-level ontologies* (these are ontologies on a very abstract level, trying to capture general world knowledge without being bound to a certain knowledge domain; e.g. the Cyc project[120] or the Standard Upper Ontology SUO[121]) still bear strong references to philosophical traditions (Gómez-Pérez, Fernández-López & Corcho, 2004). Yet, the majority of ontology engineering projects for AI studies and computer science do not include sophisticated philosophical considerations:

> "[..] most of AI chose not to consider the work of the much older overlapping field of philosophical ontology, preferring instead to use the term 'on-

---

[120]   OpenCyc Ontology: http://www.opencyc.org.
[121]   Standard Upper Ontology Working Group (SUO WG): http://suo.ieee.org.

tology' as an exotic name for what they'd been doing all along – knowledge engineering." (Smith & Welty, 2001)

By now it has widely been agreed to use Ontology (with upper case O and without a plural) for philosophical discussions and ontology (with lower case o) for computer and information scientific contexts (Guarino, 1998) to distinguish the different underlying principles and aims. An introduction to the history of ontologies in computer science with respect to the philosophical background is provided by Gómez-Pérez, Fernández-López and Corcho (2004).

For our context – the Social Semantic Web – we will also consider the computational ontology's perspective with its practical focus on applicability and can only pay little attention to the philosophical roots of Ontology. Yet instead, we have added our particular information scientific background. For this chapter, this means that after presenting some classical and recent definitions in the next section we will discuss elements and structures of ontologies in comparison with classical knowledge organization systems.

2.1.2 Ontology Definitions

One of the first definitions of ontology in its new context of computer science was by Neches, Fikes et al. (1991):

> "An ontology defines the basic terms and relations comprising the vocabu-
> lary of a topic area as well as the rules for combining terms and relations to
> define extensions to the vocabulary." (Neches, Fikes et al., 1991)

The most commonly quoted definition by Tom Gruber, which describes an ontology as an "explicit specification of a conceptualization" (1993), has been modified several times, for example by Borst (1997), who has stated a little more precisely that "Ontologies are defined as a formal specification of a shared conceptualization."

Studer, Benjamins and Fensel (1998) summed up both of these definitions and explained the characteristics "explicitly", "formality" and "shared conceptualization". They pointed out that an ontology should be machine-readable and should capture consensual knowledge. Another famous early definition was provided by Uschold and Grüninger (1996):

> "An ontology may take a variety of forms, but necessarily it will include a
> vocabulary of terms, and some specification of their meaning. This includes
> definitions and an indication of how concepts are inter-related which collec-
> tively impose a structure on the domain and constrain the possible interpre-
> tations of terms." (Uschold & Grüninger, 1996)

Even more so than the previous ones, this definition makes it difficult to distinguish ontologies from other KOS. It even defines the term ontology in a way that allows to incormporate most other knowledge representation systems, such as thesauri and classifications – and thus lets it become a gencric term for all (or most) KOS. Yet this is problematic in our context of knowledge representation on the Social Semantic Web, where (as we have seen in the previous chapter) various types of KOS co-exist. A more concrete definition of ontology is needed.

While Studer, Benjamins and Fensel (1998) have already identified machine-readability as a peculiarity of ontologies, the discussion of specific features of ontologies has moved on. On their website, the IEEE committee on the Standard Upper Ontology SUO has addressed the problem of different degrees of specificity in ontologies as follows:

> "In knowledge representation, ontology is the study of the categories of things in some domain of interest to a community of agents. The types in the ontology represent the entities and relations of the domain. Ontologies are distinguished along a spectrum of formality. An informal ontology contains a list of types that are either undefined or defined only by statements in a natural language. A formal ontology or taxonomy is specified by a set of types with constraints for subtyping, covering and partition. An axiomatized ontology is a formal ontology that uses first order logic for a richer expression of the constraints between the entity and relation types." (IEEE SUO, 2003)

Sometimes the terms 'lightweight ontology' and 'heavyweight ontology' are used to capture the varying degrees of complexity in different KOS, as described by Corcho, Fernández-López and Gómez-Pérez (2003):

> "The ontology community distinguishes ontologies that are mainly taxonomies from ontologies that model the domain in a deeper way and provide more restrictions on domain semantics. The community calls them lightweight and heavyweight ontologies respectively. On the one hand, lightweight include concepts, concept taxonomies, relationships between concepts and properties that describe concepts. On the other hand, heavyweight ontologies add axioms and constraints to lightweight ontologies." (Corcho, Fernández-López & Gómez-Pérez, 2003)

Nicola Guarino, who has also criticized and refined Gruber's definition[122], considers ontology as a general term that comprises models of different expressiveness:

> "In the simplest case, an ontology describes a hierarchy of concepts related by subsumption relationships; in more sophisticated cases, suitable axioms are added in order to express other relationships between concepts and to constrain their intended interpretation." (Guarino, 1998)

For us, these different approaches to distinguishing types of ontologies have one shared flaw: they do not allow one to easily consider ontologies in co-existence with traditional KOS.

---

[122] Guarino (1998) presented the following alternative definition and described an ontology as "[…] an engineering artifact, constituted by a specific vocabulary used to describe a certain reality plus a set of explicit assumptions regarding the intended meaning of the vocabulary words."

It has been pointed out several times during the last few years of ontology research that current definitions lack a shared consensus. In the early years of ontology research, Guarino and Giaretta (1995) already identified seven different interpretations of the term ontology. The problem still remains, as Martin Hepp (2008) so aptly sums up:

> "Surprisingly, people from various research field communities often use the term ontology with different, partly incompatible meanings in mind. In fact, it is a kind of paradox that the seed term of a novel field of research, which aims at reducing ambiguity about the intended meaning of symbols, is understood and used so inconsistently." (Hepp, 2008)

This unsteadiness particularly hampers communications across different disciplines. In our context of knowledge representation and document indexing, we are principally confronted with two distinct notions of the term ontology: a) ontology as a generic concept, subsuming all kinds of existing knowledge organization systems – or at least all that use fixed concept-relation-structures; and b) ontology as an individual type of knowledge organization system, that expands the possibilities of traditional methods.

Although the first option is more frequently used, we prefer the second one for our considerations, as it allows one to distinguish semantically richer systems from thesauri, classifications and nomenclatures.

Of course, it may be argued that a unique and unambiguous definition for ontologies and other KOS is not necessary, as long as a given knowledge model serves its intended purpose and that we may well speak indifferently of ontologies in regard of all possible knowledge models. Yet, there is a growing need for more specific definitions and classifications of types of ontologies and other KOS, if we want to be able to efficiently use and reuse them across applications and purposes. In this case, specifications are needed to precisely locate the existing knowledge model which best matches the given requirements. In this chapter (and particularly in Section 2.2), we will provide a detailed introduction to the structure and elements of ontologies. This will serve as a basis for an approach to distinguishing KOS types (mainly based on semantic relations) which is proposed in Section 2.3, and a new meta ontology that is introduced in Section 3.4.2.

While the distinction between ontologies and other KOS is a main issue of information science, discussions in computer science have come up concerning the distinction between ontologies and (relational) databases. Many ontologies that collect facts about a certain domain of interest can also be easily stored and displayed in relational databases. Yet this is only feasible for ontologies that do not make use of formal definitions and axioms and mainly focus on the abstract representation of a domain. We will not elaborate on this topic, but only refer to two quotations for a brief insight. On the one hand, Pan (2007) counts database conceptualizations as simple ontologies:

> "Database conceptual schemas [...] can be seen as ontologies, as they capture the important entities and relationships in an application domain and specify constraints on the entities and relationships." (Pan, 2007)

But he also points out that ontologies carry some additional features in comparison to databases; they add a novel semantic layer and make use of representation structures enabling the checking of query consistency (syntactically). They can also be used as global schemas to query against multiple related data sources (Pan, 2007). Gruber (2009) argues:

> "In the context of database systems, ontology can be viewed as a level of abstraction of data models, analogous to hierarchical and relational models, but intended for modeling knowledge about individuals, their attributes, and their relationships to other individuals. Ontologies are typically specified in languages that allow abstraction away from data structures and implementation strategies; in practice, the languages of ontologies are closer in expressive power to first-order logic than languages used to model databases. For this reason, ontologies are said to be at the 'semantic' level, whereas database schema are models of data at the 'logical' or 'physical' level. Due to their independence from lower level data models, ontologies are used for integrating heterogeneous databases, enabling interoperability among disparate systems, and specifying interfaces to independent, knowledge-based services." (Gruber, 2009)

Hepp (2008) identifies three confrontations which represent the roots for major disagreements on what an ontology is: "truth vs. consensus" (is an ontology intended to represent reality and its true structures or 'merely' to capture some consensus on a domain of interest?), "formal logic vs. other modalities" (is the use of formal logic a constituting characteristic of an ontology or may other modalities be chosen as well?) and "specification vs. conceptual system" (is the ontology a conceptual system, an abstraction of a domain of interest in terms of concepts and relations between them, or is it the explicit specification of this abstraction in some formalism, like OWL). The last aspect concerns the question of to what degree ontology definitions depend on the usage of formal ontology languages. Hepp explains:

> "In computer science, researchers assume that they can define the conceptual entities in ontologies mainly by formal means – for example, by using axioms to specify the intended meaning of domain elements. In contrast, in information systems, researchers discussing ontologies are more concerned with understanding conceptual elements and their relationships, and often specify their ontologies using only informal means, such as UML class diagrams, entity-relationship models, semantic nets, or even natural language. In such contexts, a collection of named conceptual entities with a natural language definition – that is, a controlled vocabulary – would count as an ontology." (Hepp, 2008)

Tom Gruber has also considered the conceptualization of an ontology as independent from its formal representation:

> "[...] today's W3C Semantic Web standard suggests a specific formalism for encoding ontologies (OWL), in several variants that vary in expressive

power [...]. This reflects the intent that an ontology is a specification of an abstract data model (the domain conceptualization) that is independent of its particular form." (Gruber, 2009)

Similarly, Welty and Guarino distinguish the terms 'ontology' and 'conceptual model':

> "We make a slight difference between these two terms, however [...]: a conceptual model is an actual implementation of an ontology that has to satisfy the engineering trade-offs of a running application, while the design of an ontology is independent of run-time considerations, and its only goal is to specify the conceptualization of the world underlying such an application." (Welty & Guarino, 2001)

Chandrasekaran, Josephson and Benjamins (1999) discuss the problem from an AI perspective. They point out that a reciprocal dependency exists between representation mechanisms and representation languages and good content theories or domain models that are represented:

> "Sometimes, the AI community gets excited by some mechanism such as rule systems, frame languages, neural nets, fuzzy logic, constraint propagation, or unification. [...] At other times, we realize that, however wonderful the mechanism, it cannot do much without a good content theory of the domain on which it is to work. Moreover, we often recognize that once a good content theory is available, many different mechanisms might be used equally well to implement effective systems, all using essentially the same content. [...] Ontologies are quintessentially content theories, because their main contribution is to identify specific classes of objects and relations that exist in some domain. Of course, content theories need a representation language." (Chandrasekaran, Josephson & Benjamins, 1999)

We may thus draw three conclusions: a) ontologies in the sense of a conceptual domain model are independent from a specific formal representation mechanism; b) but to be useful in practical application settings (such as the Social Semantic Web), a conceptual ontology has to be transferred to a formal representation; and c) various formal mechanisms are available and suitable for capturing an ontology conceptualization (and it is mainly the pursuit of interoperability which has led to the preference of several specific ontology languages).

The developing team of the Ontology Metadata Vocabulary (OMV) has introduced the distinction of *Ontology Base* (OB) and *Ontology Document* (OD): the ontology base is the abstract idea of an ontology, its core or conceptualization as considered independently of any implementation details; the ontology document is any specific realization of an ontology base, such as an implementation in a certain ontology language (Hartmann, Suarez-Figueroa et al., 2005). This distinction is also particularly useful for handling different release versions of one ontology.

Gómez-Pérez, Fernández-López & Corcho (2004) distinguish different degrees of formality which an ontology may obtain – based on the use of formalization languages:

"Ontologies can be highly informal if they are expressed in natural language; semi-informal if expressed in a restricted and structured form of natural language; semi-formal if expressed in an artificial and formally defined language (i.e., Ontolingua [...], 1997), OWL [...]); and rigorously formal if they provide meticulously defined terms with formal semantics, theorems and proofs of properties such as soundness and completeness."
(Gómcz-Pérez, Fernández-López & Corcho, 2004)

In any case, ontologies are – in contrast to other KOS – closely coupled to standardized technical implementations and particularly depend on the different formal languages used in ontology engineering. Terms cannot be formally and explicitly defined without formal representation languages. The character of a particular ontology is to a certain degree bound to the rules of the specific ontology language it has been implemented in. Thus, it is sometimes necessary to discuss statements which are only valid for 'OWL-ontologies,' or even only 'OWL-DL-ontologies.' This of course has influenced the definitions of ontologies and may be one of the reasons why definitions have become rather too general.

Hitzler, Krötzsch et al. (2008) on the other hand even go as far as to state that the use of a formal ontology language such as OWL or RDF(S) is enough to characterize an ontology:

"Der Begriff Ontologie ist in unserem Zusammenhang als äquivalent zum Begriff *Wissensbasis* zu verstehen und beschreibt schlicht ein in RDF(S) oder OWL erstelltes Dokument, welches Wissen einer Anwendungsdomäne modelliert." (Hitzler, Krötzsch et al., 2008).

"In our context, the term ontology is equivalent to the term knowledge base and simply describes a document formalized in RDF(S) or OWL which models the knowledge of a domain of application." [Author's translation]

Focusing on the actual formalization technique harbors the danger of neglecting the actual *knowledge* inside a knowledge organization system. Very careful considerations have to be made with respect to the underlying conceptualization (or the ontology base) of an ontology, before one starts implementing it in an ontology language. Considering an ontology base as an independent construct can help to sensitize the growing community of ontology engineers to basic problems of knowledge representation – apart from specific requirements in OWL or any other ontology language.

And still, the formalization is of great importance for realizing the Semantic Web. An ontology base has little practical impact without its formal implementation as an ontology document. The possibility of performing automatic reasoning is frequently discussed as a unique and typical feature of ontologies if compared with other KOS, e. g. by Horrocks and Sattler (2001):

"As we have seen, ontologies are set to play a key rôle in the Semantic Web, where they will provide a source of shared and precisely defined terms for use in descriptions of web resources. Moreover, such descriptions should be amenable to automated reasoning if they are to be used effectively by automated processes." (Horrocks & Sattler, 2001)

Or by Berners-Lee, Hendler and Lassila (2001):

> "The most typical kind of ontology for the Web has a taxonomy and a set of inference rules. The taxonomy defines classes of objects and relations among them." (Berners-Lee, Hendler & Lassila, 2001)

Stock and Stock (2008) name the support of automatic reasoning mechanisms as one of four criteria for distinguishing ontologies from classical KOS.

This request for automatic reasoning definitely implicates the use of some formal representation with standardized languages. And from our perspective in comparing Semantic Web developments with classical document indexing, the aspect of reasoning is indeed one that is completely new and a peculiarity of ontologies. Hence, what is unique to ontologies when compared to former KOS and to the entire approach of information science's knowledge representation is that they are intended to provide a knowledge base for humans as well as for human-computer and even computer-computer interactions.

Ontologies should unambiguously represent shared background knowledge that helps people within a community of interest to understand each other. And they should make computer-readable indexing of information possible on the Web. All this has not been the case for traditional KOS and is an important innovation. We will now see how this is actually achieved in ontologies and how the different elements of ontologies can capture semantics for the Web.

2.2 Structure and Elements of Ontologies

2.2.1 Basic Elements of Ontologies

Typical and basic elements of ontologies which can be captured by the different ontology languages are classes, instances, and relations between them (in form of properties specifying classes and their instances)[123]. The structure of an ontology

---

[123] In ontology engineering practice, there are different naming and spelling conventions for the different elements of ontologies. In many ontology editors it is not possible to write compounds or phrases with blanks between the words, therefore underscores and CamelCases have become frequently used. During our discussions on ontology elements and ontology engineering, we will use a special font type for examples of ontology elements. Furthermore, we will apply the following naming conventions: Classes and instances begin with a capital letter and phrases or compounds are combined to CamelCaseWords; e.g. `KnowledgeRepresentation`. Properties (relations) are written in lower case letters and phrases or compounds are combined with underscores; e.g. `is_part_of`. Such spelling conventions are frequently applied to ontology elements. Within single discussions on actual concepts – not the classes representing them – concepts will be written in *italics*. Note that examples cited from other authors may use other spelling conventions.

can furthermore be modeled through restrictions representing axioms. Comments and other annotations can provide additional information via informal semantics.

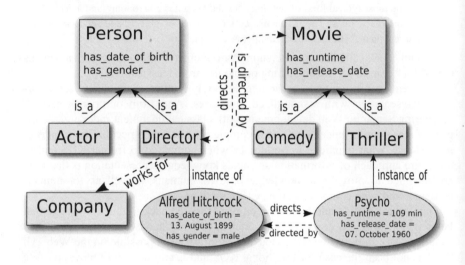

Figure 2.1.   A simplified model of basic ontology elements.

Figure 2.1 shows a simplified model of an ontology, including concepts (depicted as square boxes), two exemplary instances (depicted as round boxes) and relations between them (depicted as arrows; continuous arrows are used for hierarchical relations, a dashed line represents a self-defined semantic relation). Classes represent *general concepts* or knowledge categories and form the basic structure of the ontology. Instances represent *individual concepts* and are grouped into superordinate classes; and properties are used to represent relations between classes as well as to specify their typical attributes. The classes `Person` and `Movie` in our example also possess datatype properties (like `has_runtime, has_date_of_birth`) which do not relate to other classes but specify class attributes. They can be directly filled with values which are not formal parts of the ontology.

```
<?xml version="1.0"?>

<!DOCTYPE rdf:RDF [
    <!ENTITY owl "http://www.w3.org/2002/07/owl#" >
    <!ENTITY xsd "http://www.w3.org/2001/XMLSchema#" >
    <!ENTITY rdfs "http://www.w3.org/2000/01/rdf-schema#" >
    <!ENTITY rdf "http://www.w3.org/1999/02/22-rdf-syntax-ns#" >
]>

<rdf:RDF xmlns="http://www.owl-ontologies.com/Ontology1247819746.owl#"
     xml:base="http://www.owl-ontologies.com/Ontology1247819746.owl"
     xmlns:xsd="http://www.w3.org/2001/XMLSchema#"
     xmlns:rdfs="http://www.w3.org/2000/01/rdf-schema#"
     xmlns:rdf="http://www.w3.org/1999/02/22-rdf-syntax-ns#"
     xmlns:owl="http://www.w3.org/2002/07/owl#">
    <owl:Ontology rdf:about=""/>
    <owl:Class rdf:ID="Actor">
        <rdfs:subClassOf rdf:resource="#Person"/>
    </owl:Class>
    <Person rdf:ID="Alfred_Hitchcock">
        <has_date_of_birth rdf:datatype="&xsd;date">1899-08-13</has_date_of_birth>
        <has_gender rdf:datatype="&xsd;string">male</has_gender>
        <directs rdf:resource="#Psycho"/>
    </Person>
    <owl:Class rdf:ID="Comedy">
        <rdfs:subClassOf rdf:resource="#Movie"/>
    </owl:Class>
    <owl:Class rdf:ID="Company"/>
    <owl:Class rdf:ID="Director">
        <rdfs:subClassOf rdf:resource="#Person"/>
    </owl:Class>
    <owl:ObjectProperty rdf:ID="directs">
        <rdfs:domain rdf:resource="#Person"/>
        <rdfs:range rdf:resource="#Movie"/>
        <owl:inverseOf rdf:resource="#is_directed_by"/>
    </owl:ObjectProperty>
    <owl:DatatypeProperty rdf:ID="has_date_of_birth">
        <rdfs:domain rdf:resource="#Person"/>
        <rdfs:range rdf:resource="&xsd;date"/>
    </owl:DatatypeProperty>
    <owl:DatatypeProperty rdf:ID="has_gender">
        <rdfs:domain rdf:resource="#Person"/>
    </owl:DatatypeProperty>
    <owl:DatatypeProperty rdf:ID="has_release_date">
        <rdfs:domain rdf:resource="#Movie"/>
        <rdfs:range rdf:resource="&xsd;date"/>
    </owl:DatatypeProperty>
    <owl:DatatypeProperty rdf:ID="has_runtime">
        <rdfs:domain rdf:resource="#Movie"/>
        <rdfs:range rdf:resource="&xsd;string"/>
    </owl:DatatypeProperty>
    <owl:ObjectProperty rdf:ID="is_directed_by">
        <rdfs:domain rdf:resource="#Movie"/>
        <rdfs:range rdf:resource="#Person"/>
        <owl:inverseOf rdf:resource="#directs"/>
    </owl:ObjectProperty>
    <owl:Class rdf:ID="Movie"/>
    <owl:Class rdf:ID="Person"/>
    <Thriller rdf:ID="Psycho">
        <has_runtime rdf:datatype="&xsd;string">109 min</has_runtime>
        <has_release_date rdf:datatype="&xsd;date">1960-10-07</has_release_date>
        <is_directed_by rdf:resource="#Alfred_Hitchcock"/>
    </Thriller>
    <owl:Class rdf:ID="Thriller">
        <rdfs:subClassOf rdf:resource="#Movie"/>
    </owl:Class>
</rdf:RDF>
```

Figure 2.2.   The example of a movie ontology (as depicted in Figure 2.1) transferred to
OWL/RDF.

To illustrate the basic elements of formal ontologies, we have used this schematic
movie ontology in order to create a very simple exemplary ontology. Figure 2.2
shows how this very small exemplary excerpt will look like in the formal OWL
representation.

Other, more detailed introductions to exemplary ontologies are provided, for the domain 'pizza', by Horridge, Knublauch et al. (2004), for the domain 'wine' by Noy and McGuinness (2001) and most recently, for the domain of 'Harry Potter', by Horrocks (2008).

We will pay the most attention to semantic relations as elements of ontologies. This is because relations greatly influence the structure of any KOS and will thus play an important role in the upcoming sections on distinguishing types of KOS (2.3) and on semantic upgrades of KOS (3.3).

Ontology Elements and Different Ontology Languages

The foundational elements of ontologies (concepts, instances, properties) are typical, but their exact specifications may vary across different ontology languages, depending on the underlying knowledge model[124]. Axioms are not supported by every ontology language[125]. The terminology for discussing the different ontology elements also varies slightly. The representation of knowledge in the form of concepts/classes, instances and relations/properties enriched with restrictions is typical for many ontology languages. A different terminology for the basic elements of ontologies is used, for example, within *frame*-based representation systems[126]. These approaches have been used at the beginnings of computational ontology research and are founded on various theoretical, philosophical and linguistic discussions (e.g. Barsalou, 1992; Fillmore, 1982; Minsky, 1975). The ontology editor Protégé started with a frame-based version before supporting RDF and OWL (Noy, Fergerson & Musen, 2000). In this approach, frames are the principal building blocks of a knowledge base. A frame represents an entity in the domain of interest. An ontology based on frames consists of classes, instances, slots and facets, which are all types of frames:

> "[...] a Protégé ontology consists of classes, slots, facets, and axioms.
> Classes are concepts in the domain of discourse. Slots describe properties or
> attributes of classes. Facets describe properties of slots. Axioms specify ad-
> ditional constraints." (Noy, Fergerson & Musen, 2000)

Apart from terminological differences, frame representations and those based on description logics differ in expressivity and underlying paradigms (Wang, Noy et al., 2006). For example, frame-based systems like Protégé Frames work with a *Unique Name Assumption*; this means that, by default, different names refer to different things. The most prominent difference in underlying paradigms is the

---

[124] For a discussion of different knowledge models and their effects on ontology engineering and different ontology editors see Gómez-Pérez, Fernández-López and Corcho (2004).

[125] Gómez-Pérez & Corcho (2002) consider the absence or availability of axioms as a distinctive feature for separating lightweight from heavyweight ontologies.

[126] Artale, Franconi et al. (1996) regard the term *class* as used in object-oriented systems as a synonym of *frame* in frame-based languages, *entity* in E-R data models, *node* in Semantic Networks and *concept* in Description Logics. They consider the term *attribute* as synonymous with *slot*, *link* and *role*.

Closed World Assumption versus the Open World Assumption. The Closed World Assumption (which is the paradigm of Protégé Frames) states that everything not directly stated in the ontology is assumed to be false; "everything is prohibited until it is permitted" (Wang, 2006). In contrast, the Open World Assumption (which is used in OWL, for example) holds that everything is only false if it contradicts already formalized facts; "everything is permitted until it is prohibited" (Wang, 2006).

With the enormous success of RDF and OWL the support of frame-based languages like Protégé Frames, the OKBC frame language[127], XOL[128] or SHOE[129] have lost importance and are currently less considered in Semantic Web research.

Furthermore, the various other existing ontology languages particularly differ with regard to the following characteristics (Gómez-Pérez & Corcho, 2002):

- Whether they support informal concept definitions or not (where the standard is to support informal definitions and documentations).
- Whether there are formal constraints on the naming of ontology elements (e.g. can two different elements within one ontology carry the same character string as their name; are special characters allowed or not).
- Which formal specifications may be applied to define concepts (e.g. can concepts be defined as disjoint in order to represent exact partitions).
- Whether properties can be specified for instances only or for both instances and concepts.
- Which types of restrictions may be placed on concept properties (e.g. may they be filled with default values, do they support cardinality restrictions).
- How many arguments can be interlinked with one property (typically only binary relations are supported).
- Whether the ontology may represent not only facts about instances but also *claims*, i.e. statements that have not been or cannot be verified (while most ontology languages do not allow one to model claims or hypotheses).
- Whether supportive editors and reasoners are available or not.

Many of our considerations in the next sections are abstracted views, uncoupled from particular ontology languages. Questions about how to define a class or about what semantic relations may hold between concepts are to a large degree independent from the actual ontology languages. Yet in general, one has to know the capabilities of a certain language before one may use it to model knowledge in a certain way, as some particular constructions may not be supported in every case. We will demonstrate some of these cases exemplarily for the language OWL-DL

---

[127] OKBC Open Knowledge Base Connectivity:
http://www.ai.sri.com/~okbc/spec/okbc2/okbc2.html.
[128] XOL Ontology Exchange Language: http://www.ai.sri.com/pkarp/xol/.
[129] SHOE Simple HTML Ontology Extensions:
http://www.cs.umd.edu/projects/plus/SHOE/.

(yet we do not aim to introduce all the capabilities of OWL), visualized in the interface of the ontology editor Protégé[130].

This is on the one hand due to reasons of feasibility, since comparing the realization of ontologies in different representation formats in detail is beyond the scope of this book. On the other hand, we focus deliberately on a more general consideration of representing knowledge with ontologies based on the meaningful elements of ontologies. In the context of a Social Semantic Web, this basic discussion is of major importance: As ontologies should be built and applied by broad communities of interest we need easily adaptive approaches to ontology engineering on the one hand and well-founded conceptualizations on the other. Motivating communities to contribute expert knowledge for shared information systems is already a challenging task. If potential communities are required to learn different formalization languages before they may contribute to the Social Semantic Web, this will constitute an additional barrier for user contributions. Thus a focus on one standard representation language will be reasonable in order to establish the foundations of knowledge representation on the Social Semantic Web. Translations into other formal languages for specific purposes and applications can still be established subsequently by experienced ontology engineers or Semantic Web professionals. OWL has a fair chance of becoming such a standard representation language[131], though an even simpler language like RDF can also be imagined to become a common foundation for social contributions to semantic knowledge representations. We will focus on OWL rather than RDF in this chapter as it allows us to better point out specific features of ontologies in contrast to other KOS.

As we experienced during our work (both during students' courses on ontology engineering and in analyzing publicly available ontologies), problems in building usable knowledge organization systems start at a very basic conceptual level. We will mention some of these very basic problems over the next sections (deliberately focusing on mistakes by inexperienced ontology builders, not trained knowledge engineers). Modeling errors are to some extent grounded in insufficient considerations of the actual nature of a domain of interest and of appropriate concept names and structures. On top of this, other modeling errors occur which can be ascribed to misinterpretations of formal language specifications.

For large-scale collaborative ontology engineering projects on the Web, the key challenge will be to establish a basic understanding of principles of knowledge representation. This may well be learned exemplarily for one common ontology language – or probably even in absence of an ontology language.

---

[130] If not indicated otherwise, all screenshots in the following sections are taken from Protégé, release 3.2.1, using the OWL version.

[131] Alhough it has to be noted that the motivation in developing OWL was not to establish a universal standard language. Consequently, it may not be the *ideal* representation language for the Semantic Web as it still has certain shortcomings (e.g. not being able to represent uncertainty).

2.2.2 Concepts and Instances

Concepts / Classes

The basic elements KOS are *concepts*; they are the foundation for the actual vocabulary in a knowledge organization system. In ontology engineering, concepts are often represented as *classes*[132]. The terms 'concept' and 'class' can be regarded as quasi-synonyms for most aspects of practical ontology engineering, although they should be clearly distinguished for theoretical foundations in knowledge representation. Sometimes they are also called *objects* or *categories* (Gómez-Pérez & Corcho, 2002).

Fundamentally, concepts are abstract thoughts about (or references to) objects in the world, expressed with words or other symbols. This definition is based on the *semiotic triangle* (also referred to as *triangle of meaning, triangle of reference*) as introduced by Ogden and Richards (1969 [1923]) (Figure 2.3). The semiotic triangle originally describes the use of language in general, where a word acts as a *symbol* to describe a real world object, the *referent*. Although a word or symbol stands for a real world object (or refers to it/ represents it) there is no direct relation between symbol and referent. The relation between them is only enabled by a *thought* (also called *reference*) in the human brain, which links symbols with references.

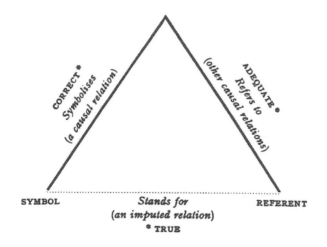

Figure 2.3. The semiotic triangle. Source: Ogden & Richards, 1969 [1923].

This triangle has been modified and transferred to knowledge representation in information science by Stock and Stock (2008), for instance (Figure 2.4). The *con-*

---

[132] For example, concepts are modelled in classes in Protégé OWL.

cept has taken over the place formerly held by the "inherent thought or reference" in Ogden and Richards' model, and instead of being defined as a thought or reference (which is a psychologistic view), the concept is defined by means of set theory. Thus concepts are understood as sets/classes of elements; either in the form of a list of elements (extensional concept definition) or as a set of elements sharing the same characteristic features (intensional concept definition). We will discuss these two options of concept definition in more detail in the section "Concepts and Attributes" below.

Concepts interlink real world *objects* with their *representations* or denotations (i.e. words or symbols used to describe a concept). For many concepts, there exists more than one word which refers to it. In knowledge representations these should ideally be interlinked as synonyms.

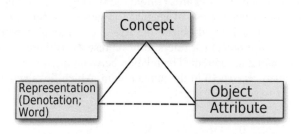

Figure 2.4.   The semiotic triangle in information science. Source: Modified from Stock & Stock, 2008.

This triangle is an important theoretical foundation for knowledge representation in information science. Yet in practice, this strict distinction between concepts and their denotations is not always adhered to. In KOS engineering, the term 'concept' is typically used for what is precisely the linguistic denotation or representation of the actual concept[133].

Concepts (as they are based on set theory) do not usually refer to exactly one concrete real-world object but are an abstraction of a set of objects with shared characteristic attributes (Figure 2.5). Thus a concept would be *Church* rather than *St. Paul's Cathedral* (the latter would typically be represented as an instance of the concept church, as will be demonstrated below).

---

[133]   And as this has become common practice, we may also do so within this book and sometimes use class and concept as synonymous expressions for the respective elements in ontologies.

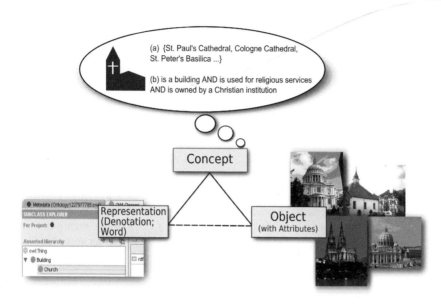

Figure 2.5. The semiotic triangle in ontology engineering with examples for the concept church. Source: Photos of churches from Wikipedia, Screenshot from Protégé.

Principally, there are no limits to what can be represented as a concept:

> "Concepts can be abstract or concrete, elementary or composite, real or fictitious; in short, a concept can be anything about which something is said, and, therefore, could also be the description of a task, function, action, strategy, reasoning process, and so on." (Gómez-Pérez & Corcho, 2002)

Thus ontologies contain concepts of uneven quality. Not only tangible objects can be represented as concepts and a concept does not always need to be represented by nouns. Some concepts cannot be described by exactly one word but have to be paraphrased.

Furthermore, concepts can have different degrees of specificity or abstraction. They can be simple terms as well as complex compounds. KOS can hold highly general concepts like *Science* as well as very specific ones like *Chinese Shrew Mole* or, as found in examples by Broughton (2002), "distribution of long wave photoreceptors in the compound eye of the honey bee," "non-visual migration orientation of the European robin" and "effect of ionizing radiation on the chromosomes in meiotic and mitotic cells."

In the context of their prototype theory, Rosch and her colleagues (Rosch, Mervis et al., 1976) distinguish three abstraction levels for concepts, called the subordinate, basic and superordinate levels. They consider the basic level to be the most important: It captures concepts of medium specificity such as *chair* or *car*, which constitute categories for various real-world objects with highly similar attributes. These basic level concepts are specified by subordinate level concepts and abstracted to superordinate level concepts.

> "[…] categories one level more abstract [author's note: than the examples chair and car on the basic level] will be superordinate categories (e.g., furniture, vehicle) whose members share only a few attributes among each other. Categories below the basic level will be subordinate categories (e.g. kitchen chair, sports car) which are also bundles of predictable attributes and functions, but contain many attributes which overlap with other categories (for example, kitchen chair shares most of its attributes with other kinds of chairs)." (Rosch, Mervis et al., 1976, 385)

Such considerations are important theoretical foundations for knowledge representation and concept structures. In practice, ontologies may of course also work with more than three levels of abstraction – and often do so[134]. For the mentioned example, we may for example add a concept `Artifact` as a broader term for both *Furniture* and *Vehicles*.

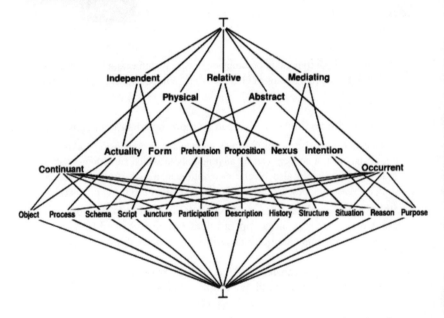

Figure 2.6.   Sowa's top-level ontology. Source: http://www.jfsowa.com/ontology/
              toplevel.htm.

---

[134] The number of levels of categorization as well as the level of detail depends on the actual domain and scope of an ontology (which is the same for almost all other KOS).

So-called *upper ontologies* in particular deal with the highest possible abstraction levels to provide the basic foundations of knowledge representation modeling (Gómez-Pérez, Fernández-López & Corcho, 2004, 71 ff.). Sowa's top-level ontology (Figure 2.6) consists of 27 fundamental concepts, which have been derived from a variety of sources in logic, linguistics and philosophy (Sowa, 2000).

Most domain- or application-specific ontologies do not distinguish concepts with respect to these fundamental differences at a top level of abstraction[135]. Referring to a shared upper ontology should facilitate a better mediation among domain ontologies. The basic problem in the upper ontology approach is that one has to agree on the most fundamental categories of existence. This again leads us back to philosophical Ontology. Various reputable philosophers have proposed and discussed fundamental categories, e.g. Aristotle, Lullus and Kant, but the results have always been different categories with one shared set everyone could agree on. To establish a categorization that is not dependent on one certain philosophical background (or one specific domain of interest) seems almost impossible.

Those single aspects from upper ontology engineering most frequently taken on in domain ontology engineering concern the distinction of objects and roles (e.g., Hepp, 2008; Mizoguchi, 2004; Sunagawa, Kozaki et al., 2004), or of objects and events (e.g., Jain, 2008). Both address the problem that some information remains constant over of time while other information is subject to changes. For example, a given person will always be considered as belonging to a class Human (or Person) – but he or she may change their *role*, e.g. from being a Student to being a Teacher. The ontology editor HOZO[136] explicitly distinguishes between concepts and roles during the ontology engineering process (Mizoguchi, 2004; Sunagawa, Kozaki et al., 2004).

The DOLCE[137] ontology (developed as a part of the WonderWeb Project[138], which was initiated to provide a foundational ontology infrastructure for the Semantic Web) pays much attention to the philosophical foundations of ontology. It works with very high-level concepts as basic categories (Figure 2.7) and clearly distinguishes between *endurants* and *perdurants* (Masolo, Borgo et al., 2003):

> "DOLCE is based on a fundamental distinction between *enduring* and *perduring* entities, i.e. between what philosophers usually call *continuants* and *occurrents* [...]. Classically, the difference between enduring and perduring entities (which we shall also call *endurants* and *perdurants*) is related to their behavior in time. Endurants are *wholly* present (i.e., all their proper parts are present) at any time they are present. Perdurants, on the other hand, just extend in time by accumulating different temporal parts, so that, at any time they are present, they are only *partially* present, in the sense that

---

[135] Although it has sometimes been recommended to use upper ontologies as an initiative model when building a domain ontology.

[136] HOZO: http://www.hozo.jp/.

[137] DOLCE Descriptive Ontology for Linguistic and Cognitive Engineering: http://www.loa-cnr.it/DOLCE.html.

[138] WonderWeb Project: http://wonderweb.semanticweb.org/.

some of their proper temporal parts (e.g., their previous or future phases) may be not present. E.g., the piece of paper you are reading now is wholly present, while some temporal parts of your reading are not present any more. Philosophers say that endurants are entities that *are in time*, while lacking however temporal parts (so to speak, all their parts flow with them in time). Perdurants, on the other hand, are entities that *happen in time*, and can have temporal parts (all their parts are fixed in time)." (Masolo, Borgo et al., 2003)

"Leaf" Basic Category	Examples
Abstract Quality	*the value of an asset*
Abstract Region	*the (conventional) value of 1 Euro*
Accomplishment	*a conference, an ascent, a performance*
Achievement	*reaching the summit of K2, a departure, a death*
Agentive Physical Object	*a human person (as opposed to legal person)*
Amount of Matter	*some air, some gold, some cement*
Arbitrary Sum	*my left foot and my car*
Feature	*a hole, a gulf, an opening, a boundary*
Mental Object	*a percept, a sense datum*
Non-agentive Physical Object	*a hammer, a house, a computer, a human body*
Non-agentive Social Object	*a law, an economic system, a currency, an asset*
Physical Quality	*the weight of a pen, the color of an apple*
Physical Region	*the physical space, an area in the color spectrum, 80Kg*
Process	*running, writing*
Social Agent	*a (legal) person, a contractant*
Society	*Fiat, Apple, the Bank of Italy*
State	*being sitting, being open, being happy, being red*
Temporal Quality	*the duration of World War I, the starting time of the 2000 Olympics*
Temporal Region	*the time axis, 22 june 2002, one second*

Figure 2.7. DOLCE leaf basic categories. Source: Masolo, Borgo et al., 2003.

Furthermore, endurants may undergo changes; e.g. an endurant `Paper` can change its color from white to yellow. Such aspects will have to be covered in the form of concept attributes within ontologies. We will discuss the phenomenon of *genidentity* below, which is an attempt of capturing changes in concepts of classical KOS.

In direct comparisons (for example by Chandrasekaran, Josephson & Benjamins, 1999), different existing upper ontologies turn out to have fundamental differences in structure. Yet Chandrasekaran, Josephson and Benjamins (1999) list some generally shared assumptions:

"Although differences exist within ontologies, general agreement exists between ontologies on many issues:

- There are *objects* in the world.
- Objects have *properties* or *attributes* that can take *values*.
- Objects can exist in various *relations* with each other.
- Properties and relations can change over *time*.

- There are *events* that occur at different *time instants*.
- There are *processes* in which objects participate and that occur over time.
- The world and its objects can be in different *states*.
- Events can *cause* other events or states as *effects*.
- Objects can have *parts*." (Chandrasekaran, Josephson & Benjamins, 1999)

Yet even though these assumptions are widely accepted, their practical realization in ontology engineering still causes problems in many cases. There are no shared agreements as to how some of these facts can be consistently represented in ontologies, e.g. for properties that change over time.

Concepts and Attributes
One major challenge in ontology engineering is the identification of the most appropriate classes for representing a domain of interest. Many approaches are based on or coupled to philosophical discussions. And in most cases, the characteristic *attributes* of objects play an important role in defining a concept. Concepts are abstractions representing collections of objects with shared or similar attributes.

As pointed out by Stock and Stock (2008), we may fundamentally distinguish definitional approaches that use the concept's *extension* from those that focus on its *intension*. An extensional definition of a concept is a list of all objects that are members of a specific set. Thus a class is defined by an enumeration of all its members. In contrast, an intensional definition specifies the necessary and sufficient characteristics for an object to be a member of a certain class. An intensional definition aims at explicitly capturing the essential features of a concept.

Let us consider this for the example *UEFA Champions League Winners*[139]. For this concept, the extensional definition would be an enumeration of all the football clubs who have won the UEFA Champions League:

UEFA Champions League Winners ≡ {Manchester United, AC Milan, FC Barcelona, Liverpool FC, …, Olympique Marseille}

The intensional definition would be a (textual) definition specifying the conditional features of all members of this class:

UEFA Champions League Winners ≡ "is a football club" AND "has won the UEFA Champions League at least once"

Extensional definitions are most feasible for small and finite sets like StatesOf-Germany. Ideally, these sets should not be subject to changes over time (e.g. this type of definition is less usable for *UEFA Champions League Winners*, as the extension is growing continuously). For intensional definitions, the main challenge is to actually identify the core attributes of a concept; those features that enable us to precisely judge an object as belonging to a class and another as being excluded.

---

[139] Another example has already been provided for the concept *church* in Figure 2.5.

This can be critical, even for relatively simple concepts such as *chair*. What actually makes up the characteristic attributes of a chair? As Black (1937) has pointed out in his exemplary vision of a chair museum, it is not easy to distinguish chairs from other objects one may sit on:

> "One can imagine an exhibition in some unlikely museum of applied logic of a series of 'chairs' differing in quality by least noticeable amounts. At the one end of a long line, containing perhaps thousands of exhibits, might be a Chippendale chair, at the other, a small nondescript lump of wood. Any 'normal' observer inspecting the series finds extreme difficulty in 'drawing the line' between chairs and not-chairs." (Black, 1937)

In other cases, there even lack shared attributes for all members of a class, although a certain similarity of objects is given, justifying the consideration as one overall concept. Wittgenstein (1953) has already coined the term *family resemblances* for this phenomenon. His popular example for a concept whose members do not carry clearly shared characteristics is *game*. Games can be of various natures; some have winners and losers and others do not, some require certain techniques or equipment, others not.

> "Consider for example the proceedings that we call 'games'. I mean board-games, card-games, ball-games, Olympic games, and so on. What is common to them all? [...] For if you look at them you will not see something that is common to *all*, but similarities, relationships, and a whole series of them at that. [...] And the result of that examination is: we see a complicated network of similarities overlapping and criss-crossing: sometimes overall similarities, sometimes similarities of detail. I can think of no better expression to characterize these similarities than 'family resemblances'; for the various resemblances between members of a family: build, features, color of eyes, gait, temperament, etc. etc. overlap and criss-cross in the same way." (Wittgenstein, 1953)

It is almost impossible to grasp the essential characteristics of games in order to provide an intensional concept definition. Rosch and Mervis (1975) have summed up the problem of family resemblance as follows:

> "A family resemblance relationship consists of a set of items in the Form AB, BC, CD, DE. That is, each item has at least one, and probably several, elements in common with one or more other items, but no, or few, elements are common to all items." (Rosch & Mervis, 1975)

Following the considerations of family resemblance, Rosch and colleagues discuss the idea of a prototype theory: For any concept, there are always some objects that can be seen as prototypes, i.e. as the clearest or most typical representative of a class. Rosch and Mervis define prototypical members of a class as those with the most attributes in common with other members of that category and those with the least attributes in common with other categories (Rosch & Mervis, 1975). During some experimental instructions they have provided few illustrative examples:

"Let's take the word *red* as an example. Close your eyes and imagine a true red. Now imagine an orangish red … imagine a purple red. Although you might still name the orange-red or the purple-red with the term *red*, they are not as good examples of red (as clear cases of what *red* refers to) as the clear 'true' red. In short, some reds are redder than others. The same is true for other kinds of categories. Think of dogs. You all have some notion of what a 'real dog', a 'doggy dog' is. To me a Retriever or a German Shepherd is a very doggy dog while a Pekinese is a less doggy dog." (Rosch & Mervis, 1975)

Similarly the concept *bird* may be chosen to ask for the most prototypical bird, and people would probably agree on a robin, a blackbird or a sparrow as prototypical birds (Figure 2.8). In contrast, an ostrich or a penguin would hardly be regarded as prototypes for the concept *bird* (Jörgensen, 2003, p. 40): they fail to fly, which is common to most birds. Rosch and Mervis (1975) performed several experiments to show that family resemblance would prove to be significantly correlated with the prototypicality of items. The result confirmed their hypothesis that the most prototypical members of a category are those which bear the greatest family resemblance to other members of their own category and have the least overlap with other categories.

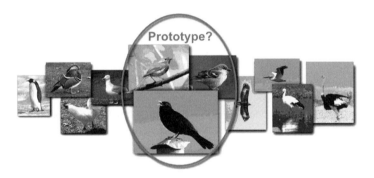

Figure 2.8.   Exemplary members of the class bird: Which one is the prototype? Source: Individual photos from Wikipedia.

This, of course, perfectly explains why penguins are not suitable as the prototype of a bird and it leaves us with the conclusion that we may not rely on the principle of shared attributes for all members of a class. This, in turn, poses a major challenge for ontology engineering: up to now the problem remains of how to handle class membership in knowledge representation models. Referring to a prototype may be a useful substitute for discussions about concepts in most cases, but it is not an entirely sufficient solution in ontology engineering, where we aim at explicit specifications. In classical KOS the concepts' attributes are either embedded in their names (e.g. `GreenApple`, `GermanChancellor`) or not included at all. Thus it is not documented which considerations have led to the construction of a particular class and to the collection of certain class members. This is different in ontologies, where concept properties can (and should) be explicitly expressed to help provide precise definitions and reasoning mechanisms.

Objects without clearly shared attributes can hardly be represented as explicitly and formally defined ontology concepts. The case of how to define the concept `Bird` while capturing both facts that a) prototypical birds can fly and b) a penguin cannot fly but still is a bird has thus become a typical example for the problem of reasoning with contradicting pieces of information (Huang, van Harmelen & ten Teije, 2006).

In sum, concept attributes have a big influence on ontology structures. Considerations of concept attributes not only influence the definition of single concepts but – as we have already noted – are also needed to specify the members of a class. In turn, this is the foundation for establishing a fundamental structure of an ontology in hierarchical order. Furthermore, concept attributes are essential for establishing additional cross-references within the ontology in the form of relations or properties.

Concept Hierarchies

In many cases, the most fundamental structure of a knowledge organization system is a hierarchical order of concepts; starting with a top term, the most general concept, which is refined stepwise. Strict concept hierarchies create tree structures in KOS.

Few discussions are available to explain why hierarchy is the most fundamental ordering principle (not only in knowledge organization). One noteworthy exception is Durkheim (2001):

> "[…] the purpose of classification is to establish relations of subordination and coordination, and man would never have thought to order his knowledge in this way if he had not already known what a hierarchy is. Neither the spectacle of physical nature nor the mechanism of mental association could provide us with this idea. Hierarchy is strictly a social thing. Only in society are there superiors, inferiors and equals. As a result, even if the facts were not yet conclusive, the analysis of these notions would be sufficient to reveal their source. We have borrowed them from society and projected them onto our representation of the world." (Durkheim, 2001)

Concepts of different abstraction levels are typically organized in hierarchies based on *hyponymy*. This means that a subclass is related to an upper class via the IS-A relation (Brachmann, 1983). KOS in biological domains rely almost exclusively on categorizations in hyponymies: For example, we may have a class `Bird` with subclasses such as `Duck` and `Lark`.

In most cases, the construction of hierarchies in KOS is based on the identification of attributes that can be used for distinguishing different objects and group together classes of objects. Ideally, a subclass should share all defining characteristics of its superclass (i.e. it inherits all properties of its superclass) and should further be specified by at least one additional characteristic (Brachmann, 1983). Thus concepts at the top of the hierarchical ladder need only a few shared characteristics, while the number increases for lower-level concepts.

As we have just seen, the identification of consistent class-defining features is not always easy. In practical KOS engineering it is also often ambiguous, i.e. there are different ways of defining subclasses. The creation of class hierarchies is one of the main challenges in creating classification systems (Batley, 2005; Bowker & Star, 2000; Hunter, 2002; Marcella & Newton, 1994; Stock & Stock, 2008) – it also plays a major role within ontology engineering and is exacerbated by the problems of identifying additional concept relations as discussed below. The process of building class hierarchies requires lots of cognitive work, as we cannot assume that a *natural* hierarchical structure of the world exists (Stock & Stock, 2008). Let us consider the following three objects from an example by Hjørland and Pedersen (2005):

If we now want to sort these objects into classes, we may decide to either group them by shape or by color. In the first case, we would create a class for Rectangles and one for Triangles. In the second case, we would create a class for BlackFigures and one for WhiteFigures. Hjørland and Pedersen (2005) conclude:

> "There is no natural or best way to decide whether form or colour is the most important property to apply when classifying the figures; whether squares should form a class while triangles are excluded or whether black figures should form a class while white figures are excluded. It simply depends on the purpose of the classification." (Hjørland and Pedersen, 2005)

In the initial example in Figure 2.1, we see two hyponymic hierarchies: Person with the subclasses Actor and Director, and Movie with the subclasses Thriller and Comedy. The class Movie in particular could have been specified in many other ways, e.g. regarding length (ShortFilm and FeatureFilm) or production techniques (ColorFilm and BlackAndWhiteFilm or also Silent-Movie). This illustrates the difficulty in agreeing on one specific hierarchical representation, as many other variations would also be applicable:

> "In principle, the number of classification criteria and distinct subtypes is unlimited, because the number of possible dimensions along which to develop subcategories cannot be exhaustively specified." (Chandrasekaran, Josephson & Benjamins, 1999)

When several object characteristics are regarded simultaneously for the different subclasses of one concept, we speak of *polydimensionality* (Bertram, 2002; Stock & Stock, 2008). A small example for polydimensional subclasses of Movie would be:

```
Movie
      Thriller
      Comedy
      ShortFilm
      SilentFilm
      SoundFilm
      ColorFilm
      BlackAndWhiteFilm
      ...
```

In contrast, in a strictly *monodimensional* KOS only one feature dimension may be regarded for dividing a class into subclasses. In order to turn a polydimensional representation into a monodimensional one, we can introduce intermediate classes to separate the dimensions (DIN 2331:1980). If we wanted to turn the previous example into a monodimensional representation, it could look like this:

```
Movie
      MovieByGenre
              Thriller
              Comedy
      MovieByLength
              ShortFilm
              FeatureLengthFilm
      MovieByProductionTechnique
              MovieBySoundTechnique
                      SilentFilm
                      SoundFilm
              MovieByColorTechnique
                      ColorFilm
                      BlackAndWhiteFilm
```

Furthermore, we may distinguish between *polyhierarchic* and *monohierarchic* knowledge organization systems: Some systems provide for the establishing of polyhierarchies, where one class may be assigned to different parent classes. For example, in one KOS about sports a class `WaterPolo` may be established as a subclass of both `WaterSport` and of `BallGame`. In contrast, monohierarchy requires that every concept must not have more than one superclass.

Typically, ontologies are expected to represent a *Directed Acyclic Graph* (DAG), which means that no cycles are allowed in the hierarchical concept structure (Lussier & Bodenreider, 2007). In rare cases, ontology languages (namely OIL and DAML+OIL) explicitly allow one to state that a single class is `not_a_subclass_of` another (Gómez-Pérez & Corcho, 2002).

Our movie example in its current state would certainly need to allow for polyhierarchies, as a single movie may be a member of the class `Comedy` and of `Col-`

orFilm at the same time. Yet this would lead to quite complex and unwieldy constructions. In the following example, we have started to resolve polyhierarchy while keeping monodimensionality for every hierarchical level:

```
Movie
  Thriller
    ThrillerInTechnicolor
        ThrillerInTechnicolorWithSound
            ShortFilmThrillerInTechnicolorWithSound
            FeatureLengthThrillerInTechnicolorWithSound
        ThrillerInTechnicolorAsSilentFilm
            ShortFilmThrillerinTechnicolorAsSilentFilm
            FeatureLengthThrillerinTechnicolorAsSilentFilm
      ThrillerInBlackAndWhite
        ThrillerInBlackAndWhiteWithSound
            ShortFilmThrillerInBlackAndWhiteWithSound
            FeatureLengthThrillerInBlackAndWhiteWithSound
        ThrillerInBlackAndWhiteAsSilentFilm
            ShortFilmThrillerInBlackAndWhiteAsSilentFilm
             FeatureLengthThrillerInBlackAndWhiteAsSi-
            lentFilm
  Comedy
    ComedyInTechnicolor
        ComedyInTechnicolorWithSound
            ShortFilmComedyInTechnicolorWithSound
            FeatureLenghtComedyInTechnicolorWithSound
        ComedyInTechnicolorAsSilentFilm
            ShortFilmComedyinTechnicolorAsSilentFilm
            FeatureLengthComedyinTechnicolorAsSilentFilm
      ComedyInBlackAndWhite
        ComedyInBlackAndWhiteWithSound
            ShortFilmComedyInBlackAndWhiteWithSound
            FeatureLengthComedyInBlackAndWhiteWithSound
        ComedyInBlackAndWhiteAsSilentFilm
            ShortFilmComedyInBlackAndWhiteAsSilentFilm
            FeatureLengthComedyInBlackAndWhiteAsSilentFilm
```

Still (or perhaps as a consequence), the construction seems rather unhandy. It strongly resembles the sock example discussed above in the section about classifications. And just as in the sock example, in a case where many dimensions are considered a faceted approach may be more appropriate for the specification of subclasses. Facets are used not only in classifications – the same principle can be applied to other KOS as well (Stock & Stock, 2008, Chapter 15). For our example, the unbundling into facets (which then enables us to create the classes on demand, through combination) could look like this:

Genre	SoundTechnique	ColorTechnique	Length
Thriller	Silent	Black and White	Short
Comedy	Sound	Technicolor	Feature Length
...	...		

In fact, ontology engineers intuitively make use of faceted constructions rather than of a continuous hierarchy. Hierarchical structures play a less exclusive role in ontologies than they do in classifications and thesauri (although they are still a fundamental design principle). This is due to the availability of other means to establish concept interrelations and thus to specify concept attributes, namely via properties which will be introduced in detail below. In a movie ontology, a class `Movies` could be described by properties stating that a movie has some `MovieGenre` and is made in some kind of `MovieColorTechnique` respectively (with `MovieGenre` and `MovieColorTechnique` as classes in the ontology). This is comparable to a faceted classification scheme of movies, which allows for the combination of the different aspects length, genre, sound and color technique etc. to classify a movie[140]. We may therefore recommend the previous works on faceted KOS to be considered in more detail in the ontology engineering community.

> "Facet analysis is regarded as a powerful methodology for the creation of structures appropriate to specific retrieval requirements in a range of contexts, with emphasis on the problems of complex subject description in retrieval and multidimensionality." (Broughton, 2002)

Broughton describes faceted approaches as a bottom-up KOS construction (starting with the individual terms or specific concepts and their characteristics) rather than one working from the top down (starting with the most general categories).

Comparable to upper ontologies, there are some approaches to developing very high-level standard facets (sometimes also called metaclasses or categories). Ranganathan originally introduced five top categories (Personality, Matter, Energy, Space and Time). On this basis, the Bliss Bibliographic Classification working group has identified 13 fundamental categories: Thing/Entity, Kind, Part, Property, Material, Process, Operation, Patient, Product, By-Product, Agent, Space, Time (Broughton, 2002).

If integrated to information systems, facets can also be used as field schemas for search query formulation, as Schwarz (2005) also points out: "Each facet can be seen as a metadata field of a resource with which a value gets associated. [...] It leads to a particular style of interaction in the user interface [...]." In this way facets can – to a certain degree – substitute fine-grained semantic relations in non-ontological KOS.

---

[140] As faceted classifications have a clear focus on the application context in document indexing, they have established clear rules for combining facets into classes (via the facet formula). Something like this is not given in ontologies.

Instances / Individuals

So far, these discussions on classes as ontology elements are not exclusively valid for ontologies. The considerations are, to a large degree, the same for every other elaborated knowledge organization system. Yet *instances* are indeed a special element of ontologies:

Instances in an ontology constitute the lowest level of a hierarchical chain. They should not represent abstract concepts but rather concrete entities, e.g. persons (like Vincent Van Gogh) or institutions (like Heinrich Heine University) – and are thus also called *individuals*[141]. Usually they can be regarded as *individual concepts* in the sense that they are concepts the extension of which covers exactly one element (Stock & Stock, 2008). Other KOS (mainly thesauri) also include individual concepts next to general concepts. Yet the distinction between individuals and classes is not made formally explicit in other KOS except in ontologies, meaning that individual concepts in thesauri are treated exactly like other concepts. Within an ontology, an instance is formally distinguished from a concept.

In practice, the interpretation of what is to be modeled as an instance may vary for different ontologies, depending on the intended use and application. Theoretically, it should not be possible to decompose instances into smaller units (in terms of hyponymy) – but this is not always feasible in ontology engineering. The configuration of the lowest hierarchical level is bound to the planned application area; in a movie ontology the lowest level may be single movie titles (e.g. 'Psycho') or single release versions of one movie (e.g. 'The Lord of the Rings: The Fellowship of the Ring' can be specified to its normal and special extended edition as well as to release versions in different languages)[142]. For reasons of practicability it may be useful to represent the color `Blue` as an instance, although in other contexts it may be specified to `Aquamarine`, `RoyalBlue` and `ChinaBlue`.

Instances are not always considered to be actual elements *belonging to* ontologies. In a way, the inclusion of instances in an ontology means that the process of indexing is to a certain extent incorporated in the ontology engineering process. In the example of a movie ontology, the individual films would normally be regarded as the documentary units that should be indexed. With ontology editors and modeling languages, the film titles may directly be included as instances in the ontology.

This is due to practical application aims; some ontologies are not primarily designed for the detailed description of external knowledge sources, but are meant to collect complex and detailed information interrelations to describe facts about a certain domain of interest. This construction may resemble databases rather than vocabularies – and is often referred to as a *knowledge base*. Furthermore, in-

---

[141] We will use the terms 'instance' and 'individual' as synonyms. In order to be precise, one would have to specify that an individual is only called 'instance' if it is an associated member of at least one class.

[142] Another example: in an automobile ontology the lowest level may in some cases be single car models (e.g. Fiat Cinquecento) but also single tangible cars, like a specific Cinquecento with a given licence plate.

stances are sometimes not viewed as parts of an ontology but as an appendix which – together with the ontology – constitutes such a knowledge base:

> "An ontology together with a set of individual instances of classes constitutes a knowledge base. In reality, there is a fine line where the ontology ends and the knowledge base begins." (Noy & McGuinness, 2001)

Martin Hepp (2008) shares this point of view and also ascribes the confusion between ontologies and knowledge bases to the fact that many ontology editors and ontology languages do not follow any clear distinctions and seamlessly support the construction of both.

> "Ontologies are the *vocabulary* and the formal specification of the vocabulary only, which can be *used for* expressing a knowledge base. It should be stressed that one initial motivation for ontologies was achieving interoperability between multiple knowledge bases. So, in practice, an ontology may specify the concepts 'man' and 'woman' and express that both are mutually exclusive – but the individuals Peter, Paul, and Mary are normally not part of the ontology. Consequently, not every OWL file is an ontology, since OWL files can also be used for representing a knowledge base." (Hepp, 2008)

Hepp further points out that individuals can be of differing quality and distinguishes "ontological individuals" from "data individuals":

> "[…] individuals (instances) sometimes belong to the ontology and sometimes do not. Only those individuals that are part of the specification of the domain and not pure facts within that domain belong to the ontology. Sometimes it depends on the scope and purpose of an ontology which individuals belong to it, and which are mere data. For example, the city of Innsbruck as an instance of the class 'city' would belong to a tourism ontology, but a particular train connection would not. We suggest speaking of *ontological individuals* and *data individuals*. With ontological individuals we mean such that are part of the specification of a domain, and with data individuals, we mean such being part of a knowledge base within that domain." (Hepp, 2008)

We agree with this basic distinction of ontological and data individuals, although it is hard to differentiate both types in practice. Furthermore we want to point out that ontological individuals are fundamental parts of ontologies. The explicit representation of individuals in contrast to general concepts is an exclusive feature of ontologies as the most elaborated type of knowledge organization systems.

2.2.3 Relations and Properties

Semantic Relations in Knowledge Organization Systems

We have already seen that hyponymic relations are fundamental for the structuring of ontology classes as hierarchies. Yet classes and their instances are not only organized by hierarchical structures, but should also be interrelated in other ways in order to precisely represent the domain of interest. We generally speak of (*semantic*) *relations* to refer to such concept interconnections within different KOS.

In knowledge representation, two fundamental types of semantic relations can be distinguished, based on their strength in bonding together terms (Khoo & Na, 2006): *Paradigmatic relations* are fixed, rigidly coupled concept relations applied to controlled vocabularies. An example would be the hierarchical relation between `Vehicle` and `Bicycle` formalized within a classification scheme. *Syntagmatic relations* are not attached to concepts but originate merely in the actual co-occurrence of terms within a certain setting. Thus syntagmatic relations may for instance exist between two expressions within a single document or between two keywords assigned to a document. These relations can be captured and expressed in the form of networks (Stock, 2007). They are particularly interesting in analyses of folksonomies – as a source for new paradigmatic relations (Peters, 2009; Peters & Weller, 2008, see also below in Section 3.3.1). In the context of information retrieval applications, both syntagmatic and paradigmatic relations help the user to browse concept systems for appropriate search terms and enable query expansion.

Broughton (2002) further mentions a third type of relations appearing in knowledge organization systems, namely *syntactic relationships*:

> "These are relationships between terms that are not significant in terms of hierarchy or meaning. Commonest examples are the relationships between the component words of compound terms and subjects e.g. heart surgery, fashion photography. These relationships are essentially impermanent i.e. they do not state a necessary, continuing, or dependent relationship between component terms; the relationship is that of an *object* and an *operation* on it [...]. It is sometimes the case that these intersections give rise to unique terms; for instance the combination of 'bones' and 'inflammation' creates the concept of 'arthritis' [...]. From the indexers point of view, these terms need to be identified and acknowledged [...]." (Broughton, 2002)

The more complex a compound class name, the more relations can be found between the different constituting elements. Yet such types of relation are hardly ever discussed and analyzed.

> "[...] conventional library classification and indexing schemes [...] frequently fail to make adequate distinction between permanent hierarchical relationships, and relationships of syntactic association in complexes. As a result, structures are not logical (since the analysis is not rigorous), positioning of compound subjects is not predictable (since no operating rules for combination are normally present), and retrieval is unreliable." (Broughton, 2002)

For the representation of rich semantics, paradigmatic relations are essential. We regard them as necessary elements of advanced KOS[143] and therefore place a special focus on them within the context of ontologies. But syntagmatic and syntactic

---

[143] Simple KOS such as folksonomies contain only syntagmatic relations.

relations are a valuable source for detecting hidden relations that should actually be turned into paradigmatic ones.

Generalizable relations play a decisive role; these are paradigmatic relations that can be meaningfully used in all (or most) general or domain-specific knowledge organization models. Markowitz, Nutter and Evens (1992) speak of conceptual relations, which can be considered as opposite to generalizable relations, since they are only valid for narrow domains of interest:

> "We also exclude *conceptual links* that are bound to limited, well-defined domains. For example, work with medical lexicons supports the link dysfunction (which represents the relationship between aphasia and speech) as an important and widely used link in medicine; but it has little relevance for most other domains." (Markowitz, Nutter & Evens, 1992)

The relations currently considered to be generally applicable and implemented in practice are (Bean & Green, 2001): relations of equivalence, hierarchies, and (unspecified) associative relations.

* *Relations of equivalence.* Synonyms and quasi-synonyms have (almost) the same meaning and are therefore exchangeable in a given context, e. g. Car and Automobile are synonyms (Löbner, 2002). Control over synonyms is particularly important for indexing and documentation purposes, in order to enable the consistent use of a vocabulary and enhance recall in information retrieval.
* *Hierarchical relations.* Two concepts are hierarchically related if one concept includes the extension of the other concept. This comprises meronymy (sometimes also called part-of relation, part-whole relation, partonomy, while mereology refers to the theory of parts and wholes) (Gerstl & Pribbenow, 1995 and 1996; Pribbenow, 2002) and hyponymy (kind-of-relation, taxonomic relation, taxonomy[144], relation of inclusion, relation of subsumption) (Cruse, 2002), i.e. Lens is a meronym of Camera; Thriller is a hyponym of Movie. The different sub-concepts for a shared broader concept are siblings (e.g. if Thriller and Comedy are both sub-concepts of Movie, then they are siblings).
* *Associative relations.* They are unspecified connections of concepts that can have any kind of relation (except synonymy and hierarchical relations). Associative relations are undirected and reversible.

While these relation types are standardized for certain KOS (e.g. DIN 1463/1:1987), ontology editors enable the construction of freely defined new types of concept interrelations. They may cover the qualities of traditional KOS relations, but may also extend them arbitrarily. This provides for rich semantic domain representations and is one major advancement of ontologies as knowledge

---

[144] Some regard taxonomy as a special type of hyponymy. For example, Cruse (2002) distinguishes the "is kind of" structures of taxonomy from "simple hyponymy". See also Khoo and Na (2006).

organization systems. We may further distinguish between different KOS types on the basis of the relations they use (Weller & Peters, 2007; Peters & Weller, 2008). We will discuss this in more detail in Section 2.3.

Concept Properties as Relations in Ontologies

In ontology engineering, *properties* usually take over the role of semantic relations. Properties are the explicit specifications of the characteristics of classes. In practice, they are a means of specifying the meaning and the semantic surroundings of each concept. Schwarz (2005) has pointed out the following distinction in using properties:

> "Properties are a fundamental construct of modeling ontologies. They are either attributes of a class, or they define the relationship between two classes." (Schwarz, 2005)

In classical KOS, we will only find properties of the latter kind defining "the relationship between two classes" (we therefore speak of semantic relations and not of properties). In ontologies, these may for example be classical relations like hierarchies (e.g. `Thriller is_a Movie`), as well as self-defined specified relations such as `Movie is_produced_by Director`.

Properties that specify "attributes of a class" (like color, shape, location etc.) cannot be found in classical KOS. The only way to include this kind of information in other KOS is via syntactic relations in compound terms (like in `FractureOfTheTibia`, which includes information about the location). In this way, ontologies definitely extend the expressivity for richer semantics in knowledge representation.

In ontologies, the actual concept characteristics will also typically be modeled as concepts – which will then be *related* to the reference concepts via properties. For example, an ontology of vehicles contains the concept `Car` and the concept `Color` (which is needed to specify the color properties of cars); these two concepts can then be related via a property such as `has_color`.

This distinction between different purposes of concept properties often remains unnoticed in practical ontology engineering as it is usually handled without problems by experienced ontology engineers. On the other hand, it is highly difficult for novices in ontology engineering to learn the principles of relationship modeling. For our context, the question arises of how naïve users, in the sense of the Social Semantic Web, can be provided with guidance in choosing appropriate concept-relationship-structures. For the guiding or teaching of novices in ontology engineering it may be useful to provide a visible distinction of *object concepts* (concepts which are actually regarded as objects in the domain of interest) and *attribute concepts* (concepts which are merely needed to specify concept characteristics). We assume that attribute concepts are more likely to be reusable across domains. An interesting open research issue would thus be to collect typical concept properties and generate a collection of attribute concepts that can be shared and reused across different ontologies.

Object and Datatype Properties

There is another distinction of property types, which is even explicitly supported by some ontology languages. In OWL we find the two types of properties, namely *object properties* and *datatype properties*:

> "Note that there are two distinguished types of properties: (i) object properties, which are binary relations between instances of two classes; (ii) datatype properties, which are binary relations between instances of a class and a datatype." (Pan, 2007)

For both of the purposes we have just discussed, one uses *object properties*, as these are properties that connect concepts in an ontology. Thus they represent a type of connection between different concepts of the domain – and between their different instances[145]. Ontologies usually contain binary relations; the first argument is known as the *domain* of the relation, and the second argument as its *range*[146]. The binary relation produces between Director and Movie, as depicted in our initial example in Figure 2.1, is an object property; Director is the domain and Movie the range of the object property produces.

Datatype properties are a unique feature of ontologies and cannot be found in other KOS. They are not relations between different classes but represent attributes attached to single classes of the ontology (and therefore only serve the purpose of properties as class attributes without representing class relations). Their range is a *value* that is not part of a formal class of the ontology. Values can be numbers, strings, Boolean values, etc.

On the instance level, properties establish "facts or individual axioms" (Pan, 2007). An example for such factual information included in the ontology by interrelating individuals through object properties would be: Alfred Hitchcock (who would be represented as an instance_of the class Director) produces Psycho (which is an instance of the class Thriller, which is itself a subclass of Movie). Facts expressed with datatype properties could be: Psycho has_runtime 109 (minutes) or has_year_of_release 1960 – while the values 109 and 1960 are not modeled as instances but added as numbers without further specification. A class Movie could be characterized by a property is_a_silent_movie, with the Boolean values 'false' and 'true' as possible choices.

The use of datatype properties is another aspect that shows the small degree separating ontologies and knowledge bases. With the use of datatype properties, ontologies integrate facts about individuals in a way that cannot be found in any classical knowledge organization system.

Within hyponymic class hierarchies, subclasses inherit the properties of their superclasses. For our example in Figure 2.1 (above) this means that if we state that

---

[145]   Object properties (in OWL) can also relate to *value partitions*, i.e. an exhaustive list of predefined values representing possible options for the property to relate to (Horridge, Knublauch et al., 2004).

[146]   See Rector, Drummond et al., 2004 for a discussion of typical difficulties with modeling OWL domain and range expressions.

a person has a date of birth (e.g. via a datatype property), this will also hold for the subclasses – and thus actors and directors also have dates of birth. And not only movies in general are made by a director – this relation is also valid for the particular types of movies like thrillers and comedies.

Both object and datatype properties can be used to model semantic relations with different qualities. The ontology designer is free to choose the properties he needs for modeling the domain. Yet, so far, many ontologies so far only make use of a small number of paradigmatic semantic relations, which sometimes do not go beyond hierarchies or thesaural standard relations. The efforts to establish a *Semantic Web* call for a more sophisticated depiction of knowledge relationships – ideally supported by a broader, standardized set of specific semantic relations to be used as ontological properties.

The community of ontology designers needs further evaluation and studies on advantages and disadvantages of certain relational constructions. Knowledge engineers often have to decide on how they ought to model certain domain properties. Also, different options for representing the same statements are often possible. We think that some guidelines that provide help for this modeling conflict can be derived from analyzing semantic relations in more detail, as has also been proposed by Hovy (2002).

Some detailed and highly professional theoretical reflections on relationships are currently available from fields such as information science, knowledge engineering, linguistics, artificial intelligence studies and related disciplines, e.g. Green, Bean and Myaeng (2002), Löbner (2002), Khoo and Na (2006), Storey (1993), Sun and Zheng (2005). They provide in-depth insights into the semantics of concept interrelations, but do not consider the practical context of ontology engineering environments. Other studies focus on how certain ontology languages can be designed and improved in order to enable a better representation of certain relational constructs, e.g. Artale, Franconi and Guarino (1996) or Guarino and Welty (2000a).

However, little attention is paid to the aspects of how users handle these techniques. We suggest broad analyses of the nature of semantic relations based on exploiting the relationships which are actually applied in ontologies (Peters & Weller, 2008). This should lead to new views on how relations can be distinguished, which might also be of use for other knowledge representation methods.

To illustrate both the expressivity of semantic KOS as well as the difficulties in applying them in practical KOS engineering, we will now provide a detailed overview on theoretical discussions on different types of semantic relations as well as some exemplary details on they can be realized in ontologies.

Hierarchical Relations in Ontologies: Meronymy and Hyponymy
While hyponymy structures hierarchical concepts according to logical aspects, meronymy reflects a physical point of view (Khoo & Na, 2006). In hyponymy, concepts are structured as general concepts (*hyperonym*) which are divided into different specific sub-concepts (*hyponyms*). In meronymy, concepts are subdivided according to their components; a hierarchical structure exists between a

concept representing a wholeness (*holonym*) as the upper class and concepts representing parts of it as lower classes (*meronyms*) (Stock & Stock, 2008).

> "Knowledge about parts is usually represented by 'part-of' relations which induce corresponding partial orders, generally called partonomies. Similar to the taxonomies formed by means of 'is-a' or 'is-kind-of' relations, partonomies reflect important aspects of the structure of a domain, and often they make it possible to organize knowledge in an efficient and economical way." (Guarino, Pribbenow & Vieu, 1996, 257)

Most ontologies make use of hyponymy and meronymy, as they usually constitute the basic structure of a KOS.

> "Is_a and part_of have established themselves as foundational to current ontologies. They have a central role in almost all domain ontologies [...]." (Smith, Ceusters et al., 2005)

In ontologies, hierarchical relationships are often labeled is_a (for hyponymy) and part_of (for meronymy), but may also be named differently, e.g. subclass_of, kind_of, is, subset_of, etc. This variety of naming relations in ontologies is one of the difficulties in using different ontologies together and in reusing existing ontologies.

As we have already mentioned, ontology editors and ontology languages allow one to establish a variety of specific semantic relations via object properties. Yet there are some knowledge models that are built in formal languages but (almost) only use hierarchical structures. This has already led to some discussion about whether such models should be regarded as 'full' ontologies (Weller, 2007). One may certainly say that although ontologies provide the methods for exploiting specified semantic relations, there still is a dominance of hierarchical relationships. The reasons for this are not very well defined, but it is likely caused by the long tradition of using hierarchical structures for classifying and structuring (as is also the case in folder structures on personal desktops, for example) and by the difficulties and challenges in using other differentiated relations posed to beginners in KOS engineering.

Furthermore, hyponymy is the only relation to be typically treated as a first-class relation in ontology languages. This means, for example, that in OWL we can find predefined is-a relations, while all other relations have to be established by the user through concept properties.

Consequently, most ontology editors (and the respective ontology visualization tools) separate hyponymy from other relations. Tools for editing ontologies are usually based on a tree-structure establishing the representation of a domain model. Visualizations also often focus on the hierarchical structures within an ontology. This may be another explanation for the phenomenon of novices in ontology engineering (naïve users on their first attempts to build an ontology) often working exclusively with hyponymy.

Let us demonstrate the construction of hierarchies exemplarily for the popular ontology editor Protégé. Is-a relations are predefined within OWL and can be modeled with the 'Class Editor' in the Protégé interface (Figure 2.9). The editor interface visualizes classes and subclasses in the 'Subclass Explorer'. If a subclass is created within this class hierarchy, it will be related to its upper class via the is-a relation.

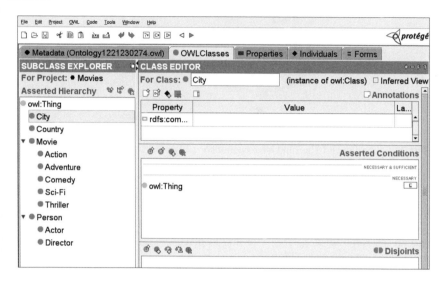

Figure 2.9. Hierarchical concept structure in Protégé. Concepts are organized in the hyponymic hierarchy section on the left. We see that, for example, Thriller is defined as subclass of Movie; Actor and Director are subclasses of Person. Other concept interrelations can be established via the 'Properties' tab.

Meronymic relations cannot be established in the asserted hierarchy section in Protégé. They have to be created as self-defined object properties via the 'Properties' tab.

This leads to some confusion for novices in ontology engineering and is therefore an essential part of ontology engineering training courses. In the beginning it is difficult to differentiate in which cases the hierarchy section is appropriate and how concept names have to be modeled, in order to match a hyponymic relationship. Naïve users tend to use the default hierarchy for both hyponymy and meronymy – forgetting that it creates an is_a relation on the formal level[147].

This yields erroneous constructs as shown in Figure 2.10: the concept England was established with the subclasses London and Sheffield. This, of course, is incorrect, as it states that London (and Sheffield) is a kind of England – although the relation between England and London is a meronymic one. London *is part of* England.

---

147 Such problems can also be found in other KOS, as Bechhofer and Goble (2001) point out for the ICONCLASS thesaurus.

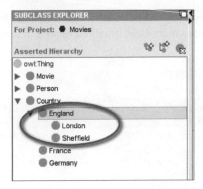

Figure 2.10. London and Sheffield have been incorrectly modeled as hyponymic subclasses of England.

One way of adequately modeling the meronymic relation of London and England with Protégé consists of three steps: The first step would be to create a new class City on the same level as Country and to place London and Sheffield as instances into this new class (Figure 2.11).

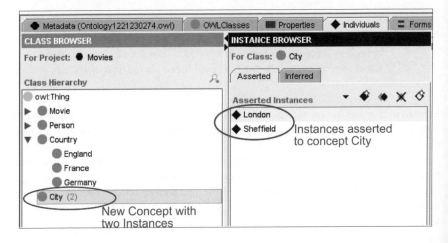

Figure 2.11. First step to establishing a meronymic relation for countries and cities: creating a concept City in addition to Country; asserting the instances London and Sheffield to City.

We can then establish a new property capturing the fact that a City is_part_of a Country (Figure). This relation should then be generally valid for all cities and countries.

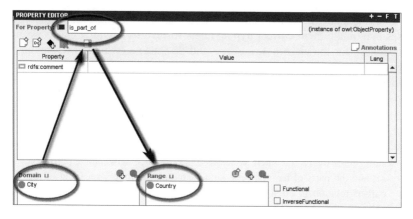

Figure 2.12. Second step to establishing a meronymic relation for countries and cities: creating the property `is_part_of` between the concepts `City` and `Country`.

If we also represent `England` (as well as, e.g., `France` and `Germany`) as an instance of `Country`, we can finally include the fact that `London is_part_of England` (Figure 2.13).

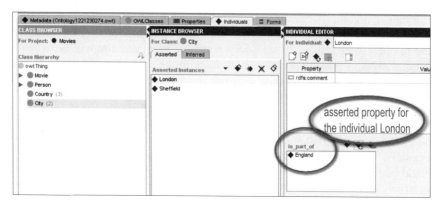

Figure 2.13. Third step to establishing a meronymic relation for countries and cities: interrelating the instances `London` and `England` via the `is_part_of` relation.

Geographical meronymies are particularly susceptible to these modeling errors – as they seem to embody 'natural' hierarchies at first sight, people are particularly tempted to model geographical information within the default hierarchy in Protégé. But similar errors may appear in almost every context. In some cases, a simpler solution than the remodeling just described can be achieved: renaming the classes may make them correct hyponymies. Instead of having a class `Computer` as superclass for the classes `Hardware` and `Software` (which is wrong as hardware is not a type of computer) one may rename the class `ComputerComponents` in order to resolve the problem (`Hardware` and `Software` *are* `ComputerComponents`).

> "It is often difficult for beginners in ontological analysis to distinguish between the part-of and the subclass relation. This is due to the fact that subclass is analogous to subset, and a subset of a set is a part of it. This confusion can be overcome when we realize the difference between the parts of a set and the parts of its members. Understanding the proper meaning of the part-of relation is often what ontological analysis is all about. However, even people who understand the distinction, often misuse subsumption to represent part-of; they are both partial ordering relations after all, and when we draw diagrams showing subclass relationships we get a picture that looks the same as a diagram representing the decomposition of something."
> (Guarino & Welty, 2002)

But it is not only the differentiation of meronymy and hyponymy that leads to modeling problems. A genuine difficulty lies in determining which other relations should be modeled instead of or in addition to hierarchies. Of course these kinds of mistake (and the examples that will follow in the next sections) are based on an uncertainty that will mainly be found with novices in ontology engineering, not with trained ontologists. Training and experience should help to avoid these problems – but this is a time-consuming task and hardly feasible for huge communities. And in order to establish a broad Social Semantic Web, one aim will be to enable as many users as possible to easily contribute to the creation and maintenance of ontologies. It will be necessary to examine the particular difficulties and expectations of this desired user community. An extensive training of users will hardly be possible. Furthermore, there are no guidelines for effectively teaching novices how to build ontologies, e.g. how to distinguish part-of from is-a relations. User surveys or experiments are needed in order to gain a better insight into their expectations and needs. Furthermore, if broad communities in a Web 2.0 sense should be incorporated in the ontology engineering process, solutions for facilitating a more intuitive use of ontology editors have to be provided additionally.

There is of course a notable research community aiming towards improving current ontology editors or developing entirely new tools for ontology engineering (see Section 3.1.2). Yet these developments do not necessarily focus on simpler solutions for community-based ontology engineering. In fact, many approaches do not consider naïve users at all but address a community of experts in ontology engineering first and foremost. In practice, there is a certain tradeoff between the users' demand for easy and intuitive tools and the Semantic Web research community's longing for better (in the sense of more elaborated) formal semantic models.

In the case of modeling hierarchies the major difficulties lie in distinguishing hyponymy and meronymy. Additional challenges concern the appropriate use of self-defined properties in addition to hierarchical structures.

The inclusion of part-of relations as another predefined element of ontology languages (e.g. OWL) can only be achieved through intensive effort and would require some more specific research regarding its usefulness and practicability:

> "Given the outstanding importance of part-whole relations, many researchers argue in favour of a first-class citizen status for part-whole relations, similar to taxonomic relations. From a conceptual modeling point of view, this necessitates both an in-depth ontological study of the specific characteristics which distinguish the part-whole relations from 'ordinary' relations such as has-color or drugs-prescribed, in addition to dedicated mechanisms by which the results of this ontological investigation can be expressed at the formal knowledge representation language level." (Schulz & Hahn, 2005)

Thus one cannot just provide tools which directly enable the user to establish a part-of relation with just one click. Alternatively, one may decide to not distinguish different types of hierarchies at all. In some classical KOS, no distinction between is-a and part-of relations is made, terms are merely related as broader and narrower classes. Ontology languages would have to be modified to enable unspecific hierarchies, as currently a subclass is strictly defined as embodying an is-a relation[148]. But such a change would constitute a step backwards in the sense of richer semantics.

Yet a feasible solution may be to provide novel visualization interfaces, in order to better demonstrate the consequences of certain modeling activities: For example, adding a concept in the class hierarchy may activate a field in which the current action is stated in natural language (e.g. "You have just included the statement that London is a kind of England. Do you want to confirm this?").

During the developing phase of the Ontoverse ontology engineering platform (Mainz, Weller et al., 2008; Paulsen, Mainz et al., 2007), the ontology editor was enriched with a SmartTree hierarchy (Figure 2.14) (El Jerroudi & Ziegler, 2007; El Jerroudi, Weinbrenner et al., 2008; Malzahn, Weinbrenner et al., 2007). It not only displays the typical hyponymic structure but also the other interrelations which have already been formalized for a concept. This may enhance the users' awareness of other properties apart from hierarchical structures. More ideas and approaches in this regard are needed in the future.

---

[148] This approach is taken in SKOS (Miles & Brickley, 2005) ontologies, see also section 3.4.3 of this book.

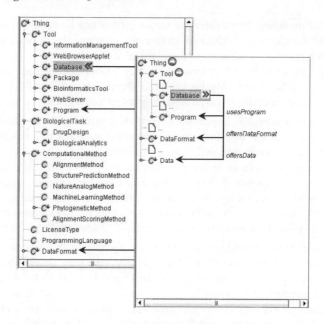

Figure 2.14. SmartTree for hierarchical navigation and approach to including additional
information on concept interrelations, part of the Ontoverse platform
(http://ontoverse.cs.uni-duesseldorf.de). Source: El Jerroudi, Weinbrenner et
al., 2008; example taken from the BIO2Me ontology (Mainz, 2006; Mainz,
2008; Mainz, Paulsen et al., 2008).

2.2.4 Selected Types of Specified Semantic Relations

All of the semantic relations mentioned so far (hyponymy, meronymy, equivalence and association) may be refined to more specific semantic relations. We now
want to discuss some approaches to specifying and classifying types of semantic
relations. In practical ontology engineering, one important challenge is the choice
of appropriate semantic relations in the form of properties. In individual cases, we
will therefore already point out how different semantic relations can be used in ontologies.

Types of Hyponymy

Although the idea of is-a relations is quite simple and seems unambiguous at first
sight, it is actually the conflation of several (though cognate) meanings. Brachmann (1983) goes so far as to say that "[t]here are almost as many meanings for
the IS-A link as there are knowledge representation systems." He has identified
four major variations of IS-A relations: Subset/superset relations, generaliza-
tion/specialization relations, AKO (a kind of, kind-of) relations, and conceptual

containment. In this argumentation, a subset/superset relation is defined as follows:

> "[...] when nodes are taken to represent sets, the connection between two generic nodes represent the subset relation. For example, when Nuke.Subs and Submarines are construed to represent the sets of all nuclear-powered submarines and all submarines, respectively, 'a Nuke.Sub is a Submarine' means 'for every entity x if x is a member of Nuke.Subs, then x is a member of Submarines'." (Brachmann, 1983)

For Brachmann, the most common way of interpreting is-a relations is in terms of generalization/specialization in the following sense:

> "[...] Generalization, a relation between predicates, seems expressible as a simple conditional. For instance, if Submarine (x) is a predicate taken to be a generalization of Nuke.Sub (x), then an IS-A between them means 'for every entity x if Nuke.Sub(x) then Submarine(x).' This interpretation of IS-A link, offered by Hayes, is probably the most prevalent semantic net connector [...]." (Brachmann, 1983)

The kind-of relation[149] is probably the most discussed subtype of hyponymy (to a certain extent because the question of whether there actually exists something like natural kinds is discussed in philosophy). Natural kinds refer to natural class-groupings, in contrast to artificially grouped classes (i.e. classes that are only given, if a human has defined them):

> "AKO is intended to stand for the relation between 'camel' and 'mammal' in 'the camel is a kind of mammal.' Although AKO has much in common with generalization, it implies 'kind' status for the nodes it connects, whereas generalization relates arbitrary predicates." (Brachmann, 1983)

Finally, Brachmann defines the notion of conceptual containment:

> "[...] in some cases, the intent of an IS-A connection is to express the fact that one description includes another. Instead of reading 'a triangle is a polygon' as a simple generalization (that is, there are triangles and there are polygons, and this happens to be a relation between them), we want to read it as 'to be a triangle is to be a polygon with three sides.' This is the IS-A of lambda-abstraction, wherein one predicate is used in defining another." (Brachmann, 1983)

Guarino and Welty (2000b) also argue that "[...] the intuitive simplicity of taxonomic relations has led to widespread misuse, making clear the need for rigorous analysis techniques." They have analyzed certain examples of poorly structured taxonomies to reveal invalid constructions, and they developed a methodology for clarifying taxonomic characteristics based on philosophical techniques. The results are several characteristics (namely identity, unity, essence and dependence) that can be used for ontological analysis as well as for judging the appropriateness of taxonomic links. In their analysis, an apple cannot be regarded as a proper sub-

---

[149] As mentioned above, this relation is sometimes also called taxonymy.

class of food – because not all apples are necessarily food. However, they point out that their analysis does not necessarily reveal wrong statements but mainly logical inconsistencies. Guarino and Welty have elaborated their methodology (Guarino and Welty, 2000a and 2000b, Welty & Guarino, 2001) and it became the foundation for the OntoClean methodology for evaluating hierarchies (Guarino & Welty, 2002).

This very strong notion of taxonomy is only rarely applied in practical ontology engineering, where it is often the final application scenarios affecting the modeling choices rather than precise ontological analyses. As we will see in the next sections, the differentiation of is-a relations is much less intuitive and requires more background knowledge in philosophy than the differentiation of part-of and associative relations.

Individuals in Hierarchies

Another specific and typical hierarchical relation within ontologies is the connection between classes and their instances. Although relations between instances and classes are sometimes also labeled is_a, they should be viewed as a different type of hyponymy. Instances are specific exemplars of a certain class, not subclasses – which should clearly be stated in the relation in order to avoid loss of information. Instances share all characteristics of the class they belong to, but ideally do not carry new, *class-defining* features, as would be the case for subclasses. This means that ideally an individual would not carry characteristics that require the establishing of a new intermediate class. Of course individuals possess individual characteristic features which make them different from other individuals in the same class. In ontology engineering this means mainly, that no new properties can be linked to instances of a class which have not been established for the class itself. But for every instance, a property should be filled with its respective value in order to state the actual individual characteristics.

A specific label like instance_of should be used for hierarchies between concepts and individuals (and actually is applied in practice, e.g. in OWL). Brachmann (1983) has pointed this out as a fundamental issue to clarify fuzziness in is-a relations:

> "That generic nodes can be more specific or less specific than other generic nodes gives semantic nets their network structure. Individual nodes tend to be at the same level of specificity. Thus, all internal nodes in the network are generic, while the leaves are individual. We can then immediately divide the IS-A relation into two major subtypes – one relating two generic nodes, and the other relating an individual and a generic." (Brachmann, 1983)

Brachmann (1983) furthermore differentiates four types of instance-of relations: set membership, predication, conceptual containment and abstraction. Typically, ontological instances can be viewed as members of a class (or a set of individuals). Brachmann refers to this as *membership*. He mentions the following example: "Clyde is a camel" means "Clyde is a member of (the set of) camels." The *predi-*

cation relation basically refers to the same case, but is modeled slightly different in semantic networks as defined by Brachmann. Furthermore, some individuals are not represented in form of named entities, but as structured descriptions. These relate to more generic concepts via *conceptual containment*: In Brachmann's examples, this is the relationship between 'king' and 'the king of France'. Finally, Brachmann describes *abstraction* as a specific case of instance-of relationships:

> "[...] a generic type is abstracted into an individual, evidenced in natural-language constructs such as 'the eagle' in 'the eagle is an endangered species.' The relation holds between the individual, The-Eagle, and the (generic) predicate or type, Eagle." (Brachmann, 1983)

Some modeling pitfalls derive from real world structures and everyday speech, which have to be reconsidered in ontology formalization: Within the domain of German politics we may, for example, intuitively consider the current German chancellor 'Angela Merkel' as an instance of 'CDU', the political party she belongs to. Within an ontology, the interconnection between Angela Merkel and the CDU will have to be viewed from the formal modeling perspective and a specified relation will have to be used to represent that Angela Merkel is a `member_of` (and not an instance of) CDU. 'CDU' itself would ideally be represented as an individual at the lowest hierarchical level in the ontology of German politics, e.g. as an instance of a class `PoliticalParty`. Angela Merkel could then be represented as an `instance_of` a class `Person`; persons and parties would then have to be related with a `member_of` relation. This way we can state that Angela Merkel is indeed a member of the CDU. Again, this is a typical modeling error made by novices in ontology engineering and should not happen after some time of training.

Types of Meronymy

To subdivide a concept into its components, only constitutive characteristics should be the determining factor. Yet these constitutive characteristics may have different qualities which in turn may produce different kinds of partitive relations. Several theoretical discussions deal with the question of how different types of meronymy may be distinguished (e.g. Gerstl & Pribbenow, 1996; Markowitz, Nutter & Evens, 1992; Varzi, 1996; Winston, Chaffin & Herrmann, 1987). Additional debates address the various challenges of how these different part-of relations should be handled appropriately in formal representation languages (e.g. Artale, Franconi & Guarino, 1996; Artale, Franconi et al., 1996; Sattler, 1995). We will introduce only some of the approaches to specifying meronymy, and of the resulting relations which have been identified so far.

Winston, Chaffin and Herrmann (1987) distinguish types of meronymic relations based on the three criteria *functionality*, *homeomericity* and *separability*:

> "[...] Functional parts are restricted, by their function, in their spatial or temporal location. For example, the handle of a cup can only be placed in a limited number of positions if it is to function as a handle. Homeomerous parts are of the same kind of thing as their wholes, for example 'slice-pie',

while non-homeomerous parts are different from their wholes, for example, 'tree-forest'. Separable parts can, in principle, be separated from the whole, for example, 'handle-cup', while inseparable parts cannot, for example 'steel-bike'." (Winston, Chaffin & Herrmann, 1987)

According to Gerstl and Pribbenow we may further define two general classes of partitions: parts of structured objects (internally defined parts) and parts of non-structured objects (arbitrary parts) (Gerstl & Pribbenow, 1996; Pribbenow, 2002). Part-whole relations of structured objects refer to precisely given and permanent partitions inherent to objects (e.g. chapters in books, months in a year). In contrast, non-structured objects do not provide fixed segmentations and are rather arbitrarily split up (e.g. a portion of some food) or can be defined according to different external criteria (e.g. wooden parts of a house).

Examples for specific types of meronymic relations that have already been identified are the following: Geographical entities typically require meronymy in the form of *geographical* (administrative) *units* and their *subunits*, e.g. a city and its districts. The *member-collection* relation is intended for non-social collections only (e.g. tree – forest, ship – fleet) (Winston, Chaffin, & Herrmann, 1987) and is distinguished from the *unit-organization* relation, which is made of social groups, down to single persons belonging to an organized group (e.g. researcher – department – faculty – university). One very common and frequent relation is that between a *complex and its components*, like wheel – car or roof – house.

Sometimes actions and processes can also be subdivided; the borders between structured and non-structured segmentations in these cases are often blurred. We use the *segment-event* relation for describing parts of pre-structured processes (e.g. different acts during a circus performance which are pre-structured in a program, like trapeze act – circus performance) and the *phase-action* relation for unstructured processes (e.g. the process of shopping, which has no predefined parts and may be divided into phases like searching, comparing, paying).

Partitions of non-structured objects often make use of external criteria, such as dimension units (e.g. milliliter – liter) or portions (e.g. slice – pie). Alternatively, internal features of an object may be considered for its segmentation (e.g. steel parts – bike) (Winston, Chaffin, & Herrmann, 1987; Gerstl & Pribbenow, 1996; Pribbenow, 2002).

There are various different approaches to specifying part-of relations. Schwarz (2005), for example, uses a more practically oriented approach and names the following relations: systems and organs of the body (e.g. brain – grey matter), geographical location (e.g. Netherlands – North Holland), discipline or field of study (e.g. history – art history – 19th century art history) and hierarchical social structure (e.g. Methodist church organization – Methodist district).

Sometimes different dimensions are applicable for dividing a concept into its parts: for example a book may be considered as consisting of single pages and a cover or – if we focus on the content – of different chapters.

Apart from this, specific interactions of parts and their wholes may be considered in detail. For example, some parts belong exclusively to one whole, i.e. they cannot be part of some other class (Sattler, 1995; Artale, Franconi et al., 1996). Artale, Franconi and Guarino (1996) sum up three important distinctions:

"Important cases are *essential parts* – the whole is generically dependent on a particular class of parts, *dependent parts* – a part is generically dependent on the whole, *exclusive parts* – there exists at most one whole containing a particular part." (Artale, Franconi & Guarino, 1996)

As an example for an essential part, the relation of Human and Brain is frequently quoted. The brain is an essential part of a human.

The different kinds of meronymic relations can be specified during the ontology engineering process by creating different object properties, respectively. This of course calls for careful considerations on the nature of specific relations (Schulz, Romacker, & Hahn, 1998). A useful overview of various approaches in developing representation languages that can capture the different cases and characteristics of part-of relations is provided by Artale, Franconi, Guarino and Pazzi (1996).

Difficulties are also encountered in the decision of how to name these different meronymic relations. No standards or conventions are available for creating specific properties. Theoretically, various names may be generated in order to describe the same semantic relations. Let us consider the example of geography. Geographical meronymy may be simply called part_of, as in Bochum is_part_of NorthRhineWestphalia, NorthRhineWestphalia is_part _of Germany. Yet one may as well create a property is_geographical_ part_of to distinguish this from other meronymic contexts, or alternatively choose to call this relation is_located_in or is_subregion_of. This makes it difficult to identify identical relations with different names (both within one ontology and across different ontologies). The same problems will grow even bigger when it comes to distinguishing different types of associative relations (see below) as they can cover a much wider variety of specific types.

Sometimes it may even become difficult to identify meronymy, as the relations do not necessarily contain the phrase 'part of'[150]. Thus they may be mixed up with other types of semantic relations.

"Among attributes, a fundamental role is often played by various forms of part-whole relations, which contribute to describe the *composite structure* of the instances of a class. The representation of such structural information usually requires a particular semantics together with specialized inference and update mechanisms, but rarely do current modeling formalisms and methodologies give it a specific, 'first-class' dignity. A common way to interpret the role played by single attributes within a class description is by the 'has-a' paraphrase: a house has an owner, a price, a location, as well as a door, a roof. [...] such a view risks to hide the nature of the relationship between an attribute and the class it applies, flattening all attributes to be

---

[150] Here, ontologies do somewhat resemble social tagging, as everyone is free to chose the denotations he prefers and there are no standard naming conventions.

> just *arbitrary* relations [...]. In this way, when modeling the characteristics
> of a whole like *house*, it is difficult to distinguish parts like *door* from other
> attributes like *price* or *color* [...]." (Artale, Franconi et al., 1996)

Artale, Franconi et al. (1996) use the following example to demonstrate how part-of relations can be hidden among other properties; the example opposes the explicit use of part names to the use of generic part attributes:

Car:	HAS-WHEEL: Wheel,	Car:	HAS-PART: Wheel,
	HAS-ENGINE: Engine,		HAS-PART: Engine,
	HAS-COLOR: Red.		HAS-COLOR: Red.

Artale, Franconi et al. (1996) conclude: "It is clear that, in order to distinguish between meronymic (like HAS-WHEEL) and non-meronymic (like HAS-COLOR) attributes, it is necessary to mark part-names used as attributes."

They further distinguish between the *implicit* and *explicit* modeling of part-whole interrelations. Implicit approaches do not actually model any `is_part_of` or `has_part` relations. The actual whole may even be absent; the parts are related via other local properties. In explicit approaches, the whole is included as an object, which is related to its parts. Consider this example for the implicit modeling of a part-of relation, where the relation between the spouses *john* and *mary* as parts of a family "is realized by an attribute in the object *john* keeping a reference to *mary* (WIFE), and vice versa via the attribute HUSBAND" (Artale, Franconi et al., 1996):

john:	AGE: 35,	*mary*:	AGE: 33,
	SEX: Male,		SEX: Female,
	HEIGHT: 175,		HEIGHT: 165,
	WIFE: *mary*.		HUSBAND: *john*.

The actual whole that belongs to the two parts *mary* and *john* is absent in the implicit approach. In an explicit approach to modeling the same connection, "the example above would be modeled by introducing an additional object – denoting Mary's and John's family (*m-j-family*) – which stands for the whole" (Artale, Franconi et al., 1996):

john:	AGE: 35,	*mary*:	AGE: 33,	*m-j-family*:	WIFE: *mary*,
	SEX: Male,		SEX: Female,		HUSBAND: *john*.
	HEIGHT: 175.		HEIGHT: 165.		

"Notice that the two attributes, WIFE and HUSBAND, appear now in the object which models the whole with a different meaning, since they model a relation which exists between a family and a particular person part of it." (Artale, Franconi et al., 1996)

This example demonstrates that part-whole relations may exist implicitly within an ontology. For some cases of reusing or extending the ontology, it may be necessary to detect such hidden part-of relations and to explicitly model the missing wholes connected to the parts. Some parts are best modeled with the explicit approach, particularly those that are closely dependent on their whole, like *Member, Center, Top, Bottom* or *Edge*:

> "They can hardly be thought of as 'stand-alone' concepts like Wheel or Engine: the reason is that they denote dependent names, in the sense that, in order for such names to denote particular objects, these objects must already be part of a whole. For instance, if x is an edge, something else of which it is a part must exist [...]."(Artale, Franconi et al., 1996)

All in all, defining the nature of a partitive relation is quite a complex task. The current collection of different types of meronymic relations has to become subject to further discussions and refinements, particularly in terms of a structured categorization. In addition to the various theoretical discussions, detailed research is needed on the nature of those semantic relations which are actually applied in practice (e.g. by evaluating a set of existing ontologies with respect to the relations used). So far, physical parts of objects, in the sense of complex and components, appear to be the most intuitive interpretation of meronymy, as in `Door is_part_of House` or `Cell is_part_of Organism`. Apart from this, geographical meronymy is also very commonly needed in knowledge representation. Precise studies on this aspect are needed in order to verify these assumptions and to provide an overview of applied meronymy. It would also be particularly interesting to examine this question with the focus on different user types.

Equivalences in Ontologies

Relations of equivalence are essential in controlled vocabularies to interrelate different names and expressions for the same concept (synonyms). This helps to regularize the vocabulary used for indexing and retrieval and therefore enhances recall in search results. Synonyms (different words that represent exactly the same concept) can be interrelated, but it is more frequently quasi-synonyms, i.e. different concepts that can be considered equivalents for a given context. Equivalents may also be abbreviations and translations in different languages.

Exact synonyms, i.e. two words that have precisely the same meaning, are rare (Löbner, 2002). Examples are 'car' and 'automobile' or the two different German words for Saturday 'Samstag' and 'Sonnabend', but also abbreviations like 'FIFA' and 'Fédération Internationale de Football Association'. In other cases, the meanings of concepts differ only slightly, so that they can be regarded as near-synonyms, quasi-synonyms or synonyms for a given context. E.g., for a broad context, one might treat 'cosmos' and 'universe' as synonyms, although they are not exactly overlapping in the more specific context of astrophysics. This is a typical phenomenon of common sense versus deep domain knowledge. Khoo and Na sum up different types of synonyms as follows:

> "Common types of synonyms are *sense-synonyms* (which share one or more senses), *near-synonyms* (which have not identical senses but are close in meaning), and *partial synonyms* (which share some senses but differ in some aspect, e.g., in the way they are used or in some dimension of mean-

ing) [...]. Sense-synonyms that share at least one sense and match in every other property for that sense are complete synonyms [...]." (Khoo & Na, 2006)

Markowitz, Nutter and Evens have discussed another type of relation which is closely related to relations of equivalence, namely *similarity*:

> "Similarity is the name we give to a link that expresses a strong correspondence between tow nodes or referents. [...] Linguistically, it is often expressed by words such as 'like' and 'resemble', as in 'A dog is like a wolf, only smaller' [...], which is why it is sometimes called 'comparison'. [...] Similarity is the messiest of the links we discuss. [...] Similarity has a hidden parameter, or set of parameters, which specify the dimensions along which the relata are claimed to be alike." (Markowitz, Nutter & Evens, 1992)

Within traditional thesauri, it is common to have one word from a range of synonyms to act as the descriptor, while all others are related to it as nondescriptors. For indexing or retrieval purposes, one may then typically only use the descriptor (the note UF, Used For, lists all non-descriptors referring to it within the thesaurus); non-descriptors are used for navigation to find the descriptor within the controlled vocabulary (via USE entries in the thesaurus) (Aitchison, Gilchrist & Bawden, 2000).

Within ontologies, which are not necessarily built for traditional indexing purposes, this distinction of descriptors and non-descriptors does not exist. Yet, one may also want to model equivalences in ontologies. Noy and McGuinness recommend the following:

> "Synonyms for the same concept do not represent different classes. Synonyms are just different names for a concept or a term. Therefore, we should not have a class called Shrimp and a class called Prawn, and, possibly a class called Crevette. Rather, there is one class, named either Shrimp or Prawn. Many systems allow associating a list of synonyms, translations, or presentation names with a class. If a system does not allow these associations, synonyms could always be listed in the class documentation." (Noy & McGuinness, 2001)

In Protégé based on OWL, however, there is no such option to easily create a list of synonyms for a concept[151]. One may state that two classes or instances represent the same (`owl:same as`), but that first requires them both to be created separately (according to the example above, we would need a class `Prawn` and a class `Shrimp`). Alternatively, one may document synonyms with the `rdfs:label` annotation property, which is frequently used.[152] Hollink et al. (2003) advert to another option for RDF(S):

---

[151] An example for a different approach to handle synonyms in ontologies can be found in SKOS, the Simple Knowledge Organization System (see section 3.4.3). In SKOS, synonyms can be added as alternate labels, similar to non-descriptors in thesauri.

[152] Alternatively, one may create customized annotation properties for this purpose.

"The revised version of RDF Schema allows cycles of subclass relations. This means that one can now represent equivalence of A and B by stating that A is a subclass of B and that B is a subclass of A." (Hollink, Schreiber et al., 2003)

Yet this cannot be accepted as a sufficient solution. It is not valid for all ontology languages and conflicts with the principle of representing ontologies as acyclic graphs. Furthermore, it is a rather unintuitive approach which will be difficult to understand for novices and criticized by experts.

In sum, the aspect of handling equivalences is much less discussed than other semantic relations in ontologies. This is interesting, as synonyms have a much higher significance in other KOS. We recommend intensifying the discussion of synonymy, and particularly of standardizing the representation of equivalences in ontology engineering. This may also help to identify similar or identical concepts across different ontologies.

Genidentity

A special case related to equivalence is *genidentity* (or gen-identity). This is the case when one individual is associated with different names at different points in time (Stock & Stock, 2008, 185f.). This may for example be the case for a city whose name has changed: The city Chemnitz in Saxonia was named Karl-Marx-Stadt from 1953-1990. We therefore might need to interrelate the concepts 'Chemnitz' and 'Karl-Marx-Stadt' within an ontology of German history or geography to make explicit that both refer to the same real-life individual. Within some knowledge representations, this is achieved by connecting concepts via chronological relations, stating for example that one concept is a *chronologically earlier version* of the other. This method is used for example in the German keyword cataloging guidelines *Regeln für den Schlagwortkatalog* (RSWK) (Umlauf, 1999).

With such systems, there is a simple rule for distinguishing genidentity and synonymy: If only the name of an object changes but not its characteristics, the different names can be considered as 'normal' synonyms. In cases where not only the name changes, but also an object's characteristics or entire context, this is a matter of genidentity (Stock & Stock, 2008, p. 185).

In ontology engineering, the treatment of genidentity is less simple, as concepts are typically embedded in a net of property relations. Thus the change in characteristics of a concept is something that will cause difficulties in modeling, particularly where several properties coupled to one concept are concerned.

For example, a person who changes his/her name after a marriage is a subject of genidentity. In an ontology, one may have to capture the new name as well as the fact that the person's family status has changed from single to married. Information about the family status can for example be captured in a datatype property `is_married` with possible values `true` and `false` or in an object property `is_married_to` with relation to another person. One approach to handling genidentity in this case would be to create two distinct instances for the names of the person, which are coupled to the respective information about their family status. These two instances could then be interrelated via a specific property like is_the_same_as. Alternatively, one could keep only the instance with the new name and relate it to the previous name via a (datatype) property like has_maiden_name or has_earlier_name. Yet this may cause difficulties if a name changes lots of times.

A general guideline for handling genidentity in ontologies is not available yet. Another idea is provided by Guarino and Welty (2000b), who discuss similar effects based on temporal effects for so-called *phased sortals*[153]:

> "Analysis of CATERPILLAR and BUTTERFLY yields interesting examples. Closer inspection of these two properties reveals a special type of property, known as a phased sortal [...]. A phased sortal is a property whose instances can change from one sortal to another and still remain the same thing, i.e. a caterpillar becomes a butterfly, or in some systems, we can imagine that a student becomes an alumnus. Our methodology requires that phased sortals be identified along with all the corresponding phases, and grouped under a rigid property that subsumes only them [...]. We add therefore LEPIDOPTERAN." (Guarino & Welty, 2000b)

Some other considerations in ontology engineering deal with the problem of time developments, but are not directly related to the semantic relation of equivalence. One example would be the case of an ontology about geopolitical information, where values of properties like has_head_of_state are subject to constant changes.

Associations in Ontologies

In traditional knowledge representation, all terms that are somehow interconnected via relations other than hierarchies or equivalents are referred to as associative relations. Usually, sibling concepts are not related through associative relations, though exceptions are sometimes made if one wants to point out very closely related sibling concepts (Aitchison, Gilchrist & Bawden, 2000). In thesauri, associations are captured as *related terms* (RT) for a given descriptor. Associative relations are typically reflexive, i.e. the relation holds in both direction between two classes.

In ontologies, specified associative relations in the form of object properties may be very narrowly defined, like has_ingredient or is_served_with in a food ontology. But they may also be new generalizable relationship types, that seem to be reusable across different domains, like is_used_for. So far, there have been few structured attempts to collect and classify the new, specific relations in practical use by exploiting current ontologies. But some discussions have analyzed the variety of possible associative relations and proposed classifications for types of associations. We will now have a look at some of them in order to better understand the spectrum of possibilities. Dextre Clarke (2001) proposes the following specifications of associative relations:

---

[153] As introduced by Wiggins (1980).

- terms with overlapping meanings: *ships – boats*,
- discipline – phenomena: *seismology – earthquakes*,
- process – instrument: *velocity measurement – speedometers*,
- occupation – person in that occupation: *accountancy – accountant*,
- action – product of the action: *roadmaking – roads*,
- action – its patient: *teaching – students*,
- concept – its origins: *water – water wells*,
- causal dependence: *erosion – wear*,
- thing / action – counter-agent: *pests – pesticides*,
- raw material – product: *hides – leather*,
- action – property associated with it: *precision measurement – accuracy*,
- concept – opposite: *tolerance – prejudice*.

Schmitz-Esser (2000) additionally differentiates between usefulness (e.g. for inter-relating *job creation – economic development*) and harmfulness (e.g. for interrelating *over-fertilization – diversity of species*) within the associative relations whereas the Standard Thesaurus Wirtschaft (Stock, 1999) makes use of relations of contextual connection (*body care – soap*) and of related branches (*coal – mining*) in economic contexts.

Some of these relations may again be subdivided into specified cases. For example, Khoo and Na (2006) discuss different variations of the cause-effect relation, particularly based on whether they represent necessary or sufficient causes. Another relation which has received much attention is that of antonymy. Antonymy is the relation of opposition (Khoo & Na, 2006). Antonyms vary in their intensity, as Khoo and Na (2006) point out:

> "Canonical antonyms constitute a special class of opposites that are stable and enjoy wide cultural currency. For example, hot/cold is a better example of antonymy than steamy/frigid, even though both pairs indicate opposite ends of the temperature scale." (Khoo & Na, 2006)

Furthermore, we may distinguish antonyms with only two *contradictory* occurrences (e.g. dead – alive) from those which cover the ends of a scale with intermediate stages (e.g. cold – warm – hot).

Some specific focus is placed on properties that concern developments over time. Schubert, Papalaskaris and Taugher (1983) have discussed problems regarding the time arrangement of events in sequences. Markowitz, Nutter and Evens have identified *queuing* as one of the most fundamental types of relations:

> "Queuing is a link that expresses order or sequence. [...] In the purest cases, these are either temporal or purely conceptual orderings with no physical association. Ordinal numbers constitute the most direct linguistic expression of queuing. English speakers also use queuing to express spatial ordering." (Markowitz, Nutter & Evens, 1992)

One challenge of ontology engineering is to find the adequate level of specificity in modeling the interrelations of concepts in a domain of interest. Just as for the differentiation of meronymy, there are no common guidelines on how to model other associative knowledge relations in ontologies effectively in practice, though discussions on this subject have begun (Hovy 2002; Schulz, Kumar & Bittner, 2006). And just as in distinguishing types of meronymy, the same problems occur when specifying relations in general: there are no standards or naming conventions for different types of associative relations. And with the great variety of different forms of association, there are also a number of variants for naming concept properties accordingly. The whole problem closely relates to the challenges in ontology *mapping*, where distinct ontologies are analyzed for overlapping contents. For the development of Semantic Web applications, identical concepts and concept interrelations have to be identified among various KOS on a large scale.

Another challenge of ontology engineering is to choose appropriate properties that complete hierarchical structures effectively. Knowledge engineers often have to decide on whether they should establish hierarchical structures or rather describe concepts through self-defined relations; a question which is difficult to answer without proper guidance and instructions. Properties are particularly useful for avoiding polydimensionality, as they allow focusing on one clean hierarchical system without loss of information. This means, that properties are useful for representing a domain if it is not clear which feature of a class should be used to divide it into subclasses. Consider the following example: For an art ontology, we may want to describe paintings both according to the epoch they belong to (e.g. impressionism, renaissance) and the painting technique that was used (e.g. oil painting, pastel). We would then have different possibilities of establishing the hierarchical structure, but it would be difficult to contain both aspects as differentiating elements in the hierarchy (similarly to the problems discussed for classifying movies, see above). We could, however, choose one of the criteria for specifying the hierarchy and add the other type of information via a property; e.g. we might have a class `Paintings` with the subclasses `OilPaintings` and `PastelPaintings` and establish a relation `was_created_in_period` for both. We may even apply no hierarchy at all, but collect all paintings in one general class `Paintings` and add `was_created_in_period` and `uses_painting_technique` as two properties for this class[154]. A comparable approach has been used in the Rosetta-Net[155] Technical Dictionary:

> "It is noteworthy that the RosettaNet Technical Dictionary, a standardized vocabulary for describing electronic components [...] does not include any hierarchy, because the participating entities could not reach consensus on

---

[154] Ontology reasoners typically comprise functionalities for classifying, i.e. for asserting a given instance to a defined class, if the instance's properties match the necessary and sufficient conditions of this class. It is thus sometimes recommended not to assign instances to multiple classes but to focus on the creation of defined classes with necessary and sufficient conditions and to enable a reasoner to judge class membership. (See the section "Formal Axioms" below for more information on defined classes and necessary and sufficient conditions).

[155] RosettaNet: http://www.rosettanet.org.

that. Instead, it consists just of about 800 flat classes augmented by about 3000 datatype properties but was still practically useful." (Hepp, 2008)

It is not a strict requirement that an ontology be monohierarchic – but a common recommendation. Some further regard the creation of clean disjoint classes in hierarchies as an important design principle for ontologies. Rector, Wroe et al. (2001) argue that this cannot be achieved if descriptions and specifications are already included in the classes' names:

> "All multiple classification and overlapping of concepts are the result of definitions and descriptions. This may involve creating artefactual concepts known as 'roles', e.g. 'doctor' is defined as a 'person who plays a doctor role' […]. This allows clean disjoint taxonomies […]." (Rector, Wroe et al., 2001)

The doctor in this example may then also play other roles – he may for example act as a patient in another context. Establishing appropriate object properties that interlink well-chosen concepts (like `Person has_role Doctor`), clearly is a way of avoiding polyhierarchies. We assume that although polyhierarchy is useful in certain contexts, it should be handled with care. As the option of using concept properties to represent information which otherwise would have to be expressed through polyhierarchies is not given in any classical KOS, the topic is rarely discussed in classical KOS literature. Additional experiments and further research are needed, concerning both ease of ontology engineering and performance in practical applications. We assume that the more characteristics of a class are to be considered, the more useful it will be to avoid polyhierarchic structures (or maybe limit them, e.g. to a maximum of two superclasses per concept) and capture information in properties instead. Let us consider the example of paintings again. We may describe a member of the class `Paintings`, e.g. the `MonaLisa`, with properties, like `was_painted_by LeonardoDaVinci, uses_painting_technique Oil, has_motive Portrait, was_created_ in_period Rennaissance`. One might alternatively decide to group it into the classes `PaintingsByLeonardoDaVinci`, `OilPaintings`, `Portraits`, and `RennaissancePaintings`. But one would probably not want to establish additional classes like `PaintingsWithSize76,8x53cm` or `PaintingsOnPoplarPanels` – although properties like `has_size` and `has_surface` could be appropriate. While this decision seems intuitive, we need more fundamental discussions on this topic as well as general guidelines.

All in all, specifying different relation types and precision in naming these concept properties are issues of sophisticated KOS modeling. Yet for practical reasons, ontology designers should also not create too many different types of properties, for all those relations and connected concepts must be handled in a knowledge representation as well as in an information retrieval system. The more formalized properties there are, the longer the reasoning processes will take. The challenge is to create as many specified semantic relations as necessary while keeping the whole system processable – yet so far there has been little investigation into best practices and benchmarks. Considering this, the urgent need for more guidance in choosing and modeling semantic relations becomes obvious. One step towards this goal would be a structured (and, ideally, standardized) set of semantic relationship types.

Classifying Types of Relations

The research community concerned with knowledge representation and artificial intelligence is particularly concerned with developing the technical means for capturing semantic relations and their specific properties effectively. This community has already reached a remarkable state both in theoretical foundation and in practical implementation (e.g. in ontology languages or editors).

On the other side, there is the user community, which is currently growing beyond the original specialized research community. By now there is already a wide interest in ontologies and semantic applications among several scientific disciplines as well as in the industry. Yet this new community is not always able (or willing) to understand the finer differences of ontology languages and to comprehend the detailed theoretical foundations of years of research in knowledge representation. As the potential user community of ontologies grows even bigger with the proceeding of a Social Semantic Web, the gap between expert ontology engineers and interested laymen will also increase. In order to participate in building the Social Semantic Web, even those laymen will have to be enabled to contribute to the ontology engineering process. This means that they will need to learn at least some basic principles of ontology design. We think that for this purpose (apart from the already achieved standardization of representation languages[156]) some standards are needed for modeling basic essentials of ontologies, such as typical and frequently-needed concept interrelations.

The variety of possible semantic relations has still not been captured exhaustively, although several attempts have been made to identify and classify the types of relationship. But none of them could be turned into a standard, or be widely accepted for practical application. Apart from the approaches already discussed in this section, some others are available.

Khoo and Na (2006) report two basic approaches to constructing a list of semantic relations: "the minimalist approach and the elaborate approach". Minimalist approaches "define a small number of general relations based on philosophical or logical principles" (Khoo and Na provide an example of an approach with only three very general relations), whereas other approaches produce rich, elaborate lists of relationship types, often grouped by some shared meaning.

Perreault (1965) has developed a classified list of 120 relationships, based on the exploitation of respective discussions by different philosophers and classification specialists. Markowitz, Nutter and Evens have worked on a taxonomic hierarchy of lexical-semantic relations (Nutter, 1989; Markowitz, Nutter & Evens, 1992). The top level of the semantic relations (which are only one part of their entire collection) are depicted in Figure 2.15.

---

[156] Kashyap, Bussler and Moran (2008) have collected existing standards in the context of the Semantic Web, covering representation and query languages, for example.

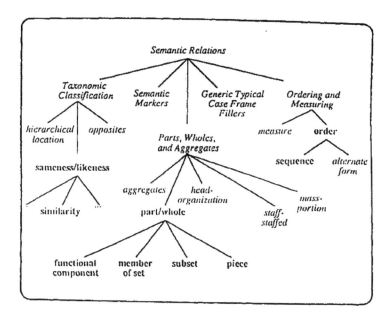

Figure 2.15. Top Levels of the semantic relations hierarchy. Source: Markowitz, Nutter & Evens (1992).

Khoo and Na (2006) quote single ontology projects that make use of predefined sets of semantic relations: The Generalized Upper Model (GUM) ontology (Bateman, Magnini & Rinaldi, 1995) has arranged several relations under the top categories participant, circumstance, process and logical-relation. The CGKAT system (Martin, 1996) uses about 200 relations hierarchically structured into nine categories (attributive relation, component relation, constraint or measure relation, relation from a situation, relation to a situation, relation from a proposition, relation referring to a process, relation with a special property, and relation used by an agent).

Various studies deal with examples and practical realizations of semantic relations for medical ontologies and related disciplines from life sciences. An early account of the state of the art of semantic relations in medical domains with a particular focus on part-whole relations is provided by Bernauer (1996). Rector (2002) analyzes interactions of meronymic and other relations for the medical domain. Rector, Wroe, Rogers and Roberts (2001) have modified typical part-of relations for use in biomedical ontologies and analyzed specific domain requirements on is-a structures amongst other aspects. Schulz and Hahn (2005) discuss part-whole structures in different biomedical ontologies and develop rules for representation and reasoning. The OBO foundry[157] has set up a set of common semantic relations which should be the basis for all OBO ontologies: the OBO Relation Ontology[158] (Smith, Ceusters et al., 2005). In connection with the Unified Medical Language System (UMLS[159], see below), much research on semantic relations has been conducted. As a result, 49 non-hierarchical relationships have been implemented in the UMLS' semantic network. These are divided into five groups (Aitchison, Gilchrist & Bawden, 2000, 183): "physical relationships (e.g., part of, consists of, contains), spatial relationships, temporal relationships (e.g., precedes, co-occurs with), functional relationships (e.g., causes, produces, effects), and conceptual relationships (e.g., measures, assesses)." There is no other domain of interest that has brought forth such rich discussions on semantic relations.

The current approaches to specifying types of semantic relations are partly overlapping or even contradictory. As a next step towards a standard model of ontology relations, one would now need to merge the different approaches and establish one shared model.

Furthermore, different types of analyses can be applied in order to identify additional types of semantic relations or to gain measures for counting the frequency of different relations. Therefore, an investigation and evaluation of existing ontologies regarding the relationships in use is needed; a challenging research task, given the diversity of currently developed and used domain ontologies. This approach may be refined by analyses of documents' full texts for investigating the relations implicitly existing between words (Sun & Zheng, 2005; Wang, Li et al., 2006). Methods of formal concept analysis (FCA) have been successfully applied (e.g. Ganter, Stumme & Wille, 2005). FCA has become an enormous research field which goes beyond the scope of this book but should be included in future works.

First experiments on analyzing Web sites or Web links for the purpose of identifying semantic relations have begun (Naing, Lim & Chiang, 2006). With the emergence of the Social Web, a new resource for gaining insight into concept interrelations has emerged: user-assigned tags in folksonomies (Peters & Weller, 2008).

Our initial unstructured investigations for the purpose of identifying generalizable relations by analyzing concept properties in existing ontologies and syntagmatic relations in folksonomies revealed unexpected parallels in current ontology engineering and social tagging (Peters & Weller, 2008). Originally, we expected ontology designers to create sophisticated and well-founded relations between concepts. This could not be confirmed for small and randomly picked ontologies (e.g. retrieved via Swoogle[160]). These test data can be considered as first prototypes of ontologies derived from the Social Semantic Web; they are built as quick approaches by interested novices rather than as sophisticated models by trained

---

[157] Open Biomedical Ontologies (OBO) foundry: http://www.obofoundry.org.
[158] OBO Relation Ontology: http://www.obofoundry.org/ro/.
[159] Unified Medical Language System (UMLS): http://www.nlm.nih.gov/research/umls/.
[160] Swoogle Semantic Web Search Engine: http://swoogle.umbc.edu/.

ontologists. Although we found different explicit concept relations in use, these are often inconsistent, of varying specificity and without any theoretical foundation. They are not expressions of a detailed analysis of real-world correlations, but display ad-hoc approaches or spontaneous ideas in order to picture a domain of interest. At least for the majority of small or application-specific ontologies (which have not been created by experienced indexers or experts in knowledge representation), the analysis of relationship types resembles the analysis of folksonomies to some degree: the creators of these ontologies are free to do what they want, no guidelines are provided, no knowledge on principles of semantic relations or background in knowledge representation is required. One major problem of this kind of ontology is that they include relations which seem to be specified associations at first sight but do not provide any additional information when compared to traditional unspecified associative relations. For example, they often interrelate concepts without describing the nature of the relationship: Within an ontology about travelling (Travel Ontology), we found the statement `Destination has_accomodation Accomodation`. This only indicates that there is some kind of relation between `Destination` and `Accommodation`, and fails to explain at all the nature of this relation. Relations of this kind can be found frequently, probably due to a lack of consciousness in the community. They are insubstantial, and may thus even dilute the expressiveness of ontologies. The underlying intention behind these relations will have to be captured in order to refine the spectrum of useful semantic relations (still, it may not always be possible to capture the underlying ideas). This example also highlights the importance of new guidelines for amateur ontology engineers. Of course, large and renowned ontology projects provide relationship types of different (higher) quality.

In the end, we will need new views on how relationships can be distinguished (which might be of use for other knowledge representation methods as well). Ideally, we will end up with an "ontology of relations", a structured collection of frequently used semantic relations. This should also contain a standardized set of names that can be used for modeling the respective relations in practical ontology engineering. Furthermore, research is needed on best practices for integrating different types of relations into ontologies, and on the effects of ontologies enriched with semantic relations in practical applications.

2.2.5 Attributes of Semantic Relations

Semantic relations in KOS may themselves also be specified by certain attributes, which are mainly (but not exclusively) the following: reflexivity, symmetry and transitivity (with the respective opposites: irreflexivity, asymmetry and intransitivity). Figure 2.16 shows the logical definitions of the logical properties transitivity, symmetry and reflexivity defined mathematically.

Property		Definition
R is Transitive	*iff*	∀ x,y,z[(R(x,y) ∧ R(y,z)) → R(x,z)]
R is Symmetric	*iff*	∀ x,y[R(x,y) → R(y,x)]
R is Reflexive	*iff*	∀ x R(x,x)

Figure 2.16. Definitions of logical properties. Source: Markowitz, Nutter & Evens, 1992.

In other words: Given that x, y, z are concepts and ρ is a semantic relation, we can define these characteristics as follows (Stock & Stock, 2008).

- Reflexivity: the relation ρ is reflexive iff x ρ x.
  This means that the relation holds between a concept and itself. One example would be x is_identical_with x. Reflexive relations are rather rare in ontologies.
- Symmetry: the relation ρ is symmetric iff (x ρ y) → (y ρ x).
  This means that two concepts are related from two sides with the same relation – the domain and range of a property are interchangeable.
  Synonymy is the most prominent example of symmetric relations: if concept x is_synonym_to y, then y is_synonym_to x. More domain-specific examples would be has_neighbour or has_sibling.
- Transitivity: the relation ρ is transitive iff [(x ρ y) ∧ (y ρ z)] → (x ρ z).
  An example for transitivity is given in the relation-chain 'racing cars ρ automobiles ρ vehicles' (with ρ indicating an is_kind_of relation): a racing car is a kind of automobile, an automobile is a kind of vehicle, and we may skip one level in this hierarchy as a racing car is also a kind of vehicle. Figure 2.17 is a schematic depiction of another example for transitivity: the relation has_ancestor.
  Some relations are transitive, others are not. It is not exclusively detected what determines the transitivity or intransitivity of relations. Hyponymy can be regarded as transitive. However, it has been pointed out that principles of hyponymy have to be followed strictly for this purpose, noticing that there is a lack of guidelines for deciding which characteristics justify establishing a kind-of relation (Cruse, 2002). Meronymy cannot generally be considered as transitive or intransitive. Both cases can be found in different examples. These effects have been discussed various times – often resulting in the explanation that there is not one single part-of relation but a family of similar relations, some of which are transitive and some are not, which should not be mixed up (Artale, Franconi et al., 1996; Iris, Litowitz & Evens, 1988; Pribbenow, 2002; Sattler, 1995). Weller and Stock (2008) conclude that intransitive part-of relations are compounds of several relations with different quali-

ties which can be decomposed into their single (transitive) elements[161]. Synonymy is only transitive for true synonyms, but not necessarily for synonyms with only a partial overlap of meaning (Markowitz, Nutter & Evens, 1992).

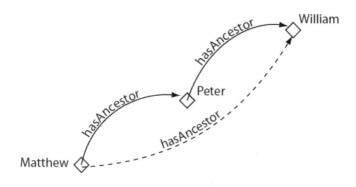

Figure 2.17. The transitive property has_ancestor. Source: Horridge, Knublauch et al., 2004.

Understanding the nature of different semantic relations helps to create more accurate knowledge representations and to use them appropriately for information retrieval purposes. Knowledge about transitivity between concepts is particularly needed to enable query expansion mechanisms for concepts from more than one step in a semantic net (Stock, 2007; Weller & Stock, 2008).

In ontologies, some features of properties can be formalized for enhanced reasoning mechanisms, depending on the ontology language and the editor in use. Exemplarily, we will consider the specific property features in OWL-DL; Figure 2.18 shows the interface for creating properties and specifying them in Protégé. Single relations may be complemented by an *inverse* relation, which is its direct counterpart. For example a relation has_subclass can have an inverse property is_subclass_of. The domain of the first is the range of the second and vice versa. Inverse relations can easily be connected in Protégé. In the properties tab, one may also indicate symmetry and transitivity. Reflexivity cannot be stated explicitly.

---

[161] Although for some application scenarios one may need one general intransitive part-of relation instead of various specified transitive sub-types of meronymy.

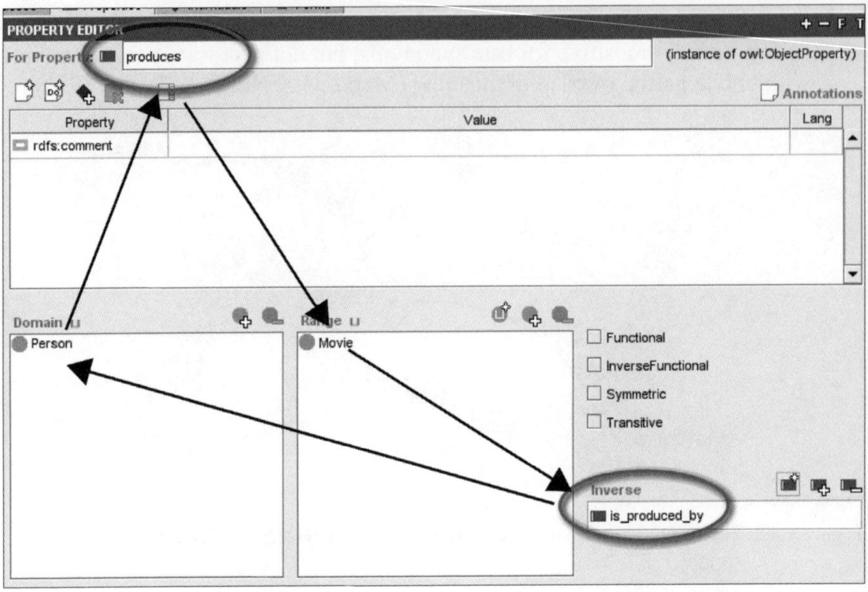

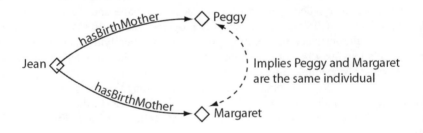

Figure 2.18. The property editing interface of the ontology editor Protégé (version 3.2.1). The relation 'produces' between 'Person' and 'Movie' has an assigned inverse property 'is_produced_by'.

Figure 2.19. The functional relation has_birth_mother. Source: Horridge, Knublauch et al., 2004.

Yet one may further define properties as being *functional*. The notion of functionality is derived from linguistics (Löbner, 1981). Functional properties are those which allow for exactly one value or instance as their range. An example is has_date_of_birth as a property of Person, because every person can only have one date of birth. Another example would be has_birth_mother, as every person can only have exactly one biological mother. Establishing functional relations in ontologies enables certain conclusions for reasoners, as Horridge, Knublauch et al. point out for the latter example (Figure 2.19):

> "If we say that the individual *Jean hasBirthMother Peggy* and we also say that the individual *Jean hasBirthMother Margaret* [footnote: The name Peggy is a diminutive form for the name Margaret], then because *hasBirthMother* is a functional property, we can infer that *Peggy* and *Margaret* must be the same individual. It should be noted however, that if *Peggy* and *Margaret* were explicitly stated to be two different individuals then the above statement would lead to an inconsistency." (Horridge, Knublauch et al., 2004)

In ontology engineering, functional properties are also known as *single valued properties* or as *features* (Horridge, Knublauch et al., 2004). The inverse property of a functional property is called *inverse functional*. For the preceding example of biological mothers, the inverse functional property could be is_birth_mother_of. Of course this inverse functional relation may relate to more than one argument (e.g. a woman can be birth mother of several children).

Further properties of relations have also been collected and discussed by Khoo & Na (2006); among them are variability, prototypicality and predictability. Guarino and Welty (2000a and 2000b) discuss the philosophical notions of *rigidity, identity, unity* and *dependency* as fundamental aspects of ontological properties. A property is rigid if it is necessarily essential to all its instances (e.g. being a *person* is rigid, while being a *student* is not). The notions of identity and unity are closely related:

> "Strictly speaking, identity is related to the problem of distinguishing a specific instance of a certain class from other instances of that class by means of a *characteristic property*, which is unique for *it* (that *whole* instance). Unity, on the other hand, is related to the problem of distinguishing the parts of an instance from the rest of the world by means of a unifying relation that binds the part together, and nothing else. For example, asking, 'Is that my dog?' would be a problem of identity, whereas asking, 'Is the collar part of my dog?' would be a problem of unity." (Guarino & Welty, 2000b)

For the notion of dependence, Guarino and Welty (2000b) distinguish extrinsic and intrinsic properties, "according to whether they depend or not on other objects besides their own instances."

N-ary Relations

Relations as discussed so far are typically binary, i.e. they interrelate two concepts/instances or an instance and a value. The construction of binary relations in ontologies is thus the default case. Yet some contexts require tertiary relations or even more complex interconnections. A W3C working group has addressed the issue of n-ary relations in Semantic Web ontologies and summed up some of the use cases (Noy & Rector, 2006). They have identified four typical cases of n-ary relations:

> *"1. Christine has breast tumor with high probability.* There is a binary relation between the person `Christine` and diagnosis `Breast_Tumor_Christine` and there is a qualitative probability value describing this relation (`high`).
>
> *2. Steve has temperature, which is high, but falling.* The individual `Steve` has two values for two different aspects of a `has_temperature` relation: its `magnitude` is `high` and its `trend` is `falling`.
>
> *3. John buys a 'Lenny the Lion' book from books.example.com for $15 as a birthday gift.* There is a relation, in which individual `John`, entity `books.example.com` and the book `Lenny_the_Lion` participate. This relation has other components as well such as the purpose (`birthday_gift`) and the amount (`$15`).
>
> *4. United Airlines flight 3177 visits the following airports: LAX, DFW, and JFK.* There is a relation between the individual flight and the three cities that it visits, `LAX`, `DFW`, `JFK`. Note that the order of the airports is important and indicates the order in which the flight visits these airports." (Noy & Rector, 2006)

These four examples differ in the way they might occur during the ontology engineering process:

> "We discover that a relation that we thought was binary, really needs a further argument – a common origin of use case 1. We discover that two binary properties always go together and should be represented as one n-ary relation – a common origin for use case 2. From the beginning, we realize that the relation is really amongst several things – a common origin for use case 3. The nature of the relation is such that one or more of the arguments is fundamentally a sequence rather than a single individual – use case 4."
> (Noy & Rector, 2006)

Traditional KOS like thesauri and classifications do not allow for n-ary relations. In ontology engineering, only the construction of binary relations is supported in most cases. In OWL ontologies it is not directly possible to relate more than one instance to another (or one instance to one value).

Yet the research community has discussed this issue for OWL and found a consensus on how to model the respective information by using intermediate classes. One property will then be modeled as an instance of this intermediate class and can then link to the different additional values, respectively. Figure 2.20 demonstrates this for the example No. 1 provided by Noy and Rector (2006). The instance `Diagonis_Relation_1` is an instance (the so-called *relation instance*) of a newly defined class `Diagonsis_Relation`.

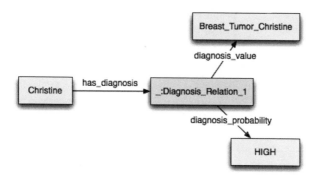

Figure 2.20. Exemplary solution for handling a tertiary relation in OWL. Source: Noy & Rector, 2006.

Figure 2.21 illustrates the modeling solution for example No. 3. As no outstanding subject could be identified in this case (all participants are of similar importance), the relation instance was chosen as Purchase_1, which was interlinked with the representants for the person who buys the book, the book, the seller, the price and the purpose of the shopping activity[162].

Another auxiliary construction would go as follows: Different sets of binary relations could be applied in order to break down the statement 'Person Peter buys BookA at Price FifteenDollars'. This tertiary relation could be turned into three binary relations: 'Person Peter buys_book BookA' (with an inverse property 'BookA is_bought_by Peter'), 'Person Peter pays_prize FifteenDollars', 'BookA has_prize FifteenDollars' (Figure 2.22). The human user may conclude that, but it requires additionally and specifically designed reasoners to enable a computer to infer this correlation[163]. If the same Person Peter buys another BookB at TenDollars, this becomes even more difficult. And if a single book is sold in several stores at different prices, the representation becomes impossible.

Concepts for a more direct approach to handling n-ary relations in semantic structures are currently being developed in the semantic wiki research community. The Semantic MediaWiki supports so-called *many-valued* properties, which resemble n-are relations. BOWiki[164], a collaborative editor for biomedical knowledge, gene functions and annotations, has extended the functionalities of the Semantic MediaWiki to include the creation of n-ary relations as suggested by the W3C.

---

[162] One may also keep additional relations between the single elements of the purchase process. For example, John is_customer_of books.example.com, or Lenny_The_Lion has_price $15.

[163] The difficulties for a machine interpretation are even intensified if the price is not modeled as an instance but as a float or integer value for a datatype property.

[164] BOWiki: http://bowiki.net/.

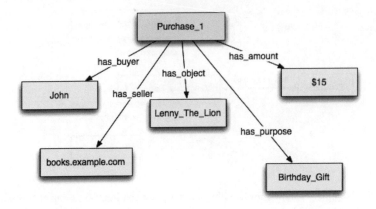

Figure 2.21. Exemplary solution for handling a n-ary relation in OWL. Source: Noy & Rector, 2006.

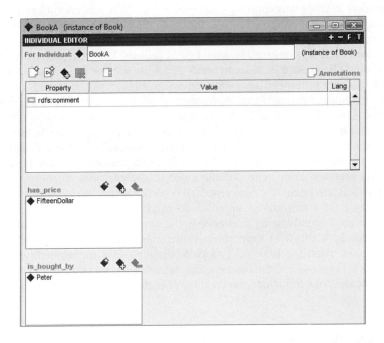

Figure 2.22. Instance BookA with properties has_price and is_bought_by. The relation between the instance Peter and the price of FifteenDollars is kept separately in a pays_price property. The entire context has to be interpreted by the human user.

Relations among Relations

Properties can also have relations among themselves (Horrocks, & Sattler, 1999), which leads to relations of relations (Stock, & Stock, 2008). Inverse relations as described above can be considered to be such relations among relations.

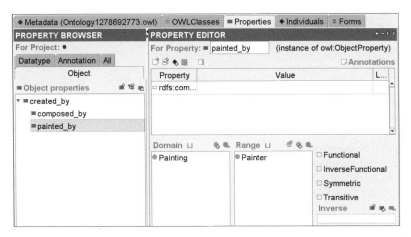

Figure 2.23. Creating sub-properties for an ontology about art in Protégé.

In most other cases, relations among relations will be hierarchies of relations: one relation is a sub-property of another one. Consider the following example: Within an ontology about art we find a property `created_by` (as the relation between a piece of art and the artist). We may now create subclasses of the concept `Artist`, e.g. `Painter` or `Composer`, and of the concept `PieceOfArt`, e.g. `Painting` or `PieceOfMusic`. In analogy, we can create sub-properties to connect the different types of art with their respective producers: `painted_by` and `composed_by` (Figure 2.23).

Inter-Ontological Relations

Apart from their use for structuring and characterizing the objects of one domain, semantic relations may also be established as interlinks between different domain models (e.g. between two ontologies or between one ontology and a thesaurus). This is a key challenge of ontology mapping (chapter 3.4.1).

OWL provides the means of interrelating the elements of two distinct ontologies. The property `owl:equivalentClass` can be used to indicate that two classes have precisely the same instances. Two properties in different ontologies may also be established as being equivalent (`owl:equivalentProperty`) or as being equal (`owl:sameAs`) (Dean & Schreiber, 2004). Smith, Welty and McGuinness warn that such inter-ontological connections have to be handled with care:

"To tie together a set of component ontologies as part of a third it is frequently useful to be able to indicate that a particular class or property in one
ontology is equivalent to a class or property in a second ontology. This capability must be used with care. If the combined ontologies are contradictory (all A's are B's vs. all A's are not B's) there will be no extension (no individuals and relations) that satisfies the resulting combination." (Smith,
Welty & McGuinness, 2004)

2.2.6 Formal and Informal Semantics

A fundamental aim of ontologies is to capture domain knowledge with formalized
semantics. Yet for some purposes, informal semantics can be a valuable addition.

Informal Semantics

Some optional components of ontologies are textual definitions (ideally in the
form of intensional definitions as discussed above). They are typically included in
OWL ontologies via `rdfs:comment` for all the previously discussed ontology
elements. In this way, one can add purely textual comments and definitions to
classes, individuals and properties – and provide a human-readable but informal
level of semantics.

"Besides providing unique identifiers only, ontologies can be augmented by
well-thought textual definitions, synonym sets, and multi-media elements
like illustrations. In fact, the intended semantics of an ontology element
cannot be conveyed by the formal specification only but requires a human-
readable documentation. In practice, we need ontologies that define elements with a narrow, real-world meaning." (Hepp, 2008)

Figure 2.24 shows how textual definitions are added to a concept in Protégé.

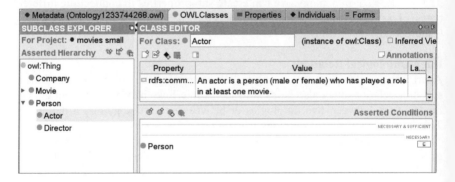

Figure 2.24. Adding a textual definition for `actor` via `rdfs:comment` in Protégé.

Providing precise and sound textual definitions in ontologies is a sophisticated intellectual task. It is certainly a way of going back to the roots of KOS. For some contexts, informal textual definitions may already be sufficient.

> "[...] such proper textual definitions can often already keep a large share of what ontologies promise. In particular when it comes to attributes and relations, specifying their intended semantics by axioms is difficult and often unfeasible, while properly chosen textual definitions are in practice sufficient for communicating the intended meaning." (Hepp, 2008)

Of course, these comments are not enough in order to make use of ontologies for reasoning and inferences. Yet textual definitions are a valuable help during the actual specification of formal definitions within ontologies and thus provide an indispensable basis for ontology engineering.

Hepp (2007) reports on some ongoing work using multimedia elements to enrich informal parts of ontology specifications – due to the experiences that "[...] ontology creators (particularly those with strong backgrounds in logic) often dedicate little effort to creating good labels and natural-language definitions."

The ontology elements rdfs:comment and rdfs:label (which was already introduced as a way of including synonyms) are types of *annotation properties*. There are some further types of annotation properties, e.g. in order to point to external resources for further definitions or to document versioning information. Furthermore, OWL allows for the creation of new, self-defined annotation properties. This may for example be useful for the creation of multilingual ontologies (one may create an annotation property to capture the translation into a specific language for every ontology element, i.e. one may annotate classes, instances and properties[165]) or for capturing certain information about how the ontology should be displayed in a practical application context.

Formal Axioms

Formal axioms are used to model sentences which are always true. Gómez-Pérez, Fernández-López and Corcho (2004) name an exemplary fact for the travelling domain "it is not possible to travel from the USA to Europe by train". Such facts may be formulated for specific domains or domain-independently. Axioms are expressed through formalized specifications of concepts and relations. They are also useful for inferring new knowledge, which is done via reasoners (or inference engines).

Figures 2.25 and 2.26 provide an overview of the formal expressiveness of OWL. We can only discuss some of the options for formalizing knowledge in

---

[165] Of course, in this case the general difficulties of multi-lingual KOS have to be kept in mind. Essentially, there are often no exact translations available. For example, a concept must be translated in such a way that neither its extension nor its intension changes.

OWL[166]; for more comprehensive explanations we may refer to Horrocks, Patel-Schneider and van Harmelen (2003), Dean and Schreiber (2004), or Smith, Welty & McGuinness (2004).

Abstract Syntax	DL Syntax
Descriptions (C)	
A (URI reference) owl:Thing owl:Nothing	A $\top$ $\bot$
intersectionOf(C_1 C_2 ...) unionOf(C_1 C_2 ...) complementOf(C) oneOf(o_1 ...)	$C_1 \sqcap C_2$ $C_1 \sqcup C_2$ $\neg C$ $\{o_1,...\}$
restriction(R someValuesFrom(C)) restriction(R allValuesFrom(C)) restriction(R hasValue(o)) restriction(R minCardinality(n)) restriction(R minCardinality(n))	$\exists R.C$ $\forall R.C$ $R:o$ $\geqslant n\,R$ $\leqslant n\,R$
restriction(U someValuesFrom(D)) restriction(U allValuesFrom(D)) restriction(U hasValue(v)) restriction(U minCardinality(n)) restriction(U maxCardinality(n))	$\exists U.D$ $\forall U.D$ $U:v$ $\geqslant n\,U$ $\leqslant n\,U$
Data Ranges (D)	
D (URI reference) oneOf(v_1 ...)	D $\{v_1,...\}$
Object Properties (R)	
R (URI reference)	R R^-
Datatype Properties (U)	
U (URI reference)	U
Individuals (o)	
o (URI reference)	o
Data Values (v)	
v (RDF literal)	v

Figure 2.25. OWL DL descriptions, data ranges, properties, individuals, and data values. Source: Horrocks, Patel-Schneider & van Harmelen, 2003.

---

[166] Also note that not all options of formal modelling are available in all three dialects. Over the next sections, we will provide an abstract overview in order to outline the principal possiblities of developing ontologies in OWL. We will not, however, discuss the differences of OWL lite, DL and full.

Abstract Syntax	DL Syntax
Class(A partial C_1 ...C_n)	$A \sqsubseteq C_1 \sqcap ... \sqcap C_n$
Class(A complete C_1 ...C_n)	$A = C_1 \sqcap ... \sqcap C_n$
EnumeratedClass(A o_1 ...o_n)	$A = \{o_1, ..., o_n\}$
SubClassOf(C_1 C_2)	$C_1 \sqsubseteq C_2$
EquivalentClasses(C_1 ...C_n)	$C_1 = ... = C_n$
DisjointClasses(C_1 ...C_n)	$C_i \sqcap C_j = \bot, i \neq j$
Datatype(D)	
DatatypeProperty(U super(U_1)...super(U_n))	$U \sqsubseteq U_i$
domain(C_1) ...domain(C_m)	$\geqslant 1 U \sqsubseteq C_i$
range(D_1) ...range(D_l)	$\top \sqsubseteq \forall U.D_i$
[Functional])	$\top \sqsubseteq \leqslant 1 U$
SubPropertyOf(U_1 U_2)	$U_1 \sqsubseteq U_2$
EquivalentProperties(U_1 ...U_n)	$U_1 = ... = U_n$
ObjectProperty(R super(R_1)...super(R_n))	$R \sqsubseteq R_i$
domain(C_1) ...domain(C_m)	$\geqslant 1 R \sqsubseteq C_i$
range(C_1) ...range(C_l)	$\top \sqsubseteq \forall R.C_i$
[inverseOf(R_0)]	$R = (^-R_0)$
[Symmetric]	$R = (^-R)$
[Functional]	$\top \sqsubseteq \leqslant 1 R$
[InverseFunctional]	$\top \sqsubseteq \leqslant 1 R^-$
[Transitive])	$Tr(R)$
SubPropertyOf(R_1 R_2)	$R_1 \sqsubseteq R_2$
EquivalentProperties(R_1 ...R_n)	$R_1 = ... = R_n$
AnnotationProperty(S)	
Individual(o type(C_1) ...type(C_n)	$o \in C_i$
value(R_1 o_1)...value(R_n o_n))	$\langle o, o_i \rangle \in R_i$
value(U_1 v_1)...value(U_n v_n))	$\langle o, v_i \rangle \in U_i$
SameIndividual(o_1 ...o_n)	$o_1 = ... = o_n$
DifferentIndividuals(o_1 ...o_n)	$o_i \neq o_j, i \neq j$

Figure 2.26. OWL DL axioms and facts. Source: Horrocks, Patel-Schneider & van Harmelen, 2003.

Formal Definitions

Formal semantics in ontologies are fundamentally based on formal concept definitions and so-called *class expressions*:

"OWL provides additional constructors with which to form classes. These constructors can be used to create so-called class expressions. OWL supports the basic set operations, namely union, intersection and complement. These are named `owl:unionOf`, `owl:intersectionOf`, and `owl:complementOf`, respectively. Additionally, classes can be enumerated. [...] And it is possible to assert that class extensions must be disjoint. Note that class expressions can be nested without requiring the creation of names for every intermediate class. This allows the use of set operations to build up complex classes from anonymous classes or classes with value restrictions." (Smith, Welty & McGuinness, 2004)

One basic aspect of defining classes is to make them *disjoint* from one another. If two classes are disjoint this means that no individual can be part of both of them. For example, if we go back to our exemplary movie ontology with the classes Movie and Person, we may make these two classes disjoint. No real world individual can be classified as being both a person and a movie. By stating disjointness for all concepts in an ontology, one would consequently decide that this ontology is monohierarchic.

The construction of *enumerated classes* allows the defining of classes by "precisely listing the individuals that are the members of this class" (Horridge, Knublauch et al., 2004). One example would be the class Months, which could be defined as comprising exactly the individuals January, February, March, April, June, July, August, September, October, November and December. This corresponds to the principle of extensional concept definition.

Classes can also be defined as the intersection or union of two (or more) already existing classes, or as the direct complement of another class (in which case they would act as contradictory antonyms).

For even more elaborated definitions, classes can be described with conditions that have to be fulfilled by every member of the class (which leads to intensional definitions). *Necessary conditions* are used to state that "if something is a member of this class then it is *necessary* to fulfill these conditions" (Horridge, Knublauch et al., 2004). Furthermore, *necessary and sufficient conditions* can be created. They constitute that "if something fulfils these conditions then it *must* be a member of this class" (Horridge, Knublauch et al., 2004). A class that is described with necessary and sufficient conditions is called a *defined class* or *complete class*; a class that is only specified by necessary conditions is known as a *primitive class* or *partial class* (Horridge, Knublauch et al., 2004).

Conditions – and thus the definitions of classes – consist of required properties for that class and *restrictions*[167] on these properties (or on their values). The expressiveness of restrictions highly depends on the specification of relations (Horrocks, & Sattler, 1999). In OWL there are three main categories of restrictions: *quantifier restrictions*, *cardinality restrictions* and *hasValue restrictions* (Horridge, Knublauch et al., 2004). Note that OWL does not support the establishment of default values for any of these restrictions, though this is possible in some other ontology languages.

> „A major function of Frame systems is to deal with default knowledge – i.e. information which is true in general but subject to exceptions. Formal description logics do not support default reasoning. However, they can provide a framework for separate default reasoner." (Rector, Wroe et al., 2001)

---

[167] One may also say that restrictions are used to model *axioms*, facts that are always true in the topic area of the ontology (Lambrix, Tan et al., 2007).

Quantifier Restrictions

Quantifier restrictions are composed of a *quantifier*, a property and a *filler* (Horridge, Knublauch et al., 2004). Two quantifiers are available: The existential quantifier ∃ can be read as *at least one* or *some*, or in OWL terminology: *some values from* (owl:someValuesFrom). The universal quantifier ∀ can be read as *only*, in OWL *all values from* (owl:allValuesFrom).

In Figure 2.24 (above) we have used an example for an informal concept definition in a movie ontology. We added the comment that an actor is a person who has played a role in at least one movie. We may now turn this into a formal definition by using the existential quantifier:

- We have a class Movie and a class Actor, which is a subclass of Person. Thus the first part of the definition (an actor is a person) is defined.
- We have a property plays_role_in with Movie as its domain and Actor as its range.
- We create a restriction on the class Actor, as shown in Figure 2.27, saying that for every member of this class the property plays_role_in is restricted to have at least one value (=the existential quantifier) from the class Movie (=the filler for the restriction). Thus the second part of the informal definition (has played a role in at least one movie) is also formalized.
- This restriction is now added as a necessary condition for the class Actor (Figure 2.28). This means that for any member of the class Actor it is *necessary* to have the property plays_role_in relating it to *at least one* instance of the class Movie.

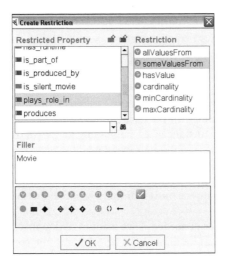

Figure 2.27. Creating a restriction to define the class Actor.

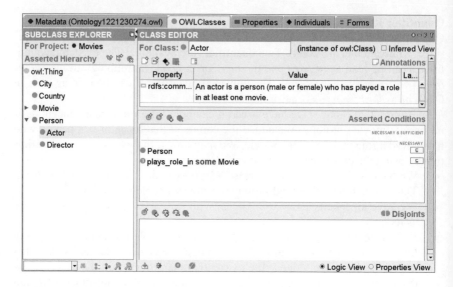

Figure 2.28. The newly created necessary condition specifies the class Actor.

Horridge, Knublauch et al. (2004) explain what the use of these restrictions means on the formal level of OWL:

> "A restriction actually describes an anonymous class (an unnamed class). The anonymous class contains all of the individuals that satisfy the restriction [...]. When restrictions are used to describe classes, they actually specify anonymous superclasses of the class being described." (Horridge, Knublauch et al., 2004)

In this way, reasoning becomes possible. A reasoner uses the information provided by the class definitions (conditions) to check the consistency and compute an *inferred* class hierarchy. In the case of necessary and sufficient conditions, the reasoner may classify instances as belonging to the defined classes. Thus we might add a fifth step to our previous example:

- We may choose to convert this necessary condition into a necessary and sufficient one. Then every random instance that fulfils our condition of having played a role in a movie *must* definitely be a member of the class actor.

The universal quantifier is needed if we want to define that the only values for the respective property must be individuals belonging to the specified filler class. Pan (2007) has provided an example of a class Herbivore, "whose members are exactly those Animals such that everything they eat is either a Plant or is a partOf a Plant". The restriction would be placed upon a property eats with the restriction that all values for this property must be taken from the classes Plant or its subclasses. This could look like the following (Pan; 2007):

```
Class (Herbivore complete
    intersectionOf (Animal
        restriction (eat allValuesFrom
            (unionOf(Plant restriction(partOf someValuesFrom(Plant)))))))
```

When creating restrictions, fillers can be combined with Boolean operators (Horridge, Knublauch et al., 2004).

Value Restrictions

Value restrictions (or hasValue restrictions) are used to describe a set of individuals who all have a property relating them to a specific *individual*. This means that the value of that particular property is restrictively fixed to a certain individual.

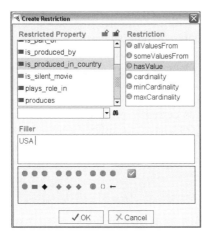

Figure 2.29. Creating a hasValue restriction to define a class AmericanMovie.

Let us imagine that we wish to define a new class `AmericanMovie` as a subclass of the class `Movie` in a movie ontology. This new class could be defined informally in the following way: "an American movie is a movie that has been produced in the USA." To turn this into a formal definition, we will need a class `Country` with `USA` among its instances, and a relation `is_produced_in` between the classes `Movie` and `Country`. The class `AmericanMovie` could now be defined as having *only* the USA (as an instance of the class `Country`) as the filler for the `is_produced_in` property (Figure 2.29)[168]. Value restrictions may also be constructed with datatype properties.

---

[168] In this case, a movie that is produced in the USA and Great Britain would not count as an American Movie, but probably as a coproduction. One could also define an American movie as any movie that has *at least* the USA as filler for the `is_produced_in` property.

Cardinality Restrictions

Cardinality restrictions provide the means of specifying the number of individuals that can be attached to a property for a given class. There are three types of cardinality restrictions: Minimum cardinality demands that at least the preset number of individuals must be asserted for a given property. Maximum cardinality demands that at most the preset number of individuals must be asserted for a given property. Pure cardinality demands that exactly the preset number of individuals must be asserted for a given property. In case the cardinality is set to exactly one value it becomes equivalent to functional properties. Not all types of cardinalities are supported by all three OWL dialects.

We have now introduced the most important elements of ontologies: concepts, instances, relations and restrictions. Again, we want to remind you that this chapter does not provide an exhaustive insight into the expressivity of OWL, and that it does not include all possibilities of formal information structuring with ontologies, as the vast variety of representation languages with their specifications is not the subject of this book. Our aim is to provide a general insight into the variety of options for modeling knowledge in ontologies (compared to classical KOS) and to highlight some of the fundamental considerations of modeling decisions appearing during the ontology engineering process. In the context of the Social Semantic Web, ontology languages currently provide the framework for establishing rich semantics. Traditional KOS have not offered such extensive options for knowledge representation. This section has illustrated how semantics may look like in a Web environment – given that enough manpower can be gathered to put these theories into practice.

2.3 Ontologies as Knowledge Organization Systems

After this insight into the structure and elements of ontologies, we will focus once more on a comparison and differentiation of ontologies and other forms of knowledge organization systems. The complex structure of formal ontologies may not be achieved in every context of the WWW. The Social Semantic Web will surely need high-quality ontologies, but these will not be the only KOS in practice. Other, less formal types will also have to be considered for future use.

In the first chapter, our focus was on the practical application of different KOS and on the motivations for using them – now we will reconsider them from a different perspective, and have a closer look on their structural differences, with the aim of providing better unique specifications for Types of KOS. For this purpose, we will start with a presentation of several examples of well-known ontologies.

2.3.1 Selected Popular and Important Ontologies

This section will present a selection of important or highly prominent ontologies. We have grouped them roughly according to their domains of interest or their application areas. Different overviews on existing ontologies are also provided by

Gómez-Pérez, Fernández-López and Corcho (2004), Feliu, Vivaldi & Cabré (2002), and Noy and Hafner (1997).

Upper Ontologies

As we have mentioned earlier, upper ontologies (also named upper-level ontologies, top-level ontologies or foundational ontologies) capture knowledge on a very high level of abstraction and typically share the aim of providing a framework or reference for the development of more specific domain ontologies. The following definition of 'upper ontology' is provided by the Standard Upper Ontology Working Group (SUO WG) on their website[169]:

> "An upper ontology is limited to concepts that are meta, generic, abstract and philosophical, and therefore are general enough to address (at a high level) a broad range of domain areas. Concepts specific to given domains will not be included; however, this standard will provide a structure and a set of general concepts upon which domain ontologies (e.g. medical, financial, engineering, etc.) could be constructed."

Upper ontologies usually have origins with very strong philosophical contexts. Most of the famous upper ontologies were developed in the early years of research in computational ontologies. The most widely recognized upper ontologies are Cyc, BFO, SUO/SUMO, Sowa's Top Level Ontology, DOLCE, PROTON and GFO. They may all differ fundamentally in the way they define world knowledge:

> "The organization of a top-level ontology contains a number of problems, similar to the problems that surround ontology in philosophy. For example, many ontologies have *thing* or *entity* as their root class. However, [...] thing and entity start to diverge at the next level. For example, CYC's *thing* has the subcategories *individual object, intangible,* and *represented thing*; The Generalized Upper Model's (GUM) *um-thing* has the subcategories *configuration, element,* and *sequence*; Wordnet's *thing* has the subcategories *living thing* and *nonliving thing,* and Sowa's root *T* has the subcategories *concrete, process, object,* and *abstract.* (Chandrasekaran, Josephson and Benjamins, 1999)

Comparisons of different top-level ontologies are provided by Grenon (2003), Herre, Heller et al. (2006), Mascardi, Cordi and Rosso (2007) and Semy, Pulvermacher and Obrst (2004), for example. Let us have a closer look at some of the important top level ontologies:

- Sowa's Top Level Ontology (Sowa, 2000): In Figure 2.6 above, we have already seen a visualization of Sowa's top-level construction. Sowa has introduced three top-level distinctions: a) physical vs. independent (concrete vs. abstract), b) form vs. role vs. mediation (firstness vs. secondness vs. thirdness), c) continuant vs. occurrent (object vs. process). These distinctions are combined to generate the 27 categories of his ontology (as can be seen in the illustration).

---

[169] Standard Upper Ontology Working Group (SUO WG): http://suo.ieee.org.

- Standard Upper Ontology (SUO) and Suggested Upper Merged Ontology (SUMO) (Niles & Pease, 2001): The Standard Upper Ontology is a large project promoted by the IEEE[170]. The Standard Upper Merged Ontology is one of its two major components (besides the Information Flow Framework, IFF). SUMO was designed to become a comprehensive and consistent top-level ontology. Therefore other existing upper ontologies and certain philosophical theories were combined to form SUMO.

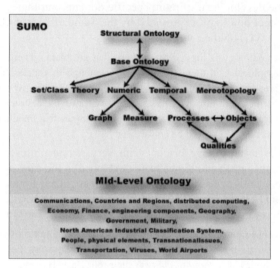

Figure 2.30. SUMO and its components at three levels of specificity. Source:
http://www.ontologyportal.org/.

SUMO is now a modular ontology, consisting of a top-level ontology (SUMO), an intermediate level (Mid-Level Ontology MILO) and certain domain ontologies. Figure 2.30 illustrates the different components of SUMO. Together, they form the largest formal public ontology today: SUMO and its several domain ontologies contain about 20,000 terms and 70,000 axioms. The concepts are informally (Figure 2.31) and formally defined. SUMO is formalized in a customized ontology language (SUMO-KIF), a specific editor and a reasoning tool have been developed. Multilingual expansion includes Czech, German, Italian, (simplified) Chinese, and Hindi. Furthermore, SUMO has established mappings to WordNet (a linguistic thesaurus discussed below) (Figure 2.32). Current efforts of enhancing SUMO already move towards the Social Semantic Web: Developers have started to enrich instance content for SUMO based on DBPedia's data about persons and on Wikipedia.

---

[170] IEEE (Formerly: Institute of Electrical and Electronics Engineers): http://www.ieee.org.

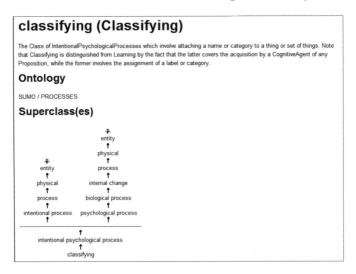

Figure 2.31. The SUMO concept 'classifying': definition and superclasses. Source: http://virtual.cvut.cz/kifb/en/concepts/_classifying.html.

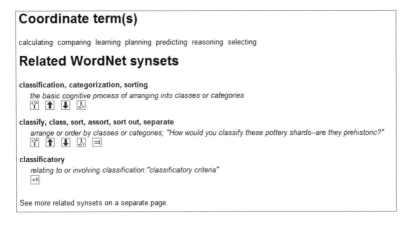

Figure 2.32. The SUMO concept 'classifying': associated concepts and mappings to WordNet. Source: http://virtual.cvut.cz/kifb/en/concepts/_classifying.html.

- Cyc[171] (Lenat, 1995; Matuszek, Cabral et al., 2006): The Cyc ontology is a very large knowledge base, which makes it different from the previous and more classical upper ontologies. It is less desirable for use as an abstract

---

[171]   Cyc: http://www.cyc.com.

framework for specific domain ontologies. Rather it can be viewed as an attempt to capture world knowledge at various degrees of specificity. One might call it a *universal ontology* as it collects universal knowledge (it also contains an upper-level ontology). However, we have included it in this section on upper ontologies as it differs from most other ontologies by not focusing on one specific domain or application. The Cyc knowledge base has been developed by Cycorp for more than 20 years now – together with a respective inference engine, the CycL ontology language, machine learning components and different other tools for handling the ontology data. It aims at building a foundation of basic common-sense knowledge which can be used for reasoning in knowledge-intensive applications or on the WWW. It has already been applied for word sense disambiguation (Curtis, Baxter and Cabral, 2006), question answering (Curtis, Matthews and Baxter, 2005) and in a knowledge base on terrorism and related information[172] (Deaton, Shepard et al., 2005). As stated on the Cyc Website in May 2009, the current version of the Cyc KB contains nearly two hundred thousand terms as well as several dozen manually entered assertions about/involving each term. Mappings to WordNet are also included. New assertions are continually being added to the KB by human knowledge engineers, but research also concerns the automatic enrichment of the knowledge base. OpenCyc[173] is a freely available subset of the Cyc knowledge base. Parts of Cyc can also be exported to an OWL format via a specific editor.

- Descriptive Ontology for Linguistic and Cognitive Engineering[174] (DOLCE) (Masolo, Borgo, et al., 2003). DOLCE is a project of the Laboratory for Applied Ontology (headed by Nicola Guarino) and part of the WonderWeb project on "Ontology Infrastructures for the Semantic Web". As such, DOLCE was initiated as the starting point for comparing and analyzing other (domain) ontologies. It is still being maintained, even after the original project has ended. DOLCE aims at capturing "ontological categories underlying natural language and human commonsense" (Mascardi, Cordi & Rosso, 2007). Above, we have already seen the basic categories of DOLCE (Figure 2.7) and how the ontology distinguishes between endurants and perdurants. Furthermore, DOLCE highlights the explicit distinction of particulars and universals, and focuses much more on the inclusion of particulars, i.e. individual concepts.

- Basic Formal Ontology[175] (BFO) (Grenon, 2003): The Basic Formal Ontology (BFO) is an upper-level framework for assisting in the organization and

---

[172] The Terrorism Knowledge Base (TKB), which aims at containing all relevant knowledge about terrorist groups, their members, leaders, ideology, founders, tactics, events etc.

[173] OpenCyc: http://www.opencyc.com.

[174] Descriptive Ontology for Linguistic and Cognitive Engineering (DOLCE): http://www.loa-cnr.it/DOLCE.html.

[175] Basic Formal Ontology (BFO): http://www.ifomis.org/bfo.

integration of biomedical information. It thus focuses on applications for the biomedical domain (Grenon, Smith & Goldberg, 2004). It is developed by the IFOMIS[176] group at Saarland University. BFO consists of two essential parts aiming to represent both entities existing at any given time and processes unfolding through time:
"BFO has two components. A SNAP ontology of endurants which is reproduced at each moment of time and is used to characterize static views of the world on the side of endurants. This view is motivated by an underlying presentist metaphysics of time (all which exists exists at the present time). No temporal consideration is germane to the SNAP ontology in this very elementary sense. SNAP, then, in order to be used in a manageable way in temporal contexts requires a temporal logic of a certain grade." (Grenon, 2003)
The history of BFO goes back to 1998, when its theoretical foundations were developed by Smith and Grenon. Recently, it has also been transferred to OWL[177].

- PROTON[178] (PROTo ONtology) (Terziev, Kiryakov & Manov, 2003): PROTON is part of the SEKT[179] project, is derived from the KIMO ontology, and was formerly called BULO (Base Upper-Level Ontology). It aims at providing the general concepts necessary for different tasks, including semantic annotation, indexing, and the retrieval of documents. PROTON is organized in three layers consisting of four modules. It contains about 300 classes and 100 properties.

- General Formal Ontology[180] (GFO) (Herre, Heller, et al., 2006): The GFO is developed by the Onto-Med Research Group[181] at the University of Leipzig – together with a domain specific extension of the ontology for biomedicine (GFO-bio). The GFO elaborates on categories like objects, processes, time and space, properties, relations, roles, functions, facts and situations. It seeks to provide novel approaches to capturing reality, particularly in material, mental and social areas. It consists of three layers: a meta ontology, a core level and a basic level. An OWL version of GFO is available.

Upper ontologies might, then, also play an important role for interlinking different domain ontologies over the Web. The ideal reference ontology for this purpose would be one shared upper ontology. We will return to this aspect of handling the diversity of ontologies in Section 3.4.

---

[176] Institute for Formal Ontology and Medical Information Science (IFOMIS): http://www.ifomis.org/.
[177] The BFO 1.0 version can be downloaded as an OWL file from: http://www.ifomis.org/bfo/1.0.
[178] PROTON (PROTo ONtology): http://proton.semanticweb.org.
[179] Semantically Enabled Knowledge Technologies (SEKT): http://www.sekt-project.com.
[180] General Formal Ontology (GFO): http://www.onto-med.de/ontologies/gfo/index.jsp.
[181] Research Group Ontologies in Medicine (Onto-Med): http://www.onto-med.de.

Linguistic and Lexical Ontologies

Ontologies also play an important role in research on computational linguistics, particularly for natural language processing (NLP) and information extraction (IE). In this application area, ontologies are used as knowledge bases which provide background information for machine processing of texts. They are usually not bound to a certain domain but capture universal knowledge, and thus resemble upper ontologies in this respect. Yet their focus is less on representing the essence of the world but on capturing linguistic behavior and lexical surroundings of concepts. The structure of linguistic ontologies may differ from the typical structure of concepts, instances, relations and axioms as discussed for ontologies; although they typically use hyponymic structures as a backbone and enrich them with additional concept relations. Single linguistic ontologies have recently also been transferred to the OWL format.

Used in combination with information extraction systems, linguistic ontologies can be applied in order to gather factual data for the semi-automatic construction of other (domain) ontologies. They may further be used as synonym collections and dictionaries or as a major mapping reference vocabulary. Some projects also focus on supporting machine translation.

Linguistic ontologies have arisen quite early in the course of computational ontology studies. The following projects all have their origins in the 1990s; Katherine Dahlgreen presented a linguistically motivated ontology in 1988 (Dahlgreen, 1988). The WordNet project in particular (but also the General Upper Ontology) receives high attention up until this day.

- WordNet (Fellbaum, 1999; Miller, 1990): WordNet is hard to classify as a type of KOS; it has been called a linguistic thesaurus, an ontology, an has also beencounted among the upper ontologies due to its broad coverage. Probably the most adequate definition is to describe WordNet as a lexical reference system or linguistic database. The lexical objects within WordNet are structured with various semantic links, and particularly with very rich synonym collections – which also makes it very useful for different Semantic Web application scenarios. Most centrally, synonyms in WordNet are grouped together in so-called *synsets*. The synsets are organized in hierarchies and interlinked via other types of semantic relations. Separate databases exist for nouns, verbs and adjectives, each with its own set of relations. The EC Telematics Project produces Euro WordNet for different European language versions. The WordNet website provides statistics on the size of the database, stating that it currently covers more than 155,000 unique synset strings.

- Mikrokosmos Ontology[182] (Mahesh & Nirenburg, 1995): This ontology was built for use in an NLP system. The Mikrokosmos project team was developing a multilingual knowledge-based machine translation (KBMT) system, with the central goal of developing a tool produceing a comprehensive Text Meaning Representation (TMR) for an input text in any of a set of source lan-

---

[182] Mikrocosmos Ontology: http://crl.nmsu.edu/Research/Projects/mikro/htmls/ontology-htmls/onto.index.html.

guages. Therefore, they needed an interlingual meaning representation, e.g. for handling word sense disambiguation, recognizing metonymy or metaphors and for inferencing absent parts of information. Although concepts are named in English, it has not been built for use with one specific language. It consists of a basic taxonomy and other specified semantic relations.

- Generalized Upper Model[183] (GUM) (Bateman, Magnini & Rinaldi, 1995): GUM is a task and domain independent knowledge model with linguistic motivations. It is designed to support sophisticated natural language processing in different languages by providing semantics for natural language expressions. Since 2007, it has been maintained in OWL and the Common Algebraic Specification Language (CASL). An extension is provided especially for spatial language constructs.

- SENSUS (Swartout, Ramesh, et al., 1996): SENSUS was formerly called Pangloss and was developed as part of the Pangloss machine translation project. It contains representations for approximately 70,000 common objects, processes, qualities and relations. The ontology was constructed by reusing and merging different online dictionaries, bilingual resources and semantic networks (among them WordNet and other linguistic ontologies) via semiautomatic methods.

Knowledge Representation Ontologies

Gómez-Pérez, Fernández-López and Corcho (2004) also name *knowledge representation ontologies* (KR ontologies) as an important type of ontology. Their purposes differ fundamentally from the examples discussed so far. They are used to gather the modeling primitives which are used in a specific knowledge representation paradigm, in the sense of different knowledge representation formalisms or languages. An important exponent of this type is thus the Frame Ontology (Gruber, 1993), designed for capturing knowledge representation conventions under a frame-based approach (for the Ontolingua[184] project). Similarly, languages like CycL and OCML (based on combinations of frames and first order logic) are supported by their own KR ontologies (Gómez-Pérez, Fernández-López & Corcho, 2004). Unlike the ontologies discussed so far, KR ontologies do not capture any kind of real-world or domain knowledge. In our context, the name 'knowledge representation ontologies' may however cause some irritation, as we consider all ontologies as methods of knowledge representation. This irritation is based on the different denotations of knowledge representation within the different disciplines of information science, computer science and philosophy.

Quite similarly, Fonseca (2007) distinguishes "ontologies of information systems" and "ontologies for information systems". The former are ontologies that describe information systems and are used to support the creation of modeling

---

[183] Generalized Upper Model (GUM): http://www.fb10.uni-bremen.de/anglistik/langpro/webspace/jb/gum/ and http://www.ontospace.uni-bremen.de/ontology/gum.html.

[184] Ontolingua: http://www.ksl.stanford.edu/software/ontolingua/.

tools. The latter can be considered as knowledge bases used in information systems.

Ontologies for the Life Sciences

Biology and bioinformatics can be regarded as the scientific disciplines with the highest interest in ontologies outside of computer science and information science, resulting in elaborated considerations on the topic (e.g. Bodenreider & Stevens, 2006; Rojas, Ratsch et al., 2003; Stevens, Goble & Bechhofer, 2000; Stevens, Wroe, et al., 2004), as well as in different bio-ontologies, use cases and applications (e.g. Mainz, Weller et al., 2008; Smith, Ashburner et al., 2007). Widely recognized are the TAMBIS Ontology, the RiboWeb Ontology (Altman, Bada et al., 1999), the Ontology for Molecular Biology, the Schulze-Kremer Ontology for Molecular Biology (MBO) (Schulze-Kremer, 2002), EcoCyc[185] (Karp & Paley, 1998; Karp, Riley et al., 1998) and the Open Biomedical Ontologies[186] (OBO) collection, which covers a range of bio-ontologies including the Gene Ontology (GO). We will describe some of them in more detail below.

There have been some attempts to explain the particular and ever growing interest in ontologies within the life sciences: More than most other scientific disciplines, the life sciences experience an exponential growth of data and publications; researchers are increasingly becoming overstrained with data survey, aggregation and integration. This coerces the scientific community into finding sophisticated structuring, accessibility, context information and information integration solutions. Furthermore, domains in the life sciences themselves are very complex. Concepts and classifications are subject to constant evolution (Rojas, Ratsch, et al., 2003) because new findings could possibly entail new classifications. Classifications or taxonomies have thus long been an important issue for documenting shared knowledge in disciplines such as zoology (Bodenreider & Stevens, 2006), starting with Carolus Linneaus' hierarchical classification of the flora and fauna. We have already discussed some of the current KOS applied in the domain of health care in Section 1.1.3. Ontologies continue this tradition but also shift the focus of interest. They provide the means of structuring recent findings and represent knowledge in an organized way; they enable the consistent indexing of biological objects, database management and query formulation (Stevens, Wroe et al., 2004). Approaches to unifying terminologies are also urgently needed, as there are often different vocabularies in use within different sub-disciplines of the life sciences. Schulz and Hahn (2005) explain:

> "Biology and medicine both share a long-standing tradition for structuring their domain knowledge in terms of taxonomies, classifications, and thesauri. These terminological resources have been developed and put into practice mainly from the perspective of their utility for disease encoding, health care statistics, gene annotation, document retrieval, or accountancy practices, while ontological considerations never played a considerable role

---

[185]   EcoCyc: http://ecocyc.org.
[186]   Open Biomedical Ontologies (OBO): http://www.obofoundry.org.

in organizing terms and their (shared) meaning. With increasing demands for more 'intelligent' support of research and routine work in terms of planning, diagnostic reasoning, decision support, and natural language processing, requirements for more sophisticated forms of computationally adequate domain representations have shaped." (Schulz & Hahn, 2005)

This long tradition of approaches to structuring the domain of interest in the life sciences has brought forward a variety of systems which cannot be easily classified as one particular type of KOS. Today, the tendency is to name every knowledge model in the life sciences 'ontology'; including those that have formerly been called 'thesaurus' (e.g. UMLS, see below) and which hardly use any formal structures besides taxonomies. Ontologies, and not only in the life sciences, should therefore themselves become a subject of reclassification; many of them ought rather to be regarded as a different type of KOS. In many cases, the producers of bio-ontologies have ranked functionality and applications above ontologically well-formed structures. The quality of popular bio-ontologies has been discussed, e.g. by Soldatova and King (2005) as well as by Schulz and Hahn (2005), who criticize UMLS for its "vague semantics" and for mixing up is-a and part-of relations:

> "For the current routine uses of large-scale biomedical vocabularies, such as lexicon look-up, enforcement of a controlled language (terminology service), or term expansion for information retrieval, the underlying representation structures turn out to be useful in most cases. For 'intelligent' applications requiring inferential computations on conceptual structures, the informal approach is doomed to failure, because semantically vague or even inconsistent assertions may lead to a broad range of inadequate, or even invalid, deductions." (Schulz & Hahn, 2005)

We will now provide a short introduction to single ontologies and an overview over their different scopes and backgrounds.

*   The Gene Ontology[187] (GO) (Ashburner, Ball et al., 2000): The GO was started by the Gene Ontology Consortium as a collaborative effort to address the need for consistent descriptions of gene products in different databases[188]. With currently approximately 100 applications that use the GO, it is one of the most prominent indications of the growing importance of KOS for the further development of bioinformatics. The GO is part of the OBO collection. It consists of three sub-ontologies *cellular component, biological process* and *molecular function*.
    A huge effort is placed on clear definitions of concepts, to ensure consistent indexing of gene products. The structure of GO comprises pure is-a and part-of relations. GO terms can now also be interlinked with `regulates`, `positively_regulates` and `negatively_regulates` in order to describe in-

---

[187] Gene Ontology (GO): http://www.geneontology.org/.
[188] This process is referred to as annotation in the respective community; we may also call this process the indexing of gene products.

teractions between biological processes and other biological processes, molecular functions or biological qualities. Mappings exist for diverse external database schemas. As of June 5, 2009, the GO contains 27,569 terms, 98.8% of them with definitions.

- Unified Medical Language System (UMLS): The UMLS is produced by the United States National Library of Medicine[189], together with a set of associated software tools. It is not developed for one single application, but aims at supporting tools for different purposes like information systems for patient records, scientific literature, guidelines and public health data.

  The UMLS consists of three essential parts: the Metathesaurus, the Semantic Network and the SPECIALIST Lexicon. The Metathesaurus is a thesaurus that represents important concepts from the domain of biomedicine and health, collects their synonyms and interrelations of different concepts. It has been built by reusing and merging various other knowledge resources. The Semantic Network is an external resource which includes fine-grained semantic relations for the Metathesaurus. Together, these two resources can actually be counted as an ontology.

  The SPECIALIST Lexicon has been developed as a lexical information source for implementation in a natural language processing system. It covers both general English and specific biomedical terms, arranged in lexicon entries with the syntactic, morphological, and orthographical information needed by the SPECIALIST NLP System.

- Systematized Nomenclature of Medicine-Clinical Terms[190] (SNOMED-CT): SNOMED-CT was originally created by the College of American Pathologists by combining SNOMED RT and a computer based nomenclature called Clinical Terms Version 3. It is now promoted by the International Health Terminology Standards Development Organisation[191] (IHTSDO) as a comprehensive, multilingual clinical healthcare terminology for easing communication and interoperability in an electronic health data exchange. The current version (released January 2008) comprises about 311,000 unique concepts (800,000 including synonyms) organized in hierarchies via is-a links. Together, there are approximately 1,360,000 semantic links, including is-a and certain associative relationships like CAUSATIVE AGENT (for cause-effect relations), FINDING SITE (for locations) and ASSOCIATED MORPHOLOGY/PROCEDURE MORPHOLOGY. SNOMED-CT includes mappings to ICD-10 and other medical classifications.

---

[189] National Library of Medicine: http://www.nlm.nih.gov/.
[190] Systematized Nomenclature of Medicine-Clinical Terms (SNOMED-CT): http://www.ihtsdo.org/snomed-ct/. It can also be accessed via the VTSL SNOMED CT Core Browser at Virginia-Maryland Regional College of Veterinary Medicine: http://terminology.vetmed.vt.edu/SCT/menu.cfm.
[191] International Health Terminology Standards Development Organisation (IHTSDO): http://www.ihtsdo.org/.

- GALEN Common Reference Model[192] (Rector, Wroe et al., 2001): The GALEN Programme is developing a clinical terminology – the GALEN Common Reference Model – to represent medical concepts. A specific modeling language was developed for this purpose, known as GRAIL, the GALEN Representation And Integration Language.

  The intent of the GALEN team is to provide the GALEN Common Reference Model as a KOS component that can be implemented in various clinical applications. The focus was on designing a re-usable, application-independent and language-independent model of medical concepts. The Drug Ontology developed within the UK NHS Prodigy project has been created on the basis of the standards of the GALEN model.

- Transparent Access to Multiple Biological Information Sources Ontology (TAMBIS Ontology, TaO) (Baker, Goble et al., 1999): TAMBIS was a research project meant to establish a centralized access point for biological information sources around the world. The TAMBIS Ontology was developed as a part of this project in order to mediate between the different sources: a user would formulate search queries with the ontology, and the system would then transfer them to requests appropriate for the single resources. Thus the TaO captures biological and bioinformatics knowledge in a way that is meant to be understandable both by the end users and by machines. It was originally formalized in the GRAIL concept modeling language; translations to DAML+OIL and OWL are now available.

  An interesting point is that TaO does not contain any instances. The TaO contains knowledge about bioinformatics and molecular biology concepts and their relationships: the respective instances they represent reside in the external databases. TaO includes a rich set of specific semantic relationships.

  TaO consists of levels with different degrees of specificity and is available in three releases of different complexity. Parts of TaO are based on knowledge models from the GALEN project.

- MGED Ontology[193] (Stoeckrt & Parkinson, 2003): The MGED Ontology was developed by the Microarray Gene Expression Data society (MGED)[194] to capture information about microarray experiments in a structured way. MGED has a set of guidelines to collect the Minimal Information About a Microarray Experiment (MIAME). The purpose of the ontology is to provide a controlled vocabulary to follow the MIAME guidelines. It includes types of organisms and their structures, for example.

---

[192] OpenGALEN: http://www.opengalen.org.
[193] MGED Ontology: http://mged.sourceforge.net/ontologies/index.php.
[194] Microarray Gene Expression Data society (MGED): http://www.mged.org/.

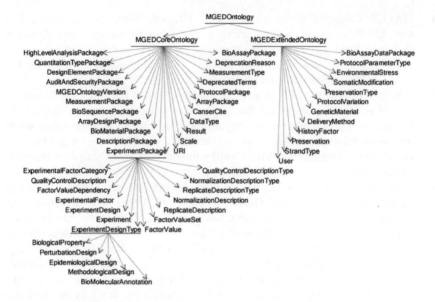

Figure 2.33. Fragment from the MGED Ontology, showing the concept hierarchy for
ExperimentPackage and ExperimentDesignType. Source: Soldatova & King,
2005.

The MGED ontology and its surrounding projects are among the first attempts to formalize the description of experiments in biology. MGED is subdivided into a core ontology and an extended ontology (Figure 2.33). It is
freely available in OWL format. Soldatova and King (2005) have collected
some shortcomings and modeling problems of MGED (e.g. inappropriate
concept names, lack of distinction between classes and individuals and problematic concept definitions), which may be the reason why it has not been
applied more widely.

- National Cancer Institute Ontology[195] (NCI Ontology/NCI Thesaurus)
  (Goldbeck, Fragoso, et al., 2003): The NCI Thesaurus evolved from the NCI
  Metathesaurus, which in turn is based upon UMLS. The NCI Thesaurus thus
  still contains ULMS concordances, as well as mappings to other resources. It
  is produced and maintained by the National Cancer Institute.
  Goldbeck, Fragoso et al. (2003) describe it as a "nomenclature with ontologic
  features". It contains detailed semantic relations among concepts such as
  genes, diseases, drugs and chemicals, anatomy, organisms and proteins. For
  example, diseases are interlinked with anatomical parts via the Dis-
  ease_Has_Associated_Anatomic_Site relation. An OWL version of the

---

[195] NCI Terminologies: http://nciterms.nci.nih.gov.

NCI Thesaurus has been developed in order to bring about new forms of applications.

Ontologies for Industry

In the surroundings of industrial applications, there are different usage scenarios for ontologies. Industry's interest in semantic technologies concerns the fields of (intra-company) knowledge management and content management as well as improvements or standardizations for e-commerce and e-learning technologies (e.g. Davies, Fensel & van Harmelen, 2002; Fensel, 2004).

In the field of knowledge management, ontologies may be applied in order to enable new retrieval functionalities, personalization of services or knowledge visualization, and can support organizational memories or communities of practice (Abecker & van Elst, 2004; Mika, Iosif et al., 2004). They can be used for managing ideas and organizing knowledge, for the management of competencies, for organizing inter-company communication and process optimization (Blumauer & Fundneider, 2006). The semantic desktop (see above) is one vision of how semantic technologies can support daily work.

For e-commerce, ontologies should act as standard models that classify products or services (Ding, Fensel et al., 2004). For this domain, we have already introduced some classifications of products and industries (like NACE and UNSPSC) that have similar aims (Section 1.1.3). We also got to know the eClassOWL as one example of an industrial ontology (Section 1.2.2). Furthermore, ontologies should be applied to e-commerce for corporative product search and intelligent product catalogs (Fensel, 2004).

Gómez-Pérez, Fernández-López and Corcho (2004) further discuss enterprise ontologies as a type of ontology that is "usually created to define and organize relevant knowledge about activities, processes, organizations, strategies, marketing etc."

For industrial settings, the underlying knowledge models are less important than the respective applications. Research focuses on the development of intelligent tools that make use of underlying semantic models. Thus in the following, we will present two early attempts for enterprise ontologies as well as two projects that focus on the integration of semantic technologies in business workflows.

- Toronto Virtual Enterprise[196] (TOVE) ontology project (Fox, 1992): The aim of the TOVE project was to develop a set of integrated ontologies for the modeling of both commercial and public enterprises. The TOVE project has produced two foundational ontologies (Activity and Resource) and four domain-specific ontologies (Organization, Product and Requirements, ISO9000 Quality and Activity-Based Costing).

---

[196] Toronto Virtual Enterprise (TOVE) ontology project: http://www.eil. utoronto.ca/enterprise-modelling/tove/.

- The Enterprise Ontology[197] (Uschold, King et al., 1998): The Enterprise Ontology was developed in the Enterprise Project by the Artificial Intelligence Applications Institute at the University of Edinburgh[198], together with several partners from industry. It comprises terms and definitions relevant to business enterprises, organized under five top-level concepts: Activity, Organization, Strategy, Marketing and Time. It has been built in the Ontolingua format.

- On-To-Knowledge Project[199]: The On-To-Knowledge project's aim was to develop tools and methods for the support of knowledge management. These tools should be based upon shared and reusable knowledge ontologies. Ontologies were used for the purposes of information integration and mediation. Usage scenarios and applications included the organizational memory of a large company, the help desk functionality of a call centre, as well as knowledge management in a virtual enterprise. Among the results of this project were the ontology language OIL (Fensel, Horrocks et al., 2001) and a methodology for ontology engineering.

2.3.2 From Vocabulary to Ontology: Towards an Analytical Description of Knowledge Organization Systems

We have now encountered several ontologies and projects that use ontological models. Some of them cannot easily be told apart from traditional KOS. For example, the Gene Ontology seems to be little more than a scientific thesaurus.

Additionally, it is difficult to distinguish specific types among the several ontologies. So far, we have structured ontologies according to their domain of interest or of application. But this is not the only dimension for subdividing types of ontologies. Which other criteria can and should be used for describing and classifying types of ontologies as well as types of KOS?

As we have seen in Chapter 1, classical knowledge organization systems differ in structure and format. International agreements exist for several standardized knowledge organization systems. But what are the specific features that let us distinguish between different types of KOS?

We have already mentioned the ongoing dissatisfaction of the Semantic Web community concerning missing shared definitions, and have quoted Martin Hepp (2008) who stated that "people from various research communities often use the term ontology with different, partly incompatible meanings in mind". Similarly, there are no exact definitions for the different types of KOS that unambiguously

---

[197] Enterprise Ontology:
http://www.aiai.ed.ac.uk/project/enterprise/enterprise/ontology.html.
[198] Artificial Intelligence Applications Institute, University of Edinburgh:
http://www.aiai.ed.ac.uk/.
[199] On-To-Knowledge: http://www.ontoknowledge.org.

circumscribe their differences. This lack has been pointed out several times, which demonstrates the need for a shared terminology across domains:

"There is a lack of clarity when discussing the following three terms: classifications, taxonomies, and ontologies. A general cause of confusion is caused by a trend [...] to use the most fashionable of the three terms: 'ontology', without further clarifications." (van Rees, 2003)

"The term, ontology, is sometimes used loosely for any knowledge organization system, particularly if it is represented using Semantic Web standards, such as RDF. However as intended for AI modeling and inferencing purposes, ontologies tend to have the most precise and formal definition of relationships of the knowledge systems discussed here." (Tudhope, Koch & Heery, 2006)

Hill, Buchel et al. (2002) have pointed out the need for definitions of KOS types in digital library settings and argue that precise definitions are also a precondition for accessing available KOS and reusing them across applications:

"Collections, KOSs, and services need to work together in DL [author's note: Digital Libraries] architectures. KOSs play a part in collection building, discovery and searching, navigation, evaluation, and visualization. A formal and consistent set of definitions for KOS types, methods for identifying, locating, and referring to individual KOS resources, and protocols for their use will integrate these valuable resources into the overall DL environment. The KOS resources preferred by different communities will be accessible outside of that community for the increasing necessity of cross-domain access to information. The existence of free-standing and accessible KOS resources will counter the tendency to build such systems into particular metadata standards and service protocols." (Hill, Buchel et al., 2002)

There are different explanations for this lack of shared definitions. The most fundamental one is that the community dealing with KOS is very large and heterogeneous, with lots of different backgrounds, perspectives and expectations (on the other hand, this is of course also the strongest argument for why discussions about shared definitions are needed: they can enable cross-discipline communication and collaboration). The second explanation is that the different KOS do not always adhere to strict standards and sometimes mix the peculiarities of several approaches. For example, the principles of classifications and thesauri can be conflated in various ways; in other cases thesauri are transferred to OWL and thus cross the border of formal semantics. Such developments generate new fuzzy types of KOS. The borders between different types of KOS become blurred. Thus the only way to handle this and create a shared set of definitions for KOS types is probably to focus on prototypical exponents for each of them. The whole problem is augmented as various criteria may be used for comparing KOS.

"Descriptions and comparisons of different types of vocabularies are often confusing because the terminology is not controlled and there is also a fair degree of overlap. Furthermore, systems can be compared across different criteria. For example vocabularies differ in structure and levels of complexity but also in the application purposes for which they are designed." (Tudhope, Koch & Heery, 2006)

Of course, several approaches to classifying types of KOS have already been made, e.g. by Hodge (2000a and b), Schwarz (2005), Tudhope, Koch & Heery (2006), Ullrich, Maier & Angele (2003), Uschold and Jasper (1999), Van Rees (2003), Voß (2004 and 2007) and Zheng (2000).

Complexity, Expressivity and Specificity: The Role of Semantic Relations
One basic criterion for distinguishing KOS types is whether they apply vocabulary control or not. Tudhope, Koch and Heery (2006) speak of Terminology Services (TS) instead of KOS; more precisely, they use TS as a generic term for both KOS and folksonomies:

> "Terminology Services (TS) are a set of services that present and apply vocabularies, both controlled and uncontrolled, including their member terms, concepts and relationships. This is done for the purpose of searching, browsing, discovery, translation, mapping, semantic reasoning, subject indexing and classification, harvesting, alerting etc." (Tudhope, Koch & Heery, 2006)

In general, systems that apply vocabulary control are more complex than uncontrolled vocabularies, and the former may again be of varying complexity. The aspect of complexity is most frequently chosen to distinguish KOS, but it is not always applied and defined in the same way and thus does not always lead to the same results.

Tudhope, Koch & Heery (2006) distinguish the following types by "increasing structural complexity and types of relationship:" term lists, taxonomies, subject headings and relationship-based KOS. Zheng (2000) considers different approaches for distinguishing types of KOS, particularly "characteristics such as structure and complexity, the relationships between terms, and historical function". She distinguishes term lists, classification and categorization, and relationship groups. Schwarz (2005) has analyzed the application of KOS in twelve case studies with information retrieval purposes. She distinguishes between taxonomy, thesaurus and ontology based on how precisely they model information: "These 3 types of models differ mainly in their degree of precision. The more precise a model is, the more effort goes into making it, and the more features it offers." This aspect of precision is directly related to the complexity of the available structures in different KOS. Ullrich, Maier and Angele (2003) discuss taxonomies, thesauri, topic maps and ontologies as systems with different degrees of representational power or expressivity – this can also be considered as a different approach to complexity. Based on both complexity and historical function, Hodge (2000a) distinguishes "term lists, which emphasize lists of terms often with definitions; classifications and categories, which emphasize the creation of subject sets; and relationship lists, which emphasize the connections between terms and concepts." Sometimes the specificity of terms (the more specific a concept, the less ambiguous it is) is also counted as a criterion of complexity. Tudhope, Koch and Heery (2006) discuss the notion of specificity and exhaustivity in KOS as follows:

> "While the structure of a classification system and a thesaurus may be fairly similar, in that both consist of hierarchical structures of concepts, they will tend to differ in the *exhaustivity* and *specificity* of their application to information items. Thus an information item will generally tend to be classified by fewer, more general concepts from a classification system and conversely will tend to be indexed by several, more specific concepts from a thesaurus." (Tudhope, Koch & Heery, 2006)

We will take these different approaches as our basis and propose an overview of KOS types based on increasing complexity. Complexity, in our definition, is most fundamentally based on the use of semantic relations as a method of vocabulary control and an expression of meaning. This concerns both the types of relations in use and their specific properties and capabilities. Let us consider the prototypical KOS types we have introduced so far (folksonomies, nomenclatures, classifications, thesauri and ontologies) and their use of semantic relations, respectively.

- Folksonomies do not include any type of paradigmatic relations (and thus provide no control over such as synonyms, homonyms and related terms). Yet one may exploit folksonomies for implicit relations, for example by computing co-occurrences.
- Nomenclatures focus on capturing synonyms for controlling the vocabulary (the relation of equivalence is the most important one in this type of KOS). They may be enriched with unspecified associations. In the case that single hierarchical relations are included, the system is not a clear nomenclature but has started to evolve into a thesaurus.
- Classifications aim at organizing the whole knowledge of a domain of interest (or captured in a database) in a uniform and language-independent way and display it in a proper structure. Classifications are structured mono-hierarchically, without further distinguishing between different types of hierarchies. Synonyms are usually captured by listing them in a class' name.
- Thesauri pay a lot of attention to the relation of equivalence, which results in a collection of synonyms as non-descriptors. Furthermore, thesauri are organized poly-hierarchically. They may distinguish hyponymy and meronymy, and they make use of (entirely undifferentiated) associative relations. In the majority of cases, for every descriptor its relations to other elements of a thesaurus are captured in its term record.
- Ontologies are based on concept hyponymies, and further have the capability to represent other types of specified hierarchies as well as freely defined semantic relations. As we have seen, properties can be semantic relations between concepts and may also be filled with values for one concept. Attributes of relations (e.g. transitivity) can be represented formally.

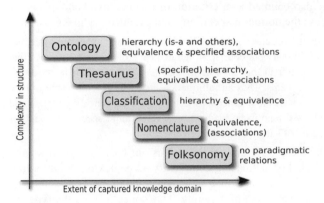

Figure 2.34. KOS types with increasing complexity measured by available semantic relations. Source: Modified from Weller, 2007.

Let us remember the introduction of different KOS in Chapter 1; we have already stated that there is an increasing structural complexity from folksonomies to ontologies. The original illustration in Figure 1.2 may now be enriched with information about semantic relations that make up for the complexity (Figure 2.34). Again, we want to point out that fine-grained relation-modeling will only be possible for limited domains of interest (in exceptional cases also for universal domains if the representation is not very deep). The ontologies we got to know in the previous sections were either designed for specific narrow domains or, in the case of upper ontologies, for broad universal domains with little depth.

The possibility of using self-defined knowledge relations that specify the general relationship types is one major characteristic of ontologies. Yet this is mainly a matter of standards. Technically, a thesaurus might also use more specific types of relation; but, as we have seen, the use of relations in standardized classifications and thesauri are regulated by national as well as international norms. This ensures the interoperability of different KOS. A comparable standard would be desirable for ontologies on the Social Semantic Web. It would also be of advantage to maintain several standards for the different KOS types with increasing structural complexity. This would support the mediation between different models and facilitate *semantic enrichment* (which will be discussed in more detail in Section 3.3).

On the other hand, the structural complexity of KOS types like thesauri may also be enhanced by means of their application environments. Wielinga, Schreiber et al. (2001) point out that the field structure of an advanced retrieval system combined with a thesaurus will also generate novel concept-value pairs. Consider a database of pieces of art, located in different museums: one search field may be 'location'. Documents in that database will thus also contain an index field 'location', filled with geographical names from the respective thesaurus. This can be interpreted as a semantic relation between the document (a particular piece of art) and its location. Furthermore, some thesauri work with qualifiers, or auxiliary descriptors, which can be used in combination with a certain set of given descriptors. The Medical Subject Headings (MeSH) contains 83 qualifiers that can be used in conjunction with certain descriptors. For example, indexing a document with *liver/drug effects* (where *liver* is a MeSH descriptor and *drug effects* a qualifier) indicates that the document in question is not about the liver in general, but about the effect of drugs on the liver. Such allowable qualifiers are thus a kind of pre-stage to ontologies' specified concept properties.

Another aspect of semantic relations in ontologies is indeed a novel technical innovation: relations in ontologies can be formally defined (e.g. as being functional or transitive), and they can be used to construct formal concept definitions. This is enabled by the use of formal representation languages, which in turn allows for reasoning and inferencing.

The complexity of ontologies is thus to a large degree based upon types and attributes of semantic relations. But other aspects are also involved in the notion of complexity or expressivity, e.g. the clear differentiation of individuals (as instances) from general concepts. This is another feature unique to ontologies, not found in traditional KOS[200].

To summarize, ontologies differ from traditional KOS in the following ways (modified from Stock & Stock, 2008):

- They are machine-readable (make use of representation languages), which also enables automatic reasoning over their content. Certain types of implicit information may be inferred.
- Various types of semantic relations (properties) can be freely defined.
- Datatype properties may also link values to concepts.
- Properties may be specified by additional attributes, like transitivity or reflexivity.
- Individual concepts can be formally distinguished from general concepts (via instances).
- Ontologies can be designed for purposes other than pure document indexing (as will be discussed below).

We want to propose these aspects as key differences for distinguishing ontologies from other KOS and thus consider as prototypical ontologies those KOS which make use of all these possibilities.

Existing ontology editors and ontology languages can be easily used for designing simple as well as complex knowledge organization systems. Yet ontology editors do not support the output of standardized thesaurus formats (with descriptors and term lists) or classifications (with notations).

On the other hand, the fact that a KOS has been developed with a certain editor in a certain ontology language does not guarantee that it will achieve the complexity

---

[200] Although traditional KOS, like thesauri, may well be transferred to ontology languages, as will be discussed below.

of a prototypical ontology (as just defined). They constitute the counterpart for controlled vocabularies with semantic structures.

Supportive Resources for Knowledge Organization and Indexing
So far, we have focused on the most common types of knowledge organization systems – and left some other approaches which support them unattended. We will now provide a structured list of terminology services, including some further approaches from different fields, with short explanations. In particular, this collection is based upon the approaches of Hodge (2000a and b), Tudhope, Koch & Heery (2006) and Ullrich, Maier and Angele (2003).

At the highest level one typically distinguishes uncontrolled terminologies from controlled terminologies; Christiaens (2006) opposes free and restricted metadata mechanisms. We will slightly modify this distinction and group uncontrolled and weakly controlled vocabularies together with encyclopaedic resources and approaches for categorization.

A Uncontrolled and Weakly Controlled Vocabularies, Linguistic and
Encyclopaedic Resources
Uncontrolled terminologies cannot actually be counted as knowledge organization systems, as they do not work with elaborated concept structures indicated by semantic relations. Yet in some contexts, they can perform similar tasks to KOS, or they can be applied in combination with KOS. They may further be valuable resources that can be used as starting points for building a new ontology – and are thus important in any discussion on reuse as a part of ontology engineering (see Sections 3.3 and 3.4).

A.1 Term Lists: Linguistic and Encyclopaedic Resources
Hodge (2000a) and Tudhope, Koch and Heery (2006) list several types of term lists that play a role in information systems – although these are not directly used for content-descriptive indexing. Term lists are often linguistic resources and applied on tools for linguistic processing within information systems. If they include extensive definitions, they can be considered as encyclopedic resources.
- Authority files: Authority files (also called name authority files, name authorities, named entity list) control variants of named items, such as personal, organizational or place names, typically in alphabetical order[201]. They are often needed to unify the use of names for formal metadata.
- Gazetteers: A gazetteer is a list of place names and may include coordinate information on locations.
- Glossaries: A glossary is a list of terms for a domain of interest with accompanying definitions.

---

[201] For example, the Library of Congress Name Authority File (LCNAF). For more examples see Tudhope, Koch & Heery (2006), p 30 ff.

- Dictionaries: A dictionary is typically more general than a glossary. It contains different senses of a word meaning and may also include information on word origins.
- Encyclopaedia: An encyclopaedia is an alphabetical list of terms for a domain of interest or world knowledge with rich definitions and explanations in natural language. It may include cross-references to related terms (*see also*).
- Lexical thesauri: In some contexts, a thesaurus simply denotes a collection of synonyms. Probably the most well-known lexical thesaurus is the one embedded in the text processing software Microsoft Word. In other cases, one also speaks of synonym rings (as a term list consisting of synonymous expressions for every term). Such collections of synonyms can be used to support free text search engines. They are only weakly controlled vocabularies, as there are no preferred terms for a set of synonyms.

A.2 Social Indexing

- Folksonomies: The folksonomy is the embodiment of social indexing principles. Although they do not include any vocabulary control, folksonomies exploit the social dimensions of indexing (the links between indexer/user, resource and keyword) in such an effective way that various new options for browsing and searching can be applied.
- Authors' index terms: Freely chosen keywords that are assigned to publications by their respective authors are also a 'lightweight' form of social indexing. Author keywords are not as comprehensively exploited and visualized as folksonomies. Closely related to author keywords are the title tags of a website.

A.3 Categories and Headings

We will, finally, include simple categories and headings in this collection of unstructured and weakly structured resources. In particular, we are thinking of field structures that are used to easily group related contents. Categories can mostly be found in various online resources, e.g. database field schemata, folder structures, navigation bars and search forms. Typically, simple categories and headings consist of small sets which have very shallow hierarchies (or none at all) and are not interrelated.

- Search fields. Field structures of search engines in databases can be counted as simple categories.
- Subject categories. Subject categories can mean every list of grouped documents. Categories can also be a part of wikis. An elaborated list of categories can, for example, be found in Wikipedia.

B Controlled Vocabularies and Semantic Networks

This section covers the approaches which we have already introduced as KOS, as well as single additional methods.

B.1 Synonymy-based Controlled Vocabularies

- Nomenclatures: As we have discussed above, nomenclatures primarily focus on capturing different synonymous expressions. But the vocabulary in a nomenclature may be interlinked via additional associative relations and even single hierarchies. Nomenclatures thus mark our border from miscellaneous terminology services to elaborated KOS.

B.2 Hierarchy-based Controlled Vocabularies

- Taxonomies: A taxonomy can be regarded as a simpler form of classification scheme. The term taxonomy is used with different meanings in different communities, as Tudhope, Koch and Heery (2006) point out: "Taxonomy is a particularly loose term, with a wide usage even within terminology circles, varying from relatively simple menu systems to complex corporate knowledge bases. Taxonomy is associated within (at least) three different communities: scientific taxonomic systems, website designers, corporate taxonomies." We may add natural sciences, where taxonomy is the classification of plants and animals according to their presumed natural relationships. Taxonomy as a form of controlled vocabulary is exclusively dependent on hyponymy. Sometimes the term taxonomy is also used to denote the hierarchical part of another KOS, e.g. the hierarchical section of an ontology.
- Classification Schemes: The hierarchies in classifications are usually more complex and well-defined than in taxonomies. As we have discussed, classification systems fundamentally rely on hierarchical structures, but also contain synonyms.

B.3 Faceted Knowledge Organization Systems
The principle of faceted knowledge organization can be applied to different types of KOS, although faceted classifications are the most common form. Tudhope, Koch & Heery sum up the basic features of faceted approaches:

> "Faceted systems apply facet analysis to the process of synthesizing complex descriptions from atomic elements. The term, facet, is used in different ways which gives rise to some confusion. In this context, it normally refers to a set of fundamental categories (as appropriate to an application domain) and their combination according to rules. Each fundamental category might itself be a class hierarchy. Most commonly the different facet dimensions are mutually exclusive. Single concepts from different facets are combined together when indexing an object – or forming a query. Often this is a simpler and more logical organization than attempting to form a single hierarchy that encompasses all different possible combinations of (e.g.) objects and materials and agents." (Tudhope, Koch & Heery, 2006)

- Faceted Classification Schemes. Faceted classifications are the classical examples of faceted KOS. We have already discussed their characteristics above.

- Faceted Thesauri. One example of a faceted thesaurus is the Getty Art and Architecture Thesaurus (AAT)[202].

- Qualifiers and Subject Headings: Qualifiers (sometimes also called subject headings) are controlled keyword lists with broad coverage and shallow hierarchies. Tudhope, Koch and Heery (2006) explain: "They usually allow for 'coordinated', composite headings, formed by combining single subject terms according to rules. These rules may be more restrictive than a faceted classification." Similar to facets, qualifiers and subject headings are a design principle that can be applied to a knowledge organization system. They are typically used to extend the expressivity of thesauri. The Library of Congress Subject Headings (LCSH) and Medical Subject Headings (MeSH) are popular examples of thesauri that make use of qualifiers. The main headings can be combined with a set of qualifiers. Subject headings are a more elaborated form of categories.

B.4 Relationship-based Controlled Vocabularies or Semantic Networks

- Thesauri: In thesauri, all three types of applied semantic relations are of functional importance, even though hierarchies can be considered as the backbone structure. We have therefore decided to list thesauri among the relationship-based (and not hierarchy-based) controlled vocabularies.

- Lexical reference systems/linguistic databases: Some linguistic terminology services go beyond pure term lists and embed every term into a complex network of semantic relationships. The most popular example is WordNet (see above).

- Topic maps (Garshol, 2004; Pepper, 2002): Topic maps are sometimes discussed as a type of KOS but more frequently as an effective technology for handling rich semantic KOS in a standardized way (particularly ontologies). The International Standard Organization has proposed the ISO/IEC 13250 topic maps standard (ISO 13250:2003). The ISO/IEC provides the following short definition:

  > "Topic Maps is a technology for encoding knowledge and connecting this encoded knowledge to relevant information resources. Topic maps are organized around topics, which represent subjects of discourse; associations, representing relationships between the subjects; and occurrences, which connect the subjects to pertinent information resources." (Garshol, Moore & JTC1/SC43, 2008)

  Garshol (2002) explains the semantic structure of topic maps as "[…] several overlapping hierarchies which are rich with semantic cross-links like 'Part X is critical to procedure V'."

---

[202] Getty Art and Architecture Thesaurus (AAT):
http://www.getty.edu/research/conducting_research/vocabularies/aat/.

- Ontologies: Finally, we again end up with ontologies as the most elaborated type of KOS, combining class hierarchies with complex formal concept properties and instances.

Other Dimensions to Comparing KOS
Apart from different approaches to measuring complexity, some other criteria can be applied to KOS. The most frequently used dimensions are domain of interest (as applied above), size, formality, usage and general modeling principles.

Size
The size of a KOS can be measured by the number of concepts, the number of relations or the levels in the hierarchy. Ideally, these aspects would be combined to compare KOS. In ontologies, one sometimes also counts the number of formal axioms or included facts.

Formality
The degree of formality is sometimes rated 'informal', 'lightweight' and 'heavyweight'. Uschold and Jasper (1999) distinguish between 'highly informal', 'structured-informal', 'semi-formal' and 'rigorously formal'. They explain 'highly informal' as "expressed loosely in natural language, e.g. many glossaries fit into this category." Structured-informal KOS are "expressed in a restricted and structured form of natural language, greatly increasing clarity by reducing ambiguity, e.g. the text version of the 'Enterprise Ontology' [...]." A semi-formal KOS is "expressed in an artificial, formally defined language, e.g. the Ontolingua version of the Enterprise Ontology". And finally, those KOS can be judged rigorously formal which make use of "meticulously defined terms with formal semantics, theorems and proofs of such properties as soundness and completeness, e.g. TOVE" (Uschold & Jasper, 1999).

We want to adopt this approach with slight modifications and introduce a fifth level: Those KOS that make use of a formally defined ontology language should be rated as 'formal'. Meanwhile, semi-formal KOS are those that make use of standardized structuring principles (mainly semantic relations) without applying a formal language, e.g. classifications and thesauri.

For inter-personal communication, KOS may well be informal. Human-computer interactions require at least semi-formal models. And computer-computer communication calls for formal models.

As we have seen, formal and informal semantics can (and should) be combined in ontologies. While informal definitions can be provided, e.g. via `rdfs:comment`, relations combined with restrictions generate formal definitions. Similarly, thesauri include informal definitions in scope notes, while the interrelation of concepts constitutes the semi-formal definitions.

General Modeling Principles
One may also discuss certain modeling principles (or whether they are supported or not) to compare KOS types. Yet this comparison is more sensible on the level

of comparing actual examples of certain KOS, as their presence or absence is not explicitly defined for most types of KOS[203]. These aspects focus on the contrasting principles of mono- vs. polyhierarchy, mono- vs. multidimensionality and pre-combination vs. post-coordination[204].

Purpose and Usage

Most traditional KOS are almost exclusively designed for indexing and retrieval purposes. They enable us to describe documents with unified vocabularies, support query formulation and reformulation (e.g. query expansion) or the navigating and browsing through document collections (e.g. in case of the Yahoo! Web directory). And – often as a side-effect – they help us to gain an overview of a domain of interest in that they provide a structured visualization.

Schwarz (2005) has analyzed several use cases of different KOS types. She found some examples where thesauri were combined with classifications (taxonomies) because each of them supports different functions: "In these cases the role of the thesaurus is to manage the vocabulary, the role of the taxonomy is to structure the domain."

One may also discuss different sub-purposes which all support the task of information retrieval:

> "Information retrieval KOS are intended primarily to assist retrieval of resources, originally from bibliographic databases and library catalogues and now from Digital Libraries and the Web. [...] These include classification and indexing, search (including browsing, query and various forms of 'intelligent' searching), mapping between KOS (mono and multi-lingual), providing a framework for learning a subject domain or exploring it in order to refine a (re)search question (defining concepts and setting them in context). A KOS might be used both for classification/indexing and searching, or just searching." (Tudhope, Koch & Heery, 2006)

Other than this, we got to know classical KOS which mainly aim at a standardized encoding of information in order to facilitate an exchange of documents or to gather statistical data, e.g. many of the health care and industrial classifications discussed above.

Some other KOS are mainly built for linguistic purposes, e.g. as resources for various natural language text processing techniques (automatic or intellectual), like machine-assisted translation, language engineering (named entity recognition or extraction, text mining, summarization). These usage scenarios are not typical

---

[203] Although there may be certain conventions; for example, thesauri may well be mono- or polyhierarchic, whereas classification systems are expected to use pure monohierarchies.

[204] Pre-combination is the principle of combining single meaningful concept units rigidly within the KOS. In contrast, post-coordination means that components of concepts are kept individually within the KOS and are only combined if needed during searching. Additionally, in pre-coordination the composition of single concept units is done during indexing (Stock & Stock, 2008).

for classical standard KOS. The research community in question more likely produces its own vocabulary structures, often referred to as 'terminologies' (Tudhope, Koch & Heery, 2006). As we have just seen, different ontology projects also have language-related purposes.

As discussed in Chapter 1, we may also distinguish between the usage of classical KOS according to the different application fields which make use of them, like library catalogues, health care organizations, museums and media archives (Section 1.1.3). With the advent of the Social Semantic Web, applications for eLearning and eScience are also turning into important application areas.

We may also consider the documents which are to be indexed (and/or retrieved) with the help of a certain KOS. They are closely coupled to the application scenario and – as we have already seen – cover a range from broken bones to works of art.

Folksonomies and ontologies as novel approaches in knowledge representation differ from classical KOS both in their typical purposes and in the documents they are associated with. They were primarily invented for indexing digital objects on the Web and to facilitate better retrieval and navigation in WWW applications. Tudhope, Koch and Heery (2006) point out that "[...] social tagging is predominantly associated with publications outside traditional channels such as pictures, music, blogs and news." In many social software applications that make use of folksonomies, we may further consider the users themselves as some special kind of document. Folksonomies are used for indexing purposes, but they address this issue very differently and rather playfully – as already indicated by the lack of vocabulary control. Folksonomy tags can serve various purposes besides classical content indexing, e.g. annotation with bibliographical or other formal metadata (e.g. the camera that was used to shoot a certain photo), personal information management and task organization (e.g. *toread* as a tag for a document), and communication (e.g. *for_peter*).

Ontologies by Purpose

Ontologies do not exclusively have to be created for indexing purposes (at least not in the strict sense of indexing), although some of them are used exactly like that. In most other cases, indexing has to be interpreted in a different way; this is the case if ontologies are mainly created as knowledge bases to which include facts about a domain of interest. In these cases, the main purpose is to represent these facts in a straightforward way. Furthermore, the Semantic Web has also largely broadened the scope of what a document on the Web can be, as also pointed out by Schwartz (2005): "The Semantic Web extends the information that is searchable from digital resources to real world objects. All resources, both digital files and real world objects, are referred to with unique IDs." Thus URIs are often the documents to be indexed by ontologies, and they can again represent various types of objects.

Guha, McCool and Miller (2003) describe two typical pieces of the WWW and identify the respective Semantic Web documents within them: an auction of a music album by Yo-Yo Ma, and information about the scientific author Eric Miller (Figure 2.35):

> "The Semantic Web is not a Web of documents, but a Web of relations between resources denoting real world objects, i.e., objects such as people, places and events. In the first example we have objects such as the city of Paris, the musician Yo-Yo Ma, an auction event, the music album Appalachian Journey, etc. In the second example, we have the person Eric Miller, the W3C Semantic Web Activity, the organization W3C, the city of Dublin, Ohio, etc." (Guha, McCool & Miller, 2003)

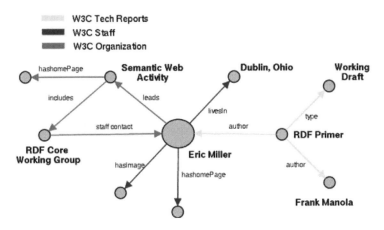

Figure 2.35. A segment of the semantic Web for the 'document' Eric Miller and its relations to other documents. Source: Guha, McCool & Miller, 2003.

Several other potential purposes of ontologies have been discussed in the literature: Stevens, Wroe et al. (2004) distinguish between annotation (as in the case of the Gene Ontology), query formulation (TAMBIS), schema definition and service discovery (referring to the myGrid Service Ontology). Chandrasekaran, Josephson and Benjamins (1999) name three main purposes: ontology as vocabulary, ontology as content theory, and ontologies for natural language understanding. Uschold and Jasper (1999) sum up the different purposes of ontologies as follows:

> "Fundamentally, ontologies are used to improve communication between either humans or computers. Broadly, these may be grouped into the following three areas: to assist in communication between human agents, to achieve interoperability, or to improve the process and/or quality of engineering software systems." (Uschold & Jasper, 1999)

Grüninger and Lee (2002) summariz three fundamental purposes of ontologies: A) ontologies may be used for communication (between implemented computational systems / between humans / between humans and implemented computational systems); B) ontologies can be used for computational inference (e.g. for analyzing the internal structures, algorithms, inputs and outputs of implemented systems in theoretical and conceptual terms); and C) they can be a means for reuse (and organization) of knowledge (e.g. for structuring or organizing libraries or repositories of plans, for planning and domain information).

Ontologies are used as background knowledge in information extraction technologies. They can also act as models for metadata fields: If ontologies are used to model the top level of a domain, "they are comparable to conceptual database models which also serve to model the elements and relationships of a domain on a high level" (Schwarz, 2005). They may be used for database schema integration.

In other cases, ontologies are proposed for capturing currently accepted (scientific) knowledge or for structured analysis of data and even for the detection of new pieces of information (through reasoning). In AI research, ontologies are desired as a support for knowledge-based problem solving, at least in limited application areas. Applications that can make use of ontologies can be found in the field of knowledge management business tools, as well as for e-science and virtual knowledge networks.

And yet, despite these various differentiations, the support for finding the right information is the main purpose of ontologies in a Semantic Web scenario (though one speaks of search rather than of retrieval). Ontology-mediated *Semantic Search* has itself become a research field with various ongoing activities (Guha, McCool & Miller, 2003).

As already noted above, we may also distinguish ontologies by their domain of interest (e.g. life science) – and may even fundamentally discriminate between domain ontologies and universal (or top-level) ontologies. Just like with all KOS, there are again some further dimensions which make up the character of one particular ontology.

Other Dimensions to Distinguishing Ontology Types and to Describing an Ontology

Uschold and Grüninger (1996) were among the first to compare a set of ontologies. They used the following principles for comparison: formality (from highly formal to rigorously formal), purpose (what the ontology is used for), and subject matter (the nature of the domain that the ontology is characterizing). Noy and Hafner (1997) have analyzed ten ontologies with the final aim creating a framework for comparing ontology projects; they created a sort of little portrait for every ontology, comprising the following aspects:

> "The comparison framework includes general characteristics, such as the purpose of an ontology, its coverage (general or domain specific), its size, and the formalism used. It also includes the design process used in creating an ontology and the methods used to evaluate it. Characteristics that describe the content of an ontology include taxonomic organization, types of concepts covered, top-level divisions, internal structure of concepts, representation of part-whole relations, and the presence and nature of additional

axioms. Finally we consider what experiments or applications have used the ontologies." (Noy & Hafner, 1997)

They further describe their structural analysis of the set of ontologies as follows:

"In comparing the content of ontologies, we discuss three different levels: (1) an is-a taxonomy of concepts, (2) the internal concept structure and relations between concepts, and (3) the presence or absence of explicit axioms. Taxonomy is the center part of most ontologies. Taxonomy organization can vary greatly: All concepts can be in one large taxonomy, or there can be a number of smaller hierarchies, or there can be no explicit taxonomy at all. [...] In taxonomy, we compare top-level categories of the ontologies. The next level of comparison is internal concept structure [...]. Internal structure can be realized by properties and roles. Concepts in some ontologies are atomic and might not have any properties or roles or any other internal structure associated with them. [...] We specifically study the treatment of part-whole relations in these ontologies. The third level in the comparison is the presence or absence or explicit axioms and the associated inference mechanisms (if any). We consider what the ontologies' use of formal axioms is and whether they go beyond first order-logic." (Noy & Hafner, 1997)

In their comparison of upper ontologies, Mascardi, Cordi and Rosso (2007) apply the following features (which can also be used for characterizing domain ontologies): dimension (i.e. size), implementation language(s), modularity (i.e. whether the ontology consists of separate building blocks), developed applications that use the ontology, available alignments to other knowledge models (in this case, they only looked for alignments with WordNet), and information about licensing (e.g., is it freely available and reusable). Further information collected for every ontology was a supportive homepage, the name of the (group of) developers and some information about its history.

From One Ontology to Many Ontologies

Having now discussed the question 'What is an *ontology*?' in quite some detail, there still remains another essential question: What is *one* ontology? There does not yet exist one perfect answer to this question; therefore, we will now provide a short insight into the different challenges associated with it. Difficulties in identifying a single ontology are particularly coupled to the aspects of versioning, integration and modularization. Can the different versions of an ontology be considered as *one*? If we combine two distant ontologies, what is the result? In which cases can we speak of sub-ontologies as parts of one ontology, and when do we have to consider them as discrete objects?

In a Semantic Web context, the vision of one all-embracing ontology has long been replaced by the development of various, application-specific ontologies acting in concert. The Semantic Web will have to be a network of multiple ontologies. Upper ontologies may be one way of establishing the interlinking of different domain ontologies. Yet for the overall scenario, additional research is needed in order to handle the multiplicity of individual knowledge models – both ontologies and other KOS. Their number even increases if we consider versions and parts of ontologies as independent elements.

Versions
Can we sum up all available versions of one ontology? Or is each version to be considered as a full-fledged ontology? Versions of an ontology occur for several reasons. First of all, there may be different release versions over the course of time. Just as with classical KOS, the development of an ontology cannot be finished at one point. There is always the need for maintaining a KOS after its release, to remove errors, to update certain aspects. By and by, updated and refined versions will have to be released. This is known from classical KOS, where release versions are usually considered as individual models and are somehow labeled for identification.

For example, the ICD classification is now available in its tenth release version, the ICD-10; the current IPC version is the IPC-2009.01. Identifying the release versions is important, because they are typically not upwards-compatible: a new release version does not only contain additional terms but may also have been remodeled and changed in structure. Different release versions of one ontology can thus differ in size and structure. There are usually no changes in terms of usage and purpose or domain of interest. In exceptional cases, there may also be changes in structural complexity, i.e. new forms of semantic relations may be explicitly defined. An example would be a thesaurus that is *semantically enriched* to become an ontology (Section 3.3.3). We therefore encourage the accounting of every release version of a KOS as an individual object.

Another common practice of KOS maintenance poses additional challenges: in thesauri or nomenclatures, there may not be explicit release versions, yet changes are performed constantly. The CAS Registry has approximately 4,000 new keyword entries per day (Stock & Stock, 2008). Such constant changes are usually handled by adding additional information on the 'date of activation' for every new descriptor (and a 'date of expiration' if a keyword is deactivated).

Furthermore, one may have different language versions of an ontology, i.e. the ontology may be translated into different natural languages. This is, again, comparable to language versions in classical KOS (e.g., the ICD-10-GM, the German Modification of the ICD-10). We should distinguish two different cases: a) the translations are directly bound to single elements of a KOS, i.e. every concept, relation and instance has a translation attached to it; and b) there are different language versions which also may have small structural differences (e.g., the Klassifikation der Wirtschaftszweige[205], WZ, is the German version of NACE; yet although it is based upon NACE, it contains one additional hierarchical level and

[205] Klassifikation der Wirstchaftszweige (WZ 2008): http://www.destatis.de/jetspeed/portal/cms/Sites/destatis/Internet/DE/Content/Klassifikationen/GueterWirtschaftklassifikationen/Content75/KlassifikationWZ08,templateId=renderPrint.psml.

thus differs in structure). In the first case, we may speak of one multilingual ontology, while in the second case we should speak of a collection of distinct ontologies.

And finally, ontologies may also be available in different ontology languages. This case is not to be found in classical KOS. As the ontology language is particularly important for the actual character of the ontology, implementations of one model in different ontology languages should be registered as different ontologies.

The different versions of one ontology should be summed up as one *ontology family* – or we may use the terminology of Hartmann, Suarez-Figueroa et al. (2005) and speak of an ontology base realized in different ontology documents.

Integration

For the co-existence of different KOS in the Semantic Web scenario, methods for mediation and interconnection are needed. We will discuss methods of combining ontologies (merging) and mediating between them (mapping) in Section 3.4. For now, it is important to point out that the closer two ontologies are connected, the more difficult is it to decide where one ontology stops and the other one begins. In extreme cases, two formerly distinct ontologies may be completely merged to form one new and inseparable ontology. Furthermore, ontologies (or parts of ontologies) may be reused as starting points for a new ontology project and become totally integrated to this new model.

Modules, Facets and Layers

Finally, an ontology may be explicitly subdivided into single units. Such approaches are also known from classical KOS. The TESE thesaurus, for example, is subdivided into 17 *microthesauri* and 4 additional lists (among them a list of names and auxiliary descriptors which can only be applied in combination with others). Single facets in faceted classifications can also generally be considered as subparts of the whole classification system.

For ontologies, there is not yet a shared terminology in respect of subdivisions and subparts. In case of the Gene Ontology, one speaks of *sub-ontologies*. The SIOC project team uses the term *ontology modules*:

> "SIOC follows a modular design where additional ontology modules can be created for specializing and further extending classes and properties contained within the SIOC Core ontology. Currently there are two modules defined: (1) SIOC Services module and (2) SIOC Types module." (Bojars, Breslin et al., 2008)

This approach already provides an outlook on future research on the Social Semantic Web. Modular ontologies may be designed with the actual objective of recombination and expansion. One may think of single, very specific domain ontologies as modules that are actually designed with the objective of being combined with others. If ontology modules are indeed becoming kinds of "building blocks", to be used and reused for the creation of new ontologies in the form of (re-)combinations, some more research must be done with regard to the identification of modules or the separation of single elements from an ontology. Recently, research in this areas has been begun, e.g. by Stecher, Niederée, Nejdl and Bouquet (2008):

> "The discovery of the 'right' ontology or ontology part is a central ingredient for effective ontology re-use. We present an approach for supporting a form of adaptive re-use of sub-ontologies, where the ontologies are deeply integrated beyond pure referencing." (Stecher, Niederée et al., 2008)

Sometimes it may be difficult to distinguish between a module/facet and the classes on the highest hierarchical level; i.e. some people regard all top level concepts as equivalent to modules. We would like to propose the definition that a module (or facet) has to be a separate, disjoint construct, without overlaps and interconnections with other parts of the ontology. It should be easy to uncouple a module from the rest of the ontology and make it available for reuse.

On the other hand, modules and facets are typically designed for use in combination in order to unfold their full potential. This aspect is even stronger for facets in the traditional sense of KOS, where facets have to be combined in order to obtain adequate index terms. We may thus differentiate between facets as elements of a KOS and modules that can either be parts of one specific ontology, or which can be provided as loose building blocks for various (re-)combinations.

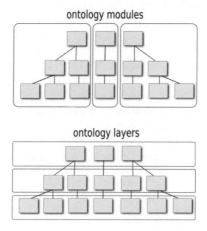

Figure 2.36. Modules and layers.

Another different approach is layered ontologies (Stuckenschmidt & van Harmelen, 2005, Chapter 10), as for example the PROTON ontology with its three layers. While modules and facets split an ontology vertically to separate different topics of interest, layers split an ontology horizontally to divide different levels of specification (Figure 2.36).

2.3.3 Requirements for Ontologies in the Social Semantic Web

We conclude this chapter about ontologies by returning to our initial question: What is the role of ontologies in a Social Semantic Web environment? The aspect of semantics, as demanded by the Social Semantic Web, can surely be covered by ontologies. Ontologies provide the means for a detailed specification of domain knowledge. More than any of the earlier KOS, they can represent complex concept structures and provide formal concept definitions. Using standardized ontology languages makes the domain model computer-readable and processable for new ways of supporting Web navigation, search and visualization.

The emergence of Social Semantic Web structures poses new challenges to the entire area of ontology engineering:

- User commitment: broad user communities should be enabled to contribute to ontologies. For this purpose, new tools are needed for ontology engineering (as will be discussed in more detail in the upcoming chapter), as well as guidelines that allow novices to enter the field of ontology engineering, and standards that support the unification of contributions of non-experts.
- Reuse: as far as possible, existing KOS should be reused as starting points for new ontologies. To make this possible, easy access to existing knowledge models will be required. Existing ontologies must be collected and classified according to various characteristics such as domain, purpose, size, complexity, availability and modularity.
- Mediation and Interaction: user contributions on a large scale will result in a multitude of novel ontologies. Solutions have to be found for how computer systems can mediate between this variety of single KOS. A sizeable research community is already concerned with developing methods and tools for merging and mapping ontologies. So far, there has been almost no research on how user communities may enter this process as well.

With the emergence of social dimensions in Semantic Web research, the definition of what an ontology is will have to be discussed even more than before; novel dimensions have to be added to the definition of ontologies on the Social Semantic Web. We therefore want to state some fundamental differences in discussing a) Ontology with a philosophical focus, b) ontologies as formal knowledge representation, c) Semantic Web ontologies, and d) Social Semantic Web ontologies. All these areas will need their own definition of 'ontology'.

a) Ontology in philosophy is a field concerned with the nature of existence, aiming to derive appropriate categories for All That Is. The focus is on discussing and establishing one general world knowledge model.

b) Formal knowledge representation – as an interdisciplinary research field on the intersection of computer science and AI, psychology, philosophy and (computational) linguistics – has adopted ontologies as a problem of applied philosophy. The focus in this area is on understanding the fundamentals of semantic structures and on developing formal mechanisms that can capture them effectively (thus the focus is primarily on theoretical considerations and on formal models that can capture them, and less on practical implementations and usage scenarios).

c) In the classical Semantic Web context, ontologies are all kinds of knowledge models that can improve indexing and search mechanisms, provide shared vocabularies or metadata schemes. The focus is on machine-readability, on reasoning over structured data and on the implementation in smart applications (thus the focus is on the technical aspects of ontology engineering and application at first).

d) And finally, in the Social Semantic Web, we define ontologies as the most complex form of available KOS to have to interact with various other knowledge resources (particularly with classical KOS and folksonomies). Main foci are social contributions to achieving large-scale coverage, reuse and integration, and mediation between different approaches. Ontologies, in this sense of a Social Semantic Web, differ from classical knowledge organization systems in information science in the following aspects: they are typically applied in a formal ontology language that enables reasoning and inferencing, they formally distinguish instances and general concepts, they support the construction of various self-defined and formalized concept properties (including datatype properties) and provide the means for formal concept definitions. Thus concept properties as the realization of semantic relations become a key feature of ontologies – and are also the key to semantics on the Social Semantic Web.

The Role of Semantic Relations in the Social Semantic Web
Khoo and Na (2006) not only provide a very detailed overview of the different semantic relations used in information science, but also on their usefulness for different application scenarios. They highlight the fundamental importance of semantic relations for information systems, particularly for use in information retrieval, query expansion and natural language processing.

> "Research and development in information science have focused on concepts and terms, but the focus will increasingly shift to the identification, processing, and management of relations to achieve greater effectiveness and refinement in information science techniques." (Khoo & Na, 2006)

Semantic relations not only play an important role in retrieval systems (e.g. to enable the automatic inclusion of sub-concepts or synonyms if a search does not retrieve enough documents), they are also an important aspect in document indexing – which again can lead to better retrieval or better judgments about a documents relevance. Currently, the situation in indexing usually appears to be as described by Khoo and Na (2006):

> "The index terms are generally not precoordinated, in other words, the index terms are assigned as separate terms and there is no indication whether two or more concepts are related in a particularly way in the document. For example, if a document is assigned the terms *information retrieval, user interface*, and *evaluation*, there is no indication whether evaluation is related to information retrieval or to user interface. [...] In some indexing languages, the index terms are precoordinated, in other words, the human in-

dexer indicates an association between two ore more concepts in the document by using the syntax of the language and placing the terms in a particular order. However, the type of association is not specified but is implied by the context." (Khoo & Na, 2006)

Some projects already develop systems where index terms for a document can be applied with semantic relations between them in order to more precisely describe the document's content. Examples can be found mainly in the field of image search (e.g. Hollink, Schreiber et al., 2003; Schreiber, Dubbeldam et al., 2001), where some approaches also involve the system's users, e.g. ImageNotion (Walter & Nagypal, 2007) and IKen (Mainz, Weller & Mainz, 2008).

For the dimension of activating semantics on the Social Semantic Web, fine-grained relations thus play an important role. While the modeling of concepts (and instances) is initially a matter of unifying a vocabulary, relations between concepts are fundamental for representing shared meanings. They are generally of importance for meaning-based navigation in a network of Web links, for example in the context of links between Wikipedia articles.

The inclusion of social activities on the Web affects the topic of semantic relations in two ways: On the one hand, we have to ask how users can learn to apply semantic relations in an effective and useful way. On the other hand, research on the foundations of semantic relations can profit from user activities. Typical Web 2.0 users already produce diverse data which implicitly include semantic information, most notably tags in folksonomy-based systems which can be exploited by means of co-occurrence analysis. In the upcoming chapters, we will examine both how non-expert users can contribute to complex KOS and how simple user activities can be mined for new input.

Finally, knowledge about semantic relations is of high relevance for the Social Semantic Web, as it is needed to provide better mediation between KOS of different complexity. Only if the structural differences are understood, can semantic enrichment based on more detailed semantic relations become possible.

Conclusion

We have now got to know the most important elements of ontologies (concepts, instances, properties and relations) and seen how they form the structure of an ontology, or how they can be used for representing knowledge in general. We have pointed out how formalized semantics help ontologies gaining rich expressivity. We have done this partly on an abstracted level, without focusing on the capabilities of single ontology languages and, in part, exemplarily for some specific capabilities of the language OWL or the ontology editor Protégé. Thus some problems encountered so far are due to the realization of OWL in Protégé, some are intrinsic to OWL – and thus some aspects may not be of importance in other ontology languages and editors. Yet it was never the aim of this book to compare the characteristics of single ontology languages and we may thus point to the detailed literature from roughly 20 years of research in this field for details on these aspects. Our attempt was to highlight the novel features of ontologies in comparison with other KOS and to at least indicate the complexity of possibilities in knowledge representation.

Another aim was to sensitize a growing community (in the sense of a Social Semantic Web) to the difficulties and challenges of knowledge representation with ontologies. Therefore, some design principles or basic considerations of conceptual modeling were introduced.

Based on all this, we have formulated a definition of "ontology" which fits our background of information science and which is useful for the context of knowledge organization systems and document indexing in the Social Semantic Web. In addition to the first chapter, some new types of KOS were considered and some more examples of existing ontologies were briefly touched on.

We have pointed out that understanding the nature of semantic relations is an important aspect of ontology design: the richness of semantic relations constitutes a major dimension for differentiating types of KOS. On a conceptual (non-technical) level, specified semantic relations are the turning point from traditional KOS to rich semantics for the Web and to formal ontologies. Properties in ontologies offer a broad range of modeling choices and are closely related to formal axiomatization (as they help us formally define concepts and can in turn be specified by respective attributes).

Thus the fine-grained properties of ontologies are the essence of conceptual ontology engineering. A basic understanding of the nature of semantic relations is important for creating semantic representations. A list of standard types of semantic relations would thus be useful in different ways: It could help novices to learn ontology engineering. Furthermore, it can provide a unified basis for ontology mediation (e.g. mapping). Generally, semantic relations are of major importance for a Semantic Web based on meanings.

Some research questions arose during this chapter which will have to be discussed in more detail and should be solved further down in the future. In particular, there are no precise user studies on how users learn to model ontologies or how they may be guided in formalizing semantic relations and restrictions. Respective research questions could be: How long does it take users to distinguish between hyponymy and meronymy? How can we help them do this faster? A methodology that helps users to use properties appropriately is needed, together with tools that make use of this methodology. Although some research has been executed in the field of relational structures, a lot more work is needed in order to generate standards for the use of semantic relations in Web ontologies, e.g. standardized expressions for the most frequent types of relations.

Altogether, this chapter has shown us how *semantics* may look in a Social Semantic Web. The next chapters will have to address the questions of how *social* technologies can support the creation and application of these kinds of semantics in the WWW. In Chapter 3, we will discuss the principles of ontology engineering, which will now have to be placed into the context of the Social Semantic Web.

References

Abecker, A., & van Elst, L. (2004). Ontologies for Knowledge Management. In S. Staab & R. Studer (Eds.), Handbook on Ontologies (pp. 435–454). Berlin, Heidelberg, New York: Springer.

Aitchison, J., Gilchrist, A., & Bawden, D. (2000). Thesaurus Construction and Use (4th Edition). London: Aslib.

Altman, R., Bada, M., Chai, X. J., Whirl Carillo, M., Chen, R. O., & Abernethy, N. F. (1999). RiboWeb: An Ontology-Based System for Collaborative Molecular Biology. IEEE Intelligent Systems, 14(5), 68–76.

Artale, A., Franconi, E., & Guarino, N. (1996). Open Problems with Part-Whole Relations. In L. Padgham; E. Franconi; M. Gehrke; D. L. McGuinness, & P. F. Patel-Schneider (Eds.), Proceedings of the 1996 International Workshop on Description Logics, Cambridge, MA, USA (pp. 70–73). Cambridge: AAAI Press.

Artale, A., Franconi, E., Guarino, N., & Pazzi, L. (1996). Part-Whole Relations in Object-Centered Systems: An Overview. Data & Knowledge Engineering, 20(3), 347–383.

Ashburner, M., Ball, C. A., Blake, J. A., Botstein, D., Butler, H., & Cherry, J. M., et al. (2000). Gene Ontology: Tool for the Unification of Biology. Nature Genetics, 25, 25–29.

Baker, P.G., Goble, C.A., Bechhofer, S., Paton, N.W., Stevens, R., Brass, A. (1999). An Ontology for Bioinformatics Applications. Bioinformatics, 15(6), 510–520.

Barsalou, L. W. (1992). Frames, Concepts, and Conceptual Fields. In A. Lehrer & E. F. Kittay (Eds.), Frames, Fields and Contrasts: New Essays in Semantic and Lexical Organization (pp. 21–74). Hillsdale: Lawrence Erlbaum Associates.

Bateman, J., Magnini, B., & Rinaldi, F. (1995). The Generalized Upper Model Knowledge Base: Organization and Use. In N. Mars (Ed.), Towards Very Large Knowledge Bases: Knowledge Building & Knowledge Sharing. Proceedings of the International Conference on Building and Sharing Very Large-Scale Knowledge Bases (pp. 60–72). IOS Press.

Batley, S. (2005). Classification in Theory and Practice. Oxford: Chandos.

Bean, C. A., & Green, R. (Eds.) (2001). Relationships in the Organization of Knowledge. Dordrecht: Kluwer.

Bechhofer, S., & Goble, C. (2001). Thesaurus Construction Through Knowledge Representation. Data & Knowledge Engineering, 37(1), 25–45.

Bernauer, J. (1996). Analysis of Part-Whole Relation and Subsumption in the Medical Domain. Data & Knowledge Engineering, 20, 405–415.

Berners-Lee, T., Hendler, J., & Lassila, O. (2001). The Semantic Web. Scientific American, 284(5), 34–43.

Bertram, J. (2005). Einführung in die inhaltliche Erschließung: Grundlagen, Methoden, Instrumente. Content and Communication, Vol. 2. Würzburg: Ergon.

Black, M. (1937). Vagueness: An Exercise in Philosophical Analysis. Philosophy of Science, 4, 427–455.

Blumauer, A., & Fundneider, T. (2006). Semantische Technologien in integrierten Wissensmanagement-Systemen. In T. Pellegrini & A. Blumauer (Eds.), Semantic Web: Wege zur vernetzten Wissensgesellschaft (pp. 227–239). Berlin, Heidelberg: Springer.

Bodenreider, O., & Stevens, R. (2006). Bio-Ontologies: Current Trends and Future Directions. Briefings in Bioinformatics, 7(3), 256–274.

Bojars, U., Breslin, J. G., Finn, A., & Decker, S. (2008). Using the Semantic Web for Linking and Reusing Data Across Web 2.0 Communities. Journal of Web Semantics, 6(1), 21–28.

Borst, W. (1997). Construction of Engineering Ontologies for Knowledge Sharing and Reuse. PhD Thesis, University of Twente, Nederlands. Retrieved from http://doc.utwente.nl/17864/.

Bowker, G. C., & Star, S. L. (2000). Sorting Things Out: Classification and its Consequences. Cambridge: MIT Press.

Brachman, R. (1983). What IS-A Is and Isn't: An Analysis of Taxonomic Links in Semantic Networks. IEEE Computer, 16(10), 30–36.

Brickley, D. (2001). Post on the W3C RDF-Interest Mailing List [Posted: April 20, 2001]. Retrieved from http://lists.w3.org/Archives/Public/www-rdf-interest/2001Apr/0356.html.

Broughton, V. (2002). Faceted Classification as a Basis for Knowledge Organization in a Digital Environment: The Bliss Bibliographic Classification as a Model for Vocabulary Management and the Creation of Multidimensional Knowledge Structures. The New Review of Hypermedia and Multimedia, 7(1), 67–102.

Chandrasekaran, B., Josephson, J. R., & Benjamins, V. (1999). What Are Ontologies, and Why Do We Need Them? IEEE Intelligent Systems, 14(1), 20–26.

Christiaens, S. (2006). Metadata Mechanisms: From Ontology to Folksonomy … and Back. Lecture Notes in Computer Science, 4277, 199-207.

Corcho, O., Fernández-López, M., & Gómez-Pérez, A. (2003). Methodologies, Tools and Languages for Building Ontologies: Where is Their Meeting Point? Data & Knowledge Engineering, 46, 41–64.

Cruse, D. A. (2002). Hyponymy and Its Varieties. In R. Green; C. A. Bean, & S. H. Myaeng (Eds.), The Semantics of Relationships (pp. 3–21). Dordrecht: Kluwer.

Curtis, J., Baxter, D., & Cabral J. (2006). On the Application of the Cyc Ontology to Word Sense Disambiguation. In Sutcliffe, G. C. J. & Goebel, R. G. (Eds.), Proceedings of the Nineteenth International Florida Artificial Intelligence Research Society Conference (FLAIRS 2006) (pp. 652–657). Menlo Park: AAAI Press.

Curtis, J., Matthews, G., & Baxter, D. (2005). On the Effective Use of Cyc in a Question Answering System. In F. Benamara & Moens, Marie-Francine, Saint-Dizier, Patrick (Eds.), Knowledge and Reasoning for Answering Questions

(KRAQ'05): Proceedings of the Workshop associated with IJCAI05, Edinburgh, Scotland (pp. 61–70). Retrieved from http://www.irit.fr/recherches/ILPL/kraq05V1.pdf.

Dahlgren, K. (1988). Naive Semantics for Natural Language Understanding. Boston: Kluwer.

Davies, J., Fensel, D., & van Harmelen, F. (Eds.) (2004). Towards the Semantic Web: Ontology-Driven Knowledge Management. Chichester: Wiley.

Dean, M., & Schreiber, G. (Eds.) (2004). OWL Web Ontology Language Reference: W3C Recommendation February 10, 2004. Retrieved from http://www.w3.org/TR/owl-ref/.

Deaton, C., Shepard, B., Klein, C., Mayans, C., Summers, B., Brusseau, A., Witbrock, M., & Lenat, D. (2005). The Comprehensive Terrorism Knowledge Base in Cyc. In Proceedings of the 2005 International Conference on Intelligence Analysis. Retrieved from https://analysis.mitre.org/proceedings/index.html.

Dextre Clarke, S. G. (2001). Thesaural Relationships. In C. A. Bean & R. Green (Eds.), Relationships in the Organization of Knowledge (pp. 37–52). Dordrecht: Kluwer.

DIN 1463/1:1987. Erstellung und Weiterentwicklung von Thesauri. Einsprachige Thesauri. Berlin: Beuth.

DIN 2331:1980. Begriffssysteme und ihre Darstellung. Berlin: Beuth.

Ding, Y., Fensel, D., Klein, M., Omelayenko, B., & Schulten, E. (2004). The Role of Ontologies in eCommerce. In S. Staab & R. Studer (Eds.), Handbook on Ontologies (pp. 593–615). Berlin, Heidelberg, New York: Springer.

Durkheim, E. (2001). The Elementary Forms of Religious Life. Oxford world's classics. Oxford, New York: Oxford University Press.

El Jerroudi, Z., Weinbrenner, S., Mainz, D., & Weller, K. (2008). Kollaborative Ontologieentwicklung mit interaktiver visueller Unterstützung. In M. Herczeg & M. C. Kindsmüller (Eds.). Mensch & Computer 2008, 8. fachübergreifende Konferenz für interaktive und kooperative Medien: Viel mehr Interaktion (pp. 87–96). München: Oldenbourg.

El Jerroudi, Z., & Ziegler, J. (2007). Interaktives Vergleichen und Zusammenführen von Ontologien. i-com. Zeitschrift für interaktive und kooperative Medien, 2007(3), 44–49.

Feliu, J., Vivaldi, J., & Cabré, M. T. (2002). Ontologies: A Review. Sèrie Informes No. 34. Universitat Pompeu Fabra, Barcelona, Spain. Retrieved from http://repositori.upf.edu/handle/10230/1295.

Fellbaum, C. (1999). WordNet: An Electronic Lexical Database (2nd printing). Cambridge: MIT Press.

Fensel, D. (2004). Ontologies: A Silver Bullet for Knowledge Management and Electronic Commerce (2nd Edition). Chichester: Springer.

Fensel, D., Horrocks, I., van Harmelen, F., Decker, S., Erdmann, M., & Klein, M. (2000). OIL in a Nutshell. In R. Dieng & O. Corby (Eds.), Knowledge Engineering and Knowledge Management: Methods, Models and Tools.

Proceedings of the 12th International Conference (EKAW 2000), Juan-les-Pins, France (pp. 1–16). Berlin et al.: Springer.

Fillmore, C. J. (1982). Frame Semantics. In Linguistics in the Morning Calm (pp. 111–137). Seoul: Hanshin Publishing Co.

Fonseca, F. (2007). The Double Role of Ontologies in Information Science Research. Journal of the American Society for Information Science and Technology, 58(6), 786–801.

Fox, M. S. (1992). The TOVE Project: A Common-sense Model of the Enterprise. In F. Belli & F. J. Radermacher (Eds.), Industrial and Engineering Applications of Artificial Intelligence and Expert Systems (pp. 25–34). Berlin: Springer.

Ganter, B., Stumme, G., & Wille, R. (Eds.) (2005). Formal Concept Analysis: Foundations and Applications. Berlin, New York: Springer.

Garshol, L. M. (2002). What are Topic Maps? Retrieved from http://www.xml.com/pub/a/2002/09/11/topicmaps.html.

Garshol, L. M. (2004). Metadata? Thesauri? Taxonomies? Topic maps! Journal of Information Science: Making Sense of it All. Journal of Information Science, 30(4), 378–391.

Garshol, L. M., Moore, G., & JTC1/SC34 (Eds.) (2008). Topic Maps: Data Model (ISO/IEC JTC1/SC34 Draft). Retrieved from http://www.isotopicmaps.org/sam/sam-model/.

Gerstl, P., & Pribbenow, S. (1995). Midwinters, end games, and body parts: A classification of part-whole relations. International Journal of Human-Computer Studies, 43, 865–889.

Gerstl, P., & Pribbenow, S. (1996). A conceptual theory of part-whole relations and its applications. Data & Knowledge Engineering, 20, 305–322.

Goldbeck, J., Fragoso, G., Hartel, F., Hendler, J., Parsia, B., & Oberthaler, J. (2003). The National Cancer Institute's Thesaurus and Ontology. Journal of Web Semantics, 1(1), 75–80.

Gómez-Pérez, A., & Corcho, O. (2002). Ontology Languages for the Semantic Web. IEEE Intelligent Systems, 17(1), 54–60.

Gómez-Pérez, A., Fernández-López, M., & Corcho, O. (2004). Ontological Engineering: Advanced Information and Knowledge Processing (3rd Print). London: Springer.

Green, R., Bean, C. A., & Myaeng, S. H. (Eds.) (2002). The Semantics of Relationships. Dordrecht: Kluwer.

Grenon, P. (2003). BFO in a Nutshell: A Bi-categorial Axiomatization of BFO and Comparison with DOLCE (IFOMIS Reports No. 06/2003). Institute for Formal Ontology and Medical Information Science (IFOMIS), University of Leipzig.

Grenon, P., Smith, B., & Goldberg, L. (2004). Biodynamic Ontology: Applying BFO in the Biomedical Domain. In D. M. Pisanelli (Ed.), Ontologies in Medicine: Studies in Health Technologies and Informatics (pp. 20–38). Amsterdam: IOS Press.

Gruber, T. (1993). A Translation Approach to Portable Ontology Specification. Knowledge Acquisition, 2(5), 199–220.

Gruber, T. (2009). Ontology. In L. Liu & M. T. Özsu (Eds.), Encyclopedia of Database Systems (pp. 1963–1965). Berlin: Springer.

Grüninger, M., & Lee, J. (2002). Ontology Applications and Design. Communications of the ACM, 45(2), 39–41.

Guarino, N. (1995). Formal Ontology, Conceptual Analysis and Knowledge Representation. International Journal of Human-Computer Studies, 43(5-6), 624–640.

Guarino, N. (1998). Formal Ontology and Information Systems. In Formal Ontology in Information Systems: Proceedings of FOIS'98, Trento, Italy (pp. 3–15). Trento, Amsterdam: IOS Press.

Guarino, N., & Giaretta, P. (1995). Ontologies and Knowledge Bases: Towards a Terminological Clarification. In N. Mars (Ed.), Towards Very Large Knowledge Bases: Knowledge Building and Knowledge Sharing (KBKS`95), Enschede, The Netherlands (pp. 25–32). Amsterdam: IOS Press.

Guarino, N., Pribbenow, S., & Vieu, L. (1996). Modeling Parts and Wholes. Data & Knowledge Engineering, 20(3), 257–258.

Guarino, N., & Welty, C. (2000a). A Formal Ontology of Properties. In R. Dieng & O. Corby (Eds.), Knowledge Engineering and Knowledge Management: Methods, Models and Tools. Proceedings of the 12th International Conference (EKAW 2000), Juan-les-Pins, France (pp. 97–112). Berlin et al.: Springer.

Guarino, N., & Welty, C. (2000b). Ontological Analysis of Taxonomic Relationships. In Conceptual Modeling: ER 2000. Proceedings of the 19th Conference on Conceptual Modeling, Salt Lake City, Utah, USA (pp. 210–224). Berlin et al.: Springer.

Guarino, N., & Welty, C. (2002). Evaluating Ontological Decisions with OntoClean. Communications of the ACM, 45(2), 61–65.

Guha, R., McCool, R., & Miller, E. (2003). Semantic Search. In G. Hencsey & B. White (Eds.), WWW 2003: Proceedings of the Twelfth International World Wide Web Conference, Budapest, Hungary (pp. 700–709). New York: ACM.

Hartmann, J., Suarez-Figueroa, M. C., Palma, R., Sure, Y., & Haase, P. (2005). OMV: Ontology Metadata Vocabulary. In C. Welty (Ed.), Ontology Patterns for the Semantic Web (OPSW-05): Workshop at the International Semantic Web Conference (ISWC 2005). Galway, Ireland.

Hepp, M. (2007). Possible Ontologies: How Reality Constrains the Development of Relevant Ontologies. IEEE Internet Computing, 11(1), 90–96.

Hepp, M. (2008). Ontologies: State of the Art, Business Potential, and Grand Challenges. In M. Hepp; P. de Leenheer; A. de Moor, & Y. Sure (Eds.), Ontology Management: Semantic Web, Semantic Web Services, and Business Applications (pp. 3–22). Boston: Springer.

Herre, H., Heller, B., Burek, P., Hoehndorf, R., Loebe, F., & Michalek, H. (2006). General Formal Ontology (GFO): A Foundational Ontology Integrating Objects and Processes. Part I: Basic Principles (Onto-Med Report No. 8, Version 1.0). Research Group Ontologies in Medicine (Onto-Med), University of Leipzig. Retrieved from http://www.onto-med.de/Archiv/ontomed2002/en/publications/scientific-reports/om-report-no8.pdf.

Hill, L., Buchel, O., Janée, G., & Zeng, M. (2002). Integration of Knowledge Organization Systems into Digital Library Architectures. In 13th ASIS&T SIG/CR Workshop, Reconceptualizing Classification Research, Philadelphia, Pennsylvania, USA.

Hitzler, P., Krötzsch, M., Rudolph, S., & Sure, Y. (2008). Semantic Web. Berlin, Heidelberg: Springer.

Hjørland, B., & Pedersen, K. N. (2005). A Substantive Theory of Classification for Information Retrieval. Journal of Documentation, 61, 582–597.

Hodge, G. (2000a). Systems of Knowledge Organization: Beyond Traditional Authority Files (Report for the Digital Library Federation Council on Library and Information Resources). Retrieved from http://www.clir.org/pubs/abstract/pub91abst.html.

Hodge, G. (2000b). Taxonomy of Knowledge Organization Sources/Systems. Retrieved from http://nkos.slis.kent.edu/KOS_taxonomy.htm.

Hollink, L., Schreiber, G., Wielemaker, J., & Wielinga, B. (2003). Semantic Annotation of Image Collections. In Proceedings of the KCAP'03 Workshop on Knowledge Capture and Semantic Annotation, Florida, USA.

Horridge, M., Knublauch, H., Rector, A., Stevens, R., & Wroe, C. (2004). A Practical Guide to Building OWL Ontologies Using The Protégé-OWL Plugin and CO-ODE Tools: Edition 1.0. Retrieved from http://www.co-ode.org/resources/tutorials/ProtegeOWLTutorial.pdf.

Horrocks, I. (2008). Ontologies and the Semantic Web: How Ontologies Provide the Semantics, as Explained Here with the Help of Harry Potter and his Owl Hedwig. Communications of the ACM, 51(12), 58–67.

Horrocks, I., Patel-Schneider, P. F., & van Harmelen, F. (2003). From SHIQ and RDF to OWL: The Making of a Web Ontology Language. Journal of Web Semantics, 1(1), 7–26.

Horrocks, I., & Sattler, U. (1999). A Description Logic With Transitive and Inverse Roles and Role Hierarchies. Journal of Logic and Computation, 9(3), 385–410.

Horrocks, I., & Sattler, U. (2001). Ontology Reasoning in the SHOQ(D) Description Logic. In Proceedings of the 17th International Joint Conference on Artificial Intelligence (IJCAI 2001), Seattle, Washington, USA (pp. 199–204). Los Altos: Morgan Kaufmann.

Hovy, E. (2002). Comparing Sets of Semantic Relations in Ontologies. In R. Green; C. A. Bean, & S. H. Myaeng (Eds.), The Semantics of Relationships (pp. 91–110). Dordrecht: Kluwer.

Huang, Z., van Harmelen, F., & ten Teije, A. (2006). Reasoning With Inconsistent Ontologies: Framework, Prototype, and Experiment. In J. Davies; R. Studer, & P. Warren (Eds.), Semantic Web Technologies: Trends and Research in Ontology-Based Systems (pp. 71–93). Chichester: Wiley.

Hunter, E. J. (2002). Classification Made Simple (2nd Edtion). Aldershot: Ashgate.

IEEE SUO (2003). Glossary of the Standard Upper Ontology Working Group (SUO WG). Retrieved from http://suo.ieee.org/IFF/glossary.html.

ISO 13250:2003. Topic Maps. Genf: International Organization for Standardization.

Iris, M., Litowitz, B., & Evens, M. W. (1988). Problems of the Part-Whole Relation. In M. W. Evens (Ed.), Relational Models of the Lexicon (pp. 261–288). Cambridge: Cambridge University Press.

Jain, R. (2008). Multimedia Semantic Web: Keynote Talk at the International Semantic Web Conference (ISWC2008), Karlsruhe, October 28, 2008. Retrieved from http://ngs.ics.uci.edu/presentations/Multimedia_Semantic_Web_ 081028.ppt.

Jörgensen, C. (2003). Image Retrieval: Theory and Research. Lanham: Scarecrow.

Karp, P., & Paley, S. (1998) Integrated Access to Metabolic and Genomic Data. Journal of Computational Biology, 3(1), 191–212.

Karp, P. D., Riley, M., Paley, S. M., Pellegrini-Toole, A., & Krummenacker, M. (1998). EcoCyc: Encyclopedia of Escherichia Coli Genes and Metabolism. Nucleic Acids Research, 26(1), 50–53.

Kashyap, V., Bussler, C., & Moran, M. (2008). The Semantic Web: Semantics for Data and Services on the Web. Berlin, Heidelberg: Springer.

Khoo, C. S. G., & Na, J. C. (2006). Semantic Relations in Information Science. Annual Review of Information Science and Technology, 40, 157–228.

Lambrix, P., Tan, H., Jakoniene, V., & Strömbäck, L. (2007). Biological Ontologies. In C. J. O. Baker & K.-H. Cheung (Eds.), Semantic Web: Revolutionizing Knowledge Discovery in the Life Sciences (pp. 85–99). Boston: Springer.

Lenat, D. B. (1995). Cyc: A Large Scale Investment in Knowledge Infrastructure. Communications of the ACM, 38(11), 33–38.

Löbner, S. (1981). Intensional Verbs and Functional Concepts: More on the "Rising Temperature" Problem. Linguistic Inquiry, 12, 471–477.

Löbner, S. (2002). Understanding Semantics. London: Edward Arnold Publishers.

Lussier, Y. A., & Bodenreider, O. (2007). Clinical Ontologies for Discovery Applications. In C. J. O. Baker & K.-H. Cheung (Eds.), Semantic Web: Revolutionizing Knowledge Discovery in the Life Sciences (pp. 102–119). Boston: Springer.

Mahesh, K., & Nirenburg, S. (1995). A Situated Ontology for Practical NLP. In Basic Ontological Issues in Knowledge Sharing, Workshop at the Fourteenth International Joint Conference on Artificial Intelligence (IJCAI 95), Montréal, Québec, Canada. Retrieved from http://crl.nmsu.edu/Research/Projects/ mikro/htmls/ijcai95-htmls/ijcai95.html.

Mainz, D., Paulsen, I., Mainz, I., Weller, K., Kohl, J., & von Haeseler, A. (2008). Knowledge Acquisition Focused Cooperative Development of Bio-Ontologies: A Case Study with BIO2Me. In Elloumi, M., et al. (Ed.), Bioinformatics Research and Development. Second International Conference, BIRD 2008. Vienna, Austria. Communications in Computer and Information Science: Vol. 13. (pp. 258–272). Berlin, Heidelberg: Springer.

Mainz, D., Weller, K., & Mainz, J. (2008). Semantic Image Annotation and Retrieval with IKen. In C. Bizer & A. Joshi (Eds.), ISWC2008 Posters and

Demonstrations. Proceedings of the Poster and Demonstration Session at the 7th International Semantic Web Conference (ISWC2008), Karlsruhe, Germany. CEUR Workshop Proceedings: Vol. 401.

Mainz, I. (2006). Entwicklung einer Prototypontologie für bioinformatische Werkzeuge. Bachelor Thesis, Heinrich-Heine-University, Düsseldorf, Germany.

Mainz, I. (2008). Development and Implementation of Techniques for Ontology Engineering and an Ontology-based Search for Bioinformatics Tools and Methods. PhD Thesis, Heinrich-Heine-University, Düsseldorf, Germany.

Mainz, I., Weller, K., Paulsen, I., Mainz, D., Kohl, J., & Haeseler, A. von (2008). Ontoverse: Collaborative Ontology Engineering for the Life Sciences. Information Wissenschaft & Praxis, 59(2), 91–99.

Malzahn, N., Weinbrenner, S., Hüsken, P., Ziegler, J., & Hoppe, H. U. (2007). Collaborative Ontology Development: Distributed Architecture and Visualization. In Proceedings of the German eScience Conference 2007. Max Planck Digital Library, ID: 315470.0.

Marcella, R., & Newton, R. (1994). A New Manual of Classification. Aldershot: Gower.

Markowitz, J. A., Nutter, J. T., & Evens, M. W. (1992). Beyond Is-A and Part-Whole: More Semantic Network Links. Computers & Mathematics with Applications, 23(6-9), 377–390.

Martins, P. (1996). Knowledge Acquisition using Documents, Conceptual Graphs and a Semantically Structured Dictionary. In Proceedings of Tenth Knowledge Acquisition for Knowledge-Based Systems Workshop (KAW96), Banff, Canada (pp. 1–19).

Mascardi, V., Cordi, V., & Rosso, P. (2007). A Comparison of Upper Ontologies. Dipartimenta di Informatica e Scienze dell'Informazione (DISI), Università di Genova (DISI Technical Report DISI-TR-06-21). Retrieved from http://www.disi.unige.it/research/expand-techrep?id_tr=44.

Masolo, C., Borgo, S., Gangemi, A., Guarino, N., Oltramari, A., & Schneider, L. (2003). WonderWeb Deliverable D17: The WonderWeb Library of Foundational Ontologies. Preliminary Report. Retrieved from http://www.loa-cnr.it/DOLCE.html.

Matuszek, C., Cabral, J., Witbrock, M., & DeOliveira, J. (2006). An Introduction to the Syntax and Content of Cyc. In C. Baral (Ed.), Formalizing and Compiling Background Knowledge and Its Applications to Knowledge Representation and Question Answering: Proceedings of the 2006 AAAI Spring Symposium, Stanford, CA, USA (pp. 44–49). Menlo Park: AAAI Press.

Mika, P., Iosif, V., Sure, Y., & Akkermans, H. (2004). Ontology-based Content Management in a Virtual Organization. In S. Staab & R. Studer (Eds.), Handbook on Ontologies (pp. 455–475). Berlin, Heidelberg, New York: Springer.

Miles, A., & Brickley, D. (Eds.) (2005). SKOS Core Guide: W3C Working Draft 2 November 2005. Retrieved from http://www.w3.org/TR/2005/WD-swbp-skos-core-guide-20051102/.

Miller, G. A. (1990). Wordnet: An On-line Lexical Database. International Journal of Lexicography, 3(4), 235–312.

Minsky, M. (1975). A Framework for Representing Knowledge. In P. H. Winston (Ed.), The Psychology of Computer Vision (pp. 211–277). New York: McGraw-Hill.

Mizoguchi, R. (2004). Ontology Engineering Environments. In S. Staab & R. Studer (Eds.), Handbook on Ontologies (pp. 275–296). Berlin, Heidelberg, New York: Springer.

Naing, M. M., Lim, E. P., & Chiang, R. H. L. (2006). Extracting Link Chains of Relationship Instances from a Web Site. Journal of the American Society for Information Science and Technology, 57, 1590–1605.

Neches, R., Fikes, R. E., Finin T., Gruber, T., Senator, T., & Swartout, W. R. (1991). Enabling Technology for Knowledge Sharing. AI Magazin, 12(3), 36–56.

Niles, I., & Pease, R. A. (2001). Towards a Standard Upper Ontology. In C. Welty & B. Smith (Eds.), Formal Ontology in Information Systems: Collected Papers from the Second International Conference (FOIS 2001) (pp. 2–9). New York: ACM.

Noy, N. F., Fergerson, R. W., & Musen, M. A. (2000). The Knowledge Model of Protégé–2000: Combining Interoperability and Flexibility. In R. Dieng (Ed.), Knowledge Engineering and Knowledge Management: Methods, Models, and Tools. 12th International Conference (EKAW 2000), Juan-les-Pins, France (pp. 97–112). Berlin: Springer.

Noy, N. F., & Hafner, C. D. (1997). The State of the Art in Ontology Design: A Survey and Comparative Review. AI Magazine, 18(3), 53–74.

Noy, N. F., & McGuinness, D. F. (2001). Ontology Development 101: A Guide to Creating Your First Ontology. Stanford Knowledge Systems Laboratory Technical Report KSL-01-05 and Stanford Medical Informatics Technical Report SMI-2001-0880, March 2001. Retrieved from http://protege.stanford.edu/publications/ontology_development/ontology 101-noy-mcguinness.html.

Noy, N. F., & Rector, A. (Eds.) (2006). Defining N-ary Relations on the Semantic Web: W3C Working Group Note 12 April 2006. Retrieved from http://www.w3.org/TR/swbp-n-aryRelations/.

Nutter, J. T. (1989). A Lexical Relation Hierarchy: Technical Report TR-89-06. Computer Science, Virginia Polytechnic Institute and State University. Retrieved from http://eprints.cs.vt.edu/archive/00000143/01/TR-89-06.pdf.

Ogden, C. K., & Richards, I. A. (1969 [1923]). The Meaning of Meaning: A Study of the Influence of Language Upon Thought and of the Science of Symbolism (10th Edition). London: Routledge & Kegan Paul.

Pan, J. Z. (2007). OWL for the Novice: A Logical Perspective. In C. J. O. Baker & K.-H. Cheung (Eds.), Semantic Web: Revolutionizing Knowledge Discovery in the Life Sciences (pp. 159–182). Boston: Springer.

Paulsen, I., Mainz, D., Weller, K., Mainz, I., Kohl, J., & von Haeseler, A. (2007). Ontoverse. Collaborative Knowledge Management in the Life Science

Network. In Proceedings of the German eScience Conference 2007. Max Planck Digital Library, ID 316588.0.

Pepper, S. (2002). The TAO of Topic Maps: Finding the Way in the Age of Infoglut. Retrieved from http://www.ontopia.net/topicmaps/materials/tao.html.

Perreault, J. (1965). Categories and Relators: A New Schema. Revue Internationale de la Documentation, 32(4), 136–144.

Peters, I. (2009). Folksonomies: Indexing and Retrieval in Web 2.0. Berlin: De Gruyter Saur.

Peters, I., & Weller, K. (2008). Paradigmatic and Syntagmatic Relations in Knowledge Organization Systems. Information – Wissenschaft & Praxis, 59(2), 100–107.

Presutti, V., & Gangemi, A. (2008). Content Ontology Design Patterns as Practical Building Blocks for Web Ontologies. In Q. Li; S. Spaccapietra; E. Yu, & A. Olivé (Eds.), Conceptual Modeling ER 2008: Proceedings of the 27th International Conference on Conceptual Modeling, Barcelona, Spain (pp. 128–141). Berlin: Springer.

Pribbenow, S. (2002). From Classical Mereology to Complex Part-Whole-Relations. In R. Green; C. A. Bean, & S. H. Myaeng (Eds.), The Semantics of Relationships (pp. 35–50). Dordrecht: Kluwer.

Quine, W. v. O. (1974). Methods of Logic (3rd Edition). London: Routledge & Kegan.

Rector, A. (2002). Analysis of Propagation along Transitive Roles: Formalisation of the GALEN Experience with Medical Ontologies. In I. Horrocks & S. Tessaris (Eds.), International Workshop on Description Logics (DL2002), Toulouse, France. CEUR Workshop Proceedings: Vol. 53.

Rector, A., Drummond, N., Horridge, M., Rogers, J., Knublauch, H., & Stevens, R., et al. (2004). OWL Pizzas: Practical Experience of Teaching OWL-DS. Common Errors & Common Patterns. In E. Motta; N. Shadbolt; A. Stutt, & N. Gibbins (Eds.), Engineering Knowledge in the Age of the Semantic Web: Proceedings of th 14th International Conference (EKAW 2004), Whittlebury Hall, UK (pp. 63–81). Berlin: Springer.

Rector, A., Wroe, C., Rogers, J., & Roberts, A. (2001). Untangling Taxonomies and Relationships: Personal and Practical Problems in Loosely Coupled Development of Large Ontologies. In Y. Gil; M. Musen, & J. Shavlik (Eds.), Proceedings of the First International Conference on Knowledge Capture (K-CAP 2001), Victoria, BC, Canada (pp. 139–146). New York: ACM Press.

Rojas, I., Ratsch, E., Saric, J., Wittig, U. (2003) Notes on the Use of Ontologies in the Biochemical Domain. In Silico Biology 4, 0009.

Rosch, E., & Mervis, C. B. (1975). Family Resemblances: Studies in the Internal Structure of Categories. Cognitive Psychology, 7(4), 573–605.

Rosch, E., Mervis, C. B., Gray, W. D., Johnson, D. M., & Boyes-Bream, P. (1976). Basic Objects in Natural Categories. Cognitive Psychology, 8(3), 382–439.

Sattler, U. (1995). A Concept Language for an Engineeering Application with Part-Whole Relations. In Proceedings of the International Workshop on Description Logics. Rome, Italy (pp. 119–123).

Schmitz-Esser, W. (1999). Thesaurus and Beyond: Advanced Formula for Linguistic Engineeringd Information Retrieval. Knowledge Organization, 26, 10–22.

Schreiber, G., Dubbeldam, B., Wielemaker, J., & Wielinga, B. (2001). Ontology-Based Photo Annotation. IEEE Intelligent Systems, 16(3), 66–74.

Schubert, L. K., Papalaskaris, M. A., & Taugher, J. (1983). Determining Type, Part, Color, and Time Relationships. IEEE Computer, 16(10), 53–60.

Schulz., S., & Hahn, U. (2005). Part-Whole Representation and Reasoning in Formal Biomedical Ontologies. Artificial Intelligence in Medicine, 34(3), 179–200.

Schulz., S., Romacker, M., & Hahn, U. (1998). Part-Whole Reasoning in Medical Knowledge Bases Using Description Logics. Lecture Notes in Computer Science, 1504, 237–248.

Schulz., S., Kumar, A., & Bittner, T. (2006). Biomedical Ontologies: What Part-of Is and Isn't. Journal of Biomedical Informatics, 39, 350–361.

Schulze-Kremer, S. (2002). Ontologies for Molecular Biology and Bioinformatics. In Silico Biology, 2(3), 179–193.

Schwarz, K. (2005). Domain Model Enhanced Search: A Comparison of Taxonomy, Thesaurus and Ontology. Master Thesis, University of Utrecht, The Netherlands.

Semy, S. K., Pulvermacher, M. K., & Obrst, L. J. (2004). Toward the Use of an Upper Ontology for U.S. Government and U.S. Military domains: An Evaluation. The MITRE Corporation (Technical Report MTR 04B0000063). Retrieved from http://www.mitre.org/work/tech_papers/tech_papers_04/04_0603/.

Smith, B. (2003). Ontology. In L. Floridi (Ed.), Blackwell Guide to the Philosophy of Computing and Information (pp. 155–166). Oxford: Blackwell.

Smith, B., Ashburner, M., Rosse, C., Bard, J., Bug, W., & Ceusters, W., et al. (2007). The OBO Foundry: Coordinated Evolution of Ontologies to Support Biomedical Data Integration. Nature Biotechnology, 25, 1251–1255.

Smith, B., Ceusters, W., Klagges, B., Kohler, J., Kumar, A., Lomax, J., et al. (2005). Relations in Biomedical Ontologies. Genome Biology, 6(5), Article R46.

Smith, B., & Welty, C. (2001). Ontology: Towards a New Synthesis. In C. Welty & B. Smith (Eds.), Formal Ontology in Information Systems: Collected Papers from the Second International Conference (FOIS 2001) (pp. 3–9). New York: ACM.

Smith, M. K., Welty, C., & McGuinness, D. L. (Eds.) (2004). OWL Web Ontology Language Guide: W3C Recommendation 10 February 2004. Retrieved from http://www.w3.org/TR/2004/REC-owl-guide-20040210/.

Soldatova, L. N., & King, R. D. (2005). Are the Current Ontologies in Biology Good Ontologies? Nature Biotechnology, 23(9), 1095–1098.

Sowa, J. F. (1984). Conceptual Structures: Information Processing in Mind and Machine. Reading: Addison-Wesley.

Sowa, J. F. (2000). Knowledge Representation: Logical, Philosophical and Computational Foundations (Reprint). Pacific Grove: Brooks/Cole.

Stecher, R., Niederée, C., Nejdl, W., & Bouquet, P. (2008). Adaptive Ontology Re-use: Finding and Re-using Sub-Ontologies. International Journal of Web Information Systems, 4(2), 198–214.

Stevens, R., Goble, C.A., Bechhofer, S. (2000). Ontology-based Knowledge Representation for Bioinformatics. Briefings in Bioinformatics, 1(4), 398–416.

Stevens, R., Wroe, C., Lord, P., & Goble, C. (2004). Ontologies in Bioinformatics. In S. Staab & R. Studer (Eds.), Handbook on Ontologies (pp. 635–657). Berlin, Heidelberg, New York: Springer.

Stock, M. (1999). Standard-Thesaurus Wirtschaft: Ein neuer Standard der Wirtschaftsinformation? Password, 1999(1), 22–29.

Stock, W. G. (2007). Information Retrieval: Informationen suchen und finden. München, Wien: Oldenbourg.

Stock, W. G., & Stock, M. (2008). Wissensrepräsentation: Informationen auswerten und bereitstellen. München, Wien: Oldenbourg.

Stoeckrt, C. J., & Parkinson, H. (2003). The MGED Ontology: A Framework for Describing Functional Genomics Experiments. Comparative and Functional Genomics, 4(1), 127–132.

Storey, V. C. (1993). Understanding Semantic Relationships. The VLDB Journal - The International Journal on Very Large Data Bases, 2(4), 455–488.

Studer, R., Benjamins, V., & Fensel, D. (1998). Knowledge Engineering. Principles and Methods. IEEE Transactions on Data and Knowledge Engineering, 25(1-2), 161–197.

Sun, X., & Zheng, Q. (2005). An Approach to Acquire Semantic Relationships between Terms. In L. M. Liebrock (Ed.), Proceedings of the 2005 ACM Symposium on Applied Computing (pp. 1630–1633). New York: ACM.

Sunagawa, E., Kozaki, K., Kitamura, Y., & Mizoguchi, R. (2004). Organizing Role-concepts in Ontology Development Environment: Hozo. AI Technical Report (Artificial Intelligence Research Group, I. S. I. R., Osaka Univ.), AI-TR-04-1.

Swartout, B., Patil, R., Knight, K., & Russ, T. (1996). Toward Distributed Use of Large-Scale Ontologies. In Proceedings of Tenth Knowledge Acquisition for Knowledge-Based Systems Workshop (KAW96), Banff, Canada. Retrieved from http://ksi.cpsc.ucalgary.ca/KAW/KAW96/KAW96Proc.html.

Terziev, I., Kiryakov, A., & Manov, D. (2003). Base Upper-Level Ontology (BULO) Guidance (Sekt Project Deliverable No. D1.8.1). Retrieved from http://proton.semanticweb.org/D1_8_1.pdf.

Tudhope, D., Koch, T., & Heery, R. (2006). Terminology Services and Technology (JISC State of the Art Review). Retrieved from http://www.jisc.ac.uk/Terminology_Services_and_Technology_Review_Sep_0 6.

Ullrich, M., Maier, A., & Angele, J. (2003). Taxonomie, Thesaurus, Topic Map, Ontologie: Ein Vergleich (Ontoprise White Paper Series). Karlsruhe.

Umlauf, K. (1999). Regeln für den Schlagwortkatalog: Die Grundregeln der RSWK. Berlin: Berliner Handreichungen zur Bibliothekswissenschaft (66).

Uschold, M., & Grüninger, M. (1996). Ontologies: Principles, Methods, and Applications. Knowledge Engineering Review, 11(2), 93–155.

Uschold, M., & Jasper, R. (1999). A Framework for Understanding and Classifying Ontology Applications. In V. Benjamins, B. Chandrasekaran, A. Gómez-Pérez, N. Guarino, & M. Uschold (Eds.), Proceedings of the IJCAI-99 Workshop on Ontologies and Problem-Solving Methods (KRR5): Lessons Learned and Future Trends, Stockholm, Sweden. CEUR Workshop Proceedings: Vol. 18.

Uschold, M., King, M., Moralee, S., & Zorgios, Y. (1998). The Enterprise Ontology. Knowledge Engineering Review, 13(1), 31–89.

van Rees, R. (2003). Clarity in the Usage of the Terms Ontology, Taxonomy and Classification. In R. Amor (Ed.), Proceedings of the CIB W78's 20th International Conference on Construction IT, Construction IT Bridging the Distance (CIB Report 284), Auckland, New Zealand (pp. 432–440).

Varzi, A. C. (1996). Parts, Wholes, and Part-Whole Relations: The Prospects of Mereotopology. Data & Knowledge Engineering, 20, 259–286.

Voß, J. (2004). Begriffssysteme: Ein Vergleich verschiedener Arten von Begriffssystemen und Entwurf des integrierenden Thema-Datenmodells. Diploma Thesis, Humboldt University, Berlin.

Voß, J. (2007). Tagging, Folksonomy & Co: Renaissance of Manual Indexing? Retrieved from http://arxiv.org/abs/cs/0701072.

Wang, H. (2006). Frames and OWL Side by Side: Extended Abstract and Slides Comparing the Features of Frames and Description Logic Languages. Retrieved from http://protege.stanford.edu/conference/2006/submissions/slides/7.2wang_protege2006.pdf.

Wang, H., Noy, N. F., Rector, A., Musen, M. A., Redmond, T., Rubin, D., et al. (2006). Frames and OWL Side by Side. In 9th International Protégé Conference, Stanford, CA. Retrieved from http://protege.stanford.edu/conference/2006/submissions/abstracts/7.2_Wang_Hai_ Protege_conf.pdf.

Wang, T., Li, Y., Bontcheva, K., Cunningham, H., & Wang, J. (2006). Automatic Extraction of Hierarchical Relations from Text. In Y. Sure & J. Domingue (Eds.), The Semantic Web: Research and Applications. 3rd European Semantic Web Conference (ESWC 2006), Budva, Montenegro (pp. 215–229). Berlin, Heidelberg: Springer.

Walter, A., & Nagypal, G. (2007). IMAGENOTION: Collaborative Semantic Annotation of Images and Image Parts and Integrated Creation of Ontologies. In S. Auer, C. Bizer, C. Müller, & A. V. Zhdanova (Eds.), The Social Semantic Web 2007. Proceedings of the 1st Conference on Social Semantic Web (CSSW), September 26-28, Leipzig, Germany (pp. 161–166). GI-EditionProceedings: Vol. 113. Bonn: Ges. für Informatik.

Weller, K. (2007). Folksonomies and Ontologies: Two New Players in Indexing and Knowledge Representation. In H. Jezzard (Ed.), Applying Web 2.0: Innovation, Impact and Implementation. Proceedings of the Online Information Conference, London, Great Britain (pp. 108–115). London: Learned Information Europe.

Weller, K., & Peters, I. (2007). Reconsidering Relationships for Knowledge Representation. In K. Tochtermann & H. Maurer (Eds.), International Conference on Knowledge Management: Proceedings of I-Know 07. Graz, Austria (pp. 493–496). Graz: J.UCS.

Weller, K., & Stock, W. G. (2008). Transitive Meronymy: Automatic Concept-based Query Expansion Using Weighted Transitive Part-Whole Relations. Information – Wissenschaft & Praxis, 59(3), 165–170.

Welty, C., & Guarino, N. (2001). Supporting Ontological Analysis of Taxonomic Relationships. Data & Knowledge Engineering, 39(1), 51–75.

Wielinga, B., Schreiber, G., Wielemaker, J., & Sandberg, J. A. C. (2001). From Thesaurus to Ontology. In Y. Gil; M. A. Musen, & J. Shavlik (Eds.), First International Conference on Knowledge Capture (KCAP'01). Victoria, Canada (pp. 194–201). New York: ACM.

Wiggins, D. (1980) Sameness and Substance. Blackwell: Oxford.

Winston, M. E., Chaffin, R., & Herrmann, D. (1987). A Taxonomy of Part-Whole Relations. Cognitive Science, 11(4), 417–444.

Wittgenstein, L. (1953). Philosophical Investigations (Translated by G.E.M. Anscombe). New York: Macmillan.

Zheng, M. L. (2000). Taxonomy of Knowledge Organization Sources/Systems. Retrieved from http://nkos.slis.kent.edu/KOS_taxonomy.htm.

Chapter 3

Ontology Engineering in the Era of the Social Semantic Web

Now that we have gotten to know the expressivity of ontologies, the next step is to discuss how such rich semantic models can be built and applied to achieve practical benefit. It has often been asked whether the vision of a Semantic Web based on sophisticated ontologies will ever become reality. Supporters of the Social Semantic Web idea should reply that – even though the entire vision of a Semantic Web as proposed by Berners-Lee and his colleagues of the W3C will not become true in near future – less formal semantics may soon become applicable for large parts of the Web, as user communities may take over much of the necessary work.

The Semantic Web initiatives have two major critical areas – which have so far hampered a true take-off of semantic technologies: At first, ontologies are difficult to *build*. Representing complex knowledge structures with formal languages requires some training and expert skills. But experts in knowledge engineering are rather rare and will thus probably never be able to provide the world wide ontology infrastructure which is needed for an all-over Semantic Web – due to the enormous size of the WWW.

Second, *indexing* with ontologies so far only plays a minor role in Semantic Web research. But the actual process of indexing Web documents with semantic metadata is crucial for practical applications.

Within this chapter we will mainly address the first of these two aspects and have a look at how Social Web strategies may influence ontology engineering processes. The converging of semantics and user collaboration into a Social Semantic Web opens new directions for research on knowledge representation – and will hopefully include the key to the solution of current problems. The directions of research include: a) the development and provision of tools and technical means to enable groups of people to collaborate in ontology engineering or in the construction of other elaborated KOS; and b) ways and approaches to reuse and upgrade already existing, less formal semantic models and exploit and interlink various knowledge resources.

We will see that ontology engineering is no longer a process of building one single ontology in a clean setting with a beginning and an end. Instead, ontology engineering is converting to a broader framework of KOS engineering, where different models can not only influence each other but are also interlinked to form a knowledge organization network.

3.1 Ontology Engineering

In the previous chapter, we have seen the main elements of ontologies and how they may be arranged to represent knowledge in a formal way. Due to their complex expressiveness, the development of ontologies which make use of all semantic elements (from concept hierarchies and individuals to fine-grained concept properties and restrictions) is a demanding and time-consuming task. It requires technical skill and careful considerations of the appropriate representation of the domain of interest. Consequently, ontology engineering – the process of building an ontology – is sometimes considered to be an "art" rather than a process of "engineering", e.g. by Soldatova and King:

> "The engineering of ontologies is still a relatively new research field. There does not yet exist a well-developed theory and technology for ontology construction, as there is for bridge construction, for example. This means that many of the steps in designing an ontology remain manual and a kind of 'art'." (Soldatova & King, 2005)

Yet some methodologies have been developed to guide this process, and some phases have been identified which are typical for developing ontologies. The laborious work of building high-quality ontologies is supported by a range of tools and some basic design guidelines.

3.1.1 Methodologies, Dimensions and Principles of Ontology Engineering

Methodologies
Creating an ontology requires careful considerations of how to represent a domain of interest adequately. Ontology engineers (people with skills in knowledge representation and formal ontology languages[206]) as well as domain experts (with expert knowledge in the particular domain of interest) are needed to work together in formalizing precise definitions within the ontology (Paulsen, Mainz et al., 2007). The process of building an ontology is rarely linear but requires iterations of refinements. Particularly in the early years of ontology research, ontologies were built from scratch without many thoughts on the most effective course of action. Step by step, methodologies have been developed inspired by role models from the field of software engineering.

We will not go into details of the several methods that have been developed but simply sum up aspects which can be considered to have reached a consensus in the scientific community. Individual methodologies that have gained much attention

---

[206] Sometimes also called *information architects*.

are, for example, METHONTOLOGY (Fernández-López, Gómez-Pérez & Juristo, 1997), DILIGENT (Tempich, Pinto et al., 2005; Vrandecic, Pinto et al., 2005) and On-To-Knowledge (Staab, Schnurr et al., 2001). A comprehensive overview of single ontology engineering methods and methodologies is given in the works of Asunción Gómez-Pérez, Mariano Fernández-López and Oscar Corcho (Corcho, Fernández-López & Gómez-Pérez, 2003; Fernández-López & Gómez-Pérez, 2002; Fernández-López, Gómez-Pérez et al., 2002; Gómez-Pérez, Fernández-López & Corcho, 2004) as well as for example by Matteo and Cuel (2005), by Sure, Tempich and Vrandecic (2006) and by Pinto and Martins (2004). Often, these methodologies indirectly assume that an ontology is built for a specific purpose by a project team or individual project members.

Typical Activities and Phases of Ontology Engineering
Gómez-Pérez, Fernández-López and Corcho (2004) identify several typical activities as part of the ontology engineering process: ontology management activities, ontology-development-oriented activities and ontology support activities. They also report how these have been grouped into phases of an ontology life cycle within several different methodologies:

> "[...] the ontology development process identifies which activities are to be performed. However it does not identify the order in which activities should be performed [...]. The ontology life cycle identifies *when* activities should be carried out, that is, it identifies the *set of stages* through which the ontology moves during its life time, describes what activities are to be performed in each stage and how the stages are related [...]." (Gómez-Pérez, Fernández-López & Corcho, 2004)

Some activities have to be done before the actual editing process can begin. This may be called the "pre-development" phase (Gómez-Pérez, Fernández-López & Corcho, 2004) or the "project setting" phase (Staab, Schnurr et al., 2001). We will regard it as the organization phase of ontology engineering. This phase includes all activities devoted to the planning of workflow and work environment, like setting up a developer team, arranging a timetable, performing environment studies (and choosing the appropriate technical support) and feasibility studies. One special activity can also be to calculate or estimate the costs of ontology engineering, methods for this are currently being developed in the Ontocom project (Simperl & Sure, 2008).

After this, the domain-specific planning can begin. We call the next steps *conceptual planning phase* and *conceptualization phase*. On a rather general level, one has to plan and define the aim and scope of the ontology as well as some shared design guidelines. This phase is crucial for agreeing upon a common view on the domain of interest, particularly if the ontology is developed by a group of people. During this planning phase, thematic discussions on the developers and the user perspective are extremely useful for capturing the characteristics of the domain. Some ways of collecting basic knowledge about the domain of interest and of limiting and specifying the scope of the planned ontology have been proposed. Grüninger and Fox (1995) propose the specification of precise application scenarios for the ontology, as well as a set of "competency questions", i.e. natural language questions regarding the domain of interest, later to be answered with the knowledge gleaned from the ontology.

Checking for available and reusable knowledge resources is also an important part of this phase in ontology engineering. Reusable knowledge may be available in the form of other ontologies, but also in less formal KOS or other informal knowledge collections.

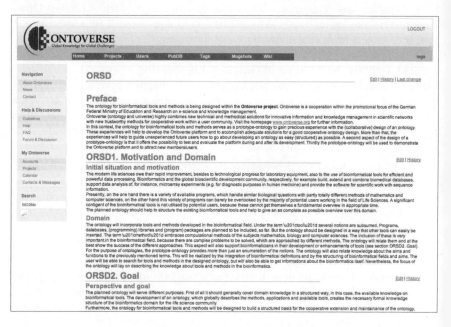

Figure 3.1. Template for an ORSD in the Ontoverse Platform. Such a document is coupled to every newly created ontology in Ontoverse. It can be edited and saved by the user community. Source: Mainz, Weller et al., 2008.

In their methodology for the On-To-Knowledge project, Staab, Schnurr, Studer and Sure (2001) point out the usefulness of an Ontology Requirement Specification Document (ORSD) for the purpose of documenting shared requirements on the planned ontology. The ORSD covers conceptual foundations like domain and goal of the ontology, design guidelines including naming conventions, available knowledge sources such as publications or experts, potential users and use cases (Staab, Schnurr et al., 2001; Sure, Staab & Studer, 2002). This ORSD can be realized as a standard form which lists the basic planning points and which can be filled in with the respective decisions and then work as a guideline for the development team. Figure 3.1 shows how an ORSD form (based on the proposal by

Staab, Schnurr et al., 2001) has been integrated into the Ontoverse[207] ontology engineering platform (Mainz, Weller et al., 2008; Paulsen, Mainz et al., 2007). Every ontology on this collaborative ontology engineering platform is supported by an ORSD form, which can be filled in with basic information about the ontology and decisions on its principles mady by the user community. The Ontoverse ORSD comprises the subsections: ORSD1 Motivation and Domain, ORSD2 Goal, ORSD3 Design Guidelines (general design criteria and naming conventions), ORSD4 Technical Requirements, ORSD5 Available Knowledge Sources and ORSD6 Competency Questionnaire.

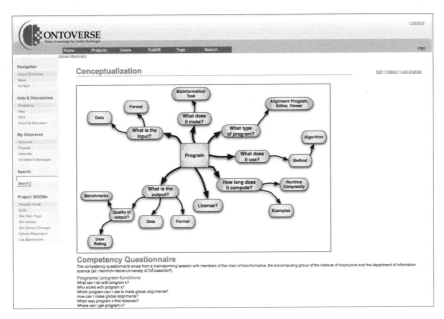

Figure 3.2.   Conceptualization of a new ontology in the Ontoverse Platform. Source: Mainz, Weller et al., 2008.

The conceptual planning phase then becomes more specific; the actual conceptualization of the domain begins[208]: a first sketch of the structure of the ontology is produced. Conceptualizations may have the form of a mere concept collection, a "baseline taxonomy" (Staab, Schnurr et al., 2001), a concept dictionary with definitions or graphical concept maps. Figure 3.2 shows a wiki for collecting informal and semi-formal knowledge as support for the conceptualization phase as part of the Ontoverse ontology engineering platform.

---

[207] Ontoverse: http://www.ontoverse.org.
[208] This has also been called the *knowledge acquisition phase* (Gómez-Pérez, Férnandez-López and Corcho 2004).

One may now enter the editing or formalization phase[209]. This is the core of the ontology engineering process. The informal knowledge collection gathered in the previous phase will now have to be formalized.

> "Once the conceptual model is built, the methodology proposes to transform the conceptual model into a formalized model, which will be implemented in an ontology implementation language. That is, along this process the ontologist is moving gradually from the knowledge level to the implementation level, increasing slowly the degree of formality of the knowledge model so that it can be understood by a machine." (Gómez-Pérez, Fernández-López & Corcho, 2004)

There is a variety of strategies for identifying concepts and formalizing the ontology. One principle distinction is made whether the process is bottom-up (from the most concrete to the most abstract elements), top-down (from the most abstract to the most concrete elements) or middle-out (starting with the most relevant parts) (Gómez-Pérez, Fernández-López & Corcho, 2004). The middle-out approach is most commonly proposed in classical methodologies (Gómez-Pérez, Fernández-López & Corcho, 2004).

The METHONTOLOGY methodology (Fernández-López, Gómez-Pérez & Juristo, 1997; Gómez-Pérez, Fernández-López & Corcho, 2004) works with the following very fine-grained formalization steps: a) build glossary of terms; b) build concept taxonomies; c) build ad hoc binary relation diagrams; d) build concept dictionary; e) describe ad hoc binary relations; f) describe instance attributes; g) describe class attributes; h) describe constants; i) describe formal axioms; j) describe rules; k) describe instances. Other approaches use less detailed but principally similar steps of successive formalization (e.g. the approach by Kashyap, Cheung et al. (2008), who describe the stepwise formalization exemplarily for the domain "Parkinson's Disease").

Typically the concept identification is followed by a hierarchical structuring phase; the resulting basic taxonomic structures are then enriched by specified properties and axioms – all, of course, with final implementations in formal ontology languages. We thus partition the formalization phase as depicted in Figure 3.3. We may conclude that this stepwise semantic enrichment is the core of the ontology engineering process. In Section 3.3, this will be picked up as the basis for new approaches of creating ontologies out of other KOS or Web 2.0 resources.

---

[209]   Also referred to as the *implementation* phase. Gómez-Pérez, Férnandez-López and Corcho (2004) also call this process the *conceptualization* phase.

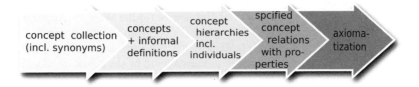

Figure 3.3.   Activities during the ontology formalization phase (which is Phase 3 in the entire ontology engineering process as depicted in Figure 3.4).

For formalization purposes, most methodologies follow the model of *evolving prototypes* (Kendall & Kendall, 1995) and thus suggest a stepwise *refinement* in terms of error correction and adjustment of the ontology during the development process. This is also referred to as *ontology evolution* (de Leenheer & Mens, 2008).

> "The formalization of ontologies is not possible completely from scratch. In particular for emerging ideas and concepts, it is not possible to directly integrate them into an ontology as they are not clearly defined, yet. That means, the development of an ontology underlies a process of continuous evolution where different levels of formality might co-exist within one ontology." (Braun, Schmidt et al., 2007)

Furthermore, the *evaluation* is often considered as an additional process. Ontology evaluation means judging the quality of the content of the ontology, and it should be performed at least once before the ontology is applied in practice. This can be done with respect to predefined requirements and competencies (Grüninger & Fox, 1995) or with the help of external domain experts. Brank, Mladenic and Grobelnik (2006) distinguish four categories of evaluation approaches: a) "based on comparing the ontology to a gold standard", b) "based on using the ontology in an application and evaluating the results", c) "approaches involving comparisons with a source of data about the domain that is to be covered by the ontology", and d) "approaches where evaluation is done by humans who try to assess how well the ontology meets a set of predefined criteria."

Brank, Grobelnik and Mladenic (2005) have reviewed certain evaluation methodologies; Gómez-Pérez, Fernández-López & Corcho (2004) provide an overview of methods for ontology evolution with a particular focus on the OntoClean method. Ontology evaluation covers the aspects of ontology *verification* (ensuring that all definitions are implemented correctly according to pre-set requirements), ontology *validation* (ensuring that the knowledge model appropriately represents the real world) and ontology *assessment* (checking whether the knowledge model fits the users' requirements and the application scenario) (Gómez-Pérez, Fernández-López & Corcho, 2004).

The field of ontology evaluation is still in need of further analysis and research. So far, there are no commonly shared and univocal quality measures for ontologies, but some current research efforts focus on this problem (e.g. in the EON Workshop series on the Evaluation of Ontologies for the Web[210]). Anyway, some design principles are considered to be generally applicable to ontologies.

As we expect ontologies to be built for a specific purpose, usually the last phase of the life cycle of every engineering process should be the actual *application and use* of the ontology for this respective purpose.

Refinement may be considered as a specific development phase after the formalization, and also as a part of the *maintenance* phase. The maintenance of ontologies mainly focuses on keeping ontologies up to date in the long term, e.g. by adding new pieces of knowledge or renaming/remodeling concepts according to changes in the domain of interest. This necessity is often underestimated, as Hepp (2007) points out:

> "Because finding ontological truth has historically been a major guideline of building ontologies in computer science, we often falsely assume that creating lasting ontologies is just a matter of proper conceptual modeling. That is, once we've discovered the correct model for a domain of discourse, the conceptualization will be stable for ages." (Hepp, 2007)

Much of the work in ontology maintenance is part of the task of adding new instances to ontology classes: although a well-founded ontology may remain stable in its basic structure over time, new individuals will appear in the real world and may have to be included as new instances. Adding instances to an ontology is referred to as *ontology instantiation* or *ontology population* (Lambrix, Tan et al., 2007). The results of refinements during the maintenance phase are typically different release versions of one ontology which have to be managed respectively. Besides their original purposes, ontologies may be reused for other than their intended purposes. This optional *reuse phase* particularly considers the adaptation of an existing ontology as a resource for a new one[211]. If ontologies are reused as starting points for new ontologies, all the phases of ontology engineering will make up an ontology life cycle as depicted in Figure 3.4[212].

Of course, the delimitation and differentiation of engineering phases is not unambiguous. The borders between different stages may also be perceived in slightly different ways and are often blurred due to necessary iterations. Some additional activities may be inserted to one specific stage or as a continuous parallel activity, particularly the *documentation* of the ontology development but also *publication, licensing* and *archiving* activities (Tudhope, Koch & Heery, 2006).

---

[210]   EON 2009 Workshop: http://www.seals-project.eu/eon2009/.

[211]   Aspects of re-engineering, reuse and collaborative ontology engineering are to be considered over the following sections.

[212]   If there is no reuse of existing ontologies as starting points for a new one, the ontology engineering process will only cover the phases 1-7 as depicted in Figure 3.4 and will not form a cycle.

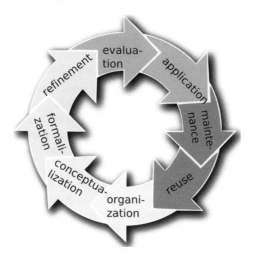

Figure 3.4. Phases of the ontology engineering process in one prototypical life-cycle constellation.

Design Principles and Engineering Requirements

Gruber (1993) has collected five basic design principles for ontologies: clarity, coherence, extendibility, minimal encoding bias and minimal ontological commitment. *Clarity* requires precise representations of meanings:

> "An ontology should communicate effectively the intended meaning of defined terms. Definitions should be objective. Definitions can be stated on formal axioms, and a complete definition (defined by necessary and sufficient conditions) is preferred over a partial definition (defined by only necessary or sufficient conditions). All definitions should be documented with natural language." (Gruber, 1993)

Furthermore, formal and informal definitions should always be *coherent;* there must not be any contradictions. This is very close to the demands for *consistency* and *soundness*, which can be found in other discussions. Gómez-Pérez, Fernández-López & Corcho (2004) explain "[...] that an ontology is sound if and only if it does not allow deducing invalid conclusions[213]."

Consistency cannot be checked for every ontology; it depends on the ontology language in use. For example, while OWL Lite and OWL DL are both decidable,

---

[213] They also define consistency in the following way: "Consistency refers to whether it is possible to obtain contradictory conclusions from valid input definitions. A given definition is consistent if and only if the individual definition is consistent and no contradictory knowledge can be inferred from other definitions and axioms" (Gómez-Pérez, Fernández-López & Corcho, 2004).

OWL Full is clearly undecidable (Pan, 2007) and thus knows no inconsistency. In other cases, representations are deliberately fuzzy and thus represent vague and imprecise knowledge which also makes it hard to check consistency or to evaluate clarity and correctness. Pan (2007) points out the need for fuzzy ontologies:

> "Such information is very useful in many applications like multimedia processing and retrieval, information fusion and many more. [...] Furthermore, in many applications, like ontology alignment and modularization, the interconnection of separate and distributed ontologies and modules is hardly ever a true or false situation, but rather a matter of confidence or relatedness degree." (Pan, 2007)

Back to Gruber's original requirements: the extendibility criterion means that "[...] one should be able to define new terms for special uses based on the existing vocabulary, in a way that does not require the revision of the existing definitions" (Gruber, 1993).

In cases where specific implementations of domain conceptualization depend on the actually used ontology language and cannot easily be transferred to other formats we speak of encoding bias. The principle of *minimal encoding bias* aims at reducing such restrictions for easy knowledge exchange, sharing and reuse.

The principle of *minimal ontological commitment* finally aims at providing a shared knowledge representation for a large community. Ontological commitment (Gruber, 1993; Gruber & Olsen, 1994) is the agreement on shared representations and definitions in a coherent and consistent way. According to Gruber, an ontology should only make minimal use of restrictive specifications; otherwise it cannot be commonly accepted. Thus he prefers social agreement to formal complexity and completeness.

> "An ontology should require the minimal ontological commitment sufficient to support the intended knowledge sharing activities. An ontology should make as few claims as possible about the world being modeled, allowing the parties committed to the ontology freedom to specialize and instantiate the ontology as needed. Since ontological commitment is based on consistent use of vocabulary, ontological commitment can be minimized by specifying the weakest theory (allowing the most models) and defining only those terms that are essential to the communication of knowledge consistent with that theory." (Gruber, 1993)

Gruber's request for minimal ontological commitment acts on certain assumptions which do not necessarily hold for all contexts of ontology engineering. He assumes that a) an ontology's primary aim is to provide a shared domain representation – and that it should be shared by the largest possible community; b) an ontology is 'only' a domain's vocabulary and not a complete knowledge base representing various facts about a domain; c) instances are independent elements which may be added to the ontology. As we have seen in the previous chapter, these preconditions are not generally accepted; ontologies may also act as complete knowledge base and include instances.

The longing for minimal ontological commitment becomes critical for very large communities such as, for example, the Web 2.0 user community. There is a trade-off between complexity in structure and social agreement on appropriate modeling: the more people have to agree on a definition, the more difficult it will be to find a consensual representation; therefore, one may only agree upon very basic structures. In a way, folksonomies are the prototypical effect of this principle. The large user communities of social software services cannot ultimately agree upon one shared vocabulary and thus simply use an open vocabulary without any fixed structure. We may thus specify the request for minimal ontological commitment; some form of explicit commitment is still needed if we want to make use of formal semantics and not to act on mere community suggestions. Della Valle, Celino and Cirezza (2008) have investigated the need for capturing statements of disagreement in knowledge representation. They also conclude that "looking for a comprehensive agreement sometimes can be useless or counter-productive, because the practice of excluding possible causes of conflict from the agreement can produce agreements that are so limited as to be almost empty, thus useless."

Some more principles for ontology development can be found in the literature. Gómez-Pérez, Fernández-López and Corcho (2004) also name "the representation of disjoint and exhaustive[214] knowledge; the minimalization of the syntactic distance between sibling concepts; and the standardization of names" as criteria for good ontology design. They also aspire towards *completeness* in ontologies:

> "We say that an ontology is complete if and only if it allows deducing all the possible valid conclusions starting from the ontology vocabulary and applying the deducing rules permitted." (Gómez-Pérez, Fernández-López & Corcho, 2004)

With this strict definition, completeness of ontologies is very hard to obtain. Braun, Schmidt et al. (2007) discuss the three design principles "appropriateness", "social agreement" and "formality", particularly with regard to collaborative engineering and usage of ontologies. *Appropriateness* may displace the ideal of completeness with regard to practical usage:

> "An ontology needs to be an appropriate representation of the domain with respect to the purpose of the ontologies required for a semantic application so that it is actually useful. This is only possible when we have a tight coupling and immediate mutual feedback between changes to the ontology and use of its elements, e.g., for search or annotations." (Braun, Schmidt et al., 2007)

The matter of *formality* aims mainly to achieve the right amount of formal definitions so that "[…] the outcome is an adequate level of formality in the ontology, avoiding both overformalization and the inability to apply semantic algorithms"

---

[214] Exhaustiveness alludes to the decomposition of superclasses. The decomposition of a class into subclasses is exhaustive if they cover all possible instances. There must not be any instances that belong to the superclass but not to one of its subclasses Gómez-Pérez, Fernández-López & Corcho, 2004).

(Braun, Schmidt et al., 2007). The request for *social agreement* also bears in mind the early definition of Borst (1997) who describes an ontology as "a formal specification of a shared conceptualization".

> "An ontology needs to represent a shared understanding among all stakeholders. Thus, successful ontology construction is a social and collaborative learning process within the communities of its users. The involved individuals deepen by and by their understanding of the real world and of an (appropriate) vocabulary to describe it." (Braun, Schmidt et al., 2007)

Gómez-Pérez, Fernández-López and Corcho (2004) likewise point out that

> "[…] it is important to remark that the model can only be considered an ontology if it is a shared and consensual knowledge model agreed by a community."

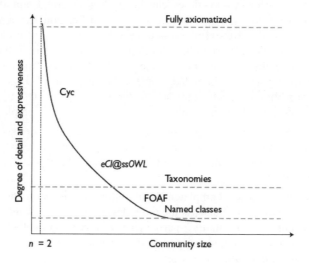

Figure 3.5. The expressivity-community-size frontier. Source: Hepp (2007).

To ensure this, intensive support of collaborative ontology engineering and evaluation is needed. On the other hand, Hepp (2007) points out that the agreement of a user community is typically coupled to a loss in expressiveness (Figure 3.5): "A trade-off exists between an ontology's degree of detail and expressiveness and the achievable community size, because the more detailed the ontology, the fewer people will be willing to dedicate the resources for reviewing it prior to adopting it." Thus a more simple Social Semantic Web ontology like FOAF is adopted by a larger community than the complex Cyc Ontology.

With regard to the work of Guarino and Welty on the OntoClean methodology (Guarino & Welty, 2002; Guarino & Welty, 2004) the principle of designing *clean* ontologies has been accepted by a number of ontology engineers. This means that inappropriate and inconsistent modeling choices should be detected in ontologies, and then be removed or remodeled. As we have already mentioned in the previous chapter (Section 2.2.4), Guarino and Welty built their definition of what a clean ontology is on several formal notions derived from philosophy, which are general enough to be used for any domain of interest. Among them is the notion of *essence*: "A property of an entity is essential to that entity if it must hold for it" (Guarino & Welty, 2002). Thus a property is not essential if is not true for an entity in all cases but may become true accidentally in some contexts.

Due to their high dependence on philosophical discussions, these notions are rather difficult to apply by non-experts in knowledge representation and are thus unlikely to be applied in WWW contexts. This leads us to a more general problem: While all these discussions on ontology design already provide important theoretical foundations, the Social Semantic Web mainly requires more practical approaches to establishing design principles. What is more, these basic design principles will have to be transferred to practice; they have to become actual guidelines for practical ontology engineering, ideally in the form of a recommended course of action.

Practical Guidelines

Practical guidelines for creating ontologies in terms of how to identify and model concepts, relations and axioms appropriately and how to ensure the compliance of design principles are rather rare; there are no comprehensive textbooks. Some introductory material is available, but it stays on a rather basic level (e.g. Noy & McGuinness, 2001). This is to a large extent due to the problem that general guidelines cannot easily be provided as the actual shape of an ontology is bound to at least the following variables: the domain, the purpose (and eventually a certain practical application tool) and the available techniques (editors and languages). Thus most considerations have to focus on the use of single ontology languages or single editing tools (e.g. Horridge, Knublauch et al., 2004).

Rector, Drummond et al. (2004) have summed up their experiences teaching OWL-DL and collected a set of typical difficulities for novices in OWL-DL. They mention the following typical modeling errors, among others:

- Failure to make all information explicit (users assume that information implicit in concept names is already explicit and thus do not perfom actions such as making concepts explicitly disjoint from each other).
- Mistaken use of universal and existential restrictions.
- Problems understanding the differences between defined and primitive classes and deciding which of the classes ought to be defined.
- Misunderstanding the underlying open world assumption (i.e. something is false only if it can be proven to contradict other information in the ontology).
- Misunderstanding underlying logical issues (e.g. the difference between "only" and "some", the difference between "and" and "or").

As a result, they have set up a list of nine guidelines for ontology engineering:

"1. Always paraphrase a description or definition before encoding it in OWL, and record the paraphrase in the comment area of the interface.
2. Make all primitives disjoint – which requires that primitives form trees.
3. Use someValuesFor as the default qualifier in restrictions.
4. Be careful to make defined classes defined – the default is primitive. The classifier will place nothing under a primitive class (except in the presence of axioms /domain/range constraints).
5. Remember the open world assumption. Insert closure restrictions if that is what you mean.
6. Be careful with domain and range constraints. Check them carefully if classification does not work as expected.
7. Be careful about the use of 'and' and 'or' (intersectionOf, unionOf).
8. To spot trivially satisfiable restrictions early, always have an existential (someValuesFor) restriction corresponding to every universal (allValues-For) restriction, either in the class or one of its superclasses (unless you specifically intend to be trivially satisfiable).
9. Run the classifier frequently, spot errors early." (Rector, Drummond, et al., 2004)

Furthermore, some considerations are available that discuss single aspects and difficulties of ontology engineering, like the discussions about endurants and perdurants introduced in Section 2.2.2. The Semantic Web Best Practices and Deployment Working Group[215] has been concerned with providing solutions to some frequent problems in ontology engineering, like 'how to represent n-ary relations in ontologies?' Kashyap, Cheung et al. (2008) discuss some modeling problems which frequently appear in ontology development – and which are not conclusively resolved. Among them are the representation of uncertainty (e.g. for representation of knowledge, such as "genetic mutations in the alpha synuclein gene *could cause* Parkinson's disease"), the use of relationship versus classes for modeling knowledge, the use of instances versus sub-classes, and the granularity of represented relationships. The OBO Foundry has set up some best practice principles which have to be fulfilled by every ontology that is accepted as a member of the OBO collection. They are mainly established on a rather general level and include directives like "[t]he ontology is in, or can be expressed in, a common shared syntax. This may be either the OBO syntax, extensions of this syntax, or OWL" or "The ontologies include textual definitions for all terms"[216]. Such general statements will not help ontology engineers in typical knowledge modeling situations. But three more OBO principles are of high interest for considerations of the Social Semantic Web. First, semantic relations have to be based on the OBO Relation Ontology and are thus to some degree standardized. And what is more, the OBO Foundry has a major interest in fostering collaborative ontology engineering in order to establish ontologies that are shared by communities, as un-

---

[215] Semantic Web Best Practices and Deployment Working Group (SWBPDWG): http://www.w3.org/2001/sw/BestPractices/.
[216] All OBO Foundry principles can be found at: http://www.obofoundry.org/crit.shtml.

derlined by the two principles "The ontology has a plurality of independent users" and "The ontology will be developed collaboratively with other OBO Foundry members." All OBO principles are subject to ongoing discussions and may be refined in the future[217].

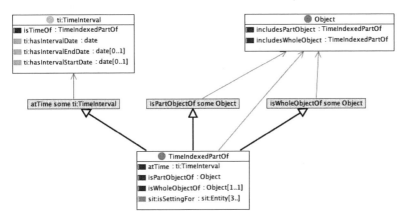

Figure 3.6.   Approach to handling part of relations that are bound to time intervals.
Source: ODP suggestion by Valentina Presutti, http://ontologydesign
patterns.org/wiki/Submissions:TimeIndexedPartOf.

More specific guidelines for ontology engineering are discussed by a research community on the Ontology Design Patterns (ODP) portal[218]. The aim of this platform is to create ontology design patterns (ODPs) for the Semantic Web, i.e. modeling solutions for typical problems of ontology engineering in the form of best practice building blocks. For example, the problem of building part-of relations is addressed in one ODP[219]. It suggests using the properties `hasPart` and its inverse property `isPartOf` in OWL ontologies in order to represent entities and their parts. Another ODP addresses the question of how to express time-related aspects of part-of relations[220]: The suggested solution for relating a time interval to a whole and its part is illustrated in Figure 3.6 (as this is also a form of tertiary relation, the approach assembles the one for n-ary relations discussed above; an intermediating class "TimeIndexedPartOf" is created as the linking element between the whole, the part and the time interval). This suggestion may now be reviewed and discussed. Currently, many ODPs are still under construction and not

---

[217]   Ongoing discussions can be found in the OBO Foundry Wiki at:
     http://obofoundry.org/wiki/index.php/OBO_Foundry_Principles.
[218]   Ontology Design Patterns (ODP): http://ontologydesignpatterns.org.
[219]   ODP for part-of relations: http://ontologydesignpatterns.org/wiki/Submissions:PartOf.
[220]   ODP for time-related part of relations:
     http://ontologydesignpatterns.org/wiki/Submissions:TimeIndexedPartOf.

yet readily available. But the overall idea is particularly important for more guidelines and standards for the Social Semantic Web and is definitely worth pursuing[221].

Finally, we may refer to some additional literature from the field of knowledge representation which deals with the practical construction of other KOS (e.g., Aitchison, Gilchrist & Bawden, 2000; Cleveland & Cleveland, 2001). These introductions may also be of use for the elementary design of ontologies, i.e. the design stages before the addition of specified properties and axioms. They mainly address issues of grammatical unification, e.g. the consistent use of grammatical forms of concept names (which will have to be transferred to property and instance names in ontology engineering), usage of articles, singular or plural forms, spelling, punctuation, capitalization, abbreviations and acronyms.

3.1.2 Tools for Ontology Engineering

A variety of tools have been developed to support the different phases of ontology engineering. Ontologies may also be constructed with other techniques and tools, e.g. adapted from software engineering or database technologies (Gómez-Pérez, Fernández-López & Corcho, 2004). Not all tools refer to the several phases of ontology engineering which have been proposed in the different methodologies, and most of them do not suggest a specific course of action to their users. Yet ontology engineering tools cover most of the identified life-cycle tasks and some tools have been developed directly in the context of a certain methodology for putting its principles into practice[222].

The terms 'ontology engineering tool', 'ontology development tool', 'ontology editor' and 'ontology management tool' are not always used as exact synonyms, but there is also no precise distinction between these different types of tool. We will thus use the term ontology editor (or in short: editor) for all tools that at least provide the means for constructing, saving and editing formal ontologies (i.e. KOS in the form of a machine-readable language format). These tools may have additional components supporting ontology management or other life-cycle activities. Some editors can be enriched in functionality by certain plug-ins or can be combined with other tools in the form of tool suites. Individual tools which can be integrated to such tool suites are typically reasoners, ontology merging and mapping tools (Noy, 2004), ontology evaluation tools and repositories[223]. They all constitute the *infrastructure* for ontology engineering.

Overviews of different editors and their functionalities have been provided several times, in the context of the history of these tools, e.g. by Corcho, Fernández-López & Gómez-Pérez (2003), Denny (2004), Duineveld, Stoter et al. (2000),

---

[221] The idea has already led to a scientific Workshop on Ontology Patterns (WOP 2009): http://ontologydesignpatterns.org/wiki/WOP2009:Main.

[222] For example the OntoEdit editor and the On-To-Knowledge methodology or the OntoStudio editor and the Activity-First Method.

[223] Like Jena or Sesame.

Fensel (2004), Gómez-Pérez, Angele et al. (2002), Gómez-Pérez, Fernández-López & Corcho (2004), Kashyap, Bussler & Moran (2008), Mizoguchi (2004) and Waterfeld, Weiten & Haase (2008). Lambrix, Habbouche & Pérez (2003) consider the use of different tools specifically for the domain of bioinformatics. Ahmad & Colomb (2007) describe the state of the art in research on *ontology servers*, which they describe as specific tools for ontology management. Dzbor and Motta (2008) focus on ontology reuse as supported by different tools.

Functionalities of Ontology Editors
Ontology editors vary in their range of functions, which are themselves dependent on the following factors:
- the supported ontology language(s),
- the underlying knowledge model (e.g. based on frames or description logics),
- single-user or multi-user mode,
- web-based or locally installed application,
- commercial or free tool,
- desired interoperability with other tools (e.g. merging and reasoning tools).

Among the classical tools for ontology engineering we find those that have to be locally installed as well as Web-based editors. Many of them support little more than one specific ontology language[224] and are designed for individual users or groups – but not for broad Web communities. Several tools are freely available, which often also means that they are being developed as part of a certain research project. They are thus in some cases still under construction, or in other cases there is no longer any user support or maintenance. The most commonly needed functions in ontology engineering, and thus typical components of ontology editors, are:
- *Basic editing functionalities*: creating, deleting and renaming concepts, instances, properties, comments and restrictions.
- *Import and export functionalities*: saving and storing ontologies in different file formats and importing ontologies in certain formats for editing and modification.
- *Inference and reasoning functionalities:* reasoners are often specific tools that may be incorporated into certain ontology editors or used in combination with them[225]. They check the consistency of the ontology, determine whether it is possible for a class to have any instances (concept satisfiability) and compute inferred class hierarchies. Sometimes they also support debugging, check against competency questions or query answering.
- *Visualization*: different techniques for visualizing the formal structures of ontologies have been developed to support ontology engineers (e.g. Fluit, Sabou

---

[224] In this regard, one may distinguish editors which have been explicitly developed for use with one certain ontology language and others that were designed as general tools and support several languages (Gómez-Pérez, Fernández-López & Corcho, 2004).

[225] The most prominent reasoning engines are Pellet, FaCT or FaCT++, KAON2, Onto-Broker, RacerPro, Cerebra Engine, and OWLIM.

& van Harmelen, 2004). Figure 3.7 exemplarily shows the Ontoviz plug-in for the Protégé editor.

*   *Task Management*: Sometimes it is possible to keep track of planned and up-coming activities within the engineering process. For example, Protégé has the option of annotating single ontology elements with "to do" labels, which can then be displayed as a to do list.

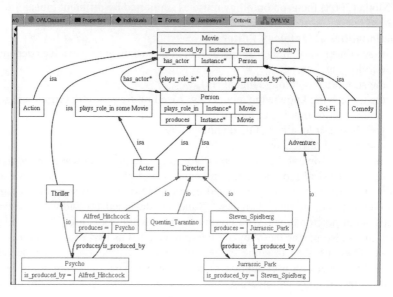

Figure 3.7. Visualization of a small ontology with the Ontoviz plug-in for Protégé.

In addition to these basic functionalities, some editors provide advanced and specialized functionalities, such as:

*   *Change tracking and versioning:* Classical ontology editors do not necessarily provide mechanisms for highlighting changes made in the ontology. Yet this is an important aspect for collaborative approaches and has thus recently received growing attention.

*   *Graphical editing:* In single cases, visualizations are not only available for analyzing and surveying an ontology, but also provide an additional interface for ontology editing. For example, Mind2Onto was designed as a plug-in to provide a graphical user interface for creating conceptualizations, directly transferable to formal representations (Mizogushi, 2004).

*   *Conceptualization and knowledge acquisition*: The conceptualization phase and support of knowledge acquisition are rarely directly incorporated into ontology editors. OntoKick supports conceptualizations in the form of competency questions (Mizogushi, 2004). As already shown in Figures 3.1 and 3.2,

the Ontoverse platform also includes specific support for informal knowledge collection and conceptualization.

- *Multi-user support*: Some editors support the collaboration of several users. Yet, as we will discuss in more detail in Section 3.2, collaboration does not necessarily mean broad Web communities but rather envisions the joint work of small working groups.

Selected Ontology Editors
Since the beginning of research efforts on ontologies in computer science, a variety of tools have been developed to handle ontological data. Shortly, we will introduce single editors that have gained and still gain attention within the Semantic Web community. Additionally, some less popular editors can also be found on the SemWebCentral[226] platform, a place where a community can publish open source tools related to the Semantic Web.

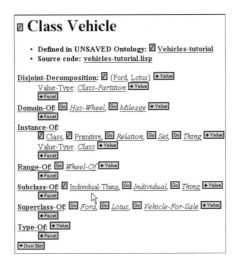

Figure 3.8.   Example for the Ontolingua editing interface. Source: http://www-ksl-svc.stanford.edu:5915/doc/frame-editor/guided-tour/notes-on-editing.html.

- Ontolingua[227] (Farquhar, Fikes & Rice, 1997a): The first tool for creating and managing ontologies was the Ontolingua Server. It was developed in the mid 1990s at Stanford University and had a simple Web interface (Figure 3.8) for editing ontologies in the Ontolingua format, as well as additional services like the support of ontology merging. In the context of this project, there al-

---

[226]   SemWebCentral: http://projects.semwebcentral.org/.
[227]   Ontolingua Server: http://www.ksl.stanford.edu/software/ontolingua/.

ready existed first approaches for the collaborative and modular construction of ontology engineering.

- Ontosaurus[228] (Swartout, Patil et al., 1996): The Ontosaurus server and editor were developed at the University of Southern California – almost at the same time as the Ontolingua server. One fundamental difference is that it is explicitly built for supporting the ontology language LOOM[229].
- WebOnto[230] (Domingue, 1998): WebOnto was developed by the Knowledge Media Institute at the Open University. It was designed as a Web-based and collaborative ontology editor for OCML[231] ontologies. An additional tool TADZEBAO was created for discussing and planning ontologies (uncoupled from the formal editing process).

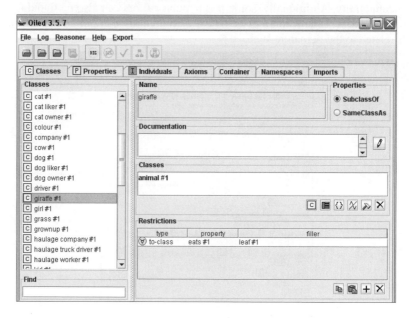

Figure 3.9.   Interface of the ontology editor OilEd version 3.5.7 (showing an exemplary ontology included in the download package).

- OilEd (Bechhofer, Horrocks et al., 2001): OilEd has been developed by the Information Management Group at the University of Manchester in connec-

---

[228]   Ontosaurus: http://www.isi.edu/isd/ontosaurus.html.
[229]   LOOM: http://www.isi.edu/isd/LOOM/.
[230]   WebOnto: http://projects.kmi.open.ac.uk/webonto/.
[231]   Operational Conceptual Modeling Language (OCML): http://technologies.kmi.open.ac.uk/ocml//.

tion with the On-To-Knowledge project. It was designed for use with OIL[232] and later DAML+OIL[233] (two ontology languages based on description logics), and can be connected to certain inference engines (like FaCT) for reasoning and consistency checking. Later, OWL and RDF support was added. OilEd has no Web-based platform but is a standalone application (Figure 3.9). The editor does not include a section for the class hierarchy (classes are listed in alphabetical order). Hierarchical structures have to be computed by the accompanying reasoner.

- ODE (Blázquez, Fernández-López et al., 1998) and WebODE (Arpirez, Corcho et al., 2001): The Ontology Design Environment (ODE) is a standalone ontology editor developed by the Ontology Group at the Universidad Politécnica de Madrid. WebODE is its Web-based successor. It allows for the import and export of several ontology language formats and explicitly supports the METHONTOLOGY methodology of ontology engineering.

- Protégé (Gennari, Musen et al., 2003; Noy, Sintek et al., 2001): The most popular ontology editor is probably Protégé, which we have also used to illustrate the examples in the previous chapter. One may use it to build ontologies in the frame-based representation format, specific to Protégé, or – which is by now more common – in OWL and RDF(S) (Knublauch, Fergerson et al., 2004).

  The basic functionalities are complemented by several plug-ins for additional tasks (e.g. version management or different visualization tools[234]). A multi-user version of Protégé, CollaborativeProtégé[235], is the most recent additional development (Tudorache, Noy et al., 2008).

- KAON[236] (Oberle, Volz et al., 2004): KAON is a tool suite developed by the FZI[237] and the AIFB[238] at the University of Karlsruhe. The integrated ontology editor is called OI-Modeler and contains a graphical user interface.

- SWOOP[239] (Kalyanpur, Parsia et al., 2005): Swoop was originally produced by the MIND lab at the University of Maryland and is now continued as an open-source project. It is intended to be used for editing OWL ontologies. The aim of Swoop was to provide a usable interface for average Web users; the design was thus inspired by the look and feel of Web browsers. Still, the interface resembles other classical editors rather than modern Web 2.0 tools.

---

[232] Ontology Inference Layer (OIL): http://www.ontoknowledge.org/oil/.
[233] DAML+OIL: http://www.daml.org/language/.
[234] An overview of available plug-ins is given on http://protege.stanford.edu/download/plugins.html.
[235] CollaborativeProtégé: http://protege.stanford.edu/doc/collab-protege/.
[236] KAON: http://kaon.semanticweb.org/.
[237] Forschungszentrum Informatik (FZI) : http://www.fzi.de.
[238] Institute of Applied Informatics and Formal Description Methods (AIFB): http://www.aifb.uni-karlsruhe.de/english.
[239] SWOOP: http://code.google.com/p/swoop/.

- Hozo (Sunagawa, Kozaki et al., 2004): Hozo is an ontology editor with visual editing support and some collaborative functionalities. An English and a Japanese version are available.
- OBO-Edit[240] (Day-Richter, Harris et al., 2007): OBO-Edit is developed by the Berkeley Bioinformatics and Ontologies Project, and is funded by the Gene Ontology Consortium. It is an open source project that particularly addresses biologists as its target users. Originally, the tool GO-Edit was exclusively designed as an editor for the Gene Ontology. As it got adapted by a growing community, its functionalities were broadened and the tool was renamed DAG-Edit, since the ontologies that could be edited were special forms of directed acyclic graphs (DAG). Later again, the tool was once more modified to support ontologies in the OBO ontology format[241] and renamed OBO-Edit. The OBO ontology format is an ontology format developed for the needs of biologists, in particular, for creating biological ontologies. It resembles OWL or DAML+OIL but is less detailed and simpler.
- DOME[242] (DERI Ontology Management Environment): DOME is developed by the Ontology Management Working Group[243] (OMWG) as an integrative tool for building, managing and mapping ontologies.
- OntoStudio[244]. OntoStudio is one of the most popular commercial ontology editors. It is produced by Ontoprise as the successor of OntoEdit (Sure, Erdmann et al., 2002). It supports F-Logic, RDF, OWL and its own internal format OXML. Furthermore, data can be imported from other than ontological resources, e.g. from Microsoft Outlook or Excel.
- TopBraid Composer[245]: TopBraid Composer is a commercial ontology editor provided by TopQuadrant[246]. It supports ontology development in OWL and RDF. The interface resembles Protégé in certain aspects (Figure 3.10), but the tool is a novel system with its own features. For example, geodata can be explicitly handled by the editor and can directly be linked to Google Maps (Figure 3.11).

---

[240] OBO-Edit: http://oboedit.org/.
[241] OBO Ontology Format: http://www.geneontology.org/GO.format.obo-1_2.shtml.
[242] DOME: http://dome.sourceforge.net.
[243] Ontology Management Working Group (OMWG): http://www.omwg.org/.
[244] OntoStudio: http://www.ontoprise.de/content/e1171/e1249/index_ger.html.
[245] TopBraid Composer: http://www.topquadrant.com/products/TB_Composer.html.
[246] TopQuadrant: http://www.topquadrant.com.

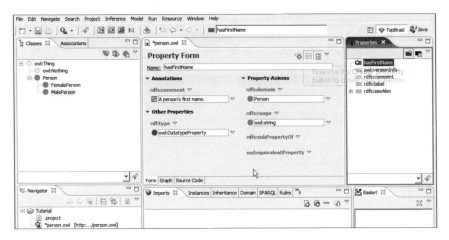

Figure 3.10. The TopBraid Composer editor interface. Source:
http://www.topquadrant.com/composer/videos/introduction.html.

Figure 3.11. TopBraid Composer: The Instance Canberra is represented with geodata that
can directly be mapped to Google Maps. Source:
http://www.topquadrant.com/composer/videos/geotravel.html.

- Altova SemanticWorks[247]: SemanticWorks is a commercial tool with a focus on graphical user interfaces and visual ontology engineering. It enables a graphical editing of ontologies in RDF(S) and OWL format (Figure 3.12).

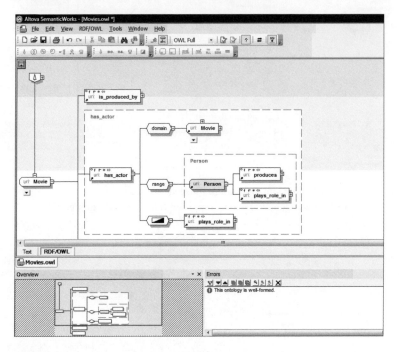

Figure 3.12. Altova SemanticWorks: The graphical ontology editor.

- NeOn[248]: The NeOn Project is a large research project with 14 participating European institutions. Their aim is to provide a novel tool that helps to handle multiple networked ontologies and to create, manage and maintain them collaboratively. For this purpose, the NeOn Toolkit is being developed: an ontology editor with various extensive plug-ins. It supports F-logic and OWL. A first preliminary version can be downloaded.

3.1.3 Recent Trends and Open Challenges in Ontology Engineering

Altogether, a lot of work is being done in developing the 'ideal' ontology editor, and more than the selected tools we have just introduced are available. Among the

---

247   Altova Semantics Work:
      http://www.altova.com/products/semanticworks/semantic_web_rdf_owl_editor.html.
248   NeOn: http://www.neon-toolkit.org/.

current works in progress, some issues receive particularly high attention – and their solutions will be a significant step towards a Social Semantic Web.

Reuse of Existing Ontologies

Developing numerous ontologies with broad domain coverage is a time-consuming task. Thus every tool and every method that helps to reduce this effort is welcome. Reuse of existing knowledge resources – both ontologies and other knowledge models – is probably the most promising solution. And yet, research concerning ease of reusability is only in its infancy. Presutti and Gangemi (2008) name the following reasons for this deficit:

> "Today, one of the most challenging and neglected areas of ontology design is reusability. The possible reasons include at least: size and complexity of the major reusable ontologies, opacity of design rationales in most ontologies, lack of criteria in the way existing knowledge resources (e.g. thesauri, database schemata, lexica) can be reengineered, and brittleness of tools that should assist ontology designers." (Presutti & Gangemi, 2008)

Thus ontology engineers who are willing to reuse existing resources are facing several problems. There is neither any guidance, nor any tool that directly addresses this issue, nor any central repository for discovering reusable knowledge resources. This also hampers the actual distribution of many ontologies on the WWW.

> "On this situation, an average user that is trying to build or reuse an ontology, or an existing knowledge resource, is typically left with limited assistance in using unfriendly logical structures, some large, hardly comprehensible ontologies, and a bunch of good practices that must be discovered from the literature. On the other hand, the success of very simple and small ontologies like FOAF and SKOS shows the potential of really portable, or 'sustainable' ontologies." (Presutti & Gangemi, 2008)

Presutti and Gangemi (2008) consequently propose the following changes: small ontologies should be developed that are both easily usable and reusable and should be prepared with explicit documentation of design rationales. Best practices are needed for issues of reengineering, and the ontologies should be implemented in repositories (or registries/ catalogs) to make them accessible. Furthermore general discussion and evaluation forums are needed, as well as a new generation of ontology design tools. We may add that modeling standards (like standardized semantic relations) can enhance reusability.

We assume that the matter of reusing ontologies and other knowledge resources will gain in importance in the upcoming years. The first steps have been taken and the topic has entered international scientific conferences[249]. This book will also discuss two of these aspects in more detail: The options of using certain KOS as

---

[249] Like the 1st International Workshop on Knowledge Reuse and Reengineering over the Semantic Web (KRRSW) at the European Semantic Web Conference (ESWC) 2008, http://babage.dia.fi.upm.es/krrsw2008/index.html.

starting points for ontology engineering (semantic upgrades, Section 3.3) or reusing other resources from the (Social) Web (Section 3.3.4); and a meta-ontology for the indexing of ontologies in order to describe their contents and make them accessible (Section 3.4.2).

Automatic Approaches in Ontology Engineering

Apart from support for the manual construction of ontologies, some research focuses on the automatic development or enrichment of ontologies. This should reduce the cost and effort needed to build ontologies. So far, there are no fully automated methods for constructing entire ontologies (and it is usually not desired to automate the whole process) but quite a few approaches for the semi-automatic enrichment of ontologies with human intervention (Ding & Foo, 2002a).

In this context, we are mainly talking of *ontology learning*[250] – a term introduced by Alexander Maedche and Steffen Staab (2001). Jäschke, Hotho et al. (2008) aptly sum up the task of ontology learning:

> "Usually machine learning or data mining algorithms are applied mostly on textual data to extract the hidden conceptualization from the data and to make it explicit. Revealing the hidden conceptualization of an author partially written in a text document can be seen as a kind of reverse engineering task [...]. All ontology learning approaches try to support the knowledge engineer by setting up the ontology." (Jäschke, Hotho et al., 2008)

Buitelaar, Cimiano and Magnini (2005) have collected comprehensive works on the topic. Automatic ontology engineering involves research from various disciplines. A particular focus is placed on works from computational linguistics and the sub-disciplines of *information extraction* or *machine learning*, which provide the means for extracting semi-structured information from text. The tasks of identifying concepts, instances or subsumption relations (hierarchies) can be considered suitable for machine-based approaches. Much more difficult is the automatic generation of other types of semantic relations (Maedche & Staab, 2000; Schutz & Buitelaar, 2005).

Only few ontology editors directly include methods of automatic extraction from texts or natural language processing. Here, there is still a lot of room for improvement. The Cmap Ontology Editor (COE, see below, footnote 274) includes some approaches to incorporating natural language processing and cluster analysis to an ontology editor. The Ontoverse Editor also supports automatic information extraction, fundamentally based on co-reference resolution (Kilbury, Bontcheva et al., 2009). This mechanism may for example be used to detect new candidates for instances, which can then be added to an ontology. Other tools provide gateways for existing IE tools like Gate[251].

The description of single techniques, methods and tools for (semi-) automatic ontology engineering goes well beyond the scope of this book and makes up a vast

---

[250] In some cases this is also referred to as *ontology population* (Cimiano, 2006).
[251] Gate: http://gate.ac.uk/ie/.

research field in itself, which will presumably grow even bigger in the near future. Also closely related to automatic approaches in ontology learning are (semi-) automatic approaches for indexing and annotation, which constitute another hot topic in ontology engineering research.

Ontology Engineering and Ontology-Based Indexing

In most cases, ontology management tools focus entirely on the development of ontologies – independently of their subsequent application and usage. Thus functionalities for semantic indexing on the basis of the ontologies are rarely directly included. Braun, Schmidt et al. (2007) speak of "shortcomings of the usual separation of creation and usage processes". But, furthermore, methods for indexing are generally underrepresented in Semantic Web research[252]. We may say that the main problems with folksonomies as a Web 2.0 approach to knowledge representation are opposite to those of ontologies for the Semantic Web: On the one hand, research in ontologies and the Semantic Web have almost inclusively focused on the process of building models for knowledge representation (providing representation languages and editing tools) while the process of indexing has been neglected. On the other hand, folkonsomy-based approaches in Web 2.0 mainly address indexing issues (enabling large user communities to index Web contents) while little or no considerations are being made concerning the underlying knowledge structures and vocabularies. With the beginning of Social Semantic Web initiatives, these two sides have started to converge.

Indexing poses a series of new challenges to ontology tools, like how to handle different versions of an ontology, how to index documents with multiple ontologies and which parts of a Web document to index[253]? These problems have been recognized and this has already resulted in some new tools combining semantic indexing for a certain document collection with the actual ontology development process. In these cases, we cannot speak of ontology editors in a strict sense but may classify them as a new type of application. They may for example be called *semantic indexing* tools or *ontology-based indexing* tools and are often also referred to as *annotation* tools.

While few systems so far rely on the users to index documents with ontologies, some tools apply semi-automatic technologies to semantic document indexing. Such techniques are basically useful for detecting named entities based on underlying ontologies. They typically correspond to instances of ontology classes. These systems usually do not display the whole spectrum of information included in complex ontologies, i.e. they do not yet make full use of the expressiveness of complex ontologies.

---

[252] Some exceptions from early Semantic Web research are CREAM (Handschuh, Staab & Maedche, 2001) or Annotea (Kahan, Koivunen et al., 2002).

[253] This would be a matter of 'What is our documentary unit?' in classical document indexing discussions.

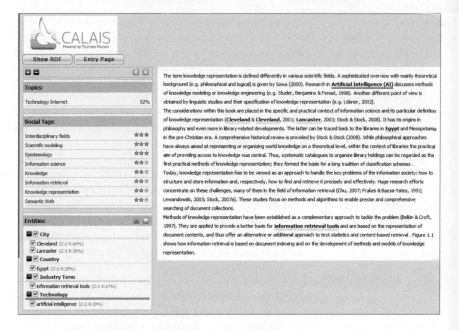

Figure 3.13. The Document Viewer, a tool for demonstrating the capabilities of
OpenCalais. Source: http://viewer.opencalais.com/.

One project that currently receives much attention is OpenCalais[254], a tool suite for
document annotation which includes a Firefox plug-in (Gnosis[255]) and solutions
for content management software. The Calais Document Viewer[256] can be used to
demonstrate the capabilities of OpenCalais. In Figure 3.13 we see an exemplary
analysis of a text chunk (in this case, the first paragraph of this book) which has
been submitted to the Document Viewer. The Document Viewer has determined
the topic of the text ("Technology Internet"), additional content-descriptive keywords (section "Social Tags" on the left part of the interface, among them "Semantic Web"), and some named entities (e.g. "Egypt" as an entity of "Country" –
whereas the names "Cleveland" and "Lancaster" have been recognized as cities,
which is not correct in this case). Currently, it cannot automatically detect connections between the single entities.

---

254   OpenCalais: http://www.opencalais.com.
255   Gnosis: http://www.opencalais.com/applications/gnosis.
256   Document Viewer: http://viewer.opencalais.com/.

In the future, such semi-automatic as well as manual indexing tools[257] will have to be closely coupled to ontology editors. This way users will be enabled to directly influence the outcome of automatic processes and will also be able to directly apply an ontology to a document collection. Walter and Nagypal (2007) also point out the need for blended solutions that combine ontology engineering and document indexing:

> "While tagging systems are user-friendly, ontology formalisms and development tools are too complicated for most users [...]. This fact normally leads to a separation of the ontology engineering process from the usage of ontology for the semantic annotation of resources. When the content of an image repository rapidly changes – and this is the case for most image repositories that are created collaboratively – this separation usually results in missing or obsolete concepts in the ontology. [...] – Second, the process of ontology development should be integrated into the process of semantic annotation." (Walter & Nagypal, 2007)

Figure 3.14. SOBOLEO editor interface. Source: http://tool.soboleo.com/editor/editor.jsp.

---

[257] One example project for manual semantic document indexing is Loomp, http://www.loomp.org/, which is still under development.

One tool that combines on-the-fly collaborative ontology engineering and indexing is SOBOLEO[258] (Zacharias & Braun, 2007), which is part of the Im Wissensnetz project[259]. SOBOLEO facilitates the simple creation, extension and maintenance of lightweight ontologies (in the SKOS[260] format, mainly hierarchical). At the same time, it supports the annotation of Web resources (bookmarks) with concepts from this ontology. Figure 3.14 shows the interface for editing the simple underlying ontology: concepts are interlinked by a general hierarchy (broader and narrower terms) and in the form of associative relations (related terms); synonyms can be added as alternative concept labels. Figure 3.15 shows the interface for indexing a document (in the form of a URL for a Website) with concepts from the underlying ontology.

Furthermore, SOBOLEO supports query expansion in information retrieval based on the underlying ontology. This means that broader, narrower or related terms may be added to reformulate a search query. This leads us directly to the next hot topic in ontology engineering: the combination of ontology editors and information retrieval tools.

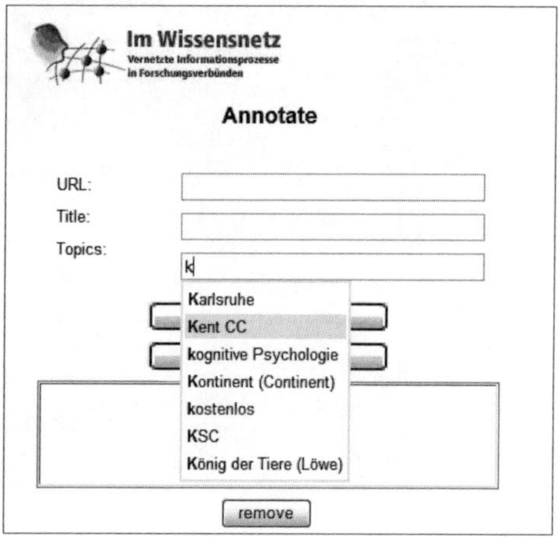

Figure 3.15. SOBOLEO indexing tool. Source: http://tool.soboleo.com.

Ontology Engineering and Semantic Search
As we have seen in the first chapter, indexing is almost intrinsically tied to information retrieval. Thus the idea of combining tools for ontology engineering, in-

---

[258] SOBOLEO: http://www.soboleo.com.
[259] Im Wissensnetz (German for: In the Knowledge Network): http://www.im-wissensnetz.de/.
[260] Simple Knowledge Organization System (SKOS): http://www.w3.org/2004/02/skos/. See also section 3.4.3 of this book.

dexing and retrieval seems only natural. So far, there are only very few tools that combine all three aspects. Schwarz (2005) has collected 30 tools that somehow support searching with underlying KOS (mainly ontologies, thesauri or classifications). Some of them also provide editing and indexing functionalities, for example the Ontopia Knowledge Suite[261] for topic maps and Convera Retrieval-Ware[262] for thesauri and lightweight ontologies.

Besides SOBOLEO, ImageNotion[263] is another tool developed at the Forschungszentrum Informatik (FZI) Karlsruhe. ImageNotion uses automatic semantic annotations for semantic image retrieval (Walter & Nagypal, 2007). Semantic search technologies generally receive high attention in the specific application area of image retrieval (e.g. Hollink, Schreiber et al., 2003; Hyvönen, Styrman & Saarela, 2002; Mainz, Weller & Mainz, 2008; Popescu, Moellic & Millet, 2007; Schreiber, Dubbeldam et al., 2001). Image and video retrieval systems are also an important point of contact between the Social and the Semantic Web. In Web 2.0, image and video collections are intensively indexed with folksonomy tags (e.g. on Flickr or YouTube). The potential for enhancing these free social tags with semantic structures are enormous, e.g. in order to bundle synonyms, separate homonyms or enable query expansion based on semantic relations.

We also assume that a lot of new projects combining folksonomy-indexed media portals with semantics will be developed in the near future. Furthermore, the combination of ontology editing and ontology-based retrieval will gain in importance in the future of Social Semantic Web research, and there is still a lot of work to be done.

User Perspectives and Collaboration

The support of user collaboration is one of the all-time hot topics in ontology engineering. As we have seen in the presentation of different editors, even some of the early ontology editors had some form of collaboration support (for example Ontolingua and WebOnto). And new approaches to enabling users to jointly edit ontologies remain popular until today (for example in the projects Ontoverse or SOBOLEO). Just like traditional KOS, ontologies are rarely developed by single individuals but by working groups and teams of developers. Gómez-Pérez, Fernández-López and Corcho have pointed out (2004):

> "[…] we can say that ontologies aim to capture consensual knowledge in a generic way, and that they may be reused and shared across software applications and by groups of people. They are usually built cooperatively by different groups of people in different locations." (Gómez-Pérez, Fernández-López & Corcho, 2004)

And yet there are differences between supporting small groups or project teams in working together and enabling a large Web community to jointly build ontologies.

---

[261] Ontopia Knowledge Suite: http://www.ontopia.net/solutions/products.html.

[262] Convera: http://www.convera.ch/.

[263] ImageNotion: http://www.imagenotion.com.

In the early years of ontology engineering, the target group of ontology editors were mainly experts in the fields of knowledge engineering and/or computer science. Thus not much attention was placed on user interfaces that are easily and intuitively usable by broad user communities. Until today, "both ontology editors and ontology languages impose high entrance barriers for potential users" (Hepp, Bachlechner & Siorpaes, 2006a). Instead of on easy usability, the focus is placed on the sophisticated support of ontology languages and engineering methodologies. Dimitrova, Denaux et al. (2008) indicate that the lack of available ontologies for Semantic Web applications is also connected to the complexity of ontology engineering tools:

> "This is due to the time and effort required to create ontologies. Most ontology construction tools aggravate this situation because they are designed to be used by specialists with appropriate knowledge engineering and logic skills, but who may lack the necessary domain expertise to create the relevant ontologies. At present, it is knowledge engineers who usually drive the ontology authoring process, which creates an extra layer of bureaucracy in the development cycle." (Dimitrova, Denaux et al., 2008)

With the growing interest in Web-wide user collaboration the focus has already started to shift to more intuitive interfaces – probably at the cost of high formality. The challenge lies in keeping the balance between feasibility and formality.

As user collaboration in ontology engineering is probably the most important aspect of ontology engineering for the Social Semantic Web, we will now discuss this topic in more detail.

3.2 Community-based Ontology Engineering

For the context of the Social Semantic Web, we will distinguish between collaborative ontology engineering and community-based ontology engineering. Collaborative ontology engineering is every process of developing an ontology that is performed by more than one ontology engineer. Thus collaborative ontology engineering may be carried out by two co-workers or a project team with several members. Typically, the participants of a collaborative ontology development process are an appointed group with a shared motivation and background (e.g. members of the same research project or co-workers). They may be located at different places. Seidenberg and Rector (2007) have collected several examples for project teams which have carried out some form of collaborative ontology construction, e.g. the GALEN project or the NCI thesaurus development.

Community-based ontology engineering is a specific form of collaborative ontology engineering based on the contribution of an open community (in contrast to a fixed team). New participants may join in, others may leave the project. People do not necessarily know each other. They may all possess different skills and expertises as well as different points of view and motivations.

3.2.1 Basic Principles of Community-based Ontology Engineering

Motivation and Objectives

One initial motivation for supporting collaborative approaches in ontology engineering is grounded in the definition of ontologies as a "shared conceptualization" (Borst, 1997). If a group of people jointly builds up an ontology, they will likely account for the requirement of representing a consensual point of view. Gómez-Pérez, Fernández-López and Corcho (2004) even claim that a "[...] model can only be considered an ontology if it is a shared and consensual knowledge model agreed on by a community." Hepp, Bachlechner and Siorpaes (2006a) state that "[...] it is important to note that ontologies are not just formal representations of a domain, but much more *community contracts* of such formal representations." On the other hand, they criticize that "[...] most available ontologies have a very weak community grounding in the sense that they are designed by single individuals or small groups of individuals, while the majority of potential users is not involved in the process of proposing new ontology elements or achieving consensus" (Hepp, Bachlechner & Siorpaes, 2006a).

To actually capture the consensus of a broad community, collaborative ontology engineering approaches have to go beyond the co-operation of specialized teams. Ontologies should not only be created by a team of information architects but by as many as possible members of the community of interest meant to finally use the ontology. People with expertise or interest in the depicted domain of an ontology should at least be enabled to easily comment on the ontology and provide suggestions for changes and enhancements. In the best case scenario, a worldwide community should be able to discuss the structure of the ontology, perform changes and maintain the ontology. Of course this poses various new challenges to ontology engineering, from handling different release versions to managing the access rights of community members. On the other hand, this approach does offer new opportunities for capturing consensual knowledge, for capturing the actual vocabulary of a user community and for harvesting collective intelligence (in the sense of: collecting knowledge from a variety of specialized experts).

> "In such settings, typically, different participants have only partial knowledge of the domain, and hence can contribute only partial ontologies of the domain. Common tasks involve refinement of a predefined ontology, and integration of several such partial ontologies to obtain a coherent ontology. Semantic mismatches and logical inconsistencies between independently developed ontologies are unavoidable. Thus, there is an urgent need for principled approaches and flexible tools for allowing individuals to collaboratively build, refine, and integrate existing ontologies as needed in specific contexts or for specific applications." (Bao & Honavar, 2004)

Another major objective for advancing collaborative ontology engineering techniques is grounded in the fact that ontology engineering is very expensive in terms of labor and time. The success of Web 2.0 applications has shown that certain laborious tasks, like image and video indexing, can be carried out by a community of volunteers. If a comparable division of labor could be achieved for ontology engineering, the aim of developing large-scale ontologies for the Semantic Web would come one step closer to being achieved.

Dimensions of Collaborative Ontology Engineering

One may consider different dimensions to discussing approaches in collaborative ontology engineering. The differentiation of collaborative and community-based ontology engineering can be located on the *person* level (ranging from small working groups to worldwide communities). Much more research needed on the effects of community-based ontology engineering is certainly needed, while other collaborative scenarios are already being heavily discussed[264].

> "Although numerous fine-grained methodologies exist for building ontologies, most reflect best practices for settings in which the individuals have agreed to build a particular ontology (as part of an academic research project, for instance)." (Hepp, 2007)

Another dimension may be discussed as the *formality* level. This may range from the community-based construction of highly formal ontologies to the development of rather primitive controlled vocabularies. Braun, Schmidt et al. (2007) have encountered a "[t]rade-off between the degree of formalization and degree of participation." Gruber, Westenthaler and Gahleitner (2006) also report difficulties in creating consistent formal knowledge models with broad communities:

> "The easiest way to create a (consistent) knowledge model is to have the model developed by an individual. In that case the individual plays both major roles: creator and user of the system. In reality, this is not the case for most knowledge based systems because they are typically used by a community of workers. Therefore, a single expert is not capable of conceptualizing the communities' required knowledge in an appropriate way. Also, different kinds of communities with different interests may want to participate in the process: the developer community (software engineers, domain experts and knowledge experts), the community of decision makers, and the targeted end-users. We found that the formality of a model is a limiting factor for its acceptance because formality tends to increase the user's perception of complexity. There are two strategies for gaining large scale acceptance: either hide the formality or remain less formal. However, the latter is not a viable option for machine-to-machine interoperation. Therefore, role-based views on the ontology, abstraction layers and visualisation methods beyond graph visualisation need to be implemented in a workbench, that realises this methodology." (Gruber, Westenthaler & Gahleitner, 2006)

---

[264] Collaborative editing has also been a topic of interest for KOS engineering before the Semantic Web entered the scene. Raschen (2005), for example, provides practical guidelines for developing a corporate taxonomy with a minimum of three co-workers.

In some contexts, it may even be appropriate to count the mere activity of document indexing as a preliminary stage for community-based ontology engineering – which means that all processes of social tagging are closely related to the construction of informal KOS. Hepp (2007) further distinguishes between actual ontology engineering as an activity, and committing to an ontology as a mere process of agreement and acceptance:

> "We can classify ontology-related tasks into two main groups: building or contributing to the development of ontologies and committing to a particular ontology. Committing to a given ontology, explicitly or implicitly, means agreeing that it properly represents the domain's conceptual elements." (Hepp, 2007)

Siorpaes and Hepp (2007) have also distinguished the dimensions of *horizontal* and *vertical* ontology engineering. Horizontal ontology engineering refers to the efforts to extend an ontology by concepts and properties but not in the level of detailed axiomatization. Vertical ontology engineering means extending an ontology by axioms. While the horizontal broadening of ontologies is a typical task for domain experts, the specification of axioms or formal semantics in vertical ontology engineering is a task for ontology engineers (Figure 3.16).

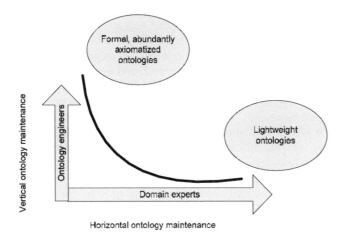

Figure 3.16. Horizontal and vertical ontology maintenance. Source: Siorpaes & Hepp, 2007.

Noy, Chugh et al. (2006) have analyzed several use cases of collaborative ontology engineering (e.g. the case of the OBO ontologies), and have identified four pairs of attributes to describe collaborative developments: "synchronous vs. asynchronous editing", "continuous vs. periodic archiving", "curation vs. no curation", and "monitored vs. non-monitored" development. While synchronous editing means that all users work on the *same* version of an ontology and all changes are immediately visible to everybody, in asynchronous editing a user checks out a part of the ontology for editing and then merges his changed version back into the common version. Continuous editing means that there is no process of archiving a particular version, all changes are made to *one* common version; a "rollback is performed using an undo operation" (Noy, Chugh et al., 2006). Alternatively, different versions may be archived periodically. Some systems work with curators, i.e. administrative persons who have to accept or reject changes (for example before a new version is archived). If a tool records all changes and possibly even assigns annotations to these changes (like a note on the type of change), we can speak of monitored editing. In non-monitored development, changes are either not logged at al, or the respective data is not made available.

For community-based ontology engineering we would generally prefer synchronous and monitored editing. Periodic archiving as well as curation may be useful for certain case, but they certainly require more sophisticated systems than continuous editing and systems without curation.

Furthermore, it is advisable to differentiate between intra-ontological and inter-ontological processes of ontology engineering (Weller, 2006). Knowledge representation and ontology engineering on the intra-ontological level deal with the challenges of constructing concepts, instances, properties and axioms within *one* single ontology (as discussed in detail in Chapter 2). In community-based approaches, the main challenges on this level are to establish modeling conventions (e.g. to agree on basic naming conventions and design principles) in order to make the ontology itself consistent and well-formed, and to represent the domain of interest in an appropriate way that can be accepted by the community.

The inter-ontological level of ontology engineering deals with the correlations between several ontologies. Inter-ontological ontology engineering comprises all activities that aim at mediating between ontologies (e.g. ontology mapping and merging) or at applying different ontologies within the same setting.

Challenges and Requirements

The aim of community-based ontology engineering is to enable broad groups of users to plan, create, maintain and manage ontologies in a convenient way. This calls for novel user interfaces that not only pay attention to all necessary functionalities of formal ontology editing but also include aspects such as user awareness, versioning control and instant information exchange (Hoppe, Malzahn & Weinbrenner, 2009). Technically, the basic requirement for collaborative ontology engineering is the support of synchronous and asynchronous information exchange via a certain platform. But this alone is not enough:

> "To support collaborations it is not sufficient to enable two users to access the same data synchronously, but also to support the awareness of other users' actions, and to enable users to discuss changes and to exchange resources and opinions." (Hoppe, Malzahn & Weinbrenner, 2009)

This alludes to some other important requirements of collaborative and community-based ontology engineering: group awareness and communication. If various users work on the same data, they need a good overview of what others are doing. Mechanisms have to be created that help to visualize the activities of the community so that each user may easily grasp what is going on. Additionally, all changes should be collected in a history tracing system to enable constant documentation of the editing process (monitored editing). This should ideally comprise a versioning mechanism and the option to undo changes and go back to a previous version.

Yet practical experience teaches us that change management and visualization are much more difficult to realize than it might seem on first sight:

> "When an ontology is created collaboratively in a larger community, it can be assumed that it will quickly become unwieldy; i.e. that the ontology becomes too large to easily display it in editors, that one user cannot follow all ongoing discussions about changes, that most users are not able or willing to understand the details of parts of the ontology of little concern to them, that there are too many changes happening in quick succession etc. So far we have tried to avoid this problem by intentionally restricting the users to only a small group from a single domain trying to achieve a single joint goal. However, traces of this problem appeared even in our small-scale evaluation when some users started to create sophisticated conceptualizations of the world of military aircraft – too specialized to be of interest to the other users." (Braun, Schmidt et al., 2007)

For actual collaborative activities, communication channels have to be directly coupled to editing functionalities. Furthermore, it may be useful to provide both private and shared workspaces – sometimes it may be desirable to create pieces of an ontology in a private workspace first, before committing it to the actual ontology. Yet such workflow scenarios lead us to the next great difficulties in providing support for community-based ontology engineering. If several users are simultaneously working on the same ontology, or if users gradually enrich an ontology, enormous challenges arise concerning the aspects of access conflict resolution or concurrency control, versioning and debugging.

Access conflicts mainly occur when several users edit the same pieces (or closely interlinked parts) of an ontology at the same time. As a solution, one may either think of systems to prevent such incidents or of systems that tolerate conflicts but provide means for managing them automatically or manually (Hoppe, Malzahn & Weinbrenner, 2009; Paulsen, Mainz et al., 2007). To support the discussion of ontology elements and the constant evolution of an ontology based on community decisions, the option of handling concurrent pieces of information and uncertainty in ontologies need lots of further research.

> "Also, we think it is important to stress that ontologies are not just formal representations of a domain, but community contracts about such representations. Given that a discourse is a dynamic, social process during which participants often modify or discard previous propositions or introduce new topics, such a community contract cannot be static, but must evolve. Also,

the respective community must be technically and skill-wise able to build or commit to the ontology [...]. For example, one cannot expect an individual or a legal entity to authorize the semantic account of an ontology without understanding what they commit to by doing so." (Hepp, 2008).

Furthermore, issues of quality ensurance have not yet been sufficiently discussed. While the community-based approach of writing an online encyclopedia (Wikipedia) has turned out to be successful and has brought forward its own mechanisms of quality control, it is still unclear whether the same will work for ontology engineering.

Another critical aspect in community-based ontology engineering is located in the formality dimension. Non-experts in ontology engineering cannot easily contribute to axiomatizing ontologies by establishing formal restrictions. They may even be overstrained with tasks such as creating properties. Siorpaes and Hepp (2007) thus focus on the collection of basic pieces of information from a broad community that are added to a fundamental ontology, the ontology meta-model:

"We need to define an ontology meta-model that is suitable for a large audience. Obviously, non-expert users are not able to build highly axiomatized ontologies; as explained above flat ontologies can be useful as well. Additionally, reasoning support is desirable which comprises limitations concerning expressivity. The meta-model must support adding concepts, properties, and relations, as well as instances and several annotation properties. In order to support the upload of more expressive ontologies, elements that are not included in the meta-model will be preserved within annotation properties." (Siorpaes & Hepp, 2007)

Finally, presumably the greatest challenge for collaborative ontology engineering research is how to motivate groups of people to work together in the sense of collective intelligence. Before we address this question and discuss some recent incentive systems, we will have a look at the actual user community and at different kinds of users.

User Communities and Types of Users

Community-based ontology engineering has to focus on a very heterogeneous user community. Ideally, contributions to an ontology should be collected from a broad spectrum of people interested in the domain of the ontology. These people may well have different background knowledge, different skills and probably also different points of view or ideologies.

On a very basic level, we may distinguish between active and passive ontology users, i.e. those who actively contribute to an ontology and those who passively commit to an ontology (for example simply by using it) (Hepp, 2007). Dzbor and Motta (2008) also distinguish normal and power users (or users and engineers).

Also common is a differentiation between domain experts (DEs) and ontology designers (ODs) (e.g. by Gruber, Westenthaler & Gahleitner, 2006; Mainz, Paulsen et al., 2008; Paulsen, Mainz et al., 2007). A community that wants to create an ontology must consist both of individuals who are knowledgeable in the domain of interest of the planned ontology and those who are trained in ontology engineering, or knowledge representation in general (while some individuals may even be skilled in both domain knowledge and knowledge representation techniques).

"Domain experts are individuals who are both experienced in and knowledgeable about, a particular area. They provide knowledge varying from highly specific understanding of e.g. particular scientific areas like medicine to 'simple' experience in professional usage of a certain software tool. [...] The integration of domain experts into the ontology creation process has a major influence on the community's acceptance of the resulting knowledge model. The more experts are involved in the construction process, the more likely it is that the model will be accepted in the community. In addition, the heterogeneity of domain experts of different disciplines leads to a network of ontologies which needs a common grounding in a foundational ontology." (Gruber, Westenthaler & Gahleitner, 2006)

The ideal collaboration scenario of ODs and DEs would be a workflow based on constant exchange. Domain experts are mainly needed for ontology instantiation, ontology maintenance and evaluation.

They may for example collect knowledge, provide it informally and discuss it, collect literature and knowledge resources relevant to actual topics of interest and tag them. They may populate ontologies and constantly enrich them with new (scientific) findings. They may reflect and benchmark existing ontologies, and they may answer domain-specific questions posed by ontology designers without the respective background knowledge (Paulsen, Mainz et al., 2007). On the other hand, ontology designers are needed to provide the actual formal representation of the ontology.

In broad communities, it may also be advantageous to have some users acting as administrators, who might coordinate discussions among DEs and ODs, or monitor the collaboration process and release versions of an ontology (Paulsen, Mainz et al., 2007).

An even more differentiated distinction can be made between "content consumers", "content providers", "content reviewers", and "super users" (among them moderators or administrators) (Siorpaes & Hepp, 2007). Rector, Wroe et al. (2001) distinguish "content contributors", "domain experts" (who capture knowledge and carry out quality assurance), "knowledge engineers" (who design and maintain the formal ontology) and "logicians" (who develop and maintain the underlying logic engines and representations). They encountered that "[...] domain experts find even knowledge-engineering languages at the level of GRAIL or OIL difficult to manage" (Rector, Wroe et al., 2001).

Much more research is needed on user types and on the specific needs of different user groups, respectively, before an ideal support of broad Web user communities can be facilitated. What is undisputable is that different types of users pose different requirements to ontology engineering tools.

For example, Pinto, Peralta and Mamede (2002) have evaluated Protégé from their power users' perspective. Dzbor, Motta et al. (2006) have performed an observational study: they have asked a group of participants with different background knowledge to perform three tasks of ontology engineering of increasing complexity and using different tools. They obtained both user feedback on the respective tools and observational data on specific user behavior. Mainz, Paulsen et al. (2008) report some experiences of ontology engineers collaborating with domain experts for the domain of bioinformatics. Tudorache, Noy et al. (2008) have evaluated Collaborative Protégé with a focus on domain experts from the domain of biomedicine. The greatest challenge they encountered in their user survey was:

> "[…] the disconnect between the produced ontology on the one hand and all the thought and discussion that went into producing this artefact on the other hand. The former was captured in Protégé, but the latter was captured in myriads of email messages, forum posts, phone conversations, and MS Access databases. When someone browsed the ontology, it was often impossible to understand the rationale that went into the design decisions, to find which references were relevant, to find the external resources that informed the modeling decisions. Conversely, when developers read a mailing list post discussing a modeling issue, they do not see the context for that post." (Tudorache, Noy et al., 2008)

From this experience, we may derive the general requirement that formal ontology engineering and discussion or documentation processes have to be very closely interlinked in community-based ontology engineering.

Also, there are only few detailed works on the behavior of novices in ontology engineering and on training mechanisms so far. We know far too less about the didactics of ontology engineering and of methodologies for education in knowledge representation principles. Rector, Wroe et al. (2001) also report their work with users untrained in formal ontology engineering (but who in some cases had previous experiences with medical taxonomies). They experienced that "[t]raining time for most workers had to be confined to no more than six days divided into two workshops" (Rector, Wroe et al., 2001).

Mike Uschold (1996) has proposed an approach to helping people untrained in knowledge engineering model part-whole relations. Target users were ecologists with little experience in mathematics, computing and artificial intelligence (and who wanted to build simulation models of ecological systems). Uschold provided the users with both a predefined ontology for guidance and an interactive computer system. He encountered difficulties in handling formal representations:

> "Of particular importance is that the constructs of the language be intuitively easy to grasp. Standard object-oriented programming systems are billed as being very natural, but they have representational shortcomings when it comes to part-whole information. We might have used a language from the KL-ONE family, but these are difficult to master, and come with no ontological guidelines as to how they are best used." (Uschold, 1996)

Uschold distinguishes three types of part-of relations: member-set, subdivision-set, and part-composite. He concludes that "[…] users must not be forced to distinguish which kind of part-whole they are referring to when no purpose is served. Yet it must be possible to infer the distinctions when needed" (Uschold, 1996). He further points out that simple, combinable elements should be used to create complex expressions, and that similar things should be represented similarly.

Good and Wilkinson (2007) have carried out some experiments with novices in ontology engineering. They performed an automatic transformation of the MeSH thesaurus to OWL format and then needed the help of a community with some expert knowledge in biomedicine to remove wrong statements and mismatches; they assumed about 40% of the automatically created subsumption relations to be incorrect. In a workshop, voluntary participants were asked to answer questions such as "is a lymphocyte a sub-class of a lymphatic system" or "is it true that a 'mast_cell' is also a 'connective_tissue_cell'?" (Good & Wilkinson, 2007). They observed that the participants could handle such tasks and encountered a typical long-tail distribution in the contributions: very few single participants carried out the large majority of the work.

Such rather random pieces of experience in user studies will need to be systematically collected in the future and transferred into an overall methodology for community-based ontology engineering.

Incentives and Obstacles for User Participation

As already indicated, probably the biggest challenge in community-based ontology engineering is to provide the incentives to motivate Web users to contribute to ontology creation processes. Understanding incentives and obstacles for user participation in online projects is closely related to understanding the general motivations for people to cooperate. Group behavior and motivations for collaboration have established a huge research field in psychology and sociology, which we cannot begin to review within the scope of this book. We may simply conclude that basic factors may be environmentally driven (expecting a reward or fearing a punishment) as well as internally driven (based on personal values, like group obligation, loyalty) (Fokker, Pouwelse & Buntine, 2006).

Some work has also been conducted with regard to collaboration in online environments. Before Web 2.0 had been detected as a trend, lots of collaborative efforts with numerous voluntary contributors could be found in conjunction with *open source*[265] projects, i.e. the development of software with open usage licenses, free access to source codes and the option to reuse and modify it (with respect to certain conditions). Within the FLOSS survey (Ghosh, Glott et al, 2002), several motivations for participation in open source development projects were accounted for. Over 78% of the 2,784 participants declared that their motivation was to "learn and develop new skills", 49.8% answered that to "share my knowledge and skills" was their primary motivation. Materialistic reasons like "make money" and "get a reputation in the […] scene" received the lowest rankings, while idealistic

---

[265] Open Source Initiative: http://www.opensource.org/.

motivations like "social software should not be a proprietary good" was named by 37.9% (Ghosh, Glott et al., 2002).

Kuznetsov (2006) reports a survey of student Wikipedia users with regard to their motivation for contributing to Wikipedia. One result was that "willingness to contribute to Wikipedia correlated with respondent's frequency of Wikipedia use". Of those participants that were willing to contribute to Wikipedia, 48.89% claimed that they would do so to "educate humanity/raise awareness"; 17.78% stated that contributing means to "feel like I'm making a difference" (Kuznetsov, 2006):

> "This data indicates that respondents are willing to contribute to Wikipedia because they want to share information, as well as to reciprocate to the Wikipedia and acquire a sense of satisfaction from contributing. [...] responses suggest that the primary reason for not contributing is the lack of time or knowledge of subject matter." (Kuznetsov, 2006)

Kuznetsov (2006) further sums up the top five motivations for contributing to collaborative online projects in general and Wikipedia in particular: altruism (i.e. aiming to benefit others without any intended personal gain), reciprocity (committing an altruistic act but also gaining some benefit in return), community (sharing a goal with a group of people, being part of a collective and working for a collective effort), reputation (being recognized, respected and appreciated for one's work) and autonomy (being free to chose one's own tasks and activities, carrying out creative work). To enable these processes to unfold, certain functionalities must be supported by the respective services. Wikipedia for example supports various acts of communication and coordination to foster the community and creates an individual page for every contributor to acknowledge the reputation factor. Marlow, Naaman et al. (2006) have also named the following motivations for participation in social tagging systems: "attract attention", "play and competition", "self expression", "opinion expression", "future retrieval", and "contribution and sharing". Peters (2009) has reviewed several studies of users' motivations for tagging Web resources. It is noticeable that purposes of personal information management (particularly information retrieval) are highly represented; aspects of community-building, communication with peers and altruistic motivations were also reported in several studies.

As community-based ontology engineering is a relatively new dimension of Web collaboration, we will have to wait for specialized studies of the motivations of Web users for contributing to ontologies. Collaborative approaches in traditional KOS engineering are barely usable for analyzing participants' motivations: in these cases we are typically dealing with organized teams who have directly been set up with the aim of building an ontology for a certain purpose – thus the motivation is directly coupled to the task. Yet some experiences can be gathered from projects in which groups of domain experts are incorporated into KOS engineering, like where knowledge engineers have to collect relevant data from experts in the field of bioinformatics in order to build a domain-specific ontology (Mainz, Paulsen et al., 2008).

The main problem in motivating people to contribute to ontology engineering is the large tradeoff between time-consuming effort and hard-to-grasp reward: Currently, huge efforts are needed not only to build an ontology but also to learn how to build an ontology (at least the basic principles of knowledge representation and of ontology elements). On the other hand, positive results of ontology-based applications will only come to the fore after some time. This is fundamentally different in Web 2.0 scenarios, where the positive effects of, say, wikis and folksonomies are directly visible and contributing to these systems requires very few technical skills.

> "[...] Web 2.0 environments provide direct rewards for user involvement, mostly in form of improved access to Web content: Users who tag objects in collaborative tagging systems immediately improve their own access to those objects, while at the same time improving the shared metadata. As for the Semantic Web, many important tasks come without a proper reward for the contributing humans: Building an ontology is a fairly abstract task and thus pretty much decoupled from immediate rewards. Also, heavyweight annotations often require a lot more time from a single skilled individual than this individual will ever save by means of the improved access." (Siorpaes & Hepp, 2008a)

Ontology engineering and ontology-based indexing are often two distinct steps, i.e. there is no visible immediate application and benefit. This is fundamentally different for folksonomies, where no actual engineering process takes place in social tagging. Furthermore, Schroll and Hafkesbrink (2009) point out that "[p]eople who are investing time in the construction of an ontology are not necessarily the ones who will benefit from it."

Another critical aspect of collaboratively creating formal ontologies is the restrictiveness of ontological structures. In contrast to social tagging with folksonomies, ontology engineering does not support the incentive principle of autonomy, i.e. the freedom of choosing one's own actions is much more limited. Collaborative ontology engineering is often a process of close co-operation bound to constant discussions and establishing agreements. For community-based ontology engineering, this process has to be made easier. New methodologies for ontology development are needed in order to that take account of the quite random behavior of Web communities. A user may not want to plan an ontology and act according to a certain life-cycle scheme. He may simply want to add one single piece of relevant information, e.g. one particular instance. Community-based ontology engineering will surely not work strictly top-down or bottom-up but will evolve as a chaotic form of middle-out engineering.

Another effect that can be observed in almost all parts of voluntary community collaboration is the *participation inequality* problem: the majority of content is contributed by the minority of actual users (Nielsen, 2006)[266].

> "User participation often more or less follows a *90-9-1 rule*: *90%* of users are *lurkers* (i.e., read or observe, but don't contribute). *9%* of users contribute *from time to time*, but other priorities dominate their time. *1%* of users participate a lot and *account for most contributions*: it can seem as if they don't have lives because they often post just minutes after whatever event they're commenting on occurs." (Nielsen, 2006)

This also means that the contributing participants of a Web community are never representative of the entire group of users. On the other hand, we may derive that in order to gain only a few active participants for a community-based ontology engineering project, we will have to address a much broader community of interested (passive) users.

Nielsen (2006) has also suggested some measures for reducing participation inequality, i.e. to attract more active users to a Web system: Contributing to a system has to be made as easy as possible, or, "[e]ven better, let users participate with zero effort by making their contributions a side effect of something else they're doing" (Nielsen, 2006). An example for user contributions as side effects are recommender systems (Perugini, Goncalves, & Fox, 2004; Riedl & Dourish, 2005; Stock, 2007), such as Amazon's book recommendations based on users' buying behavior. William Hill and colleagues (Hill, Hollan et al., 1992) have coined the term "read wear" for even tracing and profiting from reading activities (or other forms of passive usage).

Nielsen (2006) further suggests that in order to increase user participation it is advisable that "[…] users build their contributions by modifying existing templates rather than creating complete entities from scratch. Editing a template is more enticing and has a gentler learning curve than facing the horror of a blank page." Finally, Nielsen discusses the need for rewarding users for participation and enabling a form of reputation ranking, and concludes that a balance has to be found between reward and "over-reward".

For community-based ontology engineering, we need new approaches that:

- Break down the complexity of the actual task: The complex task of building an ontology should be divided into small subtasks. There should not be any need for open communities to learn OWL-DL or to understand all challenges of ontology modeling.
- Mediate between domain experts and ontology engineers: even if many domain experts could be enabled to simply collect (informal) knowledge, we will still need some experts in KOS engineering to transfer this knowledge

---

[266] The same effect has for example been noticed by Heath and Motta (2008) for review sites and was reported by Good and Wilkinson (2007) for their voluntary participants in the ontology engineering experiment.

into formal ontology languages. The challenge is to create a flow of information with as little loss and effort as possible.

- Hide the actual task: Ideally, the task of designing an ontology would be invisible to the majority of users. The creation of the ontology itself does not immediately yield any profit (profits will only come into notice after additional steps have been carried out), and therefore it would be advisable to let the users focus on other tasks instead or to provide them with an environment that can harvest semantic data from various user activities.
- Provide some form of reward: The participation in a community-based system must offer some form of benefit to the users; this may be access to information, becoming a member of a community, building up some reputation or simply having fun.

Overall, two basic ideas appear most suitable for actually integrating user communities into the creation of ontologies for the WWW: a) providing systems that break down the process of ontology engineering into small tasks and let users easily contribute single pieces of information, and b) harvesting various data that are created by users for other purposes and deriving semantic structures from them.

Both ideas touch upon each other and may even be combined. In the following section, we will introduce some ongoing works that aim to achieve large-scale consensual knowledge representations and to allow broad user communities to easily contribute to ontologies.

3.2.2 New Approaches and New Tools for Community-based Ontology Engineering

We will now have a closer look at some of the most important recent ideas on how untrained Web users can contribute their knowledge to the creation of ontologies. The advancement of such systems is one key to enabling the creation of semantic technologies with broad coverage of the WWW.

Ontology Editors with Community Support

Not all approaches to involving user communities with ontology engineering are directly related to the development of new types of ontology editors. But of course the enhancement of available tools and the development of new community-based editors is an important research field.

As we have seen above, some initiatives from the very beginnings of research already included multi-user support for collaborative ontology engineering (e.g. in the Ontolingua project). Now we will have a closer look at how new forms of community support evolve.

One notable approach comes from the developers of the most popular ontology editor, Protégé: Collaborative Protégé is an extension of the Protégé system that supports collaborative ontology editing as well as annotation of both ontology components and ontology changes (Tudorache, Noy et al., 2008). Voting mechanisms are included to let users vote for different change proposals.

Collaborative Protégé is available in a standalone and a multi-user mode. The standalone version allows multiple users to access and modify the same ontology one after the other; the multi-user mode requires an additional client-server connection and enables simultaneous collaboration – all changes made by one user are seen immediately by other users.

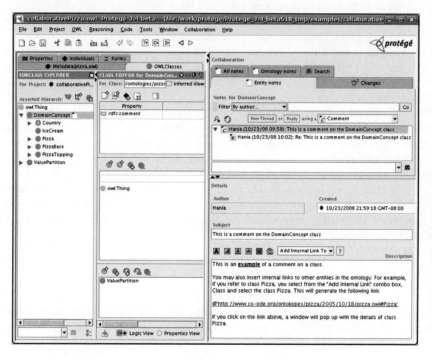

Figure 3.17. Collaborative Protégé. The right part of the interface is the collaboration
section. This image shows how a note is added to a concept. Source:
http://protegewiki.stanford.edu/index.php/Collaborative_Protege.

One main aspect of collaboration in Protégé is the support of communication processes. Notes can be created and attached to different ontology elements, like classes or instances (Figure 3.17). Within the notes, one may insert internal links to other elements of the ontology. Different types of notes are available, e.g. "comment", "advice" or "example". All notes can be searched and filtered. Additionally, an instant messaging/chat service is available for live communication.

Changes are constantly tracked and documented in the change history (for every entity in the ontology). Changes can also be commented on and labeled with different types of notes (e.g. "class creation", "renaming"). Collaborative Protégé supports two types of proposals with voting systems. Within "Agree / Disagree" proposals, users may either accept or dismiss a suggested change. In "Five Stars" votes, proposals may be rated with up to five stars.

Collaborative Protégé thus offers some important features for user groups co-operation – but is not yet fully geared to Web communities. It still focuses on groups of people who meet up with the intent of creating a specific ontology, not on general and accidental communities.

The Ontoverse project has a different aim: people with different background, different knowledge and different skills should be addressed and enabled to meet up and work together.

> "What is new in Ontoverse, is the explicit support of a social (scientific) network closely combined with a web-based ontology editor. A focus will be placed on the support of a heterogeneous community. Potential users will differ in their fields of interest and skills: On the one hand knowledge and expertise is needed from domain experts (DEs). On the other hand ontology languages can only be fully exploited by knowledge engineers — in the following called ontology designers (ODs). DEs are often unfamiliar with techniques of knowledge formalization, but contribute valuable data if they are provided with easy to use systems for knowledge input and additional help from ODs." (Paulsen, Mainz et al., 2007)

Ontoverse is a Web-based ontology editor (for OWL ontologies) embedded in a platform for sharing ontologies with a community. The fundamental idea behind the Ontoverse project was to provide a space where users are free to create, edit and modify ontologies, and to do so as a community of users with the same interests. Not only experts in ontology engineering should be able to contribute, but everybody willing to share his knowledge with the community.

A formal ontology editor is combined with (modified) basic wiki characteristics (easy to handle, web-based, multi-user support, change tracking and notifications, undoing changes, options for discussing the current state). The Ontoverse platform allows users to start new ontology projects or to join existing ones. It is thus also a repository for different (scientific) ontologies, so that another major task for an interested community will be to interlink and classify current ontology projects to make them accessible and traceable. Different access rights enable the creation of closed and open work spaces.

The important elements within Ontoverse are ontologies on the one hand and people on the other hand. The Ontoverse platform includes message boards where contacts can be established across the borders of ontology projects, and it includes a social networking component, i.e. personal profile pages for every user and the option of establishing and maintaining lists of personal contacts across the platform. One may also search for users who fulfill certain criteria, for example based on expertise or fields of interest.

As we have already indicated above, different phases of ontology development are supported in the Ontoverse platform. The wiki editor does not merely focus on the formalization phase but also provides the means for planning and collecting structure informal knowledge in the conceptualization phase (exemplary screenshots have been provided above in Figures 3.1 and 3.2). Wiki pages for conceptualization and discussion are directly interlinked with ontology entities. Other knowledge resources can be collected via the wiki. Ontoverse, in particular, is coupled to a publication database which helps users to collect scientific publications relevant for a topic of interest. For formal ontology engineering, new technical solutions are being developed to facilitate data storage and collaborative editing of data. Interactive ontology visualizations are included as well as options for integrative ontology mapping and merging (Malzahn, Weinbrenner et al., 2007; El Jerroudi & Ziegler, 2007).

Finally, the Ontoverse platform includes mechanisms for enriching an ontology semi-automatically, based on information extraction from document collections (Kilbury, Bontcheva et al., 2009). This technology is also applied for indexing publications with ontology terms.

Ontoverse is one among several projects to have spotted the usefulness of combining ontology engineering with wiki technologies. One of the earliest approaches to using wiki technology for ontology engineering is Wiki@nt (Bao & Honavar, 2004).

As we have mentioned in Section 1.4.2, there are two different ways in which wikis and semantic technologies can act together[267]. We have already provided some examples for the first method: enriching existing wiki platforms that include semantic annotations. Now we are dealing with the second type: collaborative ontology editors which have adopted certain wiki principles for ontology development. Auer, Dietzold and Riechert (2006) also point out these two different directions: some approaches "mix text editing with knowledge engineering" and integrate semantic markups into wikis, others "appl[y] the Wiki paradigm of 'making it easy to correct mistakes, rather than making it hard to make them' to collaborative knowledge engineering." Both directions are important innovations within a Social Semantic Web scenario.

Wiki systems are particularly useful as tools for ontology engineering, because they allow for the easy creation and management of informal data relating to an ontology, and even for the inclusion of images or other related files. Schaffert, Eder et al. (2009) sum up the advantages of wiki principles: Wiki systems "allow anyone to edit", "are easy to use", "support versioning", and "support all media." Hepp, Bachlechner and Siorpaes (2006a) also highlight this last aspect of media support in wikis (particularly because natural language definitions are often underestimated in current ontology engineering):

> "We especially propose the use of multimedia elements to improve the richness and disambiguity of informal concept definitions in an ontology. Also, we regard it as beneficial if the definition of a concept is not separated from the discussion that led to shaping the intension of this concept, since

---

[267]   Actually, there is a third way of how Wikis and ontologies can interact: In section 0 we will present approaches that harvest information from existing Wikis and use them for ontology engineering.

the history of a conceptualization is a valuable part of the respective definition." (Hepp, Bachlechner & Siorpaes, 2006a)

Hepp and his colleagues also suggest using unmodified wikis for ontology development (Hepp, Bachlechner & Siorpaes, 2006a and 2006b).

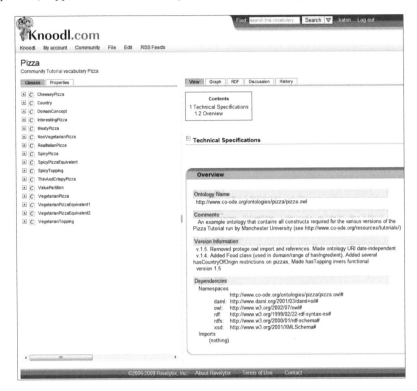

Figure 3.18. The Knoodl ontology editor. Source: http://knoodl.com/ui/groups/ Tutorial/vocab/Pizza.

Another recent system which has applied a very similar approach based on the combination of formal (OWL) ontology editing and a wiki for informal knowledge collection is Knoodl[268]. Like Ontoverse, Knoodl makes use of wiki technology in order to capture unstructured knowledge and to enable non-experts in formal ontology languages to contribute. Knoodl has a complex system of access rights and user roles in order to ensure property management. Figure 3.18 shows the Knoodle interface with the concept hierarchy on the left (a concept can be edited after clicking on it) and a section for informal or organizational information and unstructured knowledge on the right. Furthermore, queries may be formulated

---

[268]   Knoodl: http://knoodl.com.

within the system, for example to search for all instances which fulfill a certain criterion (Figure 3.19).

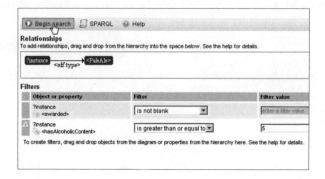

Figure 3.19. Formulating queries within Knoodl. Query elements can be combined in the
editor via the "drag and drop" principle. Source:
http://knoodl.com/ui/site/webcast/intro.jsp.

The following noteworthy approach to using wiki technology for ontology development is presented by the MyOntology[269] research project (Siorpaes & Hepp, 2007; Siorpaes, Hepp et al., 2008). The developers distinguish between two types of ontology development; engineering-oriented and community-oriented. Engineering-oriented ontology development is when a "small group of engineers carefully builds and maintains their view of the world" and then publishes the resulting ontology for further use; community-oriented ontology development lets "multiple individuals work on an ontology collaboratively" (Siorpaes & Hepp, 2007). This distinction basically corresponds to our distinction of collaborative and community-based ontology engineering.

Figure 3.20 shows the user interface of the first demo version of myOntology. The typical hierarchy section is on the left side of the screen, the remaining space being reserved for concept descriptions and properties in a wiki modus. "The domain vocabulary editing and creation forms are the same: users can add a description, synonyms, images and videos, translations, tags, a seeAlso link and concepts. Most of these attributes are enhanced by gathering data from the Web, such as Wikipedia, Flickr, YouTube, WordNet, etc." (Siorpaes, Hepp et al., 2008). The ontologies in myOntology are lightweight vocabularies, the "metamodel behind myOntology is a subset of OWL DL as a trade-off between expressiveness and suitability for lay people" (Siorpaes, Hepp et al., 2008). Some mechanisms for a semi-automatical removal of inconsistencies are included. Ontologies in community-based systems are subject to constant changes. In the myOntology system, so-

---

[269] MyOntology: http://www.myOntology.org.

called "freeze points" can be created in order to capture a stable snapshot of the current version of an ontology (plus the respective URI).

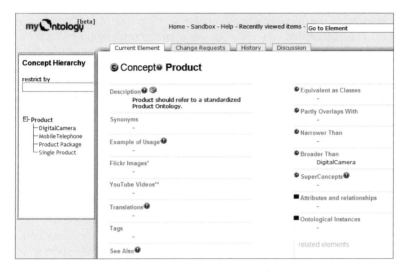

Figure 3.20. User interface of the myOntology demo version. Source:
http://myontology.sti2.at/prototype/Class/Product.

There are further related projects which we will not discuss in detail. One example is the OntoWiki project [270], which provides a tool for the flexible development of knowledge bases (Auer, Dietzold & Riechert, 2006). Furthermore, some wiki applications are available for the development of one specific knowledge organization system: WikiProteins[271] is a wiki application for authoring an ontology of proteins (Mons, Ashburner et al., 2008). Wikispecies[272] is a wiki-centric ontology for species, hosted by the Wikimedia Foundation. The BOWiki system focuses on biomedical knowledge, particularly gene functions (Hoehndorf, Bacher et al., 2009).

In future, the wiki principles are likely to be adopted by a growing number of systems. The KiWi[273] project has already entered the next stage of combining wikis and semantics: it provides a wiki-like platform that enables the community-based development of different kinds of Social Semantic Software (Schaffert, Eder et al., 2009).

Some additional initiatives exist that aim to support communities in participating in the ontology development process. Within the NeOn project, a meta-model

---

[270] OntoWiki: http://ontowiki.net.
[271] WikiProteins: http://proteins.wikiprofessional.org.
[272] Wikispecies: http://species.wikimedia.org.
[273] KiWi (Knowledge in a Wiki): http://www.kiwi-project.eu/.

is developed to guide the engineering process (Catenacci, Gangemi et al., 2007). COE[274] (Concept-Map Ontology Editor, Cmap Ontology Editor) has placed its focus on simplified user interfaces. COE is a suite of tools for displaying and editing OWL content in the form of simple node-link diagrams called "concept maps" (Cmaps). This means that concept maps are used to create models which can then be translated into OWL. On the project's Web site, it is also stated that the developer team is currently working on conventions for constructing new Cmap OWL ontologies to provide guidance for class and relationship construction. Apart from these two, several other ideas exist for how to support the community by reducing the required precognition and assumed skills. We will now have a look at a selection of them.

Support of Communication between Different Types of Users

Other current approaches focus on developing technologies that can help to transfer statements by domain experts to formal ontology languages on the one hand, and technologies that can help to translate formal ontology constructs to natural language sentences, so that domain experts can understand them, on the other hand. Both directions are two sides of the same coin and aim for better communication processes between domain experts from different fields of expertise and ontology engineers.

Controlled Natural Languages (also called Controlled Languages, CL) are among the approaches to incorporating domain experts into the ontology engineering process (Dimitrova, Denaux et al., 2008; Funk, Tablan et al., 2007; Schwitter & Tilbrook, 2004; Schwitter, Kaljurand et al., 2008). Schwitter and Tilbrook (2004) explain:

> "In a nutshell, a controlled natural language is a subset of a natural language that has been restricted with respect to its grammar and its lexicon. Grammatical restrictions result in less complex and less ambiguous sentences, while lexical restrictions reduce the size of the lexicon and the meaning of the lexical entries for a particular domain." (Schwitter & Tilbrook, 2004)

Controlled languages are based on research efforts that go back to the 1930s. In the context of ontology engineering, controlled languages are bound to a formal ontology language. Sentences which are formulated according to the rules of such controlled languages may directly be translated into ontology constructs. As any language, controlled languages have to be learned before they can be used. But learning to write CL sentences in order to express domain knowledge is considered easier than building OWL statements or editing an ontology via a formal editor.

> "Although the goal of CL tools is to assist in entering knowledge constructs, the existing tools focus solely on the CL aspect – they do not aim to provide assistance for the whole ontology construction process." (Dimitrova, Denaux et al., 2008)

---

[274] COE (Cmap Ontology Editor): http://cmap.ihmc.us/coe/.

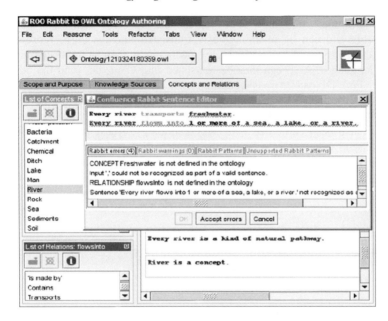

Figure 3.21. The ROO plug-in interface for entering Rabbit sentences into Protégé. Source: Dimitrova, Denaux et al., 2008.

Rabbit is a controlled language that covers OWL 1.1; ROO (Rabbit to OWL Ontology authoring) is an open-source tool developed as a Plug-in for Protégé 4 (Dimitrova, Denaux et al., 2008). The developers explain:

"ROO extends the Protégé 4 user interface by simplifying it as much as possible – hiding advanced options from the user and using what we believe to be less-confusing terminology (e.g. instead of 'classes and properties', ROO shows 'concepts' and 'relations'." (Dimitrova, Denaux et al., 2008)

Figure 3.21 shows the interface for entering Rabbit sentences via the ROO plug-in. The user has entered two Rabbit sentences describing the concept river: "every river transports freshwater" and "every river flows into 1 or more of a sea, a lake, or a river." The tool now checks whether these sentences are Rabbit-conform and then decides what changes should be made to the ontology. Freshwater is added as a new concept, flowsinto is added as a new relation.

First experiments showed that domain experts with no background knowledge in ontology engineering could be trained to use ROO, producing fair results in little time (Dimitrova, Denaux et al., 2008).

A very popular controlled language for ontology engineering is ACE[275] (Attempto Controlled English) (Fuchs & Schwitter, 1996). It is a subset of standard

---

[275] Attempto Controlled English (ACE): http://attempto.ifi.uzh.ch/site/.

English designed for knowledge representation. ACE texts are computer-processable and can be unambiguously translated into discourse representation structures (a variant of first-order logic) – which may than be translated into other formal languages. ACE can thus be translated into OWL DL (and the other way around: OWL DL can be translated into ACE).

The ACE Editor[276] has been developed to help users in creating correct ACE sentences. A plug-in for Protégé called ACE View is also available. Presently, ACE has also been combined with wiki technology: AceWiki (Kuhn, 2008) is a semantic wiki using ACE to enable the easy creation and modification of ontologies in a Web-based tool. It combines the features of community support and easy ontology authoring. Figure 3.22 shows the predictive Sentence Editor for creating ACE sentences in AceWiki; the fragment "Every area that contains a city is" has already been entered, the editor shows all possibilities for continuing this sentence (Kuhn, 2008).

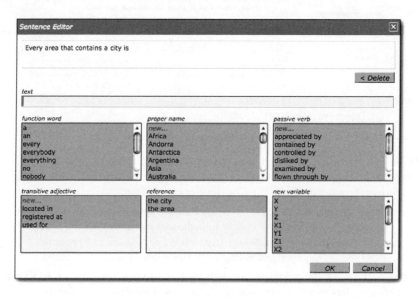

Figure 3.22. The sentence editor as part of AceWiki. Source: Kuhn, 2008.

Every ontological entity is coupled to a wiki page in AceWiki. Figure 3.23 shows the wiki page for a concept `continent`. It contains ACE sentences with collected information about this concept. ACE may further be used to formulate queries such as "Which continent contains more than 10 countries?" (Kuhn, 2008).

---

[276]   ACE Editor: http://attempto.ifi.uzh.ch/webapps/aceeditor/.

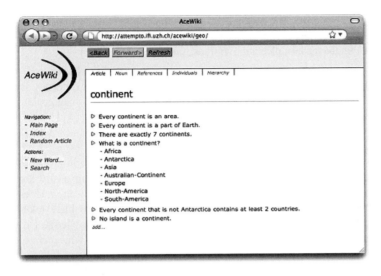

Figure 3.23. AceWiki user interface. Source: Kuhn, 2008.

Other controlled languages for ontology authoring include CLOnE (Controlled Language for Ontology Editing) (Funk, Tablan et al., 2007) and Sydney OWL Syntax (SOS) (Cregan, Schwitter & Meyer, 2007).

Besides research on controlled natural languages, some other approaches can be found that should help domain experts contribute to the development of formal ontologies more easily, or that support indexing applications. One such case is *Rules-by-Example* (RBE) (Hollink, Little & Hunter, 2005; Hunter & Little, 2004), a system that can help users formulate a kind of mapping of their own vocabulary to an ontology vocabulary:

> "This prototype enables experts to define rules specific to their domain, which map particular combinations of low-level visual features (colour, texture, shape, size etc.) to high-level semantic terms defined in their domain ontology. These semantic inferencing rules capture a domain expert's understanding of how low-level features are related to ontology terms." (Hollink, Little & Hunter, 2005)

Hollink, Little and Hunter have applied the Rules-by-Example approach to a system for the semantic indexing of cell images:

> "To overcome the difficulty that domain experts face when developing complex rules in XML format using unfamiliar terminology, a visual interface called Rules-By-Example (RBE) was developed. For example, an oncologist labelling brain scans to enable the search and retrieval of particular types of tumours, may define the following rule: IF [(color is like *this*) AND (texture is like *this*) AND (shape is like *this*)] THEN (the object is

an astrocytoma). The system assists users to construct rules with palettes of example colors, shapes defined using drawing tools, and example regions within the media collection." (Hollink, Little & Hunter, 2005)

For the future of ontology engineering, as well as semantic indexing and semantic retrieval, we expect lots of novel efforts of combining formal ontology languages with mediating systems for the benefit of people who have no background knowledge in ontologies.

Community Knowledge Bases

Community Knowledge Bases can also be counted among the approaches to providing interfaces that let non-experts in ontology engineering easily share their knowledge. These efforts are to some degree also inspired by the success of the online encyclopedia Wikipedia: community knowledge bases have taken on the Wikipedia principle of letting a community collect world knowledge (in contrast to semantic wikis, which have mainly adopted the underlying wiki technologies to create ontologies). The users of knowledge base projects are not told to build an ontology but to contribute little pieces of information to a system; the semantics may then be derived from the users' activities.

Figure 3.24. Freebase Fact Sheet for the football club 'VfL Bochum'. Source: http://www.freebase.com/view/en/vfl_bochum.

Probably the most popular recent example is Freebase[277], an open database for factual information about people, places and things. The domain is not limited and all kinds of topics of interest may be added. Like Wikipedia, users may contribute pieces of information by editing already existing topics (e.g. adding missing parts, correcting mistakes) or by starting new topics. Unlike Wikipedia, information in Freebase is not organized in the form of articles, but as fact collections/fact sheets. Mika and Greaves (2008) conclude about Freebase that "ontology editing and data acquisition can be carried out in parallel and the approach can scale to large numbers of users."

Figure 3.24 shows the Freebase page for the football club 'VfL Bochum'. It includes a reference/quotation from the Wikipedia article with the same topic and some structured facts about the club. The organization of Freebase facts resembles ontology structures in many ways: the single elements in Freebase (like VfL Bochum in our example) can be interpreted as ontology instances. Facts about them are organized in properties that may be filled with text or with links to other freebase contents. In the example, we find the properties 'founded', 'arena/stadium' and 'also known as' (for synonyms). Furthermore, VfL Bochum has been classified as a 'football team' and a 'sports team'. In Freebase, this is done by stating that something is of a certain *type*. Types are then coupled to certain properties (like 'player roster' and the team's 'colors' in the example), which can be applied to the respective 'instance'. More properties are coupled to these types in a *schema* and can be filled for a Freebase element. Figure 3.25 shows how the information about VfL Bochum's stadium has been added to the profile. Typing in the first letters reveals a list of suggestions for elements already included in the knowledge base. One may thus directly link the club to its stadium 'Ruhrstadion'.

---

[277] Freebase: http://www.freebase.com.

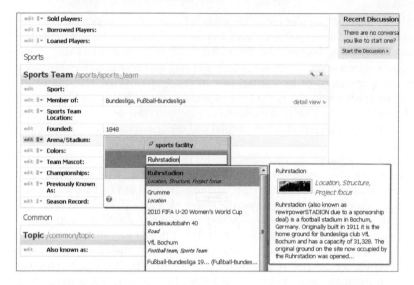

Figure 3.25. Freebase: On the page of the football club 'VfL Bochum', information on the
team's football stadium is added. Source: http://www.freebase.com/edit/topic
/en/vfl_bochum.

To edit Freebase, a user has to register and log in with a user name. Adding single
facts to individual fact sheets (as in the example in Figure 3.25) is the simplest
form of contribution. Furthermore it is quite easy to arrange single objects of a
certain type into a list. Figure 3.26 shows how the person 'Allister Carter' is added
to a list of 'snooker players'; conversely, the type 'snooker player' is added to the
profile page of Allister Carter.

The creation of new types and schemas is more complicated and requires more
careful consideration. This is the actual part of data acquisition and data modeling
that can be compared to ontology engineering processes. Freebase types loosely
correspond to ontology classes (though there is no explicit hierarchical view);
Freebase properties can be compared to ontology properties. In Figure 3.27, a new
type 'snooker tournament' has been created and is now filled with a new property
'tournament location'. The 'type of topic to link to' is the equivalent of the range
in ontology properties. It indicates that this property always has to link to elements
from Freebase which belong to a certain type (in this example, a tournament location has to be of the type 'city/town'; e.g. the 'Welsh Open' tournament has the
location 'Newport'). Other types of properties may be created to link to date/time
entries, text strings, numeric values or other entries, like external Web sites. With
the 'restrict to one value' operation, Freebase properties might also be stated as
being functional.

Figure 3.26. Freebase: Adding individual persons to a list of snooker players. Source: http://www.freebase.com/view/user/tadhg/tsport/views/snooker_player.

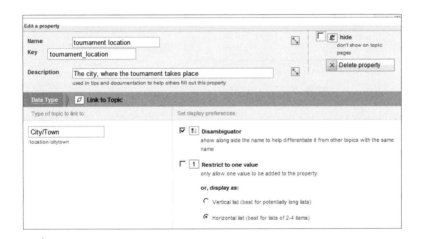

Figure 3.27. Freebase: Adding a new property for the 'snooker tournament' schema. Source: http://www.freebase.com/type/schema/user/kwelle/default_domain/ snooker_tournament.

Freebase provides some guidelines for this purpose in their online Data Modeling Guide[278], among them the following advices:

---

[278] Freebase Data Modeling Guide: http://www.freebase.com/view/en/data_modeling_guide.

- "Types should define collections of objects that share common properties."
- "Be careful to not over-develop the model."
- "The best types define collections that are useful to many people."
- "Use existing types when possible."
- "Pick property names that make sense in context."
- "Avoid types that are too abstract."

Freebase also experiments with another type of user contribution. The Freebase Typewriter[279] is an application that lets users easily judge the types of single Freebase topics. Freebase collects topics without assigned types which are likely to belong to a certain type (e.g. to the types 'location', 'politician', 'football player', 'song' or 'film actor'). Figure 3.28 shows candidates for the type 'human language'. The user may now tell the system whether each item belongs to this category or not. This application is optimized for usage with mobile iPhones and is a very simple form of game-like approach to knowledge collection. We will describe some comparable approaches in the next section about *games with a purpose*.

Figure 3.28. Freebase Typewriter: Decide whether the displayed items represent instances of 'human language' or not. Source: http://typewriter.freebaseapps.com/ queue/language/human_language.

All information collected in the Freebase database can be accessed via the API and may be reused for new applications[280]. One popular Freebase application is

---

[279]   Freebase Typewriter: http://typewriter.freebaseapps.com/.
[280]   A list of current Freebase applications is available at:
        http://www.freebase.com/view/freebase/featured_application.

Thinkbase[281], a tool for visual navigation and exploration of Freebase. Freebase articles are represented as nodes of an interactive graph.

Figure 3.29. Suggested starting points for contributing to the Open Mind Common Sense Project. Source: http://commons.media.mit.edu/en/add/.

Another interesting initiative is the Open Mind Common Sense Project[282], an ongoing research project by the Commonsense Computing Initiative at the MIT Media Lab[283]. In this case, volunteers are asked to contribute pieces of knowledge to the open-source semantic knowledge network ConceptNet[284] (Liu & Singh, 2004). ConceptNet is designed as semantic background knowledge for natural language processing and inferencing from texts. It is a large knowledge collection, comparable to Cyc or WordNet, with 1.6 million edges connecting more than 300,000 nodes in 2004.

The Open Mind Website provides users with statements like "a highway is a type of road" (Figure 3.29), which may be judged as correct or incorrect. Alternatively, one may choose one of the included concepts and judge all statements col-

---

281 Thinkbase: http://thinkbase.cs.auckland.ac.nz/.
282 Open Mind Common Sense: http://commons.media.mit.edu/en/.
283 Commonsense Computing Initiative at Massachussetts Institute of Technology (MIT) Media Lab: http://csc.media.mit.edu/.
284 ConceptNet: http://conceptnet.media.mit.edu/.

lected for this concept so far. Figure 3.30 shows the statements collected for the concept 'flower'.

Similar concepts

a person, something, a plant, flowers, fruit, a dog, a cat, a tree, water, food

Current knowledge

→ roses are flowers	by Evalise	Score: 24
→ orchids are flowers	by colm	Score: 15
→ a rose is a flower	by gros0468	Score: 12
→ Most flowers are pretty	by WhiteSun	Score: 11
→ An iris is a flower	by guru1	Score: 10
→ some plants have flowers on them	by circe3	Score: 10
→ Something you find at a park is flowers	by motminds	Score: 8

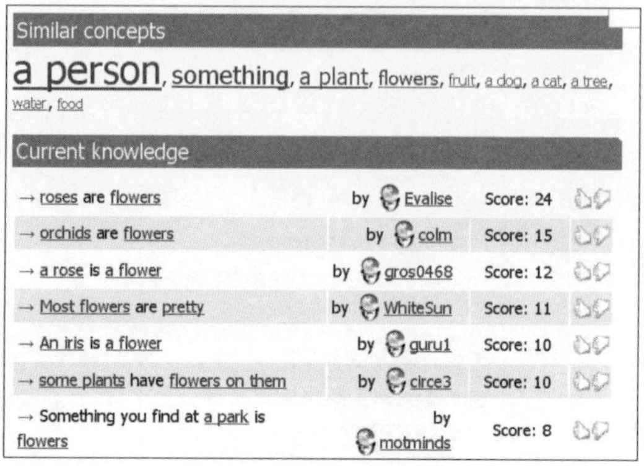

Figure 3.30. Information collected for the concept "flower" in the Open Mind Common Sense Project. Source: http://commons.media.mit.edu/en/concept/flowers/.

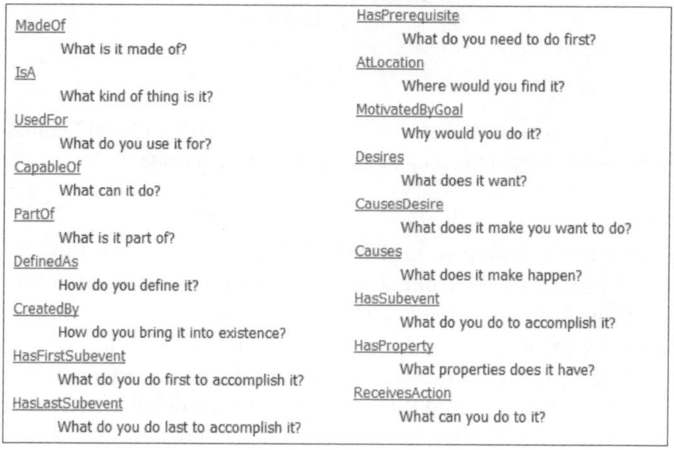

MadeOf
    What is it made of?
IsA
    What kind of thing is it?
UsedFor
    What do you use it for?
CapableOf
    What can it do?
PartOf
    What is it part of?
DefinedAs
    How do you define it?
CreatedBy
    How do you bring it into existence?
HasFirstSubevent
    What do you do first to accomplish it?
HasLastSubevent
    What do you do last to accomplish it?

HasPrerequisite
    What do you need to do first?
AtLocation
    Where would you find it?
MotivatedByGoal
    Why would you do it?
Desires
    What does it want?
CausesDesire
    What does it make you want to do?
Causes
    What does it make happen?
HasSubevent
    What do you do to accomplish it?
HasProperty
    What properties does it have?
ReceivesAction
    What can you do to it?

Figure 3.31. Predefined concept relations that can be used to enter new information in the Open Mind Common Sense Project. Source: http://commons.media.mit.edu/en/add/.

Furthermore, one may directly enter new facts in the form of concept-relation triples. Figure 3.31 shows a list of pre-defined semantic relations, which can be chosen to enter new facts to the knowledge base. Each relation is supported by some exemplary use cases to help users to submit other statements of the same kind (Figure 3.32). In this way, non-experts in ontology engineering can be enabled to contribute knowledge about instances and their relationships.

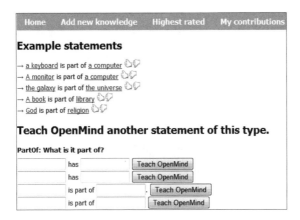

Figure 3.32. Collecting examples of part-of relations in OpenMind. Source: http://commons.media.mit.edu/en/add/21/.

Both Freebase and the Open Mind Common Sense Project are still miles away from the popularity of the community-based encyclopedia Wikipedia. Although they require much less training and introduction than ontology engineering tools, they are still less easy to use than wiki systems. On the other hand, their usefulness may not be as easy to grasp as Wikipedia. We have already seen that Freebase has applied some playful tool for collecting information from the users. Having fun while interacting with a system is an important motivation for user contributions – and it constitutes the initial driving force of our last category of recent tools and new approaches to supporting community-based ontology engineering: games with a purpose.

Games with a Purpose
The pioneer in the domain of *games with a purpose* (gwap/GWAP) is Luis von Ahn, who gained a lot of attention with his ESP Game[285] (Figure 3.33) (von Ahn, 2005; von Ahn, 2006a; von Ahn & Dabbish, 2004). Von Ahn's underlying idea is as brilliant as it is simple: people around the world spend billions of hours playing computer games – so how can we simultaneously profit from this behavior and gain something useful out of it? The ideal solution would be a computer game in which players help to solve computational problems without noticing it (von Ahn, 2006a). Of course there is a great challenge in creating games that are both useful and entertaining, Yet von Ahn claims to have solved this problem, stating about

---

[285] ESP Game: http://www.espgame.org/.

his game 'Peekaboom' that it "[...] has been played by thousands of people, some of whom have spent over 12 hours a day playing, and thus far has generated millions of data points" (von Ahn, 2006b).

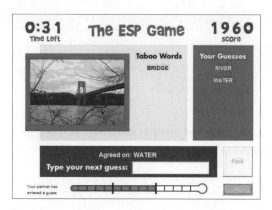

Figure 3.33. The ESP Game in 2007: playing the game. Source: http://www.espgame.org/.

For his games with a purpose, von Ahn mainly thinks of large-scale computational tasks in which humans clearly outclass computers such as, for example, image recognition. Image recognition still is one of the great challenges in Web retrieval. An enormous number of digital images are available on the WWW, but most of them are only insufficiently retrievable based on the hyperlink structure of the Web – no content-descriptive metadata are available. Approaches for automatic (content-based) image recognition are not yet mature enough.

> "Humans understand and analyze everyday images with little effort: what objects are in the image, where they are located, what is the background, what is the foreground, etc. Computers, on the other hand, still have trouble with such basic visual tasks as reading distorted text or finding where in the image a simple object is located. Although researchers have proposed and tested many impressive algorithms for computer vision, none have been made to work reliably *and* generally." (von Ahn, 2006b)

In the Web 2.0 environment, as we have seen, users tag (their own) image collections with keywords in order to make them retrievable. While they do this mainly for their own benefit in retrieval, games with a purpose go one step further and provide another incentive for image annotation: fun. While playing a gwap, index terms for images can be created as a by-product. In this regard, certain games with a purpose can be counted as a specific type of indexing in a Social Semantic Web context. Several games for image annotation are already available (many of them developed by von Ahn and his colleagues).

Figure 3.34. ESP Game in 2009: playing the game. Source: http://www.gwap.com /gwap/gamesPreview/espgame/.

Figure 3.35. The ESP Game in 2009: summing up the game. Source: http://www.gwap. com/gwap/gamesPreview/espgame/.

The ESP Game was the first one, and its principle has been adopted by Google for the Google Image Labeler[286]. In the ESP Game, two players are matched as a team and are then shown the same images. Both are asked to type in words which describe the respective image. The players cannot see the actions of their partner during the game. Every time two players assign exactly the same word to an image, they score. Furthermore, the matching word can now be assigned to the image – as a content-descriptive keyword with some basic form of documented social agreement. Within the game, the aim of the players is to gain as many points as possible in a limited time period. For most images, the system also lists a set of "taboo words", which must not be used by the players (e.g. words that have already been added during previous games by other players). Figure 3.33 shows

---

[286] Google Image Labeler: http://images.google.com/imagelabeler/.

what playing the game looked like in 2007: the player sees an image and may type in his suggestions (which are then collected on the right side of the screen, in this case 'river' and 'water'). The taboo words are presented in the middle ('bridge'). If the two players assign the same word, this will be shown to the players ('Agreed on: Water') and the game will proceed to the next picture. By now, the ESP Game has a new user interface while the principles have stayed the same (Figure 3.34). After having played one round, all images of the game are summed up and can be recapitulated (Figure 3.35).

Figure 3.36. Google Image Labeler: playing the game. Source: http://images.google. com/imagelabeler/.

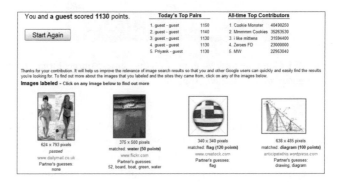

Figure 3.37. Google Image Labeler: summing up the game. Source: http://images. google.com/imagelabeler/.

Google has bought the license for applying the technology of the ESP Game to the Google Image Labeler (Figure 3.36). In this way, Google image search should be improved via user-generated keywords. Google has modified the game and does not reward all matching terms with the same score, but assigns higher scores for more specific terms. The game instructions explain this for the image of a flying bird: agreeing on 'sky' is rewarded with 50 points, 'bird' with 60, 'soaring' with 120 points, and 'frigate bird' with 150 points. This is Google's incentive for more individual and precise tags. After each round, the players may also have a look at all suggestions made by their partner during the game (Figure 3.37). So far, there have been no evaluations of the quality of index terms gained via such labeling games.

A different approach is pursued by the tool LabelMe[287] (Russell, Torralba, et al., 2008): not the whole image is labeled, but the user is asked to outline the shape of a certain object depicted in an image. The aim is to collect data for training computers to recognize objects in images. The developers point out that LabelMe is primarily "[d]esigned for object class recognition as opposed to instance recognition. To recognize an object class, one needs multiple images of different instances of the same class, as well as different viewing conditions" (Russell, Torralba, et al., 2008). LabelMe cannot directly be described as a game, as there are not yet any game-like activities like scoring or competing, and no players are grouped together as everyone is outlines and labels on his own. Instead, some experiments are being used to couple the labeled images to WordNet synsets. Figure 3.38 shows a collection of labeled images for the WordNet cluster "pedestrian, walker, footer, traveler, traveller". More work is being done with regard to sorting image structures into WordNet hierarchies.

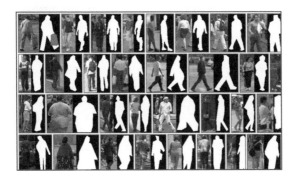

Figure 3.38. LabelMe: collection of annotated images matching the WordNet cluster "pedestrian, walker, footer, traveler, traveler". Source: http://labelme. csail.mit.edu.

The idea of Squigl[288] is similar to LabelMe, but this time two players get so see the same image and have to sketch in a certain object (like the "girl" in Figure

---

[287] LabelMe: http://labelme.csail.mit.edu/.
[288] Squigl: http://www.gwap.com/gwap/gamesPreview/squigl/.

3.39). The game computes the degree of overlap of the two players and assigns a corresponding score for each image.

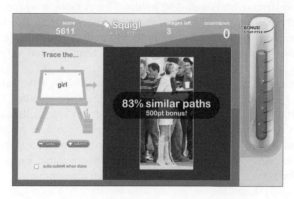

Figure 3.39. Squigl: Single objects in a photo have to be identified by two players. Source: http://www.gwap.com/gwap/gamesPreview/squigl/.

So far, the research group around von Ahn has created several other games with a purpose[289], many of them with different approaches to image annotation: Peekaboom (von Ahn, 2006b) is another example for this approach. Phetch[290] is a game in which groups of players have to look for a certain image within a data-base – based on a description entered by another player (von Ahn, Ginosar et al., 2006). The player who is first to find the described image wins. Players are in-structed to use entire sentences (and not mere keywords) to describe images. The purpose of this game is to collect complex image descriptions in order to improve Web accessibility for visually impaired Web users. Tag a Tune[291], on the other hand, is a game for music and sound annotation based on tags, and in PopVideo[292] two players can tag videos based on sound and image features.

Not a game but also closely related to this topic are CAPTCHAs[293] (von Ahn, Blum et al., 2003), or more precisely, the reCAPTCHA project (von Ahn, Maurer et al., 2008). CAPTCHAs are small tests applied in online scenarios, used to tell human users and machine agents apart, like the blurred images of texts that have to be re-typed as part of the registration for a website. As Web users already spend lots of time with CAPTCHAs, the idea was to use this time for a valuable purpose: reCAPTCHA is an application that helps to digitalize books based on CAPTCHAs. We might also think of a new type of reCAPTCHA for purposes of

---

[289] A collection of them is available on the Website http://www.gwap.com.
[290] Phetch: http://www.peekaboom.org/phetch/.
[291] Tag a Tune: http://www.gwap.com/gwap/gamesPreview/tagatune/.
[292] PopVideo: http://www.gwap.com/gwap/gamesPreview/popvideo/.
[293] CAPTCHA is short for *C*ompletely *A*utomated *P*ublic *T*uring test to tell *C*omputers and *H*umans *A*part.

semantic indexing. Users who want to register on a Website may also be asked to tag an image with content-descriptive keywords (each image should then be presented to several users, ensuring appropriate tags by community agreement. Mapping against other users' suggestions will also be needed to keep up the functionality of telling users apart from computers). As far as we know, such an approach is not yet realized in practice.

While all the games we have mentioned so far are interesting new approaches to Web document *indexing*, some other games bring with them notable ideas for ontology *engineering*. In this context the challenge is to create games that let people playfully contribute to the creation or enrichment of ontologies. So far, games that explicitly aim at building formal ontologies are not available. But some tools show us what letting Web users build up knowledge bases during games could look like.

Figure 3.40. Verbosity: describing the secret word 'day' via the phrase 'is opposite of'.
Source: http://www.gwap.com/gwap/gamesPreview/verbosity./

One of these games is another gwap by von Ahn and colleagues: Verbosity[294] (von Ahn, Kedia & Blum, 2006). Two players have to describe or guess a "secret word" in turn. This word is revealed to one player, who may then try to describe it with some predefined phrases. Figure 3.40 shows the interface for a player who has to describe the secret word "day". He may use the phrases "it is", "it is a type of", "it has", "it looks like", "it is typically near", and "it is opposite of". On the right side of the screen, the other player's guesses are then displayed. A game like this can help collect knowledge related to certain concepts (the secret words), mainly in the form of broader terms for hyponymy (it is a/ it is a type of), narrower terms for meronymy (it has) and antonymy (it is the opposite of). One could, of course, also think of other phrases to collect information about other se-

---

[294] Verbosity : http://www.gwap.com/gwap/gamesPreview/verbosity/.

mantic relations. If the partner guesses the secret word, this can be counted as a validation for the description.

A related research field is *commonsense knowledge acquisition*, which describes different projects aiming at collecting large knowledge bases of everyday facts. The Open Mind Common Sense project we have just introduced as a community knowledge base also fits this category. Moreover, these efforts may also be combined with games. Lieberman, Smith and Teeters (2007) have presented the game Common Consensus, a multi-player game that should collect and validate commonsense knowledge about everyday goals and activities:

> "The game model is similar to the television game show FamilyFeud where contestants are asked to answer a trivial, open-ended question and are rewarded based on the commonality of their answers. On the game show, the scores would be determined by pre-screening the audience; however, our game computes the score dynamically based on the answers for the given round or, if there are too few players, the answers from prior games." (Lieberman, Smith & Teeters, 2007)

The aim of this game is to create a large knowledge base of facts about everyday life in the form of goals. The domain of goals has been chosen because "[g]oals often answer the why questions about human behavior, and provide good clues as to the when, how, and other considerations. They are therefore fundamental to explanation" (Lieberman, Smith & Teeters, 2007). The authors describe a typical scenario from their game and explain how they assign scores based on the commonality of answers:

> "For example, when users were presented with the question: *What are some things you would use to: cook dinner?* Their aggregate answers gravitated toward the superordinate and basic categories [note from the author: with regard to the basic level theory by Rosch and colleagues as discussed in Section 2.2.2]. The most common answers (by the number of unique users) were: food (7), pots (3), pans (3), meat (3), knife (2), oven (2), microwave (2)... We also collected specific and atypical answers, like *garlic press* and obscure answers, like *cans* but they had a low count (in this case, 1). It should be noted that there is a trade-off involved with only using the popular answers: many good uncommon answers are neglected." (Lieberman, Smith & Teeters, 2007)

The Cycorp[295] group has also experimented with collecting information for their knowledge base Cyc (see Section 2.3.1) via an online game: FACTory[296]. The design of FACTory is rather primitive. It is a single-player game. Statements are randomly chosen from the Cyc database and presented to the user, who has to judge whether they are wrong or right (Figure 3.41). The knowledge base collects this information to validate its content based on the community judgments. The user is rewarded with points (the more he agrees with answers from previous players, the

---

[295]   Cycorp : http://www.cyc.com/.
[296]   FACTory : http://game.cyc.com/.

higher the score). After playing a round, FACTory shows some basic gaming statistics (Figure 3.42).

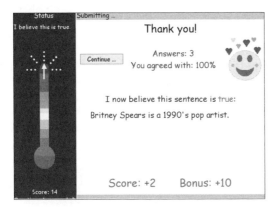

Figure 3.41. Cyc FACTory: Reaction of the game after judging a statement as right.
Source: http://game.cyc.com/game.html.

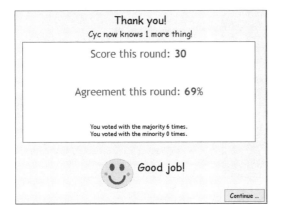

Figure 3.42. Cyc FACTory: results for one gaming round. Source: http://game.
cyc.com/game.html.

Another game that uses similar statistical methods to gather facts from its users is
20Q[297]. 20Q is based on a US-American TV and radio quiz from the 1940s called
Twenty Questions. Originally, one human candidate was challenged to identify an
envisioned object with 20 questions which could be answered "Yes" or "No". In

---

[297] 20Q: http://www.20q.net.

the 1980s, the idea was adopted by the Artificial Intelligence community and a machine took over the role of asking the question and identifying the envisioned object. Currently, it is available in several languages, with modifications for very specific domains (like the TV series "The Simpsons" or the book series "Harry Potter"). The principle is always the same. The player thinks of an object, person or place from the chosen domain of interest. The computer asks different questions which have to be answered as precisely as possible (with answers like yes, no, probably, unknown). The computer tries to identify the imaginary object with the help of 20 questions at most. Figure 3.43 shows a scene from the game where the computer has correctly identified a concept with 16 questions. Figure 3.44 shows another scene where the imagined concept has not been identified by the system.

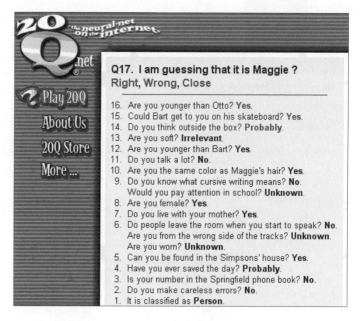

Figure 3.43. 20Q The Simpsons edition: The envisioned person "Maggie Simpson" has been correctly identified based on 16 questions. Source: http://www.20q.net/.

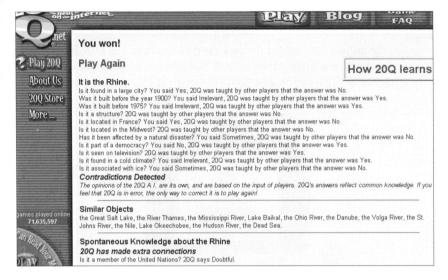

Figure 3.44. 20Q: The concept "Rhine" has not been identified. The judgments made by the player are compared with information collected in former gaming rounds. Source: http://www.20q.net/.

Although these previous examples are innovative approaches to collecting structured knowledge from communities, they are not directly linked to the Semantic Web. A more recent example for games with a purpose in a Semantic Web context is OntoGame[298] (Siorpaes & Hepp, 2008a; Siorpaes & Hepp, 2008b). The developers explain their motivation:

> "Despite significant advancement in tools and semi-automatic approaches, we still need a significant amount of human labor and intelligence for the construction of ontologies, for the annotation of data in various modalities and formats, and for aligning the conceptual elements in multiple ontologies. […] However, we observe that it is hard to motivate people to dedicate their time to those three tasks. At the same time, the amount of Web content in complex modalities (like images, videos, sounds, or Flash applets) and services exposed on the Web is increasing; such is even harder to annotate without the aid of human intelligence." (Siorpaes & Hepp, 2008a)

The following sub-tasks are described as the most important for these purposes: collecting named entities and ascribing them to the ontology, adding taxonomic and non-taxonomic relationships, modularizing the domain of discourse and providing formal and informal definitions for ontology parts (Siorpaes & Hepp, 2008a). The OntoGame team has developed approaches to collecting user contri-

---

[298] OntoGame: http://www.ontogame.org.

butions for all these subtasks, and is working on ideas for ontology alignment solutions.

So far, the project has yielded the two games OntoTube and OntoPronto, while
other applications are under development. OntoGame is designed as a generic
game infrastructure that can be extended via new plug-ins.

Figure 3.45. OntoTube. Semantic indexing of YouTube videos. Source:
http://members.sti2.at/~katharinas/ontogame/ontogame-demo.htm.

OntoTube is a game for the semantic image annotation of YouTube videos. Two
players are shown the same video from the YouTube database and are asked to
add structured metadata (both formal and content-descriptive) to it. They score
with every agreement. Figure 3.45 shows the interface of OntoTube: in this scene,
the players have to agree upon the genre of the current video. They cannot add
free tags but have to choose from predefined genres, which are based on an underlying ontology. During other stages, they will also be asked for information on the
movie's color scheme (black/white or color), as well as the language, location and
topic of the video. Entries for the latter two aspects are directly mapped to
Wikipedia articles. In Figure 3.46 we see how the topic of the video is linked to
the Wikipedia page "Snoopy vs. the Red Baron"[299].

---

[299]   Actually, in this case the linking to Wikipedia is not yet ideal: There are two Wikipedia
articles titled "Snoopy vs. the Red Baron" and "Snoopy Vs. the Red Baron", but none
of them directly refers to the comic video. The first is about a single/album by the
Royal Guardsmen, the second is about a computer game – yet both are inspired by the
cartoon. See:
http://en.wikipedia.org/wiki/Snoopy_vs._the_Red_Baron_(disambiguation).

The statements collected during the gaming sessions can then be transferred to the underlying ontology. The resulting ontology can be downloaded in the OWL format[300]. Thus OntoTube serves the semantic indexing of video files and the instantiation of the underlying ontology.

Figure 3.46. OntoTube. Describing the topic of a video with the help of Wikipedia articles.
Source: http://members.sti2.at/~katharinas/ontogame/ontogame-demo.htm.

OntoPronto, the second current game by the OntoGame developers, is designed to interlink Wikipedia articles with the PROTON Ontology (see Section 2.3.1).

> "The use of Proton is mainly motivated by two factors. First, we needed a general-purpose ontology that would make sense as an upper-level ontology above all Wikipedia entries. This ontology should already contain sufficient specializations so that the difference in the level of abstraction as compared to Wikipedia URIs was appropriate for average users. In the future, we will also consider upper ontologies such as DOLCE or SUMO." (Siorpaes & Hepp, 2008a)

In the OntoPronto game, two players get to see the first paragraph of a Wikipedia article. They are then asked to select whether this Wikipedia entry rather describes a set of objects (and thus represents a class) or a single object (an instance) (Figure 3.47). If the two players agree, they will reach the next level: they are now asked

---

[300] OWL version of OntoTube ontology (April 17, 2008):
http://www.ontogame.org/ontologies/ontotube.owl.

to decide into which class from the PROTON ontology the article may be placed (Figure 3.48).

Figure 3.47. OntoPronto. Choosing whether a Wikipedia article represents a class or an instance. Source: http://members.sti2.at/~katharinas/ontogame/ontogame-demo.htm.

The developers conclude:

> "The deeper the teams manage to go into the hierarchy, the more Wikipedia articles they play, and the more Proton abstractions they find within 2 minutes, the more points they are awarded. [...] The motivation for this game is that the URIs of the more than 1.8 Million Wikipedia entries are reliable identifiers for countless useful conceptual entities. [...] If we are able to ground those 1.8 Million conceptual elements properly in the Proton ontology, we will create the largest general interest ontology for annotating Web resources – 1.8 Million identifiers for anything from artist to high schools, from products to organizations." (Siorpaes & Hepp, 2008a)

The games developed in the OntoGame project should later be integrated into the myOntology platform.

In conclusion, games with a purpose are an interesting idea, particularly for the playful indexing of Web documents with free keywords. A certain degree of "social" control may be established if two or more players have to "agree" on an appropriate index term. We have seen that even the tasks of establishing a knowledge base and of indexing with a preset vocabulary have already been implemented in gwap scenarios. We expect some more game-like approaches to be developed in the future. Certain game elements may become directly integrated into ontology engineering tools or practical Semantic Web applications.

Figure 3.48. OntoPronto. Choosing an appropriate class from the PROTON Ontology for a
Wikipedia entry. Source: http://members.sti2.at/~katharinas/ontogame/onto
game-demo.htm.

Gwap concludes our review of current trends in community-based ontology engineering. We have seen that there are a lot of innovative approaches to encourage
broad user communities (and non-experts in ontology development) to contribute
to knowledge representation activities in the Social Semantic Web. In the next
section, we will keep in mind the same underlying question: how can we gather
the necessary data for World Wide Web knowledge representation, with as little
effort as possible but producing high quality (ensured for example by a heterogeneous community of experts)? But this time, approaches do not focus on novel incentives for user contribution; they are rather based on the exploitation of data that
are already available and may be reused and modified for ontology engineering.

3.3 Semantic Upgrades & Tag Gardening

This section introduces some recent approaches which may help to reuse existing
KOS data for the creation of ontologies. For this purpose, one may reuse both data
collected in indexing processes (particularly in social tagging activities) as well as
existing, less formal KOS like thesauri or classifications. We will first discuss *tag
gardening*: the process of structuring folksonomies in order to obtain richer KOS
models. Then we will have a look at some projects that have performed semantic
upgrades. Finally, we will complete the section with some considerations on additional knowledge resources for ontology gardening.

3.3.1 From Tagging to Ontologies

Methods of organizing and structuring tags in folksonomy-based systems have recently been arousing interest in the research community. Such activities of editing and structuring tags have been described as "tag gardening" (Governor, 2006; Peters & Weller, 2008b; Weller & Peters, 2008).

The initial motivation behind this idea is grounded in the different shortcomings of folksonomies. Despite the enormous success of folksonomies for Web indexing, certain problems of folksonomies have constantly been pointed out (e.g. by Peters, 2006; Peters, 2009; Peters & Stock, 2007)[301]. Many critiques of folksonomies are somehow based on a comparison of folksonomies with traditional methods of knowledge organization and professional indexing. In turn, many suggestions for improving folksonomies are also inspired by classical KOS. As we have seen in the previous sections, the boundaries between different types of KOS are not at all solid but rather blurred. This also means that one may modify an existing system, for example by *upgrading* it to become a more complex type. In this way, folksonomies can adopt some of the principal guidelines available for traditional KOS and may gradually be enriched with some elements of vocabulary control and semantics.

In the context of ontology engineering there is a second perspective on tag gardening. Incentives for user participation are still a problematic issue in collaborative ontology engineering, as there are rarely any large communities forming up for ontology engineering or semantic indexing purposes. In contrast, social tagging applications have long succeeded in gathering large user communities and are registering enormous user activities. Consequently, the other side of tag gardening is the question of how these very lightweight semantics provided by Web users may be "harvested" for ontology engineering. We will soon demonstrate that folksonomies provide a useful basis for the step-by-step creation of semantically richer KOS and for the refinement of existing classifications, thesauri or ontologies.

Thus, on the one hand, gradual refinement of folksonomy tags and a gradual application of additional vocabulary control and semantic structure to tagging systems is a promising approach for handling the current problems of folksonomies, such as inconsistent vocabularies and varieties of synonyms, spelling variants, misspellings, language variants and a general lack of semantics (Peters, 2009). But, on the other hand, by applying methods of semantic enrichment, folksonomies become a valuable knowledge resource for ontology engineering. This provides a means of incorporating collective indexing efforts into the broadening of ontologies.

Figure 3.49 illustrates the two perspectives of tag gardening: a) folksonomies should be semantically enriched with structures and are thus gradually upgraded to

---

[301] We have already discussed problems of folksonomies above, in Section 1.3.2, and an overview of problems and advantages of folksonomies was provided in Figure 1.38.

more elaborated KOS types, or b) an existing formal KOS may be enriched with terms harvested from a folksonomy in order to broaden it with community terms.

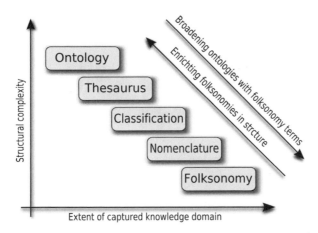

Figure 3.49. Two sides of tag gardening.

Thus the image of tag gardening is used to illustrate processes of manipulating and re-engineering folksonomy tags in order to make them more productive and effective or in order to use them as foundations or enrichments for more elaborated KOS, such as ontologies. For this gardening metaphor[302], we first have to imagine a document collection indexed with a folksonomy. This folksonomy now becomes our *garden*, each tag being a different *plant*. Currently, most folksonomy gardens are rather savage: different types of plants all grow wildly (see Figure 3.50). Some receive high attention, others almost none. Some are useful for the community and for retrieval tasks, others are not, being highly personal or rather inappropriate for indexing purposes (for example the tag 'me', or tags with spelling mistakes). Tanasescu and Streibel (2007) have criticized folksonomies for being a "mess". Wu, Zubair and Mair (2006) stress that "[t]he tags in some large tagging systems have become non-navigable and not even searchable due to the sheer volume of the tags/documents and the low quality of the tags."

Tag clouds can be considered to be the very first approach to making folksonomies more easily accessible, but they are "not sufficient as the sole means of navigation for a folksonomy-based dataset" (Sinclair & Cardew-Hall, 2008). Additional structures are needed as navigational pathways.

---

[302] The image of gardening has also been applied in the research context of knowledge management (Harun & Noor, 2007; Udel, 2004; Vollmar, 2005).

Figure 3.50. The folksonomy tag garden. Source: Peters & Weller, 2008b.

We can envision an improvement of folksonomies based on tag gardening on different levels (Weller & Peters, 2008):

- *Document collection vs. single document level*: Should the collection of all tags within a platform be edited in total, or does one only want to change the tags of one single document?
- *Personal vs. collaborative level*: We may consider tag gardening as being performed individually by single users for the personal tags they use within a system. This may also be called the personomy level; a personomy is defined as the tag collection belonging to one single user (Hotho, Jäschke et al., 2006). Alternatively, one may think of systems that enable the whole user community to collectively or collaboratively edit and maintain all tags in use (which could be called the folksonomy level).
- *Intra- and cross-platform level*: Usually, a folksonomy is defined as the collection of tags within one platform or system. Yet for some cases, the use of consistent tags across different platforms will be useful. We will discuss this in more detail below.

Seeding, Weeding, Fertilizing: Tag Gardening for Folksonomy Enrichment
In our previous works (Peters & Weller, 2008b; Weller & Peters, 2008), we have introduced different gardening activities which symbolize the steps needed to enhance folksonomies and to enrich them with basic semantic structures: weeding, seeding, landscape architecture and fertilizing. These activities are to some extent based on common procedures for building classical KOS.

Weeding
The first activity of tag gardening is dedicated to the basic formatting of tags. One general problem of folksonomies is that there is no guarantee for the correct spelling or consistent formatting of tags (Guy & Tonkin, 2006). We call this very first activity in tag gardening *weeding*: Tag weeding in general is the process of removing or revising 'bad tags'; it can be considered a primitive form of vocabulary con-

trol. Bad tags might for example be tags with spelling mistakes. But as in real gardens, the identification of *weeds* (or bad tags) is not always easy.

Eliminating spam tags (Heymann, Koutrika & Garcia-Molina, 2007) should be the simplest form of tag weeding, and can to some degree even be performed automatically. Spamming is a serious problem in social tagging applications, and the hosts of folksonomy-based systems are trying to find solutions that allow for the removal of spam without any loss of valuable information. For example, one has to consider whether some tags should be (permanently) removed from the entire folksonomy (e.g. explicit curse words) or whether some tags should only be removed from certain documents. This is a general challenge for tag weeding.

Spelling mistakes are another relatively simple form of folksonomy weeds. Automatic spell checking algorithms could help to replace or edit incorrect tags. Yet one has to consider that some words may seem misspelled – but are actually neologisms or word creations by the user community which carry important information and thus have to be preserved.

Another occurrence of 'bad tags' is due to the nature of many folksonomy tools which do not allow for adding multi word concepts as tags; as a consequence, the systems contain inconsistent makeshifts such as 'semanticweb', 'semanticWeb' or 'semantic_web'. This is problematic, because currently all possible variants also have to be considered in retrieval, i.e. they have to be manually added to a search query. In this case, tag gardening aims at making the folksonomy more consistent and to format all multi word tags in the same manner. This could be achieved if one format (e.g. the underscore spelling variant) were chosen as the preferred version and all alternative forms were re-edited accordingly. One alternative to re-editing existing tags would be to provide some general formatting guidelines to the tagging community in advance. However, both re-editing and obeying guidelines will require additional advertence by the users. Another alternative would be to collect spelling variants (automatically or manually by ambitious power users) and offer them as suggestions – either during the tagging process or as query expansion terms during search. This would be a lightweight form of treating spelling variants as synonyms.

Comparable problems exist for the handling of different word forms, e.g. singular and plural forms or nouns and their corresponding verb forms. The reduction of current variants to only singular nouns may be useful for enhancing recall, e.g. in publication databases (if both singular and plural forms are allowed, one would miss documents tagged with "thesauri" when searching for "thesaurus"), while it would bring about a loss of information in other cases, e.g. for photo databases (where one may, for example, explicitly want to look for a photo showing more than one cow and would therefore need the plural "cows"). It is thus not generally advisable to reduce tags to either singular or plural and to delete all different variants during the tag weeding process, but it may be an option for certain application contexts.

Peters and Stock (2007) have collected some suggestions on how the formatting problems of folksonomies may be automatically resolved via methods of Natural Language Processing (NLP). In most cases, problems still arise with user generated tags that cannot be found in (multi-lingual) thesauri or dictionaries. Laniado, Eynard and Colombetti (2007b), who used WordNet as a lexical base for identifying folksonomy tags report that "only about 8% of the different tags used are contained in the lexicon" (Laniado, Eynard & Colombetti, 2007b). These unknown tags cannot be directly edited via methods of NLP. Their processing has to be handed over to the users themselves. Thus a folksonomy based system will profit from editing functionalities which allow users to delete or edit the tags assigned to single documents. In some cases, one may even consider allowing users to (carefully) remove certain tags from the whole system. Additionally, some formatting guidelines may be provided to (or discussed by) the users, to enhance the consistency of tagging behavior.

We suggest the following procedure for handling weed tags (Peters, 2009; Peters & Weller, 2008b; Weller & Peters, 2008):

- Basic editing functionalities should be provided in order to enable users to easily correct misspellings and to perform other types of correction on their own tags.
- Automatic algorithms should check all tags for potential misspellings, spelling variants and spam tags. Identified spelling variants, typical misspellings, singular and plural forms etc. should be collected by the system.
- Based on this, tag suggestions can be provided to the user, e.g. in the form of type-ahead functionalities during the tagging process or in the form of suggestions for additional tags (like "did you mean ...?" / "do you also want to add ...?").
- Words identified as typical spelling variants or corresponding singular-plural variants can also be suggested as query expansion terms during search.
- Definite spam tags should be collected as a 'blacklist' and be directly removed. Spam tag candidates may be collected and judged by the community.
- Advanced editing options may be exclusively provided to authorized users – like removing tags from the entire folksonomy, marking tags as spam, removing or editing tags from other users' documents. In this case, a specific group of users would act as gardeners. This should ideally be power users or those that have gained some kind of reputation within the platform, comparable to administrators in Wikipedia[303].
- Guidelines for optimized tagging behavior and retrieval strategies should be set up, either by the provider of a folksonomy-based system or by the user community. This is most feasible for systems with comparatively small user groups (e.g. in a corporate tagging system) and will become more difficult with the growing size of the intended user community.

Seeding
Frequently, the most popular tags within a folksonomy-based system are highlighted, most typically in the form of tag clouds, where the most common tags are

---

suggested as entry points to browsing the document collection. Tag suggestions for indexing may also be based on tag frequencies, though. Tag popularity is thus highly appreciated at the moment. On the other hand, high-frequently tags discriminate less in describing documents; in some cases, the most popular tags are too general to render precise and useful retrieval results, e.g. resulting in enormously large hit lists (Muller, 2007; Paolillo & Penumarthy, 2007; Peters, 2009).

In this case it might be necessary to explicitly *seed* new, more specific tags into the tag garden, which can help narrow down the search results and strengthen the expressivity of the folksonomy. Such infrequent but specific and discriminating tags can be called *seedlings*. Seedlings require specific attention and care, so as to do not get lost among the bigger plants. Peters (2009) suggests evaluating the "long tail" tags (i.e. low-frequency tags, see Section 1.3.3) as potential seed tags. We recommend the following seeding measures, which are all based on automatic processes integrated into a folksonomy-based system (Peters, 2009; Peters & Weller, 2008b; Weller & Peters, 2008):

- An inverse tag cloud (showing rarely used tags in bigger font sizes) can be used to display some very rarely used tags and provide an additional access point to the document collection[304].
- Other than the most frequent tags should be highlighted in a certain area (as a kind of "greenhouse"), for example the most recently added tags, new tags that have never been added before, or trend tags.
- Seedlings in the form of infrequent or new tags should not only be highlighted for browsing the document collection, but could also be integrated into a tag suggestion system during the indexing phase.

The main purpose of seeding during tag gardening is to enhance the expressivity of a folksonomy in order to obtain more precise search results.

Landscape Architecture

After the basic formatting problems have been solved, the actual "vocabulary problem" (Furnas, Landauer et al., 1987) of folksonomies can be tackled. In folksonomies

- synonyms are not bound together (thus someone searching a photo portal for pictures of 'bicycles' would also have to use the tag 'bike', and probably even translations into other languages for a comprehensive search and higher recall),
- homonyms are not distinguished (searching for "jaguar" will retrieve pictures of the animal as well as the car),
- there are no explicit relations enabling a semantic navigation between search or index terms (thus for example, a search for photos of 'cats' cannot auto-

---

[304] These aspects have also been discussed in the Workshop "Good Tags – Bad Tags. Social Tagging in der Wissensorganisation", February 21st and 22nd, 2008, Institut für Wissensmedien, Tübingen, Germany. A similar concept to "seedlings" was discussed by the participants as "baby tags".

matically be broadened to include 'siamese', 'european shorthair', 'birman' etc.).
This lack of vocabulary control is the price that must be paid for facile usability, flexibility and the representation of active and dynamic language. Yet the additional and subsequent editing of folksonomies may be the key to allowing free tagging as well as basic control functionalities over the vocabulary in use. Folksonomy users are becoming more and more aware of these effects – which is the basis for introducing gardening techniques to enable the user to improve their tags.

We have imagined the step-by-step establishment of vocabulary control as *landscape architecture* in gardening (Peters & Weller, 2008b; Weller & Peters, 2008). In our folksonomy garden we have some plants that look alike but are not the same (homonyms), some plants which can be found in different variations and are sometimes difficult to recognize as one *species* (synonyms) and others which are somehow related or should be combined. Thus we have to apply some garden design or landscape architecture to turn our savage garden into a structured, cultivated one. Landscape architecture aims at establishing semantic structures in folksonomies. We need some additional structure and direct accessibility in order to provide additional forms of (semantic) navigation (besides navigation based on tag clouds, most popular tags or tag-user relations).

For this purpose, one may use *labels* for the homonyms, and establish *flower beds* as well as *paths* between them and *pointers* or *sign posts* to show us the way along the synonyms, hierarchies and other semantic interrelations. Within classical KOS, homonyms are often distinguished by additional specifications (e.g. 'bank (finance)' vs. 'bank (river)') or unique identifiers (e.g. notations in classification systems). Synonyms can be interlinked to form a set of synonyms, and sometimes *preferred terms* are chosen which have to be used exclusively to represent the whole set. Some folksonomy systems already provide functionalities for deriving *clusters* or *related tags*, which mainly rely on information about co-occurrence and term frequencies (see below). Apart from these automatic approaches, options for the individual manual manipulation of tags are needed. This is particularly useful for personal tag management, where categories, taxonomies and cross-references of tags can be built and maintained for individually customized information management.

Another peculiarity of folksonomies is that tags can be intended to fulfill different purposes. Not all tags describe a document's content, they may also refer to its author, origin, data format etc. Some tags are intended for personal (e.g. 'toread') and interpersonal (e.g. '@peter') work management (Kipp, 2006a). Currently, all these tags are handled indifferently in folksonomy systems. This means that in the tag garden we have different plants used for different purposes, wildly thrown together (e.g. economic plants mixed with ornamental plants and medical herbs) – which of course makes it hard to find exactly what we need. Thus the garden would need some additional structuring and – most of all – labeling. We need a way to distinguish the different tag qualities and label the tags accordingly (we may even decide to have different gardens, one for agriculture placed next to a flower garden and a herb garden and probably even a vineyard). Thus structuring folksonomies in landscape architecture activities may not only focus on the meaning of tags (e.g. by capturing hierarchies or synonyms), but may also include an additional level regarding the different purposes of tags.

In practice, this distinction of different tag qualities might be accomplished in the form of facets, categories or fields. For each document, different fields may be provided for tagging according to the different tag functionalities, e.g. one for content-descriptive tags, one for formal tags (or more specifically, one for the author, one for the file type etc.), and one for organizational tags (e.g. task organization, reference to projects). Alternatively, complex naming conventions could be established to specify the purpose of non-content-descriptive tags. Certain conventions are already being established to use specific formats for labeling different tag purposes (like the '@' in '@name'-tags which are attached to documents to be forwarded to a colleague or friend). But such conventions are, again, more feasible for smaller or closed communities. In summary, the following steps should be taken in the landscape architecture process of tag gardening:

- conflation of multi-language tags,
- summarization of synonyms,
- distinction of homonyms,
- establishment of semantic relations between tags,
- field-based tagging.

These activities should enhance the expressivity of a folksonomy; semantic structures and tag purposes will become explicit and can be used for more elaborated information retrieval models (e.g. with query expansion or field-based search forms).

Fertilizing

Some of the problems with missing vocabulary control can also be approached by combining Folksonomies with other, more complex knowledge organization systems, which would then act as fertilizers. Largely unnoticed by the folksonomy users, KOS like thesauri or ontologies may be used behind the scenes of a folksonomy, e.g. for query expansion or query disambiguation (Au Yeung, Gibbins & Shadbolt, 2007). Search queries over folksonomy tags may be (automatically) enhanced with semantically related terms, derived from an existing KOS, for example.

WordFlickr uses relational structures from WordNet to expand query terms in the Flickr database (Kolbitsch, 2007). Users submitting a query to WordFlickr may choose which types of relations (e.g. synonyms, hyperonyms, hyponyms, holonyms or meronyms) should be used for expanding the query. Thus if a user searches for 'shoes', the query may be expanded with the hyponyms 'slippers' and 'trainers' to retrieve pictures tagged with these subtypes of shoes from the Flickr collection.

Furthermore, an existing KOS can be used within a tag recommendation process, i.e. the users are provided with suggestions for possible tags during the tagging process (either suggestions for additional tags to the ones which have been already entered for a resource or suggestions in the form of type-ahead functionalities). Currently, such recommendations are typically computed on the basis of tag co-occurrences. In a KOS-based approach, the nature of the suggested tags could be made explicit, which would help the user to judge its appropriateness. For example, if a user types the tag 'Tottenham', a KOS-based system might suggest to also use the *broader terms* 'London' and 'United Kingdom'; another user choosing the tag 'folksonomy' might be provided with the information that a folksonomy *is_used_by* 'social software' and that an almost synonymous expression is 'social tagging', and can then decide whether these tags should be added to the document as well.

Fertilizing folksonomies with existing KOS is a promising approach to providing semantic enrichment – but it is heavily dependent on the availability of high-quality KOS, which also have to cover the respective domain of interest. Furthermore, much more research is needed in order to facilitate reliable mappings between folksonomy tags and terms from a controlled vocabulary. Angeletou, Sabou et al. (2007), who have developed algorithms for the automatic mapping of folksonomy tags to ontologies, which are currently available on the Web in order to make semantic relations between tags explicit, conclude: "[…] that it is indeed possible to automate the semantic enrichment of folksonomy tag spaces by harvesting online ontologies" (Angeletou, Sabou et al., 2007). Their work is a small fragment of a large research area dealing not only with mappings between folksonomies and ontologies but with all forms of cross-references and cross-walks between different individual KOS.

We have now introduced the main activities of tag gardening, namely weeding, seeding, landscape architecture and fertilizing. Of course these metaphors are only used to illustrate the underlying idea of improving folksonomies with unifying formattings, new discriminating tags, (semantic) tag structures and coupling to elaborated KOS. All tag gardening activities aim toward enhancing the efficiency of folksonomy-based systems while keeping as much as possible of the easy usability which addresses a broad community. Some may argue that tag gardening conflicts with the basic principle of folksonomies, which states that tags have to be added by a free and unaffected community, as otherwise they will no longer capture the true user-centric point of view, or the authentic user vocabulary. This is of course a justified objection, which we will not dispute. Rather, this fact is readily accepted, as tag gardening must maintain the balance between capturing the users' terminology and unifying the vocabulary for better retrieval results. Thus, tag gardening clearly goes beyond the initial motivations of social tagging, always actuated by the basic question of how to combine the dynamics of freely chosen tags with the steadiness and complexity of controlled vocabularies.

It appears that a gradual refinement of folksonomy tags and a step-by-step application of additional structure to folksonomies is a promising approach for this problem. And we suggest that, whenever possible, tag gardening activities should be established on top of existing folksonomies rather than in advance of the tagging process.

Related Work and Examples for Tag Gardening in Practice

The literature is full of works that are closely related to the idea of tag gardening. A very broad overview on this topic is presented by Peters (2009). A lot of research concentrates on the automatic clustering of tags and different clustering algorithms, respectively (e.g., Begelman, Keller & Smadja, 2006; Schmitz 2006). Some of them are directly bound to systems for tag suggestions, which may also act as seeding mechanisms (Sen, Lam et al., 2006). Methods for automatically distinguishing homonyms in folksonomies based on context information (users, documents, tags) are also being developed (Au Yeung, Gibbins & Shadboldt, 2007).

Theoretical approaches for the structural enhancement of folksonomies are also related to the current discussions on "emergent semantics" (Aberer, Cudré-Mauroux et al., 2004; Staab, Santini et al., 2002; Zhang, Wu & Yu, 2006), "ontology maturing" (Braun, Schmidt et al., 2007), "semantic upgrades" or "semantic enrichments" (Angeletou, Sabou et al., 2007).

Some folksonomy-based systems have already implemented certain functionalities that may be used for tag gardening purposes. For example, Flickr uses tag clusters to distinguish homonymous tags (Figure 3.51), Delicious computes related tags for a given search tag, and Bibsonomy offers basic functionalities for establishing connections between tags, called "relations"[305]. Users can create relations between their own tags manually (Figure 3.52) and may use them for broadening search queries.

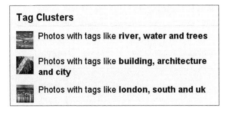

Figure 3.51. Tag clusters in Flickr for the search tag 'bank'. Source: http://www.flickr.com/search/?q=bank.

---

[305] The most popular relations in Bibsonomy can be found at http://www.bibsonomy.org/relations.

Figure 3.52. Manually established tag relations in Bibsonomy. Source: http://www.bib
sonomy.org/user/kweller.

Another approach to establishing relations between tags is discussed by Tanasescu
& Streibel (2007) as the "tagging of tags". The MOAT[306] project also aims to label tags in order to enrich their semantic expressiveness (Passant, Laublet et al.,
2009). Their approach is to enable users to label tags with URIs of Semantic Web
resources (like DBpedia or other knowledge bases). Zigtag[307] is a social bookmarking tool that aims at the enriching of information about tags, to interrelate
synonyms and to distinguish homonyms (Smith, 2008). Figure 3.53 shows how
short textual definitions are displayed for tags in a tag cloud.

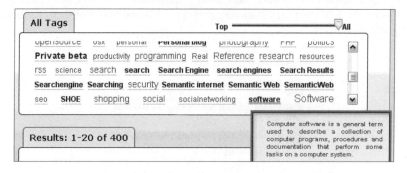

Figure 3.53. Tag Cloud in Zigtag. Moving the mouse over the blue tags displays a square
box with a short definition. Source: http://www.zigtag.com/tag/.

Several experiments can be found which consider the fertilizing of folksonomies
with controlled vocabularies, some of them have already been mentioned above.
The system FaceTag[308] intends to demonstrate how tags may be used in combination with a faceted classification scheme.
Laniado, Eynard and Colombetti (2007a and b) have enriched Delicious tags with
semantics from WordNet. Their aim is to integrate "an ontology in the navigation

---

[306] MOAT (Meaning Of A Tag): http://moat-project.org.
[307] Zigtag: http://zigtag.com.
[308] FaceTag: http://www.facetag.org/.

interface of a folksonomy, filtering tags through a predefined semantic hierarchy to improve the possibilities of searching and browsing" (Laniado, Eynard & Colombetti, 2007b). Specifically, they want to improve the suggestions of 'related tags'. The fundamental challenge they experienced in their work was to find the respective WordNet terms that matched the folksonomy tags. Only 8% of their sample tags could be found in WordNet (Laniado, Eynard & Colombetti, 2007b), others could not directly be mapped because they were adjectives, verbs, subjective or personal tags, compound terms with makeshift spellings or spam tags. They report further challenges in the disambiguation of homonyms. Nevertheless, the authors found that their method is very helpful for merging synonyms (Laniado, Eynard & Colombetti, 2007b).

3.3.2 Collaborative, Personal and Cross-Platform Tag Gardening

As we have mentioned, we distinguish between tag gardening on the personal (or personomy) level and the collaborative (or folksonomy) level.

Collaborative Tag Gardening and Professional Tag Gardeners
The previous examples mainly focus on the folksonomy level of tag gardening. They should enable a community to edit and maintain the collective tag-base, i.e. all tags in use within one platform. While approaches like tag suggestions or query expansion work well for this dimension, other gardening activities, like intellectual tag editing and compliance with tag guidelines, are rather difficult to be performed collaboratively by a large community and within a shared tag collection. Some critical questions are: Who may perform which types of edit? Which tags are spam? Which tag variants should be preferred? Can guidelines be set up?

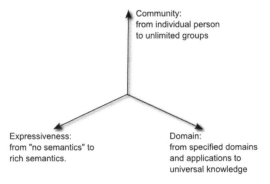

Figure 3.54. The three-dimensional knowledge space of tag gardening.

The three elements of folksonomies, resources, people and tags, constitute a three-dimensional knowledge space: domain – community – expressiveness, as depicted in Figure 3.54. Conflicts are caused if all three elements are completely or to a large extent considered simultaneously, as there is a complex interdependency between all of them.

To simplify, this means that if we have a broad community it will be easy to cover broader domains but more difficult to capture rich semantics (Figure 3.55). On the other hand, if we have a very small community (or only a single individual) there will be difficulties in handling broad domains, but it will be possible to establish rich semantics for limited domains (Figure 3.56). This corresponds to the schema depicted above in Figure 1.2, where complexity and size of domain are contrasted. The ultimate goal of social semantic knowledge representation is the construction of a KOS with highly expressive semantics and broad domain coverage. In the context of both collaborative tag gardening and community-based ontology engineering, this aim is tightly coupled to the question of the ideal size (and composition) of the community (Figure 3.57).

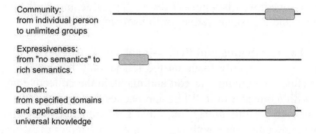

Figure 3.55. Interdependency of community, expressiveness and domain in tag gardening, part I.

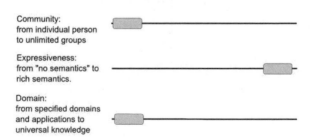

Figure 3.56. Interdependency of community, expressiveness and domain in tag gardening, part II.

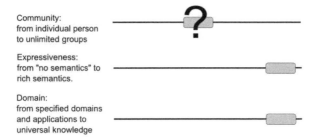

Figure 3.57. Interdependency of community, expressiveness and domain in tag gardening, part III.

Some different scenarios can be envisioned for tag gardening in communities. We will consider (relatively small and) closed communities and, in contrast, open Web communities.

Relatively small and closed communities can mainly be found within single industrial or institutional working groups, for example if a company sets up a tagging system for its intranet or if a research team builds up a shared knowledge base with tagging support. A related but less closed case would be a professional content provider/online host who wants to enable his registered customers to tag the available documents (like Elsevier's Engineering Village).

Such closed communities may soon want to enhance pure tagging with gradual vocabulary control, and they are able to agree on some form of shared vocabulary. For such scenarios, we suggest the establishment of some administrator role, e.g. in the form of single 'information architects' – or 'chief gardeners'. The majority of the community will then basically carry out the indexing activities with free tags and maybe perform some smaller editing activities; the administrator/information architect may also perform edits within the entire folksonomy, and is responsible for establishing semantic structures between tags (interlinking synonyms, establishing basic hierarchies and applying additional semantic relations). Additionally, he may monitor the other users' tagging behavior and suggest certain guidelines for unifying formatting variants.

Open Web communities may also profit from chief gardeners who take over the main work in tag gardening. To establish user roles (with specific rights) in an existing community is more difficult than in closed group settings, yet in broad communities establishing such administrative gardeners is probably the only way of performing platform-wide changes to the folksonomy. Other than that, the editing and weeding of tags should only be performed on a personal level by each user. And even with chief gardeners, there is always the danger that one user might destroy the arrangements another has made, or that someone regards certain tags as weed while others consider them pretty flowers. This will again require new tools that explicitly support collaboration and thus go beyond the current collective approaches of tagging systems. Users will have to be supported by communication channels and workspaces apart from the tagging application itself.

As folksonomies may consist of thousands of tags and even a personomy may comprise hundreds of tags[309], the administrator or the user needs some support during the tag gardening activities. Which tag should be considered first? Are any tags somehow related and may I use this connection for something? These are questions a user or administrator is faced with. Thus it makes sense to choose some candidates from the entire folksonomy which can be used as tag gardening starting points. They should be extracted automatically given the huge number of tags, while the actual tag gardening activity has to be carried out by the administrator/user intellectually. We have discussed so-called "power tags" as tag gardening candidates (Peters & Weller, 2008b).

Personal and Cross-Platform Tag Gardening
Social tagging applications are often used for personal information management (PIM) and are in this sense collective rather than collaborative services. Every user is entirely free to use a folksonomy-based system the way he wants, and there is rarely any advice on how to most efficiently make use of tags. The typical user of a folksonomy-based system has to come up with his own strategies for handling his own personal tags. Many personal tagging vocabularies thus grow into savage tag gardens. It is not unusual that a single user accidently applies different spelling variants of the same word (e.g. 'InformationRetrieval', 'informationretrieval' and 'information_retrieval') or different synonyms (e.g. 'Web2.0' and 'Social Web') to different documents in his collection. This causes additional expenses when searching personal document collections. Searching for all documents on the topics *Web 2.0* and *Information Retrieval* would now require the user to enter all his spelling variants and synonyms as search terms. This may be the case for a user's tags within one single folksonomy-based platform – but the problem may even grow bigger if a user actively tags within different platforms. With the growing number of tags and services it is getting more and more difficult to keep track of one's own personal preferred tags and to achieve some tagging consistency. Consequently, Oldenburg, Garbe and Cap (2008) ask:

> "Nowadays users can interact with more than one tagging service in parallel. As these services typically provide non-interoperable tagging features, users cannot be sure to apply the same tagging behaviour in all services. [...] How can a variety of services be efficiently used by users in such way, that they do not have to cope with service specific features, and that they can transparently apply their tagging behavior not regarding the service in background?" (Oldenburg, Garbe, & Cap, 2008)

Without an additional structuring approach, tags are of limited use for efficient personal information management. Someone using different folksonomy-based

---

[309]   Peters and Weller (2008) present an example of a Delicious user with 1,175 bookmarks and a very large personal tag collection.

tools in parallel will particulary profit from using his own terminology very consistently.

The inconsistent tagging behavior of users' within their own personomy has been described by Muller (2007). De Chiara, Fish and Ruocco (2008), as well as Panke and Gaiser (2008), conclude from their studies that users need better systems for managing their tags. Vander Wal (2008) also points out the need for a tag management tool:

> "An unsolved issue hampering the personal benefit is the portability of tagging data between different web services, which would allow to aggregate and manage all my tags from different systems in one interface." (Vander Wal, 2008)

We have thus thought of a cross-platform tag gardening application meant to help a user take care of his tags within one or several tagging systems: tagCare.

tagCare: A Personal Tag Garden

tagCare[310] (Dittmann, Dittmann et al., 2009; Golov, Weller & Peters, 2008) is a tool designed to help users apply their tags consistently across different platforms, and to structure a personal tagging vocabulary. A user can assemble all the tags he has used within different tagging systems and should further be supported in creating his own vocabulary hierarchy, synonym collections and cross-references to related terms in order to establish some basic form of controlled vocabulary. The system lets users import, manage and edit their tags. It will in future also include a meta retrieval system for using the tags to search the supported social software applications (where the tags originally came from). Furthermore, documents in the supported services may be directly tagged via tagCare.

tagCare currently supports Flickr and Delicious, i.e. it allows a user to import his personal tags from these platforms into tagCare and to maintain them all in one place. Other folksonomy-based tools are currently being integrated[311].

The central gardening activities as described above are transferred to the personomy level, to allow individual users to handle their tags. Beyond that, the indexing and editing behavior of all tagCare users may be evaluated to provide single users with suggestions for gardening activities based on certain types of frequencies. Figure 3.58 shows the personal user interface of tagCare for a user who has

---

[310] tagCare: http://www.tagcare.org. tagCare is work in progress. It is based on an idea by Katrin Weller and is currently being developed in several students' projects at the Dept. of Information Science, Heinrich-Heine-University Düsseldorf. Acknowledgements for their contributions go to Carsten Dittmann, Marc Dittmann, Evgeni Golov, Stefan Götz, Denis Anuschewski, Oliver Hanraths, Yunus Kaplan, Gabriel Nativo, Stephan Zalewski and Isabella Peters.

[311] This will probably also enable us to gather data on actual user behavior: which different tagging platforms are used by an overlapping community? How many different personomies across systems does a user maintain? Which systems are likely to require an overlapping tagging vocabulary?

just logged in; Figure 3.59 is a detail of this screenshot showing the suggestions for editing activities based on the user's own editing history, statistics of all users' actions, automatic spell checking mechanisms and general guidelines (e.g. for capitalization and the handling of compound terms). The interface also includes a personal tag cloud, an overview on the number of images and tags within the different platforms (in the right section) and a presentation of the most recently added documents (at the bottom of the page).

Figure 3.58. Demo version of tagCare. Source: www.tagcare.org.

Another simple form of suggestion is provided with type-ahead functionalities during the tagging process: typing the first letters of a word displays words with the same beginning that have already been used. Basic statistics are provided on how often the user has applied single tags on different systems. Possible future refinements of this feature may be:

- Exorbitant use of a single tag may be detected and the user may be warned to specify it. A respective threshold value will have to be detected first: How often may a tag be used within a personomy before it becomes indiscriminate and useless?

- If a user has applied several tags only once, these will be highly discriminating for search purposes – but, on the other hand, the extensive use of 'one-time-tags' may lead to overcrowded personomies. This will in turn increase the need for structuring mechanisms, which help, for example, to subsume single terms under a common broader term.
- An inverse tag cloud should be implemented, or alternatively, a ranking of the least frequently used tags. This can help to detect rarely used tags that should be handled as seedlings – or alternatively be bundled with others (in some cases, such rarely used tags are simply non-preferred synonyms).

Figure 3.59. Suggestions for tag gardening activities in tagCare. Source: www.tagcare.org.

Based on such tag statistics and editing suggestions, the user may start to edit his tags. tagCare offers different functionalities for the editing and structuring of tags. Basic editing functionalities for tags comprise the renaming and deleting of tags as well as directly creating new terms in tagCare. Changes can be directly[312] submitted to the respective services, i.e. the user does not have to perform a certain change on every single platform he uses but can edit a tag once in tagCare and see the change carried out on the cross-platform level. Furthermore, synonyms can be grouped together under a preferred tag. All changes are recorded in a history, previous versions of edited tags are saved and collected and may thus later be used as non-descriptors for query expansion. External services like Google Translate[313], as well as statistics of tag co-occurrences, will be integrated used to suggest candidates for relations of equivalence.

In future, tagCare will also include advanced editing options for the organization of tags with semantic relations and for fertilizing the personomy with other KOS. The resulting structures help the individual user to gain a better overview of his tags. Furthermore, broader, narrower or related terms may be suggested as additional tags during tagging or as additional search terms during retrieval. If semantic relations are used for tag suggestions during tagging, and are thus applied as additional tags, the accessibility of the resource will also be enhanced for other users.

---

[312] Some services support a live update, others are regurlarly updated.
[313] Google Translate: http://translate.google.com.

For the detection of homonyms, tagCare will also need external services (e.g. Flickr Cluster[314]). Homonym candidates can then be pointed out to the user, who may specify them as needed.

Apart from consistent tagging, tagCare will be extended with retrieval features to search several services with a personal tag vocabulary. Established tag interrelations may be used for query expansion, e.g. adding synonyms via disjunction (OR).

The particular approach of tagCare is to support tag gardening and semantic enrichment for single users on the personomy level. The result is a simple, personal knowledge organization system which goes beyond free keywords. Our intention was to enable the gradual refinement of personal tags into what may be called a persontology, i.e. a small personal ontology. Of course actual ontology features as outlined in the previous chapter (e.g. formal concept definitions and reasoning support) are not yet included and are still a distant vision.

Furthermore, the person-centric approach may be criticized for not being appropriate for fulfilling the "shared conceptualization" requirement. We have pursued this approach as a potential alternative to community-based ontologies. We assume that the personal development of KOS based on tag enrichment will lead to an improved 'tag literacy'. Participating in social tagging services has already started to sensitize broad user communities to the principal effects of document indexing for retrieval and information management. This might be fostered, if users would simply enrich their own tags (without the need to discuss changes with a community at this stage) in easy usable systems and thus learn about the basic effects of vocabulary control; this may encourage users to contribute to community ontologies at a later stage.

Until then, the community of taggers will also profit slightly from tags which are improved on a personal basis: spell checks and suggestions for additional broader, narrower, related and synonymous terms can already improve the quality of tags added to a document – which, in return, has a positive effect on its retrievability. Identified semantic relations between terms can be presented to the whole community for query expansion or refinement.

In the long term, we may think of ways of combining different personal tag vocabularies with a shared terminology and of exchanging tagging vocabularies between different tagCare users.

3.3.3 Ontology Gardening: Engineering Based on Semantic Enrichment

Enhancing folksonomies with semantics (e.g. from other KOS) and enriching ontologies with folksonomy terms are two sides of the same coin. Let us now switch our perspective to the question of how social tagging applications can contribute to the construction or maintenance of ontologies. Two basic methods may be distinguished: a) building an ontology from scratch based on a collection of tags, and b) enriching an ontology with terms collected from a tagging system.

---

[314] Flickr Cluster: http://www.flickr.com/photos/tags/homonym/clusters.

While tags are one useful way of performing semantic enrichment of KOS, we may more generally say that every less structured KOS may be enriched in terms of semantic structure. Thus semantic enrichment includes all the processes of structurally enhancing a given vocabulary.

Ontology Gardening Activities
In analogy to tag gardening, we want to suggest the following activities for ontology gardening:

Weeding & Seeding:
Weeding and seeding in ontology gardening are quite similar to the respective activities in tag gardening. They are mainly activities of ontology maintenance and refer to the elimination of those concepts in the ontology that are less useful, as well as the introduction of new concepts, respectively.

Fertilizing
In tag gardening, fertilizing was defined as the enhancement of a running folksonomy with semantic structures derived from another, external KOS. In ontology gardening, we may already possess a semantically rich ontology and wish to fertilize it with social information from folksonomies. This is a different type of fertilizing. Ontologies may be fertilized with social information included in folksonomies, e.g. tag popularities (How often has a tag been used? Which users have applied a certain tag?) and tag co-occurrences.

Harvesting
Closely related to fertilizing is another ontology gardening activity, namely *harvesting*[315]. Harvesting is the process of investigating external resources and extracting information from them which can be used to enhance the ontology. While fertilizing is focused on enriching an ontology with social dimensions (which may be obtained from a folksonomy), harvesting is about gathering terms (or other ontology elements, like relations) from other sources. Folksonomies are one such source which may be harvested, i.e. the development and updating of structured KOS can profit from folksonomies: tag distributions and tag frequencies are sources for new KOS terms and may encourage term modifications (Christiaens, 2006; Gendarmi & Lanubile, 2006; Macgregor & McCulloch, 2006; Mika, 2007; Mikroyannidis, 2007). They allow for fast responses to changes and innovations in a domain vocabulary. The most interesting aspect of harvesting folksonomies is that social tagging provides empirical data on the user's (not the expert's) language use in terms of knowledge representation, in the sense of a "bottom-up categorization" (Vander Wal, 2004). The tags are produced by a community – which may reach enormous sizes in popular folksonomy-based systems. The community members do not have to communicate or interact explicitly, which

---

[315] The image of harvesting folksonomies is also mentioned by Wu, Zubair & Maly (2006).

means that incentives for participation are mainly based on objectives of personal benefit. The information is taken from the collection of the different users' tags. These tags include data on how non-experts in knowledge representation compose content-descriptive keywords, which should be evaluated to gain a better understanding of the underlying ideas. Some studies have already been performed to reveal structures in users' tagging behavior (an overview is given by Peters, 2009). For example, it is accepted that about 90% of applied tags are nouns (Guy & Tonkin, 2006). This resembles the preference for nouns to be used in controlled vocabularies and makes it possible to regard most tags as candidates for ontology concepts and their co-occurrences as candidates for semantic relations.

Weeding processes may be needed in advance to harvesting. Again the fundamental precondition for using tags in ontology engineering is to eliminate "bad tags"; particularly spam tags, misspellings, spelling variants etc. Van Damme, Coenen and Vandijck (2008) refer to this process as "cleaning the tags".

Related Work
Some related work deals with aspects of how ontologies can be built upon or enriched with folksonomy terms. One example is the "ontology maturing" approach (Braun, Schmidt et al., 2007). In this context the tool SOBOLEO (see above) is used as a platform for establishing lightweight ontologies based on tagging behavior. The aim of the DBin project was to "[…] enable a group of users to share their del.icio.us tags and organize them in to a cooperatively built RDFS ontology" (Tummarello & Morbidoni, 2007). Van Damme, Coenen and Vandijck (2008) report their experiences of using tags as the basis of a lightweight controlled vocabulary in a corporate setting.

Wu, Zubair and Maly (2006) not only consider tags for harvesting semantics but also use tagging behavior to detect communities of common interest and information leaders (comparable to domain experts). The Annotea project (Koivunen, 2005) also considers the whole process of organizing documents in a bookmarking process as a valuable basis for the creation of rich metadata.

Harvesting Semantic Relations from Folksonomies
One particular task of harvesting information from folksonomies is the detection of hidden, implicit semantic relations. The support of differentiated semantic relations is essential for the upgrading of a given KOS to a more complex type (particularly if it should become an ontology). Folksonomies can act as a means of analyzing the social dimensions of semantic relations:

As there are no explicit structures provided in folksonomies, all relations between tags are by definition syntagmatic ones, i.e. they implicitly exist in the *co-occurrence* of tags. Relationships between tags are not labeled at all; they are not even discussed by the users. And we can still assume that a user does keep the idea of certain relationships in mind during the process of tagging. For example, a certain picture on Flickr might be tagged with 'Germany, Rheinland, Düsseldorf' another with 'Brasil, Brazil' or 'countryside, landscape', which implicitly includes a part-of relation in the first case and kinds of synonymy in the latter examples. If these implicit semantic relations between tags in folksonomies can be detected and made explicit, we can use them to upgrade the structure of KOS. We call this the *harvesting* of semantics from folksonomies for ontology engineering.

Automatic approaches

The automatic derivation of semantic structures (e.g. hierarchies) has established itself as a popular research topic (e.g., Benz & Hotho, 2007; Fan, Gao & Luo, 2007; Grahl, Hotho & Stumme., 2007; Heymann & Garcia-Molina, 2006; Schmitz, 2006). Some studies also focus on the automatic extraction of specific semantic information like "place" or "event" (Rattenbury, Good & Naaman, 2007). The underlying principles for current approaches are statistical evaluations of the co-occurrence of tags, which can be computed in different ways.

Al-Khalifa and Davis (2007a) discover that folksonomies are appropriate sources for the extraction of new terms which can then be implemented in existing ontologies. The authors state that this is due to the "latent (implicit) semantics embedded in the tags" (Al-Khalifa & Davis, 2007a). A subsequent study of Al-Khalifa and Davis (2007b) verifies this assumption. They find out that the following semantic relations exist between tags: 1) same (spelling variants or acronyms), 2) synonymy, 3) broader term, 4) narrower term, 5) related term (of a comparable thesaurus descriptor) and 6) related (an unspecific relation). Knowledge of these relations can be used for the refinement and expansion of ontologies or KOS. Angeletou, Sabou et al. (2007) mostly confirm the findings of Al-Khalifa and Davis (2007b). Kipp (2006b) is also able to demonstrate that relations between tags do exist, which had been defined as associative relations in KOS, but were valuable sources for more fine-grained semantic relations in both folksonomies and KOS.

Cattuto, Benz et al. (2008a) have investigated the use of similarity measures for deriving semantics from Folksonomies. They have, for example, induced a hierarchical representation of music genres based on tags from the social music platform Last.FM (Figures 3.60 and 3.61) (Cattuto, Benz et al., 2008b).

These different ways of automatically detecting tag relations and tag clusters are interesting approaches to enhancing folksonomies for everyday usage, and they provide the basis for harvesting richer semantics for more fine-grained KOS. Yet for the creation of elaborated ontologies, intellectual refinement is needed. Automatic tag analysis and clustering does not lead to full ontologies (mostly not even to full classifications), but regarded as a *statistical KOS* (e.g. statistical classification), they are of enormous value for KOS engineering. The main problem of automatic approaches is the differentiation of the various associative relations or of different kinds of hierarchical relations.

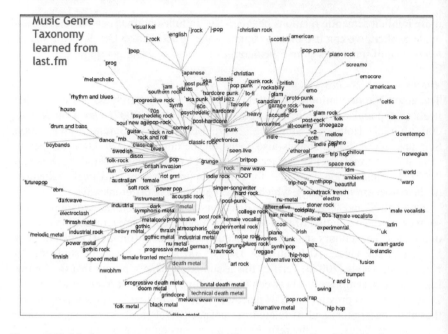

Figure 3.60. Music genre taxonomy automatically created from Last.FM tags. Source: Cattuto, Benz et al., 2008b.

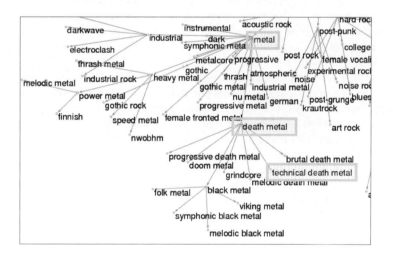

Figure 3.61. Zoom into a music genre taxonomy. Source: Cattuto, Benz et al., 2008b.

Intellectual approaches
In previous works, we have exemplarily investigated the options for *intellectually* identifying semantic relations in folksonomies (Peters & Weller, 2008a; Weller & Peters, 2007).

For this purpose, we have used co-occurrences of tags as indicators for existing relations. The actual quality of the underlying tags has then been judged by humans. Figure 3.62 shows an example of a Flickr photo and its associated tags. The following are manually identified semantic relations: A relation of location is given as 'cloud gate' *is_located_in* 'Millennium Park' or 'Millennium Park' *is_located_in* 'chicago'. A relation of production/fabrication can be found in 'sculpture' *is_made_of* 'metal'. There is an attributive relation regarding the sculpture's format, e.g. 'sculpture' *has_shape* 'bean'. Standard relations like synonymy ('vacation', 'trip' and 'travel') and both relations of hierarchy, hyponymy ('cloud gate' *is_a* 'sculpture') and meronymy ('chicago' *is_part_of* 'america') can be found as well. Of course such manual harvesting of semantic relations from folksonomies is laborious and time-consuming. They should thus be combined with automatic approaches. We have also suggested a method for using power tags as candidates for further investigation (Peters & Weller, 2008b).

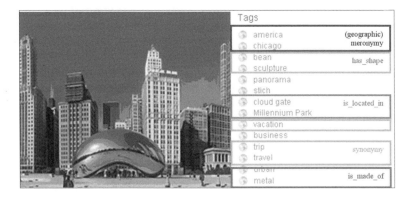

Figure 3.62. A photo on Flickr and its associated tags. Specified semantic relations between tags have been identified manually. Source: Peters & Weller, 2008a.

KOS Enrichment

As mentioned above, semantic enrichment does not have to focus exclusively on folksonomies. Other KOS may also be enriched or upgraded. For example, a nomenclature may be enriched with hierarchical structures to become a thesaurus (and the SWD has begun to do so). Aitchison (1986) describes how the Bliss Bibliographic Classification has become the source for a thesaurus. In chapter 1.2.2 we have introduced eClassOWL, which is an ontology developed by upgrading a classification system (Hepp, 2006a and b). Hepp & de Bruijn (2007) report some difficulties in and solutions for transferring classifications and thesauri into ontologies, with a focus on eClassOWL and an OWL version of UNSPSC. The Museo Suomi[316] has also launched a project for transferring the Finnish cultural thesaurus MASA into an ontology, resulting in the MAO ontology (Hyvoenen, Salminen et al., 2004). Closely related are attempts to remodel existing KOS in formal languages (e.g. van Assem, Malaise et al., 2006; van Assem, Gangemi & Schreiber, 2006). Another exemplary project deals with transferring the NCI Thesaurus to OWL (Noy, Coronado et al., 2008).

Basically, all systems introduced in Section 2.3.2 can be used for semantic upgrades, but little research is dedicated to the less obvious among them, like lexicons. Hepp & de Bruijn (2007) conclude:

> "Hierarchical classification standards, thesauri, and such taxonomies that were not initially designed to be used as ontologies exist in many domains. They are likely the most promising sources for the creation of domain ontologies at reasonable costs, because they reflect some degree of community consensus and contain, readily available, a wealth of category definitions plus a hierarchy." (Hepp & de Bruijn, 2007)

We think that, among all KOS, thesauri are most suited to being upgraded to become an ontology because they are closest to ontologies in terms of their structure.

3.3.4 Additional Knowledge Resources for Ontology Gardening

Apart from KOS, other resources may also be harvested to support ontology engineering. Among them are, of course, the novel approaches for community-based ontology engineering as discussed above, mainly community knowledge bases and games with a purpose.

Harvesting Wikipedia

Wikipedia has been recognized as a valuable source for ontology engineering as well as background knowledge for semantic applications.

> "Now we can observe on the one hand that there are very few real domain ontologies available; a large share of ontologies published on the Web are outdated, dead collections created in some academic research context. On the other hand, the English version of Wikipedia contains more than 850,000 entries, which means it holds unique identifiers for 850,000 concepts." (Hepp, Bachlechner & Siorpaes, 2006a)

Wikipedia is constructed by a free online community and thus constitutes probably the most valuable community knowledge collection on the Web. It is only logical that this source should be explored for other knowledge-based applications

---

[316] Museo Suomi: http://museosuomi.cs.helsinki.fi/.

as well. Ponzetto and Strube (2007b) declare that "we overcome the well-known knowledge acquisition bottleneck by deriving a knowledge resource from a very large, collaboratively created encyclopedia."

One important idea is to use Wikipedia articles as unique identifiers for concept references (Hepp, Bachlechner & Siorpaes, 2006a and 2007). Yet this is not entirely problem-free. Hepp, Bachlechner and Siorpaes (2006a) point out that Wikipedia entries may be changed over the course of time – meaning that there is no conceptual consistency of a URI over time.

> "It is possible that the concept represented by a URI changes substantially over time, rendering old annotations inconsistent. This is especially a problem when so called 'disambiguation pages' are introduced, which happens when the community realizes that the same word is a homonym and used in very different senses in different contexts. In such cases, the original page is turned into a disambiguation page that contains separate links to the multiple context-specific entries." (Hepp, Bachlechner & Siorpaes, 2006a)

In a first evaluation Hepp, Bachlechner and Siorpaes (2006a) revealed that 94% of their sample pages were stable during the considered period, only 3% have been turned into disambiguation pages and another 3% subject to other changes in meaning.

> "The data from our experiment shows quite clearly that for the vast majority of Wikipedia entries, there is community consensus about the meaning of the URI from the very beginning to the most recent version. In other words, communities seem to be able to achieve consensus about named classes as very lightweight ontological agreements in an unsupervised fashion and with only the known mechanisms for preventing destructive changes of standard Wiki software. As shown above, we can estimate that each month, about 2,465,000 change operations are made by Wikipedia users, but only 5 % of concepts change in a major sense during their lifespan. We think this is a fundamental argument in favor of community-centric ontology building." (Hepp, Bachlechner & Siorpaes, 2006a)

Another challenge is caused by redundancy in Wikipedia, as "it can happen easily that multiple entries for the same concept are created" (Hepp, Bachlechner & Siorpaes, 2006a). If such cases are detected in Wikipedia, users may merge the different pages by using the 'redirect" function ("#redirect [[PAGENAME]]"). This redirections will also have to be considered, ideally by turning the merged pages into synonyms within an ontology (Hepp, Bachlechner & Siorpaes, 2006a).

Much attention is also paid to Wikipedia's category system. Voß (2006 and 2007) compares Wikipedia categories to a thesaurus and labels them as a particular type of tagging with a controlled vocabulary:

> "A special kind of tagging system is the category system of Wikipedia. The free encyclopedia is probably the first application of collaborative tagging with a thesaurus. The extent of contribution in Wikipedia is distributed very inhomogeneously [...] this also applies for the category system. Everyone is

allowed to change and add categories but most authors only edit the article text instead of tagging articles and even less authors change and add the category system. Furthermore, each article is not tagged independently by every user but users have to agree on a set of categories per article. So tagging in Wikipedia is somewhere between indexing with a controlled vocabulary and free keywords. Most of the time authors just use the categories that exist but they can also switch to editing the vocabulary at any time." (Voß, 2007)

YAGO[317] is a large, light-weight ontology (formalized in a specific extension of RDFS, the YAGO model, and also available in RDFS[318]) with high topical coverage (Kasneci, Ramanath et al., 2008; Suchanek, Kasneci & Weikum, 2007). In 2007, YAGO contained more than 1 million entities (like persons, organizations, cities, etc.) and 5 million facts (Suchanek, Kasneci & Weikum, 2007), by now it has grown to more than 2 million entities and 20 million facts about these entities[319]. It includes hyponymic as well as specified associative relationships. What is so special about YAGO is that it has been automatically extracted from Wikipedia and unified with WordNet.

"The resulting knowledge base is a major step beyond WordNet: in quality by adding knowledge about individuals like persons, organizations, products, etc. with their semantic relationships – and in quantity by increasing the number of facts by more than an order of magnitude." (Suchanek, Kasneci & Weikum, 2007)

The YAGO project was motivated by observations indicating that many upcoming semantic applications used either Wikipedia or WordNet as a knowledge resource. Such systems could "boost their performance, if a huge ontology with knowledge from several sources was available" (Suchanek, Kasneci & Weikum, 2007).

It does not – as other approaches (e.g. Ruiz-Casado, Alfonseca & Castells, 2006) – apply methods of information extraction, but rather utilizes Wikipedia's *category pages*:

"Category pages are lists of articles that belong to a specific category (e.g., Zidane is in the category of French football players). These lists give us candidates for entities (e.g. Zidane), candidates for concepts (e.g. IsA(Zidane, FootballPlayer)) [...] and candidates for relations (e.g. isCitizenOf(Zidane, France))." (Suchanek, Kasneci & Weikum, 2007)

Yet the YAGO developers found out that the category hierarchies provided by Wikipedia are not useful enough for the construction of an ontology; they do not consist of clean hyponymy relations, resulting in misconstructions such as "Zidane is a Football in France". They thus decided to combine Wikipedia categories with

---

[317] YAGO: http://www.mpi-inf.mpg.de/yago-naga/yago/.
[318] The YAGO ontology can be downloaded from: http://www.mpi-inf.mpg.de/yago-naga/yago/downloads.html.
[319] As stated on the YAGO website on August 24th, 2009. Facts are defined as triples in the form of entity – relation – entity.

the clean hierarchical structure of WordNet. For this purpose, a specific method was needed, as Wikipedia categories hardly have any direct counterparts in WordNet. They claim that their unification of Wikipedia facts and WordNet terms is achieved with an accuracy of 97% (Suchanek, Kasneci & Weikum, 2007).

All in all, the YAGO project aims at providing a comprehensive knowledge base[320] as well as "logical reasoning capabilities and rich support for querying" (Kasneci, Ramanath et al., 2008). A demo version[321] of YAGO can be used to query the database. Figure 3.63 shows an exemplary query with four search arguments.

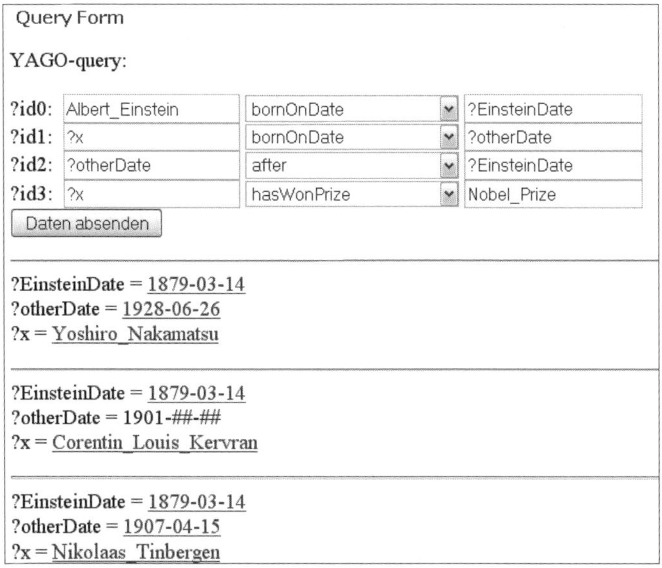

Figure 3.63. Querying the YAGO Database for Nobel prize winners who were born after Albert Einstein (not all results are displayed in this screenshot). Source: http://www.mpi-inf.mpg.de/yago-naga/yago/demo.html.

A variety of other works deal with attempts to extract semantic information from Wikipedia. Wikipedia is particularly suitable for harvesting ontology classes or instances, as Wikipedia articles typically belong to one of these types. Qualified properties/relations are not made explicit in Wikipedia.

---

[320] On the project's Website (http://www.mpi-inf.mpg.de/yago-naga/), they define their vision as the "confluence of Semantic Web (Ontologies), Social Web (Web 2.0) and Statistical Web (Information Extraction) assets towards a comprehensive repository of human knowledge".

[321] YAGO demonstration: http://www.mpi-inf.mpg.de/yago-naga/yago/demo.html.

In current research, one particular focus in harvesting Wikipedia for ontology engineering is placed on the question whether a Wikipedia article refers to a class or an individual.

> "Since there is no explicit knowledge representation model in the background, a Wiki entry can be anything; it is not clear whether it refers to an instance, a concept, or a property. By social convention, Wikipedia contains mostly entries that are proper nouns and does not include relationships and properties [...]. So it must be clarified whether a Wiki entry is to be treated as a class or as an instance, at least if the ontology model requires a choice between these two." (Hepp, Bachlechner & Siorpaes, 2006a)

We have already mentioned the gwap approach of OntoPronto (Siorpaes & Hepp, 2008a), which aims exactly at solving this task.

Zirn, Nastase and Strube (2008) developed methods for automatically distinguishing between instances and classes in Wikipedia. They state that "[i]t may seem intuitive that categories in Wikipedia are all classes, but that is not the case. For example, UNITED NATIONS, an instance of the class ORGANIZATIONS, appears both as a page and as a category in Wikipedia" (Zirn, Nastase & Strube, 2008). In their method, they work with automatic named entity analysis (amongst others), and profit from Wikipedia conventions for capitalization and plural usage. They achieved up to 90.92% precision in distinguishing instances and classes with combined methods.

It is more difficult to investigate qualified semantic relations from Wikipedia, as "we cannot find properties and relationship entries in Wikipedia" (Hepp, Bachlechner & Siorpaes, 2006a). As we have seen, the YAGO project uses the WordNet hierarchy instead of computing hierarchies directly from Wikipedia. Others have developed approaches to also extract semantic relations from Wikipedia itself.

Ponzetto and Strube (2007a) have developed a method to extract subsumption hierarchies out of the English Wikipedia. They use the category system as a semi-structured starting point: "This provides us with pairs of related concepts whose semantic relation is unspecified. The task of creating a subsumption hierarchy then boils down to distinguishing between isa and notisa relations" (Ponzetto & Strube, 2007a). For this purpose, they applied methods of head matching[322] (amongst others) for detecting is-a relations and modifier matching[323] for not-is-a relations. They have evaluated their results by comparing it to ResearchCyc[324] as a gold standard. Furthermore, the authors have extended their research to works about deriving semantic relatedness, which is defined as the degree of "how much two

---

[322] That is, labelling pairs of categories that share the same head, e.g. "British Computer Scientists" and "Computer Scientists" (Ponzetto & Strube, 2007a).

[323] Category pairs are labelled as not-is-a in "case the stem of the lexical head of one of the categories as given by the Porter stemmer [...], occurs in non-head position in the other category. This is to rule out thematic categorization links such as CRIME COMICS and CRIME or ISLAMIC MYSTICISM and ISLAM" (Ponzetto & Strube, 2007a).

[324] ResearchCyc: http://research.cyc.com.

concepts are semantically distant in a network or taxonomy by using all relations between them" (Ponzetto & Strube, 2007b). They point out that Wikipedia implicitly includes relations of synonymy (via the redirect pages), distinguishes homonymy (via disambiguation pages) and a variety of unspecified cross-references (internal links) between the articles, which indicate some kind of relation. They do not directly aim at identifying the quality of these relations, but use them as a source for computing how closely two concepts are semantically related.

There are other works that actually focus on the nature of the respective semantic relations. For example, Nguyen, Matsuo and Ishizuka (2007) aim at "locating interesting entities and identifying relations among them" with automatical NLP methods. Wang, Yu & Zhu (2007) introduce the PORE method for extracting semantic relations from Wikipedia. With their automatic approach, they could for example detect relations between music albums and artists, firms and directors, universities and cities or bands and band members. Milne, Medelyan and Witten (2006) use "Wikipedia as a source of manually defined terms and relations" to build a domain-specific thesaurus. They also note that "[h]yperlinks between articles capture many of the same semantic relations as defined in the international standard for thesauri (ISO 2788)", namely relations of equivalence, hierarchy and association. They suggest methods for indentifying these three relationship types in Wikipedia, and they use their methodology to develop an experimental thesaurus for the domain of agriculture. In an evaluation phase they compare their resulting thesaurus with the AGROVOC[325] thesaurus, which should act as a gold standard for this domain.

While instances, classes, basic hierarchies and some semantic relations may be derived from Wikipedia, there is no chance of harvesting the information needed for more elaborated reasoning tasks. Hepp, Bachlechner and Siorpaes (2006a) conclude that only "very simple ontology metamodels" can be derived in this way. Consequently, they focus on future work in enriching community-based and harvested ontologies:

> "Our future research will focus on how this skeleton can be extended towards a richer ontology meta-model without introducing new entrance barriers for users. We think for example of clever voting mechanisms with thresholds that make a subsumption relationship subject to community voting." (Hepp, Bachlechner and Siorpaes, 2006a)

With the ongoing efforts of creating a semantic version of Wikipedia (Völkel, Krötzsch et al., 2006), new interesting perspectives for integrating Wikipedia into ontology engineering purposes will emerge.

Harvesting other Knowledge Resources from the Web

In sum, lots of existing Web resources may be considered as potential resources for providing knowledge structures useful for ontology engineering. In the context of the Social Semantic Web, those services that are based on some kind of com-

---

[325]   AGROVOC Thesaurus: http://aims.fao.org/website/AGROVOC-Thesaurus/sub.

munity activity (like Freebase, which was discussed above) are regarded as the most valuable ones. But other 'traditional' Web applications may be useful as well. Not much work is being done toward providing a (comprehensive) overview of the variety of possible knowledge resources (some first attempts are, for example, presented by García-Silva, Gómez-Pérez et al., 2008) – and unfortunately, it is beyond the scope of this book to do so. We may exemplarily recommend the following services as subjects for future work on harvesting semantics from the Web, however:

- The Encyclopedia of Life[326] (EOL): The EOL is an online reference and database for living species. It currently holds about 1.8 million species currently known to science. So far, the encyclopedia has been developed in a largely collaborative (but curated) approach by a variety of domain experts. It is planned to let an open Web community allow the adding of images, descriptions or sighting reports for the different species. Besides information in the form of topical articles and images it includes a biological taxonomy of living species[327] for navigation and context information.

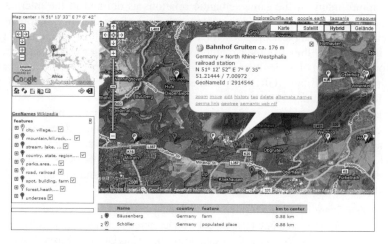

Figure 3.64. The GeoNames entry for the railroad station in Gruiten. Source: http://www.geonames.org/maps/google_51.214_7.01.html.

- GeoNames[328]: GeoNames is a free of charge geographical database. It currently contains over eight million geographical names[329]. Users may edit the data, correct mistakes or add new names. Figure 3.64 shows a Google map with GeoNames entries. For the selected location, some additional geo-

---

326 Encyclopedia of Life (EOL): http://www.eol.org.
327 Integrated Taxonomic Information System (ITIS): http://www.itis.gov/.
328 GeoNames: http://www.geonames.org.
329 As stated on the Website http://www.geonames.org/about.html on August 27th, 2009.

graphical information is displayed which may be edited by the users. Different types of location are marked in different colors. They are furthermore specified with one of the 645 GeoNames feature codes[330], a kind of classification of location types.

- Product categories or shopping portals: A valuable resource for creating, enriching or updating KOS in the domain of economics can be the product categories of major Web shopping portals, such as eBay[331] (also suggested by Hepp & de Bruijn, 2007), Amazon[332] or Shopping.com[333]. This will become even more interesting if the systems also include users' tags (as Amazon does, Figure 3.65), as both tags and categories may then be evaluated in combination.

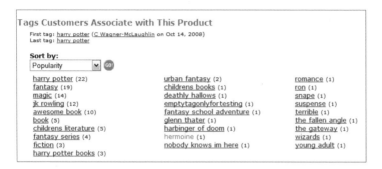

Figure 3.65. Customers' tags on Amazon.com for the book "Harry Potter and the Deathly Hallows". Source: http://www.amazon.com/.

- Internet Movie Database (IMDb): The IMDb is a large online database for movies as well as a general information and entertainment portal. IMDb started off as a fan project, then turned into a company and was finally bought by Amazon.com. Due to its size and coverage, it may well act as a unique reference (i.e. providing unique identifiers) for the domain of movies. Furthermore, it includes relations (via Weblinks) between movies, actors, directors, writers etc. Users are encouraged to contribute new content to the database.

Harvesting Knowledge from Indexing and Abstracting Activities
If we consider tags as valuable resources for ontology engineering, many of these approaches might also be transferred to other indexing and abstracting activities. Of course, as discussed above, every KOS is a valuable resource per se and may

---

[330] GeoNames feature codes: http://www.geonames.org/export/codes.html.
[331] eBay: http://www.ebay.com.
[332] Amazon: http://www.amazon.com.
[333] Shopping.com: http://www.shopping.com.

become subject to semantic enrichment. But furthermore, new dimensions arise from the actual process of applying a KOS during an indexing activity. Structured KOS of course obtain paradigmatic semantic relations between terms, but if single terms from among these are applied to documents during indexing, there will also be syntagmatic relations based on co-occurrences, which may be interpreted similarly to tagging data (with the limitation that typically no information about the person who provided a keyword is included). In simple terms, we may say that KOS which already include elaborated semantic structures may be used in ontology engineering via methods of semantic enrichment; and all KOS which are practically used for indexing can be analyzed and mined for co-occurrences.

Folksonomies occupy an exceptional position: they are almost exclusively focused on the indexing process and (in their purest form) pay virtually no attention to the establishment of knowledge structures. That is exactly why folksonomies are not always considered to be actual types of KOS (as mentioned above, footnote 9). Quite the opposite – ontology research has long been primarily focused on the engineering part and has often neglected the indexing perspective. So in this respect, folksonomies and ontologies may again be considered as opposites.

Another option for indexing documents without a KOS but based on the terms actually used within the document is Henrichs' *Textwortmethode*[334] (Henrichs, 1970). The textwortmethode was explicitly developed as an alternative draft to controlled vocabularies. It was meant for indexing publications in philosophy – a discipline which does not cling to a set terminology and, even more, heavily depends upon the freedom of the used vocabulary for its discourse of arguments. Henrichs thus proposed an indexing method that accounts for the exact terminology of a document's author: only words which actually appear in a document may act as index terms. After choosing the appropriate text terms, they are thematically interlinked via syntactical indexing. This means that a specific indexing syntax is applied to denote the contexts of individual terms. Henrichs does this by creating thematical term chains (marked with index numbers). As a result, one gets chains of index terms which state, for example, that a document deals with a 'definition' of 'knowledge representation' by 'Sowa'. Term frequencies and co-occurrences within term chains can be used for computing indexing weights (Stock & Stock, 2008).

Knautz (2008) has pointed out some similarities between folksonomies and the textwortmethode. She proposes a method for deriving a "statistical thesaurus" from a document collection indexed with the textwortmethode. She uses statistical analyses to calculate term coincidences and weightings for term importance. Similarly, she computes "tag clusters" from documents indexed with a folksonomy. All term relationships gathered by these methods are unqualified (i.e. they only indicate that *some* kind of relation exists) but may be used as starting points for building a KOS with explicit semantic relations.

Pepper (2002) highlights some features of book indexes which make them interesting for the purposes of harvesting information for ontology engineering.

---

[334] Which may approximately be translated as 'text term method' or 'text word method'.

Fundamentally, terms in an index are provided with numbers which indicate their appearance within a book – and which may thus also be mined for co-occurrences. The use of cross-references between index terms ('see also') and sub-entries may be investigated for semantic relatedness, and some indexes may include "explanatory labels" for distinguishing homonyms (Pepper, 2002). Furthermore, some indexes apply typographical conventions to distinguish between different types of entries; Pepper (2002) names the example of an index from a book about opera, where all names of operas are typed in italics. Some books also contain multiple indexes, for example separate indexes for names and places.

Furthermore, one may envision the investigation of tables of contents or chapter headings, or abstracts with automatic information extraction methods, as profitable additions to the ontology engineering process. The research field of examining indexing data for ontology enrichment still leaves much room for future work.

There is thus a variety of resources that may be reused for ontology engineering. We expect many more approaches and methods to be developed in the future. For the reuse of various existing sources in collaborative or community-based ontology engineering, a structured overview of appropriate resource collections is needed – and some more continuous work will have to be conducted in this direction. This book may provide the first step for such a project: in the next section, we will introduce our basic approach to metadata for KOS within the Social Semantic Web.

3.4 Co-Existence of Knowledge Organization Systems

With all the different KOS we have discussed in this book so far, the next big challenge of Web knowledge representation becomes obvious: how can all these different approaches act in concert to enable the broadest possible coverage of semantics for the Web? With respect to the Social Semantic Web, we may phrase the matter differently: different user communities establish different semantic models for their particular purposes; but how can we ensure that these communities will understand each other? Can we mediate between divergent points of view? Depending on the purpose of a KOS, the size of the respective user community may vary, and we have even seen that there are cases of individual KOS (like the personomy within a folksonomy) which are based on one single user's point of view. These different KOS may thus consist of overlapping information – which may also contradict each other in some cases.

All these matters can be considered as the inter-ontological level of ontology engineering as mentioned above. With the growing importance of inter-ontology engineering, we may also say that the task of ontology engineering has reached a new meta-level. It will have to be addressed by many research endeavors in the near future if ontologies are to help structure the growing amounts of data on the Web and not to become part of the information overload themselves. This new inter-ontological meta-level of ontology engineering has two major goals: a) the mediation between different KOS, e.g. by referring to equivalent concepts within different KOS, and b) the reuse of available knowledge resources, e.g. in the form of ontology integration, ontology merging or semantic upgrades.

Another challenging task is directly tied to the inter-ontological level: how to store the growing number of ontologies and make them accessible and retrievable for future engineering activities? Without any ways to access available ontologies they can neither be easily reused nor interrelated.

3.4.1 Multiple Knowledge Representations on the Social Semantic Web

As we have seen in the previous chapters, various different knowledge organization systems exist. Yet currently, we can only guess *how many* individual knowledge models exist. We hardly have any overview of all available KOS, their specific characteristics, their usage and – probably least of all – their cross-references and interactions. Some Web collections exist for thesauri and classifications (an overview is given by Dextre Clarke, 2008), covering mainly influential and well-established KOS. A lot more smaller ones may still be hidden, for example in Web applications and corporate systems. Non-standardized knowledge resources (as discussed above, Section 2.3.2) are hardly covered in collections at all. The ontology search engine Swoogle[335] (Ding, Finin et al., 2004) currently claims to search more than 10,000 ontologies[336]. But these documents are mainly files in RDF or related formats; very few of them are of high quality or meet our expectations for ontologies as defined in the previous chapter. Ding, Finin et al. (2004) call them "Semantic Web documents". Thus Swoogle basically indicates that not only ontologies but also 'preliminary ontologies' and various other forms of knowledge models using formal languages are scattered over the Web.

To handle the co-existing KOS and to enable mediations between them is fundamentally dependent on a more comprehensive overview. Furthermore, a general understanding of the ways in which different KOS may interact is needed. Individual KOS may be complementing or overlap with others, some may even be contradictory and incompatible. Efforts to handle the variety of KOS will also always face the challenge of most knowledge models being subject to constant changes due to modifications and updates.

We will now first discuss several types of KOS interaction and then introduce our approach for a meta-ontology, which may help provide a broader overview of existing KOS.

Types of Interaction between KOS

Various types of interaction are already being heavily discussed and researched by a large scientific community. Stock and Stock (2008) discuss possible "crosswalks" of KOS, and indicate that the respective methods either aim at establishing compatibility (through comparability) or interoperability. Many discussions deal with the "semantic heterogeneity" of KOS and discuss forms of "ontology coordi-

---

[335] Swoogle Semantic Web Search Engine: http://swoogle.umbc.edu/.
[336] As stated on http://swoogle.umbc.edu on March 5th 2008.

nation" to overcome this state (e.g. Bouquet, Ehrig et al., 2004). Sometimes the problem of handling multiple ontologies is also discussed under the keyword "ontology mediation":

> "The use of such shared terminologies enables a certain degree of inter-operation between these data sources. This, however, does not solve the integration problem completely, because it cannot be expected that all individuals and organizations on the Semantic Web will ever agree on using one common terminology or ontology [...]. It can be expected that many different ontologies will appear and, in order to enable inter-operation, differences between these ontologies have to be reconciled. The reconciliation of these differences is called ontology mediation." (de Bruijn, Ehrig et al., 2006)

We ought to briefly introduce the most important forms of KOS interactions:

Reuse and Upgrades
One important form of interaction between KOS has already been discussed above. One (or more) existing KOS may be used as a starting point for developing a new ontology. Consequently, the newly developed ontology will have strong references to the sources. Semantic upgrades of less formal KOS are one particular case of *reuse*.

In some cases, only a part of an existing KOS may be needed for reuse. The extraction of such relevant KOS parts for further usage is sometimes referred to as "pruning" (Conesa, de Palol & Olivé, 2003; Stock & Stock, 2008). In pruning processes it is particularly necessary to include consistency checks; if only parts of a KOS are extracted, relevant context information may be excluded, possibly rendering the extracted part inconsistent.

KOS *modifications* can also be considered a particular form of reuse: an existing KOS is adapted for a new application, for which it requires slight refinements. Ideally, the modification should encompass only minor changes so that the modified KOS can still refer to its source. The FOAF vocabulary has been explicitly envisioned to support such modifications to make it more reusable:

> "The loose definition of `foaf:knows` won't fit all applications, particularly those geared to capture information about complex social and business networks. However, this doesn't mean that FOAF is unsuitable for such purposes; indeed FOAF has the potential to be an open interchange format used by many different social networking applications. The expectation is that additional vocabularies will be created to refine the general FOAF knows relationship to create something more specific. The correct way to achieve this is to declare new sub-properties of `foaf:knows`." (Dodds, 2004)

Although some theoretical research and practical experiments on KOS reuse are already available, more work on this topic will be needed in the future. Of particular use would be precise guidelines for checking the appropriateness of a certain KOS for a specific reuse task. As already pointed out by Chandrasekaran, Josephson & Benjamins (1999), "what aspects of reality are chosen for encoding in an ontology does depend on the task" and "an ontology is unlikely to cover all possible potential uses", which indicates that not every ontology is appropriate for every reuse scenario. Kashyap, Cheung et al. (2008) name some basic questions which will have to stand at the beginning of every reuse process, e.g. how specific or general the ontology to be re-used should be, and on what level of granularity concepts should be included for reuse.

Matching and Mapping
Matching is the process of finding relations and correspondences between single elements located in different KOS, e.g. equivalences of two concepts within distinct ontologies. In ontology *mapping*, the correspondences detected during matching processes are highlighted and established as links between two ontologies. The process of ontology mapping is sometimes also referred to as ontology *alignment*[337]; in the context of classical KOS, one usually speaks of *concordances*.

Overviews on ontology matching and mapping are provided by Choi, Song & Han (2003), Ding & Foo (2002b), Ehrig (2007), Ehrig, de Bruijn et al. (2004), Euzenat & Shvaiko (2007), Kalfoglou & Schorlemmer (2003), Lanzenberger & Sampson (2008), Predoiu, Feier et al. (2005), to name a few. Some of them not only consider mappings between formal ontologies but also take into account other knowledge models. Mapping scenarios in the field of traditional KOS have also been amply discussed, e.g. by BS 8723-4:2007, Mayr (2006), Walter, Mayr et al. (2006), Zheng & Chan (2004) and also in the Project ISO 25964[338] and the CARMEN[339] project[340].

Several algorithms for (automatic) ontology mapping are being developed, as well as different tools that make use of them to support the ontology engineer in the mapping of two ontologies. Euzenat and Shvaiko (2007) explain several methods for computing matching parts within two different ontologies, e.g. based on similarity or distance measures or string matching techniques. Usually at least an intellectual review is needed to confirm computed mappings. Furthermore, the quality of each mapping between two elements may be described intellectually in the form of inter-KOS semantic relations. Typically, mappings between two KOS concepts represent relations of equivalence. But not in all cases can 'ideal' mappings be found, i.e. two elements within distinct KOS with an exact overlap in meaning (Stock & Stock, 2008). Sometimes, one concept from a KOS may have to be mapped to several concepts within the second KOS or to one which is not

---

[337] For a more detailed insight into the slight distinctions in meaning of terms like ontology mapping, matching, merging, integration etc. see Euzenat & Shvaiko (2007); a terminology overview is also provided by Klein (2001).
[338] Project ISO 25964: http://www.niso.org/workrooms/iso25964.
[339] CARMEN: http://www.bibliothek.uni-regensburg.de/projects/carmen12/.
[340] Further projects are also discussed by Tudhope, Koch & Heery (2006).

exactly overlapping in meaning[341]. References between two KOS can also appear in the form of hierarchical (inter-KOS) relationships. Furthermore, mappings may not only be established as references between concepts, but also for other KOS elements, e.g. relations or instances (e.g. to declare that the relation `is_made_by` in one ontology is the same as the relation `is_produced_by` in another ontology). Klein (2001) as well as de Bruijn, Ehrig et al. (2006) discuss several problems of common mismatches in ontology mapping scenarios; Doerr (2001) considers mapping difficulties for thesauri.

In cases where more than two ontologies must be mapped, two basic approaches are typically distinguished:

> "In the first case, there is a one-to-one relationship between the ontologies, i.e. each pair of ontologies to be integrated has a mapping between them, whereas in the second case, integration is achieved through a global ontology, which is mapped to all the local ontologies." (Ehrig, de Bruijn et al., 2004)

The same two basic approaches can be found for establishing concordances between classical KOS (Nöther, 1998; Stock & Stock, 2008): each KOS within a considered collection may be mapped to every other one in this collection, or each individual KOS may be mapped to one single reference KOS, the *master*. In cases where many KOS should be mapped, using a central reference model or master seems most intuitive at first sight. But realizing this approach is not trivial:

> "Drawbacks of using a global ontology are similar to those of using any standard. For example, it is hard to reach a consensus on a standard shared by many people (it is always a lengthy process), who use different terminologies for the same domain and a standard impedes changes in an organization (because evolution of standards suffers from the same problems as the development of standards)." (Ehrig, de Bruijn et al., 2004)

A global master KOS will usually have to be built from scratch for this particular purpose, though in some cases it might be possible to reuse an existing one.

Mapping is one of the most common kinds of interaction between different KOS, and some illustrative examples for successful mappings between two KOS can be found in practical applications. Let us have a look at two examples for concordances between classifications. Figure 3.66 shows one example; the United States Patent and Trademark Office provides a table that indicates the mappings between the USPC and the IPC. Figure 3.67 shows an example for concordances between NAICS and SIC[342], as provided by Dun & Bradstreet (D&B).

---

[341] To some degree, mapping challenges can be compared to the main problems in establishing different language versions for one KOS.

[342] Particularly, the Dun & Bradstreet version of SIC, D&B SIC-8.

US to IPC8 Concordance for Class 473 GAMES USING TANGIBLE PROJECTILE					
Printable Version(PDF) See notes regarding proper use of US-to-IPC Concordances.					
U.S. Subclass	IPC8 Subclass			IPC8 Group	
1 - 47	A	63	D	15	/ 00
1 - 47	A	63	F	9	/ 24
1 - 47	G	06	F	17	/ 00
1 - 47	G	06	F	19	/ 00
5	A	63	D	13	/ 00
10 - 14	A	47	C	17	/ 62
10 - 14	A	63	D	15	/ 04
15 - 16	A	63	D	13	/ 00
15 - 16	A	63	D	15	/ 02
17	A	63	D	15	/ 20
18 - 19	A	63	D	15	/ 02
19	A	63	D	13	/ 00
21	A	63	D	13	/ 00
22 - 27	A	63	D	15	/ 20
28	A	63	D	13	/ 00

Figure 3.66. Excerpt from a mapping table for concordances between USPC and IPC for the USPC class 473/2. Source: http://www.uspto.gov/web/patents/classifi cation/uspc473/us473toipc8.htm.

SIC Division Title	NAICS Sector Title
-Agriculture, Forestry and Fishing	Agriculture, Forestry, Fishing and Hunting
-Mining	-Mining
-Construction	-Construction
-Manufacturing	-Manufacturing
-Transportation, Communications, and Public Utilities	-Utilities -Transportation and Warehousing
-Wholesale Trade	-Wholesale Trade
-Retail Trade	-Retail Trade
-Finance, Insurance, and Real Estate	-Finance and Insurance -Real Estate and Rental and Leasing
-Services	-Informations -Professional, Scientific, and Technical Services -Education Services -Health Care and Social Assistance -Arts, Entertainment, and Recreation -Other Services
-Public Administration	-Public Administration
-None (Previously categories within each division)	-Management of Companies and Enterprises

Figure 3.67. Concordances between SIC and NAICS. Source: https://www.dnb.com/ market/hmarket6.htm.

Once such concordances are established they can be used for information retrieval, e.g. across different databases that make use of the different mapped classification systems. The user may formulate a query with one KOS and the system may translate this query (via the concordance relations) into another KOS' vocabulary (Stock & Stock, 2008).

Merging and Integration
While mapping techniques establish points of reference between two distinct KOS, merging goes one step further and describes the creation of one new KOS from two (or more) source models:

> "Ontology merging is the creation of a new ontology from two, possibly overlapping, source ontologies. The initial ontologies remain unaltered. The merged ontology is supposed to contain the knowledge of the initial ontologies, e.g., consequences of each ontology are consequences of the merge." (Euzenat & Shvaiko, 2007)

Or in other words:

> "When performing ontology merging, a new ontology is created which is the union of the source ontologies. The merged ontology captures all the knowledge from the original ontologies. The challenge in ontology merging is to ensure that all correspondences and differences between the ontologies are reflected in the merged ontology." (de Bruijn, Ehrig et al., 2006)

De Bruijn, Ehrig et al. (2006) distinguish merging and mapping processes (and aligning) as follows:

> "Summarizing, ontology mapping is mostly concerned with the representation of correspondences between ontologies; ontology alignment is concerned with the discovery of these correspondences; and ontology merging is concerned with creating the union of ontologies, based on correspondences between the ontologies." (de Bruijn, Ehrig et al., 2006)

Thus ontology mapping is often included in ontology merging as a preparatory phase. Merging is further closely related to the process of integration and to reuse. Euzenat and Shvaiko (2007) explain the difference between merging and integration as follows: in merging, both initial ontologies remain unaltered; in integration, one ontology remains the same while the other is modified during the integration process. We may add that during reuse processes, only parts of ontologies might be integrated and that both ontologies might actually be altered during these processes.

In research on ontology engineering, merging techniques play an important role. Several algorithms for (semi-) automatic approaches are being developed (Fernández-López, Gómez-Pérez et al., 2002) and a variety of tools are designed to support the mapping and merging process in ontology engineering (Kalfoglou & Schorlemmer, 2003; Noy, 2004). Examples are PROMPT (Noy & Musen, 2003), GLUE (Doan, Madhavan et al., 2002), OBSERVER (Mena, Illarramendi et al., 2000) and FCA-Merge (Stumme & Maedche, 2001).
In the domain of classical knowledge organization system, merging techniques gain much less attention.

Scenarios for Handling Multiple KOS

Reuse, mapping and merging (and their mentioned variations) are the most fundamental types of ontology interaction. We will now go one step further and sketch a few scenarios to illustrate how KOS interactions might be realized in practice. The inter-ontological level does not only apply to the actual process of building ontologies but also to their application in different usage scenarios, where they may complement one another.

This is not an exhaustive list; various settings that combine mapping, merging and reuse methodologies in different ways are currently being developed (see for example de Bruijn, Ehrig et al. (2006) for a combined approach). We would rather like to point out some examples that may disclose the variety of options – which deserve more attention in future research.

References to Upper Ontologies

Referring to an upper ontology may be considered a complementary approach to ontology mapping. As we have explained above (Section 2.3), upper ontologies capture knowledge on a very high level of abstraction. They often intend to provide a point of reference for domain ontologies, or to act as an abstract guidance in developing new domain ontologies. Referring to a shared upper ontology is to some degree comparable to referring to a shared master in mapping scenarios: different single ontologies should be geared to the one upper ontology. But as concepts in an upper ontology are highly abstract, domain ontologies cannot (and are not supposed to be) completely mapped to upper ontologies. The domain ontologies should rather adapt the general structure of the upper ontology as a foundation and modeling guideline. This should help render domain ontologies more comparable, so that they may also be more easily mapped among each other. Mascardi, Cordi & Rosso (2007) think that "upper Ontologies are quickly becoming a key technology for integrating heterogeneous knowledge coming from different sources. In fact, they may be exploited as a lingua franca by intelligent software agents [...]."

Several difficulties remain unsolved in this approach of using upper ontologies as guidelines and references. First of all, there is not one single community-based and shared upper ontology. We have seen that different upper ontologies exist that highly differ in structure and in their underlying philosophical assumptions. The ideal reference ontology for this purpose of interlinking different domain ontologies over the Web would be one shared general upper ontology. Some approaches have already tried to merge the different ontologies into one final upper ontology or to establish mappings between upper ontologies (Mascardi, Cordi & Rosso, 2007); e.g. during the Upper Ontology Summit[343] and within the projects COSMO[344], the Multi Source Ontology (MSO)[345] and OntoMap[346].

Furthermore, current upper ontologies are often hard to understand for common Web users, due to their strong reference to philosophical traditions. This makes them rather inapplicable for Social Semantic Web scenarios, where broad Web communities would have to be able to use them as a foundational model.

Some works on applying upper ontologies to achieve KOS-interoperability are available (e.g., Sanchez-Alonso & Garcia-Barriocanal, 2006), but more practical experiences are needed:

> "While many researchers hope that domain and application-specific ontologies will reuse the foundational ontologies, like SUMO and DOLCE, and that such reuse will indeed facilitate semantic interoperation between applications based on these ontologies, we do not yet have enough experience reports with such approaches to claim it a success. There are reports on both the successes and difficulties of such reuse." (Noy, 2009)

Distributed and Modularized Development of KOS
As we have explained above, a KOS may consist of different modules, facets or layers. This extends the dimensions of a multi-KOS world. Of course, mapping, merging and reuse may also happen on the level of ontology modules.

For example, different KOS may be collected and established as modules of a new, broader KOS. Furthermore, an existing KOS may be decomposed into modules (Cuenca Grau, Parsia et al., 2006). In ontology engineering, this form of modularization should help to prevent performance difficulties in reasoning, which often appear in huge ontologies, and to enable change management for single parts of a domain. In ontology engineering, discussions have begun concerning the usefulness of explicitly developing single ontology modules as building blocks for versatile and multiplicatory usage and reuse scenarios. And research on modular ontologies will surely play an important role in future Social Semantic Web research (Cuenca Grau, Honavar et al., 2007); experiences from software engineering may be reused and applied in the context of ontology engineering (d'Aquin, Schlicht et al., 2007).

A closely related idea is the modularized development of ontologies, also called *distributed* ontology engineering (Sunagawa, Kozaki et al., 2003). It can be considered another possible solution to supporting communities in building large-scale ontologies: different ontology engineers (or groups of ontology engineers) work on different ontology modules, which should finally be combined to one consistent ontology. Rector, Horridge et al. (2008) discuss modularization as follows: "[...] we can now implement each major tree [...] in a separate module and then provide one or more 'joining ontologies' that contain the axioms and definitions to join them together." They further suggest several usage scenarios for

---

343   Upper Ontology Summit (2006): http://ontolog.cim3.net/cgi-
      bin/wiki.pl?UpperOntologySummit.
344   COSMO: http://www.micra.com.
345   Multi Source Ontology (MSO): http://www.webkb.org/doc/MSO.html.
346   OntoMap: http://www.ontotext.com/projects/OntoMap.html.

modularized ontologies. Others also propose to develop single ontology modules and keep them separate, yet interconnected (e.g. Stuckenschmidt & Klein, 2003; Ensan & Du, 2008).

So far, there is not much technical support for modularized approaches and tools for developing and handling modular ontologies are rather rare – Farquhar, Fikes and Rice (1997b) having presented an early approach within the Ontolingua Server.

> "Collaborative ontology building demands modularized ontology representation by its very nature. Current ontology languages like OWL, while offering some degree of modularization using XML namespaces, fail to fully support modularized semantics." (Bao & Honavar, 2004)

Rector, Horridge et al. (2008) also discuss issues of using OWL for modularized ontologies. Ensan & Du (2008) propose Swoop as a tool for developing ontologies in modules.

Other current activities that are related to the topic of modularized ontologies are discussions on *ontology design patterns* (Gangemi, 2005; Presutti & Gangemi, 2008). This approach intends to develop building blocks (called Content Design Patterns), which may be used for ontology development and reuse, and is carried out within the NeOn project, which tests ways of handling networked ontologies. The project team also works on a "Library of Design Patterns for Collaborative Development of Networked Ontologies" – which may become an important step towards a repository for distributed, collective ontology engineering. Similar approaches are discussed as "knowledge patterns" (e.g. Clark, Thompson & Porter, 2000).

Multi-Representation and Faceted Approaches
Another scenario for the co-application of several KOS can be described as multi-representation. The basic idea is to use different KOS in parallel, to enable *multiple views* on a document collection. This may for example be useful in such cases where there is no shared conceptualization of a domain for all members of the respective community of interest – and thus not one shared vocabulary that may be used for indexing and retrieval. In those cases we may use two (or more) vocabularies to index the same document collection.

Sintek, van Elst et al. (2007) highlight the importance of multiple views and multiple vocabularies within the Semantic Web that will mainly be a Web of several semantic applications:

> "The vision of the Semantic Web mainly aims at scenarios with multiple, distributed and autonomous information providers and consumers. However, the current standards for knowledge representation mainly see the Semantic Web as one big knowledge base without explicitly acknowledging the distributed, social nature of knowledge in the technological basics." (Sintek, van Elst et al., 2007)

Their research group is currently developing a new representation language called NRL (NEPOMUK Representational Language) to enable the managing of multiple views and multiple semantics (Sintek, van Elst et al., 2007). A core necessity will also be allowing single applications to use specific KOS and letting them interact on a superordinate level. This is a key challenge for knowledge representation in the Social Semantic Web, and will surely attract much future interest.

Another option of letting different KOS (or KOS modules) act in accord might be a kind of 'faceted approach' to multiple KOS (e.g. mentioned by Schwartz, 2005). In case we do not have different overlapping but different complementary KOS, these may act together as different facets within one application scenario. For example, a geographical thesaurus and a product classification can act as two facets within a database on industry.

In such settings, each KOS might act as a facet of a "virtual" faceted meta-KOS. A citation order will be needed for indexing documents.

Preconditions for Crosswalks and Co-Existence of KOS
Such ideas of multi-representation lead us back to the need for an improved structured overview on existing KOS. We consider this to be one fundamental precondition of supporting crosswalks and the effective co-existence of multiple KOS, because – as Ding, Finin et al. (2004) put it – "[f]ailure to easily find an appropriate ontology for a particular markup task typically leads to the creation of a new ontology [...]." Some approaches to this problem have recently emerged. In the next section, we will introduce our approach to creating a meta-ontology that may act as a means to a structured overview on existing KOS.

Some more aspects crucially affect the success of multiple-KOS scenarios. Waterfeld, Weiten et al. (2008) name the problem of preparing ontology languages to support explicit interconnections between different KOS:

> "To address distributed and networked ontology management, current ontology languages lack a number of features to explicitly express the relationships between ontologies and their elements. These features include in particular formalisms for expressing modular ontologies and mappings. Modular ontologies adopt the established notion of modules in order to separate ontologies into several parts, which can be developed and managed independently." (Waterfeld, Weiten et al., 2008)

Furthermore, there is a growing need for standards or guidelines both for KOS engineering and for usage rights and copyrights.

3.4.2 KOSO: A Meta-KOS for Knowledge Organization Systems

As a contribution to reducing the lack of a structured overview on available KOS, we have started to develop KOSO, the Knowledge Organization Systems Ontology (Weller, 2008 a and b). This ontology has two aims: a) to provide formal definitions for the different types of KOS, and b) to provide a detailed description of individual KOS, which can help bringing about a structured access to the knowledge models which are already available. For this project, a fundamental precondition is a structured organization and classification of KOS types with regard to their characteristics and qualities. We have collected much definitional work on this aspect in Chapter 2, which can provide a useful foundation. Apart from this, we need information about the position of a single KOS in relation to others. For this, we may use the information on KOS interactions as discussed above.

The driving objective for this project is to support a better knowledge sharing and reuse for ontology engineering. Apart from this, two more aspects are of major importance: to enable semantic upgrades and to provide comprehensive information on the semantic interoperability of different knowledge models.

Metadata about KOS

Some related approaches that try to establish some form of metadata for ontologies are already available. Earlier approaches to providing metadata for ontologies can be found in the KWeb project (Suarez-Figueroa, García-Castro et al., 2005) and in a project on "ontology yellow pages" (Arpirez, Gómez-Pérez et al., 2000).

Another prominent approach is the OMV (Ontology Metadata Vocabulary) project (Hartmann, Suarez-Figueroa et al., 2005), which has demonstrated that shared metadata are needed to enable the retrieval and reuse of ontologies and also develops a respective design environment called DEMO (Hartmann, Simperl et al., 2006) as well as further infrastructure (Hartmann, 2006; Hartmann, Palma et al., 2005). This work has now proceeded to the development of the Generic Ontology Repository Framework (GORF), a system that comprises mechanisms for ontology storage and *ontology retrieval* (Hartmann, Palma & Gómez-Pérez, 2009). The approach is also coupled to new ideas for handling modular ontologies and reusing them across applications:

> "[…] having modular ontologies is not enough to facilitate the reusability of ontologies if developers are not able to find them efficiently. We need an appropriate infrastructure that enables an intelligent ontology discovery and selection by end users." (Hartman, Palma & Gómez-Pérez, 2009)

Similar efforts can be found in the Open Ontology Repository Initiative (OOR)[347]. This project aims to provide easy access to quality ontologies.

Uncoupled from these metadata initiatives, there are some collections of ontologies on the Web, e.g. the DAML Ontology Library[348], the Open Biomedical Ontologies (OBO)[349], the NCBO BioPortal[350] or the SchemaWeb Directory[351]. Yet these collections are typically bound to a specific domain, a specific ontology editor or ontology language. The W3C further used to host a project called Ontaria[352],

---

[347] Open Ontology Repository Initiative (OOR): http://ontolog.cim3.net/cgi-bin/wiki.pl?OpenOntologyRepository.
[348] DAML Ontology repository, http://www.daml.org/ontologies.
[349] OBO Open Biomedical Ontologies: http://www.obofoundry.org.
[350] NCBO BioPortal: http://bioportal.bioontology.org.
[351] SchemaWeb Directory: http://www.schemaweb.info.
[352] Ontaria: http://www.w3.org/2004/ontaria/.

which was meant to become a searchable and browsable directory of semantic web data.

While the former initiatives mainly focus on ontologies and Semantic Web contexts, comparable ideas also exist for broader considerations on KOS types, e.g. presented by Tudhope (2006). The NSDL Registry[353] aims to cover metadata schemas and controlled vocabularies. Furthermore, it wants to support mappings and crosswalks among them (Hillmann, Sutton et al., 2006). Another initiative (which dates back to the 1970s) was the 'Bundes-Dachthesaurus', a project on behalf of the German minister of the interior (Belling, Brodmeier et al., 1974; Duske, Kretschmann et al., 1974). Its aim was to develop a thesaurus to mediate between the vocabularies applied in different database systems. In this setting, compatibility was also to be achieved by means of shared structures adhered to by the different KOS in use.

Basic Structure of KOSO

KOSO is work in progress, but will become an ontology with the power to help describe the characteristics of several knowledge resources. It is thus not primarily focused on ontologies, but can cover several types of KOS and some additional resources.

Typical characteristics of KOS that are already included in KOSO are: size (in terms of the number of concepts, properties, and instances), the language in use (regarding natural languages as well as formal languages), the depicted domain of interest and practical applications or implementations of a certain KOS (as many are bound to a certain platform or database).

We have further paid some attention to the quality of semantic relations as one distinctive feature of specifying types of KOS and defining them formally.

The classification and structured representation of knowledge organization systems was planned to be the core of KOSO, all major elements of the ontology having been derived by specifying the central concept KnowledgeOrganization-System. The ontology hat so far been built up manually with Protégé in OWL (DL). Some general guidelines have been set up, which should facilitate a consistent ontology engineering and design. These are mainly the following:

- Basic naming conventions have been established.
- Synonyms are included via the rdfs:label annotation. They can be strict synonyms, abbreviations, spelling variants, translations or quasi synonyms.
- Whenever possible, a definition has been provided, which explains the notion of the respective concept, property or instance.
- The TODO comment function has been used to mark preliminary constructions in need of revision.

The first release version of KOSO comprised 79 concepts, 37 properties, restrictions that defined some of the classes and about 35 exemplary instances. But KOSO is a work in progress and thus in the process being extended and modified. The next version will only be released after some further discussions on KOS dis-

---

[353] NSDL Registry: http://metadataregistry.org/.

tinctions and types and after some form of community agreement has been reached.

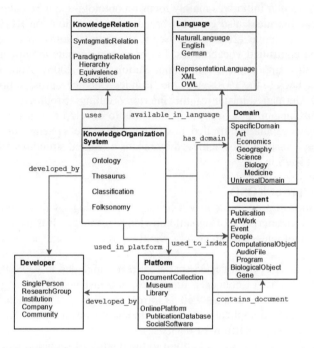

Figure 3.68. Initial version of the main concepts of KOSO with exemplary subclasses and basic interrelations. Source: Weller, 2008b.

We will now describe the initial structure of KOSO in short and hint at future plans for extension. The ontology initially started with the following seven basic modules (also see Figure 3.68):

- *Knowledge Organization System.* In the initial version, KnowledgeOrganizationSystem was intended to become the most fundamental concept. It included some first basic subclasses of KOS, namely Classification, Folksonomy, Nomenclature, Thesaurus and Ontology. For some of them, individual, more detailed subclasses have been included, e.g. BroadFolksonomy and NarrowFolksonomy as subclasses of Folksonomy, or DecimalClassification and FacetedClassification as subclasses of Classification. By now it has turned out that this first attempt was too coarse; a more fine-grained view on subtypes of KOS is needed, according to the specifications presented in Section 2.3.2. Furthermore, for a more comprehensive inclusion of other possible knowledge resources which may be valuable for constructing and refining ontologies, we plan to broaden this class. For this purpose, KnowledgeOrganizationSystem will become a subclass of a new main module `KnowledgeResource`, which can then also comprise linguistic, encyclopedic and other resources as discussed above.

- *Domain.* The domain of a knowledge resource and its intended purpose are fundamental characteristics. But a classification of possible domains leaves itself lots of room for discussion. We will prefer practicability over accuracy. No exact model of all possible real-world domains should be created, but rather a rough set of possible domains. Still, the classes should be specific enough to distinguish different application purposes. Alternatively, one may think of user-generated categories or spontaneous tagging as an additional approach (Noy, Guha & Musen, 2005).

- *Knowledge Relation.* Semantic relations are of great importance for identifying the degree of complexity of a KOS. They have thus been included as a fundamental class – and are, for example, used to formally describe KOS types (see below). In future they may also be used to refer to the expressiveness of different representation languages. The next step will be to collect a broad set of standard names for certain relation types (as specified in Chapter 2). It might be appropriate to integrate (or map to) the OBO Relation Ontology[354] (Smith, Ceusters et al., 2005).

  Again, this class should be integrated into a broader context. We intend to create an upper class called `KOSElement` to include the other components of KOS as well, and thus make possible more fine-grained formal descriptions of KOS types.

- *Language.* For the purpose of enabling efficient reuse, information about the given language of a knowledge organization system is crucial. We consider both natural languages (e.g. English, Spanish) and specific representation languages (e.g. OWL, XML, RDF). For cases in which a KOS is not bound to a certain natural language (as is the case for most folksonomies), we have added the instance `AllLanguages`. A list of available languages could be reused from existing KOS, e.g. the respective part from the Thesaurofacet (Aitchison, Gomersall & Ireland, 1969), as well as from other structured sources like Wikipedia's lists of languages[355].

- *Developer.* We state that every KOS is created by some (at least one) developer. Thus the class `Developer` comprises the subclasses `SinglePerson`, `Institution`, `Company`, `ResearchGroup` and `Community`. In future work, this class should be mapped to the class `Party` in the Ontology Metadata Vocabulary OMV. In our case, persons and groups of persons are only considered given the condition that they have been actively involved in the development of a KOS or a platform (as KOSO will be broadened, one may also relate developers to other software tools and resources). One peculiarity is the concept `Community`. It has been added to represent the fact that a folksonomy is usually bound to a user community in the context of some Web platform.

---

[354] OBO Relation Ontology: http://www.obofoundry.org/ro/.
[355] Wikipedia List of Languages, http://en.wikipedia.org/wiki/List_of_languages.

- *Document.* We distinguish between the domain of interest a KOS focuses on (e.g. biology) and the units or objects which should be organized with the help of the KOS (e.g. publications or genomic data). This refers to the concept of a *document* or *documentary unit* in library and information science (e.g. defined by Wellisch, 2000).
- *Platform.* A platform is the place where documents are stored and collected. It can be an online platform (e.g. a publications database or a social bookmarking system) as well as a real-world document collection (e.g. a library or museum). Many traditional KOS are bound to specific platforms – which also affects their actual form and structure. When other knowledge sources are included in KOSO, the concept `Platform` may have to be revisited.

Explicit Definition of KOS-Types

KOSO should not only include a hierarchical representation of KOS and other knowledge resources, it should also provide – as far as possible – formal definitions for them. This means that the different types of knowledge organization systems should be explicitly defined, if possible with necessary and sufficient conditions as offered by OWL. So far, only first attempts have been made to illustrate this idea. The actual choices will have to be discussed and refined in collaboration with the respective research community. Our starting points for definitions were the semantic relations used in different KOS:

- *Ontology*: an ontology is currently defined as a KOS using hierarchical relations to structure a domain of interest as well as specified associative relations. It has to be provided in a formal representation language (to make use of automatic reasoning). One may discuss whether the differentiation of instances and classes can and should be included in the definition.
- *Thesaurus*: is preliminary defined as a KOS which distinguishes the relation types hierarchy, association and equivalence.
- *Classification*: is so far insufficiently described as containing (unspecified) hierarchies and equivalences.
- *Folksonomy*: is defined as being developed by a community and containing no paradigmatic relations. It cannot exist without an application platform.

Example of a KOS in KOSO

With the given modules, we may now describe an existing KOS, as in this example the International Patent Classification (IPC): The IPC is a classification (which is a specific type of `KnowledgeRepresentationSystem`). Typically for classifications, it uses hierarchical relations as the main structuring elements for its vocabulary. It is not bound to a specific representation language and is available in English and French. Its `Domain` is intellectual property, it is actually used to index patents (the `Document` type). It is developed by the World Intellectual Property Organization (WIPO) and is applied mainly in the database systems of several patent offices. With this collection of information, we could make the IPC retrievable for people looking for existing resources to build an ontology on intellectual property. Still, it does not provide all information on the IPC which is presently available yet.

Properties in KOSO
A considerable number of specified interrelations between different classes have been established in the form of object properties. Furthermore, single datatype properties have been created for a more specific description of certain features of KOS. For example, the size of a KOS is captured by the datatype properties `has_number_of_classes` and `has_number_of_relations`, which both allow the adding of a value range. KOSO currently starts with seven top-level concepts. The nature of the relation between a top-level class and its subclasses may be of a different quality than that between subclasses on lower hierarchical levels – as the top-level concepts obtain a basic structuring character, rather than class-refining purpose. Besides the `is_a` hierarchies provided by OWL's natural hierarchical structure, some partitive relations have been added to represent components of concepts or other meronymic relations, e.g. a `Document` `is_part_of_platform`, a `SinglePerson` can be `part_of_institution` etc. The interdependencies of the main modules are captured with properties such as `has_domain` and `is_domain_of` (between `KnowledgeOrganizationSystem` and `Domain`), `has_developed` and `developed_by` (between `Developer` and either `KnowledgeOrganizationSystem` or `Platform`), or `is_indexed_with` and `is_used_to_index` (between `Document` and `KnowledgeOrganizationSystem`). Additional relations specify characteristics of KOS; this may be information on availability (including license types), size, address for download etc. In future, more relations are to be added that specify characteristics of other concepts (e.g. representation languages) in more detail.

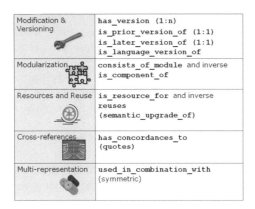

Modification & Versioning	`has_version (1:n)`
	`is_prior_version_of (1:1)`
	`is_later_version_of (1:1)`
	`is_language_version_of`

Modularization	`consists_of_module` and inverse `is_component_of`

Resources and Reuse	`is_resource_for` and inverse
	`reuses`
	`(semantic_upgrade_of)`

Cross-references	`has_concordances_to` `(quotes)`
Multi-representation	`used_in_combination_with` `(symmetric)`

Figure 3.69. Types of KOS interactions currently represented in KOSO.

Besides the objective of collecting as many useful resources for ontology engineering as possible, the second aim is to analyze the potential interoperability and already established interrelations between different systems. Thus the next step is to create and provide a classification of types of interaction between different KOS – and to collect data on actual applications as well. The broad research field of different ways of mapping, merging, modularizing, and integrating different KOS will have to be closely evaluated and structured. So far, the following aspects are included (Figure 3.69 shows how they are expressed as properties in KOSO):

- *Modifications & Versioning.* Different release versions, modified versions and language versions of the same KOS are interlinked via `is_modified_version_of` (with sub-properties `is_prior_version_of` and `is_later_version_of`). A useful approach for handling different versions of the same ontology is the distinction of OntologyBase and Ontology-Document as proposed by Hartmann, Suarez-Figueroa et al. (2005). Within KOSO, there is not yet a distinction between OntologyBase and Ontology-Document – but it should be implemented in the future. Currently, an instance should be created for every release version stating the version number and its relation to prior and later versions. For our IPC example (see above) we would need instances for several release versions and several language versions.

- *Modularization.* The properties `consists_of_modules` and its inverse `is_component_of` capture the relation between one KOS and its modules. For example, the Gene Ontology consists of three modules Biological Process, Cellular Component and Molecular Function. Future discussion is needed concerning types of modules, e.g. how facets and top level concepts can be distinguished.

- *Reuse.* Reuse is when a given KOS is used to develop a new one. Currently included in KOSO are the properties `is_resource_for` and `reuses;` they are used to represent the fact that a given resource has actually been used to build up a specific KOS.

  It may be discussed whether one should specify this to 'completely' and 'partly'. For example, SmartSUMO ontology reuses DOLCE and SUMO. Merging will have to be considered in a future version and may count as a specific type of reuse.

- *Cross-References.* KOSO can capture information about whether two (or more) KOS have established cross-references or mappings between them. This will not act on a concept level, i.e. KOSO does not cover information about what concept in one KOS is related to which other concept in another KOS.

  The property `has_established_concordances_to` simply captures information about which KOS have some kind of fixed mapping between them. For example, the Standard Thesaurus Wirtschaft has concordances to NACE. This relation is not necessarily symmetrical.

- *Multi-representation*: Multirepresentation (also called poly-representation; Larsen, Ingwersen & Kekäläinen, 2006) is defined as the case that different independent KOS are used within the same application. They may represent different points of view; an example would be if documents in one platform were professionally indexed with a thesaurus and additionally tagged with a community's folksonomy. The respective KOSO property is called `used_in_combination_with`.

Future Work

KOSO offers a first approach for a new structured access to existing knowledge organization systems, like controlled vocabularies, thesauri, classifications, folksonomies and ontologies – and their interrelations. As it is currently still a very preliminary approach, the structure will change after more instances have been added (new properties and concepts will have to be included to capture the features of individual KOS). Most of the existing top-level concepts should be stable; their subclasses have to be refined. Generally, (as discussed for languages) it should be checked more closely whether certain structures are already available and can be reused. New top-level concepts should be amended, e.g. tools, methodologies and application areas. By now, we have regarded document indexing as the core application of ontologies and other KOS. This may be too vague, particularly for high-definition ontologies. What will be needed is a specification of different tasks for ontologies, their respective actual application fields and surroundings. What is also still missing is the inclusion of methodologies used to build an ontology as well as specific tools (editors, reasoners etc.). Both can be envisioned as new modules for KOSO, which can then be interrelated with the existing modules. In addition to standardized representation languages, other standard formats that are available for KOS should be included, so that for example, thesauri which fulfill the ISO norm (ISO 2788:1986) can be labeled appropriately. Furthermore, the specificities of norms, standards and representation languages have to be represented as properties in the ontology.

The KOSO ontology has so far been developed in OWL-DL with Protégé. One future aim is to analyze whether this formalization mode is appropriate or whether one should rather implement it in another way (e.g. another formal language like RDF). In the long term, an application will be needed which can use the ontology as its knowledge base and which will then serve as a platform for retrieving KOS that fit individual needs. KOSO will also have to become more closely interrelated with established approaches to creating ontology metadata. It is planned to include mappings, particularly to the OMV Ontology Metadata Vocabulary.

In future, the KOSO ontology will of course have to be evaluated as well as revised and remodeled by a broader scientific community to guarantee that it indeed represents common needs and a shared understanding.

3.4.3 Mapping the Social Semantic Web

In this final section, we want to briefly recall some social semantic applications that have already succeeded in establishing forms of mappings between them or which may facilitate a better interoperability – with a particular focus on KOS interaction between different services.

Initiatives to Enabling KOS Interactions and Establishing Mappings

At first, we want to highlight two initiatives which are both very important for interoperability on the Social Semantic Web: the Simple Knowledge Organization System (SKOS) and the Linked Data initiative (together with the Linking Open Data project, LOD).

The SKOS developers aim at providing a framework for handling classical forms of knowledge organization system on the Semantic Web (Miles & Brickley, 2005; Miles, Matthews et al., 2005). SKOS is a family of formal representation languages that can capture thesauri, classifications and other controlled vocabularies. It is based on RDF. Thus a KOS that is represented in the SKOS format can be processed and handled by systems in a standardized way. SKOS specifications are still under development and are published and discussed as a W3C Working Draft.

Among the thesauri that have been translated to SKOS are the AGROVOC thesaurus, MeSH, GEMET[356], a multilingual thesaurus published by the European Environment Information and Observation Network (EIONET) and The Thesaurus for the Social Sciences (TheSoz)[357] (Zapilko & Sure, 2009). Isaac, Phipps and Rubin (2009) describe several use cases for SKOS vocabularies. General considerations on modeling classifications in SKOS have been collected by Panzer & Zheng (2009).

Interlinking data over the Web is the core objective of the Linked Data[358] initiatives (Bizer, Heath et al., 2007; Bizer, Heath & Berners-Lee, 2009; Heath, Hepp & Bizer, 2009):

> "Therefore, the top priority on the agenda must be techniques and patterns of social interaction that foster the publication of data on the Web and the emergence of dense linkage between data items, as well as between schemata." (Heath, Hepp & Bizer, 2009)

The links between different data on the Web should be typed, i.e. they should define the nature of the relation between the data. The Linked Data community has set up best practices for publishing and connecting structured data on the Web, which have been increasingly adopted during the last three years, "leading to the creation of a global data space containing billions of assertions – the Web of Data"

---

[356]   GEMET (GEneral Multilingual Environmental Thesaurus):
http://www.eionet.europa.eu/gemet.
[357]   Thesaurus for the Social Sciences: http://www.gesis.org/en/services/tools-standards/socialscience-thesaurus/.
[358]   Linked Data: http://linkeddata.org/.

(Bizer, Heath & Berners-Lee, 2009). Links should take the form of RDF triples, "where the subject of the triple is a URI reference in the namespace of one data set, while the object of the triple is a URI reference in the other" (Bizer, Heath & Berners-Lee, 2009). Both are interlinked with a "predicate", which corresponds to semantic relations as discussed in Chapter 2. Bizer, Heath & Berners-Lee (2009) give two examples; one of them is depicted in Figure 3.70: The data set for the movie "Pulp Fiction" within the Linked Movie Data Base[359] is connected to the data set for the same movie within DBpedia, via an owl:sameAs relation. This relation is included in the form of a reference to the OWL 2 Namespace Document[360], where owl:sameAs is defined as "The property that determines that two given individuals are equal".

```
Subject: http://data.linkedmdb.org/resource/film/77
Predicate: http://www.w3.org/2002/07/owl#sameAs
Object: http://dbpedia.org/resource/Pulp_Fiction_%28film%29
```

Figure 3.70. Example for a triple set of linked data. Source: Bizer, Heath & Berners-Lee, 2009.

The Linked Data community currently claims that any given formal vocabulary may be referred to in order to specify the type of a link:

> "Anyone is free to publish vocabularies to the Web of Data […], which in turn can be connected by RDF triples that link classes and properties in one vocabulary to those in another, thereby defining mappings between related vocabularies. […] Despite this general openness, it is considered good practice to reuse terms from well-known RDF vocabularies such as FOAF, SIOC, SKOS, DOAP, vCard, Dublin Core, OAI-ORE or GoodRelations wherever possible in order to make it easier for client applications to process Linked Data. Only if these vocabularies do not provide the required terms should data publishers define new, data source-specific terminology […]." (Bizer, Heath & Berners-Lee, 2009)

Supporting tools are also being developed, for example tools for publishing Linked Data and specific browsers and search engines.

The best-known applications of Linked Data principles originated in the Linking Open Data[361] project. The aim of each respective community is to convert as

---

[359] Linked Movie Data Base: http://www.linkedmdb.org/.
[360] OWL 2 Namespace Document: http://www.w3.org/2002/07/owl#, see also: http://www.w3.org/2007/OWL/wiki/Owl2DotOwlDevel.
[361] Linking Open Data: http://esw.w3.org/topic/SweoIG/TaskForces/CommunityProjects/LinkingOpen Data; the project is supported by the W3C Semantic Web Education and Outreach Group: http://www.w3.org/2001/sw/sweo/.

many freely available data sets to RDF as possible (i.e. to triplify them), and publish these converted data on the Web for reuse and interlinking. Figure 3.71 demonstrates the broad range of vocabularies and other knowledge resources which have been published within this context, including many scientific projects, but also contributions by major companies (like the BBC).

Furthermore, the LOD Triplification Challenge[362] is a yearly event that awards prizes to the best projects that make use of Linked Data or publish new sets of triplified data.

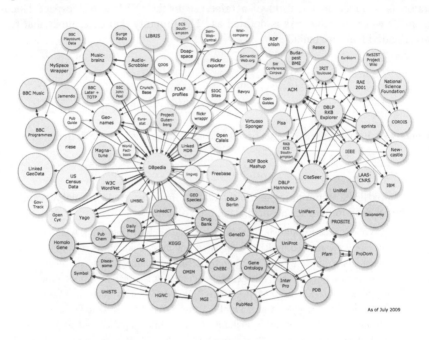

Figure 3.71. Linking Open Data Cloud. Source: http://www4.wiwiss.fu-berlin.de/bizer/
pub/lod-datasets_2009-07-14_colored.png.

Apart from these broad initiatives, a growing number of other examples can be found which, in some way or another, have interlinked vocabularies or information on the Web. This book will not try to cover all of them, but we may have a look at a few more.

Another interesting initiative is described by Kim, Breslin et al. (2009): the Social Semantic Cloud of Tags (SCOT)[363]. The aim of this project is to formally describe the structure and contents of a tagging vocabulary (e.g., users, groups of users, documents, tags, frequencies, co-occurrences) in order to facilitate reusability

---

[362] Triplification Challenge: http://triplify.org/Challenge.
[363] SCOT Project: http://scot-project.org/.

across platforms. The idea is closely related to the "ontology of folksonomy" by Gruber (2005). Kim, Breslin et al. (2009) refer to both their approach and Gruber's as "tag ontologies". This means that they are small ontologies that capture the terminology and interrelations in the domain of 'tagging': "[…] ontologies are promising in providing the tools and formalism for representing social information including users, resources, tags, and their relationships" (Kim, Breslin et al., 2009).

SCOT itself reuses elements from DC, FOAF and SIOC to ensure compatibility with these resources. An application called Int.ere.st[364] has been built on the basis of the SCOT ontology. This tool allows users to collect tagging data in the SCOT format so that the context of each tag can be stored.

One future research objective will surely be finding new simple forms of establishing mappings between different KOS. Herzog, Luger and Herzog (2007) discuss the option of "statistical mappings" for their database on tourism. In this setting, ontology concepts, too, and social tags are used to index documents in parallel. They want to compute co-occurrences between tags and ontology concepts to and consider them as substitute mappings.

The first attempts to integrate the mapping process to a game with a purpose have been made by Siorpaes and Hepp (2008a): As part of the OntoGame series, they have proposed several games for mapping single vocabularies. Among them is a game scenario for mapping the UNSPSC to the eClass ontology. As we have seen above, the game OntoPronto by the OntoGame developers aims to interlink Wikipedia articles with the PROTON Ontology, which is another example for mappings on the Social Semantic Web.

But even without specific game scenarios, Web users may contribute to the mapping processes within the Social Semantic Web – and they already do so in certain applications. Theoretical foundations on community-driven ontology matching have been provided by Conroy, O'Sullivan et al. (2008) as well as by Zhdanova and Shvaiko (2006).

Wikipedia is frequently discussed as a central resource to which other knowledge organization systems on the Web might be mapped. Recently, initiatives were started to map Wikipedia categories[365] to established classifications like UDC (Voß, 2009). Mappings are labeled as semantic relations between two resources based on the SKOS standards[366], i.e. skos:closeMatch for (quasi-) synonyms, skos:broadMatch for broader terms and skos:narrowMatch for narrower terms[367].

---

[364] Int.ere.st: http://int.ere.st/.
[365] Wikipedia template for category mappings (in German):
http://de.wikipedia.org/wiki/Vorlage:Kategorienmapping.
[366] Wikipedia note for using SKOS links (in German):
http://de.wikipedia.org/wiki/Kategorie:Vorlage:SKOSlink.
[367] Specified mappings based on SKOS standards are also applied in the myOntology project (Siorpaes, Hepp et al., 2008).

Some interesting approaches to enriching the semantic link structures over the Web can also be found within certain folksonomy-based systems, for example, on the music platform Last.FM: Music events like concerts or festivals can obtain special 'event tags' (Figure 3.72), which relate to event reports within Last.FM and may also be used to tag photos about the respective event on Flickr (Peters, 2009).

Figure 3.72. Event tag on Last.FM that may be used to tag Flickr photos.

On Flickr, these Last.FM event tags are one example of so-called 'machine tags'[368]. Machine tags consists of three parts: a 'namespace', a 'predicate' and a 'value'. Within the examplary event tag in Figure 3.72, 'lastfm' is the namespace, 'event' is the predicate, and '1089786' is the value (in this case the identification number for a Last.FM event). Other than this general syntax, there are no rules for the combination of machine tags, and generally every possible combination may be chosen. This also means that the same namespaces, predicates and values may be assigned by different people for different purposes, there being no shared semantics. It is up to the community to establish naming conventions, or to platform operators who propose certain machine tags. Events from the social calendar platform Upcoming may also be tagged with an Upcoming ID in Flickr (for example 'upcoming:event=81334'). Geotags in Flickr are another example for machine tags.

Another project of interest is TagCommons[369]; a working group with the aim of sharing and exchanging tagging data across applications and communities:

> "The TagCommons project is consciously a mapping effort rather than homogenization effort, and is focusing on clarifying the conceptual distinctions rather than the low level data models. Although its goal is to create an ontology that covers all the use cases and conceptual distinctions, a main use of this ontology will be to enable interesting mappings across existing systems, including those based on existing ontologies. [...] In a sense, the TagCommons project is attempting to create a platform for interoperability of Social Web data on the Semantic Web that is akin to the "mash-up" ecology that is celebrated in Web 2.0." (Gruber, 2008)

---

[368] Flickr discussion about machine tags:
http://www.flickr.com/groups/api/discuss/72157594497877875/.
[369] TagCommons: http://tagcommons.org/.

Furthermore, LODr[370] is an initiative to support traditional tags with URIs, for example taken from DBpedia. In this way, data can be retrieved and aggregated across several social tagging platforms. LODr is a first practical application of the MOAT[371] (Meaning Of A Tag) project.

All these examples show that the challenge of interlinking knowledge organization systems on the Web is being faced and approached in several initiatives. A lot more examples can be found for cross-references between different vocabularies, e.g. from FOAF to WordNet (Dodds, 2004).

Altogether it seems that no one believes in the creation of one single central KOS for the WWW any longer. Berners-Lee, Hendler and Lassila already announced this years ago:

> "Traditional knowledge-representation systems typically have been centralized, requiring everyone to share exactly the same definition of common concepts such as 'parent' or 'vehicle.' But central control is stifling, and increasing the size and scope of such a system rapidly becomes unmanageable. (Berners-Lee, Hendler & Lassila, 2001)

Their suggested solutions are "pointers" between equivalent terms within different systems. Today, the general Web 2.0 principle of 'mashing-up' different applications and their data has also got a hold of knowledge representation.

Conclusion

This chapter has addressed the fundamental question of how the power of communities on the Social Web can be used to establish semantics that go well beyond folksonomy tags.

Ontology engineering in the tradition of Semantic Web research is a laborious and time-consuming process that requires expert skills in ontology design as well as domain knowledge in the respective field of interest. Various approaches exist that aim at providing a sound methodology for ontology engineering, but still there are few clear practical guidelines that help the ontology engineer with design decisions. We have argued that in order to handle the complexity of designing large and broad ontologies, and to ensure a commonly shared perspective, ontology engineering should be carried out by a community. While some collaborative approaches to ontology engineering date back to the beginnings of ontology research, collaborative ontology engineering has entered new dimensions with the advent of the Social Semantic Web: Community-based ontology engineering has been introduced as a new form of Web collaboration between unlimited user communities. Community-based ontology engineering:

- can handle broad as well as specific domains,

---

[370] LODr: http://lodr.info/about.
[371] MOAT: http://moat-project.org/.

- can take over the task of ontology maintenance (missing concepts can be added by any community member),
- is the key to addressing WWW-wide ontologies,
- and can capture the point of view of the user community.

And yet, to bring together broad communities and to motivate them to contribute to rich semantic models is an enormous challenge. We have discussed several approaches that may help lower the barriers that restrain users from participating in ontology engineering projects: wiki-like ontology editors provide more usable user interfaces than classical editors and also support the collection of ideas and conceptualizations, controlled natural languages can reduce the need for learning a formal ontology language, community knowledge bases can incrementally collect ontology-like data without the user being aware of it, and finally, games with a purpose may even go one step further and collect data while the user is participating in an online game. Among the games with a purpose we have seen some that may be utilized for ontology engineering as well as others that can help to address the challenge of indexing Web documents with rich semantic metadata.

Finally, two basic ideas appeared most promising for the actual integration of user communities into the creation of ontologies for the WWW: a) encouraging users to contribute little pieces of information without much effort (or as a side effect of other online activities) which can then be combined with a large knowledge model and b) harvesting various data that have already been created by users for other purposes and integrate them to a KOS.

With regard to the second alternative, we have also introduced tag gardening as a process of re-editing and structuring folksonomy tags.

How might the ideal tool for ontology engineering in a Social Semantic Web look like? We think that it should:

- include different levels of knowledge networking, both social networks and data networks,
- support ontology engineering, semantic indexing and retrieval within one system,
- enable semantic upgrades from tags or lightweight semantics up to ontologies,
- provide incentives for easy user contribution, like playful approaches (gwap), direct profit or feedback for contributors.

Of course, lots of future work is needed before a system will fulfill all these requirements. Besides technical research, some "social" aspects will have to be investigated more closely: Future work is needed on the didactics of ontology engineering, on actual user behavior in community-based ontology engineering and on users' demands on tools and functionalities. Furthermore, standards are needed for ontology modeling choices, particularly for broad user communities on the Web.

We may now conclude that various options exist for marking the beginning of community-based KOS engineering in practice. And yet for the short term, the resulting knowledge models will probably not contain rich semantics as outlined in the previous chapter. In a Social Semantic Web, ontologies will play an important role – but it may not be the leading part they have in Semantic Web research. The use of elaborated relations and restrictions and respective reasoning might have to be postponed or restricted to single application scenarios. What can be realized are basic semantics in the form of less formal KOS provided by numerous Web users. With novel, community-centered approaches this will soon be more comprehensively realized.

In the future, probably the most important step will be handling the growing number of available KOS and facilitating mediation and interaction between them. Semantic upgrades are already one example of inter-KOS crosswalks. We have briefly outlined some other dimensions of KOS interactions as ways in which different KOS may come into contact with one another. This indicates a different understanding of ontology engineering in the Social Semantic Web: we can currently observe a shift from pure ontology engineering to general KOS engineering. Furthermore, much attention is placed upon the inter-KOS level of engineering. On the Social Semantic Web, the development of rich semantic structures in one single model is secondary to the creation of lightweight models which are heavily interlinked: URIs are aggregated from everywhere, various sources are used and reused as references. In the sense of semantic upgrades, these basic link structures may be established on the fly now, and could later be enriched with semantically typed links based on standard semantic relations.

References

Aberer, K., Cudré-Mauroux, P., Ouksel, A. M., Catarci, T., Hacid, M.-S., & Illarramendi, A., et al. (2004). Emergent Semantics Principles and Issues. In Y. Lee; J. Li; K.-Y. Whang, & D. Lee (Eds.), Database Systems for Advanced Applications: Proceedings of the 9th International Conference, Jeju Island, Korea (pp. 25–38). Berlin: Springer.

Ahmad, M. N., & Colomb, R. M. (2007). Overview of Ontology Servers Research. Webology, 4(2). Retrieved from http://www.webology.ir/2007/v4n2/a43.html.

Aitchison, J. (1986). A Classification as a Source for Thesaurus: The Bibliographic Classification of H. E. Bliss as a Source of Thesaurus Terms and Structure. Journal of Documentation, 42(30), 160–181.

Aitchison, J., Gilchrist, A., & Bawden, D. (2000). Thesaurus Construction and Use (4th Edition). London: Aslib.

Aitchison, J., Gomersall, A., & Ireland, R. (1969). Thesaurofacet: A Thesaurus and Faceted Classification for Engineering and Related Subjects. Rugby: Jolly and Barber.

Al-Khalifa, H. S., & Davis, H. C. (2007a). FAsTA: A Folksonomy-Based Automatic Metadata Generator. In E. Duval; R. Klamma, & M. Wolpers (Eds.), Creating New Learning Experiences on a Global Scale: Proceedings of the Second European Conference on Technoloy Enhanced Learning (EC-TEL 2007), Crete, Greece (pp. 414–419). Berlin: Springer.

Al-Khalifa, H. S., & Davis, H. C. (2007b). Exploring the Value of Folksonomies for Creating Semantic Metadata. International Journal on Semantic Web & Information Systems (IJSWIS), 3(1), 12–38.

Angeletou, S., Sabou, M., Specia, L., & Motta, E. (2007). Bridging the Gap Between Folksonomies and the Semantic Web: An Experience Report. In B. Hoser & A. Hotho (Eds.). Bridging the Gap between Semantic Web and Web 2.0 (SemNet 2007). International Workshop at the 4th European Semantic Web Conference, Innsbruck, Austria (pp. 30–43).

Arpirez, J. C., Gómez-Pérez, A., Lozano-Tello, A., & Pinto, H. S. (2000). Reference Ontology and (ONTO)2 Agent: The Ontology Yellow Pages. Knowledge and Information Systems, 2(4), 387–412.

Arpirez, J. C., Corcho, O., Fernández-López, M., & Gómez-Pérez, A. (2001). WebODE: A Scalable Ontological Engineering Workbench. In Y. Gil; M. A. Musen, & J. Shavlik (Eds.), First International Conference on Knowledge Capture (KCAP'01). Victoria, Canada (pp. 6–13). New York: ACM.

Auer, S., Dietzold, S., & Riechert, T. (2006). OntoWiki: A Tool for Social, Semantic Collaboration. In I. Cruz, S. Decker, & et al. (Eds.), The Semantic Web. 5th International Semantic Web Conference (ISWC 2006). Athens, GA, USA. (pp. 736–749). Berlin: Springer.

Au Yeung, C. M., Gibbins, N., & Shadbolt, N. (2007). Understanding the Semantics of Ambiguous Tags in Folksonomies. In L. Chen, P. Cudré-Mauroux, P. Haase, A. Hotho, & E. Ong (Eds.), Emergent Semantics and Ontology Evolution 2007: Proceedings of the First International Workshop on Emergent Semantics and Ontology Evolution (ESOE-2007), co-located with ISWC 2007, Busan, Korea (pp. 108–121). CEUR Workshop Proceedings: Vol. 292.

Bao, J., & Honavar, V. (2004). Collaborative Ontology Building with Wiki@nt: A Multi-agent Based Ontology Building Environment. In Y. Sure, O. Corcho, J. Euzenat, & T. Hughes (Eds.), Evaluation of Ontology-based Tools. Proceedings of the 3rd International Workshop on Evaluation of Ontology-based Tools (EON 2004) held at the 3rd International Semantic Web Conference ISWC 2004, Hiroshima, Japan (pp. 37–46). CEUR Workshop Proceedings: Vol. 128.

Bechhofer, S., Horrocks, I., Goble, C., & Stevens, R. (2001). OilEd: A Reasonable Ontology Editor for the Semantic Web. In F. Baader, G. Brewka, & T. Eiter (Eds.), Lecture Notes in Computer Science: Vol. 2174. KI 2001: Advances in Artificial Intelligence. Proceedings of the Joint German/Austrian Conference on AI. Vienna, Austria (pp. 396–408). Berlin, Heidelberg: Springer.

Begelman, G., Keller, P., & Smadja, F. (2006). Automated Tag Clustering: Improving Search and Exploration in the Tag Space. In Collaborative Web Tagging Workshop: Workshop helt at the World Wide Web Conference (WWW2006), Edinburgh, Scotland.

Belling, G., Brodmeier, B., Wersig, G., Hagen, P.-T., Joers, H., & Rolland, M.-T. (1974). Bundes-Dachthesaurus: Untersuchungen zur Vereinheitlichung der

Ordnungssysteme von Obersten Bundesbehörden und Einrichtungen des Nachgeordneten Bereichs. Teil 1: Bestandsaufnahme (Gutachten im Auftrag des Bundesminister des Inneren, Bonn).

Benz, D., & Hotho, A. (2007). Position Paper: Ontology Learning from Folksonomies. In A. Hinneburg (Ed.), Workshop Proceedings of Lernen - Wissensentdeckung - Adaptivität (LWA 2007), Martin-Luther-Universität Halle-Wittenberg, Germany (pp. 109–112).

Berners-Lee, T., Hendler, J., & Lassila, O. (2001). The Semantic Web. Scientific American, 284(5), 34–43.

Bizer, C., Heath, T., Ayers, D., & Raimond, Y. (2007). Interlinking Open Data on the Web. In Proceedings of the Demonstrations Track 4th European Semantic Web Conference (ESWC2007), Innsbruck, Austria.

Bizer, C., Heath, T., & Berners-Lee, T. (2009). Linked Data: The Story So Far. International Journal on Semantic Web & Information Systems (IJSWIS), 5(3), 1–22.

Blázquez, M., Fernández-López, M., García-Pinar, J. M., & Gómez-Pérez, A. (1998). Building Ontologies at the Knowledge Level Using the Ontology Design Environment. In B. R. Gaines & M. A. Musen (Eds.). 11th International Workshop on Knowledge Acquisition, Modeling and Management (KAW'98), Banff, Canada (pp. 1–15).

Borst, W. N. (1997). Construction of Engineering Ontologies for Knowledge Sharing and Reuse. PhD Thesis, University of Twente, Nederlands. Retrieved from http://doc.utwente.nl/17864/.

Bouquet, P., Ehrig, M., Euzenat, J., Franconi, E., Hitzler, P., & Krötzsch, M., et al. (2004). Specification of a Common Framework for Characterizing Alignment (Knowledge Web Deliverable No. 2.2.1v2).

Brank, J., Grobelnik, M., & Mladenic, D. (2005). A Survey of Ontology Evaluation Techniques. In Conference on Data Mining and Data Warehouses (SiKDD 2005), held at 7th International Multi-conference on Information Society (IS'05), Ljubljana, Slovenia.

Brank, J., Mladenic, D., & Grobelnik, M. (2006). Golden Standard Based Ontology Evaluation Using Instance Assignment. In D. Vrandecic, M. C. Suarez-Figueroa, A. Gangemi, & Y. Sure (Eds.), Evaluation of Ontologies for the Web. Proceedings of 4th International EON Workshop 2006 on Evaluation of Ontologies for the Web, Co-located with WWW2006, Edinburgh, UK. CEUR Workshop Proceedings: Vol. 179.

Braun, S., Schmidt, A., Walter, A., & Zacharias, V. (2007). The Ontology Maturing Approach to Collaborative and Work-Integrated Ontology Development: Evaluation Results and Future Directions. In L. Chen, P. Cudré-Mauroux, P. Haase, A. Hotho, & E. Ong (Eds.), Emergent Semantics and Ontology Evolution 2007: Proceedings of the First International Workshop on Emergent Semantics and Ontology Evolution (ESOE-2007), Co-located with ISWC 2007, Busan, Korea (pp. 5–18). CEUR Workshop Proceedings: Vol. 292.

BS 8723-4:2007. Structured Vocabularies for Information Retrieval: Guide. Interoperability between Vocabularies. London: British Standards Institution.

Buitelaar, P., Cimiano, P., & Magnini, B. (Eds.) (2005). Ontology Learning from Text: Method, Evaluation and Applications (Vol. 123). Frontiers in Artificial Intelligence and Applications, 123. Amsterdam: IOS Press.

Catenacci, C., Gangemi, A., Lehmann, J., Nissim, M., Presutti, V., & Steve, G. (2007). Design Rationales for Collaborative Development of Networked Ontologies: State of the Art and the Collaborative Ontology Design Ontology (NeOn Project Deliverable No. D2.1.1). Retrieved from http://www.aifb.uni-karlsruhe.de/Publikationen/showPublikation?publ_ id=1632.

Cattuto, C., Benz, D., Hotho, A., & Stumme, G. (2008a). Semantic Analysis of Tag Similarity Measures in Collaborative Tagging Systems. In J. Baumeister & M. Atzmüller (Eds.), Workshop-Woche: Lernen, Wissen & Adaptivität (LWA 2008), Würzburg, Germany (pp. 18–26). Technical Report 448 Department of Computer Science. Würzburg: University of Würzburg.

Cattuto, C., Benz, D., Hotho, A., & Stumme, G. (2008b). Semantic Grounding of Tag Relatedness in Social Bookmarking Systems: Presentation at the 3rd Workshop on Ontology Learning and Population (OLP3), located at ECAI 2008, Patras, Greece, from http://olp.dfki.de/olp3/Benz.pdf.

Chandrasekaran, B., Josephson, J. R., & Benjamins, V. R. (1999). What Are Ontologies, and Why Do We Need Them? IEEE Intelligent Systems, 14(1), 20–26.

Choi, N., Song, I. Y., & Han, H. (2006). A Survey on Ontology Mapping. SIGMOD Record, 35(3), 34–41.

Christiaens, S. (2006). Metadata Mechanisms: From Ontology to Folksonomy … and Back. In R. Meersman; Z. Tari, & P. Herrero (Eds.), On the Move to Meaningful Internet Systems (OTM 2006): Proceedings of the OTM Confederated International Workshops and Posters, Montpellier, France (pp. 199–207). Berlin: Springer.

Cimiano, P. (2006). Ontology Learning and Population from Text: Algorithms, Evaluation and Applications. Boston: Springer.

Clark, P., Thompson, J., & Porter, B. (2000). Knowledge Patterns. In A. G. Cohn; F. Giunchiglia, & B. Selman (Eds.), Principles of Knowledge Representation and Reasoning: Proceedings of the Seventh International Conference (KR2000), Breckenridge, Colorado, USA (pp. 591–600). Morgan Kaufmann.

Cleveland, D. B., & Cleveland, A. D. (2001). Introduction to Indexing and Abstracting (3rd Edition). Englewood: Libraries Unlimited.

Conesa, J., de Palol, X., & Olivé, A. (2003). Building Conceptual Schemas by Refining General Ontologies. In V. Marík (Ed.), Database and Expert Systems Applications. Proceedings of the 14th International Conference (DEXA 2003), Prague, Czech Republic (pp. 693–702). Berlin: Springer.

Corcho, O., Fernández-López, M., & Gómez-Pérez, A. (2003). Methodologies, Tools and Languages for Building Ontologies: Where is Their Meeting Point? Data & Knowledge Engineering, 46, 41–64.

Cregan, A., Schwitter, R., & Meyer, T. Sydney OWL Syntax: Towards a Controlled Natural Language Syntax for OWL 1.1. In C. Golbreich, A. Kalyanpur, & B. Parsia (Eds.), Proceedings of the OWLED 2007 Workshop on OWL: Experiences and Directions, Innsbruck, Austria. CEUR Workshop Proceedings: Vol. 258.

Cuenca Grau, B., Honavar, V., Schlicht, A., & Wolter, F. (Eds.) (2007). Proceedings of the 2nd International Workshop on Modular Ontologies (WoMO 2007), Whistler, Canada. CEUR Workshop Proceedings: Vol. 315.

Cuenca Grau, B., Parsia, B., Sirin, E., & Kalyanpur, A. (2006). Modularity and Web Ontologies. In P. Doherty; J. Mylopoulos, & C. Welty (Eds.), Principles of Knowledge Representation and Reasoning: Proceedings of the Tenth International Conference (KR-06), Lake District of the UK (pp. 198–209). Menlo Park: AAAI Press.

Day-Richter, J., Harris, M. A., Haendel, M., Gene Ontology OBO-Edit Working Group, & Lewis, S. (2007). OBO-Edit: An Ontology Editor for Biologists. Bioinformatics, 23(16), 2198–2200.

d'Aquin, M., Schlicht, A., Stuckenschmidt, H., & Sabou, M. (2007). Ontology Modularization for Knowledge Selection: Experiments and Evaluations. In R. Wagner; N. Revell, & G. Pernul (Eds.), Database and Expert Systems Applications: Proceedings of the 18th International Conference (DEXA 2007), Regensburg, Germany (pp. 874–883). Berlin: Springer.

de Bruijn, J., Ehrig, M., Feier, C., Martín-Recuerda, F., Scharffe, F., & Weiten, M. (2006). Ontology Mediation, Merging, and Aligning. In J. Davies; R. Studer, & P. Warren (Eds.), Semantic Web Technologies: Trends and Research in Ontology-Based Systems (pp. 95–113). Chichester: Wiley.

De Chiara, R., Fish, A., & Ruocco, S. (2008). A Novel Resource Tagging Facility Integrated with Flickr. In S. Levialdi (Ed.), Proceedings of the Working Conference on Advanced Visual Interfaces, Naples, Italy (pp. 326–330). New York: ACM.

de Leenheer, P., & Christiaens, S. (2007). Mind the Gap: Transcending the Tunnel View on Ontology Engineering. In S. Buckinham Shum, M. Lind, & H. Weigand (Eds.), Proceedings of the 2nd International Conference on Pragmatic Web, Tilburg, The Netherlands. New York: ACM.

de Leenheer, P., & Mens, T. (2008). Ontology Evolution: State of the Art and Future Directions. In M. Hepp; P. de Leenheer; A. de Moor, & Y. Sure (Eds.), Ontology Management: Semantic Web, Semantic Web Services, and Business Applications (pp. 132–176). Boston: Springer.

Della Valle, E., Celino, I., & Cerizza, D. (2008). Agreeing while Disagreeing: A Best Practice for Business Ontology Development. In W. Abramowicz & D. Fensel (Eds.), Business Information Systems: Procedings of the 11th International Conference (BIS 2008), Innsbruck, Austria (pp. 70–82). Berlin, Heidelberg: Springer.

Denny, M. (2004). Ontology Tools Survey, Revisited. Retrieved from http://www.xml.com/pub/a/2004/07/14/onto.html.

Dextre Clarke, S. G. (2008). The last 50 Years of Knowledge Organization: A Journey Through my Personal Archives. Journal of Information Science, 34(4), 427–437.

Dimitrova, V., Denaux, R., Hart, G., Dolbear, C., Holt, I., & Cohn, A. G. (2008). Involving Domain Experts in Authoring OWL Ontologies. In A. Sheth, S. Staab, M. Dean, M. Paolucci, D. Maynard, & T. Finin, et al. (Eds.), The Semantic Web: 7th International Semantic Web Conference (ISWC 2008), Karlsruhe, Germany (pp. 1–16). Berlin: Springer.

Ding, L., Finin, T., Joshi, A., Pan, R., Cost, R. S., Peng, Y., Reddivari, P., & Doshi, V., et al. (2004). Swoogle: A Search and Metadata Engine for the Semantic Web. In D. A. Evans; L. Gravano; O. Herzog; C. Zhai, & M. Rhonthaler (Eds.), Proceedings of the Thirteenth ACM Conference on Information & Knowledge Management, New Orleand, Louisiana, USA (pp. 652–659). New York: ACM Press.

Ding, Y., & Foo, S. (2002a). Ontology Research and Development: Part 1 – A Review of Ontology Generation. Journal of Information Science, 28(2), 123–136.

Ding, Y., & Foo, S. (2002b). Ontology Research and Development: Part 2 – A Review of Ontology Mapping and Evolving. Journal of Information Science, 28(5), 375–388.

Dittmann, C., Dittmann, M., Peters, I., & Weller, K. (2009). Persönliches Tag Gardening mit tagCare. In M. Ockenfeld (Ed.), Generation international: Die Zukunft von Information, Wissenschaft und Profession. Proceedings der 31. Online-Tagung der DGI, Frankfurt am Main, Germany (pp. 117–128). Frankfurt am Main: DGI.

Doan, A., Madhavan, J., Domingos, P., & Halevy, A. (2002). Learning to Map between Ontologies on the Semantic Web. In D. Lassner (Ed.), International World Wide Web Conference: Proceedings of the 11th International Conference on World Wide Web, Honolulu, Hawaii, USA (pp. 662–673). New York: ACM.

Dodds, L. (2004). An Introduction to FOAF. Retrieved from http://www.xml.com/pub/a/2004/02/04/foaf.html.

Doerr, M. (2001). Semantic Problems of Thesaurus Mapping. Journal of Digital Information, 1(8). Retrieved from http://journals.tdl.org/jodi/article/viewArticle/31.

Domingue, J. (1998). Tadzebao and WebOnto: Discussing, Browsing, and Editing Ontologies on the Web. In B. R. Gaines & M. A. Musen (Eds.). 11th International Workshop on Knowledge Acquisition, Modeling and Management (KAW'98), Banff, Canada (pp. 1–20).

Duineveld, A. J., Stoter, R., Weiden, M. R., Kenepa, B., & Benjamins, V. R. (2000). WonderTools? A Comparative Study of Ontological Engineering Tools. International Journal of Human-Computer Studies, 52, 1111–1133.

Duske, D., Kretschmann, R., Neveling, U., Seeger, T., Supper, R., & Wersig, G., et al. (1974). Bundes-Dachthesaurus: Untersuchungen zur Vereinheitlichung der Ordnungssysteme von Obersten Bundesbehörden und Einrichtungen des

Nachgeordneten Bereichs. Teil 2: Kompatibiltätsstudie (Gutachten im Auftrag des Bundesminister des Inneren, Bonn).

Dzbor, M., & Motta, E. (2008). Engineering and Customizing Ontologies. In M. Hepp; P. de Leenheer; A. de Moor, & Y. Sure (Eds.), Ontology Management: Semantic Web, Semantic Web Services, and Business Applications (pp. 25–57). Boston: Springer.

Dzbor, M., Motta, E., Buil, C., Gomez, J., Görlitz, O., & Lewen, H. (2006). Developing Ontologies in OWL: An Observational Study. In B. Cuenca Grau, P. Hitzler, C. Shankey, & E. Wallace (Eds.), Proceedings of the OWLED 2006 Workshop on OWL: Experiences and Directions, Athens (Georgia), USA. CEUR Workshop Proceedings: Vol. 216.

Ehrig, M. (2007). Ontology Alignment: Bridging the Semantic Gap. New York: Springer.

Ehrig, M., de Bruijn, J., Manov, D., & Martín-Recuerda, F. (2004). State-of-the-art Survey on Ontology Merging and Aligning V1 (Sekt Project Deliverable No. 4.2.1). DERI Innsbruck.

El Jerroudi, Z., & Ziegler, J. (2007). Interaktives Vergleichen und Zusammenführen von Ontologien. i-com. Zeitschrift für interaktive und kooperative Medien, 2007(3), 44–49.

Ensan, F., & Du, W. (2008). An Interface-Based Ontology Modularization Framework for Knowledge Encapsulation. In A. Sheth, S. Staab, M. Dean, M. Paolucci, D. Maynard, & T. Finin, et al. (Eds.), The Semantic Web. 7th International Semantic Web Conference, ISWC 2008. Karlsruhe, Germany (pp. 517–532). Berlin: Springer.

Euzenat, J., & Shvaiko, P. (2007). Ontology Matching. Berlin, Heidelberg: Springer.

Fan, J., Gao, Y., & Luo, H. (2007). Hierarchical Classification for Automatic Image Annotation. In Proceedings of the 30th Annual International ACM SIGIR Conference on Research and Development in Information Retrieval (pp. 111–118). New York: ACM.

Farquhar, A., Fikes, R., & Rice, J. (1997a). The Ontolingua Server: A Tool for Collaborative Ontology Construction. International Journal of Human-Computer Studies, 46(6), 707–727.

Farquhar, A., Fikes, R., & Rice, J. (1997b). Tools for Assembling Modular Ontologies in Ontolingua. In A. Farquhar, M. Grüninger, A. Gómez-Pérez, M. Uschold, & van der Vet, P. (Eds.), AAAI Symposium Report: AAAI'97 Spring Symposium on Ontological Engineering, Stanford University, Califormina (pp. 436–441).

Fensel, D. (2004). Ontologies: A Silver Bullet for Knowledge Management and Electronic Commerce (2nd Edition). Chichester: Springer.

Fernández-López, M., & Gómez-Pérez, A. (2002). Overview and Analysis of Methodologies for Building Ontologies. Knowledge Engineering Review, 17(2), 129–156.

Fernández-López, M., Gómez-Pérez, A., Euzenat, J., Gangemi, A., Kalfoglou, Y., & Pisanelli, D. M., et al. (2002). A Survey on Methodologies for Developing,

Maintaining and Reengineering Ontologies (OntoWeb Deliverable No. 1.4). Universidad Politecnica de Madrid.

Fernández-López, M., Gómez-Pérez, A., & Juristo, N. (1997). METHONTOLOGY: From Ontological Art Towards Ontological Engineering. In Spring Symposium on Ontological Engineering of AAAI (pp. 33–40). Stanford: Stanford University.

Fluit, C., Sabou, M., & van Harmelen, F. (2004). Supporting User Tasks through Visualisation of Light-Weight Ontologies. In S. Staab & R. Studer (Eds.), Handbook on Ontologies (pp. 275–296). Berlin, Heidelberg, New York: Springer.

Fokker, J., Pouwelse, J., & Buntine, W. (2006). Tag-Based Navigation for Peer-to-Peer Wikipedia. In Collaborative Web Tagging Workshop: Workshop helt at the World Wide Web Conference (WWW2006), Edinburgh, Scotland.

Fuchs, N., & Schwitter, R. (1996). Attempto Controlled English (ACE). In First International Workshop on Controlled Language Applications (CLAW '96), University of Leuven, Belgium.

Funk, A., Tablan, V., Bontcheva, K., Cunningham, H., Davis, B., & Handschuh, S. (2007). CLOnE: Controlled Language for Ontology Editing. In K. Aberer & et al. (Eds.), The Semantic Web. 6th International Semantic Web Conference, 2nd Asian Semantic Web Conference, (ISWC 2007 + ASWC 2007). Busan, Korea (pp. 142–155). Berlin: Springer.

Furnas, G. W., Landauer, T., Gomez, L., & Dumais, S. (1987). The Vocabulary Problem in Human-System Communication: An Analysis and a Solution. Communications of the ACM, 30, 964–971.

Gangemi, A. (2005). Ontology Design Patterns for Semantic Web Content. In V. R. Benjamins; Y. Gil; E. Motta, & M. Musen (Eds.), The Semantic Web: Proceedings of the 4th International Semantic Web Conference (ISWC 2005), Galway, Ireland (pp. 262–276). Berlin, Heidelberg: Springer.

García-Silva, A., Gómez-Pérez, A., Suarez-Figueroa, M. C., & Villazón-Terrazas, B. (2008). A Pattern Based Approach for Re-engineering Non-Ontological Resources into Ontologies. In J. Domingue & C. Anutariya (Eds.), The Semantic web: Proceedings of the 3rd Asian Semantic Web Conference (ASWC 2008), Bangkok, Thailand (pp. 167–181). Berlin: Springer.

Gendarmi, D., & Lanubile, F. (2006). Community-Driven Ontology Evolution Based on Folksonomies. In R. Meersman; Z. Tari, & P. Herrero (Eds.), On the Move to Meaningful Internet Systems (OTM 2006): Proceedings of the OTM Confederated International Workshops and Posters, Montpellier, France (pp. 181–188). Berlin: Springer.

Gennari, J. H., Musen, M. A., Fergerson, R. W., Grosso, W. E., Crubezy, M., & Eriksson, H., et al. (2003). The Evolution of Protégé: An Environment for Knowledge-Based Systems Development. International Journal of Human-Computer Studies, 58(1), 89–123.

Ghosh, R. A., Glott, R., Krieger, B., & Robles, G. (2002). Free/Libre and Open Source Software: Survey and Study (FLOSS Final Report). Part 4: Survey of Developers. International Institute of Infonomics, University of Maastricht, The

Netherlands & Berlecon Research GmbH, Berlin, Germany. Retrieved from http://www.infonomics.nl/FLOSS/report/index.htm.

Golov, E., Weller, K., & Peters, I. (2008). TagCare: A Personal Portable Tag Repository. In C. Bizer & A. Joshi (Eds.), ISWC2008 Posters and Demonstrations. Proceedings of the Poster and Demonstration Session at the 7th International Semantic Web Conference (ISWC2008), Karlsruhe, Germany. CEUR Workshop Proceedings: Vol. 401.

Gómez-Pérez, A., Angele, J., Fernández-López, M., Christophenides, V., Stutt, A., & Sure, Y. (2002). A Survey on Ontology Tools (OntoWeb Deliverable No. 1.3). Universidad Politecnica de Madrid.

Gómez-Pérez, A., Fernández-López, M., & Corcho, O. (2004). Ontological Engineering: Advanced Information and Knowledge Processing (3rd Print). London: Springer.

Good, B. M., & Wilkinson, M. D. (2007). Ontology Engineering Using Volunteer Labor. In E. Franconi; M. Kifer, & W. May (Eds.), The Semantic Web: Research and Applications: Proceedings of the 4th European Semantic Web Conference (ESWC 2007), Innsbruck, Austria (pp. 1243–1244). Berlin, Heidelberg: Springer.

Governor, J. (2006). On the Emergence of Professional Tag Gardeners. [Blog Post: January 10, 2006]. Retrieved from http://www.redmonk.com/jgovernor/2006/01/10/on-the-emergence-of-professional-tag-gardeners/.

Grahl, M., Hotho, A., & Stumme, G. (2007). Conceptual Clustering of Social Bookmarking Sites. In K. Tochtermann & H. Maurer (Eds.), International Conference on Knowledge Management: Proceedings of I-Know 07, Graz, Austria (pp. 356–364). Graz: J.UCS.

Gruber, A., Westenthaler, R., & Gahleitner, E. (2006). Supporting Domain Experts in Creating Formal Knowledge Models (Ontologies). In K. Tochtermann & H. Maurer (Eds.), Proceedings of I-KNOW '06: 6th International Conference on Knowledge Managment, Graz, Austria (pp. 252–260). Graz: J.UCS.

Gruber, T. (1993). Principles for the Design of Ontologies used for Knowledge Sharing. In N. Guarino & R. Poli (Eds.), International Workshop on Formal Ontology in Conceptual Analysis and Knowledge Representation, Padova, Italy. Derventer: Kluwer Academic Publishers.

Gruber, T. (2005). Ontology of Folksonomy: A Mash-Up of Apples and Oranges. International Journal on Semantic Web & Information Systems (IJSWIS), 3(2), 1–11.

Gruber, T. (2008). Collective Knowledge Systems: Where the Social Web meets the Semantic Web. Journal of Web Semantics, 6(1), 4–13.

Gruber, T., & Olsen, G. R. (1994). An Ontology for Engineering Mathematics. In J. Doyle; P. Torasso, & E. Sandewall (Eds.), Fourth International Conference on Principles of Knowledge Representation and Reasoning Bonn, Germany (pp. 258–269). San Francisco: Morgan Kaufmann.

Grüninger, M., & Fox, M. S. (1995). Methodology for the Design and Evaluation of Ontologies. In D. Skuce (Ed.), Workshop on Basic Ontological Issues in Knowledge Sharing. International Joint Conference on Artificial Intelligence (IJCAI 1995). Montreal, Quebec (pp. 6.1-6.10). Montreal: AAAI Press.

Guarino, N., & Welty, C. (2002). Evaluating Ontological Decisions with OntoClean. Communications of the ACM, 45(2), 61–65.

Guarino, N., & Welty, C. (2004). An Overview of OntoClean. In S. Staab & R. Studer (Eds.), Handbook on Ontologies (pp. 151–172). Berlin, Heidelberg, New York: Springer.

Guy, M., & Tonkin, E. (2006). Folksonomies: Tidying up tags? D-Lib Magazine, 12(1). Retrieved from http://www.dlib.org/dlib/january06/guy/01guy.html.

Handschuh, S., Staab, S., & Maedche, A. (2001). CREAM: Creating Relational Metadata with a Component-based, Ontology-driven Annotation Framework. In Y. Gil; M. A. Musen, & J. Shavlik (Eds.), First International Conference on Knowledge Capture (KCAP'01), Victoria, Canada (pp. 76–83). New York: ACM.

Hartmann, J. (2006). ONTHOLOGY: An Ontology Metadata Repository. In European Semantic Web Conference 2006: Demo and Poster Proceedings of ESWC 2006, Budva, Montenegro.

Hartmann, J., Palma, R., & Gómez-Pérez, A. (2009). Ontology Repositories. In S. Staab & R. Studer (Eds.), Handbook on Ontologies (pp. 551–571). Dordrecht et al.: Springer.

Hartmann, J., Palma, R., Sure, Y., Suarez-Figueroa, M. C., Haase, P., & Gómez-Pérez, A., et al. (2005). Ontology Metadata Vocabulary and Applications. In R. Meersman; Z. Tari; P. Herrero, & et al. (Eds.), International Conference on Ontologies, Databases and Applications of Semantics. In Workshop on Web Semantics (SWWS) (pp. 906–915). Berlin, Heidelberg: Springer.

Hartmann, J., Simperl, E. P. S., Palma, R., & Gómez-Pérez, A. (2006). DEMO: Design Environment for Metadata Ontologies. In Y. Sure & J. Domingue (Eds.), The Semantic Web: Research and Applications. 3rd European Semantic Web Conference (ESWC 2006). Budva, Montenegro (pp. 427–441). Berlin, Heidelberg: Springer.

Hartmann, J., Suarez-Figueroa, M. C., Palma, R., Sure, Y., & Haase, P. (2005). OMV: Ontology Metadata Vocabulary. In C. Welty (Ed.), Ontology Patterns for the Semantic Web (OPSW-05): Workshop at the International Semantic Web Conference (ISWC 2005). Galway, Ireland.

Harun, A. F., & Noor, N. L. M. (2007). User Interface for Knowledge Sharing Using Knowledge Gardening Metaphor. In M. J. Smith & G. Salvendy (Eds.), Human Interface and the Management of Information: Interacting in Information Environments. Symposium on Human Interface 2007, Held as Part of HCI International 2007, Beijing, China (pp. 319–327). Berlin: Springer.

Heath, T., Hepp, M., & Bizer, C. (Eds.) (2009). Special Issue on Linked Data. International Journal on Semantic Web & Information Systems (IJSWIS), 5(3), i-iii.

Heath, T., & Motta, E. (2008). Ease of Interaction plus Ease of Integration: Combining Web2.0 and the Semantic Web in a Reviewing Site. Journal of Web Semantics, 6(1), 76–83.

Henrichs, N. (1970). Philosophische Dokumentation: Literatur Dokumentation ohne strukturierten Thesaurus. Nachrichten für Dokumentation, 21, 20–25.

Hepp, M. (2006a). Products and Services Ontologies: A Methodology for Deriving OWL Ontologies from Industrial Categorization Standards. International Journal on Semantic Web & Information Systems (IJSWIS), 2(1), 72–99.

Hepp, M. (2006b). eClassOWL 5.1 Products and Services Ontology for e-Business: User's Guide, Version 1.0. Retrieved from http://www.heppnetz.de/projects/eclassowl/ eclassOWL-Primer-final.pdf.

Hepp, M. (2007). Possible Ontologies: How Reality Constrains the Development of Relevant Ontologies. IEEE Internet Computing, 11(1), 90–96.

Hepp, M. (2008). Ontologies: State of the Art, Business Potential, and Grand Challenges. In M. Hepp; P. de Leenheer; A. de Moor, & Y. Sure (Eds.), Ontology Management: Semantic Web, Semantic Web Services, and Business Applications (pp. 3–22). Boston, MA: Springer.

Hepp, M., Bachlechner, D., & Siorpaes, K. (2006a). Harvesting Wiki Consensus: Using Wikipedia Entries as Ontology Elements. In M. Völkel & S. Schaffert (Eds.), SemWiki2006: First Workshop on Semantic Wikis – From Wiki to Semantics. Proceedings of the First Workshop on Semantic Wikis, co-located with the ESWC2006. Budva, Montenegro. CEUR Workshop Proceedings: Vol. 206.

Hepp, M., Bachlechner, D., & Siorpaes, K. (2006b). OntoWiki: Community-driven Ontology Engineering and Ontology Usage based on Wikis. In D. Riehle & J. Noble (Eds.), International Symposium on Wikis: Proceedings of the 2006 international Symposium on Wikis (WikiSym 2006), Odense, Denmark (pp. 143–144). New York: ACM.

Hepp, M., Bachlechner, D., & Siorpaes, K. (2007). Harvesting Wiki Consensus: Using Wikipedia Entries as Ontology Elements. IEEE Internet Computing, 11(5), 54–65.

Hepp, M., & de Bruijn, J. (2007). GenTax: A Generic Methodology for Deriving OWL and RDF-S Ontologies from Hierarchical Classifications, Thesauri, and Inconsistent Taxonomies. In E. Franconi; M. Kifer, & W. May (Eds.), The Semantic Web: Research and Applications: Proceedings of the 4th European Semantic Web Conference (ESWC 2007), Innsbruck, Austria (pp. 129–144). Berlin, Heidelberg: Springer.

Herzog, C., Luger, M., & Herzog, M. (2007). Combining Social and Semantic Metadata for Search in a Document Repository. In B. Hoser & A. Hotho (Eds.). Bridging the Gap between Semantic Web and Web 2.0 (SemNet 2007). International Workshop at the 4th European Semantic Web Conference, Innsbruck, Austria (pp. 14–21).

Heymann, P., & Garcia-Molina, H. (2006). Collaborative Creation of Communal Hierarchical Taxonomies in Social Tagging Systems (Info-Lab Technical

Report   No.   2006-10).   Stanford   University.   Retrieved   from
http://dbpubs.stanford.edu:8090/pub/2006-10.

Heymann, P., Koutrika, G., & Garcia-Molina, H. (2007). Fighting Spam on Social
Websites: A Survey of Approaches and Future Challenges. IEEE Internet
Computing, 11(6), 36–45.

Hill, W. C., Hollan, J. D., Wroblewski, D., & McCandless, T. (1992). Edit Wear
and Read Wear. In P. Bauersfeld & J. Bennett (Eds.), Striking a Balance:
Conference on Human Factors in Computing Systems (SIGCHI`92), Monterey,
California (pp. 3–9). New York: ACM Press.

Hillmann, D. I., Sutton, S. A., Phipps, J., & Laundry, R. (2006). A Metadata
Registry from Vocabularies UP: The NSDL Registry Project. Retrieved from
http://arxiv.org/abs/cs.DL/0605111.

Hoehndorf, R., Bacher, J., Backhaus, M., Gregorio, S. E., Loebe, F., & Prüfer, K.,
et al. (2009). BOWiki: An Ontology-based Wiki for Annotation of Data and
Integration of Knowledge in Biology. BMC Bioinformatics, 10(S-5).

Hollink, L., Little, S., & Hunter, J. (2005). Evaluating the Application of Semantic
Inferencing Rules to Image Annotation. In P. Clark & G. Schreiber (Eds.),
Proccedings of the Third International Conference on Knowledge Capture (K-
CAP05), Banff, Canada (pp. 91–98). New York: ACM.

Hollink, L., Schreiber, G., Wielemaker, J., & Wielinga, B. (2003). Semantic
Annotation of Image Collections. In J. H. Gennari; B. Porter, & Y. Gil (Eds.),
Proceedings of the KCAP'03 Workshop on Knowledge Capture and Semantic
Annotation, Florida, USA. New York: ACM.

Hoppe, H. U., Malzahn, N., & Weinbrenner, S. (2009). Architectures for
Collaborative Ontology Development. In A. von Haeseler (Ed.), Ontoverse:
Global Knowledge for Global Challenges (Report for the BMBF Project
Ontoverse) (pp. 8–11). Krefeld: Varion.

Horridge, M., Knublauch, H., Rector, A., Stevens, R., & Wroe, C. (2004). A
Practical Guide To Building OWL Ontologies Using The Protégé-OWL Plugin
and   CO-ODE   Tools: Edition   1.0.   Retrieved   from   http://www.co-
ode.org/resources/tutorials/ProtegeOWLTutorial.pdf.

Hotho, A., Jäschke, R., Schmitz, C., & Stumme, G. (2006). Information Retrieval
in Folksonomies: Search and Ranking. Lecture Notes in Computer Science,
4011, 411–426.

Hunter, J., & Little, S. (2004). Rules-by-Example: A Novel Approach to Semantic
Indexing and Querying of Images. In S. McIlraith, D. Plexousakis, & F. van
Harmelen (Eds.), The Semantic Web. Proceedings of the 3rd International
Semantic Web Conference (ISWC 2004), Hiroshima, Japan (pp. 534–548).
Berlin, Heidelberg: Springer.

Hyvönen, E., Salminen, M., Junnila, M., & Kettula, S. (2004). A Content Creatio
Process for the Semantic Web. In Proceedings of Ontologies & Lexical
Resources in Distributed Environments (OntoLex 2004), Lisbon, Purtugal.

Hyvönen, E., Styrman, A., & Saarela, S. (2002). Ontology-based Image Retrieval
(HIIT Publications No. 2002-03). Helsinki: Helsinki Institute for Information
Technology (HIIT), pp. 15–27.

Isaac, A., Phipps, J., & Rubin, D. (Eds.) (2009). SKOS Use Cases and Requirements: W3C Working Group Note, 18 August 2009. Retrieved from http://www.w3.org/TR/skos-ucr/.

ISO 2788:1986. Documentation: Guidelines for the Establishment and Development of Monolingual Thesauri. Genf: International Organization for Standardization.

Jäschke, R., Hotho, A., Schmitz, C., Ganter, B., & Stumme, G. (2008). Discovering Shared Conceptualizations in Folksonomies. Journal of Web Semantics, 6(1), 38–53.

Kahan, J., Koivunen, M.-R., Prud'hommeaux, E., & Swick, R. (2002). Annotea: An Open RDF Infrastructure for Shared Web Annotations. Computer Networks, 39(5), 589–608.

Kalfoglou, Y., & Schorlemmer, M. (2003). Ontology Mapping: The State of the Art. Knowledge Engineering Review, 18(1), 1–31.

Kalyanpur, A., Parsia, B., Cuenca Grau, B., & Hendler, J. (2005). Swoop: A 'Web' Ontology Editing Browser. Journal of Web Semantics, 4(2), 144–153.

Kashyap, V., Bussler, C., & Moran, M. (2008). The Semantic Web: Semantics for Data and Services on the Web. Berlin, Heidelberg: Springer.

Kashyap, V., Cheung, K.-H., Doherty, D., Samwald, M., Marshall, M. S., & Luciano, J., et al. (2008). Ontology-based Data Integration for Biomedical Research. In J. Cardoso; M. Hepp, & M. D. Lytras (Eds.), The Semantic Web: Real-World Applications from Industry (pp. 97–122). Boston: Springer.

Kasneci, G., Ramanath, M., Suchanek, F., & Weikum, G. (2008). The YAGO-NAGA Approach to Knowledge Discovery. ACM SIGMOD Record, 37(4), 41–47.

Kendall, K. E., & Kendall, J. E. (1995). Systems Analysis and Design (3rd Edition). New Jersey: Prentice Hall.

Kilbury, J., Bontcheva, K., Rumpf, C., Kirstein, S., Kimm, N., & Zloch, M. (2009). Information Retrieval and Information Extraction in Ontoverse. In A. von Haeseler (Ed.), Ontoverse: Global Knowledge for Global Challenges (Report for the BMBF Project Ontoverse) (pp. 20–23). Krefeld: Varion.

Kim, H.-L., Breslin, J. G., Decker, S., & Kim, H.-G. (2009). Representing and Sharing Tagging Data Using the Social Semantic Cloud of Tags. In T. Dumova & R. Fiordo (Eds.), Handbook of Research on Social Interaction Technologies and Collaboration Software: Concepts and Trends (pp. 519–527). Hershey, New York: IGI Publishing.

Kipp, M. E. I. (2006a). @toread and cool: Tagging for Time, Task and Emotion. In 17th ASIS&T SIG/CR Classification Research Workshop: Abstracts of Posters (pp. 16–17).

Kipp, M. E. I. (2006b). Exploring the Context of User, Creator and Intermediary Tagging. Canadian Journal of Information and Library Science, 30(3), 419–436.

Klein, M. (2001). Combining and Relating Ontologies: An Analysis of Problems and Solutions. In A. Gómez-Pérez; M. Grüninger; H. Stuckenschmidt, & M. Uschold (Eds.), Workshop on Ontologies and Information Sharing: Held in conjunction with the International Joint Conference on Artificial Intelligence (IJCAI'01), Seattle, USA (pp. 53–62).

Knautz, K. (2008). Von der Tag-Cloud zum Tag Cluster: Statistischer Thesaurus auf der Basis syntagmatischer Relationen und seine mögliche Nutzung in Web 2.0-Diensten. In M. Ockenfeld (Ed.), Verfügbarkeit von Informationen: Proceedings der 30. DGI-Online-Tagung 2008, Frankfurt am Main, Germany (pp. 269–284). Frankfurt am Main: DGI.

Knublauch, H., Fergerson, R. W., Noy, N. F., & Musen, M. A. (2004). The Protégé OWL Plugin: An Open Development Environment for Semantic Web Applications. In S. McIlraith, D. Plexousakis, & F. van Harmelen (Eds.), The Semantic Web. Proceedings of the 3rd International Semantic Web Conference (ISWC 2004), Hiroshima, Japan (pp. 229–243). Berlin, Heidelberg: Springer.

Koivunen, M.-R. (2005). Annotea and Semantic Web Supported Collaboration. In M. Dzbor, H. Takeda, & M. Vargas-Vera (Eds.), UserSWeb 2005: Workshop on End Users Aspects of the Semantic Web, held at European Semantic Web Conference (ESWC 2005), Heraklion, Greece (pp. 5–18). CEUR Workshop Proceedings: Vol. 137.

Kolbitsch, J. (2007). WordFlickr: A Solution to the Vocabulary Problem in Social Tagging Systems. In K. Tochtermann; W. Haas; F. Kappe; A. Scharl; T. Pellegrini, & S. Schaffert (Eds.), International Conference on New Media Technologies and Semantic Systems: Proceedings of I-Media '07 and I-Semantics '07 (pp. 77–84). Graz: J.UCS.

Kuhn, T. (2008). Combining Semantic Wikis and Controlled Natural Language. In C. Bizer & A. Joshi (Eds.), ISWC2008 Posters and Demonstrations. Proceedings of the Poster and Demonstration Session at the 7th International Semantic Web Conference (ISWC2008). Karlsruhe, Germany. CEUR Workshop Proceedings: Vol. 401.

Kuznetsov, S. (2006). Motivations of Contributors to Wikipedia. ACM SIGCAS Computers and Society, 36(2), Article No. 1.

Lambrix, P., Habbouche, M., & Pérez, M. (2003). Evaluation of Ontology Development Tools for Bioinformatics. Bioinformatics, 19(12), 1564–1571.

Lambrix, P., Tan, H., Jakoniene, V., & Strömbäck, L. (2007). Biological Ontologies. In C. J. O. Baker & K.-H. Cheung (Eds.), Semantic Web: Revolutionizing Knowledge Discovery in the Life Sciences (pp. 85–99). Boston: Springer.

Laniado, D., Eynard, D., & Colombetti, M. (2007a). A Semantic Tool to Support Navigation in a Folksonomy. In Conference on Hypertext and Hypermedia: Proceedings of the Eighteenth Conference on Hypertext and Hypermedia, Manchester, UK (pp. 153–154). New York: ACM.

Laniado, D., Eynard, D., & Colombetti, M. (2007b). Using WordNet to Turn a Folksonomy into a Hierarchy of Concepts. In G. Semeraro, Di Sciascio, Eugenio, C. Morbidoni, & H. Stoermer (Eds.), Semantic Web Applications and Perspectives. Proceedings of the 4th Italian Semantic Web Workshop (SWAP 2007), Bari, Italy. CEUR Workshop Proceedings: Vol. 314.

Lanzenberger, M., & Sampson, J. (Ed.) (2008). Making Ontologies Talk: Knowledge Interoperability in the Semantic Web. IEEE Intelligent Systems, 23(6), 72–85.

Larsen, B., Ingwersen, P., & Kekäläinen, J. (2006). The Polyrepresentation Continuum in IR. In I. Ruthven (Ed.), Proceedings of the 1st International Conference on Information Interaction in Context (pp. 88–96). New York: ACM.

Lieberman, H., Smith, D., & Teeters, A. (2007). Common Consensus: A Web-based Game for Collecting Commonsense Goals. In Workshop on Common Sense for Intelligent Interfaces at the International Conference on Intelligent User Interfaces (IUI 2007), Hawaii, USA. New York: ACM.

Liu, H., & Singh, P. (2004). ConceptNet: A Practical Commonsense Reasoning Toolkit. BT Technology Journal, 22(4), 211–226.

Macgregor, G., & McCulloch, E. (2006). Collaborative Tagging as a Knowledge Organization and Resource Discovery Tool. Library Review, 55(5), 291–300.

Maedche, A., & Staab, S. (2000). Discovering Conceptual Relations from Text. In W. Horn (Ed.), ECAI 2000: Proceedings of the 14th European Conference on Artificial Intelligence, Berlin, Germany (pp. 321–325). Amsterdam: IOS Press.

Maedche, A., & Staab, S. (2001). Ontology Learning for the Semantic Web. IEEE Intelligent Systems, 16(2), 72–79.

Mainz, D., Paulsen, I., Mainz, I., Weller, K., Kohl, J., & von Haeseler, A. (2008). Knowledge Acquisition Focused Cooperative Development of Bio-Ontologies: A Case Study with BIO2Me. In Elloumi, M., et al. (Ed.), Communications in Computer and Information Science: Vol. 13. Bioinformatics Research and Development. Second International Conference, BIRD 2008. Vienna, Austria (pp. 258–272). Berlin, Heidelberg: Springer.

Mainz, D., Weller, K., & Mainz, J. (2008). Semantic Image Annotation and Retrieval with IKen. In C. Bizer & A. Joshi (Eds.), ISWC2008 Posters and Demonstrations. Proceedings of the Poster and Demonstration Session at the 7th International Semantic Web Conference (ISWC2008). Karlsruhe, Germany. CEUR Workshop Proceedings: Vol. 401.

Mainz, I., Weller, K., Paulsen, I., Mainz, D., Kohl, J., & von Haeseler, A. (2008). Ontoverse: Collaborative Ontology Engineering for the Life Sciences. Information – Wissenschaft & Praxis, 59(2), 91–99.

Malzahn, N., Weinbrenner, S., Hüsken, P., Ziegler, J., & Hoppe, H. U. (2007). Collaborative Ontology Development: Distributed Architecture and Visualization. In Proceedings of the German eScience Conference 2007 (Max Planck Digital Library, ID 315470.0). Max Planck Digital Library.

Marlow, C., Naaman, M., Boyd, D., & Davis, M. (2006). HT06, Tagging Paper, Taxonomy, Flickr, Academic Article, To Read. In Proceedings of the 17th Conference on Hypertext and Hypermedia (HT'06), Odense, Denmark (pp. 31–40). New York: ACM.

Mascardi, V., Cordì, V., & Rosso, P. (2007). A Comparison of Upper Ontologies. Dipartimenta di Informatica e Scienze dell'Informazione (DISI), Università di

Genova (DISI Technical Report DISI-TR-06-21). Retrieved from http://www.disi.unige.it/research/expand-techrep?id_tr=44.

Matteo, C., & Cuel, R. (2005). A Survey on Ontology Creation Methodologies. International Journal on Semantic Web & Information Systems (IJSWIS), 1(2), 49–69.

Mayr, P. (2006) Thesauri, Klassifikationen & Co: Die Renaissance der kontrollierten Vokabulare? In P. Hauke & K. Umlauf (Eds.), Beiträge zur Bibliotheks- und Informationswissenschaft: Vol. 1. Vom Wandel der Wissensorganisation im Informationszeitalter. Festschrift für Walther Umstätter zum 65. Geburtstag (pp. 151–170). Bad Honnef: Bock + Herchen Verlag.

Mena, E., Illarramendi, A., Kashyap, V., & Sheth, A. (2000). OBSERVER: An Approach for Query Processing in Global Information Systems. International Journal on Distributed and Parallel Databases, 8(2), 223–271.

Mika, P. (2007). Ontologies are Us: A Unified Model of Social Networks and Semantics. Journal of Web Semantics, 5(1), 5–15.

Mika, P., & Greaves, M. (2008). Editorial: Semantic Web & Web 2.0. Journal of Web Semantics, 6(1), 1–3.

Mikroyannidis, A. (2007). Towards a Social Semantic Web. IEEE Computer, 40(11), 113–115.

Miles, A., & Brickley, D. (Eds.) (2005). SKOS Core Guide: W3C Working Draft 2 November 2005. Retrieved from http://www.w3.org/TR/2005/WD-swbp-skos-core-guide-20051102/.

Miles, A., Matthews, B., Wilson, M., & Brickley, D. (2005). SKOS Core: Simple Knowledge Organisation for the Web. In Vocabularies in Practice: Proceedings of the International Conference on Dublin Core and Metadata (DC 2005), Madrid, Spain (pp. 3–10).

Milne, D., Medelyan, O., & Witten, I. H. (2006). Mining Domain-Specific Thesauri from Wikipedia: A Case Study. In T. Nishida (Ed.), Web Intelligence: Proceedings of the IEEE/WIC/ACM International Conference on Web Intelligence (WI 2006), Hong Kong, China (pp. 442–448). Los Alamitos: IEEE Computer Society.

Mizoguchi, R. (2004). Ontology Engineering Environments. In S. Staab & R. Studer (Eds.), Handbook on Ontologies (pp. 275–296). Berlin, Heidelberg, New York: Springer.

Mons, B., Ashburner, M., Chichester, C., van Mulligen, E., Weeber, M., & den Dunnen, J., et al. (2008). Calling on a Million Minds for Community Annotation in WikiProteins. Genome Biology, 9(5), Article R89.

Muller, M. J. (2007). Comparing Tagging Vocabularies among four Enterprise Tag-Based Services. In T. Gross & K. Inkpen (Eds.), Proceedings of the 2007 International ACM Conference on Supporting Group Work (Group'07), Sanibel Island, Florida, USA (pp. 341–350). New York: ACM.

Nguyen, D. P. T., Matsuo, Y., & Ishizuka, M. (2007). Relation Extraction from Wikipedia Using Subtree Mining. In Proceedings of the Twenty-Second AAAI Conference on Artificial Intelligence, Vancouver, British Columbia, Canada (pp. 1414–1420). Menlo Park: AAAI Press.

Nielsen, J. (2006). Participation Inequality: Encouraging More Users to Contribute. Retrieved from http://www.useit.com/alertbox/participation _inequality.html.

Nöther, I. (1998). Zurück zur Klassifikation!: Modell einer Internationalen Konkordanz-Klassifikation. In dbi-Materialien: Vol. 175. Klassifikationen für wissenschaftliche Bibliotheken. Analysen, Empfehlungen, Modelle (pp. 103–325). Berlin: Deutsches Bibliotheksinstitut.

Noy, N. F. (2004). Tools for Mapping and Merging Ontologies. In S. Staab & R. Studer (Eds.), Handbook on Ontologies (pp. 365–384). Berlin, Heidelberg, New York: Springer.

Noy, N. F. (2009). Ontology Mapping. In S. Staab & R. Studer (Eds.), Handbook on Ontologies (pp. 573–590). Dordrecht et al.: Springer.

Noy, N. F., Chugh, A., Liu, W., & Musen, M. A. (2006). A Framework for Ontology Evolution in Collaborative Environments. In I. Cruz; S. Decker, & et al. (Eds.), The Semantic Web: 5th International Semantic Web Conference (ISWC 2006), Athens, GA, USA. (pp. 544–558). Berlin: Springer.

Noy, N. F., de Coronado, S., Solbrig, H., Fragoso, G., Hartel, F., & Musen, M. A. (2008). Representing the NCI Thesaurus in OWL DL: Modeling Tools Help Modeling Languages. Applied Ontology, 3(3), 173–190.

Noy, N. F., Guha, R. V., & Musen, M. A. (2005). User Ratings of Ontologies: Who will Rate the Raters. In Proceedings of the 20th National Conference on Artificial Intelligence (AAAI-05), Pittsburgh, Pennsylvania. Menlo Park: AAAI Press.

Noy, N. F., & McGuinness, D. L. (2001). Ontology Development 101: A Guide to Creating Your First Ontology: Stanford Knowledge Systems Laboratory Technical Report KSL-01-05 and Stanford Medical Informatics Technical Report SMI-2001-0880, March 2001. Retrieved from http://protege.stanford.edu/publications/ontology_development/ ontology101-noy-mcguinness.html.

Noy, N. F., & Musen, M. A. (2003). The PROMPT Suite: Interactive Tools for Ontology Merging and Mapping. International Journal of Human-Computer Studies, 59(6), 983–1024.

Noy, N. F., Sintek, M., Decker, S., Crubezy, M., Fergerson, R. W., & Musen, M. A. (2001). Creating Semantic Web Contents with Protégé-2000. IEEE Intelligent Systems, 16(2), 60–71.

Oberle, D., Volz, R., Staab, S., & Motik, B. (2004). An Extensible Ontology Software Environment. In S. Staab & R. Studer (Eds.), Handbook on Ontologies (pp. 299–319). Berlin, Heidelberg, New York: Springer.

Oldenburg, S., Garbe, M., & Cap, C. (2008). Similarity Cross-Analysis of Tag / Co-Tag Spaces in Social Classification Systems. In I. Soboroff; E. Agichtein, & A. Kumar (Eds.), Proceeding of the 2008 ACM Workshop on Search in Social Media, Conference on Information and Knowledge Management (CIKM 2008), Napa Valley, California, USA (pp. 11–18). New York: ACM.

Pan, J. Z. (2007). OWL for the Novice: A Logical Perspective. In C. J. O. Baker & K.-H. Cheung (Eds.), Semantic Web: Revolutionizing Knowledge Discovery in the Life Sciences (pp. 159–182). Boston: Springer.

Panke, S., & Gaiser, B. (2008). With my Head up in the Clouds: Social Tagging aus Nutzersicht. In B. Gaiser, T. Hampel, & S. Panke (Eds.), Good Tags – Bad Tags. Social Tagging in der Wissensorganisation (pp. 23–35). Medien in der Wissenschaft: Vol. 47. Münster: Waxmann.

Panzer, M., & Zheng, M. L. (2009). Modeling Classification Systems in SKOS: Some Challenges and Best-Practice Recommendations. In S. Oh; S. Sugimoto, & S. A. Sutton (Eds.), International Conference on Dublin Core and Metadata Applications: Proceedings of the International Conference on Dublin Core and Metadata Applications (DC-2009), Seoul, Korea (pp. 3–14).

Paolillo, J., & Penumarthy, S. (2007). The Social Structure of Tagging Internet Video on del.icio.us. In Proceedings of the 40th Annual Hawaii International Conference on System Sciences (HICSS) (p. 85).

Passant, A., Laublet, P., Breslin, J. G., & Decker, S. (2009). A URI is Worth a Thousand Tags: From Tagging to Linked Data with MOAT. International Journal on Semantic Web & Information Systems (IJSWIS), 5(3), 71–94.

Paulsen, I., Mainz, D., Weller, K., Mainz, I., Kohl, J., & von Haeseler, A. (2007). Ontoverse: Collaborative Knowledge Management in the Life Science Network. In Proceedings of the German eScience Conference 2007 (Max Planck Digital Library, ID 316588.0). Max Planck Digital Library.

Pepper, S. (2002). The TAO of Topic Maps: Finding the Way in the Age of Infoglut. Retrieved from http://www.ontopia.net/topicmaps/materials/tao.html.

Perugini, S., Goncalves, M. A., & Fox, E. A. (2004). Recommender Systems Research: A Connection-Centric Study. Journal of Intelligent Information Systems, 23(2), 107–143.

Peters, I. (2006). Against Folksonomies: Indexing Blogs and Podcasts for Corporate Knowledge Management. In H. Jezzard (Ed.), Preparing for Information 2.0. Online Information 2006 Conference Proceedings (pp. 93–97). London: Learned Information Europe.

Peters, I. (2009). Folksonomies: Indexing and Retrieval in Web 2.0. Berlin: De Gruyter Saur.

Peters, I., & Stock, W. G. (2007). Folksonomy and Information Retrieval. In Joining Research and Practice: Social Computing and Information Science. Proceedings of the 70th Annual Meeting of the American Society for Information Science and Technology, Milwaukee, Wisconsin (pp. 1510–1542).

Peters, I., & Weller, K. (2008a). Paradigmatic and Syntagmatic Relations in Knowledge Organization Systems. Information - Wissenschaft & Praxis, 59(2), 100–107.

Peters, I., & Weller, K. (2008b). Tag Gardening for Folksonomy Enrichment and Maintenance. Webology, 5(3). Retrieved from http://www.webology.ir/2008/v5n3/a58.html.

Pinto, H. S., & Martins, J. P. (2004). Ontologies: How can They be Built? Knowledge and Information Systems, 6(4), 441–464.

Pinto, H. S., Peralta, D. N., & Mamede, N. J. (2002). Using Protégé-2000 in Reuse Processes. In J. Angele & Y. Sure (Eds.), Evaluation of Ontology-based Tools (EON 2002). Proceedings of the OntoWeb-SIG3 Workshop at the 13th International Conference on Knowledge Engineering and Knowledge Management (EKAW 2002), Siguenza, Spain (pp. 15–26). CEUR Workshop Proceedings: Vol. 62.

Ponzetto, S. P., & Strube, M. (2007a). Deriving a Large Scale Taxonomy from Wikipedia. In Proceedings of the Twenty-Second AAAI Conference on Artificial Intelligence, Vancouver, British Columbia, Canada (pp. 1440–1445). Menlo Park: AAAI Press.

Ponzetto, S. P., & Strube, M. (2007b). Knowledge Derived from Wikipedia for Computing Semantic Relatedness. Journal of Artificial Intelligence Research, 30, 181–212.

Popescu, A., Moellic, P.-A, & Millet, C. (2007). SemRetriev: An Ontology Driven Image Retrieval System. In N. Sebe & M. Worring (Eds.), Proceedings of the 6th ACM International Conference on Image and Video Retrieval, Amsterdam, The Netherlands (pp. 113–116). New York: ACM.

Predoiu, L., Feier, C., Scharffe, F., de Bruijn, J., Martín-Recuerda, F., Manov, D., & Ehrig, M. (2005). State-of-the-art survey on Ontology Merging and Aligning V2 (Sekt Project Deliverable No. D4.2.2). DERI Innsbruck.

Presutti, V., & Gangemi, A. (2008). Content Ontology Design Patterns as Practical Building Blocks for Web Ontologies. In Q. Li; S. Spaccapietra; E. Yu, & A. Olivé (Eds.), Conceptual Modeling ER 2008: Proceedings of the 27th International Conference on Conceptual Modeling, Barcelona, Spain (pp. 128–141). Berlin: Springer.

Raschen, B. (2005). A Resilent, Evolving Resource: How to Create a Taxonomy. Business Information Review, 22(3), 199–204.

Rattenbury, T., Good, N., & Naaman, M. (2007). Towards Automatic Extraction of Event and Place Semantics from Flickr Tags. In Proceedings of the 30th Annual International ACM SIGIR Conference on Research and Development in Information Retrieval (pp. 103–110). New York: ACM.

Rector, A., Drummond, N., Horridge, M., Rogers, J., Knublauch, H., & Stevens, R., et al. (2004). OWL Pizzas: Practical Experience of Teaching OWL-DS. Common Errors & Common Patterns. In E. Motta; N. Shadbolt; A. Stutt, & N. Gibbins (Eds.), Engineering Knowledge in the Age of the Semantic Web: Proceedings of th 14th International Conference (EKAW 2004), Whittlebury Hall, UK (pp. 63–81). Berlin: Springer.

Rector, A., Horridge, M., Iannone, L., & Drummond, N. (2008). Use Cases for Building OWL Ontologies as Modules: Localizing, Ontology and Programming Interfaces & Extensions. In E. F. Kendall; J. Z. Pan; M. Sabbouh; L. Stojanovic, & K. Bontcheva (Eds.), 4th International Workshop on Semantic Web Enabled Software Engineering (SWESE2008), Karlsruhe, Germany.

Rector, A., Wroe, C., Rogers, J., & Roberts, A. (2001). Untangling Taxonomies and Relationships: Personal and Practical Problems in Loosely Coupled Development of Large Ontologies. In Y. Gil; M. A. Musen, & J. Shavlik (Eds.),

First International Conference on Knowledge Capture (KCAP'01),Victoria, Canada (pp. 139–146). New York: ACM.

Riedl, J., & Dourish, P. (2005). Introduction to the Special Issue on Recommender Systems. ACM Transactions on Computer-Human-Interaction, 12, 371–373.

Ruiz-Casado, M., Alfonseca, E., & Castells, P. (2005). Automatic Extraction of Semantic Relationships for WordNet by Means of Pattern Learning from Wikipedia. In E. Métais, A. Montoyo, & R. Munoz (Eds.), Natural Language Processing and Information Systems. Proceedings of the 10th International Conference on Applications of Natural Language to Information Systems (NLDB 2005), Alicante, Spain (pp. 67–79). Berlin, Heidelberg: Springer.

Russell, B. C., Torralba, A., Murphy, K. P., & Freeman, W. T. (2008). LabelMe: A Database and Web-based Tool for Image Annotation. International Journal of Computer Vision, 77(1-3), 157–173.

Sanchez-Alonso, S., & Garcia-Barriocanal, E. (2006). Making Use of Upper Ontologies to Foster Interoperability between SKOS Concept Schemes. Online Information Review, 30(3), 263–277.

Schaffert, S., Eder, J., Grünwald, S., Kurz, T., Radulescu, M., Sint, R., & Stroka, S. (2009). KiWi: A Platform for Semantic Social Software. In C. Lange, S. Schaffert, H. Skaf-Molli, & M. Völkel (Eds.), The Semantic Wiki Web. Proceedings of the 4th Semantic Wiki Workshop (SemWiki 2009), co-located with 6th European Semantic Web Conference (ESWC 2009), Heraklion, Greece. CEUR Workshop Proceedings: Vol. 494.

Schmitz, P. (2006). Inducing Ontology from Flickr Tags. In Collaborative Web Tagging Workshop: Workshop helt at the World Wide Web Conference (WWW2006), Edinburgh, Scotland.

Schreiber, G., Dubbeldam, B., Wielemaker, J., & Wielinga, B. (2001). Ontology-Based Photo Annotation. IEEE Intelligent Systems, 16(3), 66–74.

Schroll, M., & Hafkesbrink, J. (2009). Collaborative Ontology Engineering Needs a Specific Incentive System. In A. von Haeseler (Ed.), Ontoverse: Global Knowledge for Global Challenges (Report for the BMBF Project Ontoverse) (pp. 28–29). Krefeld: Varion.

Schutz, A., & Buitelaar, P. (2005). RelExt: A Tool for Relation Extraction from Text in Ontology Extension. In V. R. Benjamins; Y. Gil; E. Motta, & M. A. Musen (Eds.), The Semantic Web: Proceedings of the 4th International Semantic Web Conference (ISWC 2005), Galway, Ireland (pp. 593–606). Berlin, Heidelberg: Springer.

Schwarz, K. (2005). Domain Model Enhanced Search: A Comparison of Taxonomy, Thesaurus and Ontology. Master Thesis, University of Utrecht, The Netherlands.

Schwitter, R., Kaljurand, K., Cregan, A., Dolbear, C., & Hart, G. (2008). A Comparison of three Controlled Natural Languages for OWL 1.1. In C. Dolbear, A. Ruttenberg, & U. Sattler (Eds.), Proceedings of the 5th International Workshop on OWL: Experiences and Directions (OWLED 2008), Collocated with the 7th International Semantic Web Conference (ISWC-2008), Karlsruhe, Germany. CEUR Workshop Proceedings: Vol. 432.

Schwitter, R., & Tilbrook, M. (2004). Controlled Natural Language Meets the Semantic Web. In A. Asudeh; C. Paris, & S. Wan (Eds.), Proceedings of the Australasian Language Technology Workshop 2004, Macquarie University, Sidney, Australia (pp. 55–62).

Seidenberg, J., & Rector, A. (2007). The State of Multi-User Ontology Engineering. In B. Cuenca Grau, V. Honavar, A. Schlicht, & F. Wolter (Eds.), Proceedings of the 2nd International Workshop on Modular Ontologies (WoMO 2007), Whistler, Canada. CEUR Workshop Proceedings: Vol. 315.

Sen, S., Lam, S. K., Rashid, A. M., Cosley, D., Frankowski, D., & Osterhouse, J., et al. (2006). Tagging, Communities, Vocabulary, Evolution. In P. Hinds & D. Martin (Eds.), Proceedings of the 2006 20th Anniversary Conference on Computer Supported Cooperative Work (CSCW 2006), Banff, Alberta, Canada (pp. 181–190). New York: ACM.

Simperl, E., & Sure, Y. (2008). The Business View: Ontology Engineering Costs. In M. Hepp; P. de Leenheer; A. de Moor, & Y. Sure (Eds.), Ontology Management: Semantic Web, Semantic Web Services, and Business Applications (pp. 207–225). Boston: Springer.

Sinclair, J., & Cardew-Hall, M. (2008). The Folksonomy Tag Cloud: When is it Useful? Journal of Information Science, 34(1), 15–29.

Sintek, M., van Elst, L., Grimnes, G., Scerri, S., & Handschuh, S. (2007). Knowledge Representation for the Distributed, Social Semantic Web: Named Graphs, Graph Roles and Views in NRL. In B. Cuenca Grau, V. Honavar, A. Schlicht, & F. Wolter (Eds.), Proceedings of the 2nd International Workshop on Modular Ontologies (WoMO 2007), Whistler, Canada. CEUR Workshop Proceedings: Vol. 315.

Siorpaes, K., & Hepp, M. (2007). myOntology: The Marriage of Ontology Engineering and Collective Intelligence. In B. Hoser & A. Hotho (Eds.). Bridging the Gap between Semantic Web and Web 2.0 (SemNet 2007). International Workshop at the 4th European Semantic Web Conference, Innsbruck, Austria (pp. 127–138).

Siorpaes, K., & Hepp, M. (2008a). OntoGame: Weaving the Semantic Web by Online Games. In S. Bechhofer; M. Hauswirth; J. Hoffmann, & M. Koubarakis (Eds.), The Semantic Web Research and Applications: Proceedings of the 5th European Semantic Web Conference (ESWC 2008), Tenerife, Canary Islands, Spain (pp. 751–766). Berlin, Heidelberg: Springer.

Siorpaes, K., & Hepp, M. (2008b). Games with a Purpose for the Semantic Web. IEEE Intelligent Systems, 23(3), 50–60.

Siorpaes, K., Hepp, M., Klotz, A., Hackl, M., & the myOntology Consortium (2008). myOntology in a Nutshell: Release Primer. Retrieved from http://myontology.sti2.at/prototype/doc/primer.html.

Smith, G. (2008). Tagging: Emerging Trends. Bulletin of the ASIST, 34(6), 14–17.

Smith, B., Ceusters, W., Klagges, B., Kohler, J., Kumar, A., & Lomax, J., et al. (2005). Relations in Biomedical Ontologies. Genome Biology, 6(5), Art. R46.

Soldatova, L. N., & King, R. D. (2005). Are the Current Ontologies in Biology Good Ontologies? Nature Biotechnology, 23(9), 1095–1098.

Staab, S., Santini, S., Nack, F., Steels, L., & Maedche, A. (2002). Emergent Semantics. IEEE Intelligent Systems, 17(1), 78–86.

Staab, S., Schnurr, H. P., Studer, R., & Sure, Y. (2001). Knowledge Processes and Ontologies. IEEE Intelligent Systems, 16(1), 26–34.

Stock, W. G. (2007). Information Retrieval: Informationen suchen und finden. München, Wien: Oldenbourg.

Stock, W. G., & Stock, M. (2008). Wissensrepräsentation: Informationen auswerten und bereitstellen. München, Wien: Oldenbourg.

Stuckenschmidt, H., & Klein, M. C. A. (2003). Integrity and Change in Modular Ontologies. In G. Gottlob (Ed.), Proceedings of the Eighteenth International Joint Conference on Artificial Intelligence (IJCAI), Acapulco, Mexico (pp. 900–908). San Francisco: Morgan Kaufmann.

Stumme, G., & Maedche, A. (2001). FCA-Merge: Bottom-Up Merging of Ontologies. In Proceedings of the 17th International Joint Conference on Artificial Intelligence (IJCAI 2001), Seattle, Washington, USA. (pp. 225–230). Los Altos: Morgan Kaufmann.

Suarez-Figueroa, M. C., García-Castro, R., Gómez-Pérez, A., Palma, R., Nixon, L. J. B., & Paslaru, E., et al. (2005). Identification of Standards on Metadata for Ontologies (KWeb Deliverable No. D1.3.2).

Suchanek, F. M., Kasneci, G., & Weikum, G. (2007). YAGO: A Core of Semantic Knowledge Unifying WordNet and Wikipedia. In 16th International World Wide Web Conference (WWW 2007), Banff, Alberta, Canada (pp. 697–706). Red Hook, NY: Curran.

Sunagawa, E., Kozaki, K., Kitamura, Y., & Mizoguchi, R. (2003). An Environment for Distributed Ontology Development Based on Dependency Management. In D. Fensel; K. Sycara, & J. Mylopoulos (Eds.), The Semantic Web: Proceedings of the Second International Semantic Web Conference (ISWC 2003), Sanibel Island, FL, USA (pp. 453–468). Berlin: Springer.

Sunagawa, E., Kozaki, K., Kitamura, Y., & Mizoguchi, R. (2004). Organizing Role-concepts in Ontology Development Environment: Hozo. AI Technical Report (Artificial Intelligence Research Group, I. S. I. R., Osaka Univ.), AI-TR-04-1.

Sure, Y., Erdmann, M., Angele, J., Staab, S., Studer, R., & Wenke, D. (2002). OntoEdit: Collaborative ONtology Engineering for the Semantic Web. In I. Horrocks & J. Hendler (Eds.), The Semantic Web: Proceedings of the First International Semantic Web Conference, Sardinia, Italy (pp. 221–235). Berlin, Heidelberg: Springer.

Sure, Y., Staab, S., & Studer, R. (2002). Methodology for Development and Employment of Ontology Based Knowledge Management Applications. ACM SIGMOD Record, Special Issue on Semantic Web and Data Management, 31(4), 18–23.

Sure, Y., Tempich, C., & Vrandecic, D. (2006). Ontology Engineering Methodologies. In J. Davies; R. Studer, & P. Warren (Eds.), Semantic Web

Technologies: Trends and Research in Ontology-Based Systems (pp. 171–190). Chichester: Wiley.

Swartout, B., Patil, R., Knight, K., & Russ, T. (1996). Toward Distributed Use of Large-Scale Ontologies. In Proceedings of Tenth Knowledge Acquisition for Knowledge-Based Systems Workshop (KAW96), Banff, Canada.

Tanasescu, V., & Streibel, O. (2007). Extreme Tagging: Emergent Semantics through the Tagging of Tags. In L. Chen, P. Cudré-Mauroux, P. Haase, A. Hotho, & E. Ong (Eds.), Emergent Semantics and Ontology Evolution 2007: Proceedings of the First International Workshop on Emergent Semantics and Ontology Evolution (ESOE-2007), co-located with ISWC 2007, Busan, Korea (pp. 84–85). CEUR Workshop Proceedings: Vol. 292.

Tempich, C., Pinto, H. S., Sure, Y., & Staab, S. (2005). An Argumentation Ontology for Distributed, Loosely-Controlled and Evolving Engineering Processes of Ontologies (DILIGENT). In A. Gómez-Pérez & J. Euzenat (Eds.), The Semantic Web: Research and Applications. Proceedings of the 2nd European Semantic Web Conference (ESWC 2005). Heraklion, Greece (pp. 241–256). Berlin, Heidelberg: Springer.

Tudhope, D. (2006). A Tentative Typology of KOS: Towards a KOS of KOS? Presentation held at the 5th European Networked Knowledge Organization Systems (NKOS) Workshop, Alicante, Spain. Co-located with ECDL 2006. Retrieved from http://www.ukoln.ac.uk/nkos/nkos2006/presentations/tudhope.ppt.

Tudhope, D., Koch, T., & Heery, R. (2006). Terminology Services and Technology (JISC State of the Art Review). Retrieved from http://www.jisc.ac.uk/Terminology_Services_and_Technology_Review_Sep_0 6.

Tudorache, T., Noy, N. F., Tu, S., & Musen, M. A. (2008). Supporting Collaborative Ontology Development in Protégé. In A. Sheth; S. Staab; M. Dean; M. Paolucci; D. Maynard; Finin T., & K. Thirunarayan (Eds.), The Semantic Web: 7th International Semantic Web Conference (ISWC 2008), Karlsruhe, Germany (pp. 17–32). Berlin: Springer.

Tummarello, G., & Morbidoni, C. (2007). Collaboratively Building Structured Knowledge with DBin: From del.icio.us Tags to an "RDFS Folksonomy". In N. F. Noy, H. Alani, G. Stumme, P. Mika, Y. Sure, & D. Vrandecic (Eds.), Proceedings of the Workshop on Social and Collaborative Construction of Structured Knowledge (CKC 2007) at the 16th International World Wide Web Conference (WWW2007) Banff, Canada. CEUR Workshop Proceedings: Vol. 273.

Udel, J. (2004). Collaborative Knowledge Gardening. [Blog Post: August 20, 2004]. Retrieved from http://www.infoworld.com/article/04/08/20/34O Pstrategic_1.html.

Uschold, M. (1996). The Use of the Typed Lambda Calculus for Guiding Naive Users in the Representation and Acquisition of Part-Whole Knowledge. Data & Knowledge Engineering, 20(3), 385–404.

van Assem, M., Gangemi, A., & Schreiber, G. (2006). RDF/OWL Representation of WordNet (W3C Working Draft). World Wide Web Consortium. Retrieved from http://www.w3.org/TR/wordnet-rdf/.

van Assem, M., Malaisé, V., Miles, A., & Schreiber, G. (2006). A Method to Convert Thesauri to SKOS. In Y. Sure (Ed.), The Semantic Web Research and Applications. Proceedings of the 3rd European Semantic Web Conference, ESWC 2006 (pp. 95–109). Berlin: Springer.

van Damme, C., Coenen, T., & Vandijck, E. (2008). Turning a Corporate Folksonomy into a Lightweight Corporate Ontology. In W. Abramowicz & D. Fensel (Eds.), Business Information Systems: Proccedings of the 11th International Conference (BIS 2008), Innsbruck, Austria (pp. 36–47). Berlin, Heidelberg: Springer.

Vander Wal, T. (2004). Feed on This [Blog Post: October 3, 2004]. Retrieved from http://www.vanderwal.net/random/entrysel.php?blog=1562.

Vander Wal, T. (2008). Welcome to the Matrix! In B. Gaiser, T. Hampel, & S. Panke (Eds.), Good Tags – Bad Tags. Social Tagging in der Wissensorganisation (pp. 7–10). Medien in der Wissenschaft: Vol. 47. Münster: Waxmann.

Völkel, M., Krötzsch, M., Vrandecic, D., Haller, H., & Studer, R. (2006). Semantic Wikipedia. In L. Carr; D. de Roure, & A. Iyengar (Eds.), International World Wide Web Conference: Proceedings of the 15th International Conference on World Wide Web, Edinburg, Schottland (pp. 585–594). New York: ACM.

Vollmar, G. (2007). Knowledge Gardening: Wissensarbeit in intelligenten Organisationen. Bielefeld: Bertelsmann.

von Ahn, L. (2005). Method for Labeling Images through a Computer Game. Patent No. US20050014118.

von Ahn, L. (2006a). Games with a Purpose. IEEE Computer, 39(6), 96–98.

von Ahn, L. (2006b). Peekaboom: A Game for Locating Objects in Images. In R. Grinter; T. Rodden, & et al. (Eds.), Proceedings of the SIGCHI Conference on Human Factors in Computing Systems (SIGCHI 2006), Montreal, Quebec, Canada (pp. 55–64). New York: ACM.

von Ahn, L., Blum, M., Hopper, N., & Langford, J. (2003). CAPTCHA: Using Hard AI Problems for Security. In E. Biham (Ed.), Advances in Cryptology: Proceedings of the International Conference on the Theory and Applications of Cryptographic Techniques (EUROCRYPT 2003), Warsaw, Poland (pp. 294–311). Berlin: Springer.

von Ahn, L., & Dabbish, L. (2004). Labeling Images with a Computer Game. In Conference on Human Factors in Computing Systems (CHI 2004): Proceedings of the SIGCHI Conference on Human Factors in Computing Systems, Vienna, Austria (pp. 319–326). New York: ACM.

von Ahn, L., Ginosar, S., Kedia, M., Liu, R., & Blum, M. (2006). Improving Accessability on the Web with a Computer Game. In R. Grinter; T. Rodden, & et al. (Eds.), Proceedings of the SIGCHI Conference on Human Factors in

Computing Systems (SIGCHI 2006), Montreal, Quebec, Canada (pp. 79–82). New York: ACM.

von Ahn, L., Kedia, M., & Blum, M. (2006). Verbosity: A Game for Collecting Common Sense Facts. In R. Grinter; T. Rodden, & et al. (Eds.), Proceedings of the SIGCHI Conference on Human Factors in Computing Systems (SIGCHI 2006), Montreal, Quebec, Canada (pp. 75–78). New York: ACM.

von Ahn, L., Maurer, B., McMillen, C., Abraham, D., & Blum, M. (2008). reCAPTCHA: Human-Based Character Recognition via Web Security Measures. Science, 321(5895), 1465–1468.

Voß, J. (2006). Collaborative Thesaurus Tagging the Wikipedia Way. Retrieved from http://arxiv.org/abs/cs/0604036.

Voß, J. (2007). Tagging, Folksonomy & Co: Renaissance of Manual Indexing? Retrieved from http://arxiv.org/abs/cs/0701072.

Voß, J. (2009). Wikipedia as Knowledge Organization System. Presentation at International UDC Seminar 2009, The Hague, Netherlands. Retrieved from http://www.slideshare.net/nichtich/wikipedia-as-knowledge-organization-system-2374373.

Vrandecic, D., Pinto, H. S., Tempich, C., & Sure, Y. (2005). The DILIGENT Knowledge Processes. Journal of Knowledge Management, 9(5), 85–96.

Walter, A., & Nagypal, G. (2007). IMAGENOTION: Collaborative Semantic Annotation of Images and Image Parts and Integrated Creation of Ontologies. In S. Auer, C. Bizer, C. Müller, & A. V. Zhdanova (Eds.), The Social Semantic Web. Proceedings of the 1st Conference on Social Semantic Web (CSSW), Leipzig, Germany (pp. 161–166). GI-Edition Proceedings: Vol. 113. Bonn: Gesellschaft für Informatik.

Walter, A.-K., Mayr, P., Stempfhuber, M., & Ballay, A. (2006). Crosskonkordanzen als Mittel der Heterogenitätsbehandlung in infoconnex. In M. Stempfhuber (Ed.), In die Zukunft publizieren: Herausforderungen an das Publizieren und die Informationsversorgung in den Wissenschaften. 11. IuK-Jahrestagung, Bonn, Germany (pp. 205–225). Bonn: IZ Sozialwissenschaften.

Wang, G., Yu, Y., & Zhu, H. (2007). PORE: Positive-Only Relation Extraction from Wikipedia Text. In K. Aberer & et al. (Eds.), The Semantic Web: 6th International Semantic Web Conference, 2nd Asian Semantic Web Conference (ISWC 2007 + ASWC 2007), Busan, Korea (pp. 580–594). Berlin: Springer.

Waterfeld, W., Weiten, M., & Haase, P. (2008). Ontology Management Infrastructures. In M. Hepp; P. de Leenheer; A. de Moor, & Y. Sure (Eds.), Ontology Management: Semantic Web, Semantic Web Services, and Business Applications (pp. 59–87). Boston: Springer.

Weller, K. (2006). Kooperativer Ontologieaufbau. In M. Ockenfeld (Ed.), Content: 28. Online Tagung der DGI, Frankfurt a.M., Germany (pp. 227–234). Frankfurt am Main: DGI.

Weller, K. (2008a). KOSO: A Metadata Ontology for Knowledge Organization Systems. In Y. Sure (Ed.), Proceedings of the Poster Track of the 5th European Semantic Web Conference (ESWC 2008), Tenerife, Spain. CEUR Workshop Proceedings: Vol. 367.

Weller, K. (2008b). KOSO: A Reference-Ontology for Reuse of Existing Knowledge Organization Systems. In Proceedings of the 1st Workshop on Knowledge Reuse and Reengineering over the Semantic Web (KRRSW 08), held at the European Semantic Web Conference (ESWC 2008), Tenerife, Spain (pp. 31–40).

Weller, K., & Peters, I. (2007). Reconsidering Relationships for Knowledge Representation. In K. Tochtermann & H. Maurer (Eds.), International Conference on Knowledge Management: Proceedings of I-Know 07, Graz, Austria (pp. 493–496). Graz: J.UCS.

Weller, K., & Peters, I. (2008). Seeding, Weeding, Fertilizing: Different Tag Gardening Activities for Folksonomy Maintenance and Enrichment. In S. Auer; S. Schaffert, & T. Pellegrini (Eds.), Proceedings of I-SEMANTICS'08: International Conference on Semantic Systems, Graz, Austria (pp. 110–117). Graz: J.UCS.

Wellisch, H. H. (2000). Glossary of Terminology in Abstracting, Classification, Indexing, and Thesaurus Construction. Medford: Information Today.

Wu, H., Zubair, M., & Maly, K. (2006). Harvesting Social Knowledge from Folksonomies. In Proceedings of the 17th Conference on Hypertext and Hypermedia (HT'06), Odense, Denmark (pp. 111–114). New York: ACM.

Zacharias, V., & Braun, S. (2007). SOBOLEO: Social Bookmarking and Lightweight Ontology Engineering. In N. F. Noy, H. Alani, G. Stumme, P. Mika, Y. Sure, & D. Vrandecic (Eds.), Proceedings of the Workshop on Social and Collaborative Construction of Structured Knowledge (CKC 2007) at the 16th International World Wide Web Conference (WWW2007), Banff, Canada. CEUR Workshop Proceedings: Vol. 273.

Zapilko, B., & Sure, Y. (2009). Converting the TheSoz to SKOS (GESIS-Technical Reports No. 2009-07). Bonn: GESIS Leibniz-Institut für Sozialwissenschaften.

Zhang, L., Wu, X., & Yu, Y. (2006). Emergent Semantics from Folksonomies: A Quantitative Study. Lecture Notes in Computer Science, 4090, 168–186.

Zhdanova, A. V., & Shvaiko, P. (2006). Community-Driven Ontology Matching. In Y. Sure & J. Domingue (Eds.), The Semantic Web: Research and Applications. 3rd European Semantic Web Conference (ESWC 2006), Budva, Montenegro (pp. 34–49). Berlin, Heidelberg: Springer.

Zheng, M. L., & Chan, L. M. (2004). Trends and Issues in Establishing Interoperability among Knowledge Organization Systems. Journal of the American Society for Information Science and Technology, 55(5), 377–395.

Zirn, C., Nastase, V., & Strube, M. (2008). Distinguishing between Instances and Classes in the Wikipedia Taxonomy. In S. Bechhofer; M. Hauswirth; J. Hoffmann, & M. Koubarakis (Eds.), The Semantic Web Research and Applications: Proceedings of the 5th European Semantic Web Conference (ESWC 2008), Tenerife, Canary Islands, Spain (pp. 376–387). Berlin, Heidelberg: Springer.

Conclusion & Outlook

All that we have to do is to merge and leverage
emerging and traditional tools to improve findability.
Somewhere in the intersection of those two models
is a more powerful framework
for identifying, sharing, and finding information

Emanuele Quintarelli (2005)

What sounds so perfectly simple in Quintarelli's quotation is indeed probably the biggest challenge concerning knowledge representation for the World Wide Web. As we have shown in this book, one aim of the Social Semantic Web may be described as combining "emerging and traditional tools to improve findability" (Quintarelli, 2005). Community-based applications should be combined with semantic technologies that enable the indexing, linking and retrieval of information as well as reasoning and recombination. For this purpose, classical forms of knowledge organization systems may be used in combination with both formal ontologies and community-based folksonomies. But to find the perfect "intersection" of all these models is a laborious, complex and challenging task. This book has provided a comprehensive overview on the aspects of knowledge representation within the emerging Social Semantic Web. It has brought together various aspects of knowledge representation and indexing in classical information science, in ontology engineering and in social tagging applications. And still there is much room left for discussion. We will now sum up the most important conclusions of this book and highlight aspects to be addressed in future works.

Lessons Learned & Contribution of this Book

The convergence of Web 2.0 and the Semantic Web has begun and is proceeding significantly with developments such as semantic wikis and semantic blogging. The most elementary components of the Social Semantic Web are:

- Communities of users who want to post information on the Web – for themselves or for the benefit of others.

- Technologies which enable broad communities to share information easily.
- Links between tools and between 'instances' of different tools, e.g. between users or documents.
- Identifiers for those instances, mainly in the form of URIs.
- Knowledge organization systems to describe these instances and to specify the links between them.
- Mash-ups and re-combinations of data and tools.

Knowledge organization systems in this situation have to adapt to a variety of contexts and data. Classical goals of document indexing and retrieval are one context, but not the only perspective. Some scenarios rather focus on semantic link structures of Websites, on browsing and navigation, or on inferencing new information from given resources.

This also means that knowledge representation in the Social Semantic Web has to be based on a variety of KOS types. We have given an overview on existing KOS types that can be of different complexity and based upon different standards. The more elaborated a KOS is, the more users will profit from concept interrelations and richer semantics. But of course the effort of creating and applying such complex KOS is also higher. Ontologies are the most complex type of KOS for the Web so far. We have seen that ontology languages provide the means of formalizing rich semantic models and facilitating the inferencing of implicit information. Advanced features of ontologies in comparison with other KOS have been outlined to indicate the complexity of possibilities in knowledge representation for the Web. But it has also become clear that such complex semantics are laborious to create and difficult to apply: A closer look at current ontologies revealed that quite a few of them do not make intensive use of formal definitions or specified properties and thus still leave much room for richer semantics. The capacities of the Web Ontology Language OWL are not exhausted, but lightweight representations in the form of RDF or SKOS are gaining in popularity. Among the examples for traditional KOS in practice, there were some of thesauri that were recently translated into such representation languages.

Presumably, future KOS for the Web will also not be directly published in the form of fully-grown ontologies. We have seen that upgrades of less formal sources provide a workable solution for the gradual creation of semantics for the Web.

A particular focus may be placed on the structural enrichment of folksonomies. They have gained enormous popularity among normal Web users (i.e. non-experts in knowledge representation and indexing). Therefore, they offer a valuable insight into the users' collective vocabulary. Folksonomies take an exceptional position among knowledge organization systems as they are completely unstructured and thus do not provide any vocabulary control or features of semantic navigation at all. But they do include the possibility for social navigation via shared documents or other users, and they may be gradually enriched with aspects of vocabulary control; single applications that make use of clustering or tag gardening approaches were discussed.

Apart from folksonomies, other Web 2.0 resources may be used for harvesting the collected knowledge of a community. The most prominent example for this is Wikipedia, which includes classificational structures and various instances with unique identifiers. But apart from this, a variety of other resources may still be explored for their applicability in KOS development. We had a first look at some of them, e.g. community knowledge bases or games with a purpose.

The most important conclusion of this book is: all existing approaches in knowledge organization and indexing must interact. On its own, each single approach is too weak to resolve the challenge of handling the enormous amounts of (unstructured) data on the WWW. The different approaches either lack in semantic structure, in domain coverage or in community commitment.

This book has mainly contributed the following aspects to the general discussion on knowledge representation in the Social Semantic Web:

In general, it has outlined the development of knowledge representation from classical (non-Web) contexts to the Semantic Web vision, to social indexing in Web 2.0 and finally to the combined approaches of the Social Semantic Web. Chapter 1 showed that some basic underlying ideas have stayed the same over the years (mainly, the idea of using metadata to support search), others have emerged with the change of the Web (e.g. the demand for machine readable data in the Semantic Web).

We have further provided a comprehensive overview of existing KOS types and other terminological resources in Chapter 2, and we have included several examples of ontologies (2.3.1) and other KOS in practice (1.1.3). Based on all this, a definition of 'ontology' was set up, which fits our background of information science and is useful for the context of the Social Semantic Web. In this context, we define ontologies as the most complex form of available KOS, which make use of specific representation languages, specified semantic relations and formal definitions of concepts. These ontologies have to interact with various other knowledge resources, mainly with classical KOS and folksonomies.

This book has focused on conceptual problems of ontology design rather than technical solutions. In Chapter 2, such conceptual problems of ontology design were intensively discussed, for example the foundations of concept definitions. The main focus has been placed on semantic relations within ontologies. They form the basis for the semantic richness of KOS. Semantic relations are the elements within KOS which mainly realize the aspect of vocabulary control and which may be used for defining the meaning of concepts. Thus understanding their nature and capabilities is critical for establishing formal semantics on the Web.

The third chapter has contributed several novel aspects to the discussion on the Social Semantic Web. It included an outlook on recent issues in ontology engineering and ontology editors and particularly focused on the aspect of community-based ontology engineering. Community-based ontology engineering is an expanded form of collaborative ontology engineering and incorporates not only closed groups of people but also broad and open communities. Of course this open approach to ontology engineering poses new challenges, which have been outlined here and will also have to be closely investigated in future works. Some approaches were introduced which already address the needs of community-based ontology engineering: ontology editors with new forms of community support, controlled natural languages, community knowledge bases and games with a purpose may all help to gather knowledge from broad user communities and transfer it to knowledge representation models.

Chapter 3 also discusses options of enriching less formal KOS with semantic structures in order to generate ontologies. We have explained the principles of tag gardening to facilitate such forms of semantic upgrades of KOS. Tag gardening can be used for two different purposes: for gradually enriching and enhancing the performances of folksonomies on the one hand, and for collecting folksonomy terms in order to broaden another existing KOS with them on the other hand. Tag gardening for structuring and improving tags may not only be applied to folksonomies but also to personomies as personal tag collections. Our approach to addressing the personomy level of tag gardening has resulted in the development of tagCare which is described in Section 3.3.1. The image of tag gardening has also been transferred to the area of ontology engineering and named ontology gardening. In this regard, the main interest lies in several Web resources which may be harvested during ontology engineering; the most popular one among them being Wikipedia.

The last part of Chapter 3 then provided an outlook on the most challenging aspect of KOS in the Social Semantic Web: The question of how ontologies may seamlessly be related and how they may interact will surely be among the most important and difficult topics of future Social Semantic Web research. As one contribution to this particular discussion, we have begun to develop KOSO, a meta-ontology that may be used to classify and describe knowledge organization systems.

Ongoing Challenges

Throughout the book, we have also encountered various open challenges for knowledge representation in the Social Semantic Web, which will have to be reconsidered in the future. The three most important ones should now be summed up again:

Standards for Web Knowledge Representation

While classical KOS originating in library and information science already have well-established sets of standards (e.g. in the form of international norms), similar agreements are not yet available for the context of the WWW.

In folksonomies, missing standards are the most obvious and, to a large degree, they are even welcome. Ontologies, on the other hand, have some well-developed technical standards, mainly in the form of formal representation languages. Above this technical level, ontology engineers are almost as free in modeling choices as users are in social tagging environments. For example, no suggestions exist on how to name concepts or properties in a uniform way. Thus mappings and ontology interactions also become more difficult. We want to highlight once more the importance of a standard set of semantic relations as a basic foundation for KOS on the Web.

On the other hand, classical KOS, like classifications and thesauri, may also use the technical standards of ontology languages in order to enhance machine-readability. Although first examples are available, much more work will be needed in this field.

And finally, another level of missing standards has also been addressed in this book directly concerning the definition of different KOS types: The Social Semantic Web depends on a variety of KOS types – but so far, it lacks any precise overviews on available KOS and their actual characteristics. There are no shared standards on how to define single types of KOS, their specificities and requirements. A respective overview would be enormously helpful for finding appropriate resources for reuse and semantic upgrades. Hopefully this book will encourage future discussions on KOS types based on the suggested overview presented here.

Indexing in the Social Semantic Web

Knowledge representation in general concerns the development of knowledge organization systems as well as their practical application, typically in the form of document indexing. This book has mainly focused on the aspect of developing KOS (particularly in Chapters 2 and 3), though it also sought to include aspects of practical application and indexing (mainly in Chapter 1).

Current activities in the Semantic Web research community have a dominant focus on KOS development. So far, most initiatives have concentrated on ontology *engineering*, i.e. on the creation of semantic representations. The issues and challenges of indexing in practice are rather underrepresented in these considerations and hardly any comprehensive proposals for the Web exist. In contrast, social tagging applications are all about document indexing, while they pay no attention at all to creating a controlled vocabulary in advance.

Thus the Social and Semantic Web not only differ in terms of applied vocabularies but, more fundamentally, also in their attitude towards indexing practice. A convergence in this regard will be crucial for the success of the Social Semantic Web and will be among the ongoing research challenges. We expect that the future of indexing the Social Semantic Web will lie somewhere in the intersection of community-created informal keywords, expert-generated semantic enrichment and automatically computed index terms.

The Role of Web Users for Knowledge Representation in the Social Semantic Web

Throughout this book it was argued that broad Web user communities are a valuable and important basis for novel applications in Web 2.0. It was shown that they already provide useful resources to be harvested for KOS development. Furthermore, they should be incorporated even more actively into the processes of developing KOS for the Web, e.g. within community-based ontology engineering scenarios.

Yet despite their enormous importance for the Social Semantic Web in general and for knowledge representation in particular, only little is known about actual user behavior and users' needs, expectations and motivations. For example, there are no comprehensive studies on how users learn to model KOS and how they may be guided in formalizing knowledge models. In this context, new interdisciplinary research efforts must emerge in order to fill the gap.

Future Perspectives & Related Topics

In future, the Social Semantic Web will require the joint efforts of researchers across disciplines more than any other era on the Web: The Web is no longer only a topic for computer scientists who develop technical applications. The social evolution of the Web has enormous effects on society. It has been changing our ways of communicating, how we go shopping, how we perceive entertainment, how we learn. And it will continue to influence people's daily lives on a large scale, including aspects of education, economy, trust and legal issues. The semantic movements on the Web are also closely connected to other disciplines: understanding the nature of semantics relates to linguistics as well as to philosophy, representing semantic knowledge is a main issue in library and information science and the automatization of these processes is approached in computational linguistics.

Consequently, research on Web technologies has left the boundaries of computer science. The Social Web with its focus on user communities and interactions has also found its way into social sciences and humanities. Semantic Web efforts have started in computer science but have also, from their early days on, included research activities in related disciplines like computational linguistics and philosophy; library and information science have joined in relatively late.

Future Web developers should collaborate even more intensely with experts in additional disciplines like sociology, psychology, educational science, (business) economics or law. Such broad collaborative research efforts have already begun and have only recently been subsumed under the novel term "Web Science" (Hendler, Shadbolt et al., 2008; O'Hara & Hall, 2008).

Within this book, we have started to add the background and expertise of information science to the overall discussion on the Social Semantic Web development. In this respect, the book focuses on the aspect of knowledge representation and knowledge organization systems, which have long traditions in library and information science. We placed this background into the context of the most recent developments in the Social Semantic Web. For this purpose, we obtained a rather conceptual focus throughout our discussion. We set priorities on comparing key features of different KOS, on analyzing KOS elements to represent knowledge, on collecting approaches and methods for developing semantically rich KOS, and generally on describing the overall connection between KOS, their social and semantic characteristics and the Web.

This also means that we paid only minor attention to technical realizations and computational approaches in this context; i.e. we deliberately left a number of topics that are currently on the agenda for several other disciplines unattended. Among the aspects which play an important role for developing the Social Semantic Web on a technical level are social and semantic search, information extraction, merging and mapping algorithms, clustering algorithms, reasoning mechanisms, methods of natural language processing and formal concept analysis, as well as the development of Web services. All these are highly active related research fields and are crucial for the ongoing development of the Web. Future work should thus be dedicated to interrelating these different topics and to integrating the singular aspects into a global research environment.

Conclusion

A new era of the Internet is still in its infancy but already offers new chances for its users as well as new challenges for its developers. The Social Semantic Web is a huge playground and everyone may participate in combining, interrelating and mashing up existing sources and services to create novel applications out of them. Knowledge representation methods in these new Web dimensions will have to be more flexible than ever before. With a range of controlled vocabularies like thesauri and classifications, with social tagging based on communities and with elaborated semantic ontologies, we already possess the necessary basis for putting knowledge representation in the Social Semantic Web into practice. In the near future, there will surely be a variety of novel approaches that make combined use of these KOS, that establish mappings between them or reuse available resources across applications and make use of community power to index the Web or to build new vocabularies. Knowledge representation for the Social Semantic Web has only just begun.

References

Hendler, J., Shadbolt, N., Hall, W., Berners-Lee, T., & Weitzner, D. (2008). Web Science: An Interdisciplinary Approach to Understanding the Web. Communications of the ACM, 51(7), 60–69.

O'Hara, K., & Hall, W. (2008). Web Science. Association of Learning Technologies Newsletter, 12. Retrieved from http://newsweaver.co.uk/alt/e_article001068553.cfm?x=b11,0,w.

Quintarelli, E. (2005). Power to the People. Presented at the ISKO Italy UniMIB Meeting, Milan, Italy. Retrieved from http://www.iskoi.org/doc/folksonomies.htm.

Index of Names

Subject Index